A TRIAL F

Studies in Latter-day Saint History

An imprint of BYU Studies and the
Joseph Fielding Smith Institute for Latter-day Saint History

Brigham Young University
Provo, Utah

A TRIAL FURNACE

Southern Utah's Iron Mission

Morris A. Shirts
Kathryn H. Shirts

Brigham Young University Press
Provo, Utah

To Maxine

This volume is part of the Smith Institute and BYU Studies series
Studies in Latter-day Saint History.

Also in this series
Nearly Everything Imaginable:
The Everyday Life of Utah's Mormon Pioneers

Voyages of Faith:
Explorations in Mormon Pacific History

Library of Congress Cataloging-in-Publication Data
Shirts, Morris A.
A trial furnace : southern Utah's iron mission / Morris A. Shirts,
Kathryn H. Shirts
p. cm.—(Studies in Latter-day Saint history)
Includes bibliographical references and index.
ISBN 0-8425-2487-8 (alk. paper)—ISBN 0-8425-2488-6 (pbk. : alk.
paper)
1. Mormon pioneers—Utah—Iron County—History—19th century. 2.
Frontier and pioneer life—Utah—Iron County. 3. Iron
foundries—Utah—Iron County—History—19th century. 4. Iron County
(Utah)—History—19th century. 5. Iron County (Utah)—Church
history—19th century. 6. Mormon missionaries—Utah—Iron
County—History—19th century. 7. Mormon
Church—Missions—Utah—History—19th century. I. Shirts, Kathryn H. ,
1948- II. Title. III. Series.
F832.I6 S48 2001
979.2'4702'0922—dc21
2001001971

Printed in the United States of America
10 9 8 7 6 5 4 3 2 1

Contents

Illustrations   vii

Foreword   xi

Acknowledgments   xv

Introduction   xix

Part I: "Iron We Must Have"

  1   Prelude to the Iron Mission, 1847–1849   3

  2   The Iron Mission Trail, December 1850–January 1851   25

Part II: Settling In

  3   Fort Louisa, January–May 1851   69

  4   Community Farms and Buildings, February–May 1851   97

  5   Parowan City, May–November 1851   117

  6   On to Cedar City, November 1851   139

  7   Settling Cedar City, Winter 1851–Winter 1852   163

Part III: Trying Iron

  8   The Pioneer Iron Works, February–May 1852   193

  9   First Fruits of the Furnace, May–October 1852   223

  10   The Deseret Iron Company, April–November 1852   251

  11   Change in the Townsite, Growth in the Company,
Fall 1852–Summer 1853   285

  12   Forting up during the Walker War, 1853–1854   317

  13   The Noble Furnace, 1854–1855   343

Part IV: Facing Failure

14   The Iron Works in Decline, 1855–1861   371
15   In Retrospect: Why the Iron Works Failed   409

Appendices

1   Mormon Way-Bill and Advice to Emigrants   421
2   Iron Missionaries, December 1850–June 1851   425
3   Examples of Lots Assigned in Fort Louisa/Fort Parowan:
     1851–1853 (based on surveys by William H. Dame)   445
4   Cedar City Settlers, 11 November–31 December 1851   451
5   Brigham Young's Address to the Saints in Parowan and
     Cedar City, May 1852   455
6   Shareholders and Officers in the Deseret Iron Company   461
7   Articles of Incorporation of the Deseret Iron Company,
     1852 and 1853   467
8   Cedar City Lot Entitlements, Plat A   473
9   Excerpts from an Address by President Brigham Young,
     Delivered in the Tabernacle, Great Salt Lake City,
     27 May 1855   479
10   Cedar City Lot Entitlements, Plat B   483
11   Utah Territorial Militia (Nauvoo Legion): 10th Regiment,
     Battalion and Company Muster Rolls, 10 October 1857   491

Bibliography   499
Index   507

Illustrations

Overland Routes from St. Louis to Southern California   7

Charles C. Rich   8

Iron Ore Outcropping near the Old Pioneer Trail in the
     Iron Springs Area   9

Wakara, Chief of the Ute Indians   12

Cedar City and Environs   14

George A. Smith   17

Henry Lunt   26

Anson Call   27

John D. Lee   28

Iron Mission Campsites from Fort Utah to Parowan   30

Joseph Horne   49

Dame's First Survey (1851) of Fort Louisa (later Parowan)   83

Photograph of Bart Mortenson's Pen-and-Ink Drawing of
     William Major's Oil Painting of Fort Parowan, 1852   85

Zilpha Stark Smith   89

Early Parowan Farm Allocations   103

Pioneer Tree-Trunk Harrow with Wooden Pegs for Teeth   105

Peter Shirts   112

William H. Dame's Second Survey of Fort Louisa   130

Parowan's Old Rock Church   131

Jesse N. Smith Home   132

William H. Dame's 1851 and 1853 Surveys Superimposed over
     Modern Parowan   134

David Bulloch   143

William Palmer's Sketch of the Wagon-Box Camp   165

The "Wagon-Box Camp" Illustration from Palmer's March 1851
     Improvement Era Article   167

Composite of Dame's 1851–1854 Cedar City Surveys 169
George and Mary Davies Wood Cabin 173
Dovetailing on the George and Mary Davies Wood Cabin 172
Randomly Sized Holes in George and Mary Davies Wood Cabin 173
John Pidding Jones Cabin, Shortly before Demolition 173
William Palmer's Sketch of the First Fort at Cedar City 173
Big Field and Compact Fort Layout 174
Diagram Based on William Palmer's Sketch of the
    Coal Creek Survey Site 181
Pioneer Salt Shaker Found near Compact Fort Site 183
Ellen Whittaker Lunt 187
1852 Deseret Iron Company Bar of Pig Iron 195
Charcoal Oven Processing 196
Coke Oven Processing 196
Maramec Undershot Waterwheel and Gearing 199
Blast Furnace Interior 200
Blast Furnace Exterior 201
Joseph Walker 205
Emma Smith Walker 205
Thomas Bladen 206
John Lyman Smith 207
James Whittaker Tally from Iron Works Account Book 209
James A. Little 213
Philip Klingensmith 215
James Ferguson 218
Thomas Bladen's Blast Furnace Model 232
Mine Sites in the Coal Creek Canyon Area 235
Mining Activity on "High Mountain" 238
John Steele 241
Thomas Cartwright 244
Erastus Snow 255
Franklin D. Richards 255
Christopher Arthur's Stock Certificate 257
Charles Jordan's 1852 Blowing Machine Design 259
Jacob Hamblin 276
Dame's 1852 Survey of Plat A 291
West Garden Lot Allocations 293
Pioneer Andirons 304
Plat A Fort Layout 328
Plat A Lot Owners 331

Pioneer Street References on Cedar City Signpost   334
Remnants of Plat A Fort Wall Foundation   335
Morris Shirts and York Jones Placing Brass Cap No. 7.   336
Isaac C. Haight   346
George Croft's Rendering of the Noble Furnace   352
George Croft's Rendering of Furnace Cross-Section   352
Christopher Jones Arthur   357
Caroline Haight Arthur   357
Deseret Iron Company Bell   363
John M. Higbee   372
Dame's 1855 Survey of Plat B   374
Daniel H. Wells   381
Wide-angle View of Mountain Meadows   389
Cedar City Street Excavations, 1982   413
Diagram of Deseret Iron Company Blast Furnace Site   414
Damaged Brick from Blast Furnace Site   415

Foreword

The American West has always been a contested land, a field of
battle and conquest. Through most of the twentieth-century,
writers and historians have glorified the American triumph in
"winning" the West, portraying its settlers as victors of civilization who
subdued and ordered the land and its peoples, wresting abundance and
wealth from its hitherto barren mountains and valleys. But in recent
years, new western historians, such as Donald Worster, Patricia Limerick
and Richard White, have emphasized not the heroic but the rapacious
character of western settlers of European descent, seeing them princi-
pally as despoilers of the land and its peoples.

Strangely, this discourse has virtually ignored what some have called
the hole in the vast donut of the American West—the Mormon presence.
Why would this be? How could astute and sophisticated scholars lavish
years of toil examining mining camps, ranching, prostitution, company
towns, struggles over water, range wars, women homesteaders, outlaw
gangs and corporate greed, and somehow ignore in all this the presence of
the Mormons, who, right from the beginning, turn up almost everywhere,
interacting with the whole varied procession of other westering folk?

Morris Shirts provides an implicit answer to that puzzle in this long-
awaited study of the Iron Mission completed after his death by his daughter-in-law Kathryn. *A Trial Furnace* is a full and compelling account of
the enormous effort Mormons put into developing an iron industry in the
Great Basin in the early 1850s. It is a story that chronicles the beginnings
of Mormon settlement in the Far West, the development of the "called"
mission concept, and the techniques of its mobilization and application.
The effort was headed initially by the much-loved Apostle George A.
Smith—the wry, rotund and sometimes irreverent J. Golden Kimball of
his time. The mission was the model for subsequent "called" settlements,

the nucleus from which the Mormon domain emerged. It is an epic story that on every page gives the reader fresh insights into how the peopling of the Mormon West was accomplished and how in that process the Mormons were being "made saints"—undergoing a cultural metamorphosis that began to set them apart from the rest of the West.

Consider, for example, that epic moment when the missionaries fired up their small blast furnace, erected on Coal Creek in present-day Cedar City, after months of bickering, disappointments and backbreaking toil. Rhoda Matheson Wood and Belle Armstrong's colorful account reports that on the eve of the pour, the whole town surrounded the furnace, said prayers invoking God's blessing, and listened to brief sermons. Then, at dawn, an iron worker "took a long rod and knocked out the clay plug, to let a stream of fiery metal pour out. . . . Shouts of 'Hosannah!' broke from tired, sleepy throats." Henry Lunt wrote more prosaically, "Tap[p]ed the furnace about Six oclock A.M. The Metal run out and we all gave three hearty cheers. When the Mettle was cold, on examination it was not found to be so good as might be wished."

It is not the invocation of divine blessing that is unusual in this account. It was common, in fact, for nineteenth-century industrialists to inaugurate their enterprises with such ceremonies. What is unusual is the community gathering, the all-night vigil, the shouting of hosanna when the metal poured forth. The workers were not so much employees of a company as members of a close-knit family and the iron-making effort was pursued not to enrich an Andrew Carnegie but to provide metal vital to the founding of a commonwealth they saw as theirs.

But there was an even more important goal. Lunt's concern about the quality of iron reveals but one of a number of thorny problems the iron missionaries had tried to lay down. The enterprise had gone slowly and with much fractiousness. Even as the furnace was being tapped, an apostolic delegation was on its way from Salt Lake City to try to set things aright. When they arrived, as they reported to the *Deseret News,* "we found a Scotch party, a Welch party, an English party, and an American party, and we turned iron masters and undertook to put all these parties through the furnace, and run out a party of Saints for building up the Kingdom of God." The message was clear. As important as the material accomplishment of producing iron might be, it was secondary to the spiritual accomplishment of "making saints," of creating a harmonious, cooperative community.

The story of the Iron Mission, as the authors tell it, is poignant. We see pettiness, shortsightedness and backbiting along with stoic, even heroic, dedication. The goal of fostering a successful iron industry eluded these true pioneers, yet theirs is a human story, where real "flesh-and-blood people" tried to stretch their limited human capacities to span the reach of their lofty vision. And despite hurts, resentments and grumbling, they persisted, their doggedness leading them willy-nilly to accomplish their primary goal, the making not of iron, but of Saints.

It is that communal ethic, the willingness to forego material rewards and individual satisfactions for the community good, that sets these folks apart, making them an anomaly in the West. Like Israelis in the Middle East, the Mormons seem to their neighbors to be cut from a different cloth, a source of bafflement and bewilderment, and hence ignored, shunned or at times even despised. Morris and Kathryn Shirts have brought together their story with a care and richness of detail that gives it life and meaning. Theirs is a solid and enduring accomplishment, an appropriate marker for the 150th anniversary of the commencement of the Iron Mission.

—Dean May
University of Utah

Acknowledgments

Pioneer manuscripts are the key to understanding this story. The archives of the LDS Church Historical Department, Utah State Historical Society, Southern Utah University, Brigham Young University and University of Utah have yielded many such documents time after time, thanks to the interest and willing cooperation of their staff members. Individual families in southern Utah have also been generous in sharing family records. Fortunately, Special Collections, Sherratt Library, Southern Utah University, acquired the files of historian William R. Palmer from his family, thus preserving many critical sources on early iron-making operations. Like him, I have shared in the sheer excitement of finding hitherto-unknown journals that shed light on aspects of the Iron Mission.

The search for answers also introduced me to the records of the Deseret Iron Company, to scholarly works dealing with the history and techniques of iron- and steel-making back to the eighteenth century, to LDS Church records, to historical works about Utah and to the deed books of the Iron County Recorder's Office. The institutions that have been especially helpful are the Southern Utah University and Brigham Young University libraries, the Utah State Historical Society, St. James Foundation, LDS Church Historical Department, Utah State Archives and Records Service and the Iron Mission State Park.

Concerning my own efforts, I have walked or driven over the trails by which the pioneers entered and left the area, including the roads they built into the canyons for coal and iron. I have personally examined the townsites and holdings of the Deseret Iron Company and corresponded with historians and scientists at learned societies and universities in the British Isles (including Edinburgh, Glasgow and Leeds) and with American iron- and steel-making organizations. I have interviewed curators of preserved and restored blast-furnace sites, professional geologists, chemists and physicists from the University of Utah, Brigham Young University, University of Missouri (Rolla) and Southern Utah University, and spoken to them about operational blast furnaces and refractories. Further, I carefully examined the restored Maramec Spring Iron Works, St. James, Missouri, and would like to thank the staff of the Maramec Spring Historical Park whose preservation of the iron works there provided crucial clues to many secrets of the Deseret Iron Company's operations.

During the preparation of this book, I made many visits to the old iron works in Iron County. In fall 1982, when city road crews partially uncovered the pioneer blast furnace site at 100 East 400 North in Cedar City, I obtained specimens of brick, furnace lining, cinders and slag. Dr. William T. Parry, professor of geology and geophysics at the University of Utah, analyzed them and coauthored an article with me ["The Demise of the Deseret Iron Company: Failure of the Brick Furnace Lining Technology," *Utah Historical Quarterly* 56 (winter 1988): 23–35].

I express appreciation to Southern Utah University, which generously granted me permission for sabbatical leave in spring 1982 to work on this project, not technically in my professional field. Even with major assistance, preparing the manuscript has consumed every summer and free evening since that time and, following my retirement in 1985, has been my full-time task, precluding alternate and probably less-expensive interests.

I likewise express deep appreciation to scores of individuals and organizations who provided important clues and bits of information that have helped document the work. Many individuals have willingly shared their time and talents in answering my inquiries. Although they are too numerous to include here in full, I must single out Leonard J. Arrington, Blanche Clegg, Janet Seegmiller, Alva and Zella Matheson, Lavina Fielding Anderson, Val Wilson, P. T. Reilley, Inez Cooper, A. Thomas Challis, Norm Forbush, Robert Elgin and particularly York Jones, whose specific contributions to my understanding of the structural layout of Cedar City's Plat A fort were essential to interpreting the whole history.

Gratitude is too pale a word to express my feelings for my wife, Maxine, and our children—Russell, Randy, Andrea, Robert and Steven— who willingly took "vacations" in the libraries and fields of most of the western states and in areas as far away as Missouri, Illinois and Nebraska; who saw family funds go for photocopies instead of ice-cream cones; and who regularly saw their father disappear into his files. They have remained interested and supportive even during my most obsessive moments. Special recognition is also given to Kathryn Hanson Shirts, daughter-in-law and editor par excellence, without whom the project would never have been completed.

I hope that this product of 30 years' research will prove helpful to other historical and genealogical researchers interested in understanding the faith, courage and sacrifice of those who helped subdue this wild and beautiful land.

—Morris A. Shirts

Coauthor's Acknowledgments

In 1994 my father-in-law, Morris A. Shirts, suffered health problems that made it difficult for him to continue working toward the publication of *A Trial Furnace: Southern Utah's Iron Mission.* At this point, because of my interest in his research and my admiration for what he had accomplished, we began collaborating to finish the book. Although Dr. Shirts had researched the production of iron after the initial furnace run in southern Utah in fall 1852, he had not yet written the corresponding chapters. Relying on his notes as well as on my own additional research, I completed the story through the decline of the Iron Mission. In November 1996, two months before he died, Dr. Shirts read over the new draft chapters and gave his approval.

The sections "Preparing for War" and "Disaster at Mountain Meadows" in chapter 14 are based on the following unpublished draft articles by Dr. Shirts: "Conditions Which May Have Triggered the Mountain Meadows Massacre," August 1993; "Mountain Meadows Massacre—Another Look," March 1991; "The Old Spanish Trail and the California Road through Mountain Meadows," January 1990, 15 February 1990 and 21 February 1990; and "Cane Springs: Its Physical and Historical Relationship to Mountain Meadows," 1 May 1989. They are located in Morris A. Shirts Collected Papers, L. Tom Perry Special Collections, Harold B. Lee Library, Brigham Young University, Provo, Utah. Dr. Shirts's extensive research into sites at Mountain Meadows lies beyond the scope of this book, but his insights are presented in Morris A. Shirts and Frances A. Smeath, "Historical Topography: A New Look at Old Sites on Mountain Meadows" (to be published by Southern Utah University Press). The concluding chapter on the causes for the failure of the iron works was adapted from a talk presented by Dr. Shirts to the Mormon History Association on 3 May 1986 as well as from the paper he coauthored with Dr. William Parry on the weakness of the furnace lining, published in the *Utah Historical Quarterly* (as noted earlier).

Within the book, spelling, grammar and sentence structures from the primary sources have been retained to preserve the integrity of the pioneer point of view and minimize the risk of inaccurate interpretation. If a quoted source is secondary rather than primary, we have tried to identify it as such and place it in historical context. To that end, the editorial talents of Frances A. Smeath were brought on board to check all endnotes against their respective sources. She also monitored the text for internal consistency, chapter to chapter, and continually reviewed primary source content to insure it was accurately and consistently interpreted in the text. Finally, she worked with me on revising the structure of the early chapters to flow in a clearer chronological and geographical sequence. Her insight and expertise were invaluable.

Unless otherwise noted, photographs in this book were supplied by Morris Shirts. Wherever mention is made of religious membership or ordinances, the reference applies to The Church of Jesus Christ of Latter-day Saints.

I would particularly like to acknowledge the help and encouragement of Janet Seegmiller, present curator of Special Collections at the Sherratt Library at Southern Utah University. Randy Dixon of the LDS Church Archives has, throughout the project, been equally supportive, providing the guidance needed to solve a number of key research questions. Valuable assistance was also provided by Eve Weipert, curator at the Iron Mission State Park; Russ Taylor at Perry Special Collections; Jeff Johnson and Val Wilson at the Utah State Archives and Records Service; Kent Powell, field service coordinator of the Utah State Historical Society; LaKay Weber, curator at the Daughters of Utah Pioneers Museum in Cedar City; Dixie Matheson of the Iron County Recorder's Office (especially for her painstaking work on chapter 4 documentation); and Russell Shirts, my brother-in-law and Washington County Recorder. York Jones and Rick Fish graciously provided valuable commentary on draft chapters of the project. My husband Randy has been unfailingly helpful in seeing his father's work to completion, accompanying me on trips to Cedar City, taking additional photographs, reviewing chemical data and tracking down unsolved research problems. Finally, I am most grateful to Heather M. Seferovich and the staff of BYU Studies for their continuing and enthusiastic support.

—Kathryn H. Shirts

Introduction

Only three years after the first Mormon pioneers arrived in Salt Lake Valley, a number of them were called to establish an iron works in southern Utah. Like their biblical counterparts, these modern Saints would shortly find themselves undergoing a trial of faith in the furnace of their own desert wilderness. They would have to struggle not only to secure food, clothing and shelter but focus simultaneously on founding what Brigham Young hoped would become the leading industrial enterprise of the region.

The venture began in December 1849, when the General Assembly of Deseret (the provisional legislature organized in what is now the state of Utah) authorized sending an expedition south, first to evaluate numerous reports of iron deposits there and then to begin iron production if feasible. Within the month, over the winter of 1849–50, Parley P. Pratt led 50 men on an expedition. His report was favorable and the returning party suggested a settlement on the banks of the stream they named "Center Creek"—the site of present-day Parowan. This location fit well into Brigham Young's plan to place Mormon settlements on all strategic approaches to the Great Basin.

Apostle George A. Smith, selected to head up the new settlement, solicited volunteers in June 1850, this time to establish an iron works in the unfamiliar wilds of what is now southern Utah. Initially, the struggling settlers in Salt Lake City and surrounding areas demonstrated little interest in volunteering. Church leaders subsequently began issuing, to a predetermined cadre of Saints who appeared to have the needed skills, one-year "callings" to the "Iron County Mission." It is correct to label this group "missionaries" because they were specifically commissioned by their leaders to found and stabilize an ecclesiastical society in the Great Basin. Nevertheless, their objective was more secular than religious, since they were primarily charged with exploring, surveying, settling and farming as well as manufacturing iron.

The iron missionaries were primarily men with frontier survival skills—many from the British Isles with mining and iron-making experience—totaling approximately 120, many accompanied by wives and children. Traveling almost a month through snow and bitter cold, they arrived at Center Creek on 13 January 1851. Their objective was to determine if the local iron ore could be successfully reduced to pig iron and useful articles made from it.

Although this gritty little group could not know it, the project was doomed from the start—not because they lacked courage or commitment, but because of circumstances they did not understand and could not control. Other than a few experimental items like cast-iron pots, crank shafts, gears, andirons, flat irons and fire grates, nothing of any commercial quality or quantity was ever made. The amount of pig iron produced by the iron works, expressed in tonnage over very short periods of blast furnace operation, impressed many but was, in fact, insignificant. This unique pioneering experiment ended on 8 October 1858, although the assets of the Deseret Iron Company were not liquidated until 20 December 1861, when the remaining holdings were disposed of at public auction.

Little physical evidence remains to suggest that this area was once destined to become the "Pittsburgh of the West." The Iron Mission State Park houses a few museum artifacts and maintains remnants of pioneer-era buildings. Beyond these, mostly unpublished family histories and brief descriptions in historical reference works only hint at the full story of this adventure in courage.

Initially, the pioneers must have thought that everything necessary for success was at hand. In southern Utah, deposits of iron ore seemed to be everywhere, along with the wood, coal and limestone needed to smelt them. Capable iron mongers from Europe were eager to bring the Iron Mission from dream to reality. Moreover, the entire project was motivated by intense religious zeal that did not stop short of heart-wrenching sacrifice. Why, under these favorable circumstances and after years of tremendous effort and sacrifice, did such a well-planned and much-needed project fail? The story begins with the first Spanish explorers to discover iron ore near present-day Cedar City and traces, before its end, the settlement of an entire region whose history continues to unfold.

Part I

"Iron We Must Have"

1

Prelude to the Iron Mission

1847–1849

The settlers called to smelt iron near the canyonlands of southern Utah were part of Brigham Young's plan to create and maintain a self-sufficient empire in the West from the Rocky Mountains to the Pacific Coast. Explorers as early as the Dominguez-Escalante party reported iron deposits in the area. Mountain men and adventurers found its natural resources worth developing.[1] The iron missionaries planned to go far beyond this. Their vision was no less than establishing a center of industry in the wilderness.

Driven from Nauvoo, Illinois, in February 1846 for their religious beliefs, the Latter-day Saints determined to leave the boundaries of the United States and seek refuge in the Great Basin extending from the Wasatch Mountains to the Sierra Nevada (see illus. 1-1). The first party reached the valley of the Great Salt Lake on 23 July 1847. Many Mormon pioneers, however, wearied by the 1,000 mile journey to the new city quickly rising there, found only a temporary haven. As early as 1848, the First Presidency of The Church of Jesus Christ of Latter-day Saints called men and women to begin establishing outposts north and south of the original colony. Unlike the haphazard settling of other Western communities—especially mining towns—each new Mormon community was carefully planned, following Joseph Smith's instructions for Jackson County, Missouri, and Nauvoo. The settlements along the Mormon Corridor, which stretched north to Idaho and southwest to California, absorbed new Saints as they gathered to Zion and helped claim large tracts of land as bastions against the threat of continuing persecution.

To further the goal of economic independence, some settlements had more specific assignments. The Iron Mission to southern Utah was one of the first of these. Cedar City in Iron County not only became Utah's southern gateway, but also took up the challenge of manufacturing iron in a wilderness. As iron historian James D. Norris has observed, "Unlike most frontier industries, the manufacture of iron required a large amount of capital, a highly skilled labor force, and some of the most advanced technology of the nineteenth century."[2] Although they were poor, the Mormons could draw on the resources of the entire community through tithing and special requisition to underwrite economic development. The Latter-day Saint missionary effort in Great Britain had already attracted experienced iron workers. Adapting production techniques mastered in England to conditions in the American West required flexibility, but the Mormon pioneers were used to making the most of what they had on hand.

Before the American Revolution, the colonies had been prohibited from importing equipment from Great Britain's foundries to preserve their dependence on the mother country. Nevertheless, all but Georgia had managed to smelt bog iron. Using charcoal from America's abundant forests, the next generation of ironmongers worked the rich vein of magnetite ore running from western Massachusetts to New Jersey. Foundries spread west to Pennsylvania, which became the heart of nineteenth-century America's iron industry, and then south to Ohio, Kentucky and Tennessee. In 1825, Thomas James, an entrepreneur from Ohio, learned of red hematite deposits near an abundant water source, the Maramec Spring in southeast Missouri. There, the following year, he founded the first large-scale iron works west of the Mississippi.[3] It was the "discovery" of iron deposits in southern Utah in 1849 which gave the Mormons the opportunity to attempt their own venture.

Discovering Iron along the Old Spanish Trail

In October 1776, an expedition led by Francisco Dominguez and Silvestre Vélez de Escalante, two Spanish Franciscans, left Santa Fe searching for an overland route to Monterey. They traveled as far north as Utah Lake, there encountering the Timpanogos Utes, but an early winter storm between present Milford and Cedar City forced them to abandon the attempt to reach California. Instead, they traveled south through the Cedar Valley area where Vélez de Escalante reported rocks containing almost 70 percent iron as well as large lode deposits close to the trail. The exploring party continued down Ash Creek before heading east along the Virgin River to the Colorado River, fording just north of the current Arizona border. They returned home in January 1777. Although the Spaniards lacked resources to found settlements along the

Dominguez-Escalante trail, Spanish traders roamed north, trafficking in Native American women and children who were then sold as slaves in Mexico. Ute tribes participated in this commerce, raiding less warlike neighbors for human booty to be traded for horses and guns.[4]

In the same year Dominguez and Vélez de Escalante were charting southern Utah, Father Francisco Garcés traveled from southern Arizona across the Mojave Desert to Mission San Gabriel, near Los Angeles. Fifty years later, in 1826 and 1827, the explorations of trapper Jedediah Smith covered terrain which linked the Dominguez-Escalante and the Garcés trails together, thus creating a route all the way from Sante Fe to the California coast.[5] Called the Old Spanish Trail, it was heavily used in the 1830s and 1840s by traders, trappers, couriers and adventurers, such as Kit Carson, George Brewerton, George Yount, Peter Skene Odgen, J. J. Warner and William Wolfskill.[6] The southwestern leg of the trail became known as the California Road. From southern Utah, the road followed the Santa Clara and Virgin Rivers to Las Vegas and thence to the Cajon Pass, San Bernardino and Los Angeles.

Some Mormon pioneers became familiar with the California Road after serving as members of the Mormon Battalion. The Mormon Battalion was a cadre of volunteers who fought for the United States in the Mexican War in exchange for much-needed cash to help the main body of Mormon emigrants move west. After its long march across the southwest, the Mormon Battalion mustered out in southern California on 16 July 1847, only eight days before Brigham Young's advance party entered the Salt Lake Valley. Jefferson Hunt, the battalion's highest-ranking LDS officer, led a party of 240 men from the Los Angeles area to Sacramento, thinking the pioneers were planning to settle in California. There he learned that Samuel Brannan, having arrived on the ship *Brooklyn* with a large company of immigrants, was en route to the Salt Lake Valley. Hunt, with a few men, the battalion pay and some seed grain, followed Brannan to the Great Salt Lake, leaving most of the other volunteers behind. It was some of these former battalion members who, employed by wealthy Swiss emigrant-farmer John Sutter, discovered traces of gold in his tail race and precipitated the gold rush.[7]

Brigham Young had already returned to the pioneers' Winter Quarters in Nebraska by the time Hunt reached the infant Salt Lake City in October 1847, but Hunt's description of fertile California convinced those left in charge to send him back there for more seed grain and supplies. On first traveling to Utah, Hunt had taken a northern route eastward from Sacramento along the Humboldt River. Returning south, he led a group of 19 along the portion of the Old Spanish Trail called the California Road, departing 18 November 1847 (see illus. 1-1). None had been over the trail before. They planned a 30-day trip, but it took 45, forcing them to kill horses for food before arriving in present-day San Bernardino on Christmas Day.[8]

After recovering, they made their return to Salt Lake Valley, leaving in mid-February with seed grain, 40 bulls and 200 cows. The bulls and half the cows died before the party arrived in May. A month behind Hunt was a second party of 25 former battalion members with a supply wagon and herd of 135 mules. This entourage, reaching Salt Lake City on 5 June 1848, proved the California Road a passable route for the wagon trains yet to follow.[9]

In October 1849, with the California gold rush in full spate, Jefferson Hunt's familiarity with the southern route brought his services into great demand. With Brigham Young's encouragement, Hunt accepted an offer of $1,000 to guide a company of 500 to California and then explore the area, looking for a suitable site for a Mormon outpost. Amasa M. Lyman, of the LDS Quorum of the Twelve Apostles, was already there on the same assignment. With Hunt was Apostle Charles C. Rich (see illus. 1-2), called to help Lyman, and three missionaries headed for the Society Islands. These were joined by a party of "gold missionaries" captained by J. M. Flake, a non-Mormon guide. The "gold missionaries" were sent as a special contingent by Brigham Young to enhance Zion's economy without luring the majority of Mormons away from their settlement tasks. The expanded wagon train continued on to Beaver Creek, 200 miles south of Salt Lake City, where Captain O. K. Smith, with 20 to 30 prospectors calling themselves Jayhawkers, also joined the company.[10]

Captain Smith flourished a map describing "Walker's Cut-Off," which would, he claimed, reduce the journey by some 500 miles. This won the confidence of a number of the travelers who headed off with Smith into the desert. Charles C. Rich and some of his missionaries followed Smith's group to keep them from perishing. When the combined party became lost and disoriented from lack of water, however, Rich broke with Smith, leading all the missionaries and two of the Jayhawkers back to the Old Spanish Trail where they reunited with Hunt. Some of those who followed Captain Smith into the desert did not survive. In their memory, Walker's Cut-off was given a new name: Death Valley. Hunt's party safely arrived in San Bernardino on 27 December, having lost only one ox.[11]

It was on this harrowing journey that Charles C. Rich became the first Mormon known to take note of the iron deposits along the Old

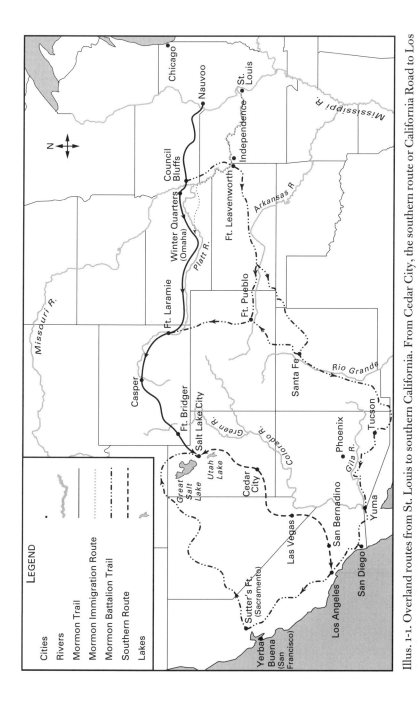

Illus. 1-1. Overland routes from St. Louis to southern California. From Cedar City, the southern route or California Road to Los Angeles generally followed the Old Spanish Trail.

Courtesy LDS Church Archives

Illus. 1-2. Charles C. Rich (1809–83) of the Quorum of the Twelve Apostles was the first Mormon to note iron deposits in southern Utah.

Spanish Trail. These were the natural resources soon to prompt the creation of the Iron Mission. Rich's journal reads:

> MONDAY 29th [October 1849] after traveling 8 miles came to a good spring at the point of a mountain in the south end of the Valley, 6 miles further came to Little Muddy [or "Coal Creek," the future site of Cedar City] a good sized creek, plenty timber & grass 8 miles further where we came to some springs [Iron Springs]. [H]ere we found iron ore.[12]

Addison Pratt, bound for the Society Islands, also noted the metal's abundance: "1st Novr [1849]. Went to Cedar Springs [Iron Springs] and camped. In the night had a snow storm, but it melted off by daylight. Near this spring is immense quantities of rich iron ore."[13]

On 18 November, Howard Egan, another Mormon wagon master of considerable experience, left Salt Lake City to lead a small Mormon contingent to California's goldfields over the southern route.[14] His contribution was to meticulously number the stops, give distances between them and comment on water, feed and campgrounds.[15] By 1851 a "Mormon Way-Bill" described campsites from Salt Lake Valley to Los Angeles, the distance to Parowan covering some 253 miles[16] (full transcript in app. 1). In 1854, Thomas Bullock compiled a more direct route, slightly reducing the distance to 249 miles. Both routes passed conspicuous iron deposits lying just a few hundred yards from the trail (see illus. 1-3).[17]

Parley P. Pratt's Southern Exploring Expedition

The iron deposits were especially inviting because the Mormons needed them so badly. They wanted to stake out and control a large territory and develop a self-sufficient economy within its borders. Freight was $200 a ton from Missouri and the Utah settlements needed "stoves, pots, rolls for squeezing the juice out of sugar cane, castings for sawmills, as well as mold boards for plows."[18]

The first purposeful Mormon exploration of the Coal Creek/Iron Springs area occurred during the winter of 1849–50. Acting by direction of

Photograph by Morris A. Shirts

Illus. 1-3. Iron ore outcropping near the old pioneer trail in the Iron Springs area.

Brigham Young and the provisional state legislature, Apostle Parley P. Pratt organized the Southern Exploring Expedition. On 24 November 1849, 47 seasoned men, traveling with 12 wagons, 24 yoke of oxen, 38 horses and mules, a brass cannon and food for about three months left Salt Lake Valley.[19] Eight of these men (marked by an asterisk in the accompanying sidebar) would later be associated with the Iron Mission. Pratt listed the entire company in his autobiography, under his entry for 7 February 1850.

The travelers were taking chances with the weather, and they were not lucky. By the time they reached Fort Utah (Provo), there was a foot of snow on the ground. At Salt Creek (Nephi), they detoured to visit Isaac Morley's 12-day-old settlement called Manti. At the time, Manti was the fifth Mormon colony, following Salt Lake City, Sessions Settlement (Bountiful), Provo and Tooele.[20]

Pratt's party continued exploring possible townsites all along the route, mapping distances and surveying streams, farmland and water supplies. In the Sevier River Valley, the group traded with Wakara, known among settlers as Chief Walker.[21] Wakara's band was suffering from the measles and, at his request, Dan Jones and Indian interpreter Dimick Huntington prayed for the suffering Utes and "rebuke[d] their meazles, by laying hands on them in the name of Jesus."[22]

Wakara's people were a significant presence in the area. After avenging his father, killed by the Timpanogos Utes, Wakara had moved south to the Sanpete Valley, establishing his base there. During the winter months, Wakara customarily moved further south along the Sevier River

THE SOUTHERN EXPLORING EXPEDITION OF 1849–50

Parley P. Pratt, president
W. W. Phelps and D. Fulmer, counselors
(Phelps also listed as topographical engineer)
Robert L. Campbell, clerk

First Ten
*Captain Isaac C. Haight, Parley P. Pratt, William Wadsworth, *Rufus Allen, Chauncey West, Dan. Jones, Hial K. Gay, George B. Mabson, *Samuel Gould, *Wm. P. Vance.

Second Ten
Captain Joseph Matthews, John Brown (also "captain of sixty"), Nathan Tanner, Sterling G. Driggs, *Homer Duncan, Wm. Matthews, Schuyler Jennings, John H. Bankhead, John D. Holiday, Robert M. Smith.

Third Ten
*Captain Joseph Horn, Wm. Brown, George Nebiker, Benjamin F. Stewart, Alexander Wright, *James Farrer, Henry Heath, Seth B. Tanner, Alexander Lemon, David Fulmer.

Fourth Ten
Captain Ephraim Green, Wm. W. Phelps, *Charles Hopkins, Sidney Willis, Andrew Blodgett, Wm. Henry, Peter Dustin, Thomas Ricks, Robert Campbell, Isaac H. Brown.

Fifth Ten
Captain Josiah Arnold, Jonathan Packer, Christopher Williams, Stephen Taylor, Isaac B. Hatch, John C. Armstrong and Dimick B. Huntington.

Source: Pratt, *Autobiography,* 365–66. The spellings are Pratt's.

to the Parowan basin, also home to the southern Paiutes. "Parowan" is a Paiute name meaning "bad, salty, or harmful water," referring to a small lake in the valley which has since dried up.[23]

The Utes and the Paiutes, although speaking different dialects, shared a language system with the Shoshoni Indians in northern Utah and Idaho. While the Paiutes, often called "Piedes" by the Mormons, were peaceful seed-gatherers traveling in small family groups, the Utes had acquired horses from the Spaniards, giving them greater power to hunt and trade. Wakara was especially ambitious, raiding ranches as far away as California for horses and capturing Paiute women and children to sell as slaves in Spanish territory.[24]

Wakara's first face-to-face encounter with the Mormons had been in September 1848 when he came with several hundred Utes, including the peacemaker Chief Sowiete, into Salt Lake City hoping to sell California horses and learn more about the settlers (see illus. 1-4). In June 1849, Wakara met with Brigham Young and other Mormon leaders in the Council House on the present site of Temple Square. Wakara was eager to establish a good relationship with the Mormon settlers, both to facilitate trade and to strengthen his position relative to the other Indian tribes. Aware of increasingly scarce natural resources in his homeland, Wakara also expressed an interest in having Mormons teach his people to raise their own food and livestock.[25]

With these considerations in mind, Wakara invited Brigham Young to send colonists to settle in his lands and live among his people. It is uncertain whether his invitation was to the Sanpete Valley, to his winter camp in the Parowan basin or to both.[26] When Parley P. Pratt and his company passed through the Sevier River Valley in December, Wakara was willing to show them lands to the southeast available for immediate settlement. Guided by Wakara's brother Ammomah, the expedition made note of a particularly good site at "Merry vale" (later Marysvale) before continuing their journey. Then, struggling through drifted snow against knifing winds, they battled forward three or four miles a day across the mountains separating Sevier River Valley from the Parowan basin. Because the basin had ramparts of mountains to the east and a small salty lake like the Great Salt Lake, the pioneers named it Little Salt Lake Valley (see illus. 1-5).[27]

Isaac C. Haight noted their difficult approach to the valley. On 18 December 1849 he wrote, "The snow two feet deep and drifted in heaps . . . Stormed continually." The next day, he reported that

> with much labor and toil we got our wagons all together upon the summit of the mountain and came three miles and camped as usual without

Illus. 1-4. Wakara (c. 1815–55) was chief of the Ute Indians based in the Sanpete Valley.

water. Our cattle almost exhausted for want of food and water. The cold was intense. Every man froze his feet more or less.[28]

In the comparative respite of Little Salt Lake Valley (present-day Parowan Valley), Pratt decided to let the exhausted oxen recuperate while an advance party went on, riding the mules and horses that were still fit. He and 20 men left the day after Christmas to go over the south rim of the Great Basin while the others established a base camp at the mouth of the canyon, where feed and fuel were more abundant. Continuing on a few miles, Pratt's forward company traveled through the area where the city of Parowan is now located, judging it to be a favorable place for a settlement because of its rich soil and water. On 27 December the group camped 20 miles further southwest, on the banks of the Little Muddy (or Coal Creek), the future site of Cedar City. In the official report to the territorial legislature, Parley P. Pratt and camp clerk Robert Campbell enthusiastically observed:

> But the best of all remains to be told, near the large body of good land on the Southwestern borders are thousands of acres of cedar contributing an almost inexhaustible supply of fuel which makes excellent coal. In the centre of these forests rises a hill of the richest Iron ore.[29]

Pratt and Campbell estimated that the combined resources of Little Salt Lake Valley and the land to the southwest could support 50,000 to 100,000 people.[30]

Although the group did not explore the "hill of iron," the forward party collected ore samples (described as "first rate" and "beautiful") over the next few days.[31] They then continued on to the area just south of present-day St. George. Advised by Native Americans from a village on the Santa Clara that the country further south was not suitable for settlement, they returned to the main camp in Little Salt Lake Valley.

Arriving on 8 January 1850, the men raised a liberty pole and prepared a feast. According to Isaac Haight, they picnicked on a wagon cover on the ground, "enjoying roast beef, mince and pumpkin pie, apple pies, sauce, coffee, etc."[32] The next day, he wrote:

> I shall leave this place with regret. It is one of the most lovely places in the Great Basin. On the East high towering mountains covered with evergreen forests and one of the most beautiful creeks running from them. On the west and south a large valley of the most beautiful lands. Little Salt Lake bordering the valley on the west and beyond a range of hills covered with verdure and backed with high towering mountains covered with eternal snows, all of which contributed to beautify the scenery and

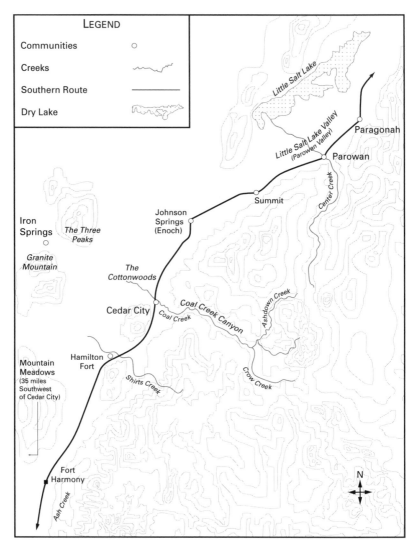

Illus. 1-5. Cedar City and Environs.

while the clouds hang heavily on the mountains and the storms and tempests are rearing [roaring] the valley enjoys a beautiful serenity.[33]

His nostalgia was not misplaced. The weather was ferocious all the way back to Salt Lake City (along a route comparable to modern I-15, west of the trail they had followed on the way down). Their animals, exhausted and tenderfooted from floundering through snow, almost starved for lack of forage. Finally, near present-day Fillmore, it became obvious the whole company could not reach home without help. They decided to leave the wagons with the younger men while the older men and those with families awaiting them would go on with the strongest horses.[34]

Pratt, along with 24 men and 26 horses, left on 22 January. On the south slope of the elevation later called Scipio Pass, drifts reached over 10 feet. The men broke trail for the horses, rotating to the rear as they became too tired to breast the drifts. Two horses gave out and had to be abandoned. Near the summit, the men shoveled down to make a fire pit and resting space, then wrapped themselves in blankets and tried to sleep. The next morning they took their hungry horses to the wind-swept hills where the animals could forage for dry grass.[35]

By the following evening, the party had crossed Round Valley (Scipio), fighting snow all the way into the pass about four miles south of the Sevier River, east of the present highway. That night it snowed again. Pratt's journal reveals his delightful sense of whimsy under difficult circumstances:

> In the morning we found ourselves so completely buried in snow that no one could distinguish the place where we lay. Some one rising, began shoveling the others out. This being found too tedious a business, I raised my voice like a trumpet, and commanded them to arise; when all at once there was a shaking among the snow piles, the graves were opened, and all came forth! We called this Resurrection Camp.[36]

On Sunday, 27 January, they again divided their forces for survival. Pratt, Chauncey West and Dimick Huntington took the strongest animals and struck out for Fort Utah (Provo) still some 50 miles away. Huntington, too weak to go on, had to turn back to camp. West and Pratt continued, taking turns breaking trail through knee-deep snow. They reached Summit Creek (Santaquin) at 11:00 P.M. and, extremely hungry, feet frozen, decided to stop for the night. They made a fire but still had "the coldest night we ever experienced, and after trying in vain to thaw out our frozen shoes, stockings and the bottoms of our drawers and pants, we rolled ourselves in our blankets, and lay trembling with cold a few hours." Rising well before daylight, they "bit a few mouthfuls off the last black frozen biscuit remaining," mounted their animals and, after traveling another weary day "living on a piece of biscuit not so large as our fist," they reached Fort Utah at dusk. Quickly reporting their dilemma, they asked for a posse of men and fresh animals. This was fitted out and sent right away, to bring in the rest of Pratt's men.[37]

Isaac C. Haight, 20 miles back on the trail, apparently had a thermometer, for he recorded that the temperature on the morning of 28 January was 30 degrees below zero. The rescue party found Stephen Taylor, who had left the main camp to follow Pratt, lying helpless in the snow about eight miles from Provo. He survived but had limited use of his limbs. The remainder of the party near the south end of the valley had weathered the night and the young men near Fillmore simply waited there until the worst weather passed, then came on to Salt Lake City in March.[38]

Called to the Iron Mission

Pratt's report helped the leaders in Salt Lake City determine southern settlement plans. Little Salt Lake Valley, which had so impressed Isaac C. Haight, became a priority site. At the April 1850 general conference, tentative possibilities took on a definite shape and purpose. George A. Smith (see illus. 1-6) was appointed to head the colonizing of Little Salt Lake Valley and build an iron works there.[39]

As a member of the Quorum of Twelve Apostles, Smith was part of the governing body of the LDS Church, second in authority only to the First Presidency (consisting of Brigham Young and his counselors). Not only were Apostles assigned to lead proselyting missions, they were also the vital force heading the colonization effort. By fall 1849, Ezra Taft Benson was directing the settlement of Tooele Valley on the Great Salt Lake's south shore. In February 1851, Apostles Charles C. Rich and Amasa Lyman would found an outpost in San Bernardino, California. After his mission in Europe, Rich would establish a community in northern Utah near Bear Lake. Apostle Orson Hyde would head settlements in Green River, Wyoming; Carson Valley, Nevada; and Sanpete County, Utah, while Lorenzo Snow, on returning from Italy, would oversee Brigham City, Utah. Although alternating service abroad with service at home could disrupt leadership continuity, it nevertheless gave members of the Twelve a broad overview of the needs of the Kingdom.[40]

Although such seasoned leadership was important, success of the colonization program depended upon the rank and file. The first recruiting announcement for the Iron Mission appeared in the columns of the *Deseret News* on 27 July 1850:

> Brethren of Great Salt Lake City, and vicinity, who are full of faith and good works; who have been blest with means; who want more means, and are willing to labor & toil to obtain those means, are informed by the Presidency of the Church, that a Colony is wanted at Little Salt Lake this fall; That fifty or more good, effective men with teams and waggons provisions and clothing for one year;
>
> Seed grain in abundance, and tools in all their variety for a new colony, are wanted to start from this place immediately after the fall, (Friday, 4th of Sept.) Conference; to repair to the valley of the Little Salt Lake; without delay; there to sow, build and fence; erect a saw and grist mill; establish an iron foundry as speedily as possible; and do all other acts and things necessary for the preservation & safety of an infant settlement among indians;—for the furnishing of provisions and lumber the coming year for a large number of emigrants, with their own families, and castings of all kinds for all the mountain settlements the coming Spring.—Farmers, Blacksmiths, Carpenters, Joiners, Mill Wrights, Bloomers, Moulders, Smelters, &c. Stone Cutters, Brick Layers, Stone Masons, one Shoemaker, one Tailor, &c. &c., in variety of occupations, who have the means, and are willing to sacrifice the society of wives and children for one year; believing that he who forsakes wife and children for the Kingdom of Heaven's sake shall receive an hundred fold, are requested to give their names, in writing, together with their occupation, residence, strength of team, wagons, grain, tools &c., for an outfit, without delay, and without further notice, to Br. Thomas Bullock, or leave the same at the Post Office, directed to WILLARD RICHARDS, Gen. Church Recorder.[41]

Courtesy LDS Church Archives

Illus. 1-6. George A. Smith (1817–75) of the Quorum of the Twelve Apostles was called to lead the Iron Mission.

When volunteers were not forthcoming, the announcement was repeated in general conference on 6 October.[42] Timing was critical. The new settlers could not afford the luxury of traveling in good weather. They first had to harvest their crops at home, then travel south over the winter so they would be ready to plow and plant their new fields when spring arrived.

George A. Smith took personal action, analyzing needed manpower and logistical skills and issuing calls to qualified men. At a 26 October 1850 meeting of the Seventies in the Bowery on Temple Square, he called 100 men by name to join the proposed 12-month mission to southern Utah. As Brigham Young explained:

> We want to plant a colony there and we don't want men to take families or little children. Those who are feeble or who suffer with lung complaints will be healthier here than there. We want to plant colonies from here to the Pacific Ocean.[43]

Brigham Young personally recruited John D. Lee a few days later, but Lee resisted. He had his house in Cottonwood Canyon "up to square," a family to care for and winter was about to set in. He offered to pay $2,000 for someone to take his place. But Young refused this offer and Lee reluctantly joined the company.[44] Nor was Lee's hesitation to accept this call unique. At Fort Utah, Isaac Higbee later told George A. Smith, he had, at Brigham Young's request, scoured the country for 10 volunteers to join the Iron County expedition and none would go.[45] Those called by George A. Smith were listed in the *Deseret News* of 16 November, along with an elegant plea for more volunteers:

> Brother Geo. A. Smith, the president of the mission to L. S. Lake calls for 50 volunteers, and it is right . . . that brethren who can, should respond to the call, and not press him, in the multitude of his cares, to run about the country to pick them up. Some of the brethren may have a delicacy in volunteering their services, and would say "I am ready to go if I have a call, but I don't like to volunteer; if the president wants me he will lay his hand on me and I am ready to go." Just right, brethren, exactly right; fifty of you not advertised in this paper, who can go (and you could all go if a mob were at your heels,) come forward and volunteer, for you not only have a call but the president's hand is on you, and you are wanted. The mission is an important one, as thousands of the saints will be ready to testify when they have spent a few years in the mountains without a stove to cook by, or keep themselves warm; a kettle to boil soap in; or a mill to grind their wheat, because there were no castings or iron by which it might be constructed. No mob is wanting to fill such a glorious mission, warm hearts will stimulate the whole. Come brethren, volunteer, and get ready.[46]

Identifying every Iron Mission pioneer is complex. Besides the call list in the article just cited, another in the *Deseret News,* published 11 January 1851, records "Names of persons over 14 years of age, on 21st December, gone to Iron county." The two versions are not identical;

OCCUPATIONS OF THE IRON MISSION COLONIZERS

Iron and Stone Workers		Woodworkers	
Blacksmiths	5	Joiner	1
Brick Masons	4	Ship's Joiner	1
Stone Cutters	2	Chairmaker	1
Forgeman	1	Coopers	2
Miner	1	Wheelwright	1
Collier	1	Millwright	1
Iron Maker	1		7
Machinist/Engineer	1		
	16	Farmers	32

General Service		Professional	
Tailors	2	Physicians	2
Storekeepers	2	School Teachers	2
Merchants	2	Surveyor	1
Butcher	1	Engineer	1
Shoemaker	1		6
Coal merchant	1		
"Woolenman"	1	Other	
Tinsmith	1	Yeomen	2
	11	Sailor	1
		Interpreter	1
		Currier	1
		Fishermen	4
			9

Source: List of occupations compiled from the May 1851 U.S. Census (see n. 46).

Apostle Ezra Taft Benson, for instance—who appears on the "call list" as company co-president with George A. Smith but nowhere on the "departure list"—was sent instead to Pottawattami County, Iowa, to organize the Saints who were still emigrating.[47] Chapman Duncan, too ill to go, joined the company later, as did Peter M. Fife and Daniel Carn.[48]

Another tally is Andrew Jenson's "arrival list" of 13 January 1851, which evidently drew from both the *Deseret News* articles.[49] The longest list is in Utah's contribution to the 1850 U.S. Census, begun in Iron County as early as 1 April 1851 but not formally enumerated until May.

By then the original population had almost tripled, primarily because many wives and children left behind for the winter joined their menfolk that spring. The accuracy of this census, however, is problematic. Names were spelled phonetically, polygamous families ambiguously entered and children under 14 often omitted[50] (see app. 2 for a comprehensive list of Iron Mission participants, collated from key primary and related secondary sources).

All four lists account in different ways for stragglers, late arrivals and dropouts. Despite instructions to the contrary, some 30 women—11 of them pregnant—and 10 or so children under 14 years of age also made the trip. Together the four lists create a relatively complete tally of Iron Mission members by occupation, as shown in the sidebar on page 19.

While most of these occupations are self-explanatory, two categories are puzzling: "fishermen" (Peter Shirts and sons George, Darius and Don Carlos) and "yeoman" (George A. Smith and Almon Fulmer). Peter Shirts had been called with others by Joseph Smith to provide fish for the needy Saints of Nauvoo.[51] Perhaps he humorously claimed it as his occupation in 1848 or wanted to indicate his pride in it. Why the two "yeomen" were distinguished from the farmers is unclear.

With Parley P. Pratt's Southern Exploring Expedition having prepared the way, George A. Smith's "volunteers" were ready to move south, bent on establishing an iron works that would supply all the territory's needs, from wagon wheels to andirons. The iron missionaries would be traveling over a fairly well-marked but snow-covered road where the hardships of winter travel would test their courage. Despite the initial reluctance with which many received their callings, they would, once committed, give the cause of the Iron Mission their best efforts.

As Jan Shipps noted in *Mormonism: The Story of A New Religious Tradition,* Latter-day Saints of the nineteenth century expressed their religious devotion differently from their modern counterparts. Attendance at formal Sunday meetings was irregular and copies of the Bible and Book of Mormon were scarce on the frontier. Obeying the Word of Wisdom, including abstinence from alcohol, tobacco, coffee and tea, was not yet considered essential to full fellowship. For the pioneer Mormon, sanctity meant sacrificing whatever was necessary to build up the Kingdom of God on earth.[52] Raising fences, irrigating fields, digging coal, and quarrying rock were tangible demonstrations of true spirituality. If called by their prophet to leave home and family in the middle of winter and found a new settlement, the pioneers were ready to do so. In the process, they found themselves transformed from ordinary farmers, blacksmiths, carpenters, millwrights, teamsters and forgemen into citizen-saints of Zion.

Endnotes

1. Rick J. Fish, "The Southern Utah Expedition of Parley P. Pratt, 1849–1850" (master's thesis, Brigham Young University, 1992), 5–17, 87–88; Ted J. Warner, "The Spanish Epoch," in Richard D. Poll, Thomas G. Alexander, Eugene E. Campbell and David E. Miller, eds., *Utah's History* (Logan: Utah State University Press, 1989), 35–49; William B. Smart and Donna T. Smart, *Over the Rim: The Parley P. Pratt Exploring Expedition to Southern Utah, 1849–50* (Logan: Utah State University Press, 1999), 3–7.

2. James D. Norris, *Frontier Iron: The Maramec Iron Works, 1826–1876* (Madison, Wis.: State Historical Society of Wisconsin, 1964), V.

3. Norris, ibid., V, 4, 11–12; Peter Temin, *Iron and Steel in Nineteenth-Century America: An Economic Inquiry* (Boston, Mass.: MIT Press, 1964), 20; Samuel Eliot Morison, Henry Steele Commager and William Leuchtenberg, *The Growth of the American Republic,* 7th ed., 2 vols. (New York: Oxford University Press, 1980), 1:101; Harold Underwood Faulkner, *American Economic History,* 6th ed. (New York: Harper and Brothers, 1949), 262.

4. Warner, "Spanish Epoch," 35–49; Fish, "Southern Utah Expedition," 87–88; Nels Anderson, *Desert Saints: The Mormon Frontier in Utah,* 2nd ed. (Chicago: University of Chicago Press, 1966), 124–25.

5. LeRoy R. Hafen and Ann W. Hafen, eds., *Old Spanish Trail: Santa Fe to Los Angeles,* vol. 1 of Far West and the Rockies (Glendale, Calif.:Arthur H. Clark, 1954), 109–119, 129.

6. Smart and Smart, *Over the Rim,* 3–7; Morris A. Shirts, "The Old Spanish Trail in Utah," 1–2, 17 Feb 1990; Morris A. Shirts, "The Old Spanish Trail and the California Road through Mountain Meadows," 1–9, Jan, Feb 1990: unpublished papers in Morris A. Shirts Collection, L. Tom Perry Special Collections, Harold B. Lee Library, Brigham Young University (hereafter cited as Perry Special Collections), Provo, Utah.

7. Anderson, *Desert Saints,* 72–73.

8. Milton R. Hunter, *Utah: The Story of Her People* (Salt Lake City: Deseret News Press, 1946), 102–3; B. H. Roberts, *A Comprehensive History of The Church of Jesus Christ of Latter-day Saints, Century One,* 6 vols. (Salt Lake City: Deseret News Press, 1930), 3:337.

9. LeRoy R. Hafen and Ann W. Hafen, eds., *Journals of Forty-Niners—Salt Lake to Los Angeles, 1820–1875,* vol. 2 of Far West and the Rockies, (Glendale, Calif.: Arthur H. Clark, 1954), 26; Smart and Smart, *Over the Rim,* 9.

10. Leonard J. Arrington, *Charles C. Rich: Mormon General and Western Frontiersman* (Provo, Utah: Brigham Young University Press, 1974), 138–41; see also Hafen and Hafen, ibid., 2:307–19.

11. James S. Brown, "Life of a Pioneer," in Hafen and Hafen, ibid., 2:118–123; Arrington, ibid., 141–48.

12. "Charles C. Rich Diary," in Hafen and Hafen, ibid., 2:184. Coal Creek was first named the Little Muddy, in honor of the Muddy River in Nevada. It was also known as the "Cottonwood" during the early months of settlement. "Coal Creek" was the established name by May 1851. For geographical references, see ch. 1, illus. 1-5, "Cedar City and Environs," and ch. 2, sidebar "Place Names along the Mormon Corridor."

13. S. George Ellsworth, *The Journals of Addison Pratt* (Salt Lake City: University of Utah Press, 1990), 385.

14. J. Kenneth Davies, *Mormon Gold* (Salt Lake City: Olympus Publishing, 1984), 201–7.

15. Hafen and Hafen, *Forty-Niners*, 2:307–19.

16. Joseph Cain and A. C. Brower, *Mormon Way-Bill* (Salt Lake City: W. Richards, 1851), reprinted in Hafen and Hafen, ibid., 2:321–24.

17. Thomas Bullock, "Table of Distances from Salt Lake City to Harmony" in Journal History of the Church, 19 May 1854, Archives Division, Historical Department, The Church of Jesus Christ of Latter-day Saints, Salt Lake City (hereafter cited as LDS Church Archives), microfilm copy in Perry Special Collections.

18. Anderson, *Desert Saints*, 121.

19. Smart and Smart, *Over the Rim*, 10–12.

20. Ibid., 8.

21. Ibid., 37–41.

22. Ibid., 45.

23. Ronald Walker and Dean Jessee, "First Contacts in Utah," draft chapter in *Brigham Young's Indian Correspondence* (publication forthcoming); John W. Van Cott, *Utah Place Names* (Salt Lake City: University of Utah Press, 1990), 288.

24. Walker and Jessee, ibid., "First Contacts in Utah" and "Settling Parowan"; Eugene E. Campbell, *Establishing Zion: The Mormon Church in the American West, 1847–1869* (Salt Lake City: Signature Books, 1988), 95–98.

25. Walker and Jessee, "First Contacts in Utah"; Campbell, ibid., 98.

26. Walker and Jessee, ibid.

27. Smart and Smart, *Over the Rim*, 45–52.

28. Isaac C. Haight, journal (part 1: 7 Jun 1842–Aug 1852; part 2: 9 Aug 1852–Jan 1862), typescript, 18 Dec 1849 Special Collections, Gerald R. Sherratt Library, Southern Utah University, Cedar City, Utah (hereafter cited as SUU Archives); original in possession of Herbert Haight, Cedar City, Utah.

29. Smart and Smart, *Over the Rim,* 109, 179.

30. Ibid., 179.

31. Ibid., 102, 104, 106.

32. Fish, "Southern Utah Expedition," 87–93; Haight, journal, 8 Jan 1850.

33. Haight, journal, 19 Jan 1850.

34. Ibid., 21 Jan 1850.

35. Ibid., 23 Jan 1850.

36. Parley P. Pratt Jr., *The Autobiography of Parley P. Pratt,* 4th ed. (Salt Lake City: Deseret Book, 1985), 368.

37. Ibid., 369.

38. Ibid., 369–370; Haight, journal, 28 Jan 1850. The remainder of Haight's terse comment reads: "We almost perished with cold. Came 12 miles; camped on Summit Creek. Had a little flour stirred in boiling water" (punctuation added).

39. Zora Smith Jarvis, *Ancestry, Biography, and Family of George A. Smith* (Provo: Brigham Young University Press, 1962), 146–47.

40. Campbell, *Establishing Zion,* 64–65, 70–71.

41. Willard Richards, "Little Salt Lake," *Deseret News,* 27 Jul 1850, 50.

42. Anderson, *Desert Saints,* 103.

43. Jarvis, *Ancestry,* 146.

44. Juanita Brooks, *John Doyle Lee: Zealot, Pioneer Builder, Scapegoat* (Glendale, Calif.: Arthur H. Clark, 1962), 154.

45. "Journal of George A. Smith, President of the Iron County Mission" (hereafter cited as Smith, journal), vol. 1 (7 Dec 1850–7 Apr 1851) and vol. 2 (8 Apr 1851–ca. 18 Nov 1851), LDS Church Archives. See 16 Dec 1850. As handwriting samples from Smith's personal letters show, the two volumes of this journal are not penned by him. The handwriting of Henry Lunt, who was Smith's officially appointed "private clerk" for the journey south, and who kept his own record of it, is similar to the hand in Smith's journals. Comparing these to Lunt's own diary strengthens the inference that he was the scribe, especially given the duplication of phrasing between the two records. Presumably, Smith not only dictated passages to Lunt as opportunity arose, but had Lunt write up entries in Lunt's own words. That Henry was generally the penman is confirmed by Smith in the entry for Monday, 17 Feb 1851, which closes with the comment "Bro. Henry Lunt wrote up my journal about 10 o'clock this evening." Note that typed transcripts of these journals exist, headed "Journal of George Albert Smith (1817–1875); Principal Residence during This Period (1850–51) Parowan, Utah." The initial typescript was originally in possession of Mrs. Luella A. Dalton, Parowan, Utah. BYU Library copied this in 1956, creating a second typescript now in Perry Special Collections. (A carbon copy of the 1956 typescript is in the Rock Church, Parowan, Utah.) The Dalton transcription, incorporating both volumes into one typescript, does not consistently preserve the

language forms and punctuation of the originals and in places even creates content errors. It should not be used as a primary source.

46. "Volunteers," *Deseret News,* 16 Nov 1850, 154–55.

47. Andrew Jenson, *Latter-day Saint Biographical Encyclopedia: A Compilation of Biographical Sketches of Prominent Men and Women in The Church of Jesus Christ of Latter-day Saints,* 4 vols. (Salt Lake City: Andrew Jenson History, 1901–36), 1:101.

48. "Biography of Chapman Duncan: 1812–1900," pp. 11A–12, under heading "Great Salt Lake this year 1850," in 1952 bound typescript, item 2, vol. 15, "Mormon Diaries," Perry Special Collections (subtitled "Parowan City, June 22nd, 1852," 2–3; copy in Shirts Collection).

49. Andrew Jenson, "Parowan Ward History, 1849–1900," 4–6, citing bound typescript, Perry Special Collections ("BYU copy"), made from MS loaned by Mrs. Luella A. Dalton. A note inside front cover of BYU copy describes the original: double-spaced, 134 sheets, single-sided, 14 by 8½ inches, inch-wide left margin punched to hold four binding screws; covers of medium-weight binder board in gray buckram with hinge bored to fit margin holes, but only two screws used (ca. 7 mm., too long to hold the document firmly). A BYU copy was made, table of contents and name index also compiled, the whole hardbound. Another copy of "Parowan Ward History" is on microfilm, SUU Archives. Jenson's authorship of this document is attributed by William R. Palmer, which is logical since it is typed in the same pica font as that on Jenson's Royal typewriter, which he used for many years. All cites in this book are from BYU copy.

50. George O. Zabriskie and Dorothy Louise Robinson, "U.S. Census for Utah, 1851," *Utah Genealogical Magazine* 29 (Apr 1938): 65–72; (Jul 1938): 130–42. Copy in Family History Library, The Church of Jesus Christ of Latter-day Saints, Salt Lake City. Note that Utah's census enumerations were not taken until 1851 but were later collated with the national census of 1850. A second transcript, made by William Bowen, collates entire territory census alphabetically (also in Family History Library, but not checked against microfilm of original by authors).

51. Journal History, 15 Jul 1844. Peter Shirts is the great-great-grandfather of author Morris Shirts.

52. Jan Shipps, *Mormonism: The Story of a New Religious Tradition* (Urbana: University of Illinois Press, 1984), 109–11, 124–25.

2

The Iron Mission Trail

December 1850–January 1851

By choosing to travel in winter, the iron missionaries were able to gather their fall harvest and still reach the new settlement site in time to plant spring crops. Early in November 1850, George A. Smith, as head of the Iron Mission, issued instructions for everyone in the company to rendezvous at Fort Utah during the first two weeks in December.[1] This short notice gave the colonists very little time to make final arrangements for their anticipated stay of at least one year.

Smith himself was so busy that it was almost dark on 7 December when he left Salt Lake City. On 3 December he had sent on ahead his fourth wife, Zilpha Stark Smith, in wagons handled by a hired teamster, 17-year-old Joseph Millett. Zilpha's two children had died, making her a logical choice to accompany Smith. Millett had agreed to work for eight months at $16 a month. He drove the baggage wagon and also held the candlestick for Henry Lunt whenever Lunt updated the trail journal, sitting in front of Zilpha's wagon with the camp stove close by to cut the winter chill. Twenty-six-year-old Henry Lunt, unmarried like Millett, was driving the other wagon. He was helped by a boy identified as Peter A. Smith, who may have been either an adoptive son of George A. Smith's or simply living with the Smith family. Millett refers to him as "Peter A. Smith (or Dibble)."[2]

In the next few days, George A. bought or traded for a yoke of oxen, a bushel of "seven-headed" wheat, two and a half bushels of oats, two of barley and 140 pounds of flour from a Brother Ferguson, handsomely supplemented by 1,200 pounds of flour from Alva Kellen, who lived in the area.[3] Smith caught up with some of the iron missionaries at Dry Creek (Lehi), about a day's journey northwest of Provo. John D. Lee, having left Salt Lake City on 11 December, arrived at Dry Creek on the 12th, noting that "at this Point a No of Families were encamped waiting for the co to gather."[4]

The entire company finally united at Fort Utah on 15 December 1850. The choice of rendezvous was sound. Abundant grass on the eastern shores of Utah Lake permitted the stock to rest ("recruit," the pioneers called it) and gain weight for the trip. Plenty of open land remained where travelers could stop to make last-minute adjustments on equipment without trespassing on private property. Jefferson Hunt, the Flake-Rich party and Howard Egan's group, all bound for California in October and November 1849, had left from here.[5]

Courtesy Daughters of Utah Pioneers, Cedar City, Utah

Illus. 2-1. Henry Lunt (1824–1902), George A. Smith's private clerk on the trek south, later led the settlement of Cedar City.

On 15 December, George A. Smith had the wagons circle around a fire. Standing on the running gear of a wagon, he addressed the assembly, naming the camp the "Iron County Mission" and declaring they were "as much on a mission as though we were sent to Preach the Gospel." He asked for their sustaining vote, affirming his appointment by the First Presidency to lead them, and all raised hands, saying "aye" in united response. President Smith insisted that all swearing and gambling cease and prophesied that "if this camp would be united hearken to council & remember the Lord when they lay down & when they [arose] in the morning & cease to profane his Name—that they shall go & perform their mission in Peace return in safety & not one of them should fall." Smith then appointed Elisha H. Groves as a superintending bishop to mediate any differences that should arise in camp. Other bishops with their counselors had been called to "Preside in meetings & to administer the Sacrament & to be like fathers to the camp."[6]

Company organization was typical. Joseph Horne, who had come north along the route the winter before on the return leg of Parley P. Pratt's southern exploring trek, would pilot the settlers. Henry Lunt (see illus. 2-1) would act as Smith's "private clerk" while John D. Lee would be "general clerk of the camp." Since the wagon train would comprise some 100 wagons, once it reached full strength, it was organized into two companies of 50 or so each. Anson Call was appointed captain of the "1st 50" and Simon Baker captain of the "2nd 50" (see illus. 2-2). These groups were further divided into "10s" (subgroups of 10 wagons each), as shown in the Traveling Company Organization sidebar.[7]

Although Henry Lunt seems to make no mention of them, both George A. Smith and John D. Lee frequently refer to "horse teams," but without further description. Context certainly implies horses hitched to wagons, but their exact relationship to the ox-drawn wagons generally and the 1st 50 and 2nd 50 specifically is never made clear. Since they are most often sent ahead of the main body for one reason or another, we can assume they were the fastest and most versatile component of the train. Whatever the precise configuration, members of the Iron County Mission left Fort Utah on 16 December and headed south, marked only by Henry Lunt's understated journal entry, "Started at 9 A.M."[8]

Courtesy LDS Church Archives

Illus. 2-2. Anson Call (1810–90), captain of the 1st 50, who shared duties on the trail with Simon Baker (1811–1864), captain of the 2nd 50.

Since the iron missionaries were generally following the route taken by Jefferson Hunt and Parley P. Pratt, signs of these earlier trains would still be visible. Virgin meadow and tree stands untouched by pioneer axes could easily be distinguished from soil rutted by hundreds of wagons and trod upon by scores of horses and oxen—even if the trail lay under several inches of snow. Heavily laden wagons quickly cut through topsoil, creating deeper ruts with each passage. Succeeding trains could pass to either side of the deepest grooves, terrain permitting, but even the widest roadways could sometimes cause extreme difficulties for wagons, especially when being driven through heavy rain or snow.[9]

TRAVELING COMPANY ORGANIZATION

Anson Call's Fifty	Simon Baker's Fifty
Aaron B. Cherry (captain 1st Ten)	Wm. C. Mitchell (captain 1st Ten)
Elijah F. Sheets (captain 2nd Ten)	Tarlton Lewis (captain 2nd Ten)
Elijah Newman (captain 3rd Ten)	John Barnard (captain 3rd Ten)
William H. Dame (captain 4th Ten)	Andrew Love (captain 4th Ten)
Orson B. Adams (captain 5th Ten)	Samuel Bringhurst (captain 5th Ten)

Source: Lee, Iron Mission journal, 15 Dec 1850.

Winter conditions kept the iron missionaries on the road for over four weeks. They had to take seed to plant in the spring and enough food to survive on until first harvest. Anything needed had to be brought; thus the wagon train also carried chickens, dogs, cats, geese, grain, corn, flour, guns, knives, ammunition, farming implements, tools for making iron, quilts, cooking pots, clothes, medicines, tonics and dishes. Most of the route was snow-covered. Although many of the travelers probably wrapped burlap over their boots for insulation, frostbite was common. Wagon stoves provided a little warmth when fuel was available. Later, as coal fields were identified, travelers heated their wagons by filling large tin tubs with glowing coals.

Courtesy LDS Church Archives

Illus. 2-3. John D. Lee (1812–77) kept a detailed journal of the Iron County expedition, and later founded Fort Harmony, southwest of Cedar City.

Winter travel was hard on the draft animals. The horse-drawn vehicles, presumably acting as advance parties, at times broke trail, but most of the wagons were pulled by slow, powerful oxen. Ice and rocks made even these sturdy beasts tender-footed and when they broke snow crusts for water their mouths became sore. Forage was scarce and they had to paw away snow to find winter-killed grass. They also ate sagebrush tips and browsed among cedar trees. Occasionally they received an allowance of precious grain.

The journals documenting the trip do not answer all our questions about the difficulties of daily life. There is little, for instance, about cooking meals over damp sagebrush or willow sprigs in sub-zero temperatures, about maintaining even the most basic level of hygiene among close-quartered travelers or about handling not only routine medical needs but also sudden, even life-threatening, crises on the trail. Nevertheless, it is intriguing to retrace, day by day, the long winter journey of the iron missionaries in such records as the Journal History of the LDS Church and the diaries of George A. Smith, Henry Lunt and John D. Lee (see illus. 2-3). For the most part, these sources agree. Minor discrepancies appear because daily entries were not always possible. The practical demands of wagon train life left precious little time and energy for journal-keeping.

Of central importance, nevertheless, are the perspectives of the three diarists. As a recent emigrant from England, Lunt did not concentrate on trail conditions as Lee and Smith did, yet he was more sensitive to problems of comfort and convenience than the task-focused leaders. Smith's journal and Lunt's diary frequently contain the same phrases. We assume Smith copied from Lunt on occasion, since Lunt was Smith's private clerk and would keep the official record up to date, Smith having too many claims on his time to do so. Compared to the somewhat general entries made by Lunt and Smith, Lee's phrasing is more distinct, containing many syntax and spelling variations but also additional detail.

A daily log of the trek south, collated from the three accounts, follows. It includes each day's camping place, with weather, trail condition and natural feature observations. Campsites and trails can be located with considerable confidence, using site descriptions and mileage records from the primary sources (see illus. 2-4). To help the reader follow the journey south, an accompanying sidebar provides a list of pioneer place names with their modern equivalents.

TRAVEL LOG

Camp 1. Sunday, 15 December 1850: Fort Utah (Provo).
Wind:	south
Morning temperature:	30 degrees
Noon temperature:	42 degrees
Evening temperature:	30 degrees
Distance traveled:	5 miles
Weather:	slight snowfall

Iron missionaries from Salt Lake and Utah Valleys had been assembling since 7 December at Fort Utah. It was here, on 15 December, that George A. Smith organized the pioneers into two traveling companies. Sometime during the night, Lunt noted, wolves killed one of the camp's ponies. After a discussion with Isaac Higbee of the local bishopric, Smith secured the services of young Thomas Wheeler, fluent in "the Utah language," to accompany the iron missionaries as interpreter during expected encounters with Native Americans.[10]

When the Mormons settled in the Salt Lake Valley, they found an area realtively uninhabited by Indians, although the Shoshoni from the north met there to trade with the Utes from the south. Utah Valley, on the other hand, was the home of the Timpanogos Utes and a rendezvous for other groups as well. Utah Lake teemed with fish and wildlife was abundant.[11] Because

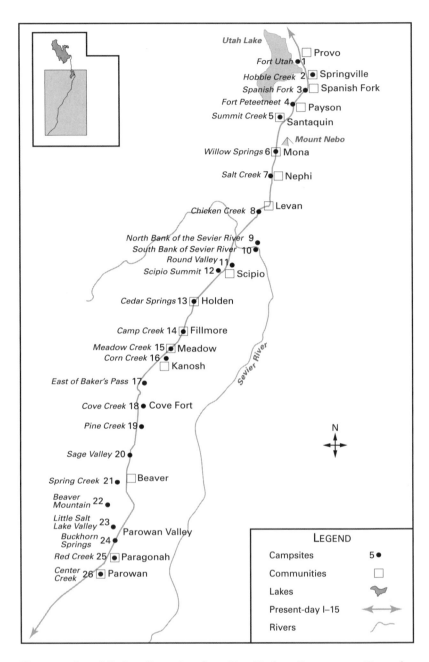

Illus. 2-4. Iron Mission Campsites from Fort Utah to Parowan, 15 December 1850–13 January 1851.

the valley was strategically located along the Mormon Corridor to California, Brigham Young was anxious to plant a colony there even though the Timpanogos Indians were constantly fighting each other. In April 1849, 33 pioneers settled on the Provo River (named for explorer Etienne Provost). By the time Pratt's Southern Exploring Expedition passed by that November, Fort Utah had expanded to 57 log houses.[12]

The uneasy co-existence between natives and newcomers exploded into conflict when, in January 1850, three Mormons killed an Indian

---

PLACE NAMES ALONG THE MORMON CORRIDOR
(From north to south)

Pioneer	Modern
Fort Utah	Provo
Hobble Creek	Springville
Spanish Fork	Spanish Fork
Peteetneet	Payson
Summit Creek	Santaquin
Clear Creek	Spring Lake
Willow Springs	Mona
Salt Creek	Nephi
Chicken Creek	Chicken Creek
Sevier River	Sevier River
Round Valley	Scipio
Cedar Springs/Buttermilk	Fort Holden
Camp Creek/Chalk Creek	Fillmore
Meadow/Meadow Creek	Meadow/Meadow Creek
Corn Creek	Hatton, near Kanosh
Baker's Pass	Baker's Canyon
Cove Creek	Cove Fort
Pine Creek	Pine Creek
Sage Valley	Wildcat Canyon
Spring Creek	Dry Creek
Beaver Mountain	Beaver Mountain
Buckhorn Springs	Buckhorn Springs
Red Creek	Paragonah
Little Salt Lake Valley	Parowan Valley
Center Creek/Fort Louisa	Parowan
Little Muddy/Coal Creek/Cottonwood	Cedar City

accused of stealing a shirt and, filling the body with stones, threw it into the Provo River. In retaliation the Utes attacked the fort and threatened to eliminate the settlement. Brigham Young, informed of the Indian hostilities, but not of the murder which aroused them, ordered the pioneer militia to drive the Indians out of Utah Valley. Over 30 Indian braves were killed, with others escaping to the Spanish Fork River. Although peace was negotiated with the remaining Utes, George A. Smith knew his expedition was traveling over disputed territory.[13]

Camp 2. Monday, 16 December 1850: Hobble Creek (Springville).[14]

Wind:	northwest
Morning temperature:	20 degrees
Noon temperature:	44 degrees
Evening temperature:	34 degrees
Distance traveled:	6 miles
Weather:	very muddy roads

According to Lunt, the two companies left Fort Utah at 9:00 A.M. They could rarely leave earlier—the long winter meant late dawns and early sunsets, often allowing only five or six hours of travel before seeking the next campsite.[15] The first stop was Hobble Creek, where they camped on the south bank at 5:30 P.M. Oliver B. Huntington and Barney Ward had explored the area in February 1849 as far south as the Spanish Fork River. During their night's camp, the bell horse broke its hobbles and strayed northward. They found it, hobbles still attached, near modern Springville, which they first named Hobble Creek.

When the iron missionaries stopped at Springville, the fortified settlement was just three months old. Only John D. Lee mentions it—perhaps because the train passed some distance to the west. Their route roughly parallels modern I-15.

Camp 3. Tuesday, 17 December 1850: Spanish Fork.

Wind:	southeast
Morning temperature:	32 degree
Noon temperature:	42 degrees
Evening temperature:	36 degrees
Distance traveled:	6 miles
Weather:	2 inches of snow that quickly melted, leaving the road muddy

The party left Hobble Creek at 10:30 A.M. In attempting to cross the Spanish Fork River around 2:00 P.M., they found themselves in a deep quagmire. The swampy passage was so difficult that Matthew Carruthers's wagon became completely trapped. Meanwhile, men worked to free other wagons, which, according to Lee, "required 9 yokes of oxen to get them through the sloughs."[16] Once they camped at 4:00 P.M. (or perhaps on the day following), the leaders considered the possibility of diverting the river into a more fordable channel and bridging it for future travelers. The route continued to roughly parallel present-day I-15.

Camp 4. Wednesday–Thursday, 18–19 December 1850: Fort Peteetneet (Payson).

Wind:	southeast
Morning temperature:	29 degrees
Noon temperature:	44 degrees
Evening temperature:	30 degrees
Distance traveled:	5 miles
Weather:	3 inches of snow

On horseback, George A. Smith, with Lunt and Lee in their respective offices of private clerk and clerk of camp, left ahead of the main body and detoured to Fort Peteetneet, so-named for a local Ute chief, Wakara's uncle. The wagon train broke camp on the Spanish Fork River at 10:30 A.M. and wound its way along the still-swampy route to make its next camp at 2:06 P.M. near the fort at the northwest corner of present-day Payson. James Pace, who hosted the Iron Mission leaders, had begun the colony with only 25 settlers. In March 1851, while visiting the Utah Valley settlements, Brigham Young would rename Peteetneet in honor of its founding settler. First known as "Pacen," the spelling evolved into "Payson," by which the town is known today.[17]

The first three days of the journey had been a useful shakedown. The pioneers shifted loads, made adjustments and waited for trailing wagons, knowing an extended line of march would be a liability as they entered Indian territory. For Smith, Lunt and Lee, much of the time was spent in writing. Smith drew up a petition for a bridge over the impassable slough and another regarding timber and irrigation rights. He dictated numerous letters, including one to Brigham Young, and took an inventory of equipment and supplies (see sidebar "Iron Mission Caravan Inventory," following Camp 5 entry, below). He also organized a militia for Iron County (see related sidebar) with himself as major and John D. Lee as adjutant. Nor had Smith forgotten Matthew Carruthers's wagon, still mired in the slough. He ordered an empty wagon and sufficient teams sent out to unload the bogged-down vehicle, insuring that Carruthers would be able to "role on, as he was wanted to go particularly as he was acquainted with manufacturing Iron."[18]

Late in 1840, the Nauvoo Charter, granted by the Illinois State Legislature, had authorized a city militia called the Nauvoo Legion, led by Joseph Smith as Lieutenant General. This military organization was reestablished in 1848, after the move across the plains, under the direction of Charles C. Rich, and was sentimentally called the Nauvoo Legion after its predecessor. On 28 April 1849 the provisional State of Deseret reorganized the Nauvoo Legion, consisting then of 11 companies (six cavalry and five infantry), into geographical military districts.[19]

John D. Lee recorded that the men of the Iron Mission also organized themselves into four military companies (distinct from the traveling companies already formed).[20] As George A. Smith explained in his letter to Brigham Young, written at Fort Peteetneet:

> Our military organization may appear strange to some of the officers of the Nauvoo Legion, and in fact some of the Iron County officers thought it rather odd. But it was organized to suit the wants of the Camp under our present circumstances.
>
> Taking the census of Iron County and also organizing and appointing and qualifying a Judge to preside over it before there is a single soul in it would to parlimentary men seem equally as odd. Should not this organization meet with your approbation, please write, and any change you may suggest, will be promptly attended to.[21]

While camped at Fort Peteetneet, Smith had received a letter from Brigham Young written 16 December 1850 outlining some contingency plans if the weather were to stop their southward progress:

> . . . we would recommend to you, if you cannot get further than Salt Creek, that we want a good settlement there; if you can get as far as Beaver Creek and should get hemmed in with winter, we also want a good settlement there, and as soon as the winter disappears, you can then lead out for Iron county, to fulfil your present instructions.
>
> Should you be hemmed in by winter at either of the before mentioned places, it will be well for you to build a fort, make yourselves secure, and when you leave in the spring, leave from ten to twenty men in each or either Fort until more assistance can reach them from this place. There is not the least fear but that your cattle will do well any where on the sides of the mountains, for feed is everywhere abundant

and fuel can be obtained at a very short distance from any point. The reason that we are so very explicit is, that you may not hurry, or kill any of your cattle, but preserve them and yourselves, and accomplish all the good you can. And may the God of Israel bless and prosper you, in all that you put your hand to do, and that you may return in safety to the bosom of your family and the society of those whom you love dearly in the kingdom of our Lord Jesus Christ.

Brigham Young

CITIZEN MILITIAS

The use of a militia (citizen soldiers) for defensive purposes and for the management of crises caused by natural disasters has long been an American tradition. Militias differed from other military forces in that they were composed of citizens who met periodically to drill, receive instructions and learn the discipline necessary to perform effectively in emergencies. A local militia force was necessary in the development of the western American frontier and was, for the most part, the only organized law enforcement agency in frontier areas. Congress provided for the establishment of militia units throughout the various states and territories, setting age limits of 18–45 years and prescribing the equipment each man was required to provide himself.

1850 Militia Organization for Iron County

Cavalry Company (35 men):	Light Infantry Unit (34 men):
Almon Fulmer, captain	Edson Whipple, captain
Thomas Smith, first lieutenant	Elijah Elmer, first lieutenant
James Lewis, second lieutenant	Orson B. Adams, second lieutenant
William H. Dame, first sergeant	Samuel A. Wooley, first sergeant
Rifle Company (35 men):	Artillery Unit (15 men):
James A. Little, captain	Jacob Hoffeins, captain
Elijah F. Sheets, first lieutenant	James Lausen, first lieutenant
John C. Steele, second lieutenant	[no second lieutenant]
Isaac N. Goodale, first sergeant	Asa W. Sabbin, first sergeant

Source: Ralph Hansen, "Administrative History of the Nauvoo Legion in Utah" (master's thesis, Brigham Young University, 1954).

Source: Lee, Iron Mission journal, 19 Dec 1850. Original spelling retained.

Source: Baugh, *Call to Arms*, ch. 3.

P.S. Please make out a schedule of your camp and leave with <u>James Pace</u> at the Peteetneet to enable me to take the census.[22]

Here at Peteetneet, two and a half years later, on 18 July 1853, the first shot in an escalating conflict between Wakara's Utes and the Mormon settlers would be fired. It would become known as the Walker War.[23]

Camp 5. Friday, 20 December 1850: Summit Creek (Santaquin).

Wind:	southwest
Morning temperature:	20 degrees
Noon temperature:	34 degrees
Evening temperature:	22 degrees
Distance traveled:	7 miles
Weather:	5–8 inches crusted snow on the ground

By this day, some members of the party were eager to move on. Smith sent riders out to check on straggling wagons but finally gave permission for the main company to proceed. Smith, Lee and Lunt remained at James Pace's, working until midnight on the travel roster and fair copy of the inventory of supplies and equipment.

Most of the camp moved out by 9:00 A.M., probably under the direction of Anson Call and Simon Baker, the two captains of 50, and pilot Joseph Horne. A letter from George A. Smith, printed in the *Millennial Star*, gives a colorful summary of the departure:

> We numbered one hundred wagons, and a number of carriages, and I assure you it was a sight to behold, to see this number of wagons winding among the hills and mountains, with each wagon having a stove pipe smoking, looked like a line of steamboats, the ground being at various depths, covered with snow.[24]

The wagon train traveled three and a half miles through five to eight inches of crusted snow on its way to "Summit Creek" where, Lee says, the men made camp around 4:00 P.M. Gustive Larson, who edited Lee's journal for publication, believes this is either a reference to Clear Creek (modern Spring Lake) or an inadvertent mileage error, since Summit Creek (modern Santaquin) is some six miles from Payson, the previous camp.[25]

Meanwhile, a Brother Gardner, apparently posted on top of James Pace's house to observe the road back to Spanish Fork River, reported the approach of the straggling wagons.[26] Eight arrived in the evening while three others were still in trouble at the slough. Once again, "an empty waggon & some 5 or 6 yoke of oxen" had to be sent back to rescue them. Despite these frustrations, the company made progress, all three journals agreeing that most of the wagon train traveled seven miles from Peteetneet (Payson) to Summit Creek (Santaquin), while Lee adds a comment on Saturday that shows they passed through Clear Creek (Spring Lake) as well.[27]

IRON MISSION CARAVAN INVENTORY
20 December 1850

Missionaries		Tools & Implements	
Men over 14 years old	119	Sets carpenter tools	9½
Women over 14 years old	30	Sets blacksmith tools	3½
Children under 14	18	Sawmill apparatus	1
		Pit saws	3
General outfit of the pioneers		Crosscut saws	4
Wagons	101	Plows	57
Carriages	2	Axes	137
Oxen	368	Spades & shovels	110
Horses	100	Hoes	98
Mules	12	Scythes & cradles	72
Cows	146	Grass scythes	45
Beef cattle	20	Sickles	45
Dogs	14	Lights of glass (window panes)	436
Cats	18	Nails	190 lbs.
Chickens	121	Stoves	55

Seed Grains & Food Stuffs		Arms, Ammunition	
Seed Wheat	35,370 lbs.	& Accouterments	
Corn	3,486 lbs.	Brass Cannon 6 pounder	1
Oats	2,163 lbs.	Guns	129
Seed Barley	1,267 lbs.	Pistols	52
Seed Potatoes	54 bushels	Swords	9
Groceries	1,228 lbs.	Ammunition	1,001 lbs.
Flour	56,922 lbs.	Saddles	44

Source: Lee, Iron Mission journal, 19 Dec 1850.

Camp 6. Saturday, 21 December 1850: Willow Springs (Mona).

Wind:	north
Morning temperature:	19 degrees
Noon temperature:	30 degrees
Evening temperature:	22 degrees
Distance traveled:	12 miles
Weather:	4 inches of snow

The main party left Summit Creek at 9 A.M., closely paralleling U.S. Highway 91 (no longer in use), traveling to a site Henry Lunt identified as Willow Creek or Willow Springs. George A. Smith and his clerks waited no longer for the 11 straggling wagons (presumably those of Captain Bringhurst), but headed out to catch up with the main company at this site, which Smith calls "Jewab Creek." (He is the only journal-keeper to mention passing, around 10:00 A.M., "a man, the name of Jones" going in the opposite direction. This was William Jones, the only iron missionary to defect from the southward journey and return to Salt Lake.) The three riders reached Summit Creek camp, which the main party had already vacated, and met up with them at "Jewab Creek." *Juab* was the white settlers' version of a Ute word, *Yoab,* pronounced *Jew-ab,* meaning flat and level. Smith gives their travel distance from Fort Peteetneet to this camp as 19 miles; Lunt, tracking the main party's mileage, puts their progress on the 21st from Summit Creek to "Juab Creek (now Willow Creek)" as 12 miles. These measurements place Camp 6 near the site of present-day Mona.[28]

Camp 7. Sunday, 22 December 1850: Salt Creek (Nephi).

Wind:	west
Morning temperature:	17 degrees
Noon temperature:	24 degrees
Evening temperature:	20 degrees
Distance traveled:	8 miles
Weather:	cloudy; afternoon snowstorm

Because of the cold weather (17 degrees) and absence of good firewood, George A. Smith authorized a Sunday drive to Salt Creek, 12 miles away. Leaving a note for the stragglers, which included a reminder to keep their wagons together and guard their teams, the main body moved on, reaching its destination between 2:00 and 3:00 P.M., camping on the south side of the creek where the pioneers found "First rate Bunch Grass water & wood." At 4 P.M., Smith called a meeting to explain "that he did not aprove of Traveling on the Sabbath but that circumstances advised us to do so at this time & when necessity required us to travel on Sunday he believed that the Teams—should have a time through the week to rest."

A major debate arose over Smith's plan to have a bridge built over Salt Creek, anticipating Brigham Young's visit south that coming spring. "The majority of the camp thought it useless to stop & Bridge the stream as it would likely never be past Fording," recorded Lee, but Smith repeated the need to carry out President Young's wishes. This was sufficiently convincing and the camp sanctioned the plan.[29]

Their route this day would have paralleled old U.S. Highway 91 from Mona to Nephi, scarcely eight miles, yet Lunt gives the distance as 11 and Lee says it was 12.[30] Examining the evidence, we can question their accuracy here. The group traveled six or seven hours, starting at 8 A.M. and stopping at 2:00 or 3:00 P.M., depending on the journal cited. The trail was frozen and slippery with three inches of snow. All these conditions would have made 12 miles an extraordinary achievement for the short wintry day.

Camp 8. Monday, 23 December 1850: Chicken Creek.

Wind:	northeast
Morning temperature:	16 degrees
Noon temperature:	46 degrees
Evening temperature:	21 degrees
Distance traveled:	15 miles
Weather:	cold; low clouds; snowing in the mountains

After breakfast, "as many men as could be employed to advantage. . . laboured till 9 when the ox teams roled on & the Horse Teams remained on the ground & finished the Bridge." This entry from Lee's journal is the first to mention horse teams as a distinct unit. Lee also notes that George A. Smith stayed behind to see the work through. Stragglers were beginning to catch up, for Smith writes that "[t]he rear Ten which we left at Capt. Paces crossed it, and pronounced it a good bridge. We called it the Rear Bridge." The day was dull and cloudy, the road slick and muddy, but past the small summit south of Nephi the track was mostly downhill. The ox-team company camped at Chicken Creek at 4:30 P.M., a quarter of a mile east of the road, at a fine spring.[31] Lee notes that "about Sun Set the rear of the camp roled in caral," bringing the Iron Mission as close to full strength as it had been thus far. All three journals record the distance from Nephi (Salt Creek) as 15 miles.[32]

Chicken Creek was a day's travel from Nephi, heading south, and the same from the Sevier River ford, heading north. There were no traditional campsites along these trails; wagon masters and individual travelers preferred to make their own. Favored sites had grass for the animals, a generous spring and firewood on the west hillsides, but also enough open area to reduce the risk of Indian attack. Probably any location between the Juab rail siding and present-day Chicken Creek Reservoir Dam would be a candidate for this particular stop.[33]

According to modern survey maps, various springs can be seen in Sections 16, 17, 20, 29 and 30 of T15S, R1W.[34] The Juab siding is very close to 15 miles from Nephi. Given this distance plus Smith's description, the Chicken Creek campsite may have been in Section 9 or 10, T15S R1W.

Camp 9. Tuesday, 24 December, 1850: north bank of the Sevier River.

Wind:	northeast
Morning temperature:	10 degrees
Noon temperature:	34 degrees
Evening temperature:	6 degrees
Distance traveled:	16 miles
Weather:	clear and cold

Three inches of snow fell on the camp during the night of 23–24 December. The travellers were already facing a new swamp, this one between the campsite and Chicken Creek. George A. Smith, concerned about the Sevier River crossing nine miles south, dispatched four experienced men that morning—Anson Call, Elijah Newman, Tarlton Lewis and William Leany—to explore ahead and consider bridging the river, while Simon Baker and Joseph Horne sought a passage around the swamp.[35]

Baker and Horne returned to the camp about 8:00 A.M. the same day and recommended swinging east around the head of the springs, then turning south, adding seven miles to the journey but avoiding the swamp.[36] The four men sent to appraise the Sevier River returned to report that the stream was "at least 150 feet wide & no material for building a Bridge excepting ceder . . . not Much tauler than sage."[37]

The company's drive to the intended crossing took a whole day of unpleasant travel "over a barron Hilly broken country covered with greesewood sage &c but no feed" until the Sevier River. To reach a camp-site near its banks, they descended a steep hill that was slippery and dangerous for the wagons and teams.[38]

This route apparently followed the southward drainage of Juab Valley to its southwestern tip, then went through the low-lying pass known today as Chris Creek. The "steep hill" would have been the bluff overlooking the northwestern tip of the Sevier Bridge Reservoir. Although the temperature had risen to 34 degrees by noon, it began "freezing very sharp" by 5:00 P.M. One hour later, when the wagons reached the river, the thermometer read six degrees.[39] The teams slithered down to the snow-covered, muddy bank and prepared to spend a cold night there.

Camp 10a. Wednesday, 25 December 1850: south bank of the Sevier River; one-half mile below the ford.

Wind:	south
Morning temperature:	-12 degrees
Noon temperature:	32 degrees
Evening temperature:	4 degrees
Distance traveled:	one-half mile
Weather:	clear; hard frost

Christmas Eve had been their most chilling night yet. As they got underway Christmas morning, the temperature was 12 degrees below zero. Sagebrush fires were hardly adequate against the piercing south wind. The party celebrated Christmas by cutting down the bank of the river enough to begin fording by 11:00 A.M. Reluctantly, oxen and horses inched into the ice-laden stream, the water coming almost to the animals' bellies and the bottoms of the wagon boxes. The exit point across the stream was a steep yellow bluff, especially slick for the unshod oxen. Even so, "all but two wagons were crossed this day; no accident occur[r]ed." According to Lee, the fording took from midday to just past sundown.[40]

As they climbed up the south bank, the wagons moved downstream half a mile to camp in better shelter, although feed was poor and the animals had to be pastured away from camp. As night fell, the main party saw 11 more wagons arriving on the north bank. It was Captain Bringhurst's stragglers who had been in the rear since leaving Peteetneet.[41]

Camp 10b. Thursday, 26 December 1850: Sevier River.

Wind:	southeast

Morning temperature:	**–16 degrees**
Noon temperature:	**28 degrees**
Evening temperature:	**4 degrees**
Distance traveled:	**none**
Weather:	**clear; hard frost**

Christmas night was even colder than the record-breaking Christmas Eve. The settlers had turned their oxen loose to graze for the night, but some, including two of George A. Smith's, were missing the next morning. While the wagons still on the north bank prepared for their own slow task of fording, men were dispatched up and down river to look for the oxen. An Indian camp was reported four miles downstream, but Henry Lunt discovered the tracks of "two head of cattle and two Indians" leading toward the mountains.[42]

This was the Iron Mission's first encounter with local tribesmen. To be on the safe side, Smith ordered 20 armed men, under Captain Fulmer, to go with Lunt. About 1:00 P.M., they returned with Smith's oxen, Bright and Balley, both with arrow wounds. Bright had been shot twice in the shoulder, but Old Balley had 11 wounds. Smith had the wounds dressed with turpentine and salt, but when it became apparent that these measures could not save his life, George A. had him mercifully dispatched, penning an affectionate tribute:

> The Oxen they had wounded were favourites with our family and had been in our Service ever Since we left Nauvoo and had travelled the road from their to the Gt Salt Lake Valley, three times over. They were at present owned by my brother, who loaned them to me for the Trip. They moved his family across the Plains and mine[,] ever faithful in all bad places, and perfectly handy and gentle, and willing to draw. I had formed an attachment for them, that is hardly conceivable to exist between man and beast. And when Old Balley goaded with eleven wounds, came up to my waggon tongue and lay down, groaning with pain and looking so wishfully to me for help myself and wife could not refrain from shedding tears. After dressing his wounds offering him food and giving him water which we had warmed, covered him with a Buffalo Robe. I felt that I could inflict almost any punishment on the head of his savage enemies, but when I come to see them [a father and 12-year-old son] two thirds naked (Thermometer below Zero,) half-starved and more than a third scared to death first thing I did was to give them some bread to eat, and place them under Guard until morning.[43]

In addition to losing what amounted to a personal friend, Smith had also lost an irreplaceable draft animal. But priorities had to be maintained.

While the missing animals were searched for and brought back to camp, the wagons still on the north bank were examined by Smith and Baker and pronounced fit to begin fording. At the end of his long journal entry covering the unusual day, Smith noted that "Capt. Bringhursts Co. crost safely over the River and formed into our Carell into Capt. Bakers 50." The whole of the camp was together.[44]

Camp 11. Friday 27 December 1850: Round Valley (Scipio).

Wind:	southeast
Morning temperature:	–8 degrees
Noon temperature:	36 degrees
Evening temperature:	3 degrees
Distance traveled:	9 miles
Weather:	9 inches of snow on the ground; a clear day; hard frost

The morning dawned clear and cold. After thoughtful consideration, George A. Smith passed judgment on the two thieves: with the help of the young interpreter, Thomas Wheeler, he claimed the boy in compensation for the dead ox, to which the father agreed, as the boy appeared willing. Smith had the boy dressed, fed and given to William Empey to rear, warning the father that no further misbehavior would be tolerated.[45]

He then moved the camp up the draw, south of the river crossing. The road was "slippery and sidling." Lunt recorded that near the summit the men had to grip the wagons physically to keep them from tipping over. Their route can be seen from the modern road and requires little imagination to confirm the description. This troublesome pass was the site of Pratt's Resurrection Camp the previous January, where two feet of snow had fallen in one night.

On the other side of the pass was Round Valley. According to Lunt, the group camped at 4:30 P.M. east of present-day Scipio, at a site providing plenty of cedar (half a mile away) and good bunch-grass for the stock, nine miles from their previous crossing.[46] There was no water, but since the snow was some 10 inches deep[47] they could easily melt it to drink.

Following camp assembly around 6:00 P.M., Smith consulted with the bishops, underscoring the policy that the horse teams would break trail and locate the most feasible routes to next water, while the heavier ox-drawn main body moved forward at a pace consistent with the strength of the animals and availability of forage.[48]

Camp 12. Saturday, 28 December 1850: Scipio Summit.

Wind:	southeast
Morning temperature:	3 degrees
Noon temperature:	36 degrees
Evening temperature:	4 degrees
Distance traveled:	6–7 miles
Weather:	old snow 12–14 inches deep on the ground

This day's journey, one of the most strenuous, began at 8:00 A.M. in subzero weather and took the party to the top of what is now called Scipio Pass. About 14 of the horse-drawn wagons moved ahead, while the rest, mostly ox-drawn, struggled with delays. After only two miles, the party had to cross a deep ravine. Here, the "forward irons" broke on A. B. Cherry's wagon. Repairs were made by lashing an iron bar across the break to form a splint. A wheel on Gideon Wood's wagon also broke, "but necessity being the Mother of invention a Plough Beam was lashed on the under side of the wheel which served as a sleigh runner."[49]

About two miles farther on they entered a canyon covered with scrub cedar and worked upward through deepening snow. To avoid another deep ravine, the party ascended the right side of the mountain. Simon Baker's 2nd 50 stopped "a short distance back" to repair another wheel apparently broken on the climb, while the "forward 50" moved slowly ahead. About 3:30 P.M., they reached the summit "where we had a fair view of the Powvan Valley."[50] There was not enough daylight for the tired ox teams to descend the southern slope to Cedar Springs (also known then as Pioneer Spring and Explorer Springs, but now as Holden), so they made a dry camp in a little valley near some cedars.

Some of the exhausted oxen were left by the wayside between the summit and the evening camp. Lee makes a special point of recording the close relationship between George A. Smith and his slowly recovering ox, Bright:

> Pres. G. A. Smith with his own hand took a camp kettle & by a Log heap Fire Melted Snow & watered his favorite ox which had been wounded at the Severe River by the Indians, the old fellow new well his Master's waggon & frequently when Traveling would voluntarily walk in front [of] his waggon & crowd himself against the team as though he wished to assist by taking his place in Rank, others followed the Example, melted snow & watered their weak cattle.[51]

Camp 13. Sunday, 29 December 1850: Cedar Springs or Buttermilk Fort[52] (Holden).

Morning temperature:	12 degrees
Noon temperature:	30 degrees
Evening temperature:	14 degrees
Distance traveled:	6 miles
Weather:	6 inches of snow; fine and frosty

The colonists roused very early. Smith gives the starting hour as 7:00 A.M., Lee even earlier, saying the cattle were yoked and the camp on the move by 6:30. Part of the group, presumably the ox teams, reached Cedar Springs[53] at 1:00 P.M., as Smith says they overtook the horse teams there. Baker's company came in around 5:00 P.M. The snow dwindled from two feet in the canyon to six inches at Cedar Springs.[54] Here they had plenty of water, firewood and feed for the stock. Everyone felt a sense of achievement and relaxed after the strenuous trip over the summit. Smith records storytelling, talking and listening to music from violins and accordions while sitting around the campfires that night. With heartfelt satisfaction, he closed that evening's journal entry, writing that

> The perfect good humour which prevails and good health in the Company, notwithstanding the severe cold and deep Snows which we have had to encounter whilst passing over high Mountains which would be no small obstacle even in Summer, is really remarkable.[55]

Camp 14. Monday, 30 December 1850: Camp Creek or Chalk Creek (Fillmore).

Morning temperature:	16 degrees
Noon temperature:	32 degrees
Evening temperature:	18 degrees
Distance traveled:	12 miles
Weather:	3 inches of snow on ground; frosty day

The party resumed its trek south at 9:00 A.M. The hind axle broke on Andrew Love's wagon near Pioneer Creek and Elijah Sheets, captain of the 2nd 10 in Call's company, was sent back to help Love redistribute his load and tow the broken wagon to Camp Creek, some six miles ahead. Lee records that the name came from Pratt's Southern Exploring Expedition having camped there, while Lunt and Smith describe the same location, now Fillmore, as Chalk Creek because of abundant chalk deposits nearby. Not for the last time, George A. Smith noted the snow glare: "At midday . . . its effect on my eyes is almost unbearable." Long exposure triggered severe headaches and near-blindness.[56]

The party had hoped to find enough large timber to bridge Camp Creek but there was none, so they forded instead. After camping at 4:00 P.M., they immediately began making charcoal so that blacksmith Burr Frost could mend Love's axle. This involved splitting dry cedar and then burning it in a covered pit for about eight hours without letting it blaze, probably by keeping it lightly covered with dirt. Smith issued the instructions, estimating they could produce about 15 bushels of charcoal overnight. Around dark, Love, the wagons of his 10, and his "rescuer" Elijah Sheets, with his 10, brought Love's broken wagon into camp.[57]

Camp 15a. Tuesday, 31 December 1850: Meadow/Meadow Creek.

Morning temperature:	22 degrees
Noon temperature:	32 degrees
Evening temperature:	22 degrees
Distance traveled:	5–7 miles
Weather:	cloudy; cold; frosty

The morning was busy. Men from each company cut down the creek banks to improve the crossing, others helped prepare the temporary forge, some rounded up cattle and a few went with Elijah Newman in search of chalk. The charcoal-making efforts were successful and Burr Frost welded a reforged axle back onto Andrew Love's wagon. The horse teams "remained on the ground" until repairs were done, but by 10:00 A.M. the rest of the camp had moved out. Smith notes that "Brother Shirts went down Meadow Creek for about eight miles hunting deer. He reported some cottonwood on the creek stream rapid, and as large as that of Camp Creek. It sinks at this place and forms a large meadow, excellent soil of a dark reddish color." Although it was cloudy, Smith spent most of the day in his wagon, his sore eyes covered from the light.[58]

At 3:00 P.M., the brigade camped on Meadow Creek, a mile west of the present-day town of Meadow. The riders were impressed with the richness of the soil and the water, but the site lacked a nearby wood supply. At midnight, Edson Whipple, in his official capacity as Officer of the Guard, loudly wished the camp "Happy New Year!"[59]

Camp 15b. Wednesday, 1 January 1851: Meadow/Meadow Creek.

Morning temperature:	22 degrees
Noon temperature:	36 degrees
Evening temperature:	22 degrees
Distance traveled:	none; day of rest
Weather:	morning clear

Because Christmas Day had been taken up with the struggle at the Sevier, the company voted to lay over for New Year's Day. Some of the men procured cedar from nearby hills while others rested. Still hunting deer, Peter Shirts went upstream, probably taking his sons with him. According to Smith, Shirts optimistically reported:

> The Land excellent all the way accept about ½ mile of Sage Brush, went up the mountain which (he says is composed of red Sand Stone) about 3 miles; he could see an open Valley as far as the eye could extend, also a Lake which he thinks is 70 miles long, and many bodies of Ceadars on the Plains.[60]

Smith spent the day in his wagon listening to John D. Lee read *The Poor Cousins,* a "romance." Meanwhile the wives of the journal writers—Zilpha Smith, Mary (Polly) Lee and Lovina Lee—prepared a festive dinner for their families.[61] Joseph Millett records that he ate with the Smith family in their tent, also joined by "Pul-wah," a French teamster working for John D. Lee.[62] Lee identifies this individual as Paul Royls, and he is included in the Iron Mission roster both as "Pull Wah" and "Paul Ray." Joseph Millet's account also mentions Peter A. Smith (Dibble), the driver of Zilpha Smith's wagon, as a teamster.[63] By the light of a cedar bonfire, the pioneers held a dance that evening. Zilpha did not attend, "being some what fatigued from exercise." The "exercise" was probably cooking all day around the campfire.[64]

Camp 16. Thursday, 2 January 1851: Corn Creek (Hatton, near Kanosh).

Morning temperature:	18 degrees
Noon temperature:	34 degrees
Evening temperature:	18 degrees
Distance traveled:	5 miles
Weather:	cloudy and frosty

The camp set off at 10:00 A.M., traveled five miles over relatively easy terrain toward the lava-strewn area to the southwest and stopped at Corn

Creek between noon and 12:30, leaving the remainder of the day for exploring. The site derived its name from the surprising discovery of land already under cultivation. John D. Lee recorded that

> about 2 acres of land was fenced with willow poles sticking them in the ground at the distance of about 3 feet apart & with bark tied willow poles horrizontally across them & in those little gardens or patches corn wheat & Beans had been cultivated Brought to maturity & harvested this present season (that is now past) & from the appearance of stocks cobs & stubble the crops were of a Rich strong growth. . . . [O]n the North Side of this Stream near the field refered too, were signs of an heavy Encampment of Indians—from appearance had been encamped during harvest time & had left some time in Autumn—from the no[.] of Wickeups it was supposed that there must have been near 500 Indians.[65]

Peter Shirts once again made a foray up Corn Creek, finding "straight & handsome" cedar trees and "considerable Oak & some Maple." "Above all," he found "Iron ore of the best quality." Shirts felt the canyon could be easily reached and its waters properly harnessed for powering "Mills & Machineries." President Smith was particularly encouraged by this unexpected evidence of a land rich enough in resources and fertility to support a large population.[66]

Camp 17. Friday, 3 January 1851: east of Baker's Pass.

Morning temperature:	12 degrees
Noon temperature:	28 degrees
Evening temperature:	10 degrees
Weather:	dense fog; low-hanging clouds; no wind; 3 inches of snow on the ground; 10–15 inches on the summit

The journal accounts for this day do not exactly correspond, but from them we can make a fair composite of events. President George A. Smith instructed Barnard's 10 and six teams of Bringhurst's 10 (both of Baker's 2nd 50) to accompany the horse teams, all of which were sent on ahead with Joseph Horne, the pilot. They were to break trail for the slower ox teams and find water as soon as possible—most likely Cove Creek, which lay some 20 miles ahead.

William Palmer, an early chronicler of southern Utah history, expressed the opinion in his personal writings that Baker's 2nd 50 forged ahead at this point in an attempt to beat Anson Call's 1st 50 into the Little Salt Lake Valley. The fact that President Smith himself ordered Baker's men to advance with the horse teams belies the notion that the companies were engaged in an ox team race. On the contrary, as Lee notes, it was established policy "to change fronts" so that the physical strain on men, beasts and wagons might be distributed as equally as possible. All three journals note dense fog or heavy cloud this day. Lee documents an extinct volcano to their left, graphically describing its

Courtesy Daughters of Utah Pioneers Museum, Salt Lake City

Illus. 2-5. Joseph Horne (1812–97) who explored southern Utah with Parley P. Pratt's expedition, acted as a trail guide for the iron missionaries.

> large mass of huge rocks & broken fragments that lay scattered in every direction—that the convulsive groans of nature had tested the firmness of it[s] deep laid foundation upon examination the whole mountain had been doubtless subjected to the action of Fire; there being the appearance among the mass of burnt Lava & Pouris [porous] stone & even the large stone that remained partly whole appeared as though at some period of time that a welding heat had been taken upon them leaving them the colour of Rich Iron ore.[67]

Today this unique feature can easily be seen east of I-15 and it definitely locates the traveling route as east of and parallel to the modern freeway.

The advance contingent from Baker's 2nd 50 under Barnard and Bringhurst traveled all day. Their pilot, Joseph Horne (see illus. 2-5), however, had never been over this trail going south. Becoming disoriented in heavy fog, he apparently mistook White Sage Flats (some 17 miles southwest of Corn Creek) for Dog Valley (almost four miles further south, to the east of the main trail). He was looking for the pass through Dog Valley to Cove Creek, but coming from the opposite direction, lost his way. As a result, he took his horse contingent into the mountains too far north to connect with the pass. Presumably it was at this point that his advance party split into two groups. All or some of the horse teams apparently continued forward in the fog, trying to regain the path. This left the ox teams of Barnard and Bringhurst partway up the northern slope of the mountainside, tiring fast, with some of them possibly near its summit. Horne sent back word "to inform the rear" that he "had taken the wrong r[oa]d he feared, & where it lead he had no idea."[68]

Camp 18a. Saturday, 4 January 1851: Cove Creek (Cove Fort).[69]

Morning temperature:	o degrees
Noon temperature:	50 degrees
Evening temperature:	28 degrees
Distance traveled:	9 miles
Weather:	15 inches of snow on the summit; cloudy and overcast.

After a night's rest, Baker, who had remained with the main company, was delegated to reconnoiter on horseback and find the route for which Horne had been searching. Returning to camp by 9:00 A.M., he "reported a pass through the mountains about ½ mile to the right"[70] of their present camp. On their way by 10:00 A.M., the party first crossed a short steep hill, then found themselves in a pass, where they "halted on a splendid spot of grass and let the teams bait about one hour."[71] The pass led directly to a little basin, through which they traveled for about five miles, finding themselves then where the "forward camp had been," supposedly still lost.

The pioneers named the pass Baker's Canyon. The basin became Dog Valley, after its prairie dog villages. Smith and the main body crossed Dog Valley and moved up a drainage area along foothills on the southeast side of the valley, ascending the hills to a second pass. The steep, dangerous trail required them to attach tow-ropes to the wagons to keep upright and maneuverable at the steepest places.[72] Toward the summit, the force of the sun caused Smith to make a special note: "Whilst passing through the narrow ravines the reflection of the sun's rays on the snow, was such that it sensibly affected our cattle and had no mercy on my weak eyes."[73]

Aside from the problems Horne's difficulties in the fog had caused, the travelers were beginning to come together. Once Horne and the horse teams reached the summit, they found themselves above the clouds, and the pilot quickly recognized where he was. About two miles past the steep passage, the main body reached a creek in a small valley resembling a cove, which they sensibly named Cove Creek. Here they found plenty of running water, good firewood and ample feed for the livestock. A little after dark, Lee noted, the rear of the company rolled into camp and "here the whole mission camped together."[74]

Camp 18b. Sunday, 5 January 1851: Cove Creek (Cove Fort).

Morning temperature:	28 degrees

Noon temperature:	40 degrees
Evening temperature:	28 degrees
Distance traveled:	none
Weather:	cloudy and thawing

On Sunday morning, Smith had the party up early checking on animals and equipment. He walked around the camp "animating and encouraging the men," intending an early departure Monday. At noon, the group assembled inside the corral of wagons to listen to President Smith preach. He reminded them why they had undertaken their challenging endeavor in the dead of winter: while the world was motivated by self-interest, the iron missionaries were united in the cause of building Zion. Because of the "Justice and Righteousness . . . written upon every man's Heart" camp rules were, as yet, unnecessary. He then offered practical advice, urging the men to be careful with firearms and to guard the precious livestock. He apologized for triggering resentment, in a previous sermon, among British members of the company by extolling American success in battles against England. "I hope never again to excite that kind of National Feelings," Smith affirmed, since "all governments on earth but one are corrupt & that is the government of God."[75]

At this meeting, Robert Wiley was appointed chorister of the "Iron County Choir," consisting of Wiley, Richard Harrison, Henry Lunt, Thomas Cartwright, Richard Benson, John Sanderson, George and Mary Wood and William C. Mitchell Jr. and Sr. That evening Henry Lunt reported a "lively appearance" in camp as everyone gathered around the campfires, singing the songs of Zion.[76]

Camp 19. Monday, 6 January 1851: Pine Creek.
Morning temperature:	28 degrees
Noon temperature:	32 degrees
Evening temperature:	28 degrees
Distance traveled:	6 miles
Weather:	cloudy and thawing; no new snow

The first task this morning was rounding up the stock, which had scattered after their full day of rest. Each journal notes how footsore the animals were, especially the oxen, who suffered from plodding relentlessly over crusted snow, frozen mud and rocks. One of George A. Smith's oxen had a wooden stub imbedded in a hoof. Smith extracted it with difficulty, filled the cavity with tar and shod the ox, pressing his healing animal, Bright, into duty as replacement. Wolves had already killed three oxen since the trip began, and a fourth, from Jacob Hofhein's span, was devoured this day.[77]

The camp got underway at 9:30 A.M., but after two miles, "the 1st 10 by order of the Pres" stopped until Edson Whipple could return from searching for his missing ox, which he found by midday. The going thereafter was relatively easy; the snow diminished rapidly. They traveled six miles, according to Lunt and Smith, seven according to Lee. The new camp offered plenty of grass and cedar for firewood. Because they could see a stand of what artist Solomon N. Carvalho later identified as "Norway pines" on a nearby mountain, they called this site Pine Creek.[78]

Camp 20. Tuesday, 7 January 1851: Sage Valley (Wild Cat Canyon).

Morning temperature:	**28 degrees**
Noon temperature:	**36 degrees**
Evening temperature:	**22 degrees**
Distance traveled:	**9 miles**
Weather:	**12–26 inches of snow on the ground with drifts; light skiff of new snow**

This day's travel was more difficult. The train moved south about five miles through sage, scrub cedars and cobblestones, which further punished the oxen. Some of the men took the hide off Hofhein's dead ox and made "moccasins" for their own beasts, an awkward and temporary remedy, but urgently needed.[79]

It is difficult to determine their exact route. Lee's comments suggest the party passed through scrub cedar and sagebrush (near the current highway rest stop) to the head of the valley—east of and roughly parallel to present-day I-15. After reaching the summit near exit 125 of I-15, they turned east to avoid the nearly perpendicular walls of upper Mud Creek Canyon, probably then filled with drifted snow.[80]

By the time they reached the divide, the group had come about six miles. The remaining three took them across the heads of a few hollows draining into Wild Cat Canyon. They followed this canyon into what they called Sage Valley, probably camping slightly north of the modern I-15 Manderfield exit (exit 120).[81]

Camp 21. Wednesday, 8 January 1851: Spring Creek (Dry Creek, near present-day Beaver).

Wind:	**high**
Morning temperature:	**24 degrees**

Noon temperature:	34 degrees
Evening temperature:	20 degrees
Distance traveled:	13 miles
Weather:	snow squall till noon; 2 inches of new snowfall during the night; long morning storm, thawing later in the day

While most of the wagons broke camp, William Dame's 4th 10 of the 1st 50 stayed behind, waiting for Dame to return from Pine Creek, where he was rounding up a missing cow. The rest moved south down a narrow sage-covered valley for about five miles and ascended to a higher table land of "green blue clay." They continued south three miles to a creek 10 feet wide with cottonwoods scattered along the bank. This is presumably Indian Creek near where I-15 crosses it today.[82]

Next they ascended a hill, probably Last Chance Bench, giving them a panoramic view of Beaver Valley, which impressed them as a desirable settlement site. After another three-mile stretch, they camped on the north bank of Spring Creek (present-day Dry Creek, a branch of the Beaver River), about three miles west of modern Beaver, a mile south of the road from Beaver to Minersville.[83]

Camp 22. Thursday, 9 January 1851: Beaver Mountain or South Hills.

Morning temperature:	13 degrees
Noon temperature:	38 degrees
Evening temperature:	7 degrees
Distance traveled:	6 miles
Weather:	8 inches of snow on the ground; thawing

Early this morning, Smith sent Baker and Horne to scout a route on the south side of the Beaver River that would avoid the swampy ground ahead. The two returned about 9:00 A.M. with recommendations. Meanwhile, Anson Call had men working to cut down the steep banks at their intended fording, while others collected teams and prepared to roll. According to Lee, "about 10 [A.M.] the horse teams commenced crossing and was followed by the 2nd 50. The 1st 50 in the rear today." A mile or more on, they came to the Beaver River, variously described as 20 to 30 feet wide and between one and two feet deep. They found a ford with a firm gravely bottom, probably a little east of Greenville and a little southwest of modern Beaver.[84]

After detouring around marshy spots and passing across good farming land, they ascended the foothills (the Greenville Bench) of South Hills, which they called Beaver Mountain.[85] Sometime in the afternoon, Lunt records, they "commenced to ascend the Beaver Mountain," passed through some scrub cedars, turned west, entered a canyon and followed it for a mile and a half to its head. In the canyon, Lee wrote, was a "smawl trail made by some of the California Emmigrants, probably last Fall."[86] Possibly the canyon Lee referred to is "California Hollow" (so identified on the U.S. Geological Survey 7.5 minute map). At least the location and the distances match. On this night, the 1st 50, led by Anson Call, plus 10 or so of the weakest wagons of Baker's 2nd 50, camped at the foot of a steep mountain about six miles from the Beaver River. The faster contingents of the 2nd 50 had moved on and were camped three miles ahead.[87]

Camp 23. Friday, 10 January 1851: Little Salt Lake Valley.

Morning temperature:	15 degrees
Noon temperature:	38 degrees
Evening temperature:	28 degrees
Distance traveled:	6 miles
Weather:	8 inches of snow on the ground

About 9:00 A.M., notes Lee, "the co doubled teams & commenced roling up the mountain promiscously . . . without regard to the organization." They climbed Beaver Mountain for about 60 rods (a little more than a fifth of a mile) where 10 inch deep snow forced them to physically hold the wagons on the trail. Some trees had to be cut to open a road, indicating they were no longer on Jefferson Hunt's route of a year ago, as the trail would already be clear had he passed that way.[88]

Near the top of the dangerous climb, Smith broke the tongue bolt on a wagon. Lee records that one of his own wagons, "by neglect of the driver," slid off the road against a dwarf pine. Lunt corroborates that "several of the wagons had the bows broken and covers torn."[89] On the summit, Smith climbed a pine tree and got his first look at Little Salt Lake Valley "through a low gap in a range of mountains."[90]

The descent was equally difficult, a "steep, road crooked winding among the timber some rocks." Lunt notes they had to rough-lock the rear wheels (chain them to the axle so they could not turn) for about half a mile.[91]

The company passed through a gap in a second range of mountains. Lee describes the "descent into the kanyon that leads into the vally" as especially rough. After journeying six miles, according to Lunt, they camped in the northeast end of the valley, which, wrote Lee, "seemed rather forbidding to a farmer especially. Scarce any thing to be seen but sage and greasewood."[92]

They were finally in Little Salt Lake Valley, where Brigham had sent them. Just before stopping at the north edge of the valley, George A. Smith sent Aaron B. Cherry and Tarlton Lewis back to notify the stragglers. The last teams arrived at the new campsite after dark, around 8:00 P.M. The forward contingent of Baker's 2nd 50 had split itself into two groups: the furthest ahead had already reached Red Creek (modern Paragonah); the rest of the forward group (about 25 wagons, then at Buckhorn Springs) were only six miles ahead of the main body.

Smith assembled this largest contingent at the foot of the mountain and, warning them that they were the "weak broken fragments of the co" and needed to be on the alert against possible Indian attack,

> [I]nstructed them to discharge their pieces and reload them. The Brethren wished to make a little noise on their arrival in the valley. They fired the Cannon and 24 stands of small arms in plattoons, followed up by 3 cheers for Iron County and 3 for the Governor [of] Deseret. Every thing was conducted in good order, and without accident.[93]

But these celebrations met with an unexpected response. Those at Buckhorn Springs heard the firing and feared the main body was under Indian attack. They immediately sent Zechariah Decker and Peter Lish to find out what was happening, at the same time sending other messengers on to Red Creek in case a relief party was needed. The Red Creek group set a strong guard on their own camp while "quite a company" of their men left immediately to ride the 15 or so miles back to the main campsite. It took until about 2:00 A.M. for everyone to be assured that no attack was underway.[94]

Camp 24. Saturday, 11 January 1851: Buckhorn Springs.[95]

Morning temperature:	28 degrees
Noon temperature:	38 degrees
Evening temperature:	24 degrees
Distance traveled:	6 miles
Weather:	thawing

Lee records breaking camp at 8:00 A.M., Smith and Call riding ahead to find an evening campsite, settling on Buckhorn Springs,

about 40 rods off the road.[96] The two men named the site for a large
buck's antler they found submerged there about four feet deep. The
trip over the summit from Cove Fort to Beaver Ridge, with snow from
eight to 15 inches deep, with some drifting, had drained their energies.
Wagons were also breaking down due to the rough terrain. Gradually
the weaker outfits dropped behind, joining an ever-increasing number
of wagons in Smith's rear echelon.[97]

The water at camp was "brackish" and there was no wood but the
animals had plenty of coarse grass. The strongest teams must have
reached Red Rock Canyon about noon or shortly afterward. The pioneers spent the afternoon shoeing lame cattle, fixing outfits and shooting
rabbits—the main ingredient for evening stew. So many oxen needed
shoeing that the company ran out of shoes and nails.[98]

Camp 25. Sunday, 12 January 1851: Red Creek (Paragonah).

Morning temperature:	24 degrees
Noon temperature:	40 degrees
Evening temperature:	26 degrees
Distance traveled:	8 miles
Weather:	fine

Lee was anxious to move on after he identified the brackish taste of the
spring as "saleratus," alkali salts in the water, poisonous in large quantities
to thirsty animals.[99] By 9:40 A.M., Smith had them all on the road—the
lame, the halt and the footsore. He and Anson Call rode ahead to prepare
Red Creek camp for the coming of the rest of the party. On arriving, the
leaders found most of the Red Creek men scattered in all directions, riding,
hunting and looking for good farm sites, which Smith felt was inappropri-
ate on Sunday. He declined an invitation to join eight of the brethren who
were even then saddling up, saying he was too weary. Lee says Smith then
"remarked cautiously" that "should they chance to meet any Bishops or
Elders of Israel by the way please remind them to return & keep the
Sabbath." This "gentle caution" apparently shamed the would-be gad-
abouts into staying in camp.[100]

The last of the wagons following Smith and Call rolled in about
3:00 P.M. It was too muddy for assembly, but Smith called the captains of
the company together for a staff meeting at 6:00 P.M. Speaking from his
wagon, the president congratulated them on their unity and good will.
Without any camp laws, except his counsel and advice, the group had

"traveled near 260 m[ile]s over mountains snow & ice, at this inclemant season, without a fight or even one single quarrel." He "hoped that the same good spirit that was with them on this mission might remain & be cherished with them always." He concluded by announcing that Brigham Young wanted them to settle on Center Creek in Little Salt Lake Valley unless the facilities there were inadequate.[101] They all agreed to move to Center Creek in the morning and begin work on a permanent settlement.

Camp 26. Monday, 13 January 1851: Center Creek/Fort Louisa (Parowan).

Morning temperature:	20 degrees (Lee); 32 degrees (Lunt)
Noon temperature:	36 degrees
Evening temperature:	24 degrees
Distance traveled:	5 miles
Weather:	"arrived at little Salt Lake" (Lunt)

Eager to reach the journey's end, the entire company was on its way by 8:00 A.M., with Anson Call's 1st 50 taking the lead. Travel over partially frozen mud and snow was not difficult and they arrived at Center Creek, five miles away, by 1:00 P.M. George A. Smith, Anson Call, Simon Baker and Tarlton Lewis rode ahead to explore the area and select a campsite, choosing one in the mouth of the canyon on the north bank. On Saturday, the 18th, they moved to the south bank to avoid the chilly canyon breeze.[102]

In Smith's words, "a great majority of our farmers who make up rye faces" complained that the soil was not suitable for farming. He immediately organized parties to explore the entire area the following morning. His focus was on identifying the natural features and resources in their immediate vicinity. Among Smith's instructions, written down by Lee, was a directive to

> let some 3 men go on the morrow up this kanyon with Bishop Lewis & examine for timber iron ore coal mill stone grit etc & bring anything that is strange & unknown—a specimen of any curiosity serves to talk about if nothing [else].[103]

Journey's End

Given the rigors and dangers of the journey, casualties had been surprisingly light. There had been no deaths, even though 11 of the 30 women traveling with the party were pregnant.[104] The only defection had been William Jones, a habitual swearer, whom Smith described on 21 December, less than a week into the trek, as a man "who got sick of a winter's mission and was returning to the Salt Lake City." Early in the journey, while staying at Peteetneet, Smith had privately estimated that at least 50 oxen would die. Much to his astonishment, out of the 368 which started the trip, only six had died along the trail, with two or three more dying after the travelers reached their destination.[105]

The successful journey augured well for the future. Despite the risks, exertions and discomforts posed by the long trek in the midst of a Utah winter, they had survived, cooperated, built bridges and cut roads for those who would follow. Brigham Young had sent a strong right arm into the southern wilderness.

Endnotes

1. Jarvis, *Ancestry*, 148.

2. Joseph Millett, "Brief Account of Artemus Millett & Family," 4, holograph in possession of Nanon (Mrs. John Reed) Corry, Cedar City, Utah, copy in SUU Archives, copy in Shirts Collection. The introduction becomes more detailed ca. Jun 1850; daily entries begin 17 Dec 1850 with muster of Iron Mission party in Provo. Daily travel account almost identical to Henry Lunt journal. Confusingly, Millett numbers both "sheets" and "pages." Wording of 9 Jan 1851 entry—"now in 1928" and "80 years ago"—suggests the beautifully penned account is a later fair copy.

3. Smith, journal, 9–10 Dec 1850; see also Jarvis, *Ancestry*, 148.

4. John D. Lee, "Journal of the Iron Co. Mission," 12 Dec 1850 (hereafter cited as Lee, journal); original in LDS Church Archives, published by Gustive O. Larson, ed., as "Journal of the Iron County Mission, John D. Lee, Clerk, December 10, 1850–March 1, 1851" in *Utah Historical Quarterly*, 20 (Apr 1952); (Aug 1953); and (Oct 1953). References are to the published version. See also Robert Glass Cleland and Juanita Brooks, eds., *A Mormon Chronicle: The Diaries of John D. Lee, 1848–1876*, 2 vols. (San Marino, Calif.: Huntington Library, 1955; reprint, Salt Lake City: University of Utah Press, 1983), 1:133.

5. Hafen and Hafen, *Forty-Niners*, 62, 70, 308.

6. Lee, journal, 15 Dec 1850. Note that, in this era of pioneer settlement, bishops were often responsible for traveling companies of riders and wagons, rather than for a stable community within a specific geographical area.

7. Ibid.; Smith, journal, on the same date. Lee, on the 15th, does mention establishing the traveling organization; Smith, on the 18th, does not.

8. Henry Lunt, *Life of Henry Lunt and Family, Together with a Portion of His Diary*, 16 Dec 1850 (hereafter cited as Lunt, diary), formerly in possession of

Paul Lunt, Cedar City, Utah. Typescript made 1955–56; now in Perry Special Collections. Separate typescript prepared and photocopies made available to family members at Lunt Reunion, 1970. The authors have closely compared this typescript to the BYU typescript. It is a close copy but occasionally inferior to the BYU typescript in content and much inferior in readability. The BYU typescript has been hardbound and stamped with the abbreviated title "Life of Henry Lunt." At the time of this printing (Feb 2001), the Sherratt Library received volumes 2, 3 and 4 of the original Lunt diary.

9. Any pioneer journal kept on the trail shows what modern readers might call preoccupation with travel conditions, but concerns were proper and real. Wet weather could turn an easy passage on level ground into a nightmare of swampy delay, risking broken wagon parts and exhausted animals. Unseasonably hot weather could mean dry creek beds and insufficient water for man and beast. Disorientation in snow or fog could cost precious time relocating the trail or even cause a complete loss of direction, increasing the risks of general panic, injury or death.

10. Lunt, diary, 15–16 Dec 1850; Smith, journal, 16 Dec 1850.

11. Campbell, *Establishing Zion*, 96; Walker and Jessee, "First Contacts in Utah," 1.

12. Campbell, ibid., 99; Walker and Jessee, ibid., 3–4; Smart and Smart, *Over the Rim*, 25.

13. Campbell, ibid., 99–100.

14. Lee, journal, 16 Dec 1850. Lee describes Hobble Creek as a "handsome Fort containing 35 Families."

15. Lee, journal; Lunt, diary: both on 16 Dec 1850. Lee says the "Leader of the camp roled out" about 10 A.M. George A. Smith, after 18 months in the Iron Mission, would be called to oversee the expanding settlements of Utah Valley.

16. Note that Lee discusses the slough on the 18th; Lunt on the 17th and 18th; Smith only on the 17th.

17. Smith, journal; Lee, journal; Lunt, diary: all on 18 Dec 1850; Madoline Cloward Dixon, *Peteetneet Town: A History of Payson, Utah* (Provo, Utah: Press Publishing, 1974), 5.

18. Smith, journal; Lee, journal; Lunt, diary: all on 19 Dec 1850. This quote is from Lee.

19. Ralph Hansen, "Administrative History of the Nauvoo Legion in Utah" (master's thesis, Brigham Young University, 1954), 12, 20, 24.

20. Lee, journal, 19 Dec 1850.

21. Journal History, 20 Dec 1850. George A. Smith is alluding to the fact that the General Assembly had already organized Iron County and elected him as its chief justice on 3 Dec, before the iron missionaries had left Salt Lake. See Gustive O. Larson's introduction to Lee, journal, 113.

22. Journal History, 16 Dec 1850.

23. Dixon, *History of Payson*, 7; Hubert Howe Bancroft, *History of Utah 1520–1886* (San Francisco, Calif.: History Company, 1890; reprint, Las Vegas: NV Publications, 1982), 474.

24. George A. Smith to Franklin D. Richards, 28 Jan 1851, published in *Millennial Star* 13 (1 Aug 1851), 238 (quoted in Jarvis, *Ancestry*, 149).

25. Lee, journal, 20 Dec 1850, n. 31.

26. Smith, journal, 20 Dec 1850. The man is probably Elias Gardner, included on the Nov 1850 "call list," but who seems to be otherwise undocumented in the Iron Mission.

27. Smith, journal; Lunt, diary: both on 20 Dec 1850; Lee, journal, 20–21 Dec 1850. The quote is from Lee.

28. Smith, journal; Lunt diary: both on 21 Dec 1850. Father Escalante had named Willow Springs the Fountain of St. Paul. See Herbert E. Bolton, *Pageant in the Wilderness: The Story of the Escalante Expedition to the Interior Basin, 1776* (Salt Lake City: Utah State Historical Society, 1950), 74. See also Alice McCune, *History of Juab County, 1847–1947* (Springville, Utah: Art City Publishing, 1947), 139. Dr. Matthew McCune, a former surgeon in the British Army, suggested the name Mona in memory of his home town on the Isle of Man.

29. Smith, journal; Lee, journal; Lunt, diary: all on 22 Dec 1850. The quotes are from Lee.

30. Lee, journal; Lunt, diary: ibid.

31. Smith, journal; Lee, journal; Lunt, diary: all on 23 Dec 1850. The quotes are from Lee and Smith, respectively.

32. Ibid. The quote is from Lee.

33. The Chicken Creek crossing was probably near the present dam site for the same reason the dam was eventually constructed there: the crossing's firm, rocky bottom. The site is now covered by the reservoir.

34. Mapping coordinates in Utah are based on a zero coordinate marker designating the "Great Salt Lake Base Line and Meridian," the base line running east-west and the meridian running north-south. From the zero or "prime" marker, located on the corner of Temple Square in Salt Lake City, "townships" are blocked off as 36-square mile units, 6 miles per side. Each township block is further divided into "sections" one square mile in area, comprising 640 acres each, further divisible into quarter-sections as needed. A code such as "T15S R1W," therefore, means "township 15 south, range 1 west," or the 15th township south of zero, at a range of one township west of the same.

35. Lee, journal, 24 Dec 1850.

36. Ibid.

37. Ibid.

38. Smith, journal; Lee, journal: both on 24 Dec 1850. The quote is from Lee.

39. Lunt, diary, 24 Dec 1850.

40. Lunt, ibid.; Lee, journal: both on 25 Dec 1850. The quote is from Lunt.

41. Smith, journal, 25 Dec 1850.

42. Lunt, diary, 26 Dec 1850.

43. Smith, journal, 26 Dec 1850.

44. Ibid.

45. Jarvis, *Ancestry*, 150–51; Smith, journal; Lunt, diary: both on 27 Dec 1850.

46. The unusual name was reportedly given by Brigham Young in 1863. His personal telegraph operator, lawyer Scipio Africanus Kenner, was standing on the corner designated for the town square when Young was casting about for a name. See Stella H. Day and Sebrina C. Ekins, comps., *Milestones of Millard: 100 Years of History of Millard County 1851–1951* (Springville, Utah: Art City Publishing, for the Millard County Daughters of Utah Pioneers, 1951), 388.

47. Lunt, diary, 27 Dec 1850.

48. Lee, journal, 27 Dec 1850.

49. Ibid., 28 Dec 1850 [misdated "Frid Dec 27th 1850," but content clearly establishes the 28th].

50. Ibid.

51. Ibid.

52. During the mid-1850s, Cedar Springs was known as Buttermilk Fort, due to the large quantities of fresh, cold buttermilk stored in the spring-houses of the settlers.

53. Cedar Springs and Pioneer Creek (identified by Lunt as "Explorer Creek," 2–3 miles south) were favorite campsites with traveling parties. Several large springs constituted Cedar Springs, an area which measured three miles in circumference. David Fulmer, one of the iron missionaries, had camped there the previous winter as part of Pratt's Southern Exploring Expedition.

54. Smith, journal; Lee, journal: both on 29 Dec 1850.

55. Smith, ibid.

56. Smith, ibid.; Lee, journal; Lunt, diary: all on 30 Dec 1850. On 21 Oct 1851, Brigham Young—and a committee who chose the location as the site of the territorial capital—renamed it Fillmore, honoring Millard Fillmore, the president who had signed the bill establishing Utah Territory. Truman O. Angell, LDS Church architect and designer of the Salt Lake Temple, drew plans for a four-winged territorial capitol building, only one wing of which was constructed. Anson Call led the settlement company and headed construction efforts. The first and only full session of the territorial legislature to be held there opened on 11 Dec 1855. The last session—the eighth—opened on 22 Dec 1858 and immediately adjourned to Salt Lake City. See Day and Ekins, *History of Millard County*, 3, 14, 150–54. Also see William L. Knecht and Peter L. Crawley, *Early Records of Utah: History of Brigham Young, 1857–1867* (Berkeley, Calif.: MassCal Associates, 1964), 268.

57. Lee, journal, 30 Dec 1850.

58. Lee, ibid.; Smith, journal: both on 31 Dec 1850. The quote is from Smith.

59. Smith, ibid.

60. Ibid., 1 Jan 1851. Local residents believe that the rock for the state capitol built in Fillmore, 1854–55, was quarried from this deposit. The "lake" was probably not Sevier Lake but surface water appearing, in the distance, to be a permanent body of water. See Larson's comment in Lee, journal, 256, n. 10.

61. Smith, journal; Lee, journal: both on 1 Jan 1851.

62. Millett, "Brief Account," 1 Jan 1851, p. 7, sheet 4.

63. Ibid, p. 4 [no "sheet" no.].

64. Lee, journal, 1 Jan 1851.

65. Ibid., 2 Jan 1851.

66. Ibid.; Smith, journal, and Lunt, diary: on the same date. Charles Hopkins of Lehi, Peter Robinson and Peter Bayes were the first white settlers here (1854). The Salisbury and Gilmore stages, which ran from Salt Lake City to Pioche, Nevada, and possibly Silver Reef, Nevada, stopped here at Corn Creek. Called Petersburg for Peter Robinson, the first postmaster, the townsite was later renamed Hatton after Richard Hatton, his successor. Several of the stage buildings still stand in the trees just east of I-15. In 1867, Brigham Young suggested resettling closer to the mountains to conserve water and avoid early frost damage to crops. The new site was named Kanosh, after the local Pahvant chief. A peace-loving man, Kanosh accepted the Mormon settlers and was baptized into their religion.

67. Regarding Palmer's opinion, see Jarvis, *Ancestry*, 151–52. See Smith, journal, 3 Jan 1851. The quotation is from Lee, journal, 3 Jan 1851.

68. Lee, ibid.; Lunt, diary, 3 Jan 1851. The quotes are from Lee.

69. The historic site of Cove Fort was a favorite among later pioneer travelers. In 1866, Charles Willden established a small stockade there which he called Fort Willden. Brigham Young instructed Ira N. Hinckley to build Cove Fort in 1867.

70. Lee, journal, 4 Jan 1851.

71. Ibid.

72. Ibid.; Lunt, diary: 4 Jan 1851.

73. Smith, journal, 4 Jan 1851.

74. Ibid.; Lee, journal, 4 Jan 1851. Smith's phrase is "The whole Company is together." It is not known how long the pioneer route from Dog Valley to Cove Creek, the site of future Cove Fort, was used. Horne's route to this camp was more difficult than an alternate might have been: around the west edge of Dog Valley, following the present route of I-15 and bypassing Cove Fort entirely.

75. Lee, journal, 5 Jan 1851.

76. Ibid.; Lunt, diary: on the same date. The list of singers appears in Lunt's diary following the entry for 2 Jan 1852.

77. Smith, journal, 6 Jan 1851.

78. Ibid.; Lee, journal, and Lunt, diary, 6 Jan 1851; Solomon Carvalho, *Incidents of Travel and Adventure in the Far West with Col. Frémont's Expedition* (New York: Derby and Jackson, 1857), 205. Carvalho, who traveled with John C. Frémont as expedition artist, was Brigham Young's guest in 1854 at the negotiations which ended the Walker War.

79. Lunt, diary, 6 Jan 1851; Smith, journal, 7 Jan 1851.

80. Lee, journal, 7 Jan 1851. "Mud Creek Canyon" is a modern place name not used in this entry.

81. Ibid. "Wild Cat Canyon" is a modern place name not used in this entry.

82. Ibid., 8 Jan 1851.

83. Ibid.; Smith, journal, 8 Jan 1851.

84. Lee, ibid., 9 Jan 1851; Smith, ibid., and Lunt, diary, 9 Jan 1851. The quote is from Lee.

85. The names vary. U.S. Geological Survey maps designate this feature as "South Hills." Some local residents use the name "South Greenville Hills," while still others call the location "Rattlesnake Hills"—after the jeep trail leading south named Rattlesnake Trail. State highway patrol officers designate the place "Beaver Ridge."

From hindsight and the topographically predictable route mapped for U.S. 91 and then I-15, some Beaver residents have assumed the Iron Mission party followed that route southeast of Beaver, up Nevershine Hollow and over the summit, there intercepting the Old Spanish Trail going west from Frémont Pass. However, the journal entries of Smith, Lee and Lunt would seem to imply that the company crossed Beaver Ridge through a low pass almost directly south of Greenville and east of the cave at the foot of what the pioneers called Black Mountain. From the Last Chance Bench north of Beaver, this pass is easily visible and, to first view, would appear to be the most logical route into Little Salt Lake Valley. It is indeed the shortest route, but it is not the easiest—at least, not for wagons.

Corroborative evidence about the route over Beaver Ridge comes from earlier explorers. Miles Goodyear, who perhaps knew the route better than any other early fur trader, had been over it several times using pack horses, a much easier method of transport than wagons. In fall 1849, Jefferson Hunt led a large train of 100 wagons to California. Journals from participants on that trek also suggest the route was over Beaver Ridge, rather than around it. Further evidence of a road over Beaver Ridge is the jeep trail on the U.S. Geological Survey 7.5 minute map series of the Greenville Bench and Buckhorn Flat quadrangles, which may be the old Iron Mission route. In Section 26, T36S, R8W, appears "California Hollow," a cedar-covered ravine 1½ miles long. Hiking and driving this trail provide ample evidence that it follows an older road.

86. Lee, journal, 9 Jan 1851.

87. Ibid.; Smith, journal, and Lunt, diary, 9 Jan 1851.

88. Smith, ibid., and Lunt, ibid.: both on 10 Jan 1851; the quote is from Lee, ibid.

89. Smith, ibid.; Lunt, ibid. and Lee, ibid., all on 10 Jan 1851.

90. Smith, ibid.

91. Smith, ibid.; Lee, journal, and Lunt, diary: also on 10 Jan 1851. The quote is from Lee.

92. Ibid.

93. All three journal-keepers record this first view of Little Salt Lake Valley on 10 Jan 1851, although Lunt does not mention Smith's climb up the pine tree. The quote is from Smith.

94. Smith, ibid.; Lunt, ibid., and Lee, ibid.: also on 10 Jan 1851. Lee identifies the two men by their full names, "Zachariah" Decker and Peter Lish; Lunt refers to them without names; Smith records them as "Z. Decker" and "P. Lish."

95. On their way from Buckhorn Springs to Red Canyon, Lee noted "at the distance of about 4 or 5 ms some mound[s] spring to the left of the road" (journal, 12 Jan 1851). According to archeologist Joel Janetski, the mounds are part of a Frémont archeological site in the area of Cedar City on the south to Paragonah on the north. They lie between U.S. 91 and I-15 and the base of the hills. See Joel Janetski, "150 Years of Utah Archeology," *Utah Historical Quarterly* 65 (spring 1997): 100–133. George A. Smith, who picnicked at the site in spring 1851, numbered the mounds at about 120, noting that

> they are all the ruins of an Indian City, composed of dirt lodges, the roof of Earth had been supported by timbers, which had decayed or been burnt away, causing an hollow at the top of the mounds. The brethren in excavating, dug up Adobois, that were very hard, Charcoal, curnals of Corn and cobs which had been partly burnt. found bones of Animals, but no human bones. many pieces of pottery. (Smith, journal, 29 May 1851.)

96. Lee, journal, 11 Jan 1851.

97. Ibid.; Smith, journal, and Lunt, diary, 11 Jan 1851.

98. Lee, ibid.

99. Ibid., 12 Jan 1851.

100. Ibid.

101. Ibid.

102. Ibid., 12–13 and 18 Jan 1851.

103. Ibid., 13 Jan 1851.

104. The following children were born to Iron Mission settlers in the first nine months of 1851 in Fort Louisa (Parowan): New Samuel Whitney, born 1 Mar, son of

Francis T. and Clarissa Whitney; Elizabeth Miller, born 25 Mar, daughter of Robert and Eliza Miller; Elizabeth Lee, born 24 Apr, daughter of John D. and Polly Lee; Susannah Steele, born 28 Apr, daughter of John and Elizabeth Steele; Margaret A. Hall, born 11 May, daughter of Charles and Elizabeth Hall; James Lewis, born 21 May, son of James and Emily Lewis; Ann W. Whipple, born 7 Jul, daughter of Edson and Harriet Whipple; John D. Whipple, born 27 Oct, son of Edson and Mary A. Whipple; Orson A. Dalton, born 17 Nov, son of Charles and Juliette Dalton; James Topham, born 27 Oct, son of John and Betsy Topham; Henrietta Lemmon, born 19 Sep, daughter of James and Susannah Lemmon (original spelling retained; punctuation adjusted). The list is reprinted in Luella Adams Dalton, *History of the Iron County Mission, Parowan, Utah* (Parowan, Utah: Privately published, 1970), 66. There she notes that it was taken "From a paper found in William C. McGregor's home when it was torn down. He was a former Bishop."

105. Outside Smith, journal, 21 Dec 1850, the sole comment found to date on William Jones is in a letter from George A. Smith which he would shortly send to Brigham Young via the *Deseret News* (written 17 Jan 1851; printed 8 Feb 1851, pp. 205–06), where Jones is described as a "promising young man" who "could not leave off swearing, and chose to go where he could exercise his liberty." The reference to oxen is from Lee, journal, 2 Feb 1851.

Part II

Settling In

3

Fort Louisa

January–May 1851

Upon arriving in Little Salt Lake Valley, the iron missionaries' immediate task was to determine whether the Center Creek site would prove feasible for their principal settlement, as Brigham Young hoped it would.[1] Their first priority, of course, was to secure food and shelter. Seed grain was precious, and replenishing it would be doubtful if the settlement site had poor soil. Timber availability also influenced site selection. Although the settlers could build adobe or stone houses or cottonwood log cabins, they still needed good quality planks large enough for doors, floors and roofs. All these needs had to be met for the new settlement even to take root. No wonder George A. Smith was "very earnest and much engaged about the present location for this Mission."[2]

A major concern was the quality of the soil at Center Creek. Some of the settlers, many of whom were from England, did not like the look of the "bloody red" soil. Their reaction was to make "roy [wry] faces and say they can see no facilities there."[3] Edson Whipple identified one of the vexed pioneers as blacksmith Burr Frost. On the day the settlers arrived at Center Creek, Frost told Whipple that "if any man said that he liked this country, if he had common sense that he was a liar; for, said he[,] it is not fit for any body to settle in, and for us to think of settling here, it was the height of folly, and he would venture to say as to iron ore there was none there." Whipple evidently did not share Frost's attitude, for he described Frost pityingly as a "sorry looking fellow not having shaved himself since he left home; his beard was long and his face was longer."[4] Although George A. Smith deemed the soil acceptable ("I found a track of land which pleased me"[5]), he evidently wanted to explore further since the final decision could mean the success or failure of the mission.

First Explorations in the Valley

The colonists' saddle blankets had hardly dried before explorers rode out on 13 January to assess settlement possibilities in the region. Tarlton Lewis and three men were dispatched to investigate the area around Center Creek Canyon, reporting on their return that Center Creek was "about one rod wide & 2 feet deep swift rapid current rock bottom & banks—Kanyon oppen for three ms which is the distance that it has been explored."[6] Aaron B. Cherry and four or five others were sent to explore the "next kanyon ahead," while a third group went west to examine the area around the Little Salt Lake.[7] Peter Shirts, apparently alone, was designated to explore Red Creek Canyon.[8]

In addition to the exploring parties, various work parties were assigned. One group was to construct a permanent bridge over the creek half a mile west of the encampment and move the camp downstream about three-quarters of a mile to the base of the knoll, where Pratt's group had erected its liberty pole. William Adams and Joseph Hovey were given the task of making grindstones from native sandstone so the men would be able to keep their tools sharp when timber-cutting began. A third group, under the direction of Jacob Hofheins, captain of the artillery company, mounted the cannon. Bishop Elisha H. Groves was left in charge so that everyone leaving camp reported to him.[9] Smith himself led the fourth and largest exploring party of some 20 men southwest of the encampment for 25 or 30 miles to get the lay of the land and appraise the resources along the Little Muddy. He took a three-day supply of food and a mounted escort consisting of Thomas Smith, Thomas Wheeler, John D. Lee, Almon Fulmer, William H. Dame, Ebenezer Brown, Anson Call, John Dalton, Charles Dalton, Leamon Bronson (also recorded as "Lemon Brunson"), Zechariah Decker, Gideon D. Wood, George Wood, James Lawson, Thomas Corbitt, Marius Ensign, Joseph Horne, Simon Baker, Charles A. Harper, John Webb and James Harmison ("Harmerson" in both Lee and Smith).[10]

Smith, Lee, Thomas Smith and Thomas Wheeler rode in Lee's four-horse carriage, which had enough room for the men, journal supplies, candles, a thermometer and a number of books (including "Comstocks Geology," almost certainly from J. L. Comstock's eight-volume *Outline of Geology* published in Hartford in 1834), which Smith perused while he jostled along.

This fourth group left at 10:00 A.M., presumably as soon as Smith was certain that everybody remaining behind was productively employed.

They traveled south-southwest along the Old Spanish Trail for about six miles, then stopped to noon at the Summit Creek crossing. Unexpectedly, they came upon a pack train of 42 animals, led by Jefferson Hunt, returning from his trek to California as guide to the large party of fall 1849. Accompanying him were Levi Fifield and his son, John Berry, James Brooks, Henry Gibson, Marshall Hunt and John Mackey. Levi Fifield and Marshall Hunt had been members of the Mormon Battalion and joyously greeted their former comrades, Decker and Dame.[11]

The northbound travelers had important news, which Lee recorded. First, there was Indian danger. A man named Isaac Brown, traveling with five animals several days ahead of the Hunt party, had disappeared and was presumed dead, a victim of Indian attack: "[T]hey saw where they supposed he met with his fate; there was signs where the horses were drove off. He also said that they saw Indians repeatedly & some were hostile but that they got through safe."[12] Second, Brigham Young had been appointed governor of Utah Territory. Gibson had in his saddlebags the *New York Tribune* issue reporting both the formation of the territory on 9 September 1850 and Young's appointment. Third, the travelers reported that the California goldfields should be no temptation to the faithful: "[N]early all the Brethren that were at the gold mines from the beginning & had made fortunes were all broke & but few of them that can get credit for a meal victuals & have become poor worthless disapated creatures."[13]

Hunt sent his seven men on to the Center Creek camp with the pack animals while he accompanied Smith in the carriage to the iron fields, with which he was familiar. Smith, Hunt and their mounted escort apparently followed Braffit's Creek and Wynn's Hollow through the hills to the Enoch-Rush Lake area, "a distance of about 14 miles, mostly sage and rabbit brush." As Lee recorded:

> about 5 ms N.E. of the Muddy [i.e., Cottonwood or Coal Creek] a low range of mountains puts in from the North & allmost divides the vally— on the west side of that range several springs brakes out & forms a lake (smawl) around it abundance of good feed & some good farming land.[14]

They camped for the night on the creek, which had plenty of cottonwood trees and grass for the animals. The site can be located fairly confidently at the cluster of mature cottonwoods north of the Cedar City airport and between the former Cedar and Cedar West LDS Stake farms, approximately between Sections 28 and 33, T35S R11W.

Smith and Lee retired to bed in Lee's carriage at 11:00 P.M. but the 29-degree weather made sleep difficult. They talked until 2:00 A.M., "consulting the interest of this people & the best policy to build up Zion," while many of the other men sat around the fire and talked over old times until daybreak.[15] That morning, Wednesday, 15 January, Almon Fulmer took four men upstream while William H. Dame led a small party downstream, presumably going north,[16] although the old Coal Creek channel went west through the Iron Springs area. George A. Smith, Thomas Smith, Jefferson Hunt and Thomas Wheeler took the carriage and headed for the iron deposits, accompanied by the rest of the group (about eight mounted men under the direction of Anson Call). They rode approximately eight miles to the southwest, examining the soil and appraising farming conditions. Near noon, they were in the small gap in the mountain range on the west side of the valley. Later, at Iron Springs, they turned their horses out to drink and graze. Leaving part of the group on guard, Smith, Lee, Hunt and eight others

> ascended one of those hills or smawl mountains of Iron Ore distance about ½ mile found large quantities of ore Some appeared to have been subjected to the action of heat & was pronounced by some to be dead. However specimens of the ore rock & to be tested by regular and proper process—in this vincity [*sic*] are 3 hills of ore & large amount of free stone suitable for buildings & ceder in great abundance.[17]

This "smawl mountain" was most likely north or northeast of Iron Springs in the region that extends northward from the spring about five miles and holds sufficient iron deposits to provide large-scale successful mining to this day. The chunks of free iron, plus outcroppings of solid ore, were plainly visible. The cedar could be used for fuel and the water impounded for blast furnace power. The "free stone" was monzanite, a form of granite suitable for building. The phrase "action of heat" may refer to the explorers' perceptions that the area had seen volcanic activity.

Suddenly, as Smith was to put in his journal that night, probably dictating to Henry Lunt, they found themselves no longer alone:

> At 5 minutes to 12, noon. Several horsemen were seen rideing towards us in ful speed abt. 3 miles off when first discovered. Soon they reached the camp and proved to be Indians of the Utah Tribe, there were 7 in number well clad and rideing good Horses they rode up and shook hands with the Interpreter and others who were well acquainted with them: the leading one was old Peteetneet, after whom Peteetneet Creek was named. From them we learned that Walker the Hawk of the Mountains was a short distance South about 25 miles near the Euinta Valley, they were quite friendly and seemed glad that we were settling in Little Salt Lake Valley. Capt. Hunt and Webb gave

them some tobacco which pleased them they then must smoke the pipe of Peace.[18]

Although this encounter was amicable, it underscored the need to select a defensible settlement site and must have occasioned no little talk once the iron missionaries returned to camp. That night, after supper, Smith called a council meeting at which the various exploring parties presumably reported their day's findings. It is likely that William H. Dame aired his negative reactions to the downstream explorations; Almon Fulmer concluded the Little Muddy lacked enough water to irrigate the amount of land needed for a sizable colony.[19] Probably a good portion of the evening was spent on appointing officials to serve the new county, so that Hunt could take the information back to Salt Lake with him.

"Sanctioned by the Convention": Organizing Iron County

The Deseret General Assembly had created Iron County on 3 December 1850, less than two weeks before the iron missionaries departed. Although Pratt had named their destination the Little Salt Lake Valley, Brigham Young had already written disapprovingly on 20 November to John M. Bernhisel, the Mormon delegate in Washington, D.C., saying "The Little Salt Lake is a misnomer; it is nothing but a little saleratus pond, about half the size of the Hot Spring lake in this valley. We have therefore altered the name of that county, and owing to its immense stores of iron ore, have named it Iron county."[20] On 16 December 1850, Young's courier had brought George A. Smith, camped at Peteetneet (Payson), a copy of the county ordinances that the legislature had created on 3 December:

AN ORDINANCE, to provide for the organization of Iron County. Passed, Dec. 3, 1850.

Sec. 1. Be it ordained by the General Assembly of the State of Deseret, that all that portion of country, lying in the southeast corner of the Great Basin; and being south of the divide between Beaver Creek and the Sevier River, and east of the Desert Range, extending south to the rim of the Basin, and east to the Wasatch Range of mountains; be and the same is hereby known and designated "Iron County."

Sec. 2. The Chief Justice of said County, is hereby appointed and authorized to organize said County. He shall cause notices of election to be made, and receive and open the returns of said election; qualify the officers elected according to law; approve of, and file their bonds in his office; and make return of his proceedings therein, as soon as practicable, being prior to the first day of June next.

Sec. 3. All officers elected and qualified under the provisions of this ordinance, shall hold their offices until super[s]eded by due course of law. This ordinance to be in force from and after its passage, any law or ordinance to the contrary notwithstanding.[21]

It was signed by Jedediah M. Grant as Speaker of the House and Heber C. Kimball as Speaker of the Senate. Brigham Young as governor approved it on 9 December. George A. Smith was the chief justice described in Section 2. In that capacity, he resolved the company into a political caucus during the evening council meeting on 15 January to nominate a complete ticket of county officials.[22] The nominating committee consisted of "Major" George A. Smith, "Lieut." Thomas Smith, "Pilot" Joseph Horne, "Capt." Anson Call and "Adjt." John D. Lee. Together they made their one-party nominations, which were accepted by unanimous vote (although John D. Lee withdrew his candidacy for recorder since he would be gone for some time moving his family from Salt Lake City to the settlement). James Lewis was nominated in his stead. Thomas Smith, Simon Baker and John Barnard were appointed election judges and the meeting adjourned for an evening of conversation. Anson Call offered the evening's prayer "around the camp fire."[23]

Choosing the Best Townsite

The next morning, Thursday, 16 January, with the temperature hovering at eight degrees, Smith sent Fulmer and four other men back up the Little Muddy to check out Fulmer's report that lack of irrigation water would handicap any colony's growth there. Lee's diary states that the party consisted of nine men: Almon Fulmer, Thomas Wheeler, Charles Dalton, John Dalton, Simon Baker, Anson Call, James Lawson, Charles A. Harper and George Wood.[24] This second examination underscores the importance of the Little Muddy in settlement deliberations. Fulmer's exploring party evidently rode east, up the Little Muddy, then retreated to its mouth and angled back north, over to Center Creek, while the main body under Smith went northeast, straight to Center Creek. Smith's party nooned at Summit Creek where Hunt showed him a cache of wagon wheels, hand saws, planes, chisels, augers, spades and so forth, which he had left the year before. Smith could use them, Hunt said, providing Hunt could have access to the tools should he return to live there. By 4:00 P.M. both parties were back at the Center Creek campsite.[25]

The second report was again unfavorable: although the water flow in the Little Muddy was as great as that in Center Creek, contrary to Fulmer's report, the canyon was narrow and building there would be difficult. Smith's journal entry agreed that the stream was as large as Center Creek but stated the canyon was "open and accessible."[26] Lee describes the pioneers' decision, taking everything into consideration, to reject the option of settling on the Little Muddy:

> after a fair & thorough examination of the surrounding country the company agreed in one thing (& that was) this creek with all its advantages and facilities the richness of its soil etc was not the home of this mission at the presant. The face of [the] country looked desolate and even the surrounding objects seemed forbidding & fearful threatening of future consequences was plainly depicted on the countenances of every man who felt the weight interest & responsibility resting on them (the building up of Zion) Therefore the spirit bid them return home it [being] the only place that seemed like home to us.[27]

By "home," Lee meant Center Creek; by "forbidding & fearful threatening of future consequences," he may have meant evidences of volcanic activity in the area. Mount Vesuvius had erupted in 1844, just six years earlier, and a Royal Observatory on its slopes had produced a series of reports that were widely circulated. Some of the pioneers, at least, may have been aware of these.

While the townsite would be on Center Creek, the leaders decided to place the foundry near Iron Springs, about eight miles northwest of the Little Muddy and about 12 miles southwest of Center Creek. John D. Lee wrote:

> The Pres advised the escort to strike for the direction of the encampment [at Center Creek;] in so doing the road would be shortened about 5 ms which would be quite an advantage to our encampment when we established an Iron foundary. We shall go back & forth occasionally as circumstances shall require.[28]

Seven factors seem to have been important in this decision:

1. With major ore deposits in the Iron Springs-Three Peaks area, workers would commute the 20-odd miles (round-trip from Center Creek) for family, social and religious activities. Building the foundry near the ore was deemed more efficient than transporting the ore to a foundry built near the settlement.

2. Cedar trees (for charcoal) and ample water near the ore deposits were further reasons for locating the foundry near Iron Springs. (The later discovery of coal on the Little Muddy would cause a major change in plans.)

3. Although the Little Muddy had the best land, there did not seem to be enough water to insure adequate irrigation. Nor did it have adequate timber for building.

4. At Center Creek, in contrast, although some of the group were dissatisfied with the land, there was an adequate water supply and the best and most easily accessible timber supply of all the canyons explored.

5. Parley P. Pratt and Jefferson Hunt had both advised settling on Center Creek.

6. Smith judged that a fort on Center Creek would provide better protection against Indian attack, although he did not specify his reasons.

7. The group had sought divine guidance and their impressions after doing so favored Center Creek.

Holding the First Iron County Election

If bringing the settlers away from civilization to a new townsite was the first task of Iron Mission leaders, the second was to begin bringing the forms of civilization back to the settlers. To this end, after the return of the exploring parties on Thursday afternoon, George A. Smith called a "convention" and presented the slate of nominations made the previous day by the Cottonwood Precinct at Little Muddy camp. The first election in Iron County would be held the next day, Friday, 17 January 1851, with John P. Barnard, Simon Baker and Thomas Smith as election judges. No other nominations were called for; apparently only one candidate was proposed for each office.

The next morning, Thomas Smith cried three times that the election was open. George A. Smith cast the first ballot, followed by the rest of the company. John Topham, butcher, dispatched an ox and the company prepared a feast. Their "tables" were white linen cloths placed over buffalo robes spread on the ground. To the sound of a trumpet, the "dignitaries" and their ladies took places of honor at the head of the "table." George A. Smith offered grace and proposed a toast with tea. After a few patriotic speeches came the roasted ox. The entire company "ate & drank with gladness & singleness of heart," recorded Lee, "& never did I behold the same No. enjoy themselves better." The meal closed with another prayer of thanks, and in 20 minutes "every man was again about his own buisiness."[29]

Lee also recorded that several explorers made additional reports, apparently on election day. Tarlton Lewis and Elijah Newman had examined Center Creek for six miles, discovering at least three separate branches. Its timber was estimated at about 4,000 saw logs, including many five feet in diameter, which were too large to handle. The timber in the bottom of the canyon could be easily reached by bridging the creek in several places. The men also reported plenty of feed, plaster of paris and rock for grindstones and building materials.[30]

A. B. Cherry reported that his party's explorations of Summit Creek had been curtailed because it was too narrow and rough to ascend for any great distance; therefore, its resources were unknown. Peter Shirts described Red Creek Canyon as containing "considerable timber . . . great quantities of aspen poles . . . & Mormon Lignam vitas," which Gustive Larson suggests might have been mountain mahogany.[31] Because the preliminary decision to settle on Center Creek with the foundry near Iron Springs had apparently been made the day before, these reports must have confirmed the choice rather than provide information on which to base it. At 6:00 P.M., Jacob Hofheins, captain of the Iron County artillery, fired a three-shot salvo from the cannon and the polls closed. Earlier, a cannonade had been fired from the top of Beaver Ridge,[32] possibly serving the extra purpose of warning off Chief Wakara and his war party. The 117 ballots were then counted and the voters celebrated with a square dance, for which Lee called the figures.[33]

The unanimously elected officials who joined the appointed chief justice included Jefferson Hunt as Iron County's representative to the territorial legislature. Hunt's election seems puzzling since he was not an iron missionary, but his offer to let George A. Smith use his tools temporarily suggests he was thinking of settling in Iron County. William Dame was not listed with the elected officials, although he had been nominated for county surveyor. The omission appears to be a clerical oversight, since he served extensively in that office, surveying being a skill he had learned in Vermont.[34]

Sending Letters and Petitions North

The Iron County settlers spent Saturday, 18 January 1851, preparing for Hunt's departure and moving their encampment to the south or west bank of the creek to avoid the cold canyon breeze. They generously resupplied Hunt's party, replacing his weaker animals with strong ones. When Jefferson left around 10:00 A.M., he carried with him the camp's good wishes, along with about a hundred letters and descriptions of the new county organization, the pioneers' general health and the location of the settlement site on Center Creek.

First Elected Officials in Iron County

Representative:	Jefferson Hunt
Associate justices:	Elisha H. Groves
	Edson Whipple
County recorder:	James Lewis
Sheriff:	James A. Little
Assessor and collector:	Joseph Horne
Supervisor of roads:	Almon L. Fulmer
Magistrates (justices of the peace):	Anson Call
	John D. Lee
	Aaron Farr
	Tarlton Lewis
Constables:	Zechariah B. Decker
	Charles Dalton
	Samuel A. Woolley
	Charles Hall
Sealer of weights and measures:	Phillip B. Lewis

Sources: Lee, Iron Mission journal, 17 Jan 1851; Lunt and Lunt, Lunt, diary, and Smith, Parowan journal, on the same date. These entries agree on the personnel named, but spellings differ in Lunt. He gives Edson Whipple as "Edwon," Joseph Horne as "Horn," Zechariah Decker as "Z.B." and Phillip Lewis as "Philip."

Presumably one of the many letters sent north was that headed "Letter from George A. Smith, Center creek, Iron county, Jan. 17, 1851. To His Excellency, Brigham Young," printed in the 8 February 1851 issue of the *Deseret News*. This letter is a report summarizing the journey to Center Creek and the first efforts to successfully establish a colony there. The letter illustrates the mix of idealism and practicality that motivated the iron missionaries. The idealism appears in a passage describing a celebration held to honor both their successful arrival and the surprising reunion with Jefferson Hunt:

> Friday, there was a scene which transpired in camp scarce ever equalled. After a little consultation, after the given signal, the whole camp sat down to an elegant repast given to Bro. Hunt and his company, who so unexpectedly dropped down among us, greeting many of their old friends. You will feel assured that the happiest feelings existed among us. The dinner passed off with many expressions of happy feelings towards their friends, and you, and those who surround you, came

up in many a burst of the hearts filled with love for their rulers, and the building up of the kingdom of God.

A few lines later, practicality takes precedence, Smith writing quite seriously that "If those who are coming in the spring would bring us a few potatoes, they would do us a great favor; by this, the colony would be blessed."[35]

In addition to the packet of letters and other messages, Jefferson Hunt also took four petitions to the legislature. These requested: (1) a state road from Peteetneet (Payson) to Iron Springs; (2) an exploratory study for a railroad from Tooele through Sevier Lake to Center Creek; (3) a railroad from Salt Lake City to Iron Springs; and (4) assignment of Center Creek's timber and water rights to George A. Smith.[36]

These petitions were significant. Smith realized that a railroad would be necessary to serve inland iron manufacture of any size. During the latter half of the nineteenth century, the nation experienced a boom in railroad construction because of the industry's efficiency in shipping goods and linking markets. Hardly a month had elapsed since Brigham Young had addressed the Deseret General Assembly on making a railroad from Salt Lake City through Iron County to San Diego.[37]

Smith's request for control of Center Creek's resources has been seen by critics, according to Dale Morgan, as evidence that the Mormon state favored a ruling clique. Early acts of the Deseret General Assembly do show a pattern of similar grants to ecclesiastical authorities. However, Morgan cites George Q. Cannon's explanation that these grants were seen as stewardships made to responsible persons who would act in the best interests of the whole community and were never meant to bestow exclusive privileges on the grantee.[38]

Appealing to the Common Interest

On Saturday, 18 January, Peteetneet and his band of some 30 braves came to trade, camping 200 yards south of the new settlement. The colonists formed a rectangular corral with their wagons and gathered wood for the Sabbath.[39] The following day, the 19th, was their first Sunday in the new location. The men of the camp (and one unnamed woman Lee records as the first female to attend a meeting in Iron County) met for worship in front of President Smith's wagon. Lee reported George A.'s remarks, including the observation that, despite the unity which prevailed on the trail, the president was concerned that "he saw a spirit & disposition by some persons in camp to build up themselves independent of the common interest of this Mission . . . [which was] to pave the way for the gathering of the House of Israel by subdueing the land & planting strong posts of defense for the protection of the surrounding settlements, that will hereafter b[e] made."[40]

The morning meeting, in near freezing weather, lasted an hour and a half. Smith's pointed remarks, implying a negative "spirit & disposition" in camp, affirm that not all Iron County colonists had accepted the location of the settlement. The president attacked the problem head-on at the afternoon meeting:

> Brethren we have after a tedious journey arrived safe here at the point of our destination. Though previous to our arrival, many have formed an opinion of the country & its facilities before seeing one foot of it, & the result was many were disappointed, & almost thrown into the French Hysterics . . . others [who] had the building up of the Kingdom in view alone were willing to put up with the country & its disadvantages—& be satisfied & thankful that it is no worse & this is the way we should all feel.[41]

Smith acknowledged that there was better farming land on the Little Muddy, which he claimed had abundant timber and enough water to irrigate 6,000 acres, but he was concerned the dense foliage would provide too many opportunities for Indians to attack the settlers. He anticipated that the area around the Little Muddy, soon to become better known as Coal Creek, would be "the grand post of farming in this country" when the area was secured, concluding that "I feel for the interest of this camp as much so as any other man can. I love every man in it, & my only object is to do for the general good & to fill the mission for which I was sent in connection with my brethren."[42]

George A.'s combination of irony, sentiment and inspiration was persuasive. As he himself notes in that day's journal entry, "The Brethren met again at 2 oclock in general Council; it was unanimously agreed to build a Meeting House & To settle in a Compack Fort and to make a road up Center Creek Kanyon."[43] While the origin of the term "compact fort" is uncertain, this quote would suggest it was used to denote both the wall surrounding a settlement and the settlement itself.[44]

A holograph record in the LDS Church Archives (which has no cover, first page/pages, date or identified author) documents the trip south from Salt Lake City. This "Iron Mission Record" gives another version of Smith's speech, suggesting that he had to work hard to overcome resistance to the idea of putting fort-building first, although he approached the men with a jocular tone:

I have proposed to go to work after a week running about to form a settlement. We are an outpost 250 miles from Salt Lake City and if any difficulty occurs with the natives we are expected to fight our own battles—make a permanent location to guard against intruders, we are here and when those who have not their families return there will be few left or the numbers in the fort will be materially lessened. the buildings we erect should be in compact form military fashion and style. by these means you provide for the safety of those outside and in. this is my advice and counsel it is unpleasant I know but it [is] unpleasant to have one's back stuck full of arrows. you are all as near to me as my own Brothers and when the country is settled and safe you then can spread out.[45]

Struggling to comply with these fort-building priorities, the pioneers apparently disagreed on how the settlement should be governed. Some wanted an ecclesiastical organization; others saw no need to disband the traveling system with captains of 50s and 10s until the colony was better established. After much discussion, the traveling organization was retained temporarily. Trading with the Indians was also discussed and an ad hoc committee, consisting of Thomas Wheeler (the 19-year-old interpreter) and Elisha H. Groves, was appointed to supervise dealings with the Indians. George A. Smith and John D. Lee went to the surveyor's camp between 8:00 and 9:00 P.M. to determine true north and establish longitude and latitude by star sightings, but everyone else turned in early.[46]

Surveying and Logging: First Labors on the Fort

The work of settlement-building began promptly Monday morning, 20 January 1851. Various tasks were set in motion. Tarlton Lewis, with eight men and overnight provisions, left on a trek to the canyon to cut and stack timber for the intended council house. Almon Fulmer, newly elected Supervisor of Roads, was assigned to build a road into the canyon. This used most of the 80-man work force. George A. Smith, John D. Lee and Philip Lewis[47] selected a site for the fort a few rods north of their new camp, back across the stream on the east bank but away from the canyon breeze, on a small rise for a good view. Water could easily be routed to the site from the upper stream.

The day before, Peteetneet and his men had ridden into camp expecting to trade. Smith, however, told them "it was the Lord's Day" and asked them to come back the next morning. Smith recorded, with satisfaction, that Peteetneet "then instructed his men not to trade today as it was the good day."[48] Members of the band, punctually obedient to Smith's invitation to trade once the Sabbath was over, arrived early on

Monday, asking for ammunition to hunt game. After some spirited debate, Smith decided it would be the lesser of two evils to break the territorial law prohibiting sales of arms to the Indians rather than risk antagonizing them.[49]

On Tuesday, George A. Smith met with surveyor William H. Dame and his crew to plan the fort survey and put the crew to work (see illus. 3-1). Groves and Lee were "stakes men," George Brimhall and Chandler Holbrook "chain carreers [carriers]," Isaac Barnard a "staff man," and William A. Morse a "stake maker." Morse and Isaac Newton Goodale numbered the lots.[50] James Lewis selected one man from each 10 in the 1st and 2nd 50s to guard the camp and stock, since on the previous day Peteetneet and his men "hung about our camp all day in considerable numbers."[51] Late Tuesday afternoon, Tarlton Lewis and crew returned, reporting that the timber was cut and showing a "small" sample, two feet in diameter.[52]

Surveying the fort site was the beginning of a sustained crescendo of activity, from building the road into the canyon, cutting and hauling timber for the council house and bastion, damming Center Creek and digging a two-mile irrigation ditch east of the fort site to erecting a blacksmith shop and making charcoal, building a sawmill in the mouth of the canyon, making and operating grindstones, raising a liberty pole, surveying farm lots, guarding the camp and stock, quarrying rock for the council house chimney and constructing a bowery and wickiup for a temporary school and meetinghouse. Lee describes how the survey team "gathered up their surveying apperatus & went on the ground[;] the committee establish[ing] the corners of the fort" as follows:

> The Fort was laid out 56 rods square, with a square in the center of 40 rods, for a public carrall, with a street 4 rods wide around the square with 4 large gates opening north & south 2 on each line, on the south east corner 4 rods square of ground is reserved for a Council House to be built 45 by 22 feet with recesses one on each side of 12 feet deep forming a bastion on that corner; & on the N. W. corner 4 rods are also reserved for a bastion, & around this square are laid out in lots 2 rods by 4. 26 lots on the 2 E. & W. lines & 2 on the 2 N. and S. lines making 92 lots in all.[53]

In other words, the fort was laid out on a square, each side of which measured 924 feet (308 yards). It had an interior square, the sides of which were 40 rods, containing 10 acres. This space was also used as a public corral. A four-rod inner square (66 by 66 feet) was reserved in the southeast corner of the public square for a flagpole and small assembly

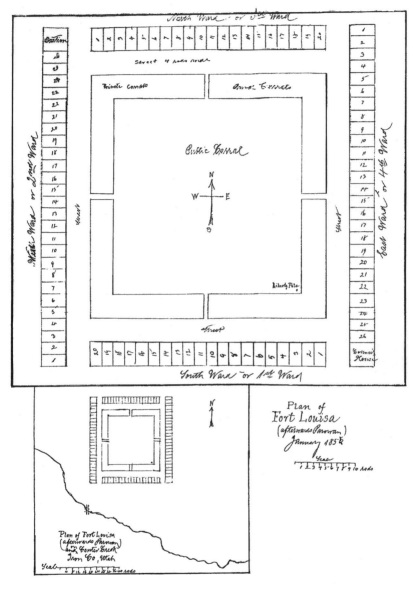

Illus. 3-1. Dame's first survey (1851) of Fort Louisa (later Parowan). See app. 3 for list of lot owner assignments in Fort Louisa.

area. Between the inner square and the houses was a street four rods wide (66 feet or 22 yards). The back wall of each house, by forming the outer perimeter of the settlement, became, in effect, the fort wall.

There were four gates, located two each on opposite sides of the north and south walls. A bastion was planned for the northwest corner and a council house (which could also serve as a bastion) for the southeast corner. From atop these two buildings, lookouts could command all approaches to the fort in an unbroken line of sight. Small individual lots formed the interior perimeter of the fort, each facing the public square. The whole plan allowed symmetrical division into four wards. The first ward consisted of 20 lots on the south (later Block 11); the second included 26 lots on the west side (Block 16); the third covered 20 lots on the north (Block 13); and the fourth included 26 lots on the east (Block 6). This totaled 92 lots, each measuring two rods by four rods.[54] These dimensions mean that individual lots were only 33 feet by 66 feet, certainly not big enough to accommodate a large house, corral, barn and garden each.

The survey was finished on Wednesday, 22 January; that evening, house lots were assigned to members of the camp (see app. 3). Since Lunt refers to the completion of the "Fort Plot" survey on this date, we can be confident that these were house lots, not the farm lots outside the townsite proper. On 23 January, Lee writes, referring to George A. Smith, that "Last evening the Pres had the camp collected togather & dealt out the lots to them as long as any man wanted one[.] all taken but 2 lots on the east line there being no demand for them the Pres said he would take them."[55] It was common practice at this time to parcel out land by drawing lots at random. Unfortunately, no comprehensive record of these and the related farm lot allocations has survived. A search of titles and abstracts reveals names and lot assignments of some original settlers, but the list is incomplete. The Deseret General Assembly had passed an ordinance dated 2 March 1850 requiring all county recorders to procure suitable record books, but the first official records of city lots in Fort Louisa were not made until June 1851 (see app. 3), and official county recording was not required by the territorial legislature until March 1852.[56]

Neither Smith nor Lee documented the garden spaces outside the fort boundaries assigned to each family, although drawings and paintings of the fort clearly show them on the east, south and west sides (see illus. 3-2). Presumably, there were spaces on the north side as well. Each settler probably had a narrow, 33-foot strip directly behind his fort lot. The only written documentation supporting these strips is a list of garden plots recorded in the front of Deed Book B,[57] as follows:

Assignee	Lot
William A. Morse	1
J. D. Lee	2
B. Watts	3
F. T. Whi[t]ney	4
L.Lewis	5
E. Whipple	6
J. L. Robinson	7
C. Holdbrook	8
E. H. Groves	9
Walker & Parks	10
Brown & Goodale	11
S. Johnson	12
M. Carruthers	13

The Council House and the Bastion

Public projects took precedence over private buildings. Among the former were the council house, bastion, public corral, irrigation canals

Rock Church Museum, Parowan, Utah

Illus. 3-2. Photograph of Bart Mortenson's pen-and-ink drawing of William Major's oil painting of Fort Parowan, 1852. Major's painting is probably the most authentic extant representation of Fort Louisa. The Mortenson drawing hangs in the Old Rock Church in Parowan; the Major painting is on display in the Lion House, Salt Lake City.

and, to some extent, the sawmill. The council house was the most important of these. The University of California's Bancroft Library manuscript, "Early Records of Utah" describes these structures as follows:

> During the year the settlers at Parowan built a fort, the houses being on the lines and the intervening spaces being filled with pickets, ten feet high. On the southeast corner of the fort a meeting house, in the form of a St. Andrew's Cross, was built of hewed logs, which projected sixteen feet over the lines, so as to form a bastion, and completely commands two sides of the fort. On the opposite or northwestern corner a pentagon bastion was erected of logs, so as to hold a cannon, and thus command the other two lines. The stockade of the public corral was built two feet in the ground and six feet above.[58]

In her *History of Iron County Mission,* Luella Dalton describes this building's uses and remodeling over some 15 years, enabling us to get a glimpse of the central place it held in community functions. Dalton's commentary is based on the reminiscences of Heber Benson:

> In the southeast corner of the Old Fort, a four rod square was reserved for building a Log Council House and on the 26th of February, 1851, the foundation was laid. This building stood a little north of where Alvin Benson's home (Elmer Lowe's) now stands [35 East 100 South], and was the first building to be started in the valley. The main building was 22 by 44 feet with two recesses twelve feet deep and sixteen feet long on the east and west sides. It was built of hewn logs and timber, the roof being covered with slabs and dirt. As soon as the shingle mill started up, the roof was raised a little making a large classroom above the auditorium and a fine substantial shingled roof covered the building. There were steps at the north and outside of the building leading to the upper classroom, which was used as a meeting room for the Priesthood quorums. The building was heated by a large fireplace in the south end. The two recesses on the east and west were used for classrooms.
>
> A stage was built in the north where the pioneer plays were produced for many years. Plays were put on here in 1851 by the Parowan Dramatic Association with Edward Dalton as President. The first plays were put on with quilts and blankets for want of curtains and scenery.
>
> The Old Council House was built for a bastian with portholes at every corner and in case of Indian attack it was large enough to hold the whole colony, but fortunately it never had to be used that way. It was built so it could be made into five large classrooms, by using canvas curtains and when drawn it was a fine big auditorium with a moveable pulpit in the center. It served as the Community Center for many years until about 1867, when the basement of the Old Rock Church was completed.[59]

Three different dimensions are given for the main structure. Lee reports the size, not counting "recesses," as 22 by 45 feet, while Dalton gives both 22 by 44 and 25 by 45 feet.[60] Nor is the completion date known. Lee's diary, which ends on 11 March 1851, does not mention the building's completion. George A. Smith's journal records meetings "at" (but not "in") the council house on 25 March and 16 May 1851.[61] His first reference to a meeting "in" the building was on 25 May 1851, nine days after the end of Brigham Young's first visit to the area.[62]

The bastion, important to the security of the community, was located on the fort's northwest corner. It was "laid with 5 Corners, logs 14 feet long," suggesting it may have been only about 14 feet square.[63] Fort Utah (Provo) had been built with a raised platform in the center for its cannon, enabling the weapon to fire over the walls in any direction but without allowing it to protect the area immediately adjacent to the fort. In contrast, the Iron County bastion's location enabled it to sweep the entire north and west approaches to the fort, while the council house guarded the east and south walls. No other description of the bastion is available. Perhaps a ramp allowed easy placement of the cannon; but since the weapon was small enough to be disassembled and carried in a wagon, a ramp may not have been required.

"Large Sticks of Timber": Building the Sawmill

Another public works project was a sawmill to provide finished timber. On 6 February 1851, work began on the public water ditch. The same day, 20 men "commenced cutting and sawing the timber for the mill." On 7 February, carpenter Richard Benson began operating a pit saw (also called a whip saw) to cut timber for gears for the sawmill. The single blade, five to 10 feet long, was usually operated by two men, one astride the log and the other in a pit below. A more sophisticated version of the tool could be driven by water power.[64]

Apparently encouraged by Benson's activity, Smith predicted two days later that "the timbers for the mill should be got out this coming week," continuing that "the necessity of a mill is imperiously felt by all at the present. The mill can be put in opperation within 4 weeks time without injuring any man. There are men who are not ready to plough, that might spend a few days on the mill just as well as not."[65]

On 10 February, Smith borrowed a horse and rode up the canyon for five miles, personally locating a mill site about three-quarters of a mile from the fort. That same day, he "engaged hands to get out the timber for the mill" frame.[66] According to Luella Dalton, this was "just below the old Lime Kiln on the right hand side of the canyon, after you cross the Mill race going up."[67] A mill appears there on William Dame's 1853 Parowan plat. Richard Benson, one of Parowan's older citizens and descendant of pioneer Richard Benson, showed Morris Shirts the site in 1980. The pit depression and millrace are still faintly visible.

Between mid-February and the beginning of May, Smith oversaw cutting and hauling timber for the mill, raising the frame and installing the machinery. On 20 February, workmen made a tailrace by rechanneling the creek; on 19 March, Burr Frost finished the mill crank; on 8 May, the mill "sawed four boards," just two days before Brigham Young arrived on a tour of inspection. Smith writes that the mill sawed 613 feet on 21 May and 750 the next day.[68]

President Smith formally petitioned the city council "for a Mill Priviledge" on 24 May,[69] and on 2 June was "Granted . . . the controll of the timber grass and Mill power in Center Creek Kanyon . . . [and] the privillidge of a Saw & Grist Mill on Center Creek."[70] Smith, who intended to operate the mill as a private venture for the public good, had previous experience with mills. In the Salt Lake Valley, he was in partnership with Archibald and Robert Gardner at West Jordan in a gristmill and had sawmill and timber rights in the Oquirrh Mountains west of the Jordan River.[71] With Smith's background, it is no wonder that he took such a personal interest in the Center Creek mill project. Smith used public labor to build and operate the mill until Brigham Young established a city government in Parowan apart from the ecclesiastical organization, at which time Smith began to hire laborers. (The Gardner mills in West Jordan were unambiguously private enterprises. The owners hired builders and millhands and charged the pioneers for their flour and lumber.)

The June reference to a gristmill raises interesting questions. While the various journals contain over 80 mill references between the settling of Parowan in January 1851 and the end of September 1852, only eight can be connected to gristmill (as opposed to sawmill) operations. One is the granting of Smith's gristmill privilege; the second reports Samuel Gould's arrival from Salt Lake City with "one milstone"; the remainder refer to the grinding of wheat. None makes any mention of constructing a gristmill separate from the sawmill or of setting some part of the sawmill aside for grinding settlers' wheat into flour. Yet the *Deseret News* of 29 November 1851 prints a 5 November

Courtesy Virginia Parsons

Illus. 3-3. Zilpha Stark
Smith (1818–87), wife of
George A. Smith, was one
of 30 women among the
original iron missionaries.

letter from George A. Smith noting that "Our saw and grist mills are in sucessful operations." The exact relationship between the two types of mills remains unclear in the journal references.[72]

A "Pleasant and Lovely Location": Fort Naming and House Building

Within a month of arriving at Center Creek, a decision had been made to name the place Fort Louisa.[73] John D. Lee mentions the name as early as 26 January when he writes of strolling with his two wives, Polly and Lovina, and with George A. Smith and his wife Zilpha "to the plat of the fort Louisa" after Sunday morning meetings. A choir, under Robert Wiley, had been organized to provide music for worship services and improve morale. Many members of the camp, unfamiliar with the English tunes Wiley chose, avoided choir practice. On 26 January, George A. Smith responded by appointing Almon L. Fulmer and Thomas S. Smith to set up an American choir. To keep peace between the two choirs, Smith alternated their performances.[74]

Apparently "Fort Louisa" was not adopted as the fort's official name until Sunday, 9 February. In an entry datelined "Iron County Mission at Louisa, Deseret," John D. Lee gives George A. credit for the name: "The Pres . . . [s]aid that we had laid out a city & he being a particular favorite of the ladies gave it the name of Louisa."[75] George A. Smith's journal entry for the day confirms that "the Brethren assembled for meeting on the lee side of the Meeting House. Organized ourselves into a Branch named Louisa Branch, I was chosen President."[76]

On 31 January, Smith allowed the men their first day off from public works to begin building their own homes, probably because the men working on the council house had run out of logs.[77] With characteristic wit, Smith describes the rush to fell timber:

[T]heir was a regular Stampede for the Kanyon every man takeing his ax and leaveing his gun, their was not half a dozen men about the Camp during the day. Every accessible tree that would make a house log within 4 miles stood a slim chance today.[78]

According to Lee, Smith thriftily assessed each eager home-builder one 14-foot log for the bastion.[79] Lee's account also includes Smith's half-scolding counsel to the men before they left the camp:

> There will be a general rush for the timber & I do not want any particular restrictions or liberty given to any man but to do right that is liberty enough for any man, to slash down any great quantity of timber would not be very prudent nor run over it & tangle it about would not produce good feelings. Within ½ hour after the liberty was granted the road was lined with chopers . . . 4 o'clock p.m. would have astonished any set of men (but Mormons) to have seen the havock that had been made within 6 hours time only. There must have been at least 1500 house logs & as many poles.[80]

In addition to getting in each others' way and stacking timber in the paths, there had been an accident. Thomas Cartwright chopped into his foot, severing one toe entirely and badly cutting two others.[81] Then on 5 March, Joseph Millet "cut off about half of his big toe in scoreing timber."[82]

Smith himself had prudently avoided the canyons, first to write a letter to Brigham Young for delivery by a small party of Mormons traveling from California to Salt Lake City[83] and then to borrow a plow and turn over a quarter acre—the first furrow turned in Iron County. He then sowed wheat, peas, carrots, parsnips, radishes and mustard seed.[84]

A few people moved onto the fort lots on 4 February but the majority—89 wagons—moved Wednesday, the fifth. "The bustle was about like May day in New York," recalled Smith.[85] The temperature was a balmy 70 degrees in the shade.[86] A week earlier, Smith had advised the settlers that "it would be well to commence putting in our wheat."[87]

They lifted their wagon boxes off the running gears and formed them into a square on the fort's interior, using their canvas as roofs and heating the interiors with stoves. Some used tents until more permanent houses could be erected. Edson Whipple's journal entry says: "arranged my wagons and put a tent in front of one of them."[88]

On 6 February, Job and Charles Hall completed the first log house in the fort. Perhaps because of his administrative duties, Smith needed considerable help completing his own house. On Monday, 17 February (his sole venture into the canyon to haul logs, no less), his team took fright and ran away, knocking the wagon to pieces.[89] By 4 February, he had laid out the foundations for two houses (presumably on his two eastern lots); by his own record, he laid the foundation for one house on 10 February.[90] On 12 February, Smith records that four men hewed logs for him. Two days later, Herman Bayles helped Smith raise two rounds of logs. On Sunday,

2 March, Bishop Miller of the Third Ward (north side) suggested that the men help Smith. The next day, seven of them hauled logs from the canyon for him; on 4 March, Robert Wiley quarried rock for the chimney, which Joseph Millett and Peter Smith (Dibble) hauled to the house. The same day, four men worked all day, three more working half a day, while an eighth man worked an hour in the evening. On Sunday, 23 March, 10 men volunteered to finish Smith's home; five finished raising it on 28 March, while two more made the window sash, frame and door.[91] Smith makes no mention of paying anyone, so presumably this labor was all volunteer. His entries also do not specify how much labor he himself contributed to the project.

On 3 April he records, "The brethren at my request moved my waggon beds to the side of my house." He apparently slept in one, for nearly a month later, he records being awakened by a cry in the night from Ruth, his four-year-old Indian foster daughter. Going "into the house" he discovered that her bedding had caught fire, but she was miraculously unhurt.[92] Such moments give the flavor of settlement life. While belatedly packing their belongings, for instance, to move from Center Creek camp to the fort on 5 February, Ebenezer and Phoebe Brown were suddenly startled to see a large wolf within a rod of them. Ebenezer seized his rifle and shot it. Smith and Peter Shirts stood guard that night, but there were no further incidents.[93]

When Nephi and Sixtus Johnson erected their log house a little over the fort line, about 40 men with hand spikes gathered late on Sunday, 16 February, to move the house back into line—without informing the Johnsons. Young Joseph Millett threatened to shoot the first man to touch the building. Richard Benson and David Brinton disarmed him. George A. Smith grabbed Millett, "shook him and throwed him on the ground which hurt him more than what I intended, and told him to go off to bed and never threaten to shoot again."[94] In unloading the gun, Smith discovered that it had wadding but no lead. He then ordered everyone to bed, advising them that the Sabbath was not a good time to move the house. A few nights later, at his request, the house was put in line "but few that was in the first Co assisted in the last opperation."[95]

Such frustrations could be expected, given the long days of labor typical of frontier living conditions. For the most part, however, the iron missionaries had pulled together remarkably well, putting community welfare first. They had erected basic housing and provided for defense. Now farming would engross the community for most of the growing season.

Endnotes

1. See discussion of Camp 25 in ch. 2 (Sunday, 12 Jan 1851).

2. Smith, journal, 15 Jan 1851.

3. Ibid., 13 Jan 1851.

4. Edson Whipple, journal, typescript, 13 Jan 1851, Perry Special Collections, 15 (section beginning 8 Dec 1850).

5. Smith, journal, 13 Jan 1851.

6. Lee, journal, 13 Jan 1851.

7. Ibid.

8. Ibid., 17 Jan 1851.

9. Ibid., 13 Jan 1851; Lunt, diary, 22 Jan 1851. Note the reference in Smith, journal, 22 Jan 1851 to "elegant made grind stones."

10. Lee, ibid., and Smith, ibid.: both on 14 Jan 1851.

11. Ibid.; Orson F. Whitney, *History of Utah,* 4 vols. (Salt Lake City: George Q. Cannon and Sons, Publishers, 1892), 1:452.

12. Lee, journal, 14 Jan 1851.

13. Ibid.; Gibson's arrival in Salt Lake City on 29 Jan 1851 was the first word of the appointment to reach the territorial capital. See Whitney, *History of Utah,* 1:452.

14. Lee, ibid., 14 Jan 1851. Gustive Larson, p. 273, n. 47, identifies the "smawl" lake as Rush Lake.

15. Lee, ibid., 15 Jan 1851; Smith, journal, 15 Jan 1851. The quote is from Lee.

16. A geological feature called the Rim of the Basin falls across southern Utah south of Cedar City. Acting to some extent as a minor continental divide, this landmark creates a watershed in which creeks "above" it flow north, while creeks "below" it drain south. With Coal Creek lying above the Rim, Dame's party, while heading downstream, would still have been traveling in a more or less northerly direction.

17. Lee, journal, 15 Jan 1851; Smith's copy of this entry, made on the same date, includes the clearer phrase: "specimens of the ore rock we brought to be tested."

18. Smith, ibid.

19. Ibid.; Lee, journal, 15 Jan 1851.

20. Journal History, 20 Nov 1850, 3d page of entry.

21. Dale L. Morgan, "State of Deseret," *Utah Historical Quarterly* 8 (Apr/Jul/Oct 1940): 195 (cited hereafter as State of Deseret).

22. Smith, journal, and Lee, journal: both on 15 Jan 1851.

23. Smith, ibid.

24. Lee, journal, 16 Jan 1851 (where Charles and John's surname is spelled "Dolton"); Smith, on the same date, records a somewhat different version.

25. Lee, ibid. The implements in Hunt's cache would have been of great value to the settlers. Unfortunately, as Smith reports on 7 Feb 1851, when he and Thomas

Wheeler rode out to Summit Creek to retrieve them, the cache was empty. No further references to the small mystery have been found.

26. Lee, journal, and Smith, journal, both on 16 Jan 1851.

27. Lee, ibid.

28. Ibid.

29. Ibid., 17 Jan 1851.

30. Ibid.

31. Ibid., 278, n. 60.

32. There are several versions of the history of this cannon. According to Louella Adams Dalton, the cannon was a "war prize" from Missouri, hidden in the mud by Missourians after the battle of Crooked River near Far West. An old sow and her piglets, rooting around, partially uncovered it. The Mormon militia dug it up, cleaned it, mounted it on wheels and took it to Nauvoo, then to Salt Lake City. It is not known how the decision was made to send the cannon to Iron County with George A. Smith in 1850–51. During the time it was in Parowan, it was known as the "Old Sow Cannon." At some point, Dalton claims, it was returned to Salt Lake City. (It may be the cannon formerly on display at the Temple Square Bureau of Information and now housed in the LDS Church Museum of History and Art.) See Dalton, *Iron County Mission,* 12. See also "Cannon Being Memorialized Has Colorful Pioneer History," *Church News,* published by *Deseret News,* 29 Jan 1994, 7, 13.

33. Smith, journal; Lee, journal; Lunt, diary: all on 17 Jan 1851.

34. Lee, ibid., p. 279, n. 61.

35. George A. Smith to Brigham Young, 17 Jan 1851, published in *Deseret News,* 8 Feb 1851, 205–6.

36. Smith, journal, 18 Jan 1851.

37. Morgan, "State of Deseret," 193.

38. Ibid., 106–7, n. 100.

39. Lee, journal, 18 Jan 1851, notes the "carall" being built on the west side of Center Creek; Lunt, diary, on the same date, records forming the wagons "in two lines on south side of Creek near the liberty pole."

40. Lee, ibid., 19 Jan 1851; Smith, journal, on the same date, writes that the "Camp . . . listened to a very interesting discourse from Anson Call, to which I bore testimony."

41. Lee, ibid.

42. Ibid.

43. Smith, journal, 19 Jan 1851.

44. See ch. 7 for discussion of the Compact Fort.

45. Anonymous, "Iron Mission Record," 1850–59, entry of Sunday, 19 Jan 1851, 6th and 7th pages. Descriptive title given by Morris Shirts to holograph (undated, unpaginated, untitled and missing the first page or pages) at the LDS

Church Archives. The record begins mid-entry: "last season about two feet higher." The next entry is Monday, 23 Dec 1850, the last *daily* entry being 16 Feb 1851, with *weekly* (or longer-interval) entries until 1 Jun 1851. The final 28 pages, probably incomplete, consist of birth, marriage, excommunication and death entries in various hands, the last entry being 28 Sep 1859. Author tentatively identifies the diarist as James Lewis because known samples of his penmanship compare favorably with the writing here and because he was clerk for both the "traveling branch" of the Iron Mission and the "Louisa Branch" organized in February 1851. The MS is 52 pages long, 19½ of diary entries and 32½ of vital statistics. It was donated to the LDS Church Archives by G. Homer Durham in 1977, with no record of where he obtained it.

46. Lee, journal, 19 Jan 1851.

47. Ibid. These three were members of the Council of Fifty, a prestigious group of trusted leaders organized in 1844 by Joseph Smith to serve as a legislative body for the theocracy established in Nauvoo. It met periodically to advise and enact "shadow" legislation until Utah became a territory in 1851. Leonard J. Arrington, *Brigham Young: American Moses* (New York: Alfred A. Knopf, 1985), 109.

48. Smith, journal, 19 Jan 1851.

49. Lee, journal, 19 Jan 1851.

50. Ibid., 22 Jan 1851. Larson's spelling is "William A. Moss."

51. Smith, journal, 20 Jan 1851.

52. Lee, journal, 21 Jan 1851.

53. Ibid.

54. Ibid.; general references in Smith, journal, 21–22 Jan 1851.

55. Lee, journal, 23 Jan 1851; Smith, journal, 22 Jan 1851. Both men record the lot drawing as having occurred on the 22nd. See also Lunt, diary, 22 Jan 1851.

56. Hunter, *Utah: The Story of Her People,* 254.

57. Deed Book B (28 Feb 1855–15 Sep 1863), Iron County Recorder's Office, Parowan, Utah. The list appears on the torn flyleaf page in the front of the book.

58. Knecht and Crawley, *Early Records of Utah,* 112.

59. Dalton, *Iron County Mission,* 34–35.

60. Lee, journal, 21 Jan 1851; Dalton, ibid., 34.

61. Smith, journal, 25 Mar, 16 May 1851.

62. Ibid., 25 May 1851.

63. Ibid., 22 Feb 1851. Compare the phrasing of Lee's journal entry on 21 Jan 1851: "on the south east corner 4 rods square of ground is reserved for a Council House . . . with recesses one on each side of 12 feet deep forming a bastion on that corner; & on the N. W. corner 4 rods are also reserved for a bastion." It is not possible to tell, by collating the journal entries, exactly what size the leaders intended the bastions to be.

64. Lee, journal. Lee gives two sizeable entries the same date: "Sund. Feb. 9th 1851." The water ditch and pit saw references come near the end of the first of these, whose internal references show that it actually covers 3 Feb through 8 Feb.

65. Ibid. This cite occurs near the end of the second passage Lee dates as "Feb. 9th."

66. Smith, journal, 10 Feb 1851.

67. Dalton, *Iron County Mission*, 411–12.

68. Smith, journal, 20 Feb, 8 Mar, 19 Mar, 8 May, 21 May and 22 May 1851.

69. Ibid., 24 May 1851. Smith had already petitioned the territorial legislature for these privileges by letter on 17 Jan 1851, which Jefferson Hunt carried north on his return to Salt Lake City.

70. Ibid., 2 Jun 1851.

71. Laws and Ordinances of the State of Deseret (Utah), Compilation 1851 (Salt Lake City: Shepard Book, 1919), 16–17, microfilm copy, series 83238, reel 1, Utah State Archives and Records Service, Salt Lake City.

72. Smith, journal, 26 Jun, 1 Aug 1851; George A. Smith, letter to editor, 5 Nov 1851, in *Deseret News*, 29 Nov 1851, 3d unnumbered page; James Whittaker Sr., journal, 12 Nov 1851, catalogued as no. WH-1–2, SUU Archives (note that James Jr. occasionally records entries in this journal). Note additional mill references in Lunt, diary, 4 May, 16 Jun, 17 Aug and 9 Sep 1852.

73. Lee, journal, 9 Feb 1851, and Larson's prior comment, at p. 364, n. 16. The origin of the fort name is not clear. None of the 30 women in the first company was named Louisa. John D. Lee implies that the fort was named in honor of Louisa Beaman, first plural wife of Joseph Smith (although there are indications that other women may have preceded her). Louisa's fairly recent death, on 16 May 1850, may have prompted George A. Smith to think of her when searching for a fort name.

74. Ibid., 26 Jan 1851.

75. Ibid., 9 Feb 1851. (The quote is taken from the second section so dated.)

76. Smith, journal, 9 Feb 1851 (mislabeled "Jany" in original). This "branch" should not be understood as equivalent to a twentieth-century branch (one unit smaller than a ward). Lee's journal entry of 9 Feb (the second so dated) reports that, immediately after the settlers agreed to name their fort "Louisa," they "laid out the city into 4 wards . . . & Bishop A. Call is a resident of the 1st ward. Bro. Tarlton Lewis of the 2nd[.] D.A. Miller of the 3rd & Bishop Jos. L. Robbinson of the 4th. J. D. Lee motioned that the above named persons act as Bishops in their respective wards the vote was taken sepperately & carried."

77. Lee, journal, 31 Jan 1851.

78. Smith, journal, 31 Jan 1851.

79. Lee, journal, 31 Jan 1851.

80. Ibid.

81. Ibid., 1 Feb 1851.

82. Smith, journal, 5 Mar 1851.

83. Ibid., 28 Jan 1851; Lee, journal, 27 Jan 1851. The six men—William P. Goddard, Gordon S. Beckstead, Jacob Winters, Henry Cook, William Bird and James Davidson—were traveling to Salt Lake City with another letter for Brigham Young, this one about the proposed purchase of the Williams Ranch near Cajon Pass in California.

84. Smith, journal, 31 Jan 1851.

85. Ibid., 5 Feb 1851.

86. Lunt, diary, 5 Feb 1851.

87. Lee, journal, 31 Jan 1851.

88. Whipple, journal, 5 Feb 1851. The whole reference from Whipple is: "This morning most of the camp moved. Some remained on the ground. Bro. Hulse and I got our wagons over, and he hauled a load of stone for underpinning my house, and I arranged my wagons and put a tent in front of one of them."

89. Smith, journal, 17 Feb 1851.

90. Ibid., 10 Feb 1851; Lee, journal, 7 Feb 1851 (misdated "Frid. The 4th" inside already-misdated "Sund. Feb. 9th 1851" section).

91. Smith, ibid., 12 Feb, 14 Feb, 2–4 Mar and 23 Mar 1851. On 24 Mar, Smith wrote that that "Br [John P.] Bernard and [William] Empy presented me with a hewed log house." The reference does not clarify whether this log structure was another house Smith had arranged to buy or trade for, or whether the two men had, on that date, finished construction work on his initial home.

92. Ibid., 3 Apr and 1 May 1851.

93. Lee, journal, 5 Feb 1851 (within the misdated "Sund. Feb. 9th 1851" section).

94. Smith, journal, 16 Feb 1851.

95. Lee, journal, 16 Feb 1851.

4

Community Farms and Buildings

February–May 1851

After providing shelter, the next most important task facing the new community was assuring a food supply. The colonists would need to decide where to locate their farms, how to fairly distribute the farm lots and exactly when to begin planting. With these specific tasks well underway, the iron missionaries could then turn their attention to more general affairs, such as building a meetinghouse, establishing a school, exploring for fuel and accommodating new arrivals.

Most likely, the settlers were able to begin producing spring vegetables in their garden plots by April. These plots, as noted in chapter 3, were located outside the fort but near the walls[1] (see sidebar: "Planning a City of Zion"). Typical of this early stage in Utah colonizing, the Mormons also planned a "big field" or communal farm. Settlers were assigned lots within these large parcels of arable land. The whole was then surrounded by a fence that was collectively maintained. Having all the farm allotments in one location improved efficiency; having a constantly maintained perimeter fence improved security. However, the initial process of locating these farm lots caused a serious division of opinion among the pioneers.[2]

Locating the Farms: Black Soil or Sandy Loam?

The settlers had their choice of two distinct soil types in the region. In the valley below and west of the fort, nearer the lake bed, grew thick wire grass in black soil, called the "bottom land." Closer to the fort on the uplands of the bench was sandy loam, the "bloody red soil" that had so displeased some of the men.

George A. Smith opened the discussion on Sunday, 26 January 1851, about 10 days before the planned move to the fort site. The camp met for

PLANNING A CITY OF ZION

The fundamental concept of the City of Zion, developed in 1838 by Joseph Smith for Far West, Missouri, provided a pattern of village residences on generous-sized lots with farms ringing the city. Isolated homesteads gave way to solid and unified communities. Streets were to be four-square, aligned with the cardinal directions, running east-west and north-south. Brigham Young had deliberately chosen a site for Salt Lake City that allowed precise orientation to the cardinal directions, with farming land close to the city in five-acre parcels, a second ring of farms in ten-acre plots and a third ring in 20-acre plots (generally speaking). This arrangement, by assuring that no single individual would own a large amount of land near the city center, effectively discouraged land speculation.

The same principles seem to have governed Dame's January–February 1851 survey. He worked within a grid system of blocks and ranges, the standard survey system used throughout the region. *Blocks* were laid out from a base line running east and west with *ranges* laid out from a common meridian running north and south. He tried to plot his base lines and meridians from the Great Salt Lake Base Line and Meridian (see chapter 2, n. 32). When plotted on current maps, Dame's grid system is fairly close to this township-and-range system. His zero point, where prime base line and meridian cross, was toward the northeast corner of Fort Louisa (currently north Main Street, midway along the west side of Block 13 in Parowan—the block abutting the north side of the original fort's central square). The modern city of Parowan is essentially superimposed upon Fort Louisa and enlarged in relation to it, so its blocks do not line up precisely with Dame's original survey boundaries, either for the town or its farm lots.

Dame's eight "outer" blocks were one-half mile wide, running east-west along his base line. His 12 ranges were one-quarter mile wide, laid out on a north-south meridian. Streets measuring either three or four rods (49.5 or 66 feet) ran along the base and meridian lines so that all farms could be easily reached. A set of smaller, "inner" city blocks began at the southeast corner of the townsite, ran north and then south, north, south and north again, and ended with Block 22 in the northwest corner (see chapter 5, illus. 5-1).

Source: For discussion of Joseph Smith's City of Zion concept, see Leonard J. Arrington, *Great Basin Kingdom: Economic History of the Latter-day Saints, 1830–1900* (Lincoln: University of Nebraska Press, 1968), 10.

worship around 1:30 P.M. After the service, Smith stated that "he would resolve this meeting into a legislative capacity (especially) for the committee to express their views & bring up their strong reasons in favor of the best spot to locate our farming interests this present season."[3]

John D. Lee's journal notes the vigor of the debate. Elisha H. Groves wanted to farm the upland near the fort because he thought it would produce just as well as the bottom land but with less labor. Anson Call warmly disagreed, saying he would rather have one acre of wire grass land than four of the upland because the yield would be so much greater.[4] Unfortunately, Lee reports no other opinions in this entry. However, the "Iron Mission Record," presumably penned by James Lewis, does. The statements documented there clearly demonstrate the eagerness of camp members to share in decision-making. For instance, Andrew Baston, 44, a farmer from Maine, wanted to accommodate everyone by having two fields, but Almon L. Fulmer, the 34-year-old newly elected road commissioner, wanted to work together on one field, saying the cattle were weak and already had too much work to do. Dr. William A. Morse, at 64 one of the oldest of the pioneers, agreed, saying "One field. Union is power." Edson Whipple was willing to farm either bottom or upland, though he preferred upland "for this season," but hoped it would be on the south side of the creek.[5]

After a dinner break, the settlers reconvened at 6:00 P.M. William H. Dame, who had led an exploring party west toward the lake, following the creek on the north side and returning on the south side, said he liked the low land, but ultimately preferred the upland by the fort, thinking it best "to farm as near home as possible." A "Bro. Miller" expressed a preference for the bottom land "for this season" since it would require only a third of the water necessary for the upland and had fewer crickets. Elisha Groves agreed that the bottom land was best, but questioned whether farming there would be "best for the present season." He felt crickets were likely anywhere, but since one man could farm more upland in a day than two could on the bottoms, the fort would be better protected by a big field closest to it.[6]

Vermont farmer Joseph L. Robinson, 49, had earlier voiced his preference for the "very handsome" bottom land, but now seconded Lee and Baston's proposals for two fields, each settler to have an allotment in both. The energetic debate continued, but neither position gained on the other. Having heard all the opinions, George A. Smith wanted more time to consider, finally announcing "I shall study the best interest of the camp."[7] Following a short break, talk resumed around a large campfire. In

Smith's words, they "continued the discussion very spiritedly until about Ten oclock."[8]

The initial debate had focused on which type of soil would produce the best crop. John D. Lee, however, in the afternoon meeting, raised an equally important point—that not all the settlers had the right tools or sufficient experience to farm the wire grass land on an equal footing. He urged that the "interest of all . . . be considered togather & not the building up of one or a few individuals." The conclusion of his 26 January journal entry underscores his wish to apply the spirit of compromise to a decision affecting the survival of the whole company:

> the wire grass land is a first rate soil & no man can prise it higer than he does but the question now resolves its self in this shape, among this co. are farmers blacksmiths, carpenters, shuwmakers, tailors, stone & brick masons silver smiths & portrait painters etc. Some have good ploughs & strong teams & could manage the wire grass land to a good advantage, to such it would be proffetable but a great many have poor ploughs & weak teams & some no ploughs at all—& what is still worse than all they lack experience, to that class it would be very unproffitable to engage in the tough hard sod this present year. But could we so manage it as to unite our interests & have a portion of both kinds of soil to cultivate this present season it certainly would better accommodate the whole & would be in my opinion the best policy.[9]

Deliberations continued for the next several days, but by 31 January 1851 lots were being surveyed and allocated. On that date, Smith says, William Dame "surveyed 30 5 acre Lots, 5 of which he condemned" on account of greasewood and sage. Later that evening, around a large campfire, "their was about 50 applications for 5 acre Lots and about 20 for 10 acre Lots."[10] John D. Lee's entry for the same day reports that "the surveyor commenced surveying the 5 acre lots to accommodate the whole camp with a small piece of land nearby for vines[,] potatoes and garden stuff." Later in the entry, however, Lee states that only "about 6 persons applied" for the 5 acre lots, another instance of the journals being less than consistent on this subject.

"Shooked Up Togather": The First Draw for Farm Lots

The inconsistency between Lee and Smith on lot allocations points out the whole problem of where the five-acre and 10-acre lots were located. Smith's entries generally imply that five-acre lots were located on the upland near the fort, while 10-acre lots were located on the wire grass or bottom land some two to three miles away. Lee, however, in one entry, claims the exact opposite. On Sunday afternoon, 2 February, at a further allocation of lots, he notes that "Names were then taken & the amount of land wanted to the amount of about 300 acres of upland in 10 acre lots & near the same amount in 5's of the wire grass something over 500 acres were petitioned for."[11]

By closely examining both journal references and Deed Book A entries we can clarify the issue. On the evening of 2 February, the five-acre lots were distributed, each being numbered by a stake placed in one corner. The name of each man who applied for a lot was placed on a ticket, and the tickets were tossed in a hat, shaken together and drawn out by Bishop Groves. Lot 1 was automatically assigned to George A. Smith. The first man whose name was drawn took Lot 2, the next man took Lot 3 and so forth until all the names were drawn. The surveyor and clerk were on hand to record the lot number and corresponding range and block assigned to each man.[12] As early as 9 February, President Smith (according to Lee) noted that 550 acres of wire grass and 1,000 acres of upland had been applied for when there were "only about 550 bushels of seed wheat in camp" along with some oats, corn, barley and potatoes. He scolded overambitious farmers, saying

> it is not good policy to overcrop ourselves—there is a great deal of work to be done always in the settlement of a new place more than what many are aware off [*sic*]. A small crop well tended is better than double the amount of land run over & half tended.[13]

Apparently, not all the settlers who claimed land in early drawings officially recorded their property. Some transactions are known to us primarily through journal references. William Dame, for instance, took 80 acres near the stream bed where water would have been easily obtained. (As surveyor, he may have had privileged selection of lots since his "salary" was in acreage, as was the custom of the day.) George A. Smith had a farm adjoining Dame's that he refers to on 10 March, writing that "Thos Wheeler and Peter Smith (Dibble) took my seed grain, plough and drag, two yoke of cattle and Wheeler's horses and went down on my farming land, a piece which Dame surveyed me, 20 acres, about 2½ miles distant."[14] And on 12 April, heading for the Pacific Islands with a group of missionaries, Parley P. Pratt asked William Dame to survey a piece of land for him on the mountainside south of the fort. This day was also Pratt's birthday, which he celebrated by sharing a "sumptuous repast" with 10 or 12 others at George A.'s house. Pratt's new land included some valuable springs and range land but not much farm land. It was gigantic by 1851 standards—84 by 240 rods, a little over one-quarter mile by three-quarters of a mile, or 130 acres[15] (see illus. 4-1).

But even these helpful descriptions do not resolve Smith and Lee's journal inconsistencies over how the five and 10-acre lots were distributed between upland and wire grass land. To answer that, we must review the earliest transactions found in Deed Book A. One insight into local geography that helps us understand the deed book entries is knowing that the change from wire grass soil to upland more or less followed the old river channel of Center Creek, west of Parowan City (in the neighborhood of the first five blocks or so of Range 4 or 5 North). By organizing the list of entries according to the range in which the respective blocks and lots are located, the problem quickly resolves itself:

Selected Lot Listings from Deed Book A

Date	Owner	Range	Block	Lot	Acres
07 Feb 1851	George A. Smith	1	1	1	5
[11 Apr 1851?]	Thomas Corbitt	1	1	4	5
24 Feb 1851	George Brimhall	1	1	9	5
07 Feb 1851	Francis Whitney	1	1	16	5
16 Mar 1851	Elisha H. Groves	2	1	4	5
11 Apr 1851	William Mitchell	2	1	6	5
27 Feb 1851	Philip Lewis	3	1	10	5
24 Feb 1851	Zedick Judd	4	1	11	5
16 Mar 1851	Elisha H. Groves	4	1	13	10
11 Apr 1851	William Mitchell	5	1	4	10
07 Feb 1851	James Lewis	5	1	8	10
24 May 1851	George A. Smith	7	5	4	10
24 May 1851	George A. Smith	7	5	5	10
24 May 1851	George A. Smith	7	5	6	10
24 Feb 1851	Zedick Judd	8	6	1	10
24 Feb 1851	Zedick Judd	8	6	8	10
16 Mar 1851	Jefferson Wright	10	6	1	10
24 Feb 1851	George Brimhall	10	7	2	10
27 Feb 1851	Peter Shirts	11	6	1	10
27 Feb 1851	Peter Shirts	11	6	7	10

Source: Deed Book A, Iron County Recorder's Office, Parowan, Utah.[16]

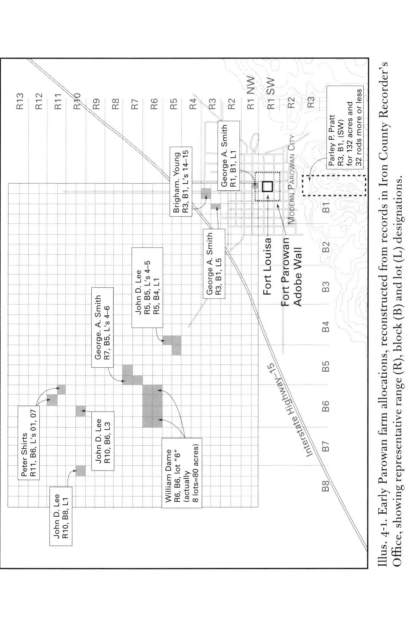

Illus. 4-1. Early Parowan farm allocations, reconstructed from records in Iron County Recorder's Office, showing representative range (R), block (B) and lot (L) designations.

It appears, even from this incomplete list, that most if not all upland lots were surveyed at five acres, while wire grass lots were surveyed at 10 acres. That Range 4 is the only location on the list showing separate records for a five and 10-acre lot each merely confirms our expectation that somewhere in that vicinity, soil type shifts from sandy upland loam to heavier, darker wire grass sod. Finally, the list tells us that Lee's journal entry of 2 February, noting 10-acre upland lots and five-acre wire grass lots, is almost certainly an error, most likely an inadvertent transposition of what he intended to write.

"The Frost . . . is Out of the Ground": Sowing Early Crops

The first planting season was difficult, although it started well. As early as 30 January, Smith wrote "The frost in some places is out of the ground sufficiently to plough." The next day (the same day Dame surveyed the five-acre lots), Smith records that he "borrowed a plough and with the assistance of Peter [Smith (Dibble)] ploughed ¼ of an Acre of land on a 5 Acre Lot." John D. Lee draws a more important conclusion to Smith's experiment, saying "the Pres. with his own hands held the plough to make the first furrow that ever [has] been made in Iron Co to our knowledge, & sowed some wheat."[17]

On 3 February 1851 Anson Call, Joseph Robinson and Daniel Miller (the committee assigned to investigate fencing the wire grass field) gave their report. They concluded that in some places Center Creek would itself be a sufficient fence to restrain the cattle. An irrigation ditch, following the lay of the land, could become the greater portion of the east line of the fence, running north and emptying into the lake bed. Only the south line would need to be picketed (a series of straight poles without any crossbars) for a distance of about 100 rods. The committee confirmed "the sod on the wire grass land to be tough & hard to break."

Smith recognized that the fence might not be completely reliable, especially since he had "recommended the brethren to establish a herd for cows" on 31 January. According to Lee, Smith reiterated this wish on Sunday, 9 February, at the afternoon meeting, saying "We should be pleased to have some faithful efficient man get up a heard of milch cows[;] a great deal of time is spent in hunting cows, which may be avoided could we get up a heard." When no volunteers came forward, Smith appointed Peter Shirts, who began his new duties on 3 March.[18] On 22 March the fence committee decided to divide responsibility for building the perimeter fence by lot assignment. Each owner, according to Smith, would be responsible for "1 rod 2 ½ feet" of fence or 19 feet per acre per man.[19]

With only 57 plows in the company, preparing the soil was largely cooperative. Since the ground had never been worked, the plows constantly jumped furrows, rebounding from hidden roots and rocks. Well-established sage and rabbit brush had to be grubbed out. The pioneers harrowed with homemade tree-trunk drags (logs studded with pegs in the bottom) to ready the soil for planting (see illus. 4-2). After harrowing, the pioneers would furrow the plots and then broadcast seed grain from bags slung over their shoulders. At the same time, they dug ditches to channel Center Creek's water through the fields, carefully routing a fair share to each farmer.

The weather remained chilly all spring. Lunt and Smith's journals are not detailed enough to let us reconstruct a planting log, but many acres had been sown by 25 March. Smith's letter of this date to Brigham Young illustrates how farming was proceeding in the settlement, despite ever changeable weather. It also reflects the spirit of compromise which John D. Lee had urged upon the pioneers when they first debated the relative merits of upland and wire grass.

> We are progressing rapidly in our farming operations, having already
> sown four hundred acres of wheat, and they will probably amount to
> one thousand. The soil is considered of the first quality, both upland
> and wire grass, by our best farmers—no division of opinion regarding

Photograph by Morris A. Shirts.

Illus. 4-2. Pioneer tree-trunk harrow with wooden pegs for teeth.

soil. There have been about sixteen hundred acres surveyed, and the probability is that it will nearly all be cultivated this season.[20]

The settlers had found a way past their differences without risk to individuals or the community at large. Now they had to solve the next problem: how to plant, manage and harvest crops in a region where unpredictable weather seemed to be the norm. On 26 March, for instance, Smith himself planted those of his potatoes that had not frozen en route, even though it snowed the night before. Settlers were plagued with wind and snow all spring; nevertheless, they planted wheat, corn, oats and barley as well as garden crops such as peas. Some crops failed when unseasonably warm weather turned chill again, requiring a second planting,[21] but the men continued plowing and planting, trying to learn the nature of the land quickly enough to make it produce the crops they needed to survive.

The School and the Bowery

Crowded into the events of this busy spring were a few weeks of school. In late February, Smith had put together a "Wickyup" or Native American shelter. He was proud of its practicality, writing that it was

> a very important establishment composed of Brush, a few slabs and 3 waggons, a fire in the Center, and a lot of milking stools benches & logs placed around, two of which are cushioned with Buffalo Robes, in answer for various purposes, Kitchen, School House, dineing room, Meeting House, Council House, Sitting Room, Reading Room, Store Room.[22]

Smith's evening grammar school had opened on 21 February, with six scholars who met nightly. He identifies them as Thomas Wheeler, 19; Joseph Millet, 17; Peter A. Smith (Dibble), 15; carpenter Richard Benson, 35; Benjamin Hulse, 36, a ship joiner; and William Mitchell, either the 44-year-old bricklayer or his 16-year-old son.[23] George A. describes his school colorfully—scholars huddled around a campfire, the thermometer at seven degrees above zero, "the wind broken off by the brush and the whole canopy of heaven for a covering . . . one side roasting while the other freezing, requiring a continual turning to keep as near as possible an equilibrium of temperature." Grammar book in hand, George A. "would give out a sentence at a time, and pass it round, notwithstanding these ci[r]cumstances, I never saw a grammar class learn faster for the time."[24]

On 23 February, two nights after opening his school, Smith records: "Br. Shirts at my request started a school this Evening in Br Millers

House. An Evening Grammar School."[25] Since an analysis of the letters Shirts wrote to Brigham Young (from Brigham's letter book) suggests that Shirts was hardly qualified to teach English grammar, he may have been teaching other subjects. Neither the names nor the number of students in the class are given. Note that the two men listed as "teacher" on the May 1851 Census, James Lewis and James A. Little, apparently were not involved in these first academic efforts.[26]

Another makeshift construction that spring was the Bowery. At first, most public meetings were held in the 24-rod square inside the fort. The wind always felt cold no matter which direction it was blowing. On 25 January, president Smith raised a bowery of cedar boughs in front of his wagon for the next day's Sunday worship. When the Louisa Branch was organized on 9 February, the settlers gathered on the lee—or south—side of the unfinished council house, to escape, in Smith's words, the "fine wind blowing from the East."[27] On Sunday, 16 February, they held "no meeting to day the weather being to[o] uncomfortable to sit in the open air,"[28] by no means the only case of inclement weather. On 19 March, Smith wrote, "The wind blowed very hard from the South, leaving no Tents standing in Camp." Nine days later came a similar entry: "The wind blew very hard all night and continued so all the day." The Cartwright wagon caught fire and burned up, a lesson not lost on Smith. "Tremendeous high wind all day," he commented two days later, on the 30th of March, "dangerous to have fires in waggons."[29]

The first Bowery was replaced by a more substantial structure in late February. Luella Adams Dalton provides the following description:

> In the spring of 1851, the settlers built the Old Bowery, 54 by 77 feet just west of the Log Council House. The roof was fifteen feet high in the center, sloping down to the sides and covered with scantlings about a foot apart, then covered with boughs from trees. The south and west walls were boarded up with scantling and boards giving some protection from the southwesterly winds. There was a large platform in the south end, which on state occasions was decorated with flowers, boughs, pictures and maps. . . . The Old Bowery was a nice cool shady place for meetings for many years. Many times, President Young's party were entertained here and the Saints on their way to San Bernardino, California met here. Meetings were still held here as late as 1865, when President Brigham Young's party came on another visit through the settlements.[30]

Arrivals and Departures

Other noteworthy events that spring were the arrivals and departures of visitors and colony members. On 17 March, in the absence of an established mail route, Smith appointed "John P. Barnard, Wm. Empy, Capt. A. L. Fullmer, Wm. Bringhurst, Charles Harper & [blank space] Harmison" as a special "express" to carry the mail to Salt Lake City.[31] The settlers spent the next few days composing official and personal communications.

Only three days later, an Indian courier identified as "Turnip" arrived from Sanpete Valley with news from Isaac Morley that Amasa Lyman and Charles C. Rich were assembling a company in Utah County, bound for California. Members of the Lyman group were assigned to form a settlement at Cajon Pass near San Bernardino to produce grapes, sugar cane and cotton.[32] As noted earlier, a group of missionaries under Parley P. Pratt was also forming. It consisted of Pratt and his wife Phoebe, Francis and Mary Jane Hammond, William and Patsy Perkins, Richard R. Hopkins and wife, John Stillman Woodbury, John Murdock, Rufus Allen, Philo Wood and Morris Miner. They were bound for Hawaii and Sydney, Australia, with Pratt and Phoebe going to Valparaiso, Chile.[33]

A few days later, on 7 April, a lone rider whom Smith identifies as "Homes" reported that the express had reached the Sevier in four days and that an advance party of the California company (the wagons of the Lyman and Pratt groups, now traveling together) was camped on the Beaver. According to George A. Smith, 10 wagons from this advance party crossed Beaver Ridge on the 8th and were accompanied by an additional "5 for this place." George A., John Calvin Lazelle Smith and Orson Drake rode out to Red Creek to meet the wagons.[34]

However, on the very next day, 9 April, Smith records that "our Settlement is increased by the arrival of eight waggons, . . . three women and eight men and a number of children," none, unfortunately, identified by name. This party brought with them 30 welcome bushels of seed potatoes, which the settlers planted on 25 April. The travelers also brought a letter from Heber C. Kimball, first counselor to Brigham Young, apparently confirming Young's plans to visit the settlement. There was also a letter from George A. Smith's wife Lucy Meservy conveying the unhappy news that another wife, Sarah Ann Libby, was very ill with tuberculosis.[35]

The combined parties of travelers created an influx of 520 people and 157 wagons, temporarily doubling the size of Fort Louisa. Some camped south of the fort, but Smith, Rich and Pratt located a large campsite five miles to the south on Summit Creek. They celebrated "Mormon-style," with several open-air meetings, usually around campfires. The choir, designated as the Louisa Choir (perhaps indicating that the English and American choirs were singing together), supplied music, and many settlers walked from Fort Louisa to Summit Creek to hear the sermons.

On Sunday, 20 April, while Smith was riding with John D. Lee and their wives in Lee's carriage, a broken rein spooked the lead team, causing them to swing sharply and overturn the carriage. Smith "curled [him]self up like a sloth and rolled out uninjured," but Lee and the ladies suffered kicks from the frightened animals and severe bruising from being thrown out of the vehicle. Despite the near disaster, they traveled on to Summit Creek after a replacement wagon was procured and held their Sunday meetings, ending the "cool and pleasant" day listening to hymns performed by the Louisa Choir of singers, "which diffused general joy throughout the meeting."[36]

New settlers and families of first settlers continued to trickle in steadily. Samuel Gould, listed in the *Deseret News* on the original 16 November 1850 "call list" but not on the 11 January 1851 "departure list," is recorded by Smith as arriving on 8 April with his wife Fanny Gould and his sons (from a previous marriage) John and William.[37] On 10 April, Parley P. Pratt, looking around with an admiring eye, praised the success of the colony:

> I found the inhabitants all well, and the settlement in a truly flourishing condition. Hundreds of acres of grain had been sown, gardens planted, etc., and the farming land nearly enclosed; together with a most substantial saw mill, and many houses of wood and of sun dried brick, built and in progress. Building materials consisting of timber of the finest quality, viz: pine, fir and cedar, together with good building stone and brick, were scattered in profusion in every direction.
>
> Water ditches were flowing for mills and irrigation purposes in many directions.
>
> Mechanics' shops were in operation; such as joiners, carpenters, millwrights, coopers, blacksmiths, shoemakers, etc.
>
> All this was the work of two or three months, in winter and early spring; not to mention a large enclosure of pickets in the centre of the fort—a council house of hewn timber, and a bastion of the same material.
>
> The number of men composing the settlement and performing all this work, did not exceed one hundred and twenty all told, including old men, boys and Indian servants.[38]

The California-bound party left on 26 April, leaving behind them three wagons whose owners were waiting for a Sister Swarthout to have her child. The 22-year-old woman died two days later and became the community's first Mormon burial, which took place "north east of Louisa in the Cedar grove."[39] With the California party went four of the Iron County pioneers: Philip B. Lewis, called as a missionary with Pratt's group; and P. George Moore, Chester Towne and Peter Lish, who, according to Smith, joined the California colonizing group after having been in the settlement "all winter."[40] On 28 April, however, there were less welcome departures: "Early this morning Thos. Corbet Denis Wynn Hiram Wolsey and Saml. Bateman left this place for the Gt Salt Lake City. Contrary to my Council."[41]

That same day, the company "found some stone coal in the Creek at Cotton Wood [i.e., the future Coal Creek], which had washed down" the streambed. The next day, Smith sent out one party to collect loose iron and another to locate the source of the coal. A day later, the first party returned with "about 150 lbs. of Iron." Three days later, 3 May, the second party "report[ed] two veins of coal made bare by a land slide 5 miles up Cotton wood Kanyon." Francis Whitney, a 46-year-old blacksmith from Maine, burned the coal in his forge, making nails and welding pieces of iron together. He pronounced the find "a good quality of Coal."[42]

Anson Call returned from Salt Lake City on either 5 or 7 May, leading a company of 16 wagons and reporting that Brigham Young would arrive soon to inspect Fort Louisa.[43] Among the new arrivals listed by George A. Smith were Call's own wife, Mary, and three other sisters joining their husbands: Mary Hofheins, Eunice Holbrook and Jane Hulse. "Miss Hall and two children" are included in Smith's list. This might refer either to 21-year-old Elizabeth Hall, wife of Charles, or 23-year-old Mary E. Hall, wife of Job P., each listed in the May 1851 Census as having two children. New arrival Juliet Dalton joined her husband, who was Charles W. Dalton, as indicated in the McGregor list (see chapter 2, n. 104).

Of the men listed as members of Anson Call's company, Chapman Duncan, Peter Fife, Priddy Meeks, James Lemmon, Gilbert Morse, Robert Owens, Harry Dalton and John Dart came with family members whom they had brought down from Salt Lake City to join the settlement. Norman Jarvice, Robert Gallisby, Henry Moggredge, Michael Shaw, George Braffit, Alphonzo Green, L. W. Potter and Ezra Clark (not all of whom were original missionaries) are listed as arriving without any family members.[44]

Along with the excitement generated by these comings and goings was increased contact with the indigenous population. Late in February 1851, Wakara's brother Amon arrived at the fort to negotiate an alliance between Wakara's band and the Fort Louisa settlers. Relations with the Mormons at Manti had soured and Wakara had sent word that he would consider relocating at Fort Louisa to raise corn. On 3 March, Wakara strode into the settlement himself and headed directly for George A. Smith, exchanging a hug for a hearty handshake. They shared a peace pipe and carried on an animated conversation through "signs and guesswork." Wakara said that he wanted to "build a house and teach his children to work." Smith concluded, after this discussion, that Wakara was as intelligent as any Indian he had met, "[n]o doubt the master spirit of the Utah Nation."[45]

The next day Wakara appeared with Peteetneet, on another diplomatic mission. They made peace overtures on behalf of Chief Taugunt, whose Paiutes had killed Isaac Brown, and reported advising all the surrounding bands not to disturb the Mormons or "even a brute of theirs." In return, the Utes wanted an opportunity to exchange horses for cattle, to which Smith agreed. The spirit of friendship was tested on 8 March, however, when Jacob Hofheins unintentionally pointed a cannon at the Indian camp. After Thomas Wheeler, the Indian interpreter, explained that the cannon was only part of a training exercise, Wakara suggested his warriors participate. In a show of good will, they donned ceremonial regalia and paraded around the corral on horseback, while Wakara and President Smith reviewed the troops.[46]

For the next week and a half, Wakara's band stayed in Fort Louisa to trade. They sold not only horses but also small children to the Mormons who hoped to rescue them from slavery in Mexico and California.[47] Finally, on 18 March, Wakara announced that he was going north to fight the Snakes, despite President Smith's suggestion that he make peace with the Shoshoni tribe. Three days later the Utes departed with much ceremony, Wakara, Peteetneet and a Paiute chief breakfasting with George A. Smith before riding out. John P. Barnard gave Smith a Paiute girl about 4 years old, exchanged for an ox. Before leaving, Wakara delivered what George A. characterized as a "Mormon sermon" to the Paiute chief, encouraging him to engage in honest trading rather than stealing.[48]

Searching for Coal

With Brigham Young expected in May, the time was right to discover an abundant fuel source of the best kind for making iron. The settlers had previously decided to build the foundry at Iron Springs and use cedar wood for fuel. By 11 March 1851, they had found a one-inch vein of "Pennal" coal near Fort Louisa and by 19 March had exposed it to its full width of six inches. They had not, apparently, considered coking it to fuel a blast furnace, but this would not be surprising if the vein turned out to be of low quality or insufficient quantity for their needs.[49]

On 5 May, Smith, Aaron Farr, Samuel Bringhurst, Burr Frost, Elijah Newman, Elisha Groves, Robert Green and Peter Shirts (see illus. 4-3) headed out with "Two waggons six horses, blankets and provisions for three days" on an exploring expedition to look for coal. Even after the long day's ride, George A. Smith's sense of humor prevailed: "after eating supper, we went to bed. br Farr and myself occupied one waggon, there were Two sides to our waggon, the in side and the out side, br. Farr and myself occupied the former and br Shirts[,] Newman & Groves the latter." The next morning, despite talking through most of the night with Smith, Aaron Farr cooked break-

Illus. 4-3. Peter Shirts (1808–82), prospector and adventurer, was always among the first sent on exploring expeditions. Frank E. Esshom, *Pioneers and Prominent Men of Utah*, 260 (Salt Lake City: Utah Pioneers Book Publishing), 1913.

fast for the camp and then left with Robert Green to bring back several horses that had strayed. The rest of the party headed up the canyon, except for Smith, who remained behind. While he kept camp and read old newspapers, the other five brought back two bushels of coal samples from several veins they had found about a mile up the creek.[50] While continuing their explorations the next day, 7 May, Smith found "a splendid sight [*sic*]" for a city on the banks of the newly renamed Coal Creek. The creek was

> a rod whide 15 inches deep very rapid stream, Rocky bed, Soft water milk and water Colour, banks studed with scrub Cedars a few Service bushs and some Spanish Soap root, abundant grass, 5 miles from Coal mines and 10 miles from Iron Mountain; and large tracks of farming land. this point must become a fine flourishing manufacturing Town. About Ten oclock we harnessed our horses, and explored a new road home we guess it at 15 miles.[51]

This "splendid sight" was the future home of Cedar City.

Endnotes

1. See ch. 3, n. 57.
2. Lee, journal, 30 Jan 1851.

3. Ibid., 26 Jan 1851.

4. Ibid.

5. "Iron Mission Record," 26 Jan 1851.

6. Ibid. The identity of "Bro. Miller" is unclear. Among the settlers were (1) Daniel A. Miller, a 41-year-old farmer from New York, present with his wife Hannah and nine children, ranging in age from 15 to one; (2) Reuben Miller, about whom nothing is known except that his name appears on the list of those called, as printed in the *Deseret News* of 16 Nov 1850; and (3) Robert Ewing Miller, a 25-year-old ship's carpenter from Scotland, present with his wife, Eliza, then six months pregnant (see app. 2).

7. Ibid.

8. Smith, journal, 26 Jan 1851.

9. Lee, journal, 26 Jan 1851.

10. Smith, journal, 31 Jan 1851. Lee, ibid., 31 Jan 1851, reports a much smaller group of applicants responding on 31 Jan, the more formal and complete lot drawing, according to Lee, not taking place until late afternoon through early evening of the following Sunday, 2 Feb 1851.

11. Lee, ibid., 2 Feb 1851.

12. Ibid.

13. Ibid., 9 Feb 1851.

14. Smith, journal, 10 Mar 1851.

15. Ibid., 12 Apr 1851; Pratt, *Autobiography,* 375. Although Smith describes Pratt's property as being 80 acres, the property description identifies it as "One hundred Thirty Acres and Thirty two Rods more or less." The entry, also dated 12 Apr 1851, is no. 17 on p. 4 of Deed Book A (7 Feb 1851–28 Feb 1855), Iron County Recorder's Office, Parowan, Utah.

16. On the Philip Lewis deed, the original appears to read "Lot 111," but as this is impossible, the numeral must be a "10" with upper and lower connecting arcs on the zero faded or worn away. This is proved by the first George A. Smith "Range 7" entry, the ink of which is still dark and readable. The zero of the "10" acre figure there also appears as two slightly curved lines, missing both its upper and lower arc.

17. Smith, journal, 30–31 Jan 1851; Lee, journal, 31 Jan 1851.

18. Smith, ibid., 31 Jan and 3 Mar 1851; Lee, ibid., 3 and 9 Feb 1851. A system of community herding developed in southern Utah as settlements became established. The village bell signaled dairy cow owners in the morning to turn out their animals, which were herded in rotation by boys usually under 12 years of age and thus too young for men's work. The boys were held strictly responsible for preventing damage to property by the cows, for keeping them from straying or being injured and even for protecting them from Indian raids. Men who had no children of an age to take a turn at herding might be assessed a cent and a half per cow per day.

19. Smith, ibid., 22 Mar 1851.

20. George A. Smith to Brigham Young, 25 Mar 1851, published in *Deseret News*, 8 Apr 1851, 237.

21. Smith, journal, 26 Mar, 22–25 Apr 1851.

22. Ibid., 3 Mar 1851. The superscripted phrase in this quotation very clearly reads "& blogs," but presumably this is no more than a momentary lapse of attention and/or slip of the pen by the writer. The word *logs* makes perfect sense in the context of the entire passage.

23. Ibid., 21 Feb 1851.

24. Ibid., 3 Mar 1851.

25. Ibid., 25 Feb 1851.

26. Zabriskie and Robinson, "U.S. Census for Utah, 1851."

27. Smith, journal, 9 Feb 1851; Lee, journal, 25 Jan and 9 Feb 1851.

28. Lee, ibid., 16 Feb 1851.

29. Smith, journal, 19 Mar, 28 Mar and 30 Mar 1851.

30. Dalton, *Iron County Mission,* 37–38.

31. Smith, journal, 17 Mar 1851. "A.L." is Almon L., "Wm." stands for William in both cases, and Harmison's first name is James.

32. In Sep 1851, they purchased a 100,000-acre farm at San Bernardino for $77,500 (Dalton, *Iron County Mission,* 39). See also Edward Leo Lyman, *San Bernardino: The Rise and Fall of a California Community* (Salt Lake City: Signature Books, 1996), ch. 2, esp. 35–36, 58.

33. Pratt, *Autobiography,* 371; R. Lanier Britsch, *Unto the Islands of the Sea: A History of the Latter-day Saints in the Pacific* (Salt Lake City: Deseret Book, 1986), 105.

34. Smith, journal, 7–8 Apr 1851.

35. Ibid., 9–10 Apr 1851. She died the following 25 Jun in Salt Lake City. Smith himself seems to have had this potentially fatal disease. On 23 Apr 1851 he records that he "bled a little at the lungs." Other sources report severe coughing, lung pain and spitting blood. See Jarvis, *Ancestry,* 261–62.

36. Smith, journal, 20 Apr 1851.

37. Ibid., 8 Apr 1851; "Volunteers," *Deseret News,* 16 Nov 1850, 154–55; departure list, *Deseret News,* 11 Jan 1851, 188–89.

38. Pratt, *Autobiography,* 374–75.

39. Smith, journal, 28 Apr 1851.

40. Ibid., 27 Apr 1851; Pratt, *Autobiography,* 384.

41. Smith, ibid., 28 Apr 1851.

42. Ibid., 28–30 Apr and 3 May 1851. Peter Shirts, Simeon Howd and George Leavitt appear to have been "the company" or at least some of them who found the stone coal on 28 Apr 1851. A typescript of excerpts taken from George Leavitt's

journal reports that he received a call while at Parowan to help Shirts, Howd "and two others" in further explorations and that, while doing so, the group found considerable iron ore and "at Cedar City, coal," which they found while eating their dinner by the creek. See George Leavitt, typescript history, SUU Archives.

43. Smith, ibid., 7–8 May and 31 May 1851; Lunt, diary, 7 May 1851. Call's arrival date remains slightly ambiguous. Lunt records the arrival of Call's company of 16 wagons on 7 May and Smith writes on 8 May that the party arrived "the day before." However, on 31 May, where Smith lists the members of this party, he begins by writing "Bro. Anson Call came in with a company and reported to me an account of the company which arrived here on the 5th day of May."

44. Smith, ibid., 31 May 1851.

45. Ibid., 27 Feb, 3 Mar 1851. It is possible that "Amon" is the settlers' name for Walker's brother Ammomah.

46. Ibid., 4 Mar, 7–8 Mar 1851.

47. Ibid., 10 Mar, 12–13 Mar 1851.

48. Ibid., 18 Mar, 21 Mar 1851.

49. Ibid., 11 Mar, 19 Mar 1851.

50. Ibid., 5–6 May 1851.

51. Ibid., 7 May 1851.

5

Parowan City

May–November 1851

Eager to inspect the progress of the Iron Mission personally, Brigham Young made the first of many annual visits south in spring 1851. His visit was to have a lasting impact on the community. Not only did President Young establish a new city government, he also called additional ecclesiastical leaders to assist George A. Smith. These new officials would help the fledgling settlement manage tasks associated with growth on the frontier, such as taking the first census and creating an irrigation system.

President Young arrived with a large party at Red Creek, the future site of Paragonah, on Friday, 9 May, just two days after George A. Smith's party completed a fairly extensive exploration of Coal Creek. Late that evening, Smith rode out to Red Creek to meet the more than 50 travelers and bring them back to Fort Louisa.[1] The sidebar provides a complete roster of this group.[2]

Although neither George A. Smith nor Brigham Young's clerk Thomas Bullock mentions that new recruits or family members of original iron missionaries accompanied Brigham Young, it would have been logical for wives and families to attach themselves to an organized group, as they did to Anson Call's, which had reached Fort Louisa, bringing mail from Salt Lake City, only a few days before the president's party arrived. Call's fellow travelers account for the tremendous increase in the settlement's population by mid-1851.

Brigham Young brought the colony "a host of letters" from friends, colleagues and family members, plus national and territorial news.[3] He was greeted by six inches of snow on the ground, a three-volley salute from the cannon, the singing of school children and the posting of colors. Young's close inspection and commendation of their efforts buoyed the spirits of these tough pioneers, who were certainly on

---

BRIGHAM YOUNG'S 1851 TRAVELING COMPANY

Brigham Young and (unnamed) wife

George Bean

E. T. Benson and wife

William Bringhurst

Thomas Bullock

Robert J. Burton

Cyrus Canfield

Daniel Carn

Miron Crandell

John S. Dunton

Horace Eldridge and wife

Ira Eldridge, wife and child

Stephen H. Goddard

George D. Grant

Jedediah M. Grant and wife

Joseph L. Heywood

Jerrius Hollister

Dimick Huntington

Benjamin F. Johnson

Heber C. Kimball, wife, and
   Heber T. Kimball

Thomas Rhodes

Abraham O. Smoot

Samuel Sprague

Levi Stewart

Seth Taft

Stephen Taylor

Hansen Walker

Daniel H. Wells

Daniel Wood

Wilford Woodruff

Brigham J. Young, Joseph A. Young
and Lorenzo Young "and others."

Source: Journal History, 2 May 1851.

---

hardship assignment. A public meeting in the Bowery on 10 or 11 May appears to have been cut short by the weather, but other get-togethers followed in the council house over the next few days.[4] President Young spent a good deal of time in private meetings, acquainting himself with the progress and problems of the settlement. He counseled those who were homesick and eager to return to Salt Lake City. He personally inspected the newly built sawmill and newly ploughed farms. On Sunday, 11 May, in the midst of "very hard" wind and rain, he met with "the brethren" and again "made arrangements for to send an exploring company to Coal creek."[5] This or possibly another exploration was made on 15 May.

On 16 May, the president and his contingent took to the road again, joined by a number of men released from their year-long mission in the south. According to George A. Smith, "about 28 of the Iron Co. Mission accompanied [Young] on his return home; part of them to get their families and the residue to attend to their private business."[6]

The Iron Mission Record names at least 30 Iron County settlers, two of whom were women, who returned to Salt Lake City at this time: Thomas Bloxom, Francis Boggs, Samuel and William Bringhurst, Ebenezer Brown, Isaac Burnham, Rich Burton [*sic*], Angus Cannon, Aaron Cherry, Ezra L. Clark, Aaron Farr, Burr Frost, Alphonzo Green, Samuel Gould, Joseph Horne, Joseph Hovey and wife, Simeon Howd, James Lawson, William Leany, George Leavitt, Emily Leavitt, Daniel A. Miller, Joseph Millett, Jonathan Pugmire, Ara W. Sabin, Thomas S. Smith, Charles Y. Webb, Gideon Wood and Samuel Woolley.[7]

Some of the departures were only temporary. Samuel Gould, often called Father Gould in deference to his age, reappeared on 26 June, bringing his "one milstone" and a report that 17 wagons were on the road behind him. Between the 26th and 27th, George A. Smith reports the return of Isaac Burnham, Washburn Chipman (not listed in the Iron Mission Record), Jonathan Pugmire and Charles Webb, with families. Also arriving were the families of Zechariah Decker, Thomas Cartwright, Elisha Groves, Elijah Elmer and Tarlton Lewis.[8]

Although there are minor differences among primary sources documenting the iron missionaries and their families, agreement is fairly close. These sources are collated to form appendix 2; differences among them are discussed there. Note that initial records like the "call list" and "departure list" focus on men officially called to form the settlement party. Later records like the May 1851 Census include wives and children, accounting for many more female settlers than the initial sources report.

Taking the Census: May 1851

On the trip down, while his party was camped near Payson, Brigham Young had sent George A. Smith instructions to take a census, and the high priority Smith gave it can be shown by the fact that he began it only two days after Brigham Young arrived.[9] This census is extremely valuable. Congress granted Utah territorial status on 9 September 1850, with the news reaching Salt Lake City 27 January 1851.[10] A quick and accurate census would be able to chart the growth of new settlements and allow communities to be given fair political representation. This one shows Iron County's population at 360, a considerable leap from approximately 168 four months before. Certainly, all 360 were not housed in the fort; many were likely camped nearby along Center Creek or on their newly acquired farms.

The May 1851 Census is not trouble-free. For instance, Darius Shirts, 18-year-old son of Peter Shirts, appears on the census records of not only Iron County but Weber and Utah counties as well. Another point of interest concerns John D. Lee, who seems to have listed his family incorrectly, even though he appears to have enumerated the census himself. Juanita Brooks concludes that he gave his plural wife Lovina's age as 15 rather than 30 in order to disguise her relationship to him by pretending she was a daughter[11] (see app. 2 for a correct listing of this family group).

Among other discrepancies are these: Edson Whipple is listed in Andrew Jenson's "arrival list"[12] as having brought two wives, Mary Ann and Harriet, but only Mary Ann appears on the census. "Mrs. Benjamin Watts" is on the "arrival list," but not on the census (where her husband is listed in the household of James McGuffie). Clarissa Whitney has five (unnamed) children in the "arrival list" but only one child in the census ("New Samuel"), suggesting a possible confusion between herself and Clarissa Hancock, who has six children in the census. John P. Barnard appears on all the sources except the census. He was one of the seven members of the express party carrying mail to Salt Lake City on 24 March. Barnard, Empey and Harmison did not make it back in time for the census, although the others in their group did.

Of those listed in the Iron Mission Record as returning north with Brigham Young's party on 16 May, Thomas Bloxom, Francis Boggs, "R. T." Burton, Angus Cannon, Ezra T. Clark, Alphonzo Green, Samuel Gould and George and Emily Leavitt are not on the census, some for obvious reasons. Alphonzo Green and Ezra Clark, for instance, tagged by the Iron Mission Record as returnees, had only been in Fort Louisa some 10 days since coming south with Anson Call's company, which had rolled into the settlement on the 5th or 7th of May. George A. Smith's journal entry for the 31st lists the two as coming with Call, immediately thereafter noting that "Alphonzo Green and Ezra Clark returned with Prest. Young." Ezra's name appears on the "call list" of November 1850 but he seems not to have traveled south until joining Anson Call's wagon train. Why both men would come so far in order to stay so short a time is not yet clear.[13]

The census names all but one of a party of iron missionaries that returned to Salt Lake City on 4 June 1851. This is the first group of pioneers to travel north from the settlement after Brigham Young's expanded party left on 16 May. Smith organized the 13 men into a traveling company on 25 May: "E. F. Sheets Captain of Company; Chandler Holbrook Seargent. John D. Lee Clerk & Recorder Anson Call. David Brinton. C. A. Harper John Dolton. James Parks Daniel Hendrix,

Leamon Brunson Jefferson Wright, Sixtus Johnson, & Thos. Wheeler."[14] Sixtus Johnson is the only one on the list whose name does *not* appear on the May 1851 Census. After traveling north with this group, John D. Lee returned to Fort Louisa in November 1851 (by then six months into its new name, Parowan), bringing his family with him.[15]

One name of interest on the May 1851 Census is that of "John Burton," a 53-year-old, Virginia-born African-American living with the Joseph Lee Robinson family. He had originally "belonged" to John Newton Burton, a wealthy plantation owner in Virginia, whose widow, Susan McCord Burton, became a Latter-day Saint and married Robinson as his plural wife in Nauvoo on 31 January 1846. When they decided to go West, Susan freed her slaves. John elected to stay with her, using the name John Burton (sometimes spelled "Barton" in pioneer records). He accompanied Brigham Young's advance party in the spring of 1847 and, on settling in Salt Lake Valley, prepared a farm for the Robinsons. When they arrived in October 1848, he had already grown a crop of corn.[16]

After coming with the Robinsons to Fort Louisa in 1851, John reportedly helped erect the Old Rock Church. James Martineau's minutes of a Thursday evening fast meeting on 5 January 1860 briefly mention John, suggesting—beyond his known attributes of loyalty and industriousness—that he was a spiritual man as well: "Br. J. P. Hall spoke in tongues, and John Barton (a slave) interpreted. The burden of Br. Hall's word was to the effect that great and important events were now being consummated in the world which we would soon hear of, and of the importance of living our religion."[17] When Susan Robinson died, John intended to return to Missouri, hoping to locate his wife. He became ill, however, after reaching Salt Lake City on the first leg of his homeward journey. He died there and is buried in City Cemetery.[18]

The May 1851 Census confirms the multi-regional, even multi-national makeup of the Iron Mission. Approximately 30 percent of those over 17 years of age came from New York, Pennsylvania, Delaware and New Jersey; about 20 percent came from New England; another 20 percent came directly from England, Scotland, Ireland or Wales. Almost 15 percent came from the Midwest and a slightly lower percentage than that from the South. Thirteen individuals came from Canada and four from Germany.[19]

From Traveling Company to City Government

Brigham Young's trip to Fort Louisa was obviously not just a pleasure jaunt. In the seven days of his stay, he set a remarkable number of activities in motion, of which the census was the first. The second was (we can infer) approving a location for the intended new settlement 20 miles to the south, near Coal Creek. Smith records that on Thursday, 15 May, Young visited the mill and farms, then rode up to Summit Creek where he and his party viewed "Coal Creek or Iron valley all of whom were delighted with the prospect."[20] Although this journal entry does not name a specific site chosen by the president or record any orders from him authorizing its colonization, Smith's words clearly imply that Brigham gave his blessing to the Coal Creek venture. Settlement there could proceed as soon as the harvest at Fort Louisa was safely gathered.

A third event, held 16 May while Brigham Young was still present, was the nomination of John Bernhisel as congressional delegate, a position he was already occupying. Also nominated were George A. Smith as "Council for the Teritory of Utah" (he later calls himself a member of the "Territorial Council") and Elisha H. Groves as candidate for legislative representative from Iron County. Formal elections were held 4 August 1851, at which all three were elected, presumably without opposition.[21]

The fourth accomplishment was organizing a formal city government to replace the ecclesiastical fiat by which George A. Smith was authorized to act as chief judge of the county and president of the mission. Ecclesiastical government first took the form of a traveling system—two companies of 50 with captains of 10 within each. It had worked well on the road. As early as 19 January 1851, John D. Lee records George A. Smith discussing whether to build the council house, survey the fort and make the canyon road, all under the administrative structure of the traveling system. While some felt that "more labour could be done under direction of Bishops than of capt[ain]s," the consensus was that the men would prefer to continue working under the system with which they were familiar.[22]

By 9 February, however (see chapter 3, N. 76), the new settlement was organized into four wards. Smith observed that the "company organization was disolved & that our future opperations would be carried on under the direction of the Bishops . . . & that it would be pleasing to him to have the Bishops all manage the affairs of their respective wards expecially the public work under same form."[23] The four bishops were Anson Call, First Ward; Tarlton Lewis, Second Ward; Daniel Miller, Third Ward; and Joseph L. Robinson, Fourth Ward. All male settlers, irrespective of their actual priesthood offices, were organized into an "Elders Quorum," including, by his own request, George A. Smith, who was a high priest.[24] Thus, the bishops were responsible to supervise not only the spiritual but also the public affairs of the community with the elders quorum acting as legislative body. This system, while suitable for the young Fort Louisa, would burden bishops unnecessarily as the town grew and cease to work once non-Mormons moved in.

While in Iron County, Brigham Young "gave some excellent instructions on government." On 16 May, under his direction, the residents organized a municipal government, which Smith listed in his journal as William H. Dame, mayor; Richard Harrison, Tarlton Lewis, John D. Lee and Matthew Carruthers, aldermen; and Andrew A. Love, Joel H. Johnson, William A. Moss, William Leany, Dr. Priddy Meeks, Elijah Newman, Robert Wiley, John Wolf and John Dolton, city council members.[25]

The territorial legislature created a county government less than two weeks before the iron missionaries left for southern Utah, but no city government was created at the same time. However, by 6 February 1851, soon after the travelers "arrived," the legislative assembly approved a charter for a city to be called "Parowan," the same day granting charters to Ogden, Manti and Provo. Salt Lake City had been granted a charter a month earlier on 9 January. That document was patterned closely after Nauvoo's, granted by the Illinois State Legislature, and the others were virtually carbon copies of Salt Lake City's. The entire Parowan charter consists of 47 sections; Sections 3 through 45 are common to all five charters.[26]

It is interesting to note that the incorporation ordinance identifies the city as "Parowan" even though no such city yet existed. Sec. 1 gave its boundaries as

> beginning at the dam, above the sawmill, in the mouth of the kanyon, on Centre creek, and running from thence north-east along the base of the mountain two miles; thence north three miles; thence west six miles; thence south to the base of the mountain; thence along the base of the mountain in a north-easterly direction, to the place of beginning.

The settlers were given a two-year exemption on road taxes beyond the city limits.[27] The dam was not even built, although construction began 6 February, the day the charter passed. Certainly the legislators did not know the dimensions of the city. Perhaps they had passed the description provisionally, pending exact information from the field. It is also possible the boundaries were written in after the fact.

What is most curious is that the first reference to Parowan in Smith's journal is not made until 9 March when he points out the Little Salt Lake on his copy of John C. Frémont's map to Chief Wakara, who tells him the

IRON MISSION LEADERSHIP

In Parowan   In Cedar City

April 1850
President, Iron Mission
George A. Smith

9 Feb 1851
Bishops of Parowan Wards
Anson Call, Tarlton Lewis,
Daniel Miller, Joseph L. Robinson

16 May 1851
Mayor of Parowan
William H. Dame

17 Aug 1851
Acting President, Iron Mission
Elisha H. Groves

28 Oct 1851
President, Iron Mission
Elisha H. Groves

1st Counselor   2nd Counselor
John Lyman Smith   Matthew Carruthers

"1st Counselor"
Henry Lunt*
"2nd Counselor"
John Easton*

12 May 1852
President, "Stake of Zion," Iron County;
General Manager, iron works
John Calvin Lazelle Smith

1st Counselor   2nd Counselor;
John Steele   Supervisor, iron works
                                                        Henry Lunt

Bishop of Parowan Ward   Bishop of Cedar Ward
Tarlton Lewis   Philip Klingensmith

18 Jun 1853
Mayor of Parowan
John Steele

26–27 Nov 1853
General Manager, Deseret Iron Company
Isaac C. Haight

6 Dec 1853
Mayor of Cedar City
Isaac C. Haight

20 May 1855
President, Cedar Stake
Isaac C. Haight
1st Counselor
Jonathan Pugmire
2nd Counselor
John M. Higbee

21 May 1855
President, Parowan Stake
John Calvin Lazelle Smith
1st Counselor
Jesse N. Smith
2nd Counselor
James H. Martineau

Spring 1856
President, Parowan Stake
William H. Dame
1st Counselor
Calvin C. Pendleton
2nd Counselor
Jesse N. Smith

31 July 1859
President, Cedar Stake;
Bishop, Cedar Ward
Henry Lunt
1st Counselor
Richard Morris
2nd Counselor
Thomas Jones

*Lunt, diary, 2 Feb 1852, records that these two "councillors" were "unanimously Elected" to assist Matthew Carruthers. This unusual step—calling counselors to a counselor—reflects the growth of the new colony in Cedar City.

correct name is Parowan Lake.[28] In fact, three days *after* the legislative assembly designated the city as Parowan, it was formally named Fort Louisa on a motion by John D. Lee. On 16 May, however, when the company finally organized the city they had been granted in the charter, they chose to name it Parowan.[29]

One result of organizing a municipal government is that George A. Smith, whose powers had been virtually unlimited, now petitioned the city council for authorization to operate his mill and the county for permission to use the canyon's timber, grass and creek water. On 12 June, he refers for the first time to employing men to work on his mill, suggesting that they had earlier donated their time as though to a public project.[30]

The fifth project which received Brigham Young's scrutiny was finding an alternate route to Beaver Ridge, an extremely rough and steep section of the road where wagons routinely had to be double-teamed. On 17 May, Smith and a small party accompanied the president's group back over this ridge ("a weary ride over the mountain") as far as Beaver River, which would have been a jarring reminder of the difficulties of freighting over that section.[31]

Evidently Brigham Young assigned Smith to find a better route; on 30 June, Smith sent Peter Shirts and Samuel Gould "to explore a rout for a State road to the Beever." They returned a day later to report "an excellant rout to the Beever, without a mountain but would cost some labour to make the road."[32] The route ran east of Beaver Ridge, entered Parowan Valley at the northeast end, turned a little left and ran over a small ridge down into Nevershine Canyon. George A. Smith was one of the first to use it when he left the Iron Mission in November 1851 for his new duties in Utah County:

> At the Elk Horn Springs, 14 units from Parowan, we took a new road, recently broke by John D. Lee & co., through a pass, which avoids the rough and steep crossing of the Beaver mountains. This road had been broken out through heavy sage, by the passing of 20 wagons of bro. Lee's company, being piloted thro' by Mr. Samuel Gould of Parowan. It is a grand improvement in the road.[33]

The Water Crisis

The months following Brigham Young's May 1851 visit to Parowan were hectic ones of reappraisal and readjustment for Smith. Every day seemed to produce a management crisis of some kind. His personal affairs needed attention and his civic, church and administrative functions demanded equal amounts of his time. He was busy overseeing completion of the mill, including the repair of the millrace and waterwheel. He was building a permanent adobe home on the south side of the public square. The fence around the Big Field, which was under his supervision, needed almost constant repair. Strong winds roared out of the canyon and a late frost nipped the gardens. Roads had to be surveyed and built, not only into the canyons but also to Coal Creek, Cedar City's future site, and through the mountains to the Beaver River. The continuing Indian presence called for regular sentry duty and militia drills. New colonists needed constant help to locate and settle in. More personally, his wife Sarah Ann Libby had died in Salt Lake City of consumption and he himself was shaken with recurring bouts of what was almost certainly the same disease.

In the midst of all the other activities, an unexpected crisis occurred. That spring, Center Creek's abundant waters suddenly and alarmingly dropped off. On Sunday, 15 June, George A. Smith "spent the evening in counciling about herding the Cattle, fencing, divideing of the water. The water was considered deficient for watering our crops. A committee was appointed to see if Red Creek or Summit Creek could be brought onto the rabbit brush or wire grass land."[34]

On 17 June, this committee (Joel H. Johnson, Tarlton Lewis and William H. Dame) reported that diversion was not possible. On the same day, Smith observed that the volumes of Coal Creek and Red Creek were also falling.[35] While the settlers had prepared for much they might find on arriving in a new country, they had no inkling that seasonal water fluctuations were tied to local weather patterns and the geology of this unfamiliar terrain. Thus, from the very beginning, the colonists were scrambling to learn the lessons of the land on which their survival would depend.

Newton Goodale, a 36-year-old farmer from New York, not satisfied with the committee's report, took his own level on Red Creek and told Smith that it would be possible to divert its waters to the Big Field "as far up as the Rabbit brush dam." Smith promptly appointed him chief engineer of the Parowan Canal Company, organized the same day, and assigned Chapman Duncan as clerk.[36] All the men in the community worked on the project, which was completed 2 July, but the ground was so dry it was difficult to get the water through it. In a report to Brigham Young published in the *Deseret News,* 26 July 1851, Smith wrote:

> To increase the water we have made a canal about seven miles in length, to bring in Red Creek, to water the lower surveys in our field. This has been quite a job, and had not the colony been weakened by the return of a part, this would have been completed one month earlier, thereby saving thousands of bushels of grain. It seems almost

incredible the amount of labor that has been done, and yet much is before us, and every man is straining every nerve to accomplish the task before him. The Wire Grass Survey which was thought by the WISEST farmers to need but little water, upon trial requires double the amount of the upland.[37]

It must have been with some relief that George A. Smith took time off on the 4th of July, although the pioneers, with their complement of Englishmen, had given scant notice to the national birthday. Smith's journal entry notes merely that he "spent the day in fus[s]ing round the mill, and reading a discription of California. All was silent, not a gun fired, nor a drunken man seen in the Streets."[38]

The 24th, however, was livelier. This day celebrated the arrival of the Mormon pioneers in Salt Lake Valley in 1847. The Parowan pioneers began the anniversary with a 7:30 A.M. flag-raising. The cannon was fired and an infantry battalion formed up, marching in drill and discharging their weapons "in plattons" while the citizens formed their own procession at 9:30 and marched to the Bowery for an oration interspersed with hymns and sentimental songs. George A. Smith reviewed pioneer explorations into the mountains, after which the settlers returned to Parowan house to a postlude of cannon fire. Smith then notes taking dinner with Orson Adams and 30 others, "an excellent feast in which the fruits of our valley formed quite a variety." By four o'clock, dancing commenced under the watchful eyes of Bishop Groves and George A. Smith and continued "until a late hour."[39]

George and Zilpha Smith were finally able to move into their partially completed house on 26 July, as he recorded with obvious satisfaction: "Worked on the house, finished the roof, and the floor, moved into it. br Webb moved into the house, I moved out of. And for the first time since I left Gt Salt Lake City slept on a bedstead." Any sense of ease that the Smiths might have felt, however, was to be short-lived, as George A. was soon to be on the road again, to attend general conference and visit his other families in Salt Lake City. But before he began the preparations for the trip, he took time, on 28 July, to perform the first marriage in the colony, uniting Robert Gallisby and Phoebe Dart, noting that the bride "married contrary to her fathers wish."[40]

George A. Smith's Return to Salt Lake City

Events were progressing well enough in the settlement to make Smith confident about leaving for general conference, scheduled to begin on

7 September 1851. On 31 July, he recorded, "I took my waggon to Pugmires [blacksmith Jonathan Pugmire] to be repaired ready for the trip back to the Gt. Salt Lake."[41] Between then and his departure on 21 August, he was busy administering colony affairs and making final preparations for the trip.

On 4 August, after the settlers elected George A. Smith to the territorial council, the 14 who were traveling to Salt Lake Valley with him met and organized themselves into a traveling company, Peter Shirts serving as captain and J. C. L. Smith as clerk. That evening the colony celebrated with another dance in Peter's Parowan house. Three days later, on 7 August, one of the greatest rainstorms of the season struck, raising Center Creek by a foot and flooding the city with water "as red as blood."[42]

Because George A. Smith's wife Zilpha was ill, many of the colony's women stepped in to help sew and bake for his trip, outfitting him along with their own husbands. Individual settlers contributed hay for the horses, 15 pounds of beef and a sage hen. Smith built a chicken coop as well as a privy, with an ash bin to control the flies and odor. He tended to a seemingly endless array of little difficulties. When the quorum passed a resolution on 10 August forbidding their Indian neighbors to glean or work in the community's Big Field, Smith revoked it, claiming that the quorum had interfered with his prerogatives as president and that the Indians were to be permitted in the fields as long as they worked.[43]

On Sunday, 17 August, as his last official act before his conference trip, Smith appointed Elisha H. Groves (elders quorum president) to act as Iron Mission president while he was gone. The people voted unanimously to write Smith a letter of recommendation for the work he had done, signed by Groves and the clerk. Smith settled his accounts, rented his mill to Richard Benson and, on 21 August, left Parowan at 9 A.M.[44]

Remnants of Pioneer Parowan in the Modern City

The original survey of Fort Louisa in February 1851 had called for lots two rods by four rods or 33 by 66 feet. By November 1852, Dame had surveyed the settlement, now Parowan, a second time and started assigning the new lots (see illus. 5-1). Zadok K. Judd received the first, dated 2 December 1852 (see app. 3). This new survey plat preserved the basic design of Fort Louisa but provided for Parowan's future growth. Dame enlarged the lots by adding 20 rods to each, making them two rods by 24 rods long, or 33 by 396 feet, creating a total of 18 new blocks. The new

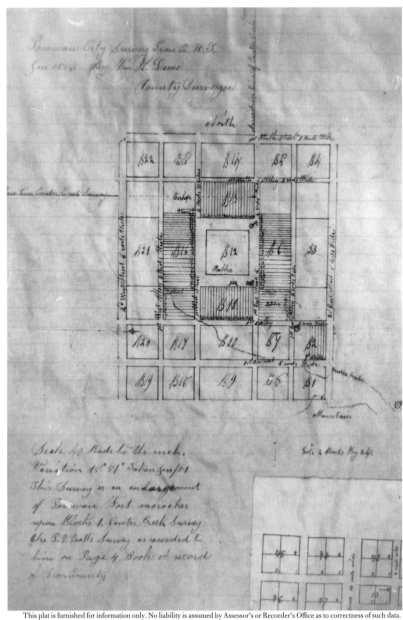

Illus. 5-1. William H. Dame's second survey of Fort Louisa, now renamed "Parowan City," dated January 1853. See app. 3 for lot owner assignments in Parowan City.

lots were, as one old-time resident put it, "damned long corn rows to weed" and were inconveniently narrow. By about 1854, two years later, the Parowan settlers had begun dividing these lots in half and building homes on opposite ends of them, facing new streets.

Fort Louisa's basic plan had, from the beginning, lent itself to division into blocks. In the new survey, the east side of the public square (the Fourth Ward) was designated as Block 6, the south side (First Ward) as Block 11, the west side (Second Ward) as Block 16 and the north side (Third Ward) as Block 13. The square itself was designated as Block 12. Dame also eliminated the council house square in the southeast corner, enlarging the bastion square in the northwest corner of the fort plat into a "bishops' square" that housed a church, a barn and a storehouse to accommodate contributions in kind.

The Old Rock Church, Parowan's most familiar LDS building, sits in the middle of the pioneer fort's public square (see illus. 5-2). All houses currently standing on blocks around the church face the square; many lots are still either 33 feet wide or just double that size. Over the years, lots facing the square have been combined through selling and trading, but many retain their original widths or multiples of 33 feet. Modern Parowan's city offices, on the southeast corner of Main and First North, are housed in the former Bank of Iron County, constructed about 1920.

Illus. 5-2. Parowan's Old Rock Church, located in the center of the public square, facing south.

Photograph by Morris A. Shirts

This building is approximately 33 by 66 feet. The building located at 13 South Main, on the east side of the square, is 66 feet wide. On the south side of the square, Block 11, the Jesse N. Smith home, which is on the state historical register, is on a lot 99 feet wide (see illus. 5-3).

George A. Smith's first lot was located on the south line of the fort, just west of the council house (First Ward, Block 11, Lot No. 1). On 30 May 1851, Smith apparently purchased a new lot, engaging with "Br. James Lewis for 10,000 dobies and his foundation on south street." The purchase took place after Smith sold his log house and one of his lots on the east line to Elijah Elmer in exchange for $200 work on the sawmill.[45] Mary Amelia Smith, the daughter of George A. and Zilpha Smith, married Peter Wimmer and the couple may have lived in the home on the Lewis lot. The Smith-Wimmer house, known locally as the old Wimmer house, stood on or adjacent to Lot 5 of the early survey. One wall of the Mortensen barbershop (still standing at 15 West 100 South, but no longer operating) was reportedly part of the Smith-Wimmer home.

A man named Morgan Richards, on a date not recorded, reportedly purchased the other Smith lot on the east side of the fort in Fourth Ward.[46] Tradition identifies this lot with Lot 9, east of the fort (Block 6),

Photograph by Morris A. Shirts

Illus. 5-3. Jesse N. Smith home, located on the south side of the public square (Block 11), facing north. It was constructed of adobe brick in 1856–1857. It has since been restored and is listed on the State Register of Historical Sites.

where Zadok K. Judd built a home at 25 South Main Street. The lot was recorded to Judd on 2 December 1852.[47]

Lots on the north side (Block 13) have been subdivided into more diverse measurements—some about 58 feet, others about 73 feet. We can also see these changes at work in some of the property transactions occurring on the west side. An analysis of Deed Book A reveals that Andrew Baston, for example, early in 1852, owned Lot 23 and part or all of the north half of Lot 22. By deed of 21 January 1852, Jacob Hofheins became "entitled" to Lot 21 and the south half of Lot 22. On 27 November 1852, Daniel Page purchased Baston's property (the word "estate" is penciled in, suggesting Baston had died by this date). Page then sold this property to Hofheins.[48] Subsequently, Robert E. Miller bought at least a portion of the Hofheins property, which he sold to William Wilcox on 27 June 1863. The pertinent deed describes the property as "the east part of lots 21 & 22 and 7½ feet on the south side of east part of lot 23 being 7½ feet front by 14 rods Parowan City Survey Block 16 Plat A."[49] Evidently, the 10 rods on the west had been sold to someone else and the combined width of Lots 21, 22 and 23 became 73½ feet.

Some lots were deeded back to the city for municipal purposes. After an adobe wall was built around the city's perimeter in 1855, it became necessary to provide streets through the center of each block surrounding the public square. Seth Rogers ceded Lot 14, Block 6 (east side), Edward Thompson ceded Lot 11, Block 11 (south), and Ross Roberts ceded Lot 10, Block 13 (north). Lot 15, providing street access on Block 16 (west side), lists no grantor.[50]

The streets on the east and north eventually reverted to private hands. The western street is still faintly visible on the property formerly owned by Wilford Durham; the south street is the only one still a public thoroughfare. By collating William Dame's first and second surveys (1851 and 1853) with the 1921 map of Parowan made by Joseph Richards, we notice that some streets were widened by condemning other lots, still identified by Dame's 1853 numbers. Center Street took Lots 3, 4 and 5 from Block 6 and Lots 24, 25 and 26 from Block 16. First South took Lots 24, 25 and 26 from Block 6 and Lots 3, 4 and 5 from Block 16. Main Street took Lot 1 from Block 11 and Lot 20 from Block 13. First West took Lot 20 from Block 11 and Lot 1 from Block 13 (see illus. 5-4).

Federal legislation, enacted by the Homestead Act of 1862 and extended to Utah in 1867, permitted the settlers of Iron County to claim, for a nominal charge, the federal lands they had occupied and improved. Probate courts, established in Iron County in 1872, processed these

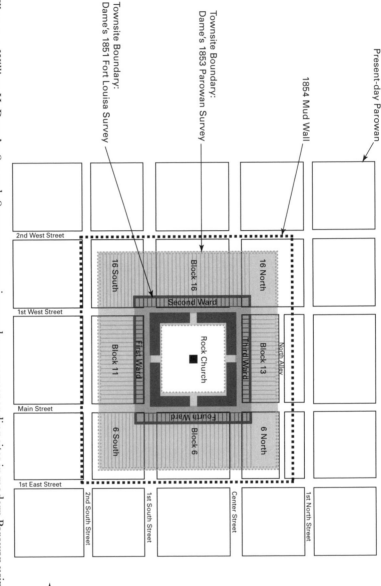

Illus. 5-4. William H. Dame's 1851 and 1853 surveys superimposed over corresponding sites in modern Parowan using the 1921 map of Joseph Richards as a base.

Townsite Boundary:
Dame's 1851 Fort Louisa Survey

Townsite Boundary:
Dame's 1853 Parowan Survey

1854 Mud Wall

Present-day Parowan

2nd West Street

1st West Street

Main Street

1st East Street

2nd South Street

1st South Street

Center Street

1st North Street

16 South

Block 16

16 North

Second Ward

First Ward

Rock Church

Block 11

Block 13

Third Ward

North Alley

6 South

Block 6

6 North

Fourth Ward

N

claims; title abstracts in the county usually begin from that year. Municipal entitlements also increased as population growth stimulated a more sophisticated response to community planning. In April 1872, for instance, Parowan City formally claimed the lots in the public square, creating a city center around which new business and professional enterprises could develop.[51] Returning the public square to community ownership for the benefit of all citizens was an action entirely in keeping with the spirit of those who founded Fort Louisa in 1851 and underscored the enduring vision connecting the modern city to its pioneer prototype.

Endnotes

1. Smith, journal, 9 May 1851.

2. Journal History, 2 May 1851, naming 57 persons comprising "Pres. Brigham Young and company," also noting 5 carriages, 15 wagons, 63 horses and 8 mules.

3. Smith, journal, 10 May 1851.

4. Lunt, diary, 11 May 1851.

5. Smith, journal, 11 May 1851.

6. Ibid., 16 May 1851.

7. Iron Mission Record, Sunday, 25 May 1851.

8. Smith, journal, 26–27 Jun 1851.

9. Zabriskie and Robinson, "U.S. Census for Utah, 1851." At that time, Utah had seven counties: Davis, Iron, Salt Lake, Sanpete, Tooele, Utah and Weber.

10. Whitney, *History of Utah,* 1:452. As noted in ch. 3 above, Jefferson Hunt revealed his important news to the iron missionaries as early as 14 Jan 1851, meeting them on the trail just as they were arriving at Little Salt Lake Valley and he was returning to Salt Lake City from California.

11. Brooks, *John Doyle Lee,* 166.

12. Found in Jenson's "Parowan Ward History" (full cite at ch. 1, n. 49).

13. Smith, journal, 31 May 1851.

14. Ibid., 25 May 1851; see Larson's commentary following entry for 1 Mar 1851 in Lee, journal, 382.

15. Brooks, *John Doyle Lee,* 169–70; Smith, journal, 25 May 1851.

16. Kate B. Carter, comp., *Our Pioneer Heritage,* 20 vols. (Salt Lake City: Daughters of Utah Pioneers, 1958–77), 8:509–10 (excerpting Joseph Lee Robinson journal).

17. James H. Martineau, Parowan Stake History, Stake Meeting Minutes, 11 Aug 1859–13 Feb 1860, entry of 5 Jan 1860, 61, film 1,666,076 (as of this writing), Family History Library, Salt Lake City.

18. Carter, *Our Pioneer Heritage,* 8:511.

19. Percentages derived from Zabriskie and Robinson's "U.S. Census for Utah, 1851."

20. Smith, journal, 15 May 1851.

21. Ibid., 16 May and 4 Aug 1851.

22. Lee, journal, 19 Jan 1851.

23. Ibid., 9 Feb 1851 (as described in the second passage so dated).

24. Ibid. Larson's commentary, at 376 nn. 33 and 35, is relevant here. See also Lee's "Elders Quorum" references on 23 Feb 1851 (misdated "Sund. 23rd March").

25. Smith, journal, 16 May 1851 (Smith's spelling of surnames retained).

26. Whitney, *History of Utah,* 1:435–41.

27. Morgan, "State of Deseret," 222–23.

28. Smith, journal, 9 Mar 1851.

29. Lunt, diary, 16 May 1851.

30. Smith, journal, 12 Jun 1851.

31. Ibid., 17 May 1851.

32. Ibid., 30 Jun–1 Jul 1851.

33. George A. Smith, letter to editor, 28 Nov 1851, published in *Deseret News,* 13 Dec 1851, 3d unnumbered page.

34. Smith, journal, 15 Jun 1851.

35. Ibid., 17 Jun 1851.

36. Ibid., 18 Jun 1851.

37. George A. Smith, letter to editor, 2 Jul 1851, published in *Deseret News,* 26 Jul 1851, 301. The phrase "return of a part" refers to those who, for whatever reason, left the Iron Mission to return to Salt Lake City, thereby draining the settlement of critically needed manpower.

38. Smith, journal, 4 Jul 1851.

39. Ibid., 24 Jul 1851. The "Parowan" house referred to by Smith is probably the "Parowan Hall" built by Peter Shirts.

40. Ibid., 26 and 28 Jul 1851.

41. Ibid., 31 Jul 1851.

42. Ibid., 7 Aug 1851.

43. Ibid., 10 Aug 1851.

44. Ibid., 17–21 Aug 1851.

45. Ibid., 30 May 1851. Elijah Elmer's surname is spelled "Elmore" by Smith.

46. The exact identity of Richards is difficult to determine. Candidates include Morgan Richards Sr. ("an artist" in plaster and concrete), Morgan Richards Jr. (clerk, later superintendent, of the co-op), and possibly a cousin, also named Morgan, all from Glamorganshire, Wales. Morgan Jr., born in 1845, later became state auditor (1896–1901); his son, Alma Richards, won the gold medal for a 6½ foot high jump in the 1912 Olympic Games in Stockholm, Sweden. See Dalton, *Iron County Mission,* 64, 304, 368–70.

47. Deed Book A (7 Feb 1851–28 Feb 1855), 104.

48. Deed Book B (28 Feb 1855–15 Sep 1863), 173–74.

49. Ibid., 186.

50. Ibid., 5, 18.

51. Lawrence B. Lee, "Homesteading in Zion," *Utah Historical Quarterly* 28 (Jan 1960): 29–30; Deed Book D (12 Aug 1863–16 Sep 1874), 253, Iron County Recorder's Office, Parowan, Utah.

6

On to Cedar City

November 1851

Meetings held in Salt Lake City in fall 1851 would directly affect the southern settlements. At the October general conference and at other special meetings that year, Brigham Young called pioneers to strengthen these outlying colonies. In the case of the Iron Mission, this would lead to the founding of a new settlement late that year which would be given the name of Cedar City.

George A. Smith, who departed Parowan 21 August 1851 to attend general conference, arrived in Salt Lake City only a week after starting out. Even with visits to friends in Nephi, Payson and Provo, his party took one-fourth as long riding north as they had on the journey south the previous December. Peter Smith (Dibble), driving George A.'s wagon, had left on 19 August, in advance of the main group. A company led by Robert Wiley, the English bricklayer, left the same day.[1]

Church leaders Brigham Young, Heber C. Kimball, E. T. Benson, Orson Hyde, George A. Smith, Wilford Woodruff, W. W. Phelps and Lorenzo Dow Young all spoke at a special gathering, 7–9 September, in the Bowery on Temple Square. Their counsel, however, was overshadowed by non-Mormon Perry E. Brocchus, federal associate territorial judge, who gave a provocative talk denouncing polygamy and absolving the U.S. government of responsibility for Mormon persecutions in Missouri and Illinois. Brigham Young immediately stood and challenged Brocchus, marking the beginning of intensifying hostilities between the U.S. government and the Mormons.[2]

General conference convened a month later, on 6 October. At that session, several items of business concerned Cedar City:

> George A. Smith made an appeal in behalf of the southern settlements and it was proposed that John D. Lee form a settlement at the junction of the Rio Virgen and Santa Clara where grapes, cotton, figs, dates,

raisins, etc., could be raised. It was also proposed to make a settlement in Coal Creek valley, 20 miles beyond Parowan City, where coal had been found in the canyons and also plenty of timber. . . . The first company was to be piloted by Peter Shirts and start next Wednesday. The second company was to start in about 2 weeks and be piloted by John A. Wolf and Andrew Love. . . . All the propositions were put to vote and unanimously sustained by the conference.[3]

Brigham Young's history confirms: "It was voted that three companies piloted respectively by Peter Shirts, John A. Woolf, and Andrew Love, should start within two weeks, to make or strengthen settlements in the Southern parts of the Territory."[4]

These terse reports only hint at the exploration and discussion that resulted in George A. Smith's proposal to create a second settlement to the south. As early as January 1851, the option of having iron workers live somewhere other than Parowan had been rejected, even though the initial foundry was to be located at Iron Springs, some 12 miles away. Coal Creek was deemed unfavorable because the canyon was narrow, making the construction of buildings difficult. It was much less accessible to wagons during winter months and the suitability of its channel for irrigation was questionable. Like Shirts Creek six miles to the south, it eventually fanned out over a broad area like a river delta, making control of the water flow difficult.

The original choice, therefore, to keep the settlement at Parowan but place the foundry at Iron Springs, seemed a good compromise. What, then, prompted the reevaluation? Almost certainly it was the April 1851 discovery of coal in the canyon east of present-day Cedar City. Finding this abundant fuel source resulted in a decision to consolidate both townsite and blast furnace on the banks of Coal Creek, near the canyon. The coal would have to be hauled only six miles—and all downhill. And even though it could not be reached during winter months, it could be stockpiled by careful management.

Although the iron ore, in contrast, would still have to be hauled eight miles, that distance was four miles closer to Coal Creek than to Parowan. After assessing all the options, George A. Smith recommended the move, pleased by the "splendid sight" he and Aaron Farr had come upon in their explorations of 7 May 1851. Brigham Young had apparently given tacit approval, during his 15 May visit, for the second colony to be founded there. Although establishing a new colony would delay the iron business another year, the failure of Center Creek to supply adequate water to the Parowan settlement must have convinced the leaders that moving to Coal Creek was the better plan. Another consequence of creating a second settlement would be the drastic change in Parowan's function in the region. Instead of being the iron manufacturing center as first envisioned, it would now take on a supporting role. The political, civic and educational needs of the area would have to be rebalanced between two communities instead of one.[5]

It is not clear when the companies called during October general conference started back for southern Utah. The three men recorded as their leaders, Peter Shirts, John Woolf and Andrew Love, all appear in the "departure list" of 21 December 1850, the May 1851 Utah Census and related "first settler" records (see app. 4). Further, on 16 May 1851, Smith records that Andrew Love and John Woolf were made counselors on the newly organized Parowan City Council. The name Peter Shirts appears frequently in George A. Smith's journal between the founding of the Iron Mission and the settling of Coal Creek almost a year later, although Lunt only mentions Shirts as the host of a ball for the 24 July celebration.[6]

On 4 August 1851, Smith organized the traveling company of those about to attend October conference in Salt Lake City and put Peter Shirts at its head, referring passingly to "Capt. Shirts" in his 22 August entry, made during the trip north.[7] Combined, the various references more than suffice to indicate that Love, Shirts and Woolf were in southern Utah until shortly before conference, when Love and Woolf must also have returned to Salt Lake City, either in the same company as Smith and Shirts or a bit earlier.

Surprisingly, John Anthony Woolf appears not to have made the expected journey back south. Separate anecdotal accounts from Woolf family histories report that, having lived in Salt Lake City since 1847, John responded to Brigham Young's call in 1852 for additional settlers in Iron County. That spring, he left his family behind and went on ahead to build a house and plant crops. He then returned north to attend conference and pick up his family. Unfortunately,

> they were destined NOT to return to Iron County. While camped on the banks of the Jordan River, all their cattle were stolen and could not be recovered. Because of the delay in searching for the cattle, and because of Sarah Ann's poor health, they found it necessary to remain in the area for the winter.

A second family history says that they wintered in a house Woolf built on the Provo River, but both agree the family tried again to go south in spring 1853, only to be preempted by Brigham Young, who asked them to settle in Mona for the time being.[8]

Some anecdotal detail is also available on Peter Shirts. According to family history, Brigham Young introduced Peter, during his attendance at general conference, to Belana Pulsipher, the newly arrived widow of Horace Burgess, one of Brigham's Nauvoo friends. Peter's first wife, Margaret Cameron, had died in 1849 on the banks of the Platte River. Belana and Peter courted during the weeks he was in Salt Lake City and then married, leaving for Parowan in early October 1851. No known document records their journey or their arrival at Coal Creek.[9] Perhaps the Scotch Independent Company or some of its members traveled south with Shirts.

The Scotch Independent Company

Members of the Scotch Independent Company had arrived in the Salt Lake Valley just before October conference and were quickly called to help establish the iron works at Cedar City. The story of the Scotch Independent Company begins in the 1840s when the Matthew Carruthers family, James and Isabella Dunn Bulloch and John and Janet Kerr Stoddard were converted to Mormonism in Scotland. Two of the sons, David Bulloch and David Kerr Stoddard, left autobiographies detailing their travels to Utah. The Bullochs, with 120 other Latter-day Saints, organized as the Franklin Richards Company, embarked from Liverpool on 20 February 1848 aboard the *Carnatic* and arrived in New Orleans in mid-April. The Stoddards reached New Orleans in October 1848 aboard the *Sailor Prince*. The Bullochs and Stoddards, with the families of Alexander Keir, James Williamson, Matthew Carruthers, John Grant and several Easton families, spent about two months traveling up the Mississippi and Missouri rivers, arriving in St. Louis just before Christmas 1848.[10]

After the party reached St. Louis, some members pushed directly on to Salt Lake Valley, while others stayed behind to earn funds for wagons, animals and supplies. The Bullochs remained almost three years, the Stoddards for two and a half. James Bulloch and Matthew Carruthers farmed together during the summers of 1849 and 1850.[11] During this time, young David Bulloch ran to see a passing mare and colt and, coming too close to the animals, was kicked unconscious by one of them. After being attended by a doctor who doubted for his life, David recalled in his memoirs, "my father [James], Mathew Cruthers and Samuel Richards administered to me and in a day or two I was able to run around at play again. The Doctor said it would have been much better if I had died as I could never be mentally efficient. This proved to be false."[12]

Carruthers was still in Scotland when he confirmed Christina Bulloch, David Bulloch's sister, after her baptism. Yet he reached Salt Lake City *before* the others, since he met with Brigham Young to "receive instructions about melting iron" on 8 November 1850.[13] He was also listed in George A. Smith's company of those who left Provo for the Iron Mission the following December, was in Iron County when the census was taken in April or May 1851 (noting his profession as "iron maker") and was already a presiding elder and militia major when the rest of the Scotch Independent Company arrived. John Chatterley reports Carruthers was in charge of the day school in Cedar City until he was called to "superintend the Iron Works."[14] Perhaps Matthew visited

Illus. 6-1. David Bulloch (1844–1928) wrote an autobiography telling the story of the Scottish immigrants to southern Utah. Esshom, *Pioneers and Prominent Men*, 280.

the Maramec Spring Iron Works southwest of St. Louis, where he could have observed how Americans constructed and operated blast furnaces, techniques that would later appear in the Iron Mission project. As the story of Carruthers makes clear, the Scottish converts did not all reach Utah in the same company.

By spring 1851, the main company of Scots still in St. Louis had enough cash and experience to set out across the plains. Bulloch recalls that each family had two yoke of oxen and two cows,[15] making a caravan of 10 or 12 wagons. David Stoddard records that they left St. Louis in April and arrived at Winter Quarters six weeks later. They were further delayed at Winter Quarters when flooding made it impossible to "take the old road up the Platte River or the old Mexican Trail." They lost time searching for a new road, Bulloch says, but at Council Bluffs, under Captain John Easton, they were

> joined by others and organized into a larger company. But in traveling in this large company we were hindered considerably. Some of the men had never driven oxen before, others had only little experience and their troubles would hinder the whole train. Therefore, after a few days of travel with the train, our Company from St. Louis broke with the main company and traveled on ahead of them to Salt Lake. We were called the Independent Scotch Company.[16]

David Stoddard also remarks on this split from the larger company:

> After a week's travel we were discouraged, as so much time was wasted.
> The captain, John Easton, called us all into council and laid before us the
> condition of affairs, asked if we were willing to travel alone as [a] company
> of ten, and leave the others. We all agreed to do this. We reached Salt Lake
> City on Friday, October 5, 1851, in Captain Cardon's Company.[17]

Stoddard's memory appears to be faulty, however, since records show
that John Easton and his group *left* Captain Cardon's company, rather
than arriving *with* it. As William Booth, a clerk in Cardon's company,
records on Saturday, 12 July 1851, a meeting was held the night before to
discuss Easton's proposal to take his part of the company on alone.
Booth's final comment was that "Captain Easton left us this morning with
his company. I fear he will repent of so doing."[18]

The next reference to the Scotch Independent Company may be this
from the Journal History of 19 August 1851: "Wilkin's merchandize train
consisting of ten wagons, with a Scotch company in the rear, were met at,
or near the same place they met Mr. Brown's company; also Gordon's."[19]
It should be noted that the *Millennial Star,* 15 October 1851, offers a
similar account. Perhaps the reference to Gordon, which sounds similar to
"Cardon," is an indication that Stoddard and his group did meet up with
Cardon's company again and arrived together, as the excerpt from his life
story would suggest (although Booth's journal does not record any such
reunion). Records of the date the Scottish company arrived in Salt Lake
City, therefore, remain vague: Wilkin's train reportedly arrived
18 September 1851, while David Stoddard put his group's arrival at
5 October.[20] David Bulloch did not give a date, but only said they arrived
"two weeks ahead of the big company of 1851."[21]

David Stoddard lists members of the company who traveled together
to Salt Lake Valley; David Bulloch lists those who said they were in that
part of the Scotch Independent Company that traveled on to Iron County.
David Bulloch was only seven when his family arrived; David Stoddard
was 21. The two did not compile their respective lists until many years
later. The lists are arranged as a sidebar into logical family groupings,
retaining spellings from each source. Family relationships have also been
supplied, where known, but pioneer punctuation injects some ambiguity.
According to David Stoddard, there were nine family groups that comprised the Scotch Independent Company journeying to Salt Lake City,[22]
while the "Life Sketch of David Bulloch" lists five family groups arriving
in Iron County in November 1851.[23] Inexplicably, the "Life Sketch" does

not include the Bulloch family in the list of first settlers. However, an additional source, "Facts Furnished by David Bulloch,"[24] does list James Bulloch, the father, and children Robert (14), Christine (13) and David (7), making a total of six family groups.[25]

Joseph Horne, who appears on David Stoddard's list, had actually preceded the rest of the group to Utah. He appears both as captain of the 3d 10 in Parley P. Pratt's Southern Exploring Expedition of 1849–50 and

---

FAMILY GROUPS IN THE SCOTCH INDEPENDENT COMPANY

David Stoddard's List
John Easton, captain, and family
James Easton and family
Robert Easton and family
Alexander Easton and family
Mrs. Easton, their mother
Two married men, George and Matthew Easton
James Williamson and family
Sandy Kear and family
Sandy Mustard and daughter
John and Andrew Burt
Joseph Horne
James [father,] Robert and David Bulloch [sons]
James Berner
John Stoddard and family [including David, the autobiographer]

David Bulloch's List
Johnie Stoddard, Jr. [*sic*] and wife; Grannie; David [the autobiographer], John Jr. [*sic*] and John 3rd
Alec Keer Sr. and wife [Mary], son Alec Jr., nephew Robert Keer
James Williamson and wife, son James Jr., son Thomas, daughters Mary [later, wife of David Stoddard] and Margaret [also called Maggie]
Robert Easton, wife [Mary] and baby; John Easton and wife and family John, Elizabeth and Barbara; Sandy Easton and wife; orphaned boy Johnie Grant Henderson family

Source: Mona Busby, "The Iron Miner," as printed in Kate Carter, *Pioneer Heritage,* 13:390–91 and David Bulloch, "The Life Sketch of David Bulloch," Cedar City Public Library, 1–2.

as an original member of the Iron Mission, 1850–51. He is also on the May 1851 Iron County Census (listed as a farmer from England). Perhaps there were two Joseph Hornes, but this is unlikely.[26] A possible inconsistency about Stoddard himself is that George A. Smith, en route to Salt Lake City two months earlier, in August 1851, records meeting three men at Corn Creek (later named Kanosh for the Pahvant Ute chief). He identifies them only as "father Gould and br Stodard and Lewis."[27]

Brigham Young's Trip South, October 1851

Shortly after the Scotch Independent Company left for Cedar City, President Young left Salt Lake City (on 21 October) to seek a more central site for the state capitol and to inspect the southern settlements. He was accompanied by his board of commissioners,[28] Orson Pratt, Albert Carrington (clerk and historian), Jesse Fox (surveyor), William Staines and Joseph Robinson. Also present were Counselor Heber C. Kimball, General Daniel H. Wells, Judge Zerubbabel Snow and Indian Agent Stephen B. Rose. In his journal entry of the same date, George A. Smith mentions that he and Bishop Joseph L. Robinson accompanied President Young. On the 22nd, he notes 15 in the company, of whom he specifically names Young, Kimball, Pratt, Wells, Carrington and Fox. He also mentions Horace Eldridge, not named in the previous list.[29]

On 28 October 1851, Brigham Young located a site for Fillmore City on Chalk Creek, "up the creek about a mile and a half from our camp," returning to Salt Lake City by 7 November, while George A. Smith's party continued on to Parowan, where they arrived 30 October. The next day, Peter Shirts hosted a welcome-home party.[30] George A. had not come back to direct the new settlement, however. In Salt Lake City, he had been called to preside over the Utah Stake in Provo and had come south only to clear up his affairs. A major obligation—the thousand dollars he owed those who had built the mill for him—dissolved when they made him a present of the bill, thus clearing the account.[31] A 28 October letter from Brigham Young and Heber C. Kimball written to the "Presidency of Parowan" implies that the appointment of Elisha H. Groves as George A. Smith's replacement had been made permanent. Since Groves would be serving annually in the territorial legislature, however, Brigham Young wanted counselors appointed to take care of the mission in his absence and suggested the names of John Lyman Smith (George A. Smith's brother, hereafter "John Lyman,") and Matthew Carruthers.[32] The letter expresses concern for the southern colonies and gives specific advice on protecting them:

When the brethren first go to Coal creek, we suggest that they leave
their families at Parowan until they build the fort at that point. We further suggest that in all your settlements the people do not stray about at
a distance alone, or only a few in company, and that you herd and coral
your cattle.[33]

Surveying the New Settlement

On 2 or 3 November, George A. Smith took his brother John Lyman,
Elisha H. Groves, Matthew Carruthers, William Dame (and others,
among whom were probably James A. Little and Henry Lunt) and traveled
to Coal Creek, where they laid out the position for a new fort and, possibly, dedicated the site for the manufacture of iron.[34] Unfortunately, none of
the presently known primary sources that record the colonizing of Coal
Creek mention a dedication of any kind.

There is, however, one reference which should be considered: the
"Early History of Cedar City and Vicinity," written by local historian John
Urie in 1880. Since Urie was not a pioneer settler of the new colony, his
comments must have been compiled from the first-hand memories of
others. The relevant passage reads as follows:

> [O]n Nov. 3rd E. A. Groves, Wm. H. Dame, James A. Little, Henry Lunt
> with George A. Smith and others arrived from Parowan on the spot
> marked out by Parley P. Pratt two years before for settlement. Next day
> Nov. 4th 1851, Cedar City was surveyed by Wm. H. Dame. It is distant
> about a mile due north from the present location. The name Cedar City
> was given because of the abundance of Cedar trees that abounded all over
> the country. Geo. A. Smith in h[u]mility before God together with the
> rest of his fellow Pioneers dedicated the ground just surveyed, the sur-
> rounding lands, the minerals in the water, the timber, the grass, to the ser-
> vice of God, in the manufacturing of Iron, machinery and that our
> necessities might be supplied and the territory built up.[35]

Urie's account helps us to interpret Cedar City's settlement date. Henry
Lunt writes that on "the 4th of November they located and surveyed a fort,
and returned to Parowan."[36] George A. Smith concurs with Lunt's diary and
Urie's reminiscence in a letter of 5 November 1851 printed in the *Deseret
News:* "Yesterday a site was surveyed for a fort and stock caral on Coal Creek,
20 miles from Parowan." Since the 5th was a Wednesday, this dates the survey
to Tuesday, the 4th. The Journal History notes, also under 5 November, that
George A. Smith's letter to Brigham Young reports a fort selected and laid off
"on the 4th inst." Surprisingly, Smith's own journal dates the survey to

Monday, not Tuesday, recording that on "November 3rd. We located a site for a fort and cattle coral. Bro. Dame surveyed it. Returned back to the city."[37] Whichever day was correct, we now have both primary and secondary sources identifying a trip by George A. Smith, just before leaving southern Utah, at which a second colony site is surveyed for the benefit of settlers who will colonize it immediately after his departure.

We can also infer a formal dedication at Coal Creek by George A. Smith, during which the site was named for its plentiful cedar trees.[38] If John Urie is reporting historical fact, then he must have meant that Smith dedicated the site shortly after Dame completed his survey. Thus (depending on which journal one accepts as the most precise), the dedication took place on Monday, 3 November, or Tuesday, 4 November, either before or after the survey but before the survey party returned to Parowan. Urie's history thus asserts a very early date for the official use of "Cedar City," superseding "Little Muddy," "Cottonwoods" and "Coal Creek" as place names (although they continued to be in use—especially Coal Creek—for some months to come). Both in recognition of this and for ease in discussing the townsite, we will use "Cedar City" hereafter, unless a different term is used in a quotation.

Organizing the Militia

Establishing the new settlement involved not only surveying a townsite but also organizing the pioneers into traveling companies structured along military lines. George A. Smith explains this in his 5 November 1851 letter, cited just above:

> Yesterday a site was surveyed for a fort and stock caral on Coal Creek, 20 miles from Parowan. To-day a company has been organized to commence operations immediately in the construction of this new post. They are mostly composed of English, Scotch and Welsh miners and iron manufacturers. They have also been organized into two companies of militia, one a horse, and the other foot, and form the 2d Battalion of Iron County. Matthew Caruthers is the Major. The company are all in fine spirits. They will commence on Monday to put up their caral, after which they will move their families which are remaining here, and encamp in their caral until their fort is completed.[39]

"Company" has two meanings here. The "company . . . organized to commence operations immediately" referred to a traveling group like any of those crossing the plains by wagon train and handcart. Smith also used the word as a military term: "they have also been organized into two companies of militia." John D. Lee's letter to Brigham Young, reporting his successful return to Parowan from Salt Lake City, clarifies the nature of military command in the Iron County district:

> on the 5th inst. the militia of Cole creek were organized into a Battalion which caused the Iron Battalion together to grow into a regiment over which Geo. A. Smith was elected colonel, James A. Little lieut. Col. and Mathew Carrathers major.[40]

In short, as military records in the Utah State Archives and Records Service confirm, a foot company and horse company of militia, constituting a new battalion (the Second) of the Iron Regiment of the Nauvoo Legion, were organized at Parowan on 5 November 1851, to be headquartered at Cedar City. According to the muster roll of 29 November (those for 5 November are missing), the foot company, Company F, consisted of 25 men commanded by Captain Henry Lunt, also identified as the "president" of the whole traveling company.[41] The cavalry, Company C, consisted of 11 men and mounts commanded by Captain Peter M. Fife.[42] Both groups included several members of the Scotch Independent Company (indicated by an asterisk in the accompanying sidebar). Combined, these two companies totaled 36 men—close to the traditional number of 35 original settlers of Cedar City,[43] although no evidence exists proving that each of the men listed in the two companies reached the Coal Creek settlement and camped together there the first night.

The March to Cedar City

On 10 November 1851, Henry Lunt's journal records that "a Company of 11 wagons started from Parowan for the purpose of making a settlement at Coal Creek; Henry Lunt having been President of the Company."[44] Lunt doesn't specify the order of march to the new site. However, the most likely premise is that one militia company preceded the other by a full day. Company C, with 10 to 13 mounted men (the roster names only 11), is probably the group which departed Parowan on 10 November, probably to secure the area and organize the campsite. Although it should have been a relatively easy one-day trip to Coal Creek, Lunt goes on to note that the party camped that evening at Summit Creek, six miles from Parowan, and reached Coal Creek the next day by 4:00 P.M.

As no member of Company C is known to have accompanied George A. Smith in selecting the Coal Creek location, how did this first party of settlers identify it? Perhaps a member of the group had been on the survey without recording it or perhaps directions were sufficiently explicit without a guide. A third and more likely possibility is that Henry Lunt, who had been a member of Smith's site-selection committee on 2–4 November and who had helped Dame make his survey, delegated leadership of Company F to someone else and accompanied Peter M. Fife's Company C to Coal Creek. Perhaps Lunt was originally assigned

---

SECOND BATTALION, IRON REGIMENT, NAUVOO LEGION

Company F (Foot)	Company C (Cavalry)
Henry Lunt, Capt.	Peter M. Fife, Capt.
Samuel West, First Lt.	Joseph Chatterly, First Lt.
James H. Martineau, First Sgt.	Alexander Easton*
James Baird, Second Sgt.	[all privates hereafter]
James Bulloch* [all privates hereafter]	John Easton*
William Stone	George Easton*
James Williamson	Robert Easton*
Alexander Kier*	William Bateman
Robert Henry	Alexander Ross
Duncan Ross	Daniel Ross
George Cassell	N. Johnson
William C. Mitchell, Jr.	S. Johnson
John Tout	
James Thorpe	
Richard Harrison	
William Woods	
James Whittaker, Sr.	
James Whittaker, Jr.	
Thomas Rowland	
William Slack	
Edward Williams	
William Evans	
John Stoddard* [Sr. or Jr. not indicated]	
Thomas Cartwright	
John Chatterley	

* Member of Scotch Independent Company

Source: Territorial Militia Muster Rolls (1851–1867), Iron County, Utah State Archives and Records Service, Salt Lake City.

to lead the foot company simply because he had no horse. In any case, his journal implies that he came to Coal Creek with the earlier Company C.

Lunt is our best source for the two-day trip, clearly recording that the group left Parowan on 10 November, arriving at 4:00 P.M. the next day, after the overnight camp at Summit Creek. The journal account, however, seems to contradict his 4 February 1852 letter to George A. Smith: "I started from Parowan on Monday, November 11th (1851) with eleven wagons for this place . . . breaking a new road nearly the whole of the way."[45] Most probably the letter, which was written in retrospect, and not the journal, contains a dating error, since Monday fell on 10, not 11, November. In any event, it would appear that Company F, consisting of 25 men, some wagons, cows, calves, two English sheep dogs and some hobbled mules, left on Tuesday, 11 November, and reached Coal Creek late the same day, probably arriving about three hours after Company C.

In 1918, at age 78, four years before his death, John Chatterley wrote an account of this trip, presumably with the foot company, which took place when he was 16 years old:

> On the 11th day of November, 1851 a company of emigrants left Parowan, Iron Co., Utah who had gathered there and came down to settle Cedar, Henry Lunt having charge of the company. They arrived here about 7 P.M. of that day. The reason they were late in arriving at the camping place on the East bank of Coal Creek, was on account of the guide Peter Shutz [i.e., Shirts] leading the company up on the South East side of the big knoll about 3 or 4 miles this side [south] of Parowan, near to the main chain of the mountains, as they, the settlers had to make road in places, the road was not used after the first trip over it, the road out in the valley North West of the knoll was made the main road. The writer of this, in company with two young men, named Duncan Ross and James Anderson, respectively drove the loose animals, cows and calves, and having two English sheperd dogs, which caused the cows to travel pretty lively, and of course cows, calves and hobble-donkeys arrived on the bank of Coal Creek hungry enough to demolish the half of a calf without an[y] cooking. There were about 13 men camped there the first night.[46]

Chatterley recalls his departure from Parowan as 11 November and arrival as late the same day—7 P.M., probably after dark. His account claims the eastward route Shirts led them on was never used again but a number of journals refer to an "upper road" and "lower road" between Cedar City and Parowan. The main, or lower road, went west near Summit and then either through the mountains to Antelope Spring or further south through the Woolsey Ranch and Pinto. The eastern, or upper road, was mentioned by Thomas Bullock as late as 1854, noting that he used it to drive from Cedar Fort to Parowan.[47]

Possibly, Shirts and the other travelers had to contend with snow along the trail. Alexander Matheson, who knew most of the Cedar City pioneers, told his son Alva that the foot company trudged in facing a snowstorm and, on arrival, took refuge in the cove on the north side of the Knoll.[48] This landmark, lying north of modern Cedar City, now topped by television and microwave relay stations, extends east to west and curls slightly north at its eastern extremity. Its western extremity has been reduced several times to provide a better approach to Cedar City's Main Street, but the cove there is still quite prominent.

To join the presumed advance party of Company C, Lunt may have felt it militarily expedient to delegate his command of Company F. Peter Shirts, who does not appear on the roster of either company but who was one of the three men designated at October conference to pilot new settlers to Cedar City, may have been pressed into service as teamster and guide. If Carruthers, as major, had led the battalion, traveling with Fife's cavalry while Lunt led his foot company, it seems unlikely that the services of Shirts would have been needed.

Although the two companies reached the Cedar City encampment the same day, 11 November, James Whittaker Sr., a member of Company F, records that (having arrived in Parowan on 29 October) he traveled from Parowan to Coal Creek on Wednesday, 12 November.[49] Lunt reports two new arrivals the same day:

> Wm. C. Mitchell and his son, Wm. C., Jr. arrived at Coal Creek from Parowan to assist in making the settlement. Bro. Mitchell stayed a few days then returned to Parowan, leaving his son to build the fort, who stayed and built a house and helped to make a public corrall and survey the first field in the valley.[50]

On 18 November, according to Whittaker, another train of 16 wagons arrived in Cedar City. Most of these settlers were Scots.[51]

Resolving Issues of Command

Major Matthew Carruthers, battalion commander of both companies as well as presiding elder of the new Cedar City settlement, is not listed on the rosters of either Company C or Company F. This strongly implies that he stayed in Parowan during the first remove to Cedar City. His presence with the advance company would more than likely have meant that he, rather than Lunt, was the appointed president of the combined traveling group. As "Elder Carruthers" presiding over the contemplated settlement and as "Major Carruthers" commanding the battalion, Carruthers had as much, if not more, status than Lunt.

On 18 November, the same day the 16 wagons of new emigrants arrived, Carruthers wrote an eloquent letter to the *Deseret News* on behalf of the Cedar City pioneers, asking for additional support for the Iron Mission:

> For us to furnish the iron necessary for the teritory, would be, in my opinion, to accomplish one of the most important objects connected with the up-building of the kingdom of God upon the earth; and we, by so doing, would secure to ourselves a name, a place and a standing among our brethren, the honor and glory of which would not once be worthy of comparing with the labor and toil which might be necessary to accomplish it. . . .
>
> Come, then, my brethren, obey the counsel of your leaders, fulfill the predictions of the prophets, and flow together to the goodness of the Lord in the valley of Coal Creek, for wheat, for corn, for potatoes, for melons, for beets, for carrots, for squashes, for pumpkins, for onions, for large cabbages, and for both the young and the old of the flock, for the wheat tithing given to the poor, and above all, to get out the coal and the iron; and if you live humble, keep the commandments, and obey counsel, your souls will be like unto a well irrigated field of goodly soil, so that there will be no necessity of your sorrowing any more at all.[52]

Henry Lunt's "election" as president of the traveling company is undocumented but probably took the usual form, in this case George A. Smith presenting him to the traveling group for a "sustaining vote." If Smith had intended Lunt to preside permanently at Cedar City, Lunt would have outranked Carruthers ecclesiastically, yet would have served as his military subordinate. The 39-year-old Carruthers definitely outranked 27-year-old Lunt, although neither of them had strong qualifications as military leaders. Lunt had been mustered into the militia as a private at Peteetneet (Payson) as the iron missionaries first traveled to Cedar City. Carruthers and Lunt were both privates in Captain Edson Whipple's foot company in Parowan as of 8 August 1851. Barely three months later, on 5 November, Carruthers was promoted to major and Lunt to captain. Neither Lunt, a middle-class Englishman, nor Carruthers, a middle or upper-class Scot, had any known prior military experience.

Journal entries and letters suggest that Lunt saw his authority as president of the traveling company extending beyond the trip from Parowan and into the first stages of settlement. In the journal entry of 10 November 1851, cited above, Lunt gives evidence he considered himself in command:

"A company of 11 wagons started from Parowan for the purpose of making a settlement at Coal Creek; Henry Lunt having been President of the Company." He also wrote to George A. Smith in February 1852, sharing his "serious reflections:"

> Twelve months had scarcely elapsed since I had the first interview with Bro. Geor. A. Smith and came on the mission to Parowan (or Iron County). Then I knew but little, what it was to help build up our Heavenly Father's Kingdom in making new settlements, and now I was leading a company myself to a large and delightful valley to form another new settlement.[53]

Matthew Carruthers acknowledged Lunt's role as commander over part of the camp at least. Two months into the settlement process, he wrote George A. Smith on 3 January 1852, saying:

> "Shortly after your departure, bro. Henry Lunt, at the head of a portion of the brethren destined for this place, went down and built a good *substantial canal*, mostly with the drift wood that lay scattered on the banks of the creek."[54]

For his own part, Henry Lunt deferred to the ecclesiastical leadership of Carruthers. The entry in Lunt's journal for Sunday, 1 February 1852 reads: "As br Carruthers was writing a letter he requested me to take charge of the meeting which I did." The next day, Lunt added:

> bro Wiley & myself . . . had considerable counsel with bro Carruthers . . . he proposed that Henry Lunt be his first councillor & John Easton 3nd he felt that these were dictated to him by the Spirit of God, they were unanimously Elected, after which H Lunt R. Wiley Josh Chatterly were chosen as a committee for public works. I was elected clerk.[55]

Appointed to fill two roles, Lunt here refers to himself in the third person as counselor but in the first person as clerk. His journal entry for 8 May 1852 is amusing in its layering of titles: "Prest Carruthers received a not[e] from Prest Groves, Parowan, saying that Prest Young had come there."[56] The title was appropriate for these men and for their counselors, since all members of a presidency are addressed as "President." But even without the complications of terminology, it is clear that authority parameters were sometimes misunderstood, a confusion which paved the way for disagreements. Later on, Carruthers became superintendent of the iron company, with Lunt as his clerk. This "cross-threaded" organization shows why pioneer leaders often found it difficult to understand their own lines of authority and even act cooperatively, let alone effectively.

More New Settlers

Even after the roles of the Scotch Independent Company and the militia companies in the move to Cedar City are clarified, questions about personnel remain. The military companies included teamsters, assigned to handle equipment and drive the supply wagons, who are not listed in the rosters. Andrew Jenson identifies two of these as Peter Filanque and Peter Shirts.[57] Gladys McConnell includes George and Darius, sons of Peter Shirts, as teamsters.[58] And John Chatterley, Joseph Chatterley's son, identifies himself, James Anderson and Duncan Ross as the young drovers in charge of loose stock.[59]

In his older years, remembering first impressions of his new wilderness home, David Bulloch wrote about traveling south from Parowan with members of the Scotch Independent Company about to settle in Cedar City. Along the trail, they met up with a Parowan man who was bringing down supplies for the newer colony on the running gears of his wagon. As David recalls,

> I jumped on his wagon with him and arrived on Coal Creek a little ahead of the main company. As I got off the wagon Brother Henry Lunt Sr. took my hat off my head and laying his hands on it said, "My boy, you have the honor of being the first white boy on this creek." He then remarked about my hair which was as white as cotton.[60]

Ellen Whittaker is another name that appears in some sources as a first settler of Cedar City. Her father, James Sr., arriving on 12 November, notes in his journal a return to Parowan on Tuesday the 25th to bring her back with him.[61] He also refers to John Lowe, a name which seems not to appear anywhere else in Iron Mission documents, writing on 4 February, that "the Co of Spaniards started for California, James Baird Duncan Ross, & John Lowe went with them." A subsequent 3 March entry laconically records: "I have heard that Amon the Indian says that Duncan Ross & the rest who went with him are killed by the Indians."[62]

Ambiguities among the various civic and family histories may have many origins: inaccurate memory, hasty and erratic journal-keeping, even the honest desire to be listed as a direct descendant of the city founders. But a close study of the extant data shows that the course of settlement on Coal Creek, unlike the arrival of the *Mayflower*, for instance, is too fluid to provide a definitive list of "first settlers." John Chatterley compiled a list of pioneers whom he remembered as being "in the first group that arrived at Cedar Fort site, November 11, 1851 & lived there 2 winters."[63]

This list (see related sidebar) was checked by other descendants of original settlers and preserved by his daughter, Nancy Walker.

While Chatterley's list is a valuable historical tool, entries from pioneer journals and other reminiscences show that it is not comprehensive. Even from the first day, the road between Parowan and the new settlement of Cedar City probably had two-way traffic and all those moving south did not arrive the same day. Even so, all these various sources record the names of men, women, boys and girls considered to be the first (or nearly first) settlers of Cedar City between 11 November and 31 December 1851 (see app. 4). Regardless of the order in which they came, each found, upon arriving, some assignment he or she could take up, either working in the

---

John Chatterley's List of Cedar City's First Settlers

Matthew Carruthers

James Whittaker, wife, 3 daughters

Joseph Chatterley, wife, 2 daughters, 2 sons

Daniel Ross, wife, 2 daughters, 2 sons

Benjamin Hulse, wife, 3 daughters, 1 son

George Wood, 2 wives, 1 daughter, 1 nephew

Richard Harrison, wife, 2 sons

James Bosnell, wife, 1 daughter, 1 son

James Pugmire, 2 wives, 1 daughter, 1 son

Joseph Walker, wife, 1 daughter, 6 sons

Wm Hunter, wife, 2 sons

Joseph Hunter, wife, 2 sons

Alexander Kier,* wife, 2 sons

Wm Henderson, 1 son

Alexander Campbell,* wife

Alexander Easton,* wife

John Easton*

James Easton*

George Easton,* wife, 2 children

Mathew Easton*

William Wood, wife

James Bullock,* wife, 1 daughter, 2 sons

Thomas Cartwright, wife

_____ [sic] Gregory, wife

Henry Lunt

Jessie Lewis

Philip Klingensmith, wife, 1 daughter, 1 son

Thomas Bladen, wife, niece, 3 daughters, 2 sons

Peter Shurtz, 3 sons

Peter Filance

William Slack, wife, 2 children

Arthur Parks, wife, 2 children

William Deakin, wife

33 of the 35 men, 26 women, 55 younger girls and boys

*Indicates member of Scotch Independent Company

Source: Cited in full at n. 63 below. Original spelling retained.

established townsite of Parowan or helping create the new site on Coal Creek. For all of them, the preeminent goal was building a secure location from which they could manufacture iron.

Endnotes

1. Smith, journal, 29 Apr and 19 Aug 1851. The 19 Aug entry reads "Peter went with my waggon," which could be interpreted to mean Peter Shirts. However, Smith's journal entries always refer to Peter Shirts by some variant of his full name, such as "Bro. Shirts," "P. Shirts," or "Capt. Shirts," while the given name "Peter" appears to be reserved for the young man living with the Smith family, sometimes referred to in pioneer records as Peter Smith and sometimes as Peter Dibble. See, for instance, 29 Apr 1851, where George A. writes that "Br Gould and Peter started out on the California road for search of some Iron," followed by "P. Shirts & W. Chipman & 3 others started exploring."

2. Knecht and Crawley, *Early Records of Utah*, 91–100.

3. Journal History, 6 Oct 1851.

4. Knecht and Crawley, *Early Records of Utah*, 109.

5. Keeping the county seat at Parowan was challenged almost immediately and people have argued about it ever since. The issue has been voted on several times. A plurality of the citizens has consistently voted to change the seat to Cedar City; however, the legal requirement of two-thirds majority has never been met. Thus, Parowan has remained the county seat.

6. Smith, journal, 16 May 1851; Lunt, diary, 24 Jul 1851.

7. Smith, ibid., 4 Aug and 22 Aug 1851; Love's own journal begins later in 1852, so it provides no assistance in dating the activities of Love, Shirts or Woolf in 1851.

8. The references come, respectively, from Edith L. Baker, "Tales of the Fore-Bears" (Bountiful, Utah: privately published, 1989), 111; and "John Anthony Woolf Family Life Histories: John Anthony Woolf and Sarah Ann Devoe, Their Children and Grandchildren" (Salt Lake City: Woolf Family Organization, 1965), n.p., copy in possession of Nancy Magleby Calkins of Springville, Utah, a direct descendent of John Anthony Woolf, to whom we are indebted for bringing these references to our attention.

9. Peter Shirts was literate, but it is not known whether he kept a journal. If he did, it may have been lost at the time of his death in New Mexico or perhaps destroyed when a fire consumed the home of his sons in Escalante, Utah, in the 1940s.

10. David Bulloch, "The Life Sketch of David Bulloch," typescript, 1–2, Historical Collection, Cedar City Public Library, Cedar City, Utah (cited here from copy in Shirts Collection). Related materials in Mona Busby, "The Iron Miner," cited in Carter, *Our Pioneer Heritage*, 13: 390–91. The company is cited variously in

these records, from Scotch Independent Company to Independent Scottish Company and so forth.

11. Bulloch, ibid., 2.

12. Ibid.

13. Journal History, 8 Nov 1850.

14. John Chatterley, "History of Cedar City," undated typescript, 3, Cedar City Public Library (cited from copy in Shirts Collection).

15. Bulloch, "Life Sketch," 2.

16. Ibid., 3.

17. Busby, "Iron Miner," 391.

18. "Journal of the 3rd Company of Ten under the Presidency of Captain Levi Hammon, William Booth, Clerk, Organized in the 2nd 50 (Captain Alfred Cordon), on Friday, the 14th day of June, 1851," n.d., n. p., typescript in Church Emigration Book, 1850–54, LDS Church Archives.

19. Anonymous update, "Later from Great Salt Lake and the Plains—Indian Depredations, &c.," *Millennial Star* 13 (15 Oct 1851): 314; Journal History, 19 Aug 1851.

20. Busby, "Iron Miner," 391.

21. Bulloch, "Life Sketch," 3.

22. Busby, "Iron Miner," 391. David Bulloch is spelled "Bullock" here.

23. Bulloch, "Life Sketch," 5.

24. Kate Palmer Macfarlane, "Facts Furnished by David Bulloch concerning Settlement of Cedar City. Dictated by David Bulloch January 25, 1920 and Received and Recorded by Kate Palmer Macfarlane," typescript, 1, Palmer Collection, SUU Archives (copy in Shirts Collection). Original spelling and punctuation retained. The list names:

> Jno. Stoddard Sr. and wife; John and David, sons, and a nephew John; Sandy Keer (or Kear); Robt. Keer, nephew, and Alexander Jr., son. . . . Mother Keer and two small daughters[;] James Williamson Sr. and wife; James Jr. and Thomas, sons[;] Maggie, daughter, and Mary, daughter, married to D. Stoddard, Jr.

> Robert Easton and wife Mary; John and wife and son, John Alexander Easton, wife and son Geo. Easton, unmarried; James and wife, Mathew [*sic*]. The men all brothers.

> James Bullock, Robert, aged 14, Christina (Sherratt) aged 13; David aged 7.

25. There are minor differences in these lists. Bulloch's "Alec Keer" is almost certainly the same as Stoddard's "Sandy Kear." David Stoddard's mother's name was Janet Keer, suggesting a likely relationship. Stoddard lists John Berner, John Burt and Andrew Burt as members of the party coming to Salt Lake City, but they appear in no Iron County record and presumably did not go south with the rest.

26. Pratt, *Autobiography*, 366; Zabriskie and Robinson, "U.S. Census for Utah, 1851."

27. Smith, journal, 23 Aug 1851.

28. Whitney, *History of Utah*, 1:482.

29. Knecht and Crawley, *Early Records of Utah*, 110; Smith, journal, 21–22 Oct 1851.

30. Smith, ibid., 28–30 Oct 1851.

31. Ibid., 4 Nov 1851.

32. Brigham Young and Heber C. Kimball, "To the Presidency of Parowan," Journal History, 28 Oct 1851.

33. Ibid.

34. On Monday, 3 Nov 1851, Lunt refers generally to Smith and "a small party of men" (Lunt, diary, 3 Nov 1851); the day before, however, Smith identifies John Lyman Smith, Elisha Groves and Matthew Carruthers as his companions, referring the following day to William Dame surveying the site, so we know Dame must have also been one of this group (Smith, journal, 2–3 Nov 1851). Little and Lunt "with others" are present as well, according to John Urie, in a passage more fully discussed and cited in n. 35. It is perhaps of interest that Lunt, in his 3 Nov entry, writes "they located" and not "we located."

35. John Urie, "Early History of Cedar City and Vicinity." There are at least eight slightly distinct versions of this quotation. Photocopies of seven of them—either full document or excerpts—are in the Shirts Collection; another complete typescript version is in Perry Special Collections at large. Originals of three of the Shirts Collection copies (all typescripts; all prepared on different machines) can be found, respectively, in the Cedar City Public Library; the Utah State Historical Society (archival information unmarked on Shirts Collection copy); and the Palmer Collection, SUU Archives. Andrew Jenson, in his "Manuscript History of Cedar City Ward" (see n. 57) incorporates Urie's quotation into his review of events in 1851 almost verbatim, which begs the question of which man borrowed from the other. A version is excerpted by Kate Carter in *Our Pioneer Heritage* but without attribution to Urie. The history is also printed in Evelyn K. Jones and York F. Jones, *Mayors of Cedar City and Histories of Cedar City* (Cedar City: Southern Utah State College [now SUU], 1986) and the passage quoted here is reprinted with slight differences in Evelyn Jones' more recent *Henry Lunt Biography and History of the Development of Southern Utah and Settling of Colonia Pacheco, Mexico* (Provo, Utah: privately printed, 1996), where she cites Kate Carter as source but does not mention Urie. The quote used here is a collation of the three Shirts Collection versions identified above and the Perry Special Collections version.

36. Lunt, diary, 3 Nov 1851.

37. Smith, letter to editor, 5 Nov 1851, published in *Deseret News*, 29 Nov 1851, 3d unnumbered page; Journal History, 5 Nov 1851, transcribing letter from John D. Lee to Brigham Young; Smith, journal, 2–5 Nov 1851.

38. Another primary source regarding the naming of Cedar City, although, like Urie's history, written much after the fact, is John Chatterley's brief "History of Cedar City," the reminiscence of his early days as a first Cedar City settler. The relevant sentence reads: "Cedar City was so named from the fact that the first day of its settlement the settlers camped in some Cedars, that were growing on the East bank of the Creek, where the North field is located at its South end [*sic*]." The source cited here is not, unfortunately, the original holograph, but a typescript of it.

39. Smith, letter to editor, cited above at n. 37.

40. Journal History, 5 Nov 1851.

41. Territorial Militia Muster Rolls (1851–67), Iron County, document #3285, acc. no. 014279, Utah State Archives and Records Service.

42. Territorial Militia Muster Rolls (1851–67), Iron County, document #3287, acc. no. 014279.

43. Many of the early militia rosters of the Nauvoo Legion in Utah are missing, but those preserved in the Utah State Archives and Records Service provide an extremely valuable resource. The 5 Nov 1851 muster rolls have not been located for Company C and Company F, who left for Cedar City only five days later on 10–11 Nov; however, there was apparently a general muster of all southern Utah units on 29 Nov, on which date Companies A, B and E mustered in Parowan and Companies C and F in Cedar City. Possibly (though doubtful), major changes took place in company personnel between 5 and 29 Nov.

44. Lunt, diary, 10 Nov 1851.

45. Lunt to Smith, 4 Feb 1852, in Journal History.

46. Chatterley, "History of Cedar City," 1.

47. Journal History, 21 May 1854. Note that the term "Cedar Fort" as used in this book always refers to the site of Cedar City in southern Utah. No reference, unless so stated, refers to the present-day Utah County town, Cedar Fort, which lies west of American Fork and southeast of Tooele.

48. Alva Matheson, interview by Morris A. Shirts, undated notes in Shirts Collection.

49. Whittaker, journal, 12 Nov 1851.

50. Lunt, diary, 12 Nov 1851.

51. Whittaker, journal, 18 Nov 1851.

52. Matthew Carruthers, letter to editor, 18 Nov 1851, published in *Deseret News*, 13 Dec 1851, 3d unnumbered page.

53. Lunt to Smith, 4 Feb 1852, in Journal History.

54. Matthew Carruthers to George A. Smith, 3 Jan 1852, published in *Deseret News*, 21 Feb 1852, 4th unnumbered page.

55. Lunt, diary, 1–2 Feb 1852.

56. Ibid., 8 May 1852.

57. Andrew Jenson [authorship attributed by William R. Palmer], "Manuscript History of Cedar City Ward," 8 [faint, hand-written numeral], LDS Church Archives (cited from copy in Shirts Collection).

58. Gladys McConnell, untitled talk on history of Cedar City, given 3 Nov 1951, typescript, 2–3, Cedar City Public Library (cited from copy in Shirts Collection).

59. Chatterley, "History of Cedar City," 1.

60. Bulloch, "Life Sketch," 4.

61. Whittaker, journal, 25 Nov 1851.

62. Ibid., 4 Feb 1852 and 3 Mar 1852.

63. John Chatterley, unsourced, undated list of Cedar Fort Pioneers, Cedar City Public Library (cited from copy in Shirts Collection). The heading reads:

> This list of names, Nancy Walker gave to me shortly before her death, saying, "This was given by my father John Chatterly, as the list of people, as he remembered them, who were in the first group that arrived at Cedar Fort site, November 11, 1851 & lived there 2 winters[.]"
>
> The list, as checked by a very small number of families enough interested to have kept track of their history, is authentic.

7

Settling Cedar City

Winter 1851–Winter 1852

The process of founding a new settlement, as Parowan demonstrated, consumed the settlers' lives and dictated priorities in the 1850s outside the Salt Lake Valley. Immediate safety, long-term security and future productivity were central to successfully inhabiting the wilderness of southern Utah. None of these concerns was left to chance. Settlers typically picked a site first and then surveyed it. Next, colonists built a corral to keep their livestock from wandering off and erected a fort to protect themselves against intruders. Laying out fields for planting and making provision for irrigation occurred simultaneously or very shortly afterward. Then individual families began building homes and cultivating their garden plots.

The Wagon-Box Camp and the "South Side" Corral

When the settlers first arrived from Parowan, on the afternoon and evening of 11 November 1851, they lifted their wagon boxes off the running gears and used the boxes as temporary shelters. By the time David Bulloch rode into Coal Creek, members of the Parowan advance party had already placed two of their wagon boxes on the ground under some cedar trees. According to Bulloch, the incoming pioneers placed their wagons "in line each one facing south" and created a "Cedar brush Wickiup" in front of each wagon, providing shelter and protecting the individual campfires.[1]

Tradition locates this camp in the cove on the north side of the 200 ft. high Knoll which lies just north of present-day Cedar City.[2] For example, Alva Matheson, recalling his father Alexander's recollections of early pioneer stories, places the Wagon-Box Camp in the cove on the north of the Knoll as the best site to provide shelter from prevailing southwest winds. Matheson believes the wagon boxes were placed on a north-south line facing east, clearly a different orientation than that remembered by David Bulloch in his "Life Sketch." Both William Palmer and his sister Kate Palmer Macfarlane interviewed Bulloch just before his death on 18 January 1928 at age 83. Macfarlane agrees with Matheson that the wagons faced east. After his own interview with Bulloch, however, William Palmer drew a sketch of the Wagon-Box Camp (see illus. 7-1) which shows the wagons placed in an east-west line facing south. Since Alexander Matheson and the Macfarlane interview come to one conclusion while Bulloch's "Life Sketch" and the Palmer interview come to the other, the question of precise orientation remains in doubt.

This is not the only example of debate over primary sources among modern commentators. Sorting through these issues depends upon an understanding of the nature of the sources themselves. The Whittaker journal, kept jointly by James Whittaker Sr. and son James Jr., gives the best information on the early weeks of the Coal Creek settlement. Henry Lunt, usually a steady journal-keeper, wrote little on the colony's first days. After recording arrivals of the first groups from Parowan on 10 and 12 November 1851, he is uncharacteristically silent. A single entry appears on 2 January 1852, after which nothing is noted until 1 February. He then skips 5–15 February, makes a single entry on the 16th and ceases recording until 26 March, after which daily entries more or less resume. This is even more surprising when we realize he made no entry concerning his own wedding, on 25 March, to James Whittaker's daughter Ellen, merely noting the next day that "Myself and wife took Breakfast with our Parowan friends."[3]

Complementing Whittaker's and Lunt's records are David Bulloch's "Life Sketch" and John Chatterley's "History of Cedar City." Each man was an eyewitness of the town's infancy and growth; each left brief but vivid and informative recollections of those years. This places them near in value to Whittaker and Lunt, but not quite equal, because both memoirs were written many years later, when details may not have been remembered accurately.

A third level of historical documentation stems from accounts like those of William R. Palmer, Katherine (Kate) Palmer Macfarlane, Gladys McConnell, Rhoda Matheson Wood, Belle Armstrong and John Urie. While providing valuable information by way of compiling the written recollections of first settlers or reporting the results of interviews with them, these sources must be handled with care because they sometimes contain undocumented assumptions. Sometimes they also depend too heavily on unconfirmed local tradition and family anecdote.

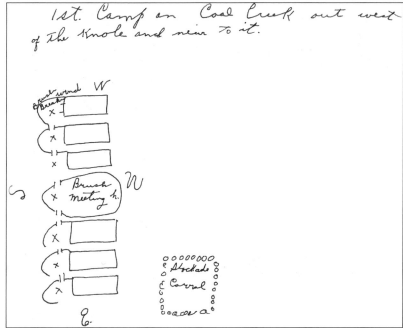

Illus. 7-1. William Palmer's sketch of the Wagon-Box Camp: the first of three drawings made by Palmer during interviews with David Bulloch, ca. 1928.

Studying two examples of source misinterpretation gives us a clearer picture of the earliest structures in Cedar City: the "Wagon-Box Camp" and the "Compact Fort." (We use these descriptive terms to distinguish one site from the other and both from later Cedar City place names.) In the *Improvement Era* of March 1951, William Palmer published an article entitled "Pioneer Fortifications." Well organized and detailed, it is based on years of research, including interviews that produced many notes and several drawings. The article contains an illustration of the Wagon-Box Camp (see illus. 7-2). Palmer writes that the wagons were placed "in a long straight line running east and west, and all fronting south," thus reaffirming the orientation of his informal sketch shown as illustration 7–1.[4] A central gathering area, midway down the line of wagon boxes, is visible in both that sketch and the *Improvement Era* drawing. In the sketch, it is labeled "Brush Meeting h.," i.e., a brush-enclosed meetinghouse; in the drawing, it is labeled "Assembly." To the drawing, however, Palmer has added an attached and gated "Livestock Stockade"—smaller, separate and ungated in the sketch—and a "Liberty Pole" on the other side of the assembly area from the stockade (not present in the sketch). Palmer describes this first encampment in the article:

On the north side and just across the sentry walk, a large stockade was built to protect the livestock. It was made by standing drift logs on end side by side in a trench, forming an arrow-tight wall. The gates were so arranged that when pulled open with a rope they bumped against posts in the wall of the meeting court. The settlers could then move from their wagon boxes to the court and on into the picket stockade and be under protection all the way.

Across the sentry walk on the south, a tall, straight liberty pole was raised. It was dedicated with solemn prayer: "To liberty, to justice, and to God." . . . Officers of the colony met in the brush court to discuss and formulate regulations and laws, but they were not of force until they were proclaimed from the liberty pole.[5]

A close reading of the primary sources reveals inconsistencies with the information published in Palmer's *Improvement Era* article. First, Palmer's description fits the larger, more permanent corral erected at the south end of the Compact Fort site—not the temporary corral that is presumed to have existed near the initial campsite. Second, Palmer adds a central assembly area not present in any of the early sketches. Third, the liberty pole, clearly noted in his text and marked on his drawing as a feature of the Wagon-Box Camp, was never located there; it was erected for the first time in the center of the Compact Fort site, which did become the place of general assembly.

Similar problems arise when using Rhoda Matheson Wood's article "In the First Fort," where she states that the wagon boxes were "set in a straight line within the surveyed 300 ft. square" and that "a wall of rock, mud, brush and cottonwood was hurriedly thrown up to provide a corral for the stock and a windbreak for the camp. Thirty-five c[a]mped there the first night."[6] As with the Palmer article, many discrepancies arise. For example, the reference to the survey area size clearly indicates Wood is confusing the initial Wagon-Box Camp with the later Compact Fort site. She gives a survey figure (300 ft. square) as though it were a known fact, when indeed the fort size is not consistent in any of the sources. Moreover, the reference to the wall being hurriedly thrown up is a collation of several journal entries, some that prove to be describing activities around the Wagon-Box Camp and some the construction of the Compact Fort. And saying that exactly 35 persons were present the first night of settlement is questionable, because the primary sources do not identify a precise number of first arrivals. Possibly she took the number 35 from John Chatterley's reminiscence in which he recorded the names of everyone he could think of who came to Cedar City on 11 November, a list that names

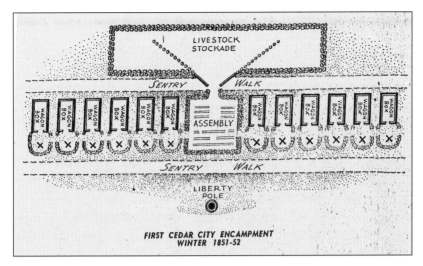

Illus. 7-2. The "Wagon-Box Camp." Illustration from William Palmer, "Pioneer Fortifications" *Improvement Era* 54 (March 1951), 149.

"33 of the 35 men" who supposedly arrived that day. Or she might have taken it from the rosters of Company C and F, which total 36 men. Her article lacks preciseness, which materially lessens its value both to the general reader and to the serious researcher on the trail of historical fact.

The primary sources themselves provide key information on the new settlement's chronology. Of first interest is distinguishing between Wagon-Box Camp and Compact Fort. We know that William Dame surveyed land at the Coal Creek site for a fort and corral on either 3 or 4 November 1851. The resulting survey map apparently no longer exists. What has survived is a composite map, dated 1853–1854 in Dame's own hand, which includes information from the 1851–1852 surveys. This composite resides in the Iron County Recorder's Office, Parowan, Utah. Its two sections are drawn on the light, blue-lined stationery common to the period. At a later date the sections were mounted on a sheet of heavier paper, using wet glue. As the glue dried, the lighter paper wrinkled. The resulting wrinkles, faded ink and blue paper have made photographic reproduction difficult. Illustration 7-3 is a further composite of Dame's survey maps, underlaid with a modern aerial photograph of the Cedar City locale.[7]

Notice that the Knoll, north of the modern city, is visible toward the upper right, with the Wagon-Box Camp labeled nearby. To the left of these lies a rectangle enclosing individual planting lots, the whole called the "Big Field." Northwest of the Big Field is an area known as "The

Cottonwoods" (not shown on illus. 7-3) which became a significant source of house logs for the settlers. Directly south of the Big Field is a square marked "Old Fort Plat." The "Compact Fort" site is shown in its northeast quadrant, as is Coal Creek, running through its southwest quadrant. Since "old fort" is used indiscriminately throughout both historical and modern records to refer to one or more locations during the first five or six years of Cedar City's existence, we have chosen to abandon that term and use "Compact Fort" to identify the second place of habitation—and first true townsite—on Coal Creek.

James Whittaker Sr., upon arriving at the settlement, first records laboring on a corral. Protecting valuable livestock was high among the settlers' priorities. The very day after his arrival, 13 November, Whittaker works on the corral; again on the 14th and 15th; breaking for Sunday, the 16th; and again on Monday through Wednesday, 17–19 November. On the 20th he reports that "a few men went for a . . . few more pickets to finish the carrell."[8] Bulloch indicates that the men hauled dry logs from "large groves of trees (cotton wood) about three miles from our camp," a statement verified by Chatterley.[9] These references could be taken to refer to wood for the temporary corral that must have existed in some form at the Wagon-Box Camp. However, additional quotes from John Chatterley and David Bulloch show that the corral being discussed is actually the larger structure built along the south line of the surveyed Compact Fort site.

John Chatterley's "History of Cedar City" records that, immediately after arrival, "the site of the Fort was looked over, which had been surveyed. . . . As future history will show[,] the first structure built was a public corral built at the south end of the Fort, the only opening was at the North and opening into the fort."[10] In his "Life Sketch," Bulloch mentions this south side corral as well as memories of the first house built at the townsite: "A fort had been planned and this meeting house was located on the east line of the fort. The cattle corral was on the south side and the public gate was on the north line." According to Bulloch, the stockade corral was "built of driftwood as there was plenty of it on the creek banks."[11] This comment about driftwood construction underscores the corral's southern location, because it indicates the enclosure was not far from the banks of Coal Creek, flowing across the southwest corner of the Old Fort plat.

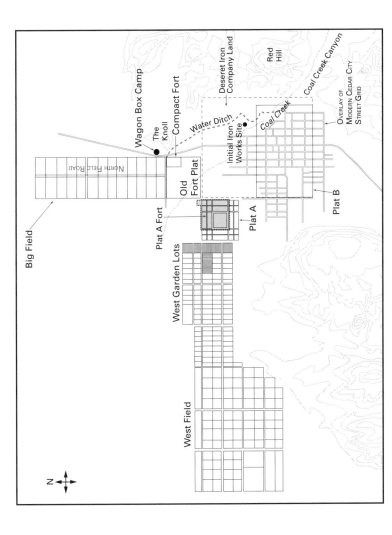

Illus. 7-3. Composite of Dame's 1851 to 1854 Cedar City surveys with additional topographic and layout details.

House-Building in the Compact Fort

Understanding the corral position helps clarify journal references to the house-building that was soon to take place. It also helps chronicle, by showing first moves onto the Compact Fort site, the steady abandonment of the Wagon-Box Camp for more permanent dwellings. On 24 November, as James Whittaker Sr. reports, "The People moved their waggons on the South Side Carrell."[12] From this point on, the Wagon-Box Camp slowly disappears, as each wagon is moved from there to the corral and from the corral, eventually, to its owner's new house lot, somewhere along the perimeter of the yet-to-be-enclosed fort. But the first day was spent, Whittaker recalls, with men and wagons jostled up close to the wall of the corral, "making it comfortable round the waggons with cedars to keep the wind from blowing on them while sitting round their little fires."[13]

On 26 November, Henry Lunt informed the men they could begin cutting logs for their own houses the next day. A week earlier, the settlers had expressed their discontent with the presiding elder, Matthew Carruthers, for hiring Lorenzo Barton to cut logs for a house for Carruthers while everyone else was required to work on the public corral. Their irritation eventually waned. Whittaker records cutting the logs for his own house between 27 November and 8 December, while from 9 to 16 December he and a neighbor, William Slack, took turns helping each other build their new homes.[14] Christmas was marked only by the terse entry "Worked at the house—very cold day snow & sleet," suggesting both how busy and how tired Whittaker was. The following Saturday's entry noted a small yet important milestone: "Worked at house. Removed waggon to the house." Occurring 45 days after Whittaker arrived in Cedar City, this move severed his last ties to the Wagon-Box Camp and documented his shift to the Compact Fort.[15]

Although no portions of the Compact Fort survive, contemporary descriptions exist. Chatterley recalls that "The houses were built along the outer wall of the Fort, and the spaces between the houses were built up with logs, chunked and daubed with mud, so it formed a solid wall about 8 feet high."[16] Picket wood, much lighter than the solid building logs, would generally be placed between houses, closing any gaps in the fort wall. An article in the *Millennial Star* of 6 January 1855, reviewing iron manufacturing in Utah, describes this construction as "put up in the form of a fort, with the intervals between the houses picketed, to serve the purposes of defence."[17]

While house logs were cut to roughly standard sizes large enough for cabin walls (see related sidebar and illustrations), almost any type and size of lumber could be used as a picket—driftwood (as Bulloch wrote), saplings, deadwood and so forth. These could be driven into the ground between houses, filled in with brush and finally daubed with mud. Insight into the process comes from a notation on William Palmer's second sketch, entitled "1st Fort at Cedar City," made during his interview with David Bulloch (see illus. 7-8). The note reads: "Dobie Walls between the houses," suggesting that the pickets set up as defensive barriers between the houses were coated with mud which, when dry, had the appearance of adobe. Chatterley's reference to "chunked and daubed" logs furthers the idea that mud was used as an insulator to protect settlers from the cold wind as well as from any stray arrows. Palmer's second sketch confirms Chatterley's and Bulloch's descriptions, noted earlier, of the fort configuration: the corral abutted the Compact Fort on the south, with a gate cut into their shared wall. Illustration 7-8 clearly shows houses built next to (or into) the outer walls of the Compact Fort.[18]

Features of the Compact Fort: Bastion and Meetinghouse

As a protective measure, the pioneers erected bastions (guardhouses) "on each side of the fort."[19] No information survives to suggest how these bastions were incorporated into the fort design. While they could have been set midway on the east and west walls, they were probably—if the settlers followed the Parowan model—built on the corners, perhaps one on the northeast corner of the fort and the other on the southwest corner of the corral. With the bastions in place, as Chatterley explains, the continuous guard duty begun at the time of the Wagon-Box Camp became more formal.

> In three weeks after settling the Fort there was a large Company of Scotch and some others, near 50 people joined the emigrants, so that guarding was a little easier, as every man had to take his turn, the writer was only 16 years of age, and he with other boys had to take their turn at guarding the same as the men. The men and boys were organized as a part of the Nauvoo Legion, and 15 of us had to go to the bastion, which was built after the public corrall was built. The nights were divided into 3 watches, 5 men on at a time with a captain of the guard, if the guards caught anyone outside the Fort, they were taken to the guard house (bastion) and kept there, some till morning, some only, until the captain of the guard would let them go.[20]

PIONEER HOUSE-BUILDING

Houses in the early days of settlement were typically small, one-bedroom log cabins with, in many cases, dirt floors. The only log house to survive from this part of Cedar City's history is the George Wood and Mary Davies Wood home, now in Iron Mission State Park, located at 585 North Main, Cedar City (see illus. 7-4). Wood reportedly built the cabin in 1851 in Parowan, then moved it to Coal Creek, where he

Photograph by Morris A. Shirts

Illus. 7-4. George and Mary Davies Wood cabin as it now appears on the grounds of the Iron Mission State Park, Cedar City, Utah.

placed it in the Compact Fort; he and his wife raised a family of nineteen in it. The house measures 14 by 16 feet and is seven feet high to the square, with a pitched roof. The apex of the gable is about six feet above the square of the house. It has a door in the middle of each side and a window next to one door. One end has a fireplace with a chimney and the other end is plain.

The logs are either spruce or fir (not cottonwood) and have been squared. The corners were dovetailed and the logs fitted closely together, requiring little chinking to make them weather-tight (see illus. 7-5). These details made the structure much sturdier than did the usual notch-and-overlap technique of the time.

The Wood cabin contains a number of round holes, drilled at random entirely through the logs, that have been the subject of considerable conjecture (see illus. 7-6). The largest is one and a half to two inches in diameter. One is located on the west end (the blank wall without a door or chimney). The east end contains 15 such holes, most of them arranged vertically in a double row near one side of the fireplace chimney. The south side of the house contains 10 holes, one low enough that it could have been a rat hole. These holes seem inappropriately spaced and too small to have served as apertures for firing a gun. One hole on the north side of the cabin, 5 by 7 inches and arched at the top, could have accommodated a stove pipe. Bits of broken pegs remain in several holes, suggesting that perhaps oak pegs were driven through to provide hangers both inside and outside the walls. Another possibility, especially in light of the holes placed near the chimney, is that they were used for ventilation.

Wood relocated the house each time Cedar City shifted its boundaries. Eventually, on 11 May 1927, the family donated it to the Daughters of Utah Pioneers, who moved it from

Photograph by Morris A. Shirts

Illus. 7-5. Closeup of the dovetail construction of the corners of the George and Mary Davies Wood cabin.

the Wood property on Main Street and Fourth North to Cedar City Park, furnished it authentically and maintained it until 29 April 1983. At that time, the DUP was forced to abandon the cabin due to vandalism and lack of finances. Its last move was from Cedar City Park to the grounds of Iron Mission State Park, where it is now maintained.

Like the Wood cabin, the John Pidding Jones cabin was originally constructed in the Compact Fort. Jones arrived in April 1853 and he also dismantled and moved his home several times. At one time, the cabin stood near the intersection of First West and Center Street in Cedar City. In 1875 it was moved for the last time to Enoch, adjacent to Cedar City on the north, where it was a family residence until 1935 or 1940, when it was destroyed. A surviving photograph (see illus. 7–7) was taken shortly before this. The bottom logs may have been cottonwood and the top logs pine. Both the Jones and Wood cabins had pitched roofs, possibly added after initial construction.

Photograph by Morris A. Shirts

Illus. 7-6. Closeup of randomly sized holes drilled through walls of George and Mary Davies Wood cabin.

Source: Iron Mission State Park; Bonnie Ellis Pryor to Morris Shirts, interview of 15 Apr 1975, notes in Shirts Collection.

Photograph taken by Eldon A. Jones, Grandson of John Pidding Jones, and provided by Bonnie Ellis Pryor

Illus. 7-7. Hyrum Jones, standing in front of the log cabin built by his father, John Pidding Jones, in 1853 at the Compact Fort, near the Knoll north of modern-day Cedar City.

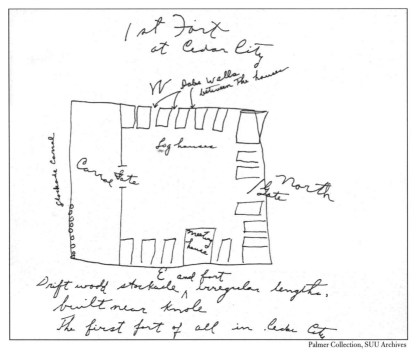

In the sketch (handwritten labels): "1st Fort at Cedar City", "Dobe walls between the houses", "Log houses", "Came gate", "Stockade Carrell", "North Gate", "meeting house", "Drift wood stockade, irregular lengths, E and fort built near knole. The first fort of all in Cedar City"

Illus. 7-8. William Palmer's sketch of the first fort at Cedar City: the second of three drawings made by Palmer during interviews with David Bulloch, ca. 1928.

Among the most historically interesting buildings constructed in the Compact Fort was that known variously as "Bro. Ross' house," the "meeting house" and the "school house." This large cabin had originally been a double-size log structure belonging to, and probably built by, the Ross brothers, Alexander, Daniel and Duncan. As noted earlier, David Bulloch recalled this cabin as the first house built in the surveyed Compact Fort site, set on its east line. William Palmer's second sketch, made following his interview with David Bulloch, also puts the meetinghouse on the east side of the fort (see illus. 7-8). Whether it was the first structure built after the "South Side Carrell" is debatable, but that is unimportant to its later history. John Chatterley sets up the story in a useful, if not totally accurate, comment in his "History of Cedar City":

> In Spring of 1852 the Ross Bros, Alexander, Daniel and Duncan after putting in their crops, concluded to leave as Aleck and Duncan did not like farming, so they sold their whole possesions to Joseph Chatterley, house with two large rooms and 84 acres of land. Bro. Chatterley had the petition cut out of the hous and fitted it up for schools and religious services of cour[s]e he was assisted by the

brethren to make seats, and desks for the day school. Elder Matthew Carruthers was the Presiding Elder, he also taught the day school until he was called to superintend the construction of the Iron Works, which were started that summer (1852) when called away John Chatterley was placed in the school as teacher.[21]

As noted in chapter 6, Duncan Ross could not have left at this time because he was, unfortunately, one of the three men identified by Whittaker in his 3 March journal entry as having been killed by Indians. Duncan and his friends, James Baird and John Lowe, had made the acquaintance of the "Co of Spaniards" passing through the area on their way to California; on 14 February the three left Cedar City and joined this party on its trek south. No comment is made concerning the fate of the Spaniards and no specifics are offered as to when or how the group was attacked. Nevertheless, Whittaker's 3 March reference tell us that Amon, one of the more friendly and communicative of the local Indians, reported the deaths of the three men to the settlers.

This must have left Alexander, Daniel and their unnamed sister badly shaken. On Monday, 28 June 1852, the remaining Ross siblings gave up their southern Utah property, left "contrary to council" and joined Wiley's party for Salt Lake City. Joseph Chatterley would have bought the home at this time. This transaction is strongly implied by both Lunt and Whittaker because, after this date, the building is never referred to again as "Bro. Ross' house," but only as "the meeting house" or "the school house."[22]

The Size of the Compact Fort

There are various reports on the size of the fort. Charles Willden said, when he arrived in Cedar City on 29 October 1852, almost a year into settlement life, that "the settlers were building their log houses in the form of a 100 yard square fort with a stockade, and assembly court and a Liberty pole in the center."[23] Since Dame surveyed the Old Fort plat at 160 rods (880 yards) wide, the fort that Willden remembered occupied only about an eighth of the total area surveyed for that site. John Lee Jones, son of iron worker John Pidding Jones, gives an even smaller size for the Compact Fort:

In the Spring of 1853, March 15th, we proceeded On our Journey to *"Iron Co"*, w[h]ere we arrived April 2nd, this Place was then Called *"Coal Creek"*, here we found a Small Fort about 20 Rods Long by 10 Rods Wide. on each Side of this Fort Log House[s] were Built & on one End Pickets were Placed in the Ground on there Ends. & a Large Gate Swung in the Center, This Was an entrance & Ingress. on the Opposite End there was a Large Corral. in w[h]ich all the Stock was placed every Night. to preserve them from the Attacks of the Lamanit[e]s.[24]

This rectangular size translates as 55 by 110 yards, just slightly larger than the playing area of a football field, which is about half as wide as Willden's recollection. George Bowering provides the only first-hand account. His journal entry on 2 May 1853 records arriving at a "small Fort of some 12 or 20 houses forted in with two big doors at the north end."[25] Perhaps the simplest way of reconciling these various references is to suggest that the basic Compact Fort survey shape was a square but that the addition of the "South-Side Carrell" changed it into a rectangle, as shown on William Palmer's second sketch (illus. 7-8).

"Ditched 'till Noon": Providing Water for the Community

After the initial survey, early in November 1851, and the building of the protective corral at the south end of the Compact Fort, the settlers had to build a ditch to divert the water of Coal Creek for irrigation. No settlement could survive without an ample supply of accessible water. Dame undoubtedly surveyed a route for water ditches between Coal Creek and the fort site, although Whittaker, on 19 November, gives Lunt and Chatterley credit for it.[26] The fact that on 20 November, within 10 days of their arrival, the settlers began work on the ditch also suggests that Dame had included it in his initial planning. Evidently it began some distance upstream, in this case south and east of the settlement (up Coal Creek Canyon).[27] As David Bulloch remembers, "After making our camp a ditch was taken out of Coal Creek. This first ditch was taken out just a little below where our present dam is. This ditch carried the water to within a few rods of the camp along the line of wagons."[28] This means the Big Field was watered by a ditch that ran from the mouth of the canyon northward along the foothills and then continued around to the foot of the Knoll (see illus. 7-3).

The dam Bulloch mentions was probably one near the mill site built later in the mouth of Coal Creek Canyon. This would place the dam between the southern tip of Red Hill[29] and the ridge of gray shale to the west of it. The ditch may have entered the settlement area just west of the Knoll, somewhere near the current KOA campground (1121 North Main Street). Possibly the stream may have been divided by the pioneers, with one branch eventually providing water for fields west of the

Compact Fort and the other routing along the east side of the fort to the garden area and Big Field. The total distance of this route, which seems very feasible, may have been over a mile and a half. Taking water out further downstream would have required the settlers to contour the ditch over or around the east side of the slight rise where the present cemetery is located. However, water could have been taken out below or near the cemetery and routed to fields west of the fort site, as is done today.

The settlers began a second ditch early in 1852. Henry Lunt recorded on 4 February 1852 that "Myself br's Wiley and Bosnell looked out a place for takeing out the water out of Coal Creek to irregate the field."[30] Both ditches were in use that first planting season. On 19 April, Lunt mentions "ditches" in his diary; on 21 May the "lower" dam washed out; and the next day the "upper" ditch broke as well. Lunt used his characteristic good humor to handle the frustration, noting merely that because the spate of water "came across my lot . . . I spent some of the afternoon in watering my wheat." Lunt inspected the ditches on 11 June and found them in very bad condition. But by 27 June he thought the men were making progress on repairs. On that date he writes a letter to the *Deseret News* describing the problem:

> The water ditch that supplies the upper part of our field has been very troublesome, owing to it washing in some places so tremendously, and again filling other places up with sand that it washed over; a great amount of labor has been spent over it, and it is now doing much better.[31]

But a heavy storm blasted the area on 16 July, striking east of the Compact Fort. Lunt himself was up in the "Kanyon" when it hit there with "tremendeous Thunder and lightning and heavy rain. . . . Rained down in the valley tremondeous for about two hours, commenced about 11 oclock. The water was 12 inches deep in some of the houses and cellars in the Fort."[32] This storm surely struck the sandy area of the upper water ditch. As Lunt notes, in mounting frustration, both dams washed out on 20 July, 29 July and 7 August.[33]

Two ditches were needed to adequately irrigate all the lots in the Big Field and still supply domestic water to the growing number of homes in the Compact Fort. On 30 July, with both dams out, "the Bishop called the brethren together in the morning for the purpose of fixing the dams in the Creek again, but because the Iron men did not go to help them they would not go, and we have now to pack our water from the Big Creek. Thunder and rain in the evening."[34] Lunt is still noting ditch repair and expansion problems in February 1853, while George Bowering records serious flood damage to the iron works, bridges and dams the following September.[35] Obviously, maintaining a safe and adequate water system demanded more than its share of time and energy during Cedar City's first uncertain years.

Surveying the Big Field

The destination for much of the water diverted into the two new ditches was the Big Field, the first major planting site of the Coal Creek settlement. As in Parowan, settlers planned to live inside the community or fort and have their farms on the perimeter. The Big Field, however, was presumably not surveyed until after the settlers arrived. We can infer this because neither George A. Smith nor Henry Lunt mentions it as a part of the initial survey.[36] Whittaker records helping Dame "to survey the field" on 23 and 24 December.[37] Most likely, this is the formal survey of the Big Field, covering approximately 500 acres, laid out in 10- and 20-acre plots north of the Compact Fort and corral.

Other surveys may have been taken after 4 November and before 23 December. Deed Book A in the Iron County Recorder's Office shows that on 19 December, four days prior to anyone else filing for a lot, Henry Lunt and Robert Wiley claimed property located in Ranges 3 and 5 (for which no map is available), paid their filing fees and presumably received a description of the property. William C. Mitchell, Thomas Cartwright and Richard Harrison paid their fees on 23 December.[38] They could not have done this unless the lots had already been surveyed. Illustration 7-9 shows those who recorded their property in the Big Field between 19 December 1851 and 14 September 1852. For some reason, the great majority of lots in the Big Field were not recorded until the latter date, almost nine months after the first five were filed. No reason is known for this large gap in time.

The Big Field was half a mile in width (Dame's survey figure is 160 rods) and 1.6 miles long. Although the leaders advised the settlers to take no more than 10 acres, the Big Field contained 26 lots of 20 acres (40 by 80 rods each; some were divided). In most of Dame's other surveys, the 10-acre lots are square: 40 by 40 rods. A scan of the Big Field area today reveals lots that are also mostly 10 acres each, 40 by 40 rods square.

According to Chatterley, the Big Field was laid out in blocks and the lots drawn. Some settlers received 10 acres and a few 20. Each man also got a one-acre lot on the south end of the Big Field to raise "garden truck for summer use" and vegetables for winter. As Whittaker notes on 17 March 1852, "Fine day, worked in the garden. Planted turnips, beets, onions, sowed some radishes, lettuce, onions."[39] (Onions must have been a valued seasoning, providing a little flavor to the often-bland pioneer fare.) There were also smaller plots, "close to the Fort," laid off for "flowers, melons, and etc."[40]

A lane, running north and south, with 20-acre lots on either side, divided the Big Field. Lanes also ran laterally between each set of lots. The remains of some of these lanes are still visible today. Many residents assume that North Field Road, running north and south, *is* the center lane dividing Dame's Big Field survey, but this is not the case. According to measurements made by the authors, the east side of present North Field Road is 111 feet east of Dame's center lane (see illus. 7-3).[41]

Why the inconsistency in measurement? Cedar City property owner Alex Rollo suggested that the present North Field Road was once the bottom of a flood channel which carried overflow waters northward to avoid inundating the fields. This, he felt, became the physical dividing line, rather than Dame's surveyed center line. Another possibility is that, after a new township survey occurred in the early 1870s, property lines were shifted to more closely match subdivision section lines. The abandonment of the

Illus. 7-9. Big Field and Compact Fort layout, with lot owners, from William H. Dame's 1853–54 survey.

George & William Hunter — 6		13
James Bosnell — 5	A. Easton	14
William C. Mitchell — 4		15
James Easton		
A. Keir — 3		16
Bladen & White — 2		1

David Stoddard — 9		10
— 8		11
— 7	J. Easton / R. Easton	12
John Chatterley — 6		13
R. Harrison / T. Cartwright — 5	Henry Lunt	14
Joseph Walker — 4	Henry Lunt	15
Joseph Walker / J. Clews — 3	Williamson / T. Bladen	16
Probably Gardens — 2	Probably Gardens	1

Compact Fort

Old Fort Plat

Compact Fort (including the roads or lands surrounding it) and its subsequent absorption into current fields no doubt contributed to the problem. Taking into consideration these minor adjustments, illustration 7-3 shows the location of the Big Field in relation to other pioneer settlement features shown on Dame's survey.

Curiously, entries in the deed books mentioning the Big Field show that some farm lots were in Ranges 2E and 5NW, but these do not appear on Dame's survey. They would have been out near The Cottonwoods, some three to four miles west of Cedar City. Since alfalfa had not yet been introduced to Utah, this land would have been valuable as a rare source of storable feed for the cattle. It probably became communal property as, evidently, everyone harvested hay from it. There are several references to hay meadows, including a particularly vivid pair of entries made by Lunt regarding Alexander "Sandy" Keir and James Bosnell:

> <u>Monday Oct. 18. 1852</u> Fine day. Mowed hay in the meadow Windy day. A fire broke out on the meadow from a little fire that was made on Saturday by Br. Keir lighting his pipe; it burned the Grass very furiously, the wind was very high, and it increased so rapidly that it appeared as though it would soon burn the whole of the Hay in the meadow, there was a large stack belonging to Br. Bosnell and also several other small stacks of hay in the meadow The fire was progressing rappidly towards Br Bosnell's stack. I fell on my knees and asked my Heave[n]ly Father to cause that the fire might stay its rageing and distruction, immediately on my rising up the fire seemed to stay its rageing and by my exertions for about two hours I succeeded in putting the whole of it out.
>
> <u>Tuesday October 19 1852</u> Fine day. Strong South wind. Mowed 2 loads of hay. Br Bosnell came to me in the morning, and said he was very much obliged to me for saving his stack of hay and said he would not promise if he should reward me any for my trouble. This afternoon the fire broke out again and Burnt Bosnell's stack of hay down to the ground and also a considerable quantity of grass.[42]

While the humorous aspects of this account will be apparent to the modern reader, it is all too easy to forget today how threatening the loss of a hay crop could be to a pioneer community. One can hope James Bosnell learned a lesson in humility and gratitude, but it would have been a costly one indeed if the price had been the destruction of the whole meadow and the burning of a precious food source on which the settlement's livestock depended. Without their animals, the pioneers would have been unable to travel, except on foot, and plowing and planting would have been nearly impossible. Lunt would have seen the rescue of the crop neither as a nuisance nor as an opportunity for personal heroics, but rather as an absolute necessity.

Many of the arguments used to locate the Big Field are also relevant in locating the site of the Compact Fort. Most people accept Dame's survey evidence, which shows the fort site slightly southwest of the Knoll. The most likely placement of the Compact Fort itself was in the northeast corner of the Old Fort plat. Palmer created a third sketch during his interview with David Bulloch that indicates this: basically, a mere outline of the fort site with a smaller segment drawn in at the northeast (upper right) corner (see illus. 7-10).

There is some evidence that one of the first houses built against the inside of the first fort wall was still in use 50 years later. It was owned by Andrew Jensen (not the historian Andrew Jenson) and stood near the present willow-lined North Field ditch, directly west of the point of the Knoll.[43] Some of the older generation still in Cedar City claim to have seen the "old Andrew Jensen home" standing just west of the irrigation

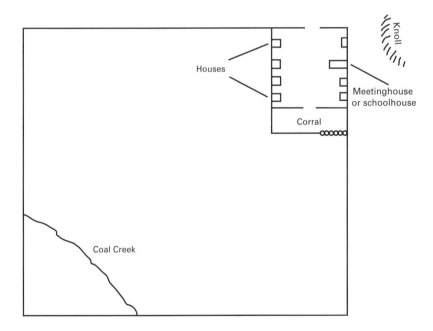

Illus. 7-10. Diagram based on William Palmer's sketch of the Coal Creek survey site: the third of three drawings made by Palmer during interviews with David Bulloch, ca. 1928.

canal behind the Southern Utah Animal Hospital and believe it was positioned just inside the old fort.

Charles R. Hunter related that as a boy he rode by this site many times, passing from the family farm northwest of Cedar City on his way to school and back. He remembered seeing old fruit trees and pieces of broken glass and other artifacts near the west bank of the irrigation ditch. He firmly believed the east line of the Compact Fort paralleled the west side of the canal.[44] Hunter is not alone in having turned up artifacts. A small piece of history—an unbroken salt shaker—was unearthed by Galen Allred in the early 1970s while excavating a sewer ditch with a backhoe for the Southern Utah Animal Hospital (see illus. 7-11). According to members of the Southern Utah University Art Department, its material, design, artwork and firing techniques are characteristic of pieces made in England in the middle 1800s.

Fencing the Big Field

As in Parowan, the Big Field for the Compact Fort settlers had to be fenced to protect it from roaming horses and cattle and from passing wagon train livestock. In the spring, new grain lured cattle to the field, so increased watchfulness was required. James Whittaker notes a community decision in his journal entry of 20 March 1852: "Attended a quorum meeting in the evening at Bro. Ross House Agreed to herd the Cattle in turns."[45] Rotating these duties among all the men, however, soon became too awkward to manage. Taking a new approach, Lunt convened another general discussion on 5 April to appoint one man to do the herding: "Called a meeting of the Brethren in the Centre of the fort in the Evening about herding the Cattle. Bro. Williams agreed to herd, and be paid in wheat at Tithing prices." Two days later, Lunt penned a hopeful note, "Williams commenced herding the Cattle." But the very next day, 8 April, the problem was back in his hands: "Williams gave up the herd last evening, he did not inform me of it. This morning I was fetched out of the field to see to sending some one wi[th] the herd."[46]

Entries reporting varied success and failure at managing the livestock continue into the summer and beyond. At the very least, such records make it clear that reconciling the ongoing conflict between raising vital crops and protecting them from livestock whose natural instinct was to eat them occupied a central role in pioneer life.[47]

Fencing the Big Field caused nearly as much trouble for the settlers as herding the cattle. However, there was a crucial difference: the Big

Field posed a finite problem that could, with enough commitment and determination, be solved. Lunt's diary entries refer to both "water ditches" and "ditches." The first, of course, carried water. The second usually refers to a method of fencing that was employed both between pioneer homes and around the Big Field.

Pioneer fence-building involved digging a ditch two or three feet deep with steep-sloping sides, approximating a V-shape. Cedar posts were set at needed intervals into the ditch bottom, connected by a single long pole or rail. Brush and various-sized tree limbs lined the bottom of the ditch between the posts and the pole, to discourage small animals like sheep or calves from breaking through. The rail height and deep, sloped ditch made it difficult for larger animals to cross over, even if they did attempt to push through the fence. The total length required to enclose the Big Field would have been nearly 22,400 feet or over four miles. Without modern materials or fence-making tools, having to rely solely on muscle power, the settlers came to see this task as one of their most back-breaking and unwelcome duties.

The Big Field was still fenced in 1870 when surveyor Joseph Gorlinski mapped the area. At that time, the field included more than the 500 acres described in contemporary journals. Perhaps some acreage was added after Dame's initial survey to accommodate a growing population. Gorlinski's survey shows the southeast corner of the Big Field west and slightly north of the Knoll, about where pioneer accounts had placed it.[48]

Photograph by Morris A. Shirts

Illus. 7-11. Pioneer salt shaker found by Galen Allred in the early 1970s near Compact Fort site.

Domestic Life in the Settlements

Social aspects of southern Utah pioneer life appear in snippets of information culled from journal entries, which usually record the more immediate demands of creating a safe and productive colony. Henry Lunt is particularly negligent in recording the little household descriptions and family anecdotes that bring settlement history to life, but this is entirely understandable given the drain on his time and energy as leader of a people who literally depended on him for their lives. His father-in-law, James Whittaker, provides domestic details a little more frequently, but often in the sparsest of prose. For example, he tells us on 10 March 1852 that he ditched until noon and then "commenced to make a table." On Friday, 12 March, he records what appears to be a companion entry: "Made some forms for seats." These are the first known comments on furniture making in Cedar City and we can wish that Whittaker had been able to look ahead and see how much his future readers would relish more information. Which wood did he choose for his table and chairs, for instance? Certainly not the softer cedar or cottonwood. The harder lumber choices (in larger widths) were piñon pine or spruce or fir from the mountains. Did he use wood-working tools or merely large or small axes? If he did own tools, did he bring them all the way from Scotland and across the plains to Utah?[49]

Lunt's first entry about domestic work occurs on 14 April 1852. Noting that he has already plowed seven acres for James Whittaker, he ends the day's report by saying, "I worked on the Chicken Coop." One's curiosity is immediately aroused. How large was this structure? Was it a true hen house or a smaller roost with latched lid or door? Since wire screening was not yet an option, Lunt's version may have been made solid on two or three sides with a slatted top or front, too small for the chickens to escape from but airy enough to provide sufficient light and ventilation. Or perhaps it was always intended that the settlement fowl would run free and the coop was only built to provide a night roost for safety against predatory animals.

Ten days later, Whittaker reports working with Lunt: "In the afternoon myself with James helped Bro Lunt to ditch having promised to help him do all his fencing & ditching for a Churn he got made for me & a door & frame."[50] The shape and size of the churn would have been interesting to know—these were often made with iron or copper hoops around the staves, similar to large packing barrels. It seems unusual that the Cedar City pioneers would have wanted to use any of the precious iron pieces already being scavenged off wagon wheels merely to make hoops for a churn. No clues are offered about the door, but almost eight months later, on 10 December, Lunt makes a comment that catches the eye: "Bro Pugmire made me some fastenings for my door and gave them unto me. I feel truly grateful to the brethren for their kindness."[51] Since we know that Jonathan Pugmire was a blacksmith, it might have been, in this case, that scrap iron was used to make the door fastenings. Another possibility is that Pugmire cut two or three fastenings out of trimmed rawhide or leather (ox, cow or deer) and used iron nails to peg each side of each flexible hinge to the proper place on door and frame.

Supplementing Lunt's and Whittaker's records, David Bulloch and John Chatterley also comment on the implements of everyday living in a pioneer age. In his "Life Sketch," Bulloch made note of the kind of weapons used by the settlers, comparing them to Native American weapons:

> The only guns we had were the old youger (powder) type. It took sometime to load these as we had no cartriges. We carried our powder in a horn which we hung from our sides. The horns were either cow or ox horns, well cleaned out inside. In the large end was placed a large cork and a very small hole was made in the small end. We filled the horn through the large hole and measured it out carefully through the small hole as powder was scarce and valuable. The powder was measured in a little measuring flask which held just the right amount. It was poured into a shell after which a wad or rag or paper was pressed to prevent the powder from losing out. Then a ball of lead was added.
>
> We were not so quick with our weapons as the red men but we were able to shoot a much longer distance than they were. I remember seeing a two year old heifer come into camp once with an arrow shot through it near the kidneys. The arrow was removed but the animal died as a result of it's [*sic*] wound. These and other kinds of minor troubles were frequent but we were blessed in not having any very serious trouble with the Indians.[52]

Chatterley's reminiscences contain at least one sentence that sounds like a direct memory from his childhood, a sentiment that every modern child would understand: "It was quite a bit of a trial to have to be deprived of sufficient sweets that was needed to fully enjoy life." The women of the colony, he reports, "boiled beets, carrots or any other produce that would boil down to a syrup," pale substitutes for sugar, but welcome as any variation would be to people who made do with the little at hand.

If sweeteners were hard to come by, materials for making soap, at least, were easy to find. Logs from the Cottonwoods, Chatterley reports, were burned to ashes and carried to the settlement, where they were "leeched in a U shaped vat and the liquid from the ashes boiled down with grease and made into soap, which answered very well, but made much labor to obtain it."

Chatterley recounted a vivid anecdote regarding one of the Ross boys, who left the settlement "contrary to counsel," not long after the death of his brother Duncan. According to Chatterley, "Daniel Ross, who left in Spring of 1852, but came back with a wife, went barefoot up Shurtz's [Shirts] canyon for logs to build a house and when he came home during the evening he would lie on his face while his wife picked the slivers out of his feet." The story ends with a nicely understated comment that "It certainly required courage and patience to build up a settlement."[53]

Not every hour of a pioneer's day, however, was burdened by the drudgeries of unending toil. According to pioneer tradition, the settlers rested from their work on one occasion when Parowan challenged Cedar City to a man-to-man ditch-digging contest. Since the ditch would be located in Parowan, this was a clever move to insure that the results would benefit the Parowan community no matter who dug the most yards. Parowan's representative was David Ward. Cedar City sent Joseph Walker, an accomplished boxer who stood 6 feet 2 inches and weighed about 220 lbs.

Walker was originally employed in the iron works at Low Moor near Bradford in Yorkshire, England. An energetic and responsible worker, he was sent by his company to Scotland to learn how to operate a power-drive trip hammer. When his arm was crushed in an accident at work, his wife, Betty, who had heard the LDS elders had the power to heal, asked if they would come and bless her husband. Joseph's arm was restored and Betty was baptized, urging her husband to take their large family to Zion along with other families from the Low Moor iron works. Although not ready to commit to the new religion, Joseph willingly moved with family and friends to a new home in America. Settling on a farm in the Mill Creek area of Salt Lake Valley, Joseph aligned himself with the Latter-day Saints soon after immigrating. In December 1850 he was called to join the iron missionaries.

According to tradition, the Parowan–Cedar City ditch-digging contest started early one morning with the crack of a pistol and continued until the noon meal. After eating, the contest resumed. Within a couple of hours, Walker had taken a substantial lead. By 4:00 P.M., David Ward threw down his shovel and acknowledged defeat. Then, as Palmer puts it, "Parowan cheerfully gave the supper and dance and in good sportsmanship credited Walker with digging enough ditch that they had to pay for it."[54]

On the whole, the iron missionaries faced life in the harsh southern Utah terrain by sharing the goal of creating a Zion community. These spiritual expectations allowed them to keep things in perspective— including the things they lacked—and provided an excellent rationale for playing as hard as they worked. Whittaker's description of the wedding of his daughter Ellen (see illus. 7-12) to Henry Lunt on 25 March 1852 beautifully illustrates the colonists' willingness to celebrate fully whatever deserved to be celebrated at all:

Illus. 7-12. Ellen Whittaker Lunt (1830–1903), first wife of Henry Lunt, was a milliner, telegraph operator and, later, Parowan Stake Relief Society president.

> Thursday March 25th 1852. Morning rather dull. hailstones after dinner, and a beautiful evening My daughter Ellen was married to Bro. Henry Lunt, myself James and Mary with several others attended the Wedding at twenty minutes to seven we left Cedar City for Parowan, in two carriages one drawn by Four horses, the other by two. as we started a Salute was fired with guns. which echoed through the Mountains and the City had the appearince of a joyfull morn, by the inhabitants being collected together to see us set off. and giving us three Cheers as we Started. . . . We arrived at Parowan at twenty minutes past nine o.clock distance twenty miles We were met at the carriages by Pres John L Smith and invited us into his house.
>
> They were married at ¼ to twelve by Bishop Lewis. Before the Ceremony we sung the 40th hymn and after it "Redeemer of Israel." after Marriage they were blessed by the Brethren with the richest of Heavens blessings. I breakfasted with Bro John D. Lee's, And left Parowan accompanied by another Carriage containing Pres. John L Smith, Bishop Lewis, John D Lee, and 4 Ladies. Arrived at Cedar City at 4 o clock when our ears were deafened with the cheering of the Saints and firing of guns when we arrived at the Assembly rooms there was a sumptuois feast prepared for about 150 persons.
>
> After dinner a number of the Brethren were amusing themselves in the centre of the Fort by running races jumping &c. Shortly after Dancing commenced and was continued until four o clock in the morning, a great variety of Songs were sung, and several Comic pieces performed. Joy and gladness seemed to be in every countenance. I never saw a party that enjoyed themselves like unto this, such order and a oneness of Spirit prevailed throughout the whole evenings entertainment. The horses in the carriages had rosetes in their bridles and white ribbons attached thereto Some 12 inches long, which added to the appearance of the fine prancing Animals.[55]

The iron missionaries had moved from the Wagon-Box Camp to a more substantial fort and improved that structure with bastions and a meetinghouse. They had laid the agricultural foundation for a second community and added domestic refinements to life on the frontier. With such an auspicious beginning, the colonists must have imagined sturdy homes, rich harvests and a flourishing iron industry merely a few months away.

Endnotes

1. Bulloch, "Life Sketch," 5–6.

2. In Nov 1981 a monument was erected at the cove to commemorate the Wagon-Box Camp.

3. Lunt, diary, 26 Mar 1852. It is important to remember that George A. Smith had left southern Utah for new duties up north and that John D. Lee had stopped keeping his journal and delegated those duties to James Lewis in Parowan. Those two essential sources of information on the southern Utah settlement process were thus no longer available, at least as far as Cedar City was concerned.

4. William R. Palmer, "Pioneer Fortifications," *Improvement Era* 54 (Mar 1951): 148–50, 183–87.

5. Ibid.

6. Rhoda Matheson Wood, "In the First Fort," 1, undated typescript of ch. 2, unpublished history of Cedar City, MS in Cedar City Public Library (cited from copy in Shirts Collection).

7. William Dame, "Coal Creek Survey Iron Co. U. T. [Utah Territory], 1853-4," Old Survey Book, Iron County Recorder's Office, Parowan, Utah. Above the date in the title the numbers "1–2" have been added, in what appears to be an early hand (prior to the turn of the twentieth century). From this, it would appear that the map includes data from 1851–52 as well as from 1853–54. The upper left corner inscription reads: "Cedar City Surveyed 1852-3[.] Lots 4 rods by 20—½ acre each. 1st Streets East and West[,] North & South 6 rods wide[.] 2d Streets 7 rods each[.] Alleys 3 rods each[.] By Wm H. Dame Iron Co. Surveyor[,] Plat A."

8. Whittaker, journal, 13–20 Nov 1851.

9. Bulloch, "Life Sketch," 6; Chatterley, "History of Cedar City," 2.

10. Chatterley, ibid., 1.

11. Bulloch, "Life Sketch," 6. The issue of the meeting house will recur in a later discussion.

12. Whittaker, journal, 24 Nov 1851.

13. Ibid., 25 Nov 1851.

14. Ibid., 19 Nov–16 Dec 1851.

15. Ibid., 25–27 Dec 1851.

16. Chatterley, "History of Cedar City," 3.

17. "Manufacture of Iron in Utah," *Millennial Star* 17 (6 Jan 1855): 1. The greater portion of this article is taken from the "Report of Erastus Snow and Franklin D. Richards, General Agents and Managers of the Deseret Iron Company," given at the first General Meeting, Cedar City, 18 Nov 1853. A less polished version, mixed with additional passages and occasional ellipses, comprises the greater part of pp. 17–30 in the Deseret Iron Company minutes. See typescript of "Minute Book of the Deseret Iron Company, 1852." Original given to LDS Church Historian's Office on 10 Jun 1937 by William R. Palmer, typescript retained in Palmer Collection, copy in Shirts Collection (hereafter cited as Deseret Iron Company, Minutes).

18. William R. Palmer, "First Forts at Cedar City, as told by David Bulloch," n.d., n.p., Palmer Collection.

19. Bulloch, "Life Sketch," 7.

20. Chatterley, "History of Cedar City," 2.

21. Ibid., 3.

22. Lunt, diary, 28 Jun 1852.

23. Jennie Jensen Hancock, "Biography of Charles Willden, 1806–1883," typescript, 15 (cited from copy in Shirts Collection provided by Willden Family; a comparable copy, "History and Diary of Charles Willden, Sr.," typescript, but differently formatted, is in Palmer Collection).

24. John Lee Jones, "Biography of John Lee Jones: Principal Residences: Cedar City and Enoch, Utah; Mission to England," bound typescript, 8, Perry Special Collections. The term "Lamanit[e]s" that the pioneers applied to Native Americans comes from an ethnic group described in the Book of Mormon.

25. George K. Bowering, journal, 161, original in possession of Bernon Auger, Salt Lake City, copy in LDS Church Archives; restricted by family (cited from photocopied excerpts in Shirts Collection).

26. Whittaker, journal, 19 Nov 1851.

27. These directions may seem inaccurate unless one remembers the unusual geography of the region. For a description of the Rim of the Basin, see ch. 3, n. 16.

28. Bulloch, "Life Sketch," 6.

29. Red Hill, so-named for the color of its sandstone, rises 1,060 ft. to the east of modern-day Cedar City, significantly taller and larger than the Knoll at the base of which the first settlers camped. Because of its distinctive features, Red Hill has become the most significant landmark associated with Cedar City.

30. Lunt, diary, 4 Feb 1852.

31. Ibid., 19 Apr, 21–22 May and 11 Jun 1852; Henry Lunt, letter to editor, 27 Jun 1852, "Interesting [News] from Iron Co.," published in *Deseret News,* 24 Jul 1852, 3d unnumbered page.

32. Lunt, diary, 16 Jul 1852.

33. Ibid., 20 Jul, 29 Jul and 7 Aug 1852.

34. Ibid., 30 Jul 1852.

35. Bowering, journal, 165.

36. Lunt, diary, 3 Nov 1851; Smith, journal, 3 Nov 1851.

37. Whittaker, journal, 23–24 Dec 1851.

38. Deed Book A: 19–21.

39. Whittaker, journal, 17 Mar 1852.

40. Chatterley, "History of Cedar City," 2.

41. Landowners interviewed in the 1980s complained that their property lines were affected by the discrepancy between the center lane as surveyed by Dame, running up the length of the Big Field, and the location of present-day North Field Road. Jay Allred, who then owned the land in the northeast corner of the Old Fort block, bought 15 acres of land and, after having it surveyed, discovered it was closer to 13 acres, because he was losing the acreage represented by the 111 feet between the old land and the modern road. Karl Keel and Alex Rollo, other property owners, have found similar problems. Cedar City Corporation engineer Matt Bulloch claimed that a four-rod strip, not included in the title abstracts, should belong to the properties that fall on the east side of North Field Road. This strip almost certainly comprises the better part of the disputed acreage. Interviews of Cedar City property owners by Morris Shirts, ca. 1985 (undated notes in Shirts Collection).

42. Lunt, diary, 18–19 Oct 1852.

43. Dalton, *Iron County Mission,* 115.

44. Charles R. Hunter, interview by Morris A. Shirts, 2 Jan 1978, notes in Shirts Collection.

45. Whittaker, journal, 20 Mar 1852.

46. Lunt, diary, 7–8 Apr 1852. Presumably, the reference is to Edward Williams, a tailor, assigned to Company F.

47. See, for instance, Lunt, ibid., 15 Apr and 1 Jun 1852; and Whittaker, journal, 2 Jul 1852.

48. Joseph Gorlinski, 1870 survey, Bureau of Land Management, photocopy in Shirts Collection.

49. Whittaker, journal, 10–12 Mar 1852.

50. Ibid., 24 Apr 1852; the minuscule phrase might mean "and a door frame" but there does appear to be a tiny ampersand between "door" and "frame."

51. Lunt, diary, 10 Dec 1852.

52. Bulloch, "Life Sketch," 7–8.

53. Chatterley, "History of Cedar City," 3–5.

54. William R. Palmer, "History of Joseph Walker and Sons," 1–2, Palmer Collection (copy in Shirts Collection).

55. Whittaker, journal, 25 Mar 1852.

Part III

Trying Iron

8

The Pioneer Iron Works

February–May 1852

Mere survival in nineteenth-century settlements in the western United States depended on access to an immediate, reliable and inexpensive source of iron. Nails, wire, shovels, hoes, hammers, bits, horseshoes, stirrups, axes, chisels, blades and hundreds of other items were costly to buy and impossible to replace without easy access to iron. It was basic to household goods, agricultural tools, construction equipment, transport vehicles and machines of all kinds. It was also so scarce, especially for home building, that a common practice, as far back as colonial days, was to burn vacant houses to the ground to salvage the nails. Pioneers searched constantly along the trails for even the smallest abandoned item of iron. As early as 1850, an attempt was made at Temple Square's public works blacksmith shop to recast "old hub cast iron boxes" into a large spur wheel for Brigham Young's mill. The smithy's forge served as a "pocket furnace." An old Pennsylvania wagon skein was used to transfer the molten ore to the ladle, which itself was made from old wagon hub-bands.[1]

Knowledge that southern Utah contained iron reserves ignited Brigham Young's dreams of a self-sufficient Great Basin kingdom. Iron County was envisioned as the center of a great iron mining and manufacturing industry. Articles in the *Millennial Star* frequently compared the territory's future to that of Great Britain after its burgeoning iron industry gave the island its manufacturing supremacy.[2] It was an ambitious, logical and defensible undertaking.

From the start, however, iron production as a working venture was beset with problems. Capricious weather, substandard resources, poverty and uncertain relations with local Indian tribes were daily realities for the iron missionaries. As Joseph Fish, an early diarist in southern Utah, poignantly wrote, "Later generations will never know what it cost the Latter-day Saints to settle the Great Basin."[3]

Nineteenth-Century Metallurgy

A basic understanding of iron-making in the 1850s is needed to more fully appreciate the process of making iron and the monumental problems facing the pioneers of the Iron Mission. This industry required some of the most advanced technology of the times. A leading authority in the field was Frederick Overman, born in Elberfelt, Germany, in 1803. He had traveled all over Europe as a consultant and superintendent at various iron manufacturing installations. Disliking the political climate in Europe, he emigrated to the United States in 1842, where he found continuous employment in iron manufacturing along the Atlantic seaboard. His book, *A Treatise on Metallurgy,* was published in 1852 and was considered by the *London Mining Journal* to be the best work on the subject. Written before the beginnings of photographic journalism, the book was illustrated by a series of woodcuts. Unfortunately, at the age of 49, Overman accidentally inhaled "arsenated hydrogen" during a chemical analysis on 7 January 1852 and was fatally poisoned. At the time of his death, only two-thirds of his manuscript had been set in type.[4]

According to Overman, there were two types of ore important in the iron industry: magnetite (Fe_3O_4) and hematite (Fe_2O_3). Magnetite, which is usually richer in iron, is highly attracted to magnets and is black, hard, brittle and opaque. It is a refractory ore, heat resistant and difficult to reduce. Magnetite was the ore discovered along the California Road 13 miles west of Cedar City and is the resource that drew the iron missionaries to the region. It was referred to by the iron workers as "West Mountain" ore or in some cases "Virgin Ore" because of its assumed purity (see illus. 1-1).

Hematite is found in various forms including *red oxide* (red hematite) and *bog ore* (brown hematite). It comprises the bulk of iron ore in the United States and throughout the world. All furnaces in America in the 1850s except one processed this type of ore. The pioneers who came to Utah's Iron County were evidently more familiar with hematite than they were with magnetite. They found a small vein of hematite ore only about a mile from their furnace site, at the base of Red Hill east of Cedar City, and mined it for use at the furnace.

Overman lists two kinds of processed iron common in the United States: *cast iron* and *wrought iron.* Cast iron is crystalline, very brittle and usually hard. It is also known as *mottled pig iron.* Molten cast iron is poured into moulds at the foundry or remelted and hammered into wrought iron, a fibrous metal, which is ductile and therefore workable

Illus. 8-1. This small bar of pig iron, produced in 1852 by the Deseret Iron Company, is on display at the Iron Mission State Park, Cedar City, Utah.

Photograph by Morris A. Shirts

into many useful forms. The iron is first heated in a refinery forge. Once red hot, it is struck many times to make it malleable. During the pioneer era, wrought iron was used extensively for wagon tires and horseshoe nails. It was called *grey pig iron* or *bar iron* because of its shape coming out of the blacksmith's forge (see illus. 8-1). Wrought iron usually contained less carbon than cast iron did. The type of ore used, impurities in the ore, furnace design, furnace temperature and other variables determined which type of iron was to be smelted.

Initially, raw iron ore was combined with a predetermined mixture of fuel and limestone to make a *charge*. A charge is like a cake recipe and a number of charges are necessary to fill or *burden* a furnace. The fuel is typically either *charcoal* or *coke* and the workers who process both are called *colliers*. Charcoal is produced when wood is burned in the absence of air. It is created by stacking raw wood in piles, usually in *pits*, and covering these with dirt, leaving openings in the piles leading to the center. When burning is controlled in such a way as to smolder for a long period of time without actually igniting, the result is charcoal. Charcoal ovens require more work to build than charcoal pits, but are more efficient (see illus. 8-2). Beehive-shaped ovens made of stone became popular in the western United States, especially in the last decades of the nineteenth century.

Coke, in comparison to charcoal, is produced when coal rather than wood is burned in the absence of air. Porous, yet having a strong structure, coke is made from coal in much the same way charcoal is made from wood—piled in stacks, usually in a pit, with flues arranged inside the pile to carry off sulfur, the whole then covered tightly and set on fire from the bottom, burning the material but not consuming it (see illus. 8-3).

Illus. 8-2. Charcoal oven processing. "Billets of wood precut to a uniform size were stacked on end around the perimeter of a pit. The collier carefully arranged succeeding billets so as to provide a system of flues to carry away smoke and gasses, the resulting wood pile was then covered, usually with dirt, and then lighted."

Caption and illus. from Overman's 1852 *Treatise on Metallurgy*

Overman's 1852 *Treatise on Metallurgy*

Illus. 8-3. Coke oven processing. These piles may or may not have been constructed in pits. Coal was carefully stacked in rows commonly 20 to 100 feet long, 3 to 5 feet high and 6 to 12 feet wide.

In 1709, Abraham Darby developed the techniques necessary to smelt iron with coke. During the next century, the British iron industry came to rely predominantly on coke, halting the depletion of Britain's limited forests and transforming the nation into an exporter of iron. Coke was not widely used in the United States until after 1850. Wood for charcoal was so plentiful that Americans did not equip their foundries to make use of the advanced technology pioneered in England. Since the iron missionaries were trained for the most part in England, they initially favored coke as fuel for iron smelting.[5] Unfortunately, the Iron County pioneers were not able to produce a high-quality coke. The local coal contained too many impurities, including sulfur, that combined with the raw ore imperfectly, leading to substandard iron.

While charcoal resulted in softer, more workable pig iron than coke, producing it ate up too much timber to make it an ideal fuel. The Maramec furnace, located 75 miles south of St. Louis, consumed over 1,600 bushels of charcoal a day at peak production in 1858.[6] When the southern Utah iron workers did not have time to make charcoal or coke, they sometimes used unprocessed coal and "raw pitchy-pine" wood or scrub cedar as fuel, neither very successfully.

Pioneer iron makers did understand the use of limestone in the smelting process. Limestone served as *flux,* a substance that assisted in melting the iron ore and then combined with undesirable elements, carrying them away from the molten iron. Iron makers used local limestone just as it came from the quarry. There is evidence that the pioneers may have *calcined* or *roasted* the limestone before adding it to the furnace.[7] This was done to drive out moisture, removing unwanted impurities. The pioneers obtained limestone in Cedar City from at least four different locations. One was the hill north of the present North Water Tank. A second was the foot of the hill near what is now the fifth hole of the Cedar City Golf Course. A third was the mouth of Squaw Cave, southeast of town. The fourth was the limestone hill on the north side of Coal Creek Canyon, immediately above the modern power station. Some of these limestone quarries were used by builders until well into the twentieth century. The pioneer iron workers had difficulty with the limestone and constantly experimented with it. Samples of yellow, grey and white limestone can still be found near the location of the pioneer blast furnace.

In general, the following mix of ingredients constituted a charge:

Limestone (the flux)	10%
Coke (the fuel)	30%
Iron ore	60%

These proportions are estimates: the *furnace master* adjusted the balance whenever he deemed necessary. Modern blast furnaces are burdened with a mix that is very accurately balanced, both chemically and physically. The precise amount of each ingredient is determined quantitatively and nothing is left to chance. This was not so with early iron makers. They experimented with a basic recipe to which they added "a little of this and a little of that" until the mix looked about right in the furnace. Once the furnace master was satisfied with his mix, several charges would be added to the furnace to make a *batch* of iron.

The actual separation of the metal from the ore depended upon the presence of heat, carbon and the weight of the metal compared to that of the oxidized substances that formed the *cinder*. We now call this *slag* and reserve the word *cinder* to describe the same material after it has cooled. The heavier molten iron would drip down through the furnace and into the hearth, or bottom level of the furnace, while the lighter molten slag floated on top of the hot, liquid iron. This was called the *fluid process* by Overman, as opposed to the *solid process* where a lump of solid iron was formed in the hearth. A pioneer furnace master had to learn by experience how the slag and the molten metal looked when the recipe was "right." Frequently, his mistakes in judgment caused the furnace to *chill* with a solidified conglomerate mass, called a *salamander* or *bear*, resulting in a long, costly and unproductive period while the furnace lining was repaired or the whole furnace rebuilt.

Fluid-iron blast furnaces were the only kind used in the United States. Blast furnace technology initially developed when men learned to build furnaces with open sides facing downhill, taking advantage of the natural uphill flow of air. This flow provided an additional draft to make the fire hotter. Later, bellows were added to provide a more reliable draft. Mechanical means (such as waterwheels) further improved furnace design, eliminating the tiresome and sometimes ineffective bellows. Such inventions not only lightened labor but also provided a stronger draft, which, by comparison with the draft produced by bellows, was a *blast* of air. Fuels like coal and coke required a greater blast than charcoal.

Two types of waterwheels were in use in the mid-nineteenth century. *Undershot* wheels, where water flowed under the wheel, pushing against paddles arranged around the perimeter, were common in England and New England. Water to drive these wheels was stored in *millponds* and released as needed, through a controlled *headgate* that regulated the amount of water striking the wheel and, thus, the wheel's speed. Undershot wheels were dependable, and exactly controllable, but produced relatively little power (see illus. 8-4).

The second wheel type was the *overshot* wheel. These were usually much more efficient than undershot wheels, utilizing not only stream flow, but also the weight of falling water, caught in the *pockets* or *buckets* formed by the perimeter spokes. At times, a long *millrace* had to be constructed a considerable distance upstream to bring water to the top of the wheel. The race included a wooden *flume* to convey the stream of water over the top of the waterwheel. A sudden flood could wipe out the creek dam, millrace and flume in seconds. In addition, the millrace could break or become "sanded up" or the flume could spring a leak, all of which would immediately shut down the system.

In the pioneer era, the blast furnace itself was a pyramid of masonry 25 to 50 feet high and commonly as wide at the base as it was high from base to mouth. It was usually constructed of rough stones cut from sandstone. Almost any stone could be used, except limestone. The bottom part of the interior was also sandstone, the upper interior, brickwork. The lower part of the furnace was termed the *hearth* or *crucible;* it was also the smallest part of the furnace. Usually square in shape, the bottom measured 20 to 60 inches, depending on the size of the furnace. The bottom of the hearth was called the *hearth stone,* just as in a fireplace. The front of the box was called the *working* or *tymp* side. The rear was simply called the *back*

Courtesy The James Foundation—St. James Missouri

Illus. 8-4. Early photograph of undershot waterwheel and gearing works for the Maramec blast furnace. Notice the large air pipes from the tandem air pumps on the right.

side. The remaining two sides were referred to as *tuyere* sides, the sides through which the air blast nozzles were placed. Thus, a 30-inch hearth had tuyeres placed 30 inches apart. A furnace smelting magnetite ore needed a larger hearth than one smelting hematite. Also, a hearth in which charcoal was to be used was generally smaller than one in which coke was the intended fuel (see illus. 8-5).

The upper part of a furnace was lined with *firebrick,* a refractory brick capable of withstanding high temperature. Manufacturing this type of brick requires special clay. Firebricks are fired in a kiln after sun-baking, much the same way as ceramic ware. If sandstone or adobe brick (sun-dried brick made from common dirt) is used for the lining, it invariably disintegrates and sloughs off, causing the furnace to *blow out.* This also happens if the furnace cools down during the smelting process. To prevent a blow out, the furnace is kept in continuous operation until the lining is burned up. Then, before the furnace can be burdened or charged again, its lining must be completely rebuilt.

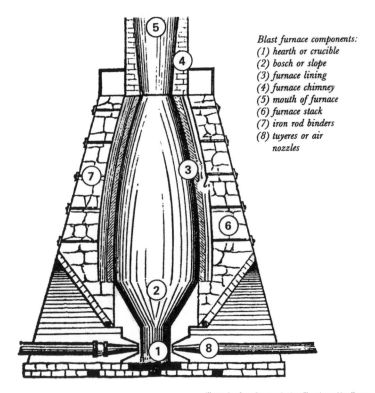

Blast furnace components:
(1) hearth or crucible
(2) bosch or slope
(3) furnace lining
(4) furnace chimney
(5) mouth of furnace
(6) furnace stack
(7) iron rod binders
(8) tuyeres or air
    nozzles

Illustration from Overman's 1852 *Treatise on Metallurgy*

Illus. 8-5. Cross-section showing interior components of the blast furnace.

Illustration from Overman's 1852 *Treatise on Metallurgy*

Illus. 8-6. Large blast furnace exterior. The covered charging house provided dry storage and a mixing area for fuel, ore and limestone.

This lining is not physically attached to the outside masonry. A space between six and eight inches wide is left between the lining and the outside wall to allow for expansion of the lining as it heats. This space is loosely filled with rough stones or in some cases, broken furnace slag. The outer sandstone wall is laid up without mortar to permit expansion. The masonry work is equipped with a series of adjustable metal binding rods, one and a half to two inches wide, which extends entirely around the outer furnace wall. As the furnace temperature changes, the binding rods are loosened or tightened by a system of *keys* at each end.

The *boshes*, or four sloping sides, extend upward and outward from the hearth, forming a hopper shaped somewhat like an inverted pyramid, upon which the cylindrical furnace lining sits. The use of the term is indicative of the influence of German iron makers on the industry and literally means "green slope." The upper rim of the boshes is the widest part of the interior of the furnace. The diameter of the upper rim and the degree of slope of the boshes are dependent upon the type of fuel and the type of ore to be used, as well as the overall size of the furnace.

The pioneer furnace mouth, sometimes called the *tunnel-head* or *trundle-head,* was often fitted with an inverted V-shaped iron cylinder whose diameter varied from 20 inches to 10 feet. If iron were unavailable, the furnace *sleeve* or *throat* was made of firebrick. One or more *doors* were provided in the throat, through which the furnace was burdened. The throat was surrounded with masonry, termed the *chimney.* A wood-frame building, the *casting house,* enclosed the furnace, while a wooden bridge ran from chimney top down to the yard where the raw materials to form the charges—ore, flux and fuel—were stored. If the bridge were covered, it was called a *charging bridge* or charging house (see illus. 8-6).

Outside access to the lower part of the furnace was necessary for furnace attendants to service the needs of the hearth. Roman arches built into the masonry wall supported its weight and provided access to the hearth. In large furnaces, these arches were interconnected by a tunnel through which furnace tenders could walk and communicate. The result of the whole process was liquid iron, which poured from the front opening of the hearth, called the *tapping*. This front opening was formed by *tymp* stones and *dam* stones plated with iron to withstand wear and tear.

The use of a *cupola* by iron workers in southern Utah is well-documented in several journals, but exactly how it was used remains somewhat of a mystery. It could have been a small experimental furnace where a single charge was tested before the large blast furnace was fully charged, thus reducing the possibility of a poor iron run and the risk of a blow out. There are also instances where the cupola was used as a reheating furnace to melt pig iron preparatory to casting or working into bar iron. Some cupolas were built on stilts with a trapdoor in the bottom so the burden could be easily removed.

Expectations and Experiments

By November 1851, when the iron missionaries arrived in Cedar City, they were a month short of having been in southern Utah for one year, a year spent in settling (then moving) their community, facing a cold spring and subsequent flooding and then dealing with a summer drought. As soon as Parowan's first harvest was in, the men of Company C and Company F left to found the new community on Coal Creek. In important ways, they had to repeat all the prior tasks of settlement; even so, some work was directly related to the central mission of producing iron.

On 2 February 1852, John Lyman Smith wrote his brother, George A., reporting the attitude of the "Coal Creek brethren," who "feel first rate and say they will have a sample of iron at Salt Lake City by 6 April; all are anxious to get the iron out from the ore."[8] No one could see this as an unrealistic expectation. They believed that iron production would begin shortly and that they would only have to rely for a few months on whatever scrap iron they could scavenge. This would be melted down by the blacksmiths and recast into the most necessary implements. Over the winter, blacksmith Burr Frost had already been attempting to make nails from scrap iron. In December 1851, he was able to report a modest success, as noted in the *Deseret News:*

Nails

We are pleased that some of the *things wanted* in our last, are, to some extent, on hand. We have been presented by elder Geo. A. Smith, with a specimen of nails, *cut nails;* sixes, eights, and brads, from Iron county; a very respectable article for a beginning. Cut? Yes! Cut out of old wagon-tire, and such like materials. True, the heads were not flattened like common nails; but left like common floor nails, or brads; which answer a good purpose, for many uses; and, if we had plenty of them, would do much towards supplying the immediate necessities of our flourishing territory; and with a little more experience, these nails may be as perfectly formed as any imported, and with as flat and perfect a head.

Will the mechanics of this valley let Iron county go ahead of them in making nails, so long as they make them of wagon-tire, and that wagon-tire has to be taken from hence, or has to pass through our city? We are told that 40 of these nails are now made in a minute, which is at the rate of 2400 per hour, or 28,000 per day, of 10 hours each. What is the use of bringing nails from foreign countries, if we can make them so fast, at home? Allowing 60 nails to the pound, the little factory at Iron county can now make 466 pounds every day, or ten hours; this multiplied by 300 days in a year, leaving sufficient for Sundays and holidays, and we have 139,800 pounds, or 1398 kegs of nails, of 100 pounds each, per annum, and if the tire can be made into nails at this place, it will save return cartage from Iron county. Great Salt Lake Valley mechanics, what do you say to this?[9]

The next month, Burr Frost ran an advertisement in the *Deseret News* for "all the old wrought and cast iron we can, for which we will pay a liberal price, either in nails, or apply the same on Tithing."[10] Although Frost's nail making used already-fabricated iron, it fulfilled one of the Iron Mission's objectives: to produce a variety of iron objects. A notice in the *Deseret News,* published two weeks after the ad just quoted, illustrates the interest and commitment felt at the time:

> The Iron and Coal mines, are in great need of blasting Powder, who has the article? materials might be collected for making a few kegs, if a manufacturer could be found; if there is such a man in the Territory, let him report to the News, without delay; for we need the coal to melt the iron, and the iron to make the stoves, pans, kettles, rail roads, steam engines, nails and fish hooks.[11]

Within a year, Frost left Iron County to set up shop in Salt Lake City, but Joseph Chatterley and Jonathan Pugmire, who remained behind, were both blacksmiths, so the colony did not suffer from Frost's absence. Early difficulties that disturbed the pioneering efforts of the iron workers included the unfortunate shooting of Jonathan Pugmire's son by his fellow herdboy, an event which shook the whole community. It was the first death among the Iron Mission settlers. As the 21 February 1852 *Deseret News* reported:

> The son of Robert Owens and the son of Jonathan Pugmire about 12 years of age each, were out herding last week, and through accident or otherwise, bro. Pugmire's son was shot through the lower part of the face—the ball going in near the right corner of the mouth; and coming out at the back of the neck.[12]

Wheelwright William Leany's diary contains some important details: "I was elected to the first city council and one of the first Magistrates and as such as coroner held the first inquest in the county on the dead body of little Jonathan pugmire [*sic*] and the jury returned a verdict of willful murder again[st] Jerome Owens for shooting him in the winter of 1852."[13] No mention is ever made in the Iron Mission journals of what punishment Jerome received or how he and his family were treated by the other settlers after the fact. We do know, at least, that Jerome was the oldest of nine children. Three sisters died at Winter Quarters and a brother died at age 15. Jerome's next youngest brother George was born in Salt Lake City on 13 December 1852, suggesting that the Owens family left the Iron Mission to avoid the stigma of Jerome's involvement in Jonathan Pugmire's death. An entry in Lunt's journal, however, on 12 September 1852, indicates that the Owens family remained a part of the community, since Lunt reports there that Jerome's father was called on a foreign mission. Most likely, Robert Owens accepted the call to serve and moved his family to Salt Lake City to await his return. Whatever the family's subsequent fortunes, young Jerome lived to marry, eventually moving to Eureka, California, where he died in 1902 at the age of 64. His wife Elizabeth survived him by 11 years and is also buried there.[14]

In addition to natural friction among the settlers, arising from their different cultural and ethnic backgrounds, the grueling nature of their hostile environment put unremitting physical demands on everyone. Disputes and defections were almost inevitable. John Lyman Smith and James Lewis hint at these problems in the same report to the *Deseret News* that carried news of the Pugmire boy's death. Although Smith and Lewis complimented the "Colony at Cedar City" for their industry in enclosing the Compact Fort, they also acknowledged some defections from the ranks: "A small company are about starting for the gold mines from this place [Parowan]—some gentiles and the rest *apostate* Mormons—though they say they are strong in the faith; yet 'by their work shall ye know them.'"[15]

Trying the Ore

That same February, problems in the overlapping administrative structures became apparent. With President Elisha R. Groves attending legislative duties in Salt Lake City, his counselor, John Lyman Smith, became *de facto* head of the mission, headquartered in Parowan. Matthew Carruthers, the other counselor, resettled in Cedar City and assumed the offices of presiding elder and major of the militia. On 2 February 1852, Carruthers had proposed that Henry Lunt, president of the now-dissolved traveling company, become first counselor in this new hierarchy, with John Easton, former captain of the Scotch Independent Company, as second counselor.[16] This decision, temporarily at least, clarified lines of authority between Lunt and Carruthers. With no president residing in the Iron Mission to settle policy issues, however, the two counselors, John Lyman Smith and Matthew Carruthers, now found themselves sometimes at odds over which practical steps to take as the iron workers began their important tasks.

On Wednesday, 4 February 1852, Lunt recorded: "In the evening wrote a letter to George A Smith[.] Br Carruthers wrote a

Courtesy Daughters of Utah Pioneers, Cedar City, Utah

Illus. 8-7. Joseph Walker (1813–81) was sent from Parowan to test the iron ore in Cedar City.

Courtesy Daughters of Utah Pioneers, Cedar City, Utah

Illus. 8-8. Emma Smith Walker (1829–96), plural wife of Joesph Walker. Her sister Betty was Walker's first wife.

Letter to Govr Brigham Young, read it to me, I approved of it, and addressed it."[17] The letter to Young, dated the next day, vividly describes the conflict arising between Matthew Carruthers and John Lyman Smith over the trying of the ore. Apparently John Lyman had sent Thomas Bladen and Joseph Walker (see illus. 8-7 and 8-8) from Parowan to test the

Daughters of Utah Pioneers, Cedar City, Utah

Illus. 8-9. Thomas Bladen (1816–97) came from a family of iron workers at the Sheffield Iron Works in England. He was the first furnace master for the pioneer iron works.

iron ore in Cedar City. Thomas Bladen (see illus. 8-9) came from a family of iron workers at the Sheffield Iron Works in England and converted while Franklin D. Richards was presiding over the LDS British Mission. Richards and Erastus Snow called Bladen, with other iron workers, to emigrate to southern Utah.[18] Also born in England, Joseph Walker (winner of the ditch-digging contest mentioned in the previous chapter) was one of the original iron missionaries. As a skilled "forgeman," he already had the experience in iron working so badly needed in southern Utah. Both men apparently reached Cedar City on 2 December 1851, James Whittaker noting that they "came into camp" on that date.[19]

Bladen and Walker asked a number of the Cedar City pioneers to help them test the ore. President Carruthers, however, felt that enclosing the fort should be the first priority, citing the counsel of George A. Smith. He resented the request from Bladen and Walker for manpower at such a crucial time. Furthermore, as he pointed out, "the canyon was locked up with snow, and we could not possibly get coal to try the experiment."

Carruthers also expressed dismay to Brigham Young that John Tout had deserted the Iron Mission. Tout was a private in Company F and is first mentioned by James Whittaker, who recorded that he was "making a public grindstone" on 19 November 1851, a week after Cedar City was settled. Tout's mechanical expertise would have been especially valuable when the time came to erect a trial furnace. Carruthers felt that "All was well with Brother Tout until a Gentile trader came along with a barrel of whiskey and a box of boots and poor John could stand the difficulties of his mission no longer and engaged to drive a few head of cattle for the gentlemen to your city and hastily took French leave."[20]

Carruthers concluded his letter with the report that a compromise had been reached. Bladen and Walker agreed to help enclose the fort, while Bladen was allowed to try a little ore with charcoal. The charcoal proved unsatisfactory, so Bladen started to build a small furnace "to try the ores and blow the bellows by water power, so that by the time the furnace is ready the canyon will be so open that we can get some coal packed down on horses' backs." Possibly lobbying Governor Young for funds, Carruthers emphasized that coal was a "spring shut up—a fountain sealed until a road is made" up the canyon.[21]

Just over two months later, on 14 March, John Lyman Smith (see illus. 8-10) wrote Brigham Young about a further conflict between Thomas Bladen and Matthew Carruthers:

> The people at Coal Creek are getting along very well. They have tried the iron as they have furnished a small specimen. Now they are divided. I am going with some of the brethren to see them to accertain their feelings and what they intend to do and any other matter, connected with the interest of the settlement.[22]

John D. Lee, who had traveled with John Lyman to Cedar City to resolve the dispute, describes the full nature of the conflict in his own letter to Brigham Young written three days later. Having agreed that trying the ore could proceed simultaneously with securing the Compact Fort, Bladen and Carruthers now disagreed over the scale of the test. Bladen wanted to build a full-sized waterwheel to power his furnace in order to give the ore a fair test. If the percentage of iron in the ore was not sufficient to justify establishing the iron works, the waterwheel could be used to power other machinery. Carruthers, on the other hand, thought it best to try the ore first with a smaller horse-powered apparatus. If the quality of the ore was high, the iron missionaries could then build on a larger scale. After learning of the differences between the two men, the brethren from Parowan prayed the Lord in the spirit of humility to help us remove all causes of difference among them and in answer to our prayers the Holy Ghost fell upon us all. Some spoke in tongues and prophecied and truly we had a time of rejoicing.

Courtesy LDS Church Archives

Illus. 8-10. John Lyman Smith (1828–98), seated, with unidentified man, served as first counselor to Elisha R. Groves and headed the Iron Mission while Groves served in the territorial legislature.

Pres. Caruthers, Bladen and all the leading men acknowledged the power of God and wept like little children and said that they would do whatever we considered was best and be one in their efforts. We advised Bro. Caruthers not to trouble Bro. Bladen, but to aid him in his opperations, in as much as they acknow[le]dge that he was acquainted with what process the ore should go through in order to test it; before we left they organized themselves to go to walk forthwith feeling warm in the cause.[23]

Lee's letter shows that the stake presidency, which had originally sent Thomas Bladen to test the ore, now confirmed his authority in the matter. Carruthers and the other settlers at Cedar City were counseled to support Bladen. Lee reports their willingness to do so, effectively ending the disharmony and confusion over what to do next. Although Carruthers had reportedly superintended an iron works in Scotland and been rushed to Salt Lake City ahead of other Scottish immigrants to consult with Brigham Young, Thomas Bladen had hands-on experience at testing ore. For the present, his were the preferred skills.

The Iron Works Account Book

Such correspondence between the iron missionaries and Brigham Young is important, not only because it reveals personal interactions within the infant settlements but also because it tracks the iron workers' first serious attempts to assess local iron. Even so, the chief sources of information on iron-related events from December 1851 through spring 1852 are Henry Lunt's journal and the Iron Works Account Book.

The "Iron Works Account Book" is a descriptive title used by Morris Shirts for an important document—it has no cover or title, consists of 34 pages of pale blue paper and measures 7¾ by 12½ inches, the whole held together by stitching as if it were once a larger notebook. Thirty-one pages, ruled into debit and credit columns, each headed by the name of an iron missionary, have survived.[24] A sample entry is shown in illustration 8-11. The pages record how much each man drew against the company (mostly in services since there are hardly any cash transactions) and how much each contributed to the project, ending with a closing balance for each. The last three pages are summaries of transactions and final additions to the register.

The Iron Works Account Book appears to have been a final audit rather than a daily record. For example, William Hunter's ledger sheet credits him with eight days' work from 16 December 1851 through June

JAMES WHITTAKER

Dr[aws]					Cr[edits]
					1852
		1852			
July 5	To Setting 4 Tire	3.00	July 9	By 70 lbs Iron 20¢	14.--
	To Herding	8.77½	July 16	By 54 " "	10.80
	"	.98	Sept	By 7 days work	14.--
				By 2 days Herding	4.--
				By 4 " Paintg Flag[1]	8.--
				By 1 Y[2] cattle 2 days	1.--
				By 1½ lbs Black Lead 40	1.50
				Waggons 2 days	.50
		12.75½			53.80
					-12.75½
					41.04½

[1]Shorthand for "painting flag"
[2]Probably "1 yoke cattle"

Illus. 8-11. Example of individual work tally from Iron Works Account Book.

1852, all included in a single entry. Thus, the account book seems to have been copied, with summarized entries, from logs kept in a daybook that has not survived. All the entries are written with the same hand and level of legibility, as if they were made the same day, with the same pen, by the same person. The handwriting is extremely similar to that of James Whittaker Sr., as it appears in his personal journal. Both James Whittaker and Matthew Carruthers are known to have helped Henry Lunt write reports of the various iron works' activities. Even though this account book is not a daily logbook, it is probably the best surviving source for identifying individual iron workers by name.

The "Iron Men"

As Lunt's diary entries show, not all those living on Coal Creek were "iron men." It is possible, using the account book, to reconstruct the personnel at the iron works with some accuracy. The 31 men whose names are identified on separate pages include:

1. Richard Harrison
2. Thomas Bladen
3. James Bosnell
4. Joseph Chatterley
5. Joseph Walker
6. Thomas Cartwright
7. George Wood
8. William Slack
9. Philip K. Smith[25]
10. Benjamin R. Hulse
11. Henry Lunt
12. John Easton
13. Robert Easton
14. James Easton
15. Alexander Keir
16. James Williamson
17. William Bateman
18. James Bullock
19. Joseph Clews
20. Jonathan Pugmire
21. David Stoddard
22. Richard Varley
23. Samuel Kershaw
24. William Hunter
25. Matthew Carruthers
26. William Stones
27. Matthew Easton
28. John White
29. John Greaves
30. James Whitaker
31. Joel H. Johnson.

The first seven names in the ledger are recognizable as those men most involved in the iron works, for their names often appear in other sources referring to iron production. John Greaves, listed on the 29th page, did no work himself, but paid the bishop for work done by the company's blacksmith. Likewise, Joel H. Johnson, bishop at Johnson Springs (modern Enoch) did not work for the company but made contributions in goods, probably from his tithing office.

At the end of the set of ledger pages, a summary of all transactions appears. Another 22 men are listed here, none of whom appear in the first group of names. Each has a debit-credit summary, suggesting that their individual ledger pages have been lost. The individuals named are:

32. Robert Henry
33. Peter Shirts
34. Alexander Easton
35. Thomas Machin
36. Edward Williams
37. William Wood
38. Charles Smith
39. William Adshead
40. Joseph Bateman
41. David B. Adams
42. Arthur Parks
43. Merius Ensign
44. John D. Lee
45. John Lyman Smith
46. Richard Benson
47. Miles Anderson
48. George Braffit
49. John Topham
50. Orson Adams
51. James Lemons
52. Edward Dalton
53. James H. Dunton.

The group includes some men who are farmers, such as John D. Lee and Peter Shirts. Several of the 22 men listed lived in Parowan but did business with the iron works, including Richard Benson, sawmill operator; James H. Dunton, farmer; and John Topham, butcher.

A third list appears on the last page of the account book. It names those who worked after the books were closed. Some of those names already appear in the main body of the book. New names include William Gough, William Roberts, Thomas T[h]orley, Robert Gallisby, Alonso Niles and stone mason Elias Morris. The list credits each man for several days of labor, frequently on a differentiated wage scale (an official wage scale was not set until November 1852). From the Iron Works Account Book it may be difficult to identify which workers spent the majority of their time in the iron works; however, the total work force of 53 comes close to Lunt's diary entry on 11 November 1852: "We now number about 60."[26]

Tracking Labor at the Iron Works

The earliest entry in the account book is on 16 December 1851. On that day, William Hunter and William Stones took their ox teams to the iron works, presumably to clear and level the site selected for the factory.[27]

According to the account book, nine men performed approximately 69 days of labor on the iron works from 16 December 1851 through April 1852: Alexander Keir, James Williamson, David Stoddard (frequently spelled Stoddart), Matthew Easton, Robert Easton, Thomas Bladen, William Hunter, William Stones and Joseph Walker. Their tasks are rarely defined, the most usual notation being "work." However, the 13 days Joseph Walker spent putting up the blacksmith shop in April and the "mining" Walker and Williamson did in the canyon are specifically noted.

Lunt's journal implies that the major focus of the community during these months was meeting survival needs. Spring 1852 was a time of unremitting toil for the residents of Cedar City. Land-leveling, ditch-making, plowing, planting, herding and building began each day at dawn and continued until dark. At times necessity kept them at work even on Sunday. Matthew Carruthers and his counselor Henry Lunt were not exempt. Iron-making was simply not the first priority at this time. Assuming that "the iron men" (distinct from other occupations) were the nine who accounted for the 69 workdays credited in the account book, the time averages out over the four-month period to about five days per man, less than one work day per month. Obviously, no one was spending full time on iron.

Lunt's first explicit reference to iron-making occurs on 5 April:

> Delightful fine day. . . . Bro. Chatterly came in from Parowan, said that Bishop Lewis and others were coming down to see us tomorrow, and wished for there to be a meeting at 4 P.M. They had been told that the Iron business was standing [i.e., idle], and public works not going on &c. These statements I can Testify are altogether false and Untrue. Peace & prosperity is in our Midst.[28]

The next day, 6 April, Tarlton Lewis, James Lewis, James A. Little, Chapman Duncan and John Steele arrived from Parowan for the 4 P.M. meeting. Of this group, only Tarlton Lewis had accompanied John Lyman Smith in March when he came to Cedar City to personally mediate the debate between Matthew Carruthers and Thomas Bladen. Lunt does not record what was said at the afternoon meeting, only noting "a meeting in Bro. Ross's house" where they were "addressed by the Parowan brethren."[29] Presumably, the group represented an investigative committee formed by John Lyman Smith to evaluate progress on the iron works. All the men were community stalwarts. Tarlton Lewis, later to become Parowan's bishop, was a busy carpenter there. James Lewis, former clerk of the University of Deseret, worked as the first clerk of Iron

Daughters of Utah Pioneers, Cedar City, Utah

Illus. 8-12. James Amasa Little (1822–1908), supervised building the steep road up Coal Creek Canyon.

County. John Steele was a surveyor and explorer. James A. Little (see illus. 8-12), Brigham Young's nephew, had already demonstrated his skills as a road builder.

On Tuesday, 13 April 1852, the week after John Lyman's committee came to Cedar City, Lunt recorded that he went to Parowan with Matthew Carruthers, Richard Harrison, Thomas Cartwright and George Wood. These men were all iron-makers, so it must be assumed that they went to Parowan on iron business, although they also participated in "electing" (i.e., sustaining the appointment of) Daniel H. Wells as lieutenant general of the Nauvoo Legion.[30] One possibility is that the men were visiting as an advisory board, reporting to John Lyman with a production plan and perhaps a schedule.

But, practically speaking, activity was limited. The only work on the iron project Lunt hints at during this time seems to have been about 6 May when he and his father-in-law, James Whittaker, planted three-fourths of an acre of wheat for Joseph Clews.[31] Clews, a brickmaker, was trading work with Lunt, a common practice in the community. Quite possibly, Clews was making adobes to be used in constructing the iron works' furnace.

Brigham Young's Annual Visit

In May 1852, Brigham Young, whose vision of the territory's industrial potential first brought the Iron Mission into being, traveled south to inspect the settlements and give momentum to the iron enterprise (see related sidebar). Almost a year and a half had passed since the colonists left Fort Utah and the samples promised for April general conference had never materialized.

On 9 May, Lunt records the arrival in Parowan of Young, Kimball, Pratt, Woodruff, Wells "and some 60 more brethren from the Gt Salt Lake valley."[32] With Brigham came George A. Smith, returning south almost exactly six months after leaving his position as Iron Mission president to become stake president in Provo. Some of the men's wives were present (probably to handle the cooking), as were children, herders, drivers and guards. The president's party had left Salt Lake City on 22 April, stopping at each settlement on the way down. The day after reaching Parowan, the visiting leaders held a conference for as many settlers as could attend.

On 10 May, driving 30 wagons and vehicles, the travelers arrived at Cedar City and were taken into various homes for food and lodging. Lunt enthusiastically notes that "Our little City was all in excitement through so great a number of visitors."[33] Later the same day, a meeting convened "in Bro Carruther's yard." There, Brigham Young and George A. Smith addressed all the settlers, both brethren and sisters. Their "principle subject was, to make Iron." After the preaching, everyone was entertained by "the delightful notes of the Brass Band" (under the direction of William Pitt, captain of martial music), which Brigham had brought along with

BRIGHAM YOUNG'S 1852 TRAVELING COMPANY

Two notices in the *Deseret News*, dated 1 May and 15 May, name members of President Young's party. Since 15 May is the more extensive listing, and no names are printed on 1 May that do not reappear on 15 May, only the 15 May list is given:

Brigham Young, President of Camp

Heber C. Kimball, 1st Counsellor

Geo. A. Smith, 2nd Counsellor

Daniel H. Wells, Captain of Camp

James Ferguson, Captain of Guard

William Clayton, Historian for Camp

S. M. Blair and John Kay, Chaplains

William Pitt, Captain of Martial Music

W. M. Andrews, Surgeon

O. Pratt and A. Carrington, Topographical Engineers

Jacob F. Hutchinson, Dancing Master

Elijah B. Ward and Miles Weaver, Interpreters

George S. Clark and J. L. Robinson, Bishops

W. W. Major, Artist

Samuel L. Sprague & Ezra G. Williams, Botanists

Geo. A. Smith, Orson Pratt, Albert Carrington [second mention each],

Z. Snow and Morgan Phelps, Geologists and Mineralogists

Wilford Woodruff, Phonographic Reporter

The camp numbers 61 men, 3 boys, 11 women, 1 girl.

Thirty wagons, 67 horses, and 12 mules.

Source: William Clayton to Franklin D. Richards on 27 Apr 1852, *Deseret News* of 15 May 1852 (vol. 2, no. 14), 2nd unnumbered page. See also Anonymous report, *Deseret News*, 1 May 1852 (vol. 2, no. 13), 3d unnumbered page.

him.[34] The next morning, Captain Lunt's militia men passed in review before Brigham Young, Lieutenant General Daniel H. Wells and Adjutant-General James Ferguson.

At 4 P.M., the "brethren only" met at Brother Ross's house, "for the purpose of organizeing an Iron Company."[35] Its name has not been preserved, if any were given, nor have many details about its structure and function. Since it was never legally incorporated, we have assigned it the name of "pioneer iron works." This will distinguish it from its immediate successor, the Parowan Iron Company, which actually survived less than two weeks, and its true successor, the Deseret Iron Company, which became a legal entity. At this 10 May 1852 meeting, Richard Harrison was appointed to superintend the iron works and Henry Lunt was made clerk. Lunt records that "Other Brethren were appointed to manage the different departments."[36] Unfortunately, he did not specify them. Richard Harrison, the new superintendent, was a moulder whose specialty was reheating iron and shaping it into useful articles. Nothing indicates Harrison had any previous experience as an iron works superintendent.

Daughters of Utah Pioneers, Cedar City, Utah

Illus. 8-13. Philip Klingensmith (1815–81), later known as P. K. Smith, was bishop of Cedar City from 1852–59.

On the evening of 11 May, Wilford Woodruff recorded that the party "took a walk on the Hill in the evening & viewed the Country. We spent the night in the fort."[37] Possibly, part of their time went to evaluating the Compact Fort's military potential. Brigham Young may have been dissatisfied with it, since Lunt and Klingensmith (see illus. 8-13) went looking for "a sight for building another Fort" on 14 May, the day after Young's departure.[38] However, nothing came of this at this time.

Two days earlier, John Kay, Albert Carrington, Barney Ward and others had gone on a short "exploring" expedition—direction not specified—returning to report "they had discovered that there were Spaniards digging Silver in the Mountains."[39] The Spanish were known to have mined silver in the Enterprise-Holts Canyon area about 40 miles west of Cedar City and possibly in the Woods Ranch area 12 miles east of Cedar City on Cedar Mountain. It is possible that Kay, Carrington and Ward were exploring iron deposits in the Iron Springs area and beyond— perhaps to evaluate ore deposits there.

"STAKE OF ZION" PRESIDENCY
IRON COUNTY, UTAH
12 MAY 1852

<u>Presidency</u>

President J. C. L. Smith, schoolteacher, living at Parowan

First Counselor John Steele, bootmaker, living at Parowan

Second Counselor Henry Lunt, merchant and store clerk, living at Cedar City

<u>High Councilors</u>

Elisha H. Groves, farmer, living at Cedar City

Matthew Carruthers, iron maker, living at Cedar City

Richard Harrison, iron moulder, living at Cedar City (wrongly identified in
  Jenson's *Manuscript History of Cedar City,* p. 27, as "Harmon")

Joseph Chatterley, wheelwright and blacksmith living at Cedar City

_____ Graham*

James A. Little, schoolteacher, living at Parowan

William H. Dame, surveyor, living at Parowan

John D. Lee, farmer, living in both Parowan and Cedar City

Samuel West, profession not known, living at Cedar City

Elijah Newman, farmer, living at Parowan

Francis T. Whitney, blacksmith, living at Parowan

Joel H. Johnson, farmer, living at Parowan

<u>Bishops</u>

Philip Klingensmith, bishop of Cedar City

Tarlton Lewis, bishop of Parowan

*No Graham is known in Iron Mission literature. John Lyman Smith records being named to the high council, yet he is not listed here. John Easton, 2nd Counselor to Matthew Carruthers in Cedar City, is also a candidate, both "Easton" and "Lyman" sharing some of the orthographic elements of "Graham."

Source: Andrew Jenson, Manuscript History of Cedar City, 27.

During his May 1852 visit, Brigham Young also clarified and stream-lined ecclesiastical and civic structure in both Parowan and Cedar City (see related sidebar), just as he had initially organized Parowan's city government on his first visit to the Iron Mission in 1851. On 12 May 1852, Young's party returned to Parowan where "Parowan and Cedar Cities were organized into one Stake of Zion," the first LDS stake in Iron County. (By date of organization, it was the fourth stake created in Utah Territory, the first three being Salt Lake City Stake, 3 October 1847; Weber Stake, 26 January 1851; and Provo Stake, 19 March 1851.)[40]

The new stake president was John Calvin Lazelle Smith (familiarly addressed as Calvin). Called to the Iron Mission in October 1850 while under contract to teach school in Salt Lake City, he had hired George Leavitt to assume his teaching duties. He arrived in Parowan in April 1852, barely a month before taking on the stake presidency.[41] He chose John Steele from Parowan as his first counselor and Henry Lunt from Cedar City as his second. The high council members were also selected from both set-tlements. All the officers shared a wide variety of occupations, but only two, Matthew Carruthers and Richard Harrison, were directly associated with iron-making. Bishops for the respective wards were also called at this time: Tarlton Lewis for Parowan and Philip Klingensmith for Cedar City.

Up to this time, Matthew Carruthers had been "presiding elder" in Cedar City (delegated these duties as second counselor to Elisha Groves in the mission presidency). Under this reorganization, he was conspicuously passed over for a seat in the stake presidency in favor of Henry Lunt, the new second counselor. John Lyman Smith, first counselor to Groves, who presided in Parowan whenever Groves was absent, appears nowhere on Andrew Jenson's list of officers in the new stake presidency. According to John Lyman's own history, however, he was called to the high council at this time.[42] In any event, he was representing Iron County in the territorial legislature four months later, so the issue of his active participation on the high council becomes moot. In his own words,

> On August 2, 1852, I was elected as representative of Iron County to the State Legislature and on the 26th of September myself and wife and two children arrived in Salt Lake City where we met my father and family. The legislative assembly convened on the 12th of December, 1852. I answered roll call every time during the session.[43]

Although the new stake presidency had no formal training in iron production, as ecclesiastical leaders the three were expected to manage all aspects of the southern Utah settlements, including the iron works.

As first counselor, Steele supervised Parowan and the settlement farms while Lunt, as second counselor, supervised Cedar City and the iron works. The high council, acting somewhat like a board of directors, represented both communities. Lunt's position is interesting: as second counselor in the presidency, he was superior to Richard Harrison, who reported on the progress of the iron works to Lunt; but as clerk of the iron works, Lunt was subordinate to Harrison, its superintendent.

Courtesy Daughters of Utah Pioneers,
Cedar City, Utah

Illus. 8-14. James Ferguson (1828–63), captain of the guard, delivered Brigham Young's May 1852 address to the Iron County Saints.

As Brigham Young understood, the success or failure of the Iron Mission rested with the workers at Cedar City. Near the conclusion of the Parowan conference, Brigham Young had James Ferguson, his captain of the guard, read an epistle that Young and Kimball had prepared for the occasion (see illus. 8-14). It seems unusual that Brigham would not deliver such an important message himself. Furthermore, the epistle is uncharacteristic of Brigham Young's style and may have been dictated to Ferguson and modified as it was transcribed. Ferguson himself, over the course of his life, sampled many professions and took on a number of civic responsibilities. He was a talented debater, a thespian in the Deseret Dramatic Association, secretary to the legislative assembly, an attorney, sheriff of Salt Lake County for several terms and a close friend of both Young and Wells.[44]

The first part of the epistle emphasized potential danger from Indians, offered general guidelines to deal with them, chastised those who felt a few head of cattle were worth the life of a Native American and rebuked (without naming them) those like Peter Shirts who had built homes outside the fort, thus tempting Indian raids. The letter lauded the settlers' sacrifice and faith, reminded them of the importance of their work and then unfolded a lengthy discourse aimed at Cedar City.

In this section, "To the Brethren at Cedar City" (see app. 5), Brigham Young emphasized the area's resources that would facilitate iron production and promised additional settlers to help "accomplish this most desirable object, the manufacture of Iron." President Young insisted that the people of the territory not be dependent on foreign countries for essential machinery and tools so they would not "labor under the present disadvantage, precarious and expensive transportation and continual drain of our money." He reminded them of their "solemn covenant" to do everything in their power to produce iron, expressing

> the fullest assurance that but a few weeks shall roll around before the cheering intelligence will salute our Ears,—"send your orders we are prepared to fill them. The Iron is piled up in our houses and in our streats send your teams and carry it away."

Brigham Young further admonished them not to let selfishness get in the way of "devoted magnanimity for the Public interest." He reminded them that it was "a gentile custom to sell Knowledge." But the principles of salvation, he noted, required that "not only our Knowledge but our talents[,] our capacity, be it great or small should be devoted to the cause of God in what Ever calling we may be engaged in, that is conducive to its interest." He insisted that manufacturing iron was part of the kingdom of God and "should be pursued as regardless of the consequences pertaining to pecuniary considerations as preaching the gospel[. I]t is as sacred as any other Mission." The southern Saints would be expected to donate produce and labor as tithing. Rather than being subsidized by the leaders in Salt Lake City, the iron workers were expected to use their own resources to begin production and then increase it as circumstances allowed. President Young concluded with a prayer for the blessings of heaven to rest on "all the faithful saints" attempting to do God's will.[45]

As a general guideline to the settlers, it was an inspiring address. Henry Lunt, the new second counselor (upon whose shoulders the burden of producing iron would soon fall), was given permission to copy the document. He retired to the home of a friend, Dr. William A. Morse, where he worked through the whole evening of 12 May until 1:00 A.M. to complete it.[46] He subsequently refers to it a number of times as support for his unending efforts, against most difficult odds, to keep the iron workers unified.

In this frontier environment, with survival always foremost, volunteer laborers for community projects were hard to come by. Leaders, struggling to govern, had trouble meeting their own needs. In 1853, John Steele was to note in his journal: "About this time I had my hands so full, I could not tell what to do first, Indian troubles, settling home matters which are generally plenty and as Calvin or the President were absent nearly all the time, the work devolved upon me."[47] Lunt would have agreed, recording on 1 May 1852 that he had "returned home very much fatigued every night this week[.] It is a very toilsome job to break up new land, and to build new settlements." An entry three weeks later, on the 21st, only underscored the amount of sheer physical toil the job demanded: "The remainder of the day myself and father Whittaker ditched on my ditching. Very much fatiegued in the Evening. The greatest portion of the lower dam, swept away by the high water. Creek still raising."[48]

Meanwhile, Brigham Young had returned to Salt Lake City, apparently satisfied with the iron ore, coal, water, soil and settlement as a whole—but not with the progress toward manufacturing iron. On 18 September 1852 the *Millennial Star* reported that President Young and the exploring company arrived "all in good health and fine spirits," speaking "highly of the industry and perseverance of the brethren . . . in their new locations."[49] Now that the basic tasks of settlement had been completed, however, the prophet expected the iron missionaries to proceed with the manufacture of iron without delay.

Endnotes

1. Temin, *Iron and Steel*, 42; John G. Crook, "The Development of Early Industry and Trade in Utah," (master's thesis, University of Utah, 1926), 30, citing *Journal of Discourses*, 26 vols. (Liverpool: F. D. Richards, 1855–86), 2:282. The "skein" is a metal collar assembly holding the axle to the wagon body.

2. See, for instance, *Millennial Star* articles in 13 (1 Apr 1851):106–7, noting the preparation of a company of about 150 to go to Little Salt Lake settlement; 13 (15 Sep 1851): 273–77, comprising Thomas Bullock's report of the "Tour of President Young and Suite"; 14 (15 May 1852): 179, inviting more brethren to "form themselves into a company to go to the Valley, and commence the manufacture of Iron"; 14 (29 May 1852): 210, "Minutes of the Special General Council" quoting Apostle Erastus Snow's comment that "our minds have been more or less occupied with the subject of the manufacture of *iron* in DESERET"; 15 (19 Feb 1853):114, "Eighth General Epistle of the Presidency of the Church of Jesus Christ of Latter-day Saints"; 15 (5 Mar 1853): 149–51, "Continuation of Minutes of General Conference of 6 October 1852," detailing a further appeal for colonists to go south; 15 (16 Jul 1853): 458–61, outlining the organization of the Deseret Iron Company; and 17 (6 Jan 1855): 1–7, comprising the article "Manufacture of Iron in Utah," cited in ch. 7, n. 17.

3. Joseph Fish, journal, 3, bound typescript, Perry Special Collections (copy in Shirts Collection: typescript of 1840–59 entries).

4. Frederick Overman, *A Treatise on Metallurgy,* 3d ed. (New York: D. Appleton, 1855). Overman's premature death is discussed in the preface, ii.

5. Temin, *Iron and Steel*, 14–15; York Jones, comp. and ed., "Iron Mining and Manufacturing in Iron County, Utah, 1850–1975," unpublished typescript, n.d., 29–30 (copy in Shirts Collection).

6. Norris, *Frontier Iron,* 42–43.

7. Calcined ore was roasted to drive out moisture and some of its impurities. The process would have required considerable labor and some kind of oven—perhaps similar to a coking pit.

8. John Lyman Smith to George A. Smith, 2 Feb 1852, Journal History.

9. "Nails," *Deseret News,* 13 Dec 1851, 2nd unnumbered page.

10. "Notice," *Deseret News,* 7 Feb 1852, 3d unnumbered page.

11. Untitled notice, *Deseret News,* 21 Feb 1852, 2nd unnumbered page.

12. John Lyman Smith and James Lewis to editor, 12 Jan 1852, published in *Deseret News,* 21 Feb 1852, 4th unnumbered page.

13. William Leany, journal, Perry Special Collections, comprising three holographic autobiographical reminiscences; this book cites the third, which begins "[Jan] 4th 1888 Harrisburg Washington Co. Utah."

14. Robert Owens family records, accessible through LDS Church, genealogy database [on-line], available from familysearch.org; see also Lunt, diary, 12 Sep 1852.

15. Smith and Lewis to editor.

16. Lunt, diary, 2 Feb 1852.

17. Ibid., 4 Feb 1852.

18. John M. Bladen, "Thomas Bladen," memoir by Bladen's grandson, copy in Shirts Collection; "Thomas Bladen," brief biography.

19. Palmer, "History of Joseph Walker and Sons"; see also Whittaker, journal, 2 Dec 1851.

20. Matthew Carruthers to Brigham Young, 5 Feb 1852, in Journal History; see also Whittaker, journal, 19 Nov 1851.

21. Carruthers to Young, ibid. An earlier letter written by Matthew Carruthers to George A. Smith on 3 Jan 1852 appears in *Deseret News,* 21 Feb 1852, 4th unnumbered page. There Carruthers says "Brother Bladen is, in my opinion, well qualified to take the charge and management of the manufacture of iron, and we ought to encourage and strengthen him as much as we possibly can," an endorsement that remained unchanged despite their administrative disagreements.

22. John Lyman Smith to Brigham Young, 14 Mar 1852, in Journal History.

23. John D. Lee to Brigham Young, 17 Mar 1852, in Journal History.

24. Iron Works Account Book, Dec 1851–Nov 1852, incomplete MS, 1–31, authorship attributed to James Whittaker Sr. and descriptive title assigned by Morris Shirts, original in Palmer Collection.

25. This individual is almost certainly Philip Klingensmith. During the spring of 1852, he began writing his name as Philip K. Smith or P. K. Smith. No reason is given, but perhaps the German name seemed cumbersome. Throughout this book, he is referred to as Philip Klingensmith, rather than P. K. Smith, to avoid confusion

with the other Iron Mission leaders surnamed Smith.

26. Lunt, diary, 11 Nov 1852.

27. Iron Works Account Book. See p. 24 for William Hunter entries and p. 26 for William Stones entries, each of which shows the earliest beginning work date for any account, 16 Dec 1851.

28. Lunt, diary, 5 Apr 1852.

29. Ibid., 6 Apr 1852.

30. Ibid., 13 Apr 1852.

31. Ibid., 6 May 1852.

32. Ibid., 8 May 1852.

33. Ibid., 10 May 1852.

34. Ibid.

35. Ibid., 11 May 1852.

36. Ibid.

37. Wilford Woodruff, *Wilford Woodruff's Journal, 1833–1898,* Typescript, ed. Scott G. Kenney, ed.; 9 vols. (Midvale, Utah: Signature Books, 1983–85), 138 (entry for 11 May 1852).

38. Lunt, diary, 14 May 1852.

39. Ibid., 12 May 1852.

40. *Deseret News Church Almanac, 1991–1992* (Salt Lake City: Deseret News, 1990), 176.

41. Fish, journal. See pp. 3–5, describing J. C. L. Smith's travels, ca. 1847–52 (J. C. L. Smith and Joseph Fish were brothers-in-law).

42. Jarvis, *Ancestry,* 36.

43. Ibid.

44. Whitney, *History of Utah,* 4:180–83.

45. Brigham Young and Heber C. Kimball, "to the Saints in Parowan and Cedar Cities," in Brigham Young Papers, Outgoing Correspondence, LDS Church Archives. See app. 5 for complete text. Circumstantial evidence places this address in the context of the May 1852 conference. "Oct–Nov 1851" appears on the back of the text, but in a different hand, believed to be that of Thomas Bullock, Brigham Young's clerk. As Cedar City was not settled until mid-Nov 1851, the speech could not have been made in Oct 1851. Most likely, Thomas Bullock was approximating the date.

46. Lunt, diary, 12 May 1852.

47. "Extracts from the Journal of John Steele," *Utah Historical Quarterly* 6 (Jan 1933): 27.

48. Lunt, diary, 1 and 21 May 1852.

49. "Arrival of Mails from the G. S. L. Valley," *Millennial Star* 14 (18 Sep 1852): 472.

9

First Fruits of the Furnace

May–October 1852

The Cedar City pioneers immediately set to work to realize Brigham Young's expectations. Their first priority was tackling the problem of how best to allocate manpower between public works, like ditch- and fence-building, and initial labor on the iron works. Efforts would also go to finding the best coal sites in the area, seeking the necessary fuel to produce useful iron implements in time for fall conference.

As second counselor in the stake presidency and thus responsible for iron production in Cedar City, Henry Lunt aptly describes in his journal the heightened interest in iron-making. On Thursday, 13 May 1852, he had been in the party escorting Brigham Young back to Parowan. Even though the return trip to Cedar City was almost half a day by wagon, Lunt and his party arrived home in time to hold a meeting. After the newly appointed bishop, Philip Klingensmith, discussed such routine matters as the repair of the water ditches, Lunt "addressed the brethren on being united, and urged them to enclose the field and finish the water ditches as a work to be done preparitory to commencing the Iron business." Even though he had already been sustained at Parowan as a member of the stake presidency, Lunt asked the Cedar City men for their sustaining vote. He spent the evening of the next day, Friday, "in Council with bro Harrison," the newly designated superintendent of the iron works, probably outlining necessary steps for iron production.[1]

Although Lunt was only 27 years old, his actions show he was serious about his calling as second counselor in the stake presidency and presiding elder in Cedar City. Not only was he eager to call a meeting but he insisted upon punctuality as a part of general discipline. Few settlers had timepieces and the community was so small that a bugle blast could reliably reach everyone. To facilitate the meeting schedule, Lunt arranged for one signal to be given at 10:30 A.M. and one at five minutes to 11:00 A.M.

to insure attendance promptly at 11:00. The horn would also sound at 10 minutes to 2:00 P.M. so that 2:00 meetings could begin on time. He neglected, however, to record the effectiveness of these measures.[2]

On 20 May, Lunt called a group of brethren together in his father-in-law's house for a council meeting. Attending were Joseph Walker, Thomas Bladen, James Bosnell, George Wood, Philip Klingensmith, Joseph Chatterley, Richard Harrison, Thomas Cartwright, Matthew Carruthers, John Easton and James Whittaker.[3] Only Whittaker and Klingensmith did not have iron-making skills but they did have an obvious ecclesiastical function, since Klingensmith was now Cedar City's bishop and Whittaker one of his counselors. Lunt refers fairly interchangeably to "the council" and "the High Council," while Richard Harrison records meeting with "the Iron Co. Councell" on the morning of Saturday, 5 June, and with "the High Councell" the same afternoon.[4] If these were indeed separate groups, as they most probably were, then at least Matthew Carruthers, Joseph Chatterley, Richard Harrison and Henry Lunt belonged to both.

Questions of Priority: Fencing the Big Field

Council meetings held in May 1852 addressed ongoing challenges posed by limited manpower. Henry Lunt never complained that the men were lazy. On the contrary, he acknowledged that they were "very busy"—but with their own spring planting, not with iron-making or the crucial public works. At least 53 men were available, yet on successive days (21 and 22 May), even when their hard-won irrigation system was threatened by spring runoff from Coal Creek, only six, of whom Lunt was one, answered Bishop Klingensmith's call to repair the water ditch.[5]

Any new irrigation system has inherent problems; here, portions of the Coal Creek ditch traversed sandy terrain. The ditch almost certainly silted up from sand carried along in the stream, a condition that sooner or later raised the water level, forcing water over the top of the bank or through cracks. Having irrigation water at all depended on the strength and effectiveness of the dams on Coal Creek. These, however, were most often small structures, composed of brush, rocks and logs—not the high, solid structures we visualize today. Located at places where the streambed was wide and the banks low, these brushwork dams extended only a short distance into the stream to divert a portion of the water into the water ditches. But high water could easily sweep the dams away. Although they were not difficult to replace, their upkeep demanded constant labor. The five who, with Lunt, answered the bishop's call to repair the ditch were most probably iron workers who were not raising grain.

Fencing the Big Field provides an even more vivid example of how the settlers were forced to choose between competing priorities, in this case protecting the source of their food supply, critical to survival, versus producing iron, their ultimate goal. On 3 May, Lunt records that he and "Bro Wiley," duly constituted since 18 April as the Committee for Laying of Public Fencing, went out and "measured off the lots for fenceing the north end of the big field."[6] The phrasing of this entry, collated with others that follow, seems to indicate that their intention was to have each Big Field lot owner fence that edge of his land which abutted the field's outer rim. Thus, everyone would be obligated to help build the fence but no individual would be overwhelmed by the size of the task.

Despite frequent urgings by Brigham Young and his fellow visitors, exhorting the settlers to solve intervening problems rapidly and move forward with iron production, Lunt's counsel of the 13th about completing the Big Field fence was essentially ignored. Whittaker mentions working on public projects on the 14th and 19th but his brief entries record no other workers.[7] At the 20 May council meeting, Lunt restated the issue, determined to get the brethren to deal with it "forth with." The iron business, he said, "was the thing that we were sent down here for to do, and the field has got to be enclosed before we can commence, so that the Crops may be secured according to council."[8]

On the 25th, still with no progress in sight, Lunt asked Bishop Klingensmith to convene a special meeting that night. Klingensmith agreed. During the meeting, Lunt counseled the people to finish the fence immediately, so the men assigned to the iron works would be free to devote themselves to that task. He was disappointed in the outcome, however, feeling that the "people generally appeared to be selfish and disunited."[9] The next day's observations confirmed his suspicions. Walking through camp, he found the brethren "all very busy, some ploughing, some planting seeds[,] some building houses, and but three putting up fence. I just felt that the devil had had his way long enough over this mission, and I was determined by the help of the Lord to stop it."[10]

Taking Joseph Walker with him, he went out to the Big Field and found Richard Harrison, the iron works superintendent, obediently building his assigned section of fence. Walker and Lunt helped him complete it and even worked together putting up a section for Thomas Cartwright. Discovering that 60 more rods of fence were needed and that 200 rods of ditching were still undone, Lunt turned to Harrison and said "go right ahead in the morning at the Iron business and I [will] put up all the fence myself, It is no use putting the thing off any longer." Harrison objected to this because previous counsel had been given to complete the fencing first and then move on to iron production. But Lunt was adamant. He knew the earlier instructions, he said, but "who is ther at work now at the fence? Scar[c]e any one. . . . The Iron works have got to be started and that right off. . . . I said much more to bro Harrison exhorting him to push the Iron works, which I do not write."[11]

Apparently not feeling he could leave the matter, Lunt again called for a general meeting that evening and spoke to the settlers in unmistakable terms:

> Brethren the field is not yet Enclosed and there is no one doing Anything at the fence save what has been done by myself and a few others. If we are to wait until that fence is finished, before the Iron works are Commenced, it will be months gone first, I say in the name of the Lord go and Commence in the Iron busniess in the morning, and not let the Sun set again before you have made a start. I will put up the fence myself and take it Altogether in my own hands.[12]

Lunt then turned the meeting over to Harrison to conduct iron business on the spot. Harrison proceeded to make "some arrangements" but not, Lunt noted, "with such a determined spirit" as he would have liked.[13]

Nevertheless, the next day at least 13 of the 30 men assigned to iron work took up that task. Lunt, meanwhile, worked on the fence with only two young men helping him. "My own fence," he penned in frustration, "has been up more than a month ago."[14] On the 29th, he finally came up with a solution no one could gainsay. He called Company F together in the center of the Compact Fort and told them their best efforts would not be in a morning's drill but rather in completing the fence. The cattle were into the crops "in a shameful manner" and there needed to be a "general push" made that day. James Williamson and Alexander Keir, two of the privates in Company F, were totally opposed to Lunt's counsel and "insulted [him] by saying they just should not do it." But Lunt persisted. He "gave them a good preach on the importance of obeying council" and, in his capacity as captain of Company F in the Second Battalion in the Nauvoo Legion, "put the whole company under Marshall Law." Few if any of the settlers were willing to argue with Lunt on such a fundamental point. He had won the day, as his entry shows: "They then went to work at the fence and finished putting it all up by about 4 oclock PM."[15]

Questions of Priority: Planting Grain or Making Iron

Henry Lunt's journal shows that Stake President J. C. L. Smith was concerned about Brigham Young's challenge to make timely and significant progress on the iron works. With his first counselor, John Steele, J. C. L. visited Cedar City the week after Young's departure. Parowan's bishop, Tarlton Lewis, and brickmaker William Bateman accompanied them. Early Sunday morning, 23 May, Lunt had gone walking with Smith, Steele and Lewis toward the mountains to water the horses. "We Sat down under a Cedar tree and [had] a good deal of most excellent talk."[16] When Presidents Smith and Steele addressed the congregation at services that morning, they counseled the brethren to cease planting any more grain. Sowing more wheat than the community needed would simply result in more time and manpower being drawn away from iron work at harvest time. The injunction was logical but it was not popular. Even so, during the afternoon meeting, after more exhortations from the leaders, Matthew Carruthers rose to express his feelings, saying that, while he had previously felt uneasy, now he had "good feelings towards all men" and was "on hand all the time for to do any thing that the Authorities might call him to do."[17]

The next morning, Monday the 24th, Smith and Steele returned to Parowan. They were barely out of sight when Matthew Carruthers hooked up a double team and began breaking more land for planting. Henry Lunt was upset and called an emergency meeting of the Cedar City high council that night. When two of the members did not come, he rescheduled for early the next morning.[18]

The 8 A.M. meeting was a stormy session, lasting six hours. Lunt garnered the strongest position for himself by opening with prayer and then dealing with Matthew Carruthers. Carruthers defended his plowing as obedience to earlier counsel. He felt "the Council was bounsing upon him too much" and asked to be released. Lunt, however, did not want Carruthers off the high council: he wanted to change his mind and gain his support. To release him for cause could have led to further discipline, even excommunication, and Lunt needed Matthew's iron-making expertise. Much of the meeting seems to have focused on Carruthers until finally he admitted himself "humbled," apologized to his brethren and shook hands all around as a sign of fellowship. The men then held a prayer circle, each praying in turn from the oldest to the youngest. Afterward, they conducted unspecified business. Lunt then gave the closing prayer, dismissed the meeting and spent the afternoon in bed, physically and emotionally drained by this direct challenge to his authority.[19]

The next few days were those during which Lunt finally solved the problem of the Big Field fence. On the 29th, as soon as the men of Company F set to work raising its final sections, Lunt left for Parowan, perhaps just for a change of scene, but more likely to counsel with J. C. L. Smith. While there, Lunt spoke in church on 30 May on the increasingly important subject of "oneness." He then met several times with members of the presidency and high council before returning to Cedar City on Monday morning. There he called his own council together for another lengthy session that lasted until midnight. By the next Thursday, 3 June, Lunt felt his "soul and spirits . . . renewed" and spoke much "on makeing Iron and exhorted the brethren to press forward in that department."[20]

Despite such appeals to unity, within a month after the grain-planting incident, Matthew Carruthers was again having difficulty "following counsel." The leaders had decided that the best way to obtain the scrap iron needed for the blast furnace was to ask for donations rather than risk men's lives sending them out to scavenge iron from discarded equipment along the California Road. This meant taking whatever iron they could spare from wagons and other gear in hopes it would soon be replaced once the iron works got underway. Evidently, Carruthers had two wagons and had promised to donate the metal parts from one of them as well as "a lot of old Iron" he had lying around. However, when Lunt and Harrison went to collect the iron on 29 June, Carruthers refused, saying he didn't have any to spare because "he thought he should go to the Gt. Salt Lake Valley."[21]

Lunt's entry on 5 August shows a further clash with Carruthers. At a Thursday fast-day meeting, Lunt invited the men to speak freely about any concerns they might want to express. Carruthers, he records, "spoke at considerable length . . . finding fault with me and several other brethren." At a meeting held that afternoon, Lunt responded for an hour and a half and reported that Carruthers appeared reconciled.[22] The following Saturday, 7 August, Carruthers traveled by buggy with Lunt, Harrison, Chatterley and John Easton to Parowan where all of them spoke at a Sunday meeting.[23]

Later that month, a group of California-bound travelers camped near the Compact Fort. They mingled freely with the iron workers and even joined their religious services. Their glowing anticipation of life in California was evidently too tempting to Carruthers and he decided to join them. On 3 September, he arranged to trade his house, a 20-acre field, some building lumber and a potato patch to Henry Lunt for two yoke of oxen. Two days later, however, Carruthers decided not to leave. He asked Lunt to cancel the deal, which Lunt readily did.[24]

This incident marks the uncertainty Carruthers felt about staying in the community. Yet in the fall, when the non-profit pioneer iron works was sold to its successor organization, the for-profit Deseret Iron Company, Matthew was one of 15 men who accepted the offer to buy into the new venture.[25] He even helped Henry Lunt "in auditing the Iron works books" at the time of this transition.[26] Furthermore, when Lunt went to Salt Lake City in March 1853 to attend general conference, he designated Carruthers to preside in his absence.[27]

The minutes of the Deseret Iron Company show that in May 1853 Matthew Carruthers was one of five men chosen as a special council to help the over-burdened J. C. L. Smith with the iron works. Erastus Snow even delegated Carruthers to take over whenever J. C. L. was unavailable.[28] Carruthers remained an active member of the stake high council as late as 9 June 1853.[29] On 18 July, Lunt's regular diary entries end, having mentioned Carruthers only five more times.[30] George Bowering's journal, which covers the weeks that follow, only mentions him in the entry for 16 August.[31] John Chatterley's reminiscences provide circumstantial evidence that Carruthers finally left southern Utah and returned to Scotland to find more profitable employment.[32]

Sustaining the Effort

The 1852 Iron Works Account Book reveals that Lunt's bid to get iron-making preparations underway that May yielded some positive results. From December 1851 to the end of April 1852, only 69 man-days had been recorded, but May alone totaled 101. Work increased dramatically through the summer—June totaled 382 man-days; July, 404; August, 293; and September, 214—but this level of work came to a sudden halt after September; October records show no work, with November totaling only 11.5 hours. These figures reflect only hours of labor performed, not the amount credited to each man for the use of his oxen, horses, tools or wagons.[33] Because this account book often summarizes labor covering two- to three-week periods (months, in some cases), implying at least one earlier, more-detailed source, other daybooks containing work tallies may still exist, merely awaiting rediscovery.

Even though the account book gives 16 December 1851 as the first date of iron-related work, Lunt, in his journal, appears to date it much later—Thursday, 27 May 1852. This may be the date on which arrangements for the actual furnace construction began. It is the day, noted earlier, on which "some 13 out of about 30" men, responding to Lunt's urgings and Harrison's somewhat less determined "arrangements," "Commenced in the Iron business, some prepairing for the Furnace, and some exploring for Coal."[34] On Friday, 4 June, Lunt himself "worked on the Iron works, Hawling rock and digging out a place for Furnace." This second reference to furnace work increases the likelihood that preliminary excavations had already been made that winter. Preparing the site required extensive labor. On 10 June, a "very warm day" according to Lunt, he labored "at diging out foundation for the machinery for the Blast furnace. . . . Very much fatiegued in the evening through the arduous duties of the day." On 7 July, a month later, he was still "hawling Rock for the bottom of the furnace."[35]

Journal references and local artifacts confirm the site as near the intersection of 400 North and 100 East in modern Cedar City. An 80-foot easterly extension of 400 North from 100 East to the streambed of Coal Creek (surveyed as a street but never completed for lack of a bridge at the creek) was set apart by the Cedar City Corporation on 10 February 1975 as a historic location. It now appears on the Utah Historic Register. In cooperation with the Daughters of Utah Pioneers and as part of the annual observance of Cedar City's anniversary of settlement (see related sidebar), the Cedar City Birthday Committee dedicated, on 11 November 1978, a 20-ton ore sample hauled to the site by Utah International, Inc., a mining company from the Iron Springs area. York Jones—company superintendent and descendant of both Henry Lunt and Thomas Jones, another iron missionary—supervised the ore transfer.

The historic site measures about 80 by 100 feet but the original site contained as many as 1,200 acres.[36] On it were the furnaces and associated machinery, as well as areas to prepare the limestone, coke, coal and charcoal needed for the operations. What is thought to be part of an iron-plated dam plate was unearthed near the south boundary of this site, indicating that the actual furnace was nearby. Samples of slag, coke, iron ore and limestone are still visible on the surface.

According to the reports of local residents, supported by circumstantial evidence, the first furnace was probably on the east side of Coal Creek, directly across from the present intersection of 100 East and 400 North. Hunter Grimshaw of Enoch, the small town six miles north of Cedar City, claims to have seen the foundation of a furnace and charcoal pits in that area when he worked for a Mr. Webster as a boy. Mr. Webster told him that what he saw were the remains of the first pioneer blast

IRON INDUSTRY MEMORIALS

A memorial plaque describes the site and shows a painting of the iron works by R. D. Adams, descendent of furnace master David Barkley Adams. The plaque reads:

Deseret Iron Works
This monument marks the spot where on September 30, 1852, the first iron was manufactured west of the Mississippi River by the Mormon Iron Missionaries sent here by Brigham Young.

This 5½ ton ore body was obtained from the Iron deposits used by the Iron Workers located about seven miles west of Cedar City in the Three Peaks area; it is about 61% Fe. The smaller specimens are some that were actually hauled by horse-drawn vehicles to this site and were found during excavations. The Blast Furnace, Foundry, Pattern Shop, Coke and Charcoal Ovens, Waterwheel and Offices of the early Pioneer Iron Works were located North, South and East of this monument.

The technology of using coke was brought by these early iron workers directly from England where the use of charcoal had been out-lawed and which was a relatively new idea, especially in American iron manufacturing. In spite of floods, which inundated the Iron Works, the undependable water source, and other natural and man-made difficulties, considerable iron was produced here until 1858, making the iron industry one of the leading factors in the economy of the Utah territory.

Dedicated November 11, 1978 (Cedar City's 127th Birthday)

The accompanying Utah State Historic Site marker reads:

Pioneer Iron Works Blast Furnace
To satisfy an urgent need for manufactured iron products, a small group of English, Welsh, Scotch, Irish and American pioneers answered a call from Brigham Young to become "Iron Missionaries" to settle Iron County and to make iron. They arrived in Parowan on January 13, 1851 and produced the first iron west of the Mississippi on September 30, 1852 on this site. Due to economics, social, environmental and technical problems, the Iron Works was closed down in October 1858.

Division of State History S-89

[original dictation and punctuation retained from both markers] furnace. Grimshaw also remembered watering his horse in what he thought was a sluice ditch.[37] At the 1978 dedication of the memorial marker on the west bank of Coal Creek, an older woman remarked that the first furnace was located on the east bank, not the west. Such a site for the original furnace makes sense, as the iron workers could have walked there from the Compact Fort near the Knoll without having to cross Coal Creek, which would have been difficult in a flood.

Little is known about the original furnace but it was probably quite small, perhaps 20 feet tall. Thomas Bladen, first furnace master, made what is thought by many to be a model of this furnace, now in the Daughters of Utah Pioneers Museum in Cedar City (see illus. 9-1). The model measures some 8½ inches square at base by 16 inches tall. Ultimately, several blast furnaces were built or reconstructed and the model could be of one of these. Furnace design depended on the amount and type of ore smelted and the type of fuel used. A furnace fueled by stone coal was designed differently from one fueled by charcoal or coke. Lunt's determined search for stone coal implies the first furnace was designed with that fuel in mind.

Photograph by Morris A. Shirts

Illus 9-1. Thomas Bladen's blast furnace model, on display at the DUP Museum, Cedar City, Utah.

Cutting a Road to the Coal Mines

Before operations at the iron works could begin, a road to access the coal deposits had to be constructed. On 18 May 1852, High Councilman James A. Little arrived from Parowan to begin building this road up Coal Creek "Kanyon." On 18 June, three of the men who had gone up the canyon the day before reported finding a vein of coal "about one mile nearer than what was discovered before."[38] The find may or may not have affected original road layout. In any event, on 21 June, more volunteers came from Parowan to work on the road.

Whittaker gives the next day, Tuesday, 22 June, as the starting date, which may be an implicit reference to the original design having been altered to take advantage of the nearer coal bed: "James and several others commenced making a road in the Kanyon." Lunt must have been one of the group because his own entry on that day says that he "laboured at working the road up the Kanyon." Interestingly, while Whittaker mentions only several men helping this day, Lunt's entry reads "About 30 hands were at work."[39]

Similar entries continue for the rest of the week, Lunt "labouring in the Kanyon" from 23 to 25 June and "on the iron works" on the 26th, a Saturday.[40] The following days brought a succession of iron-related tasks, including the hours of rock-hauling on 7 July previously mentioned.[41] On the 16th, both Whittaker and Lunt refer to road work. Whittaker merely mentions that James Jr. was up the canyon but Lunt elaborates on the same day that he himself "went up the Kanyon with 9 men to finish working the road up to the Coal." The day did not turn out as expected, as already noted in chapter 7, because a fierce summer storm hit the hills and rushed down to the settlement, flooding houses and cellars 12 inches deep in some places. Lunt appears to have been temporarily stranded at the work site. His comments on the experience are entirely in character:

> Thanks be to God for such a delightful shower, on this dry and thirsty land. Slept all night up in the Kanyon under some brush, The ground being very whet I did not have a very comfortable night lodging.[42]

Almost-daily cloudbursts continued through much of the summer. On 20 July—Henry Lunt's 28th birthday—"tremendeous storms" in the mountains

> rose the Creek 3 feet all at once, bringing down with a tremendeous rush a great quantity of logs, and rubbish and mud, for about one hour. . . . The two dams that were in the creek for taking the water to the field and Fort were both entirely swept away, and an immence quantity of wood drifted up the mouth of the ditches.[43]

Lunt makes an unusual comment about road-building on Tuesday, 10 August: a "number of the brethren went up the Kanyon to make a Rail road down from the Coal."[44] It is not certain what he meant here, since, obviously, no steel rails existed nor metal wheels to run on them. Almost certainly, they were casting about for alternatives to a conventional road, since repeated storms had played havoc with their work in the canyon. One alternative, unlikely but not impossible, is a puncheon road. Puncheons were large, straight logs hewn on one side only. They could be laid down one after another in a flattened roadbed, resulting in a surface at least somewhat easier to travel over than rocks and mud. Puncheons could certainly qualify as "rails" of a kind, but such roads were very labor-intensive and the road gradient may have been too steep to make the option practical. Nevertheless, it is a possibility worth considering.

In September, Lunt made the last of these road references. On Saturday the 18th, he "went up the Kanyon with bro Harrison and bro. Smith to cut some logs for the Iron works," an entry which might refer to cutting puncheon logs but which probably referred to logs for the iron works outbuildings. On the following Monday, his reference is more specific: "Went up the Kanyon to work a road up the Mountain to sleigh the coal down." If he meant the word literally, it might be further evidence for the use of puncheons, as sleighs or sleds could be pulled more easily over a flat wooden surface than over dirt and rock. His last two entries clearly show that, however the road was built, its creation was no easy task. On Tuesday, 21 September, Lunt "rose early, and laboured very hard at working a road up the mountain." And on the day after, he "Laboured for some 3 hours on working the road up the mountain, then packed 5 bags of coal down the mountain, and drove a load to the Iron works. Felt very much tired and fatiegued in the Evening."[45]

Regional Coal Deposits

The settlers had known about the coal deposits at Coal Creek for almost a year. In May 1851, Peter Shirts and a few others, trying to trace the path of a lump of coal found at The Cottonwoods (the cluster of mature trees still standing north of the Cedar City airport), discovered two veins that had been exposed by a landslide about four miles up the canyon. Apparently, no serious attempts were made to evaluate the deposits until 28 March 1852, Henry Lunt recording on that date eight men examined them.[46] The general locations of the deposits and their related mines are shown on illustration 9-2, based on James Martineau's 1881 map of Coal Creek Canyon mines.

Numerous outcroppings of coal can be seen near Milt's Stage Stop, a local restaurant and well-known landmark approximately five miles up Coal Creek Canyon, just east of the confluence of Coal Creek and Right Hand Canyon. Many of the deposits are visible from State Highway 14, which runs up Coal Creek Canyon. According to Otto Fife, whose father took him to visit the area as a child, the outcroppings mark the location of the first mine worked by the iron missionaries. For ease of discussion here, we have called it Mine No. 1 and marked it as (1) on illustration 9-2.

A coal bed underlies the entire area and it is still easy today to see outcroppings of various depths. In Coal Creek Canyon, the vein is usually

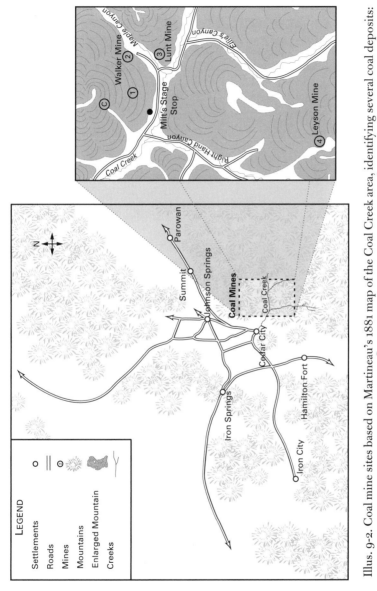

Illus. 9-2. Coal mine sites based on Martineau's 1881 map of the Coal Creek area, identifying several coal deposits: (C) marks the face of a coal vein high on the flank of the mountain; (1) marks the first pioneer coal mine, referred to as "Mine No. 1;" (2) marks the Walker Mine; (3) the Lunt Mine; and (4) the Leyson Mine.

between three and four feet thick, pitching to the southeast. At Milt's Stage Stop, coal is visible on both sides of the canyon, although south deposits (the Right Hand Canyon area) are less visible than those on the north. After the Iron Mission era, all the deposits were worked extensively, but it appears the iron missionaries worked only a few of the sites. As early as 7 February 1852, the *Deseret News* reported that the Coal Creek iron workers

> made their experiments with wood coal [charcoal], because of the difficulty in getting the stone coal, it being situated on a high mountain, or up a deep rocky gorge thereof, some four or six miles, so far as discovered, and that it will cost several thousand dollars to make a good road to it.[47]

Andrew L. Neff, quoting a somewhat later report to the territorial legislature (6 January 1860, by the Committee on Agriculture, Roads and Manufacturing), also pointed out the difficulty of reaching the mine:

> The first coal veins opened in the Territory were on Coal Creek, in the county of Iron, about seven miles from the mouth of the canyon, which was at first considered almost impassable. About fifteen thousand dollars have been expended to make a passable road to the coal. For one mile near the vein, the road is so steep, it requires a good team to haul up a heavy wagon. The vein has been worked several hundred feet, is about four and a half feet thick, and dips slightly to the southeast.[48]

To improve access to the coal, the territorial legislature appropriated $2,000 on 27 December 1852 "for the working of a road to the Coal Beds in Iron County."[49] This may have been an effort to ease the burden of road-building on the weary settlers that summer. Erastus Snow had instructions from Governor Brigham Young to carry out the winter improvements. This authority was delegated to James A. Little and Philip Klingensmith, who immediately began searching for new veins of coal. Two months later a new road had been constructed to the identified sites and coal had been mined and hauled down to the furnace. The total cost of the road amounted to $6,000.[50] On 5 January 1853, the legislature appropriated another $3,000 for more general use, "to advance the Iron interests, in Iron County."[51] The sidebar which follows identifies several of the Coal Creek Canyon landmarks and their comparative distances to the furnace site, suggesting relative lengths of road needed to bring the coal down to the iron works.

Illustration 9-3 shows the "high mountain" north of Milt's Stage Stop, with the coal vein clearly visible at the left of the photograph, marked by the (C). Apparently, the pioneers never worked this face of the

Distances from Coal Creek Landmarks to Furnace Site

Coal Location	Distance to Furnace Site
Mouth of Coal Creek Canyon*	1.0 miles
Right Hand Canyon confluence;	
coal deposit on north side of canyon	5.3 miles
Milt's Stage Stop	5.4 miles
Maple Canyon confluence	6.0 miles

*It is not possible to say what the pioneers considered to be the canyon mouth. The distance given is measured from the widest part of the canyon as it opens up just east of the city park.

vein; however, traces of the old road leading to Mine No. 1, marked by the dotted line ending in (1), can still be seen. The final sections of this road were extremely steep and rough, requiring double-teaming either with ox- or horse-drawn vehicles. Despite its near-inaccessibility, the area shows evidence of extensive mining. Steel rails protruding from the entrance to Mine No. 1 prove it was worked late in the nineteenth century and beyond, when such technology was available. A rock slide has long since covered the mine's entrance but the ends of the rails are still visible, as are other artifacts of early mining activity.

The Maple Canyon Mines

The most intense mining in the Coal Creek drainage area occurred at Maple Canyon. The Maple Canyon stream is the first to enter Coal Creek from the north, about half a mile east of Milt's Stage Stop. Mining here centered in two areas.

The first is on the west bank about half a mile upstream from Maple Canyon Bridge and is known as the Walker Mine, marked by a (2) on illustration 9-2 and shown as just off-camera to the right of illustration 9-3. The Walker Mine is marked by two abandoned tailing dumps, one of which is believed to date from pioneer times. The most easily noticed tailings lie only a few yards north of the entrance to the mine, on the canyon floor. Even after more than 140 years, this tailing dump is quite extensive, although the mine entrance is now obscured. A curious pile of rock work is still partly visible near the upper end of the dump. This tumbled heap may have been part of the August 1853 rock breastwork constructed during the Walker War by Colonel William H. Kimball's military detachment.[52]

Photograph by Morris A. Shirts

Illus. 9-3. Wide-angle view of "high mountain" taken from south of Milt's Stage Stop. The (C) shown here is identical with (C) on illus. 9-2, marking a visible coal vein apparently never worked by the pioneers. The (1) indicates Mine No. 1, at the end of a steep and dangerous wagon road (marked by the dotted line). The (2) indicates the relative position of the Walker Mine, just off-camera here, but shown on illus. 9-2. Aligning the three points confirms, as early descriptions state, that the whole deposit declines slightly southeast.

The second mine in Maple Canyon, marked (3) on illustration 9-2, is identified as the "Lunt Mine" because Henry Lunt's son, Henry Jr., assisted James Martineau with Martineau's 1881 survey and later became involved in mining operations at this site.[53] The mine is located on the east bank of Coal Creek. According to old mining claim books in the Iron County Recorder's Office, Henry Jr. claimed title to this land in 1880, two decades after the demise of the pioneer iron works.[54]

The Lunt Mine is scarcely 200 yards from modern State Highway 14, northeast of Maple Canyon Bridge. Small bits of coke found at the base of the hill in the trees near the bridge prove that coal was coked near the mine. Partially melted brick from the flue can still be found. A wooden loading dock was still visible in 1986. A small section of rock work, like that found at the Walker Mine, was also built at the Lunt Mine.

The Right Hand Canyon Mine

The coal used to fuel furnace runs during 1855–57 apparently came from Right Hand Canyon. The Deseret Iron Company "Journal" (see chapter 13) contains the first and only reference to this location; its wording implies the building of a road to bring the coal down to the blast furnace. The entry for 7 September 1855 records that Watkin Rees, John P. Smith, William Smith, Thomas Thorley, John Adams, John Gerber and

George Wood were credited "for working on road in Right Hand Canyon" from two to eight days.[55]

Notation (4) on illustration 9-2 indicates the location of this Right Hand Canyon Mine, now called the Leyson Mine, claimed by Basset G. Leyson on 9 December 1878.[56] According to Lou Webster, who operated coal mines in the area until the 1970s, the old road to this mine was an ox road probably built by pioneer coal miners. Like the trail to Mine No. 1, the last stage of this road was extremely steep and would have required double-teaming. Webster believed Leyson's to be the first mine in Right Hand Canyon. If this is true, Leyson must have taken over the Deseret Iron Company's workings there after the company failed. Coal was also coked at this mine with the same type of brick flue used at the Lunt Mine.

Henry Lunt frequently expressed concern in his journal over "stone coal," indicating that the pioneers were not satisfied with the coal from the north side of the canyon. The term *stone coal*, interpreted by some to mean anthracite, may be misleading, as anthracite is not found in this area. Eastern iron works used raw anthracite that did not have to be coked. Lunt may have been hoping to find anthracite, but more likely he was hoping for large lumps of bituminous coal, which the pioneers found by driving their tunnels further into the mountain. The experienced coal miners working there would certainly have recognized the difference between anthracite and bituminous coal. Had any of these pioneer mines contained pure anthracite, many iron-making problems would have been solved: anthracite could have been used as blast furnace fuel, thus bypassing the exhausting step of turning coal into coke.

Although the furnace was masonry, outbuildings for the machinery to run it were built of timber. Peter Shirts and French convert Peter Filanque had discovered reserves of timber earlier. An exploratory party led by Philip Klingensmith confirmed the find on 20 May 1852, Lunt recording that "Excellent pine Timber and poles" could easily be reached if a "road could be made in half a day with Ten men."[57]

Progress at the Iron Works, Summer 1852

On Monday, 7 June, Lunt called a meeting in the center of the fort to consider a plan to expedite iron production. Those who preferred iron work would be assigned exclusively to that task and those who liked farming could tend to the fields. Sixteen men chose the iron business, some "digging out a place fore the wheel to blow the blast furnace" and some going "for Timber from the Kanyon."[58] Lunt himself chose iron work, on 9 June "hawling fire clay"; on 10 June, as previously noted, "diging out foundation for the machinery for the Blast furnace"; and on 11 June digging fire clay.[59] The following Monday and Tuesday, he again "laboured on the Iron works." The next day, traveling to Parowan on personal business, he brought back lumber to be used at the works.[60]

Despite Lunt's recommendation for a strict segregation of iron-making and farming, the iron workers had to maintain gardens and some crops or they could not have survived. In the midst of the entries just cited, for instance, Lunt makes note of an intrusive problem. On 11 June, after digging for fire clay, he

> made an Examination of the water ditches in the Evening found them in a very bad condition, no water could be got on the upper side of the field. Thought it wisdom to turn out on the morrow and fix the ditches so that the crops could be watered.

The next day's entry confirms that "All hands worked on the water ditches."[61] Deed books in the Iron County Recorder's office show this constant blending of critical tasks in the many references to city building lots, garden lots and farm acreage in possession of men whose primary task at this time was iron-making. Though farmers did little physical labor at the iron works, they contributed in-kind support. Not infrequently, all able-bodied men had to work in common, most usually on the irrigation system.

At the height of the summer's work on the canyon road, dissension arose at the iron works. On 25 June, furnace mason Richard Varley went up the canyon to bring Lunt back to the Compact Fort because several men had complained about Superintendent Harrison. They requested a meeting with Lunt, Bishop Klingensmith and John Easton to air their concerns. Lunt agreed to see them early the next morning at the blacksmith's shop. There he delivered a lecture on fulfilling one's duty and not finding fault with "another man's work."[62]

How much Richard Harrison knew about furnace design, construction and operation is unknown, although his former profession of iron moulder was apparently the reason Brigham Young appointed him superintendent of the works. Most of the iron men had been through the English apprenticeship system and therefore had quite narrow specialties. Some iron workers may have openly challenged Richard Harrison's instructions on furnace building. Although we do not know the nature of the problem, it was serious enough that both Lunt and Bishop Klingensmith were needed to calm the troubled waters.

In his next journal entry, 27 June, Lunt mentions having written a letter to the *Deseret News,* as did Richard Harrison. Both letters emphasized progress at the iron works. Henry Lunt boasted that the settlement had been busily making firebrick for the furnace, cutting timber for the waterwheel, fashioning iron parts for the machinery and finishing a road to the coal. "The distance from the Iron Works to the coal is supposed to be about 8 miles," he wrote, noting the road builders were within one mile of the much-needed fuel.[63]

Illus. 9-4. John Steele (1821–1904), was J. C. L. Smith's first counselor in the Stake of Zion. Esshom, *Pioneers and Prominent Men,* 74.

Richard Harrison's letter, also written 27 June 1852, went to Brigham Young directly. The waterwheel was almost assembled, he declared. The firebricks were of the best quality clay and would be ready for use shortly. According to Harrison, the road up the canyon extended to within two miles of the coal and discoveries of new coal reserves were expected within the week. Praising the men under his supervision, he claimed:

> The work already accomplished on the iron works has been done by about half the men whose names were recorded as iron men. Those that are with me go at it determinately. Some 6 or 8 or more have been working steadily at the work ever since the field was inclosed, and others have worked as circumstances would alow them. I believe from the spirit of energy and determination manifested by the brethren engaged with me that we shall be able in four or five weeks to give an account of our stewardships satisfactorily according to your wish and desire.[64]

On 1 July, J. C. L. Smith and his first counselor John Steele (see illus. 9-4) met with second counselor Henry Lunt. It is important to note how often the three men visited each other. Even though Parowan was 20 miles away, the iron works was so important that Smith and Steele came to Cedar City eight times from May to November 1852, while Henry Lunt traveled to Parowan 11 times in the same period, both to consult with them and to grind wheat and bring back lumber. Apparently, meetings of the stake presidency, the high council and the combined group that acted as a board of directors for the iron works met on alternating Sundays at Parowan and Cedar City. They also sometimes met on the first Thursday of each month, set aside for fasting and prayer and observed as a day of rest.

On 6 July, Lunt wrote that he labored on the iron works, sawing with a whip saw and digging out the millrace.[65] Usually, a *millrace* was the ditch or canal bringing water to a wheel; a *tailrace* was the ditch carrying water away from it. The waterwheel was placed some ways away from the main streambed of Coal Creek. At this time, it was an undershot wheel, the water flowing beneath it. In the winter of 1852–53, it was replaced by an overshot wheel, the water cresting against and over the top, turning the wheel in the opposite direction from that caused by an undershot flow.[66]

On 8 July, Lunt wrote that "every thing seems to go on more prosperous, since the Iron works have been commenced." The crops were doing well; even the water ditches did not wash out as often. "It shows," he concluded, "that when saints do what they were sent to do the Lord prospers them, and the labour of their hands."[67] On the other hand, Lunt continued to be disturbed by any sign of contention among the iron workers. When further "difficulties" required a second meeting at the blacksmith's shop to talk about unspecified disagreements for two hours on 10 July, Lunt felt compelled to preach in church the next day from the epistles of Paul and James about being united in love and slow to anger.[68] On Monday he traveled to Parowan "to do some business." Since he had a "long council" with the other presidency members, J. C. L. Smith and John Steele, they probably discussed the difficulty of bringing complete harmony to the settlements.[69]

On 23 July, 10 carriages of settlers from Cedar City headed to Parowan to celebrate the fifth anniversary of the Saints' arrival in the Salt Lake Valley, 24 July 1847. A Parowan contingent came from town to escort their neighbors in with a formal procession, first saluting them with three cheers. The visitors responded by hoisting homemade flags bearing the motto "Holiness to the Lord" and the emblems of a beehive and a sheaf of wheat. Arriving at the center of the fort, the procession marched around the Liberty Pole to more cheers and the guests were then assigned hosts for their stay in Parowan. An assembly in the council house concluded with dancing until midnight.[70]

The celebration on 24 July began at 5 A.M. with an artillery salute. The battalion paraded on Artillery Square and everyone joined a procession to the church for oratory and songs, including an original composition by John Steele for the "Iron Mongers" of Iron County. Lunt recorded that John D. Lee "killed a fat sheep for the dinner" and the "rich bounties of the valley filled the table." After dinner the company met again at the church and "dancing Commenced in which the Ladies Participated largely." The festivities concluded with the song "Mountain Standard" and five cheers of "Hosannah to God and the Lamb for ever."[71]

Back at work, Lunt's entries of 27–28 July indicate that labor at the iron works extended beyond furnace construction. Workers also stockpiled materials for the first furnace run. They hauled iron from West Mountain, for instance, some eight to 10 miles to the west. They must have had some doubts, however, about the ore they planned to use. As early as 14 July, Lunt recorded that he, Matthew Carruthers and James Williamson made a trip to the known ore deposits, looked around for better quality, finally loaded up their wagon with what was available and then returned. The iron workers had begun stockpiling coal on 17 July. On the 28th, Lunt mentions a "slide" that may have been a loading chute from which the coal could be loaded onto wagons.[72]

Apparently, concerns raised by iron workers at the end of June had not been resolved. On Sunday, 1 August, J. C. L. Smith, John Steele and Henry Lunt met with the iron workers. That night Lunt wrote: "The brethren were invited to speak as they felt and a good many spoke, and exhibited a spirit of jaring and contention."[73] This is one of few recorded instances when ordinary members were asked to express themselves about iron-making; the fact that negative feelings had been building up and were so promptly expressed probably explains why such forums rarely occurred.

After Smith and Steele returned to Parowan, where Smith would leave on 8 August for a trip to Salt Lake City, Lunt met with some of his council members to consider who should be nominated for political office in the next day's election. Lunt proposed James Easton for Justice of the Peace, William Bateman for Constable, Alexander Keir for Pound Keeper, James Bulloch and Edward Williams as Fence Viewers and Richard Harrison, James Bosnell and George Wood as School Trustees.[74] At the time, territorial elections were held the second week of August, rather than in November. Because no two-party system yet operated, those in authority proposed candidates for civic duties. It would be more than a year before Cedar City would have its first mayor and city government. In the meantime, Henry Lunt was responsible for these jobs, along with his ecclesiastical duties, but received assistance from others in their various official roles.

Iron for Conference: The First Fruits of the Furnace

As the harvest season neared, work on both iron and farming tasks intensified. On 13 August, Lunt hauled five loads of adobe brick to the iron works with a diligent Indian assistant who often came to help.[75] The five loads were probably for the furnace stack, which Lunt

Illus. 9-5. Thomas Cartwright (1814–73), a blacksmith from England, helped prepare the furnace for the first iron run on 9 September 1852. Esshom, *Pioneers and Prominent Men*, 199.

described on 7 July as having a rock foundation. Evidently, the iron workers were dissatisfied with the coal being stockpiled at the furnace site. Although mined at different locations up Coal Creek "Kanyon," the coal itself was all from the same formation and generally of the same quality. Unfortunately, it was not the ideal anthracite they had hoped for.

From mid-August to 8 September, nearly everyone concentrated on the harvest. Presumably, blacksmith Thomas Cartwright continued his labors at the furnace site, a task so important that others harvested his wheat. In September, with general conference as the target date for iron production, the tempo shifted back to iron-making.

With this change in community focus came increasing frustrations. On Wednesday, 8 September, Lunt noted, "It seems with great difficulty that Harrison can get any of the men to work under him[.] Bro Harrison has almost entirely lost the confidence of the Saints[.]"[76] Some were disturbed over an innocent pig-roast party hosted by Peter Shirts at Shirts Creek, which Harrison had attended. This harvest celebration was not well received by those who were not invited. On Sunday, 12 September, Lunt preached yet again on unity, affirming that "5 men united, are better than 50 disunited."[77] On the same day, Elijah Elmer arrived from Salt Lake City with news that James Lewis and Chapman Duncan had been called on missions to China; Robert Owens, at Parowan, also received his call to an unspecified mission overseas.[78]

On 9 September, Lunt went to Parowan to mill wheat and pick up lumber. On Sunday evening, 12 September, frustrated by the ongoing lack of harmony, he rode to Parowan again, seeking counsel from the other members of the stake presidency and high council.[79] He does not identify what he wanted to know but apparently felt satisfied with their response. The news that some much-needed dry goods had been freighted to Salt Lake City by Kinkead & Company, the first big merchandisers in the territory, must have helped raise community spirits a little with the hope that some of the goods would make their way south.

Lunt's journal entries at this time mark a crescendo of efforts to meet the deadline of producing an iron sample, as Brigham Young hoped, in time for general conference. On 25 September, Lunt called a meeting in the school-house and preached "on the subject of us making Iron by Conference." Because the time left was so short, he "made arrangements for working on Sunday." This willingness to labor on the Sabbath indicates both the seriousness of Lunt's commitment and the pressure of the deadline.[80]

On Sunday, 26 September, Lunt was awakened at 2:00 A.M. by Richard Harrison, just in from Parowan, with news that J. C. L. Smith had returned there from Salt Lake City with unsettling orders from Brigham Young. Harrison, the superintendent, and Thomas Bladen, the chief engineer, were summoned to Salt Lake City by Brigham himself. Furthermore, three Apostles—Erastus Snow, John Taylor and Franklin D. Richards—would shortly be coming south with a party of new workers to take over the iron operations. Obviously, leaders in Salt Lake City were concerned that the project had not yet produced iron.

On 29 September 1852, the iron workers began charging the furnace. About noon they "put on the Blast," Lunt's phrase for the process iron technicians describe as "blowing in" the furnace. Although Lunt records no details about the charge, a review of this first furnace run, prefacing the Deseret Iron Company minute book, reports that the fuel was "stone coal coked, and dry pitch pine wood in the raw state."[81] Rhoda Matheson Wood and Belle Armstrong's account of this historic event provides a colorful, if undocumented, description:

> The whole group were excited. During the day the furnace was loaded and at evening time fired. Everyone was assembled around a huge bonfire; a service with prayer invoking God's blessing upon their efforts. Short talks reviewing their struggles, and prophesying their future, if success attended them, accompanied by the creaking and groaning of the heavy wooden water wheel, combined to make this night a time to be long remembered. As dawn began to break Robert Adams carefully arranged a sand box, then took a long rod and knocked out the clay plug, to let a stream of fiery metal pour out. Emotions had to find relief. Shouts of "Hosannah!" broke from tired, sleepy throats.[82]

Descendants of iron missionaries sometimes claim their ancestors produced the first iron made west of the Mississippi. Henry Lunt appears not to have made such a claim, probably because he knew it wasn't true. The blast furnace at Maramec Spring near St. James, Missouri (some 75 miles southwest of St. Louis), had already been in production for almost 25 years and had probably supplied the iron for wagons that carried the Mormons across the plains. Many of the pioneer iron workers passed through St. Louis on their way to departure points for the west; it is thus almost certain that they knew about or at least had heard of Maramec.

Henry Lunt's reaction on 30 September to the Iron Mission's first run was ambivalent. While giving the achievement its due, he had to admit the quality of the pig iron was disappointing:

> Tap[p]ed the furnace about Six oclock A.M. The Metal run out and we all gave three hearty cheers. When the Mettle was cold, on examination it was not found to be so good as might be wished and also of a very peculiar appearance. This was attributed to so much sulpher being in the Stone Coal.[83]

The sense of anticlimax is strong. After almost superhuman efforts for the greater part of a year, they had produced only one bar of mediocre-grade pig iron. That same day, Lunt (always the realist) asked blacksmith Thomas Cartwright to stay and help with operations in Cedar City. Cartwright, however, disregarded Lunt's counsel and left the next day for Salt Lake City to attend October general conference with Richard Harrison, Thomas Bladen, Philip Klingensmith and George Wood. Their departure gave the settlers much to ponder.

Henry Lunt did not record the questions that must have plagued him after this unprecedented but disappointing trial run. The people were, to some extent, still in rags, without shoes and short of food. How could they survive a winter that had already come early to the settlements? Would Brigham Young really understand how hard they had worked or would he scorn their foot-long bar of pig iron? Why had the president not asked Henry Lunt to come north with Harrison and Bladen to report on the status of iron-making? Did Brigham Young hold Lunt personally responsible for the lack of progress? Suddenly, the iron missionaries faced the likelihood of major changes. Their control of the iron works must have seemed in doubt. For the moment, however, they could do little but wait for Apostles Snow and Richards to arrive after conference, bringing the expected message from Brigham Young.

Endnotes

1. Lunt, diary, 14 May 1852.
2. Ibid., 16 May 1852.
3. Ibid., 20 May 1852.
4. "Diary of Richard Harrison, 1838–1867," typescript, 12, in "Diaries of Chamberlain, Cox, Crosby, Harrison, Parry & Snow," Perry Special Collections (hereafter cited as Harrison, diary). Explanatory note reads, "This copy was made

from a copy of the original found in the St. George Public Library. Permission to make this copy for Brigham Young University Library was obtained by Professor M. Wilford Poulson September 1937, thru Mrs. Roxey S. Romney, Librarian, St. George Public Library."

5. Lunt, diary, 21–22 May 1852.

6. Ibid., 3 May 1852.

7. Whittaker, journal, 14 and 19 May 1852.

8. Lunt, diary, 20 May 1852.

9. Ibid., 25 May 1852.

10. Ibid., 26 May 1852.

11. Ibid.

12. Ibid.

13. Ibid.

14. Ibid., 27 May 1852.

15. Ibid., 29 May 1852.

16. Ibid., 23 May 1852.

17. Ibid.

18. Ibid., 24 May 1852.

19. Ibid., 25 May 1852.

20. Ibid., 30–31 May and 3 Jun 1852.

21. Ibid., 29 Jun 1852.

22. Ibid., 5 Aug 1852.

23. Ibid., 7 Aug 1852.

24. Ibid., 3 and 5 Sep 1852.

25. Deseret Iron Company, Minutes, 5.

26. Lunt, diary, 29 Nov 1852.

27. Ibid., 13 Mar 1853.

28. Discussed in greater detail in ch. 12.

29. Lunt, diary, 9 Jun 1853.

30. The typescript contains an editorial note on this date to the effect that vol. 4 of Lunt's diary is missing.

31. Bowering, journal, 16 Aug 1853.

32. Chatterley, "History of Cedar City," 3. The relevant comment is, "He finally went back to Scotland as there was not any position here that would give him a living" (see ch. 13, n. 14).

33. Iron Works Account Book, 1–31.

34. Lunt, diary, 27 May 1852.

35. Ibid., 4 Jun, 10 Jun and 7 Jul 1852.

36. Dame, "Coal Creek Survey," 44, fig. 1B–1, Iron County Recorder's Office.

37. Hunter Grimshaw, interview by Morris Shirts, 6 Sep 1983, notes in Shirts Collection.

38. Lunt, diary, 18 Jun 1852.

39. Ibid., 22 Jun 1852; Whittaker, journal, 22 Jun 1852.

40. Lunt, ibid., 23–26 Jun 1852.

41. Ibid., 7 Jul 1852.

42. Ibid., 16 Jul 1852; Whittaker, journal, 16 Jul 1852.

43. Lunt, ibid., 20 Jul 1852.

44. Ibid., 10 Aug 1852.

45. Ibid., 18, 20–22 Sep 1852.

46. Ibid., 28 Mar 1852.

47. Anonymous notice, "Stone Coal," *Deseret News,* 7 Feb 1852, 3d unnumbered page.

48. Andrew L. Neff, *History of Utah: 1847–1869* (Salt Lake City: Deseret News Press, 1940), 638.

49. "RESOLUTION: In relation to a road to the Coal Beds in Iron County," 27 Dec 1852, in *Acts and Resolutions Passed at the Second Annual Session of the Legislative Assembly of the Territory of Utah* (Great Salt Lake City: 1853), 66, in the Register of the Laws of the State of Utah, 1851–, series no. 83155, reel 1, Utah State Archives and Records Service (hereafter cited as *Territorial Acts and Resolutions*).

50. Crook, "Early Industry and Trade," 58; see Henry Lunt to George A. Smith, 7 Mar 1853, published in *Deseret News,* 3 Apr 1853, 3d unnumbered page.

51. "An Act, Appropriating Money to promote the manufacturing of Iron in Iron County," 5 Jan 1853, in *Territorial Acts and Resolutions,* 13.

52. Journal History, 25 Aug 1853, recording journal entries of William H. Kimball reporting activities of "Southern Expedition No. 1."

53. James H. Martineau, 1881 Survey, General Land Office, Township 36 South, Range 10 West, Bureau of Land Management, Cedar City, Utah.

54. Mining Location Notices, Book A, 43, in Iron County Recorder's Office, Parowan, Utah.

55. Deseret Iron Company, Journal, 6 Sep 1854–5 Jan 1867, 174, in Cedar City DUP collection, on permanent loan to SUU Archives; also see "Daughters of Utah Pioneers No. 1402, Deseret Iron Company Financial Ledgers, 1854–1869" (microfilm collection, SUU Archives).

56. Mining Location Notices, Book A, 42.

57. Lunt, diary, 20 May 1852. Chatterley, in his "History of Cedar City," 1, tells of a prank played at Filanque's expense. He was apparently well known for his short stature and excitable temper. Several boys tied a cow bell high in a tree with a long string attached so they could ring the bell from their beds. Apparently, they did so well that Filanque was convinced a loose cow was wandering about after dark. He

jumped up and rushed out in his "pair of red drawers," muttering "damma da old cow" and running around trying to drive off the animal he supposed was disturbing his rest.

58. Lunt, diary, 7 Jun 1852.

59. Ibid., 9–11 Jun 1852.

60. Ibid., 14–16 Jun 1852.

61. Ibid., 11–12 Jun 1852.

62. Ibid., 25–26 Jun 1852.

63. Ibid., 27 Jun 1852; Lunt to editor, 27 Jun 1852.

64. Richard Harrison to Brigham Young, 27 Jun 1852, in Journal History.

65. Lunt, diary, 6 Jul 1852.

66. Deseret Iron Company, Minutes, 7.

67. Lunt, diary, 8 Jul 1852.

68. Ibid., 10–11 Jul 1852.

69. Ibid., 12 Jul 1852.

70. Ibid., 23 Jul 1852.

71. Ibid., 24 Jul 1852.

72. Ibid., 14, 17, 27 and 28 Jul 1852.

73. Ibid., 1 Aug 1852.

74. Ibid.

75. Ibid., 13 Aug 1852. On the following 23 Oct, Lunt identifies an Indian helper as "Pahap." This may be the "diligent assistant" who worked with him in August.

76. Ibid., 8 Sep 1852.

77. Ibid., 12 Sep 1852.

78. Ibid. Elijah Elmer appears as "Bro. Elmore" in this entry. Lewis, born 12 Jan 1814, was an 1850 iron missionary. Duncan was born 1 Jul 1812 and lived until Dec 1900. Both left for China on 3 Nov 1852; both later went on the Cotton Mission in 1861. Lewis settled in Kanab in 1871 and in 1882 went on the San Juan Mission. See Juanita Brooks, ed., *On the Mormon Frontier: The Diary of Hosea Stout: 1844–1861*, 2 vols. (Salt Lake City: University of Utah Press, 1964), 2:460, n. 17.

79. Lunt, diary, 9 and 12 Sep 1852.

80. Ibid., 25 Sep 1852. As noted in ch. 8, the Iron Works Account Book (Dec 1851–Nov 1852) records that the greatest number of hours were spent on iron work during Jun, Jul and Aug, although the average days per month per man amounted to less than one day each week. Lunt's journal seems to record that "all hands" were involved in Sep tasks but the account book shows a drop in total days for that month. Either the account book is inaccurate or Lunt, focusing exclusively on the project of greatest interest to him, ignored the fact that other workers were engaged in other tasks in the settlement.

81. Ibid., 29 Sep 1852; Deseret Iron Company, Minutes, 1 (in prefatory review of events prior to the company's formation).

82. Rhoda Matheson Wood and Belle Armstrong, "An Abbreviated Sketch of Cedar History" typescript, 8, for Cedar City Centennial, ca. 1951, SUU Archives; see also Dalton, *Iron County Mission*, 118. "Robert Adams" is a misnomer. William R. Palmer, in a series of 1951 radio talks called "Forgotten Chapters of History," refers to a David Adams punching out the clay plug to release the first run of molten iron. But even though David Barclay Adams did become the furnace master, Palmer's reference is also inaccurate. Lunt's diary does not name the person who poured the metal on 30 Sep, but even more convincing, it does record the arrival of the Adams family on 2 Nov 1852, more than a month after this run. David had both a son and grandson named Robert, but neither had yet been born. In another reference, either Wood or Armstrong if not both included "Robert Adams" as one of the signers, on 30 Nov 1852, of the Bill of Sale of the Pioneer Iron Works, but a review of the original document proves that no such name appears among the 31 signers. We believe these references are simple misinterpretations of the historical record and that no adult named "Robert Adams" lived or worked in Cedar City during the fall of 1852.

83. Lunt, diary, 30 Sep 1852.

10

The Deseret Iron Company

April–November 1852

Despite the iron missionaries' concerns about the adequacy of their efforts, the reception at general conference of the first small bar of pig iron was entirely positive. The Eighth General Epistle of the First Presidency, dated 13 October 1852, singled out the achievement for special mention:

> A specimen of pig iron, from the furnace in Iron county, was presented at the October Conference, as good as could be expected for the first; and from this time the founders will be relieved from farming to sustain themselves; and have other assistance which they need to prosecute their business; and soon we expect a good supply of iron ware, of home manufacture.[1]

The First Presidency went on to report the discovery of coal at several sites, predicting that charcoal pits to make use of the new resources would be operating soon.

During this conference, George A. Smith gave the first of two "iron sermons" recorded in the *Millennial Star*, noting that "We are almost a world by ourselves, we are a thousand miles from any other place . . . and whatever is brought here, is imported at a vast expense." He claimed that the local ore deposits could supply the needs of the entire territory, echoing the hope that trained iron workers would be relieved from farming in order to lay the foundation of economic independence. "Iron is the sinew of power," Smith insisted. "Of it your guns and your wagons are made; all the utensils in husbandry are made of iron." If the community would support the iron works, he predicted, eventually fences of iron would be cheaper than fences of wood.[2]

Erastus Snow's brother Zerubbabel, a territorial judge, seconded George A. Smith's remarks, saying that Smith had aptly named it "a Gospel sermon for the salvation of this people"—no civilized nation could ignore the manufacture of iron.[3] Other conference talks reiterated this concern over "home industry" and the need to become self-sufficient. The Eighth General Epistle, for instance, estimated "over 30,000 inhabitants in the Territory,"[4] and Heber C. Kimball, in his remarks, focused on the vital concern of feeding this increased population.[5]

While the small pig iron sample lying on the pulpit was tangible evidence of successful iron production, a stable iron industry would require more manpower. Enough workers seemed to be available. The problem was persuading them to migrate. Orson Hyde addressed himself to this challenge, claiming that Salt Lake Valley was already filled with farms and that wood, water and grass were scarce there. Hyde encouraged his listeners to go south where there was

> plenty of room for the exercise of your energies. In Iron county they are beginning to make iron, and those who live there on the manufacture of the first stove or porridge pot, their names will be had in remembrance. . . . Then don't stay here, but go to the land of clover and grapes . . . where you can get coal for the digging of it.[6]

Heber C. Kimball tried another approach. Many settlers wanted to remain in Salt Lake City to have access to the sealings and blessings of the Endowment House, both for themselves and for their families. Kimball gave such notions short shrift:

> I will tell *you*, that stay here for this purpose, you will not get your blessings as soon as those will who go and settle where they are counselled. For none of you can have these blessings until you prove yourselves worthy, by cultivating the earth, and then rendering to the Lord the first fruits thereof, the first fruits of your cattle, of your sheep, and of all your increase. This is how I understand it. Now go and get farms for yourselves while you can.[7]

An editorial in the 6 November 1852 *Deseret News* emphasized the economic imbalance between Mormon society and the outside world, because the Saints were still forced to buy from "the gentiles" much of what they needed to live on. "We do not blame the traders for coming here," the editorial continued, "nor for selling their goods as high as they can," but the Saints were placing themselves at an economic disadvantage because of their extreme need. It was clear they risked losing their independence unless they could become self-sustaining within a very short time.[8]

Plans in Europe: Creating the Deseret Iron Company

Previous chapters have already touched on the organization that came to be known as the Deseret Iron Company. Its history was tangential there, but now becomes central to the Iron Mission story. Ironically, the farmers and iron workers living in the southern settlements remained essentially unaware, as they anxiously waited to hear how their sample of iron was received at October conference, that a new entity was about to become part of their lives.

The origins of the Deseret Iron Company can be traced to Brigham Young, who knew from the first reports of ore deposits in the south that an infant iron industry would not be able to grow on missionary zeal alone. His goal was always to have a corporate structure ready to be put in place once the intended iron works became stable enough to benefit from a broader financial basis. To that end, he officially announced through the Sixth General Epistle of the Presidency, dated 22 September 1851, a program of capitalization and labor, seeking investors among the European Saints to develop a profit-making iron industry in southern Utah:

> The Valley is well-supplied with a general assortment of merchandize at the present time; but the exportation of cash having been far greater than the importation the past year, it is to be feared that many articles will remain unsold. . . . If a company of brethren could be formed in England, Wales, Sweden, or any other country, to come and make Iron from ore (magnetic ore of the best quality) and machinery for rolling, slitting, and cutting nails, and drawing off wire, it would be one of the greatest auxiliaries for advancement in building up the vallies of the mountains; and the presiding elders in those countries are instructed to examine this subject, and forward such a company with the least possible delay.[9]

The Epistle would have reached the iron missionaries in Parowan some weeks after the fact through either the *Deseret News* or the *Millennial Star,* arriving with regular mail deliveries or passed along to the settlers by occasional visitors. The concept of an investment program, however, developing outside southern Utah and merely awaiting the right time to be imported there and implemented, seems to have been unknown to the iron missionaries almost up until the time it became operational late in 1852.

Tangible outlines of such a program were becoming visible early that spring. Across the Atlantic, Apostle Franklin D. Richards was presiding over the British Conference, while Apostles John Taylor and Lorenzo D.

Young (Brigham's brother) were presiding in Europe. Their fellow Apostle Erastus Snow was mission president in Denmark from 14 June 1850 to 4 March 1852.[10] On his way home, he stopped in England. There, he and Richards began discussing the formal organization of a company to develop and support large-scale iron manufacturing in Utah. Brigham Young's correspondence to both men contains no authorization to proceed. However, providence had placed them in the British Isles, one of the greatest steel-producing regions in the world. On 31 March 1852, Erastus Snow wrote his family from Dublin, Ireland:

> We expect to meet in Conference in London April 6th. Bro. Franklin [D. Richards] and myself for scouring the churches with a view of searching out and combining the energies of the Saints with means to establish works for the manufacture of Iron and Nails, Wire &c. in Utah.[11]

According to the minutes of that conference, held 6–9 April 1852 in London, Snow gave an eloquent discourse on the need for an iron industry in Deseret:

> I was much pleased with the success which attended Elder Taylor's labours in the organizing of companies to manufacture *sugar* and *cloth,* and my prayer is that they may prove successful. . . . But when I compare these with the manufacture of *iron,* I feel that iron is of greater importance. And every year that this matter is delayed, it is thousands of pounds out of our pockets. . . . The Presidency have it in their mind . . . to establish a *furnace,* and form a company to bring the *ore* from the mountains. And the next thing is (to my mind) to have a ROLLING MILL. . . . *Nails* and *wire,* and a great many other things, cannot be made until we have a rolling mill; and the rolling out of sheet iron for many purposes; and the small bars for drawing out wire, and many other uses. Have these things, and the *stoves* and railroad irons, and nail factories, and machinery of various descriptions, and all the rest of those things necessary for the permanent establishment of iron works; and our people will save thousands of pounds.[12]

The conference subsequently resolved: "That a company of monied and faithful men be organized and sent from this land, next season, to the Valley, for the purpose of building furnaces, erecting the machinery, &c., necessary for the smelting and manufacturing of iron."[13] Erastus Snow describes traveling throughout the British Isles for the next few weeks seeking financial support:

> We commenced our operations at the Special General Conference of April 6th, 1852, in London. We here obtained of the Presiding Elders

the addresses of our wealthier brethren in different parts of the empire, and spent most of that month in visiting them, and various iron works in England, Wales, Ireland, and Scotland, obtaining all general information on the subject of making iron from magnetic and other ores, but especially labouring with our brethren who had means, the Lord labouring with us by His Spirit, to show them the importance of the work we had undertaken. We found a general readiness on their part to receive our counsel, and employ their funds as we thought best for the making of iron in these valleys.[14]

Undoubtedly, Snow (see illus. 10-1) and Richards (see illus. 10-2), pleased by the willingness of the British Saints to contribute, felt encouraged to proceed with the formation of a company. On 28–29 April 1852, nine men met in Liverpool to organize the Deseret Iron Company: Erastus Snow (chair), Franklin D. Richards (secretary), Samuel W. Richards (brother of Franklin D.), Levi Richards (brother of Dr. Willard Richards), Joseph W. Young (nephew of Brigham Young, called to serve a mission in England at the same time as Franklin D. Richards), Vincent Shurtleff (a missionary from Massachusetts, about to return home), John Weston (overseer of an iron works) and Thomas Jones and Thomas Tennant (representatives of the wealthy English Saints who intended to donate money).

The minutes of the organizational meeting, kept by Franklin D. Richards, explain that the men intended to address the vital interests of the Latter-day Saints from both a business and a spiritual perspective. Richards quoted from the Sixth

Courtesy LDS Church Archives

Illus. 10-1. Erastus Snow (1818–88), member of the Quorum of the Twelve Apostles. While on a mission in Europe, Snow recruited British Saints with iron-making experience to emigrate to Utah and join the Iron Mission.

Courtesy LDS Church Archives

Illus 10-2. Franklin D. Richards (1821–99), member of the Quorum of the Twelve Apostles. He served as president of the British Mission, where he recruited wealthy British Saints to invest in the Deseret Iron Company.

General Epistle of the First Presidency that had called for a "company of brethren" to finance the iron works established in the southern settlements and invited his fellow mission leaders and associates in Europe to organize this company as soon as possible. Richards then asked how much stock individuals were willing to buy and received three responses: Thomas Tennant pledged £2,000 (equivalent to $9,680 in U.S. currency of the time) by 1 January 1853, Thomas Jones pledged £500 by the same date and Christopher Arthur sent a letter promising the same amount by the first of the year.[15] Thomas Tennant, who was investing one-fifth of his personal assets in the company, was designated treasurer.

Plans Take Shape: Incorporating the Deseret Iron Company

Erastus Snow, Franklin D. Richards and Levi Richards were appointed to draw up the deed of agreement for the new company. These Articles of Incorporation designated the original shareholders as a board of directors with each member entitled to one vote for each share owned. A president, secretary and treasurer were to be chosen from the board. No one could withdraw stock without consent of three-quarters of the members and interest was charged on unpaid stock. The first annual meeting was scheduled for the third Monday in September 1853 in Utah Territory, although it was not held until November of that year.[16]

On Friday morning, 29 April, all nine members of the original group met to consider the articles that had been drafted (see app. 7). That afternoon they voted unanimously to admit only baptized members into the company until it was successfully established in Utah. The articles, serving as a constitution for the Deseret Iron Company, were unanimously adopted and signed by five members who subscribed for eight shares: Thomas Tennant received four shares for his pledge of £2,000 and Thomas Jones and John Weston received one share apiece for their individual pledges of £500. Franklin D. Richards and Erastus Snow received one share each as payment for their services in organizing and directing the company.[17]

The original draft included 17 articles. A week after it was adopted, Snow and Richards wrote a letter to the board of directors suggesting an additional article that would underscore the spiritual nature of the whole venture:

> Article 18th. Forasmuch as we invoke the blessings of our Heavenly father upon our capital & business, therefore resolved that each member of the Deseret Iron Company shall hallow his stock vested in

> the company unto the Lord by paying tithes thereon and that the company regularly tithe there increase ever after.[18]

Shareholder investments listed at the end of the articles show that the company incorporated with £4,000 sterling. This sum, however, appears to include the credit of £1,000, in the form of one share each, to Snow and Richards. The next to officially join the enterprise were Elias Jones and John Jones (investing £500 each) and Christopher Arthur, who made good by letter his previous offer of £500.[19] Arthur's stock certificate has been preserved (see illus. 10-3). Apparently Elias Jones, John Jones and Christopher Arthur were considered original shareholders, because their names were added to the Articles of Incorporation as they appear in the Deseret Iron Company minutes.[20] John Weston's name, although listed on the first copy of the articles, does not appear in this later version. The shareholders in general later voted to admit John Weston as a member of the company, even though he was unprepared to pay the full amount of his pledge by 1 January 1853.[21]

Taking these adjustments into consideration, the total pledged investments of the "wealthier brethren" seem to have been 11 shares (eight as indicated in the Articles plus the three purchased by Jones, Jones and Arthur), capitalizing the company at £5,500 ($26,620) due on 1 January 1853. Subtracting £1,000 for the two shares credited to Snow

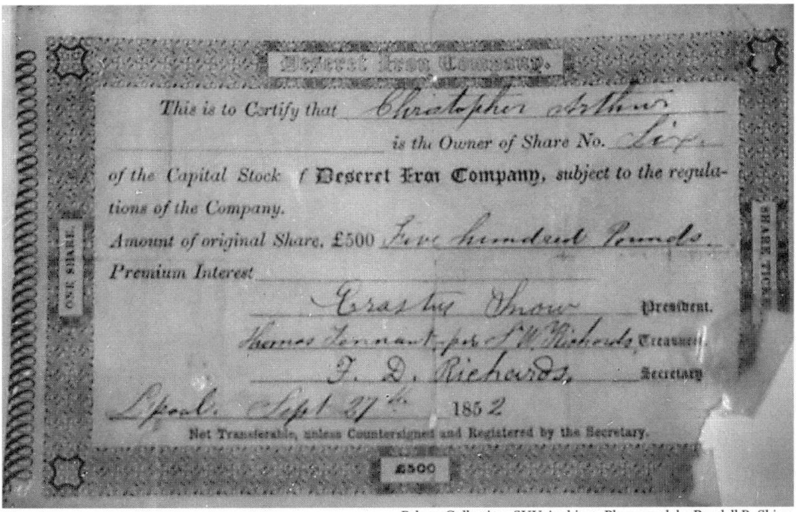
This is to Certify that Christopher Arthur
is the Owner of Share No. Six
of the Capital Stock of Deseret Iron Company, subject to the regulations of the Company.
Amount of original Share, £500 Five hundred Pounds.
Premium Interest
Erastus Snow President.
Thomas Tennant per S W Richards Treasurer.
F. D. Richards Secretary
Lpool. Sept 27th 1852
Not Transferable, unless Countersigned and Registered by the Secretary.
£500
ONE SHARE.
SHARE TICKET

Palmer Collection, SUU Archives. Photograph by Randall B. Shirts

Illus. 10-3. Deseret Iron Company stock certificate issued to Christopher Arthur in Liverpool, England, on 27 Sep 1852. This is the only certificate of its kind known to have survived.

and Richards leaves £4,500 ($21,780) as a more practical figure for the company's initial assets. Even this was an impressive sum for those times.

At least two of the original stockholders, Christopher Arthur and Thomas Tennant, emigrated to the United States. Arthur settled in Cedar City where he served as head clerk of the Deseret Iron Company. His son and namesake eventually became mayor of Cedar City. Tennant was not so fortunate. He came with his wife and a minor son but died near St. Louis on 4 October 1856. His estate was placed in the hands of Daniel Spencer, whom the Tennants had known while Spencer was on a mission in England. Upon probate, Tennant's bills were paid, including his pledge for a Deseret Iron Company share.[22]

Others also wanted to emigrate but could not liquidate their assets. Charles Jordan of Liverpool was invited to come to Cedar City and design machinery for the iron works but was forced to remain in England when Tennant was unable to borrow money for Jordan's passage. Jordan promised to send drawings that anyone could work from and suggested two millwrights, James Jones (formerly of Abordave in Glamorganshire) and Samuel Leigh (a native of Glamorganshire), who could, at least, make the wheel pit if not build the furnace. His letters indicate the detail with which men on the other side of the Atlantic were envisioning the project in Cedar City. An undated letter from Jordan, written from 15 Wilton St., Liverpool, concluded:

> I should like to know what head of water you can get as that would determine the Diam—of the wheel, if practicable, I wd advise a 15 foot wheel 5 feet wide but if a less diam—! it must be wider in proportion, that will work two Cylinders 3 feet diam and to work 5 feet stroke which wd be sufficient size to Blow one furnace and a remelting cupola[. T]his machine I have calculated to blow a high pillar of blast which would be required if you use anthracite coal[;] if bituminous coal it will be equally as suitable[. S]hould you commence with the furnace at once you should select a place convenient to the mine & coal & also a convenient place for tipping the cinders from the furnace as there will be a great quantity of it.[23]

On 27 April 1852 he wrote again, with the good news that

> According to promise I forward you the Diagram of a Blowing Machine. Having been from home since you were here am sorry I have not had time to draw it to a working scale, but it will be sufficient to show you what is necessary to blow one Furnace & a remelting Cupola.—the air chest I would propose to be made of wrought Iron on account of its being considerably light[er] than cast Iron.[24]

His diagram was attached to the letter. Drawn very neatly on light orange graph paper, it seems to be the work of an accomplished draftsman (see illus. 10-4).

Having organized an English company to invest in iron production in America, Snow and Richards now needed to take the Articles of Incorporation to Brigham Young for approval. Before they could depart, however, they had to appoint a purchasing agent for the new company who could take care of business in England and in America. They selected Vincent Shurtleff, the Massachusetts man who, with his wife, had initially gone west with the Daniel Spencer Company in 1847. Called on a mission to England in 1851, he was, by the spring of 1852, about to return home.[25] On 1 May, two days after Snow and Richards organized

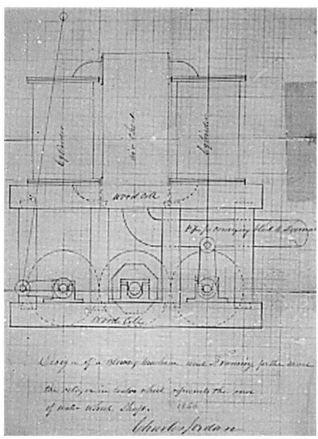

Illus. 10-4. Draftsman Charles Jordan's 1852 design for a blowing machine and frame intended for the Deseret Iron Company.

the company in Liverpool, they appointed Shurtleff and gave him a letter of authorization to purchase equipment and to collect payments on shares:

> Elder Vincent Shirtliff is hereby appointed our agent in behalf of the "Deseret Iron Company" to act under our instructions in Great Brittain or elsewhere in procuring such machinery or other articles or he may find expedient to order, or employ such workmen for the use of the company . . . and the emigration of its operatives who may be wanted, to Utah Teritory. In selecting men or machinery he will avail himself of experienced counsellors and particularly Elder John Western of Dudly Port.

> He will also visit soon as convenient Brother B. T. Clark[,] Histon Road near Cambridge[,] as well as Brothers Thomas, Jones, Arthur and others, to acquaint them with the proceedings of the company, obtain their signature to articles of Compact of Constitution, and receive their first installment on shares and deliver share tickets to those who can pay them in full.

> He will immediately deposit all funds which he may receive with the Companys treasurer; and return share tickets or treasurers receipts to those who may be entitled to them. Receipts may be signed by Thomas Tennant, treasurer or L. W. Richards assistant Tr. He will keep a faithfull account of all Receipts & expenditures that he may show himself approved as a faithful & wise Steward and he shall in nowise loose his reward.

> [F]rom the knowledge we have of Elder Shirtleff as a business man and a faithfull servant of God we warmly commend him to the confidence of all whom it may concern.[26]

There are no records that Vincent Shurtleff ever purchased a "blowing machine" in Liverpool or any other equipment in England. No doubt Snow and Richards intended, once in Utah, to construct Charles Jordan's machine from his blueprints.

Even though the share subscriptions which had been pledged were not due until 1 January 1853, some investors appear to have paid early. The stock certificate of Christopher Arthur, for instance, was dated 27 September 1852 in Liverpool, well before the deadline (and, coincidentally, three days before the first iron was made at Cedar City).

Plans in Salt Lake City: Preparing to Take the Deseret Iron Company South

By 8 May, Snow and Richards had left Great Britain. When they reached Salt Lake City the following August, they reported to Brigham Young on membership growth in Europe as well as on the newly formed Deseret Iron Company. The same August, on the 8th or 9th, J. C. L. Smith went to Salt Lake City from Parowan but spent little time there. He also met with Brigham Young (perhaps Snow and Richards were in attendance) but was speedily sent back with instructions.

Smith arrived in Parowan on Saturday, 25 September, and found iron works Superintendent Richard Harrison there. He had come to pick up a load of lumber but, possibly on Smith's orders, did not stay the night. He left for Cedar City immediately, arriving at 2:00 in the morning. We have already noted in chapter 9 how Harrison woke Lunt to tell him that Brigham Young wanted Harrison himself and furnace master Thomas Bladen to come to Salt Lake City directly. The more disquieting news was that Apostles Erastus Snow and Franklin D. Richards were scheduled to arrive in southern Utah right after October conference,[27] the implication being that they were bringing a new iron company organization with them. By that Friday, 1 October, Harrison and Bladen, accompanied by Bishop Klingensmith and Brothers Cartwright and Wood, were on their way north.

Franklin D. Richards, still in Salt Lake City, spoke in conference on 6 October. Although brief, his remarks were specific and probably constitute the unveiling of plans for a profit-making company in Iron County, a first step in realizing the goals expressed in the Sixth General Epistle. Elder Richards pronounced such a company not only necessary for the survival of the community but also a "most profitable source of investment." Further, he announced plans to go with Erastus Snow to Iron County, personally leading a train of supplies, "to unite with our brethren there" and insure the stability of investments.[28]

At this time, George A. Smith's thoughts were also turning to southern Utah. Having presided over Utah County almost since leaving Cedar City on 6 November 1851 (immediately after its initial survey and naming), Smith now had a new commission from Brigham Young, which he reports in his journal entry of 13 October 1852. Anticipating an influx of settlers, the prophet wanted George A.'s experienced eyes and ears down south, at least for the time being. He arrived in Parowan on Saturday, 23 October, the same day J. C. L. Smith, Wood, Bladen, Harrison and Cartwright returned from their hastily arranged trip to Salt Lake City.[29] The latter three spoke the next day during Sunday services, reporting on their trip to the settlers.

Plans in Cedar City: The Parowan Iron Company

Without waiting for Apostles Snow and Richards to arrive and impose on the iron works an outside organization, several of the settlers tried to create an indigenous version of their own, to be called the Parowan Iron Company. Its point of origin may have been 14 November, following Sunday services in Cedar City, at which George A. Smith preached three "most excellent" sermons. Afterward, Lunt noted, George A. requested the brethren to remain, so that they could hold a council meeting:

> Bro Smith said he wanted for to hear them express their feelings, they did so, and manifested a great disunion amongst them. Thought they had suffered very much, because some of them had to go barefoot, and others were short of good shirts[.][30]

It is difficult to tell from Lunt's wording whether the frustration expressed at the meeting was coming from overwork in a taxing environment, which intensified the sense of hardship, or from a simmering case of indignation vaguely directed toward leadership in Salt Lake City but keenly felt in the settlements as a lack of respect for the efforts made to date. In any event, the men were vocal, anxious, uncertain and divided. But two days later, James James, the chemist, had an idea he wanted to share. He showed Lunt a piece of iron that he

> had made from the ore. Talked to me about commencing a new Iron Company said he believed he could make Iron in a Pudling Furnace, and that if I was willing to join with him and a few more brethren who would be invited that we could make considerable Iron this winter. He said he had no faith to join the organized Company, and would prefer commencing a new company. I told him I would go up to Parowan in the morning and lay the matter before George A Smith.[31]

In the morning, 17 November, Lunt and James, accompanied by John Griffiths, went to Parowan, where Lunt "sat in council," apparently alone with George A. Smith, explaining the concept James had proposed. George A. received it with enthusiasm and asked Lunt to get James, J. C. L. Smith and John Steele. The five men then "counseled together," Lunt recording that "Bro G. A. Smith seemed to be full of the Spirit of God and it burned in my bones." Apostle Smith said he wished Lunt to preside over the company and "spoke a great deal on the subject." In the midst of this, Richard Varley and two others ("Benson & Davies") interrupted the meeting and "insu[l]ted Bro George A Smith and caused bro Smith's Soul to be grieved." Lunt does not record why the men were angry or how the situation ended but he does note that Smith reproved Varley and that Varley did not accept the chastisement.[32]

On the morning of the 18th, Lunt again talked with George A. Smith and then, by 11 A.M., headed off with Priddy Meeks, Samuel West, James James and William H. Dame on an "exploring expedition in search of Iron Ore." A ride up Little Creek Canyon, just north of Paragonah, proved successful and the next morning, while Lunt and George A. continued in council together, James James and John Steele constructed a "small air Furnace" to try the good ore they had found the day before. George A. Smith felt a larger burden would be worth the effort and sent Lunt up the canyon again. By half past six he was back with about 60 pounds, which was tried that very night, producing a little iron.[33]

It is important to note that these men were trying a new technology— an "air" furnace (which James called a "puddling" furnace) rather than the standard "blast" furnace. A blast furnace reduces large amounts of raw iron ore to melted iron by physical and chemical means inside the furnace. Heat is applied directly to the ore via the fuel mixed in with the ore, a blast of air helping intensify the burning of the fuel. Carbon monoxide (generated within the furnace by incomplete combustion of the fuel) combines with the oxides of iron, creating enough heat to separate out the pure metal.

In contrast, the air furnace is seldom used to reduce raw iron ore (although this is what James James was attempting to accomplish with hematite ore from Little Creek Canyon). Air furnaces, also called reverberator furnaces, reheat pig or scrap iron to make it malleable enough to be worked into various shapes. In the air furnace, pig iron or scrap metal is melted without direct contact with flame. Such a furnace requires a blast of air, as does the blast furnace, but direct contact between fire and iron has to be avoided. In air furnaces, the firebox is usually found beside the hearth, or crucible, into which the iron is placed and the heat generated in the firebox is blown across the iron. In contrast, a blast furnace fire is directly below the burden of iron.

On 19 November, while James James waited to see the outcome of his air furnace's initial trial, John Steele drafted a constitution for the Parowan Iron Company, recording it in his journal as follows:

> November 19th 1852. We the undersigned subscribers agree to form ourselves into a company for the manufacturing of iron, to be called the Parowan Iron Company, and to have a president, secretary and treasurer, and we severally agree to pay the sums annexed to our names in shares of $100 each to be appropriated in the erection of iron works.

And we further agree that we will not dispose of our intrust in the company without the consent of the same and we also agree to pay one-tenth of the increase of the company into the tithing office of the Church of Jesus Christ of Latter-Day Saints previous to a dividend being made and that we will be governed by the councils of the Church of Jesus Christ of Latter-Day Saints.[34]

The very next day, 20 November, Erastus Snow and Franklin D. Richards arrived in Parowan. Richards found George A. Smith about to leave for Salt Lake City but persuaded him to postpone his departure. The two stayed up past midnight discussing the prospects of the iron works. Franklin D.'s journal entries indicate a keen interest in the "experimental" Parowan Iron Company:

> Sat 20 . . . Br. James James has pretty conclusively shown that the Iron can be got out in an air Furnace [i.e., a puddling furnace], & the incoherence of the present Iron Co. at Coal Creek has led him to organize a Co. here for the purpose of experimenting on the air plan this Co. of 12 or 15 persons of $100.00 shares each. . . .

> Sunday, 21st . . . accompanied Br. George A. to Paragoonah then went with Br. Erastus to the Mt. in little Creek Kenyon & saw the Ore of that place returned & spoke after Br. Erastus to the house full of hearers. After meeting arranged to set the experimental Co agoing next A.M. conversed with Br. J. C. L. Smith Prest of the stake till 1 o.c.[35]

Richards also kept abreast of the activities in Cedar City, despite a heavy snow storm that delayed by four days his visit to the foundry there. He recorded hearing "that in examining the Furnace at Coal Creek the brethren found 4 or 5 crops of good Pig metal in the bottom of it—Hurrah for Iron."[36] This final comment may be a more positive version of the situation as recorded in the Deseret Iron Company minutes. J. C. L. Smith, Harrison and Bladen had returned from their Salt Lake City trip on 23 October 1852, about a month after the initial furnace run. As soon as he could, Bladen checked the furnace and found, as the minutes state,

> a lump of iron [weighing] some 400 lbs. which was very hard and tough. A recommencment of the works would have been made, but the company were informed that Erastus Snow and Franklin D. Richards were on the way here with another company of brethren from England, for to join this company, consequently it was deemed wisdom for to stop until they came and another organization was formed.[37]

Unfortunately, Lunt does not comment on Bladen's discovery of additional iron in the blast furnace at Cedar City. Likewise, Richards reports nothing further, as these are his last journal entries until 8 July 1853. His observations in November 1852, however, show that the Parowan Iron Company was not a conspiracy to undercut the mining plan organized in England and Salt Lake City. Rather it was a local project discussed openly in official circles, one about which Snow and Richards were fully informed. When the Deseret Iron Company was presented to the iron workers, the Parowan Iron Company was one of the logical alternatives.

In Cedar City, on Sunday, 21 November 1852, Henry Lunt preached at length on faith and obedience and "alluded considerable to the manufacture of Iron."[38] The visiting James James apparently convinced him to help the Parowan Iron Company secure iron ore for trial in the air furnace. James A. Little and Zadok Judd arrived on Tuesday, 23 November, to get a variety of ore samples from West Mountain. Lunt, who wished to show Little the deposits, had no horse. Joseph Walker refused to lend him one, apparently out of loyalty to the existing pioneer iron works on Coal Creek. Lunt reports Walker saying, "if you want work, we can find you plenty in our own Company." Lunt borrowed a horse elsewhere. On Wednesday the 24th, Little and Judd returned to Parowan, while Erastus Snow and Franklin D. Richards arrived in Cedar City the same day, just in time for supper.[39]

Initially, their arrival did not dishearten the Parowan Iron Company supporters. Not only had the group proved that hematite found in Little Creek Canyon could be smelted in a puddling furnace, they had also obtained magnetite from West Mountain. And there were ore samples from a separate deposit Peter Shirts had called to their attention on 1 November.[40] Although Lunt and Joel H. Johnson were preaching unity among the iron workers and diligence in following counsel, it is quite clear the organizers of the Parowan Iron Company hoped to be taken seriously not only by Snow and Richards but also by the uncommitted among their fellow iron workers, who must have wondered which company offered the best hope for a stable and profitable future.

The first trial run by James and Steele with the "small air furnace" in Parowan suggested it might be possible to simplify the iron-making process required by blast furnace technology. The remaining questions were whether the air furnace could function on a large scale and whether it would work with magnetite ore from West Mountain. Apparently the Cedar City iron men who preferred blast furnace technology believed that only a few more experiments would be needed to solve their technical problems and allow the iron workers to make full use of the region's ample magnetite ore. On the other hand, the Parowan group had shown that an air furnace, less expensive to construct and much easier to operate than a blast furnace, might prove equally efficient.

The inexorable steps that led to unity between settlers and visitors are only hinted at by Lunt but they can be traced with the help of Deseret Iron Company records. On the evening that Snow and Richards arrived in Cedar City, 24 November, a meeting was held in the schoolhouse. Lunt says only that much but it would surely be logical to assume that Snow and Richards were at the meeting and that the topic of the (subtly) competing companies was foremost. Evidently the Parowan Iron Company supporters—at least Lunt and James—were not yet ready to accept the Deseret Iron Company. They were still gathering ore samples from deposits in the area, including West Mountain and the lode Peter Shirts discovered, presumably to try the ore in an air furnace again before making a final decision. Snow and Richards, however, did not intend to wait for the outcome. The morning after their arrival, they took a ride with Lunt around the iron works and the city plat, probably evaluating water, land, fuel and ore, as well as the furnace and other structures belonging to the pioneer iron works. Afterward, Lunt hosted the Apostles at dinner in the home of his in-laws, the Whittakers. Both Snow and Richards spoke at a second general meeting that afternoon.[41]

Lunt's entry for the 26th, while saying nothing directly, implies a fundamental shift in direction. He notes being with "Bro Snow and Richards most of the day. Spent the day in makeing out the accounts of the men in the Iron works. James Whittaker assisted me most of the time."[42] As well as showing that the two Apostles were ready to assert their authority (however benignly) to initiate a review of the iron accounts, the entry reveals their—and Lunt's—awareness of the major problem attending any change to a profit-making venture: the relationship of workers to company.

From the beginning, the men had never worked for wages, despite the running summary of hours kept on the project, always considering it a *mission*. If the nature of the iron works was now moving to a *commercial* footing, what financial arrangements would be made on behalf of the men? Lunt spent the next two days with his father-in-law, James Whittaker, accounting in detail for the iron works' financial status.[43] By the evening of the second day, Saturday, 27 November, the two men had some figures to present to the iron workers. This meeting, which probably involved going over each worker's individual time sheet, lasted until 2:00 A.M.[44]

On Sunday morning, Snow "preached a most splended sermon." At 4 P.M. that afternoon, the brethren met again, this time to discuss iron business, during which many more questions were raised. Lunt records that the meeting went "very late." The next day, 29 November, Matthew Carruthers was called in to help audit the books, perhaps because Lunt was not feeling well. Even so, another meeting convened that night, lasting until 3:00 A.M.[45]

Uniting the Plans: The Deseret Iron Company Takes Over

By this time, the pioneers had apparently decided to sell the iron works to Snow and Richards on whatever terms they offered. The settlement's iron workers were all invited to become stockholders in the new company and each was to be paid wages. This appeal to a general sharing of potential profits may have been the deciding factor, as the Parowan Iron Company seems to have been conceived to benefit only the few invited to join as stockholders.

Lunt apparently yielded with good grace. On 30 November the bill of sale was signed. Erastus Snow appointed J. C. L. Smith to be general superintendent of the Deseret Iron Company, Henry Lunt as clerk, Thomas Bladen as engineer, David Barclay Adams as furnace master and Richard Harrison (superintendent of the former pioneer iron works) as superintendent of the moulding department. Basically, J. C. L. would be in charge, with Henry Lunt as his "right hand man."[46] As president of the Stake of Zion since May 1852, J. C. L. had been generally responsible for the pioneer iron works. The new Deseret Iron Company organization put him both more formally and more practically in charge.

Apparently, part of the orderly transfer of assets was an accounting of the hours each man had spent on iron production. The individual ledger sheets comprising the greater part of the Iron Works Account Book (introduced in chapter 8) are summarized at its end. This summary shows the total credits or wages owed to 53 workers as $4,171.38½. The individual balances from the summary are given in the sidebar below.

To the end of the original bill of sale, 31 men appended their signatures. Each of these men appears in the Iron Works Account Book. Against most of their signatures on the bill of sale is a penciled amount of reimbursement. A quick glance suffices to show that these reimbursements are consistently less than the amount the same worker is credited with on his ledger sheet. In the sidebar listing this information, the bill of sale reimbursements are bracketed after the ledger credits from the account book. Note that the reimbursements set against the names of those who signed the bill total only $2,211.35. This is lower than the figure of $2,865.64 stated in the bill itself. The discrepancy may or may not be accounted for by the missing reimbursement notations for several of the 31 signers.

Since only 31 men did sign, 22 of the men who appear in the account book did not. The reason for this is unclear. Some were farmers, some were from Parowan and some were iron workers—in other words, they spanned the variations within the community. Thus, no special position or place of residence seems to be a cause of their not signing the bill.

As Henry Lunt, James Whittaker and Matthew Carruthers brought the account book up to date, they also made a detailed inventory of the company's property. The list itself has not been discovered but the original bill of sale specifies some of this property:

SETTLING ACCOUNTS:
WORKER CREDITS IN THE IRON WORKS ACCOUNT BOOK
WITH BRACKETED REIMBURSEMENTS AS NOTED ON THE BILL OF SALE

Richard Harrison	183.11 ½	[67.00; 122.07]
Thomas Bladen	248.04 ½	[165.36]
James Bosnell	141.09	
Joseph Chatterley	319.88 ½	[213.25]
Joseph Walker	250.79	[167.19]
Thomas Cartwright	151.40	[6.00; 100.00]
George Wood	156.29 ½	[104.19]
William Slack	86.06 ½	[54.70]
Philip K. Smith	83.24 ½	[55.49]
Benj. R. Hulse	184.99	[123.32]
Henry Lunt	188.00	[73.76; 125.33]
John Easton	117.95	
Rob. Easton	57.52	*[—]
James Easton	131.22 ½	*[—]
Alexander Keir	155.14	[103.42]
James Williamson	160.71	[107.14]
William Bateman	36.85	[24.56]
James Bulloch	110.64 ½	*[—]
Joseph Clews	75.12 ½	[50.08]
Jonathan Pugmire	68.70	[45.80]

David Stoddart	144.59	[96.39]
Richard Varley	108.62 ½	[72.41]
Samuel Kershaw	147.59 ½	[98.39]
William Hunter	124.04	[82.69]
Matthew Carruthers	5.99 ½	[3.96]
William Stones	5.34	[43.52]
Matthew Easton	40.19 ½	[26.79]
John White	69.84	[46.56]
John Greaves	39.54½	
James Whitaker	41.05 ½	
Joel H. Johnson	41.10	
Robert Henry	8.11 ½	[5.40]
Peter Shirts	78	
Alexander Easton	14.14 ½	
Thomas Machin	18.00	[12.00]
Edward Williams	9.34	**[6.21]
William Wood	4.54	**[3.02]
Charles Smith	8.00	
William Adshead	8.10	[5.35]
Joseph Bateman	22.00	
David Barclay Adams	10.50	
Arthur Parks	2.00	
Merius Ensign	45.36 (lumber)	
John D. Lee	91.09 "	
John L. Smith	31.36 "	
Richard Benson	65.90 "	
Miles Anderson	18.75 "	
George Braffit	31.71 "	
John Topham	15.00 "	
Orson Adams	23.61 "	
James Lemon	6.69 "	
Edward Dalton	6.30 "	
James H. Dunton	8.88 "	
	$4,171.38 ½	$2,211.35

* These names have no amounts accompanying them.

** These two entries are noted as having been signed by Thomas Rowland.

Sources: Iron Works Account Book (see chapter 8, n. 26) and Deseret Iron Company Bill of Sale (see n. 47). Original spelling retained.

We the undersigned proprietors and owners of the Iron Works now erected on Coal Creek in Iron County Territory of Utah for and in consideration of the sum of twenty eight hundred & sixty-five dollars & sixty four cents to us in hand Paid or accredited to us as stock in the Deseret Iron Company the receipt whereof is hereby acknowledged to by these presents bargain, sell & convey unto Erastus Snow & Franklin D. Richards Agents for the Deseret Iron Company all our rights titles and interests in the Furnace, Blowing machine, Smith's Shop, mill sites & now situated on Coal Creek also our rights titles and interests in the Coal mines which have been discovered or worked by either or any of us which are situated in Coal Creek Kanyon and also all buildings Lumber, Tools or property of any kind thereunto belonging or in any wise appertaining and we do also hereby agree to warrant and defend the said Deseret Iron Company & Erastus Snow & Franklin D. Richards their Agents from any and all claims which may be made against them for said property by any and all persons whomsoever[.]

Witness our signatures this thirtieth day of November eighteen hundred and fifty two.[47]

All who had labored on the original iron works were invited to purchase stock in the Deseret Iron Company. Some listed in the account book bought shares; some who signed the bill of sale did so as well. The two sets of names overlap but they are not identical. Some of the men may have applied their work credits toward stock in the company. Those who did pledge to buy stock and had their names entered on the company books understood that they would be charged interest on the unpaid balance of their pledges at five percent until 1 January 1853 and at 10 percent after that date, as provided for in the constitution.

According to the Deseret Iron Company minutes, the Iron County men who both signed the bill of sale and pledged to purchase stock, becoming shareholders in the new company, included Henry Lunt, Richard Harrison, Thomas Cartwright, George Wood, Jonathan Pugmire, Benjamin R. Hulse, William Stones, Matthew Carruthers, Joseph Walker, Joseph Chatterley, Joseph Clews, David Stoddard and Samuel Kershaw. The two men who did not sign the bill of sale but did purchase stock were David Barclay Adams and Alexander Easton. All shareholders purchased a quarter share for $605 except George Wood and Joseph Chatterley, both of whom purchased a half share for $1,210. Thus, only 13 of the 31 who signed the bill of sale also purchased stock.[48] No reasons for this low percentage are identified in contemporary documents. Perhaps those who did not purchase stock were unprepared to accept a debt of up to 10 percent interest. Or perhaps they were merely not supportive of the new iron company.

In any event, the Deseret Iron Company was established in southern Utah with a total of $32,065 in pledged stock. The greater proportion of this came from the nine shares equaling $21,780 pledged by the comparatively wealthy English Saints. The remainder of the total, or $10,285, was the amount pledged by the poverty-stricken workers of Iron County. (It is important to remember, here, that the shares given to Snow and Richards for their organizational efforts were *credits* and are thus not being included here in the company's total assets.) Other investors would participate later, including the territorial legislature and Brigham Young himself (as Trustee-in-Trust for the LDS Church). It is impossible to say how many of these pledges were subscribed to in cash but apparently there was sufficient money to meet immediate expenses when Snow and Richards left for Salt Lake City on 2 December, depositing $1,400 in cash with J. C. L. Smith. Since the iron men were "paid" only by credits at the company store, they must have hoped the $1,400 would be disbursed as hard-currency wages. A month later, Lunt recorded that he "counseled the brethren to put in their means to forward the Iron works—instead of drawing cash, as there is not much cash on hand."[49] It is debatable whether any cash was ever paid out to the workers. Certainly, some resented the $1,400 being entrusted not to them but to the stake president and new superintendent, J. C. L. Smith, who lived in Parowan and had no background in iron manufacture. On 1 March 1853, J. C. L. arrived from Parowan with worse news—the cash was all gone.[50] According to one account, the $1,400 went toward the construction of an experimental "air tunnel" designed by James James to increase the efficiency of the furnace blowing system.[51] (This plan will be discussed further in the next chapter.) In general, company accounts indicate that, besides underwriting capital improvements, the money acquired from shareholders was used to stock the company store with items not produced in the settlements, such as farm equipment, turpentine, linseed oil, shoes, cloth and thread.

Buying Shares in the Company

Despite the primary sources discussed in this and previous chapters, it is difficult to compile an exact list of shareholders in the Deseret Iron Company, in part because of a continuing process of stock acquisition, transfer and withdrawal. The six original English investors, plus

Snow and Richards, added to the 15 local stockholders (13 bill of sale signers and two non-signers), all of whom joined the company in November 1852, total 23 initial investors.[52]

Minutes of the annual shareholders' meetings of the Deseret Iron Company record transfers and withdrawals by shareholders. These transactions required approval of the combined members. A pocket-sized notebook entitled "Share Register 1853, Book A" (one of the records in the Palmer Collection) suggests separate registers were kept in the names of shareholders.[53] This booklet shows the current status of 16 shareholders: Henry Lunt, Jonathan Pugmire, Benjamin R. Hulse, Joseph Walker, Joseph Chatterley (who died in September 1853), Mrs. Catherine Chatterley (Joseph's widow), Isaac C. Haight, Robert Kershaw, George Wood, James Bosnell, Thomas Cartwright (withdrawn), George A. Smith (withdrawn), James A. Little (withdrawn), Vincent Shurtleff (transferred to Christopher Arthur Jr.), Charles W. Dalton (transferred to S. D. White) and Richard Harrison. Eight of these were among the 1852 shareholders.

John G. Crook's master's thesis, "The Development of Early Industry and Trade in Utah," names from another 23 subscribers to the company: 21 men plus "Utah Territory" and Brigham Young as Trustee-in-Trust. The men are Marius Ensign, Robert Kershaw, James Bosnell, Isaac C. Haight, Charles W. Dalton, U. V. Stewart, J. C. L. Smith, Job P. Hall, John Steele, William Barton, Elias Morris, C. P. Liston, Peter M. Fife, Philip Klingensmith, Robert Reid, Henry Cook, George Coray, Ira Allen, Sam C. Pollock, William Shelton and Vincent Shurtleff. Each of these purchased a quarter share for $605, except Marius Ensign, who divided his with Benjamin R. Hulse, and Philip Klingensmith, who bought a whole share for $2,420.

The territorial legislature authorized Governor Brigham Young to buy its two shares for $4,840 on 19 January 1855. These were funded through the Perpetual Emigrating Fund Company in Salt Lake City on 31 October 1855. Brigham Young, as Trustee-in-Trust, bought another two shares for the same amount, the funding provided from tithing offices in Cedar City, Harmony and Parowan. The LDS Church paid for its shares by allowing the company to draw necessary goods from the respective office up to the given value:

Cedar Tithing Office	1,591.84	19 May 1855
Cedar Tithing Office	1,305.36	31 Oct 1855
Harmony Tithing Office	105.57	19 May 1855
Parowan Tithing Office	1,837.23	19 May 1855[54]

Over time, stockholders withdrew for various reasons. Matthew Carruthers, David Barclay Adams, David Stoddard, Alexander Easton and Thomas Cartwright left the community, either withdrawing their stock or letting it lapse as a bad debt, since they probably had not paid for it anyway. Most withdrew because they did not have the resources to pay their pledges in full and could not continue to pay interest on the amounts they still owed. Withdrawals were routinely granted to share-holders who found themselves in financial difficulty or otherwise unable to participate. For instance, when Matthew Carruthers and others withdrew from their participation in the company on 10 November 1853, the minutes record that "It was motioned and seconded and unanimously voted that the above named persons be released from their subscription on stock, with permission to dispose of and transfer the several amounts of stock which they now have in the company, to any stockholder, or to the company." As President Snow affirmed, the "real capital was bone and sinew." Good will toward the company would not be judged solely by the ability to contribute money, although men who were able to pay would be expected to fulfill their commitments. Those who could not were charitably released.[55]

In September 1854 the board of directors of the Deseret Iron Company heard through J. C. L. Smith that some Parowan residents wanted to buy stock as a group but objected to paying back-interest on stock that had been available since 1 January 1853.[56] The original constitution required that the holders of "all unpaid stock" would be required to pay 10 percent interest after 1 January 1853, even though it was unclear whether interest also accrued on unsold shares of stock. At the next general meeting, 1 November 1854, the board discussed the same problem and amended Article 8 of the constitution as follows:

> Be it resolved that the 8th section of the Constitution of the Deseret Iron Co. be so altered as to read, that 10 per cent shall be the rate of interest required, to be paid on all unpaid stock from this date only until otherwise altered by the Co.[57]

There are no other entries in the minutes to indicate whether the Parowan group went ahead with the stock purchase (see app. 6 for summary of known shareholders).

Trading at the Company Store

The Deseret Iron Company store made a significant contribution to the regional economy. Iron factories in Pennsylvania, Ohio and Missouri routinely operated company stores. Snow, Richards and possibly other iron company administrators were familiar with the concept and David Barclay Adams, the new furnace keeper, would have known about it as he had recently arrived from Iron Plantation, Pennsylvania.

The Maramec Iron Works, Maramec Spring, Missouri, which had been successfully smelting iron and manufacturing iron products for 23 years, provides a good example of a pioneer company store. This one traded with the entire community, not just iron workers. Stocks included dry goods, medicine, hardware, books, dishes, tobacco, turpentine, meat and crackers. Most everything had to be shipped great distances; with a practically nonexistent local cash flow, the company store inevitably began accepting farm produce in exchange for manufactured items. More importantly, workers were credited at the company store for their wages and could thus "purchase" needed foodstuffs and store goods. The tallies of these transactions showed up in the credit and debit columns of the individual ledger sheets kept at the store by the company bookkeeper. The store also functioned as post office, bank, credit bureau and news exchange.

The store extended credit for as much as a year to people in a cash-starved locale. When workers left the area with a credit balance, the store often extended a "note of credit" that could be cashed in another store in another community. More often, they left in debt. The mark-up on goods had to be high, for the company had a difficult time collecting bad debts. The Maramec Springs store, which had 200 to 300 individual accounts, reported annual gross sales of over $50,000. "The store served as a banking agency for the community, debts among the inhabitants often being settled by a simple bookkeeping entry transferring credit on the store books from one person to another."[58]

The Deseret Iron Company store followed the Maramec model in many respects. When Henry Lunt, the company's first bookkeeper, indicated he sold store merchandise for cash, he did not necessarily mean an exchange involving money. Hard cash was rare in the territory—hardly a sermon was preached without praising the values of "home industry," because leaders were concerned about money going out of the territory to purchase goods when little was coming in. Ledgers of the Deseret Iron Company show that most transactions involved goods traded for labor or for other goods. In fact, when Cedar City iron workers traded goods and services, the transactions were all cleared through company books in the usual form of debits and credits. If one man worked for another, the employer would "pay" by entering a credit to the employee on the company books. In this barter system, the company served as middleman.

Iron workers could subscribe to newspapers like the *Deseret News* through the Deseret Iron Company. The *Western Standard* (edited by George Q. Cannon in San Francisco) and the *Luminary* (published in St. Louis) were also ordered through the company, giving Iron County pioneers a look at the outside world.[59] Almost all the workers contributed to the company dramatic association.[60] Territorial taxes were taken directly out of workers' Deseret Iron Company accounts. Often they chose to pay off their taxes by working on community projects, such as digging irrigation ditches.[61] Several men obtained their naturalization papers with the county recorder, charging the fee to their company accounts.[62]

LDS Church members were expected to contribute one-tenth of their income to their local bishop's storehouse. These tithes, both for iron workers and for settlers with other occupations, were tallied in the Deseret Iron Company books. In 1853, for example, Peter Shirts was debited $14.00 for unpaid tithing wheat, $13.50 for unpaid tithing corn and potatoes and $6.00 for unpaid tithing butter on three cows. Charles P. Smith's account was debited $48.00 tithing in 1853 but also credited with $36.00 tithing labor. Tithing offices of the various communities were also credited with contributions on the company books.[63] For instance, Parowan, Cedar City and Harmony had formal tithing accounts. One man in Harmony might pay a grain tithing to his bishop, which would then be recorded on the man's ledger sheet. Next, its weight would be credited in the company warehouse, where it would eventually be drawn by a different man as part of his iron-making "wages."

In early Mormon culture, it was the practice of local patriarchs to charge a fee to members. Fees for patriarchal blessings were credited, for instance, to Patriarch Elisha H. Groves from the Deseret Iron Company accounts of about 10 Scandinavian iron workers. Through the company books, Groves charged for these blessings and, in turn, paid a clerk to transcribe them.[64]

The Southern Indian Mission, led by Rufus C. Allen and Jacob Hamblin (see illus. 10-5), with about 30 missionaries, was established in 1854 to preach the gospel to the Indians on the Santa Clara River and teach them how to farm. Food and clothing were provided to some of them through the Deseret Iron Company store. Thomas Dunlop Brown, recorder for the Southern Indian Mission, was also engaged on occasion to help the Deseret Iron Company with its accounting, providing a direct link between the store and the Southern Indian Mission.[65]

Courtesy LDS Church Archives

Illus. 10-5. Jacob Hamblin (1819–86) led the Southern Indian Mission, which received supplies from the Deseret Iron Company Store.

Establishing Wages and Prices

On 1 December 1852, Lunt reports the first meeting of a new committee headed by J. C. L. Smith to establish wages and price equivalents.[66] After a discussion in the blacksmith shop, the committee recommended the following: common labor would be credited at $1.25 per day; carpenters, millwrights and woodworkers would receive between $2.00 and $2.50 per day. Blacksmiths and masons would earn $2.50 per day, with an additional wage of 25¢ per hundred adobes set with their helpers ("strikers" for smiths and "tenders" for masons) earning $1.65 and $1.50 per day each. Also receiving $2.50 per day were furnace feeders (or fillers) and assistant furnace keepers, while the furnace keeper earned the highest salary of all, $3.50 per day. The labor of a span (matched pair) of horses or two yoke of oxen and a wagon were worth $1.25 per day.[67] Within the next few years, the wages for manual labor increased significantly.

Produce prices were set at $1.25 per bushel for wheat and shelled corn, while beets, carrots and parsnips brought 75¢ per bushel. Potatoes are not mentioned. The committee set 6¢ per pound for beef on the hoof and 8¢ per pound per quarter dressed. Lumber was valued at $2.50 per hundred board feet; adobes were 50¢ per hundred. Cows went at $25.00 per head, while oxen brought $60.00 to $80.00 per yoke. An interesting species of livestock on the list was cats, appraised at 75¢ each (the equivalent of about half a day's work). These prices were recommended, not only for the company, but for all Iron County citizens.[68]

Deseret Iron Company minutes indicate that Snow and Richards had "brought some 600 dollars worth of dry goods, which would help the brethren along a little, such as a few boots and shoes, shirtlings, callicoes, hats and few groceries."[69] An itemized inventory of this shipment, delivered to Cedar City by James Bulloch and James Bay in November 1852, showed a higher total—$1,087.35—than recorded in the minutes. The inventory reports additional items not listed there, such as panes of glass, nails, linseed oil and turpentine, soap, leather, candle wicking, "2 bolts Buffalo cloth," "1 bolt Blue Jeans" and "51 lbs. Saleratus." There were also books on iron and steel making. Of the $1,087.35 total, only $289.30 was reserved exclusively for the Deseret Iron Company. The remainder was for resale.[70]

When Snow and Richards left Cedar City for Salt Lake City on 2 December, they left the goods with Lunt and J. C. L. Smith, who did not make them available for purchase for nearly a week, but instead left them packed in the freight wagons. Four days after Snow and Richards left, Amasa Lyman and Charles C. Rich arrived from San Bernardino with a party of 18 bound for Salt Lake City. If the goods had been available, Lunt and Smith could hardly have denied the travelers purchase privileges and that would have been unfair to the iron workers.

Once Lyman and Rich left on 8 December, J. C. L. Smith came from Parowan, bringing some of the merchandise with him, to help Lunt "mark off the goods." The task kept them working until 1:00 A.M. There was no store building, so Lunt and Smith rented a room from James Bosnell, collecting goods that had been stored at the homes of James Easton and James Bulloch.[71]

When they opened the door on the morning of 9 December, Cedar City's people were ready. Lunt records that he was "very busily engaged all day with J C L Smith selling off the goods." He reports their value at about $500, Salt Lake Valley prices, although he felt that there were not enough items for that amount of money. Regretting there was so little to be divided among so many, he still appreciated the comfort the goods would give the struggling settlers. He himself received two pairs of boots.[72] A record of these sales must have been kept but apparently has not survived.

The activities of the pioneer iron works and the swift transition into and out of the Parowan Iron Company raise a number of questions about the more official nature of the Deseret Iron Company. The iron workers were apparently to be compensated by the Deseret Iron Company as if they owned the existing works, but did they? If they indeed owned them, did the farming members of the mission also have an interest? To whom was the $2,865.64 (offered by Snow and Richards in the bill of sale) paid? Did any cash change hands for the iron works' buildings and equipment or was the sale only a paper transaction?

We know that the Deseret Iron Company purchase included land over and above the site of the works themselves. The minutes state: "We next secured to the company a tract of land extending from Cedar City to the mountains eastward embracing the numerous water privileges on Coal Creek."[73] The Articles of Incorporation had authorized the purchase of 640 acres but the company acquired more, as an entry in Deed Book A of the Iron County Recorder's Office indicates. It was "filed" on 27 November 1852 (three days *before* the bill of sale was signed, transferring assets of the Parowan Iron Company to the Deseret Iron Company) and "filed for record" on 3 January 1853:

> Know all men by these presents that Erastus Snow & Franklin D[.] Richards are entitled to a Certain piece or parcel of land lying and being on Coal Creek Iron County U.T. viz commensing 152 Rods South of 3 Rods East of South West Corner of Lot 2 Block 1 Range 1 N & W of Coal Creek Survey Running South 480 rods Thence East 400 rods thence North 480 rods thence West 400 rods to place of beginning the Same to Contain 1200 Acres more or less[.] Surveyed by W. H. Dame.[74]

This description covers all the land east of present-day Main Street to Red Hill and south from about 400 North to 600 South.

Putting the Deseret Iron Company on Firm Legal Ground

The Deseret Iron Company compact drawn up in Liverpool in April 1852 had a number of deficiencies. For example: (1) the company had no official or legal status in England, the United States or even Utah Territory—not being a legal entity, it could not sue, be sued, hold property, sell property or legally conduct business; (2) the officers were not bonded to protect the investments of shareholders or the value of company property; and (3) the board of directors was not adequately defined. Article 2, which states that the original members of the company comprised the board of directors, was apparently in conflict with Article 10, which implies that anyone who owned shares was a member of the board of directors. The size, term of office and election procedures for the board were also not specified.

As a way to solicit European capital, the original Articles of Incorporation were useful but their failure to function legally, governing the operations of a vested company and protecting that company's workers, put the entire venture at risk. When George A. Smith left southern Utah for Salt Lake City on 21 November 1852 and Snow and Richards the following 2 December, they had clear ideas about improving the Deseret Iron Company. Soon, they submitted a bill to the legislature that officially chartered the enterprise. Some references indicate that George A. Smith, as a member of the legislature, sponsored the bill. His name is included as a member of the company.[75]

Besides granting the Deseret Iron Company legal status in the territory of Utah, the revised Articles of Incorporation clearly defined the board of directors as a separate group elected by the shareholders. The board consisted of a president, secretary and treasurer, elected for two years each, plus four trustees. In the first election, trustees would be chosen to fill terms of one, two, three and four years. Subsequently, one new trustee would be elected annually as vacancies occurred. The bill was passed by the House of Representatives and signed into law on 17 January 1853 (see app. 7).[76]

When the shareholders of the Deseret Iron Company met that November for their 1853 annual meeting, they elected a board of directors as dictated in the revised charter and approved by the legislature. Further complying with legal requirements then in operation, President Erastus Snow and Secretary Franklin D. Richards gave bonds in the sum of $10,000 each, Treasurer Thomas Tennant in the sum of $50,000 and each of the elected trustees—Isaac Haight, Vincent Shurtleff, Christopher Arthur and Jonathan Pugmire—$2,000 each.[77]

Although the territorial charter cleared up the legal deficiencies in the original Deseret Iron Company compact, it did not address aspects that still might lead to dissatisfaction among the iron workers. First, the compact did not provide for any management options or policy-making input from the iron workers themselves. Such decisions were reserved exclusively for the board of directors listed in the Articles of Incorporation. But iron production in southern Utah required the good will of the workers and, with the iron works under the direction of the Deseret Iron Company, the common laborers were even more likely to resent supervision. Many of them were there only because they saw their jobs as a mission. Knowing that the company did not have the resources to operate on a strictly cash basis must have increased their frustrations.

Second, the price of shares was too high. Almost no one in Utah could raise the £500 or $2,420 needed to purchase a full share, thus preventing virtually all the iron workers from investing in the company—the very people who had the greatest immediate interest in seeing it succeed. Further, shareholders could not vote on company policy unless they had paid for their stock in full.

Although Erastus Snow and Franklin D. Richards did not make arrangements for the workers to have a formal voice in the councils of the Deseret Iron Company, they realized they were taking over an established operation and therefore took care to acknowledge the pioneer workers' contributions. A year after coming to Cedar City, Snow and Richards reflected on the Deseret Iron Company's beginnings in a report to the workers at the company's first annual meeting, November 1853. In their report, they affirmed the wisdom of uniting all "the interests and labors of those brethren who were already endeavoring to lay a foundation for the development of the mineral resources of this county."[78]

During fall 1852, that attitude was already permeating the community with renewed feelings of unity and hope, thanks to the efforts of the two Apostles. If animosity were present, it did not dominate public meetings. Many involved in the pioneer iron works and Parowan Iron Company were supportive members of the Deseret Iron Company. Stake President J. C. L. Smith did not initially subscribe for stock in the new company but continued to act as superintendent of the works. David Barclay Adams, who did buy stock, was hired as blast furnace master because of his experience in Pennsylvania and Great Britain; James James, not a stockholder, gained permission to proceed with his air furnace experiment.[79]

Commenting on all that had been accomplished during their November 1852 visit, Erastus Snow reported that

> considerable excitement prevailed through the County, on the subject of Iron at the time of our arrival, much heightened by the arrival of those whom we had recently sent there who had been operators in the Iron business in Wales and in Pennsylvania, and we found a Scotch party, a Welch party, an English party, and an American party, and we turned Iron Masters and undertook to put all these parties through the furnace, and run out a party of Saints for building up the Kingdom of God.[80]

By weaving together theology and science, Snow was expressing his faith that the iron missionaries, for all their diverse backgrounds and varying skills, could meld themselves into a well-integrated force. He knew their efforts, united in the cause of manufacturing iron, held the key to economic independence, so vital to Latter-day Saint interests. Ironically, by creating the Deseret Iron Company—the means by which he intended to accomplish this goal—he changed the status of the iron workers from missionaries to employees with stock options.

Of course, the Deseret Iron Company was not an enterprise of strict capitalism. Church leaders still headed the iron works and iron workers still labored from a sense of religious duty. No one would question that the shareholders invested for the cause of Zion rather than for personal profit. Nevertheless, the financial principles and institutions of "gentile" society were making an impact and the economic foundations of Mormon society were shifting in response.

Endnotes

1. "Eighth General Epistle," *Millennial Star* 15 (19 Feb 1853): 114.

2. "Continuation of Minutes of General Conference," *Millennial Star* 15 (5 Mar 1853): 151.

3. Ibid., 152.

4. "Eighth General Epistle," 114.

5. "Minutes of General Conference," *Millennial Star* 15 (26 Feb 1853): 132.

6. "Continuation of Minutes," 150.

7. Heber C. Kimball, *Journal of Discourses* (7 Oct 1852), 1:295.

8. Anonymous editorial, *Deseret News,* 6 Nov 1852, 102.

9. "Sixth General Epistle of The Presidency of The Church of Jesus Christ of Latter-day Saints," *Millennial Star* 14 (15 Jan 1852): 20.

10. Andrew Karl Larson, *Erastus Snow: The Life of a Missionary and Pioneer for the Early Mormon Church* (Salt Lake City: University of Utah Press, 1971), 212, 242.

11. Ibid., 243.

12. "Minutes of the Special General Council," *Millennial Star* 14 (29 May 1852): 211–12.

13. Ibid., 212.

14. "Manufacture of Iron in Utah," 2.

15. Deseret Iron Company, Minutes, 22. Andrew Karl Larson estimates the value of the pound sterling at that time as $4.84. Larson, *Erastus Snow,* 243–44.

16. Deseret Iron Company, misc. documents: "Articles of Incorporation, 1852" (referred to in the Minutes as "Articles of Compact"), holograph, Palmer Collection. Note that Article 12 is written on a separate sheet of paper laid on top of the sheet containing Articles 13, 14 and 15.

17. Deseret Iron Company, Minutes, 22–24.

18. Erastus Snow and Franklin D. Richards to "Beloved Brethren of the Deseret Iron Company," 8 May 1852, holograph in Palmer Collection.

19. Deseret Iron Company, Minutes, 22.

20. Ibid., 5.

21. Ibid., 23.

22. Daniel Spencer invested the remainder in stocks and real estate. The estate was turned over to Thomas A. Tennant upon his coming of age in May 1876. See Thomas Tennant Estate Papers, filed under Utah District Court (Salt Lake County), "Probate Records, Estates and Guardianship, 1852–1910: An Index to Book A through F," catalogued, as of this writing, as film 0425668, 112, 140, 293, LDS Family History Library, Salt Lake City. Regarding Thomas Jones, a Thomas Jones worked in Cedar City in 1853–54 as a miner and mason, but nothing is known

to connect these references to the English investor.

23. Charles Jordan to Erastus Snow, undated letter (ca. 1852), Deseret Iron Company, miscellaneous documents.

24. Charles Jordan to "Dear Sir," 27 Apr 1852. Deseret Iron Company, miscellaneous documents. The drawing mentioned in the letter is at a separate location in the Palmer Collection, title given as "Design of a Blowing Machine and Framing for the Same." The drawing's penciled date of "1854" is incorrect; the correct date is 1852.

25. Frank E. Esshom, *Pioneers and Prominent Men of Utah* (Salt Lake City: Utah Pioneers Book Publishing, 1913; reprint, Salt Lake City: Western Epics, 1966), 123, 1160.

26. Erastus Snow and Franklin D. Richards to Vincent Shurtleff, 1 May 1852, Deseret Iron Company, miscellaneous documents. The page heading reads "Copy of a letter of instructions to the agent of Deseret Iron Company—."

27. Lunt, diary, 26 Sep 1852.

28. "Minutes of General Conference," *Millennial Star* 15 (26 Feb 1853): 133.

29. Lunt, diary, 23 Oct 1852.

30. Ibid., 14 Nov 1852.

31. Ibid., 16 Nov 1852.

32. Ibid., 17 Nov 1852.

33. Ibid., 18–19 Nov 1852.

34. "Extracts from the Journal of John Steele," *Utah Historical Quarterly* 6 (Jan 1933): 34.

35. Franklin D. Richards, journal, "May 1852 and Onward," LDS Church Archives.

36. Ibid.

37. Deseret Iron Company, Minutes, 1–2.

38. Lunt, diary, 21 Nov 1852.

39. Ibid., 23–24 Nov 1852.

40. Ibid., 1 Nov 1852.

41. Ibid., 25 Nov 1852.

42. Ibid., 26 Nov 1852.

43. Ibid., 26–27 Nov 1852.

44. Ibid.

45. Ibid., 29 Nov 1852.

46. Deseret Iron Company, Minutes, 5.

47. Bill of Sale, 30 Nov 1852, Deseret Iron Company, miscellaneous documents. Original punctuation retained.

48. Deseret Iron Company, Minutes, 5.

49. Lunt, diary, 30 Jan 1853.

50. Ibid., 1 Mar 1853.

51. "John Calvin Lazell [*sic*] Smith" typescript, Palmer Collection.

52. Deseret Iron Company, Minutes, 5, 23. The "original" (English) investors were Thomas Tennant, Thomas Jones, Elias Jones, John Jones, Christopher Arthur and John Weston.

53. *Share Register, 1853,* Book A, Deseret Iron Company, miscellaneous documents.

54. Crook, "Early Industry and Trade," 49. Crook does not provide the dates on which the other 21 subscribers purchased their shares, nor does he document from which source(s) he derived their names. Tabulating 23 "initial" investors (the 22 listed in the Minutes, 5, plus John Weston, noted in the Minutes, 23, as being "admitted a member of the company") with Crook's listing of 23 others (21 subscribers plus Utah Territory and Brigham Young as Trustee-in-Trust) results in a total of 46 shareholders. There are, however, at least nine other names connected to shareholder or company references which do not appear in Crook, but do appear later in the Minutes than on p. 5 (or, like Thomas Bladen and George A. Smith, prominently in various journals). These are Christopher Arthur Jr., Thomas Bladen, Thomas Dunlop Brown, Catherine Chatterley, Alexander Keir, James A. Little, George A. Smith, George Williams and James Williamson. This brings the known total of shareholders to 55, each of whom is represented in app. 6. For related discussions, see Leonard J. Arrington, *Great Basin Kingdom: Economic History of the Latter-Day Saints, 1830–1900* (Lincoln: University of Nebraska Press, 1968), 125–26, 453 n. 129; and app. 9.

55. Deseret Iron Company, Minutes, 14, 16.

56. Ibid., 36.

57. Ibid. 38.

58. Norris, *Frontier Iron,* 62.

59. Deseret Iron Company, Journal, 31, 125, 350–51, 451–55.

60. Ibid., 318–320.

61. Ibid., 24, 32, 205.

62. Ibid., 53.

63. Ledger, 1853–54, Deseret Iron Company, miscellaneous documents (the ledger contains one 1852 listing and several 1855 listings).

64. Deseret Iron Company, Journal, 297.

65. Deseret Iron Company, Minutes, 33; Campbell, *Establishing Zion,* 118–19.

66. Lunt, diary, 1 Dec 1852.

67. Deseret Iron Company, Minutes, 6.

68. Ibid.

69. Ibid., 5–6.

70. James Bulloch, shipping list, Salt Lake to Coal Creek, Nov 1852, Deseret

Iron Company, miscellaneous documents.

71. Lunt, diary, 8 Dec 1852.

72. Ibid., 9 Dec 1852.

73. Deseret Iron Company, Minutes, 18–19.

74. Deed Book A, 43.

75. See, for instance, Jarvis, *Ancestry,* 168: "Both of these acts were sponsored by Representative Smith." Jarvis does not, however, cite the source of that statement.

76. "An Act to Incorporate the Desert Iron Company," Jan 1853, in *Territorial Acts and Resolutions,* 14–16 (holograph signatures of Richards and Grant on original, but not reproduced on version cited here).

77. Deseret Iron Company, Minutes, 29.

78. "Manufacture of Iron in Utah," 2.

79. Erastus Snow to editor, 21 Dec 1852, published in *Deseret News,* 25 Dec 1852, 2nd unnumbered page.

80. Ibid.

11

Change in the Townsite, Growth in the Company

Fall 1852–Summer 1853

The visits of Brigham Young's three representatives, former Iron Mission president George A. Smith and his fellow Apostles Erastus Snow and Franklin D. Richards, initiated great changes in the settlements. One was the organization of the Deseret Iron Company and its acceptance by local iron workers. A second was relocating the site of the community to the south side of Coal Creek on what became known as "Plat A." The settlers would also find themselves facing an influx of newcomers who expanded the local population just as a fierce winter struck southern Utah.

As mentioned in chapter 8, Brigham Young visited Cedar City during his annual tour of the outlying colonies. On 11 May 1852, Apostle Wilford Woodruff, traveling with the President, took a walk with him to view the Compact Fort and surrounding area. Three days later, Henry Lunt and Bishop Philip Klingensmith went to "look out a sight for building another Fort."[1] The timing of these two events suggests that Brigham Young had not been totally pleased with the Compact Fort's location. It is logical, therefore, to assume that this visit in May prompted President Young to send George A. Smith back to Cedar City to oversee its relocation. Smith recorded this commission, noted in chapter 10, in his journal in October 1852:

> I took leave of President Young, who gave me instructions to visit Iron County, locate a survey on Cedar City plot, and preside over the affairs of that section, to counsel the emigration in regard to locating in the southern settlements, to locate several cattle ranches, to visit John D. Lee's settlement, and see that it was made in a safe position, as he anticipated about one hundred fifty families would go to the Iron County.[2]

Reasons for Relocating: Security Concerns

Apparently, two reasons prompted the decision to change the settlement site. First, the Compact Fort area was deemed vulnerable to Indian attack. Brigham Young's visit in May had made this all too apparent. When he and his party ascended the Knoll and viewed the landscape below, they could look directly down into the fort. Much of its interior was accessible by bow and arrow, largely nullifying the protective effect of the walls.

Although the neighboring Paiutes were generally peaceful, Cedar City and Parowan were over 200 miles from the nearest help. Wakara's extended family, including Sowiete, Peteetneet and Arapeen, led the Utes back and forth across the area on trading expeditions. The Navajos of New Mexico and Arizona often traveled north over the San Juan River to trade with the Utes. Chief Kanosh of the Pahvants, from the Fillmore area, was friendly with the Mormons but could not always control his warriors. Furthermore, the settlers had steadily lost small numbers of unguarded livestock to Indian raids.[3]

The settlers' journals record numerous confrontations with Native Americans during the spring and summer of 1852. On 12 March, James Whittaker reported that a "dozen men on horseback well armed" went to the encampment of Peter Shirts on Shirts Creek to bring him and his family back to the Compact Fort because word of a disturbance involving Paiutes had reached Cedar City. They found Shirts absent on a visit to Parowan but his family returned to Cedar City with their "rescuers." Whittaker's entry for 16 March records the outcome:

> Br Shirts came from Parowan last night, said that the Indians had shot an ox with 5 arrows, belonging to Bishop Robinson, and they were obligded to kill it. Also said that some of the Pihedes [Paiutes] had told the Brethren at Parowan that there were but four Pihede Indians that were mad and would Kill the Cattle, all the rest were friendly. He said that a Co of the Brethren intended to go out on horse back to day in pursuit of the Indians. Br Shirts went back with his family to his new farm.[4]

Early in July, John White and his family were returning from Salt Lake City. On the way, Indians stole two of their calves and wounded two others. On Saturday, 7 August, a "Pihede" brave entered John D. Lee's home and behaved "very impudent," attacking Sister Lee with a club or plank, opening a "very dangerous wound" in her head. Brother William Barton came to her aid, intervening just in time to prevent the Indian's next blow. Barton struck him and he ran off.[5]

Luella Dalton reports that Paiute Chief Ouiwonup (brother of this attacker), another Indian (apparently a Pahvant chief) and several braves met with J. C. L. Smith, John Steele, Henry Lunt and John D. Lee to work out a mutually acceptable punishment for the serious assault. Eventually, all agreed the offender should be tied to the liberty pole and given a public whipping of 40 lashes, which Ouiwonup would personally administer. On Monday, the 9th, the culprit was brought to the settlement. Ouiwonup warned his brother, on pain of death, not to retaliate for the whipping and the sentence was carried out. Afterward, they smoked a peace pipe together and the Mormon leaders gave gifts to the chiefs in token of their understanding and cooperation.[6]

Brigham Young's policy was to maintain harmonious relations with Native Americans whenever possible. In April 1852, he instructed an Indian agent, Major Holman, to

> endeavor to conciliate the Indians; also to learn their numbers, situation, usual haunts, disposition to make treaties, and obtain their consent, if possible, for a settlement upon such location as shall be most desirable for an agency and farming operations.[7]

The Mormons were also eager to proselyte. Henry Lunt reported with delight that J. C. L. Smith had baptized 58 Indians on Sunday, 18 October. On 7 November, George A. Smith wrote of this event to Franklin D. Richard's brother Samuel:

> Oiuwonup, the Pyede [Paiute] chief, in connection with fifty-seven others of Pyede parvente Indians, have been baptized at Parowan. They are becoming more industrious, and are learning to work for their bread—in the language of the chief—"we will quit stealing, and work and get an honest living." Seventeen Pyedes have been baptized at this place.[8]

Three days after the baptism, in a further expression of neighborliness, "4 Squaws and some Indian Children" assisted Lunt and his wife in harvesting potatoes, onions and beets. In the same diary entry, he notes that "Yesterday my wife commenced husking corn and some squaws came to her assistance and soon finished what was in my garden."[9]

While Brigham Young had long instructed the Saints to engage in peaceful relationships with the Indians, he also counseled that they maintain a social distance. "Stockade your fort and attend to your own affairs, and let the Indians attend to theirs. . . . the more familiar, you will find the less influence you will have with them."[10] Henry Lunt would lecture the pioneers in a similar manner in the Compact Fort in February 1853, reminding them to be careful how they treated the Indians, and told them not for to make free with them, and allow them . . . to come into their houses as they are doing but keep them at a propper distance, and if they give them anything for to have them do something first. Teach them to be industrious, and let them know that our bread is worth something, and that we have to work hard for to obtain it.[11]

Although it is true that both cultures tried, in general, to accommodate each other, they often perceived morality and justice very differently. Impatient and sometimes aggressive individuals in both camps pressed their luck, breached their own rules of ethics and dragged others into the conflict. Both groups were justifiably suspicious—and at times, afraid—of each other. The Mormons, no matter how conciliatory, had settled on the choicest lands and their guns gave them an ultimately decisive advantage. Even so, if conflict did arise and the tribes became angry enough to attack, the present position of the Compact Fort made it indefensible from too many points.

Reasons for Relocating: Increased Population

During his May 1852 visit, Brigham Young would have noticed the crowding in the Compact Fort. Even before the October conference plea for more Saints to settle in the Iron Mission, two wagons of Scottish pioneers were heading south, traveling with a group of emigrants bound for San Bernardino. Another newcomer, arriving shortly after the Scottish Saints, was Charles Willden, who worked in the steel mills of Sheffield, England, before emigrating to America. He, his wife and six children had started from Council Bluffs on 2 June, traveling in Thomas C. D. Howell's company, reaching Salt Lake City on 13 September. Once there, Charles hoped Lorenzo D. Young would employ him in farming,

> but as soon as Lorenzo heard the name Willden he wanted to know if he was Charles Willden, the steel refiner by trade. Being answered in the affirmative Lorenzo said he could not make any other arrangements as he had heard his brother Brigham speak of him and that he rather expected that his brother's intentions were to send him to Cedar City, then known as Coal Creek, to work in the iron industry there.[12]

The Willdens entered Cedar City on 29 October, having traveled down with a man named John Gregory and his wife. Three days later, a David Cook arrived with his wife and six children, along with a family named Muir (Walter, his wife and daughter) and presumed relatives David Muir, Thomas Muir and Thomas's wife.[13]

As the month turned, Joseph Bradshaw arrived, reporting that his brother and family were at Fillmore and would be in Cedar City soon. On 2 November, Lunt refers to a "Bro Adams wife and 5 children" who arrived that evening.[14] Most likely this is David Barclay Adams, whose father, James, was a foundry worker at the Carron Iron Works in Sterlingshire, Scotland. David was born there on 4 May 1814, and grew up to become a skilled furnace master in his own right. He was baptized on 6 April 1844, converting while working at the Glendon Ironworks in Pennsylvania. Like Willden, he left for Utah from Council Bluffs in June 1852, traveling in John Tidwell's company. Arriving in Salt Lake City in September, he was immediately called to help found the iron industry in southern Utah.[15] Interestingly, Willden and Adams left Council Bluffs two days apart and arrived in Salt Lake two days apart. Perhaps their separate companies traveled most of the way together and the two men became acquainted on the plains.

Within two weeks after Willden and Adams arrived, Lunt mentions "Bro. Davis and family, Miller from Gt. Salt Lake City" as coming to Cedar City, along with several other families whose names he intends to record, but apparently never does.[16] As they arrived, these newcomers were encouraged to settle on the new Plat A townsite. By 11 November 1852, Lunt placed the number of men in Cedar City (excluding their family members) at 60; on 7 November, however, George A. Smith, had already estimated "upwards of seventy families" in the settlement.[17] Since the original group of Cedar City pioneers is documented by contemporary sources to have been around 35 men, the entries made by Lunt and Smith show, in effect at least, a doubling of the population within the first year.

Planning the New City

Community leaders had to consider several factors before selecting a relocation site: it had to allow room for growth, be easily defended, be close to culinary and irrigation water for a new community field and be close to the iron works. These issues were well-understood by George A. Smith, who arrived in Parowan on 23 October to fulfill Brigham Young's commission. On the 27th, in the company of Stake President J. C. L. Smith, Bishop Tarlton Lewis, Surveyor William H. Dame and Brother Samuel Gould, George A. traveled down to Cedar City, where he soon became involved in the debate which ended in the adoption of the Deseret Iron Company. His primary directive, however, was to oversee the colony's relocation and, to that end, on the afternoon of his arrival there, he went with Lunt "and the other brethren up to the Iron works, and to look out a sight for a city."[18]

From their vantage point overlooking the Compact Fort and environs, George A. Smith and his companions decided that moving the townsite south and west would be best. As usual, William Dame was set to surveying; his perimeter placed the new city plat on the south side of Coal Creek, which meant that any fort raised there would be distant enough from the Knoll to be safe from attack by Indians (or anyone else). Dame sketched the new site on the western half of his 1853–1854 "Coal Creek Survey" (marked "Plat A" and "Plat A Fort" on illus. 7-3), drawing it as an empty square which he labeled "Cedar City Location." The northeast corner of this new survey square touches the southwest corner of the Old Fort plat. To keep the two distinct, we will use Dame's own designation—Plat A—to refer to the relocation site (see illus. 11-1). (Historically, "Cedar Fort" is the name the settlers used most often, both for the townsite as a whole and for its fort, soon to be erected in the northeast sector of Plat A.)

Plat A met the resettlement criteria well. The new townsite was located on a flat plain, controlling all approaches from all directions. Trees and tall brush were cleared from the south and west to eliminate cover for potential attackers. It was evident that water from Coal Creek could easily be channeled into both townsite and fields. Although the iron workers moving to Plat A would have to cross the creek to go to work at the first blast furnace site on the east bank, both Plat A and Compact Fort were comparably close to the iron works, so the move would not be a hardship in that regard.

Like most Mormon townships of this era, Plat A appears to have been a modification of Joseph Smith's plan for the City of Zion. Dame's survey provided for 188 individual lots[19] measuring 4 by 20 rods (66 by 330 feet), like those intended for the City of Zion, each containing a half acre. These lots, much larger than those at Parowan or in the Compact Fort, could each contain a home, a small garden, barn and corrals. Each also faced a wide street with the houses offset from it two rods (33 feet) back. Alleys three rods wide (49.5 feet) gave easy access to outbuildings behind each house, with stables facing on the alleys. This design kept barnyard areas at least 300 feet away from the nearest dwelling, yet left them easily accessible.

George A. Smith handled the distribution of these new city lots by delegating the task to Lunt, assisted by Bishop Klingensmith. On Wednesday, 27 October (the same day he arrived in Cedar City and walked out with Lunt to find the relocation site), George A. "requested

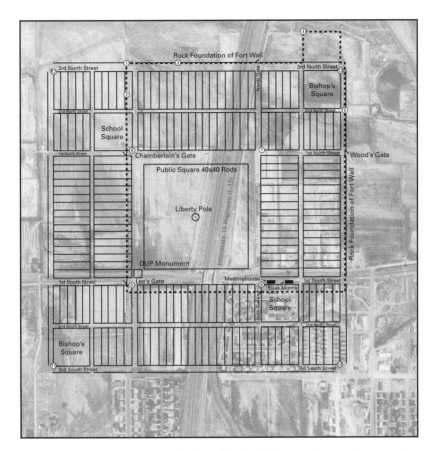

Illus. 11-1. Dame's 1852 survey of Plat A (Cedar City) superimposed over a 1985 aerial photograph. (Authors' reconstruction based on original survey in Iron County Recorder's Office.) Broken line indicates fort boundary.

those brethren who intended to build this fall on the New City plot" to give their names to Lunt. The next day, Lunt and Smith counseled together again and Smith confirmed he would "leave it to [Lunt] and the Bishop to give out the Lots in the City,"[20] although he himself remained in southern Utah for almost another month.[21]

The new site George A. Smith helped create before returning north provided space for two large school yards and two bishop's compounds (the four corners: Blocks 5, 9, 17 and 21), each 300 feet square (20 rods) or two and a half acres apiece. The large 18.8 acre, 56-rod town square in the center, called "Temple Square," was probably not intended as a temple site but rather as a space for public gatherings and worship, thus serving the same function as Temple Square in Salt Lake City. The inscription on Dame's original Plat A survey reads: "Scale 30 [?] to the inch, Outside street 7 rods, Alley 3 rods, Center Streets 6 rods, Lots 4 rods by 20, Block 13. 56 rods square, Houses front the streets, 2½ rod from the line[.] Stables on the Alleys[.] Variation N 15° 51' East[.]"

In the City of Zion plan, the public square (Block 13) would also house administrative offices; in Parowan and Cedar City, it provided enough room for a public corral. Each bishop's square was intended to contain a tithing storehouse and corral to receive in-kind tithing, including livestock. The 188 lots, two school yards, two bishop's squares and central public square were arranged into a half-mile-square master plan which could be duplicated in adjacent or nearby tracts to accommodate new settlers. The square shape also lent itself to walling in, if needed. Dame evidently altered his original plat at some point, changing the width to provide for a 10-rod "inside" street around the public square and a seven-rod "outside" street around the perimeter of the entire plat.

Magnifying the small shaded marks on illustration 11-2, which shows the area west of Plat A in Dame's 1853–54 survey, reveals them to be numbered property divisions. Iron County deed books show that these were one-acre garden lots, 4 by 40 rods each, deeded to individuals. A water ditch still runs along most of the east side of this garden area. Much of the ditch is still in use. Many of the garden lots have been consolidated, changing widths but not lengths. They now measure almost 40 rods from the head ditch to modern Airport Road, which runs down the western edge of the first garden tier (thus placing it between the east and west gardens), following the boundary line separating Robert Wiley's garden lot from those of Henry Lunt, James Whittaker and others.

In addition to the Plat A survey site, where it was expected many of the new settlers would raise their homes, Dame's survey included 1,000 acres of new farms to the west where they could grow their crops (shown on illus. 7-3). We designate this area the "West Field," in contrast to the old farming site, the Big Field, which was north of the Compact Fort. As in the first settlement days, the Plat A settlers could have three properties if they chose: a city lot (with room for a small produce garden at the back), a separate garden lot immediately west of the city survey and a larger farming lot further to the west. Iron workers were generally encouraged not to handle too much land and some of them took no farm lots at all.

None of the townsite, West Field or garden lots was registered until 28 January 1853 when the first fees were paid by 30 men and one woman (both old and new settlers) for lots in the new city.[22] These were most

Block 1 (top):

7 | 8 | 9 | 10 | 11 | 12

William Shelton	20
David Cook	19
	18
Johnathan Pugmire	17
William Hewit	16
William Greenwood	15
William Stones	14
Daniel Ross	13
Jerremiah Thomas	12
George Perry	11
Thomas Machin	10
	9
Thomas Corlett	8
Joseph Chatterley	7
William Gough	6
John Ashworth	5
	4
Wardman Holmes	3
John White	2
	1

Range 1 S & W

6 | 5 | 4 | 3 | 2 | 1

6 rod street

53 | 54 | 48 47 46 45 44 43 42 41 40 39 38 37 36 35 34 33 32 31

Charles Willden, James Adshead, John Stoddard, John Stoddard, David Stoddard, John Chatterley, John Morris, John Bradshaw, Samuel Bradshaw, George Hunter, George Hunter, Joseph Hunter, Andrew Peterson, James Bay, Richard Varley, William Bateman, Robert Wiley

Henry Lunt	30
James Whittaker	29
Matthew Easton	28
Alexander Easton	27
John Easton	26
James Easton	25
Thomas Muir	24
Walter Muir	23
Alexander Keir	22
Benjamin Rowland	21
Job Rowland	20
Thomas Rowland	19
Phillip K. Smith	18
John Key	17
John Smith II	16
	15
Robert Henry	14
	13
John Humphries	12
George Wood	11

Range 2 S & W

52 | 51 | 50 | 49 | 48 | 47

41 | 42 | 43 | 44 | 45 | 46

	10
Joseph Bateman	9
	8
John Nelson	7
Charles Smith	6
David Adams	5
John Yardley	4
Arthur Parks	3
John Griffith	2
David Muir	1

Block 3

City Gardens
Garden Lots were 4 x 40 rods

Illus. 11-2. West Garden lot allocations taken from deed books in the Iron County Recorder's Office, following Dame's 1851 to 1854 composite survey, superimposed over aerial photograph.

probably "surveying" fees, because "recording" fees for 25 of the 30 are posted in the deed books on 1 March 1853 (see app. 8 and illus. 12-2).

The Lunt's Plat A House

The complex story of the Lunt family homesites illustrates the gradual process of moving to Plat A. While gathering materials for a house in the Compact Fort, Henry Lunt and his bride had stayed in the homes of other settlers. On 28 June 1852, he records that he had "Moved in Bro Wiley's house until mine is built." Robert Wiley, the bricklayer and choir master, had gone to Salt Lake City to bring his wife back with him to Cedar City. Lunt was thus able to take Ellen to a finished home, albeit a borrowed one, while their own was being built. Through the rest of the summer, on into September and for most of October, successive diary entries report various tasks for the house, most of which concern making or "hawling" adobe bricks (some of which could have been for the iron works). Wiley returned on 14 October and Lunt must have felt obligated to vacate the house. By 26 October, Lunt records that he is "now living with my Father inlaw and am very thankful that I am so comfortable."[23]

After the October decision to relocate, however, Lunt began building again, this time on his new townsite lot. He records being pleased that this lot was less than perfect. On Monday, 1 November, although he wasn't feeling well, he took a walk and

> looked at the Lot I had selected on the plot for the City found that it was rather broken having a hollow running through it and some large rocks on it. I was well satisfied with it, Knowing that no one would envy me of it, and could not say that I had chosen one of the best Lots. I thank my Heavenly Father that I have the priviledge of having an inheritance in one of the Cities that are to be built up unto the Lord[.][24]

It would still be more than three months before the house on the new lot would be ready for occupancy. In fact, many of the brethren would pitch in and help build it, since Lunt's time was taken up with administrative tasks. Lunt expressed gratitude to his fellow settlers again and again during the long weeks of house-building. He knew that the number and nature of first priorities, all demanding immediate attention, relentlessly drained the time and strength of any new settlement group. This made him keenly appreciate those who increased their own work load on his behalf so that he could handle undistracted the leadership tasks on which the colony's survival depended. But finally, on 5 February 1853, he records with obvious delight the completion of his first home in the Iron Mission:

Removed from Father Whittakers house to my own House on the new City [lot.] Father and James [Whittaker Jr.] assisted me. . . . I have it not in my power at the presant time to pay them for their work done for me. . . . Father Whittaker has been working for me for the past week. Mother Whittaker furnished us with a number of articles necessary in housekeeping which I was entirely destitute of such as Pots and Kettles &c &c. . . . In the evening in my usual Evenings devotion, I thanked the Lord for the comfortable house that he had given me and my wife, and asked his Blessings to rest upon it; and dedicated it to the Lord. It is a dobie House 15 inch wall 15 by 16. 10 feet high well finished inside, fronts the south Lot 5 corner lot, Block 19. The first Adobie house built in Cedar City.[25]

Twenty-one days later, in a letter to the editor of the *Deseret News,* Lunt noted that the new city plat "has already on it 9 Log Houses, 2 Adobie and 10 good cellars, all inhabited." He also noted that the settlers had removed some of the fence around the Compact Fort's Big Field to begin enclosing a small field to the west of Plat A. This he expected to be completed by 1 March, "with an excellent fence all round it 6 poles high, and 2 good strong lumber gates to enter." Further, he noted, an irrigation system to water both city and field was already in place.[26]

No domestic history of the Lunts would be complete without including a most unusual event recorded in Henry's journal. He had already noted snow falling in mid-May 1853. Other journal entries confirm that the ever-unpredictable southern Utah weather was predictably displaying every mood from a "Friday that . . . Blew so tremendously" to a "Very hot day" to a "Very sharp frost last night."[27] But on Thursday, 19 May, Henry reported an unforgettable incident:

Very warm day. . . . About ½ past 4 P.M. it began to thunder and lighten over Shirts Kanyon, and in a few minutes the whole Heavens were black with clouds, and the Lightning and Thunder began to approach very near and was tremendous loud; the wind began to blow in a most terrific manner and large drops of rain decended[.] I and Ellen then went into the house. She sat down near to the fire place, and I went to the wood pile for some wood for the fire. As I came through the door, I pushed it wide open, and just as I was in the attitude of laying the wood down by the side of the fire place, The Electric Fluid struck the chimney of the house accompanied with the loudest burst of Thunder I ever before heard[.] Nocked a part of the chimney down rent the house from top to bottom blew the mantle piece to pieces took a piece out of the floor, nocked the bottome out of a Keeler which was full of water, a hole into a Box, nocked the plaster off[f] the wall, tore one of the shoes to pieces on my wife's foot, and a large hole into the other, took the use out of both of her legs for some time. I had to carry her out of the house and at the same time my own legs were burning with heat as though I had been in a fire. The house at the moment of the tremendous shock was filled with a Blaze of fire. We were both of us sensible at the time and are now that had it not been for an overruling providence which had shielded us from the danger, we most certainly should have both of us been instantly killed. It was the most awful scene I ever witnessed, and certainly will never be forgot. Praised be the Lord for his goodness unto us[.] Attended meeting in the evening.[28]

In the Fort, In the City: the Meetinghouse Expands

Providing more formal data, Lunt's diary makes it clear that people continued to live in or near the Compact Fort during and after relocation to Plat A. His journal entries frequently distinguish between the old and new townsites. On 11 February, for instance, he "gave it out in the Fort" that mail had arrived in Parowan, while he went on home "to the City," taking newspapers from that delivery given him by John Kay, whom he happened to meet on the road. On 19 February, he again went to the Compact Fort, this time to a dance held in the meetinghouse. On 2 June, he reported that a search party, returning after retrieving stolen cattle from the Indians, was greeted "at the Fort" by a large crowd.[29]

The Ross family's old home in the Compact Fort, which had become both schoolhouse and general meeting place, remained the center of the community through the summer of 1853. During Sunday meetings on 17 October 1852, Lunt had "urged the brethren to build a school house," an open-ended phrase that may have meant he was thinking of rebuilding on Plat A.[30] This did not happen, however, and by 7 November, also a Sunday, Lunt noted that the settlers "Met again in the afternoon at two oclock, meeting house densly crowded." Since the building was used as much for business meetings concerning the iron works and for various community gatherings as it was for religious services on Sundays and Thursday evenings, the situation was becoming unbearable. On Christmas night, Lunt recorded events at a holiday party but admitted that "after dancing a little while the room became so densly crowded that it was impossible for to dance with any degree of pleasure." On Sunday, 23 January 1853, he noted the "Meeting house was crowded so that some had to stand up all the while," while his entry for Sunday, 6 February, expresses both pride and frustration: "Our meetings are attended most excellent, so crowded that the house will scarsly, hold all the people."[31]

On 6 March, after ending a long day of Sunday services in cramped quarters, Lunt had had enough. He records, "I instructed the school Trustees to take measures at the evenings meeting to enlarge the School House."[32] This directive, however, went unheeded. By the end of the month, Lunt had to put his energies into an upcoming trip to Salt Lake City to attend April conference. When he returned, he was ready to have the old problem solved once and for all. On 27 April he

> instructed the brethren for to get the school house enlarged this week, and recommended bro Hewitt to take the Job, and levy a Tax on the people for to pay them for the Job. Bro Hewett and some half dozen more of the brethren are now busily engaged at the Job, and expect to have it finished this week.[33]

With a plan of action firmly in place, the work went so well that Lunt was able to record on Sunday, 1 May, that "The Brethren have made an excellent Job of the meeting House. It is now very comodius." Only the day before he had gone out "in the afternoon and looked out some lots for some brethren that have lately come in."[34] By collating the enlargement of the Compact Fort's schoolhouse with ongoing reports of new settlers moving to city lots in Plat A, we know that both sites were active and growing during the spring of 1853.

Poverty Among the Newcomers

A primary reason for relocation was to make space for new settlers, inspired by the special emphasis put on the Iron Mission during the last October's general conference in Salt Lake City. However, leaders were so successful in calling recent arrivals to take up iron production that the sheer volume of newcomers to Cedar City overwhelmed the settlement's meager resources. Arriving too late to plant and harvest, these autumn pioneers had to survive a long winter on what they brought or on what they could trade for. Purchases from other settlers were the exception, as few of the newcomers had any money to spend on even basic necessities. The Charles Willden family, for instance, set up housekeeping—exactly where isn't recorded—in their wagons and a dugout. Although the young sons herded the city's cows, there is no evidence they were paid for their time.

According to the Charles Willden family history, "Everybody was out of flour and some did not have even bran to eat. . . . [Mother was] praying and hoping all the time that a thaw would come before her family would be in need, but a thaw did not come and our family was at the starvation point."[35] Feargus O'Conner Willden, then 12 years old, later reminisced:

[We] arrived at Coal Creek on Friday the 29th of October and on the 4th day of December father took a cow herd of about 2 to 3 hundred. Me and John, my brother, sent out with them, also our sheep which had then increased to about 10 head. I was entirely bare foote and had been ever since I left Pottawattamie or better known as Council Bluffs.

We kept the herd all that winter of 1852 and 1853 with Bran Bread to eat for one month and not plenty of that. In the Spring of 1853 I dug roots and eat hands full of grass to subsist on, to keep body and soul together. For the people seemed to have nothing to pay with and bread stuff being very scarce. This I had to do every day whether rains, hail, wind or snow over hills, rocks, prickley pairs, brush and many times snow very deep and cold. North wind blowing without any sunshine. When I got home at evening I had to feed the sheep, wood to cut, water to carry in the house and milk cows.[36]

All the colonists were poor, but some were much poorer than others. Since there was little circulating currency, wages had to be paid in produce and those who had it—usually farmers—could demand almost any price for it. Henry Lunt was concerned about established settlers withholding wheat from new arrivals, like Willden, who were iron workers and had nothing yet to exchange. In response to a proclamation from Brigham Young that the first day of the new year should be a day of praise and thanksgiving, Lunt encouraged the settlers to "give liberly of their abundance to the poor, so that they might rejoice with us." The next day, he gave "a good large piece of Beef to the Bishop for the poor," and asked the "old Citizens to make a contribution" as well, "which some of them contributed to freely. The Bishop devided it out and it caused everyone to have abundance."[37]

Apparently, this exercise in practical charity was not sufficient. In February 1853, Lunt needed to instruct the farmers "not to do as the gentiles do[:] raise the price of wheat because it is likely for to be scarse." He suggested that they continue to sell wheat at one-fourth dollar per bushel.[38] Later in the month, he lamented that neither he nor President J. C. L. Smith could get any wheat for a number of men laboring at the iron works. Those in the first settlement, Parowan, who did have wheat to spare would not sell it for less than two dollars a bushel. "I am sorry," reported Lunt, "to see Saints keep their wheat locked up because they think they can make a little more of it by keeping it for a while. . . . The principle is an old Gentile Devilish principle and therefore was not good for saints."[39]

Problems of scarce supply and urgent demand were chronic in the settlements, not limited to one place, one season or one year. A letter to

George A. Smith from his wife Zilpha, written from Parowan on 24 September 1854, provides compelling evidence of one woman's struggle to survive without the most basic means to do so:

> Dear George . . . you wrote in your last letter that you saw no way to help me[. I]f you do not I do not know how I shall get along as there is neither Shoes leather or groceries in the place and there is no way to get money to send for such articles[. I]f you could send me one bottle of oil one ounce of camphor some sugar and tea and eight yards and a half of calico—the calico I had to borrow to pay a woman for washing for me[.] If you can send me these articles I Shall be very glad.[40]

Harsh Winter at the Iron Works

Although living conditions were difficult, the iron workers continued their divinely commissioned efforts. On 16 December 1852, according to Henry Lunt's diary, the iron workers tried the ore in a "small Cubelo" furnace but without success. Lunt records that the waterwheel ran all night but froze up in the morning, which suggests that they may have been blowing air into the cupola as they would into a full-sized blast furnace.[41] Another trial was made on 30 December, running about 15 hours, but again there was no iron, Lunt reporting that "it is the judgment of all that there is something in it, that eats the Iron away."[42]

Although J. C. L. Smith had been named general superintendent of the iron works, he lived in Parowan and his duties as stake president kept him busy. He visited the works every two weeks or so, Lunt managing day-to-day affairs during his absence. In mid-December, Lunt confessed that he felt "a very heavy responsibility resting upon me in regard to the Iron works."[43] On 3 January 1853, Lunt consulted with Thomas Bladen, the engineer, and David B. Adams, the furnace master, on making iron. Lunt felt encouraged enough by their optimism to trust that God would indeed help the Iron Mission accomplish its task.[44] Four days later, Lunt invited the Deseret Iron Company officers still in Cedar City to a meeting and organized them as a council similar to the ecclesiastical councils with which he was familiar. In that setting, Lunt knew that he could reconcile any difficulties that existed among leaders of the company.[45] Writing to George A. Smith, he observed wryly, "As a general thing the spirit of the Lord presides in this place. There are few cases of the common disease, viz: a swelling in the head. I would recommend as a preventative, one ounce of humility and one grain of the spirit of the Lord."[46]

The harsh winter of 1852–53 limited activity at the iron works. J. C. L. Smith wrote George A. Smith early in January that the weather had been so cold it took two or three men half a day to chop ice off the waterwheels. The superintendent lamented that "some days we could not even do that, for it was so cold that it would freeze ice to the wheels so that they would not run."[47]

When that happened, the men used the time to get ready for the next thaw. On 10 December, for instance, Lunt rode along Coal Creek, seeking the best outtake from which to run water to the wheel for powering the blast.[48] On 12 January 1853, Lunt, J. C. L. Smith and James James opened a "splended mine of bog ore [hematite] one mile north East of the Iron works."[49] Several men spent the winter hauling dry pitch pine from the mountains, while Samuel Gould labored as collier, piling the wood into pits for making charcoal.[50] One of the pits "bursted out" and Lunt, alarmed, sent "the brethren to run with Buckets," dousing the flames before the cordwood could be consumed.[51] During the winter, six men from Parowan, led by John Steele, traveled 200 miles south to the Big Muddy, searching the California Road for discarded scrap iron. They returned with two tons.[52]

The main body of the blast furnace had been constructed of adobe in the summer. During the coldest months, the bottom of the furnace was repaved with new stones and the top was raised higher. A platform was erected on the east side of the furnace so that the charge of fuel, flux and ore could be wheeled directly to the mouth of the furnace. Thomas Cartwright made tuyeres (called "tweers" by the pioneers) for the furnace under the direction of David B. Adams. Two were thought sufficient because the furnace was small.[53]

Sometime before the end of 1852, James James, whom the boys of Cedar City jokingly called "Double James," had an idea for an "air furnace" which he enthusiastically brought to J. C. L. Smith. James believed that a sufficient draft of air could be created whether the smoke stack was lying down or standing up. Instead of building a higher chimney, he suggested they construct a horizontal smoke stack lying underground to connect with the 40-foot chimney already in existence.[54] James was confident that, with the draft created by this flue, his air furnace could not only smelt iron out of untried ore but also reheat pig iron for further castings.[55] Matthew Carruthers seems to have agreed with the concept, having commented as early as 3 January 1853 that "It seems quite certain that all the ores will work in the air furnace."[56] On 8 January, Henry Lunt recorded that the iron workers, implementing the design proposed by James

James, had begun building the foundation of the "stack for an air Furnace which will also answer for 4 furnaces."[57] This new "stack" was constructed as a horizontal flue, 250 feet long and lined with brick, requiring some 40,000 abodes.[58] Lunt reported on the progress of this "excellent Air Furnace" to the *Deseret News* on 26 February.[59]

It is clear from the primary sources that trial runs were soon underway but problems were seen almost from the start. Deseret Iron Company Minutes record that, on 12 May, Erastus Snow requested "fire brick for the arch of the air furnace, as the adobies had proved a failure and would not stand the fire, in consequence of which the furnace had not yet had a fair trial."[60] Lunt notes a further trial of the air furnace (perhaps rebuilt) on 13 July, producing 40 lbs. of "good clear metal," but on 18 July he had a new failure to report:

> Another trial was made in the air Furnace, the Furnace became exceedingly hot, and about 2 oclock the arch over the grate burned through, and a small quantity fell in. Consequently nothing much was done. The arch over the fire place was built of dobies. It was of the opinion of bro James that the stack wanted to be taken higher, and the arch to be built of fire brick. . . .[61]

Lunt's phrasing here is noticeably similar to Snow's of 12 May, strongly suggesting that the Apostle's request for firebrick two months earlier had been ignored. Taken together, the comments indicate that inferior materials were certainly jeopardizing the experiment.

For whatever reason, the venture seems not to have ended well. The author of the biographical sketch on J. C. L. Smith, quoted in the previous chapter, devotes several paragraphs to James's air furnace. In his opinion,

> The project proved a costly failure. The draft was temperamental. It flowed down as often as up and it changed without any provocation or warning. The money was wasted but the mistake was as much the fault of Erastus Snow and Franklin D. Richards as of John Calvin Smith. He spent it honestly and got good value in labor and materials for it but the idea was wrong.[62]

Because one end of the underground flue surfaced near the bank of Coal Creek, it became in later years an adventuresome hideout near the swimming hole for the town's youngsters, salvaging something of use from an otherwise frustrating venture.[63]

On a more encouraging note, George A. Smith sent word on 15 January 1853 that the territorial legislature had approved $3,000 for coal and iron business in southern Utah.[64] This revenue was granted in addition to the $2,000 appropriated in December for developing roads to the coal mines. According to William R. Palmer, the Iron Mission was also awarded something of a tax break:

> The tax levy was 1 per cent—five mills for the Territory and five mills for the County. The assessor did a through job for both tax units needed money badly. The local tax valuation was $19,894, which included homes, farms, wagons, horses, oxen, clock and watches and every other kind of property found by the assessor. The total tax levied was $198.94, one-half of which ($99.47) belonged to the Territory. To clear their records and avoid showing a loss, the Territory made the generous gesture of assisting the iron industry by appropriating to them "the deliquent taxes of Iron County for the year 1852." These deliquent taxes amounted to something less than $50.00, the debtors having absconded to California.[65]

On 31 January, 40 iron workers were busily working on the supposedly improved blast furnace. In the weeks that followed, Richard Benson put up a wooden casting house and Richard Harrison laid out casting moulds on the foundry floor, ready for the next pour from the furnace.[66] Thomas Bladen repaired the blowing apparatus to work with the new overshot wheel and the wheel itself was given a new dam, millrace and flume. On 25 February, the improved system was tried and, with minor adjustments, worked satisfactorily.[67]

Trial Runs

These winter attempts to upgrade the blast furnace culminated in a trial run on Saturday, 26 February. As recorded in the Minutes of the Deseret Iron Company, the first charge consisted of the following materials:

5 bushels of charcoal	100 lbs.
iron ore (from West Mountain)	36 lbs.
bog ore	26 lbs.
limestone	15 lbs.[68]

In his letter to George A. Smith of 7 March, Henry Lunt stated that the bog ore (hematite) and West Mountain ore (magnetite) made a "first rate" combination.[69] The slag began running within half an hour after the blast was put on and continued throughout the day, with iron beginning to be visible in the slag. Despite their high hopes, however, furnace master David B. Adams discovered early Sunday morning that the iron had chilled at the bottom of the furnace. Acting immediately, Lunt and six of the iron workers began clearing the furnace. They found that the iron had indeed chilled around the tuyeres. They fired up again, hoping to create a blast hot enough to burn the iron out. The approach did not work, so all they could do was begin preparations for a new trial run.[70]

At this point, the iron workers decided that a change in furnace design might improve their luck. Thinking that perhaps blasting from two tuyeres on opposite sides of the hearth was causing the furnace to blow itself out, they "fixed both Tweers together in one Tweer hole" and rerouted the blast.[71] They also experimented with a new charge, decreasing West Mountain ore and bog ore by 6 pounds each and adding 5 pounds of limestone flux. This time they met with more success. Starting Tuesday, 1 March, the furnace ran for 18 hours and produced about 250 lbs. of iron. By Thursday, the furnace was consuming 200 bushels of charcoal every 24 hours. Thursday was supposed to be fast day, but the iron workers were too busy to observe it, everyone working feverishly to replenish the fuel supply. The next day, the furnace had to be stopped for lack of fuel. During the week, about 1,600 bushels of charcoal were consumed, resulting in approximately 2,500 lbs. of white, hard iron.[72]

"Hosannas to God": Cast Iron for April Conference, 1853

Given the fuel emergency, Lunt called a special Sunday meeting of company shareholders on 6 March to consider the best way to obtain "stone coal." Matthew Carruthers was made "Ground Bailiff" and it was decided to get the coal by letting the job out to the lowest bidder. On 10 March, crews were sent into the canyon to remove snow "some two feet deep and more" from working mines and search for new deposits although it was "snowing very fast all the time, and very cold and stormy.[73]"

Meanwhile, James James hurried north with a sample of iron, ready to report that no obstacle stood in the way of making iron as fast as coal could be obtained to fuel the blast. Willard Richards, editor of the *Deseret News,* was suitably impressed and voiced the hope that "appropriations of the Legislature will be speedily applied to the opening of the roads, mines, &c., so that the precious metal may be soon in circulation, in all its useful modes throughout our Territory."[74] Both money and equipment were needed to alleviate the fuel crisis. As early as February 1852, Matthew Carruthers had written Brigham Young begging for supplies: "If the brethren that come on this sp[r]ing would bring along boring rods, rope for sinking pits, and all the mining tools they possibly can, all the blasting powder they can, also iron and steel etc., they would confer a favor."[75]

On 15 March 1853, less than three weeks before April general conference, Lunt visited the iron works and found that several of the brethren were determined to set up the cupola furnace in order to cast a useful object for display in Salt Lake City. On the 16th, Richard Harrison, the moulder, reported having "fixed the cubelow Molded 2 Skillits and a pair of Hand Irons for fire place" (see illus. 11-3). The next day he wrote:

> T 17 [March] 1 Day Heated up the Cubelow and melted about 400 lbs of Iron. Cast a pair of Hand Irons or fire Dogs, the first pair ever cast in Iron County, State of Deseret. A number of persons on the ground at the time to see the Sight. 3 cheers was given for Iron County and the Heavens whas made to ring with Hosannas to God and the Lamb for ever & ever.[76]

Such success right before April conference was exhilarating. Lunt wrote that a "spirit of energy and enterprise seemed to be in the bosom of many of the brethren."[77] On 18 March, the cupola was raised several feet and preparations were made for another trial. On the 19th, Harrison heated the cupola and moulded a kettle, a skillet, two spider gears, two tuyeres, dam plates and another pair of andirons. Even so, he noted, "The Mettle whas very Hard and thick."[78]

The next day was Sunday. At the evening meeting, Henry Lunt, Matthew Carruthers and Richard Harrison all gave iron sermons. Lunt especially "preached a most tremendous loud discourse to the brethren on their Mission of making Iron, long to be remembered I presume by all who were sent down to this place." When he asked for those willing to

Illus. 11-3. This set of pioneer andirons (dog irons) is similar in shape and style to those produced by the Deseret Iron Works at Cedar City in the 1850s. These irons were made by historian William Palmer's father, Richard Palmer.

Photograph by Randall B. Shirts

spend full time on iron to signify their intentions, 33 men stood up.[79] They assembled in the casting house on Monday, 21 March, and were organized to carry out their tasks. They met again that evening in the fort with the farmers whose help was solicited to haul wood. Lunt felt the farmers "were very backward at promising to do anything for the Iron works" and he chastised them severely.[80]

On 22 March, Lunt recommended that they try "Raw Pitch Pine" in the cupola furnace and it worked "first rate." Harrison was able to cast a pair of pedestals, a wheel, another spider gear and tuyeres for the furnace. Leaving Matthew Carruthers in charge of the iron works, Henry Lunt and J. C. L. Smith headed for Salt Lake City, having chosen to take the andirons for conference display.[81] While their leaders rode north, the iron workers were eager to try pitch pine in the blast furnace. On 1 April, they tried a charge that produced the "best cast of iron" than any before it:

Wood	100 lbs.
Charcoal	50 lbs.
West Mountain ore	25 lbs.
Bog ore	30 lbs.
Limestone	10 lbs.

The result was "good shaped pigs" of "good grey iron." Raw wood was tried without charcoal but did not work as well. Thomas Bladen fitted the waterwheel with a fly-wheel and added a turning lathe and circular saw (presumably to cut wood for the furnace).[82]

In Salt Lake City, Henry Lunt toured the city with his wife Ellen. They were among the more than 5,000 Saints who witnessed the laying of the foundation cornerstones for the Salt Lake Temple. Lunt was impressed that "some hundreds of houses . . . and some very good ones too" had been built since he left two years earlier. He felt that the Tabernacle, the council house and the storehouse were fine buildings that "would grace the City of London." Lunt called on Brigham Young, who seemed pleased that he had brought a sample of the iron castings. George A. Smith assured Lunt that President Young would have the "Dog Irons" polished and placed on the stand during conference.[83]

On Thursday, 7 April, Henry and Ellen arose early for an 8:00 A.M. meeting in the Tabernacle. When members of the congregation were invited to speak, Lunt rose out of the audience and told about the progress of the Iron Mission in Cedar City. At this point, Dr. Festus Sprague brought the andirons out of the vestry where they had been stored and placed them on the stand. Lunt was satisfied that "the saints appeared quite excited and well pleased at the sample of cast Iron made in the mountains by the Saints."[84]

In the regular conference session later that day, George A. Smith was called on to give another "Iron Sermon," just as he had done in October 1852. As the *Deseret News* reported it, he "took in the stand one of the Fireirons, holding the same over his head, cried out, 'Stereotype edition,' and descended, amid the cheers of the Saints." It is not unreasonable to suspect that the congregation, which had been seated over five hours, eagerly stood for a rousing rendition of the closing hymn, "Praise God from Whom All Blessings Flow!"[85]

The atmosphere of success apparently encouraged some enterprising individuals to attempt making iron on their own. In spring 1853, Peter Shirts and Thomas Jones were reported to have built a smelting furnace on the outside of the fort wall to try some ore they had prospected. John D. Lee was concerned that their furnace would provide cover for Indians who might shoot at the fort. Shirts and Jones refused to pull down their furnace, so John D. Lee did it himself. John Spiers, a settler in Cedar City, stated cynically that the ruins made an even better hiding place for the Indians, "for where only ten could hide before fifty could now find ample protection."[86]

All in all, many of the settlers were engaged in iron-making throughout the spring. The daily journal of the Deseret Iron Company for 1853 lists the names of 68 men who labored at the iron works between January and April 1853, as well as the number of days they worked. Collectively, the number came to 2,106. David B. Adams, Thomas Cartwright, Joseph Walker, Thomas Bladen and Jonathan Pugmire worked over 100 days each. The entire complement of men averaged 30 days each, although about a third of them contributed only the equivalent of a week or less.[87]

Buying Merchandise for the Company Store

At the beginning of May 1853, Erastus Snow, accompanied by Amasa Lyman and Charles C. Rich, paid a second visit to Iron County. Erastus Snow informed the iron workers that they could not expect a pay check every Saturday night, but that

> we will endeavour to satisfy your wants as well as we reasonably can. I know it will be a very good thing for you to have your wages in the iron works as a bank, for if you have your money you will squander it, and if it is in the bank, it will be saved till a day of need.[88]

About the only "wages" the workers received came as goods stocked by the Deseret Iron Company store, which indeed acted as the community bank. On his recent trip to Salt Lake City for conference, Henry Lunt had met Edward Williams and his company about seven miles north of Beaver on their way to Cedar City. Williams was bringing "a few groceries" from Erastus Snow and Franklin D. Richards for the store as well as an invoice for about $900.00 worth of dry goods, which would be sent along soon.[89] This document, entitled "Invoice of goods for Iron County, No. 1," is dated 28 February 1853. It lists $869.93 worth of dry goods, mostly fabric (including alpaca, silk, flannel, muslin, Irish linen, velvet, lace, "Casimere" and "Green Barize" for veils) and $182.30 worth of books (including 80 readers, four copies of Webster's *Dictionary,* 30 of Holbrook's *Arithmetic,* 20 of Weld's *Grammar,* nine of Olney's *Geography,* two of Parker's *Philosophy* and one of Comstock's *Chemistry.*)

Lunt's "few groceries" were also listed on "Invoice No. 1" and amounted to $751.55 worth of coffee, tea, sugar, tobacco, dried fruit and soap.[90] An "Invoice No. 2" for additional delivery to Cedar City, dated March 1853, itemized several pounds of dye (indigo, Prussian blue, umber and "extract of logwood"), boots, locks and latches, lampblack, starch, borax, sand paper and 25 bottles of "Acids, &c." purchased by James James.[91]

Home from his conference trip, Henry Lunt spent 2 May opening and marking off the goods and 3 May with J. C. L. Smith selling the goods for cash.[92] Comparing a price list of items for sale with the original invoices indicates goods were sold for what they cost, with no mark-up. Iron county residents could buy a first reader for 30¢, a grammar book for $1.25, a pound of sugar for 50¢, a pound of imported tea for $2.25, a pair of men's boots for $4.50, one cravat for $2.00, a bonnet for $3.50, bar soap for 55¢, one yard silk for $2.20, a yard of linen for $1.25 or a card of hooks and eyes for 10¢.[93]

Not only did Richards and Snow supply the Deseret Iron Company store through Salt Lake City merchants such as Kinkead & Company but they also bought goods from a variety of enterprises in St. Louis. These transactions were made by purchasing agent Vincent Shurtleff on credit through the Alexander Dow Company, a kind of international clearing company that arranged for financing from England or Salt Lake City and then paid the bills. Although the ultimate goal of the Iron Mission was to make Utah Territory more independent, receipts from 8 to 14 June 1853 show that the Deseret Iron Company was, in fact, buying on a large scale in St. Louis from numerous companies (see related sidebar).[94]

A final shipment of merchandise for the year 1853 was sent to President J. C. L. Smith by Snow and Richards on 5 September. The shipment consisted primarily of boots and shoes, cloth and construction materials. As the two noted, the purpose of the shipment was to pay the company's debts and to "supply . . . the wants of the people." Smith was cautioned to keep a strict account of every item, reimbursing the account of Snow and Richards as soon as the goods were sold. The value of any unsold item was to be credited back to the Deseret Iron Company. After having sold the merchandise, Smith credited $1,475.67 to Snow and Richards and later transferred $96.79, representing the unsold goods, back to the general manager for the use of the company.[95]

Sharing the Workload: the Iron Council is Called

On 12 May 1853, two weeks after he addressed the iron workers, Apostle Snow met with the company's leadership. J. C. L. Smith pointed out that he had more work than he could handle and would be happy to be released as superintendent of the works. Snow decided to retain Smith at least until the general shareholders' meeting in the fall, but proposed that a council of five men help him. Matthew Carruthers, Henry Lunt, Richard Harrison, Thomas Bladen and David Barclay Adams were unanimously chosen to form this council. A special office was planned for the iron works, to serve as both superintendent's office and council room.

The makeup of the group is intriguing. Carruthers and Lunt would be considered management; Bladen and Adams, labor; Harrison, iron moulder and former superintendent, falls into both categories. Snow may have realized that it was time to invite workers' opinions into the decision-making process. John Chatterley, many years after his service as a foundryman, penned a strong opinion of his own about labor relations on site, using Adams as his example:

> The business would have been successful if those that had a little authority would not have interferred with the practical workmen, who had in their native homes in the old countries run out thousands upon thousands of tons of cast iron but authority would order the charges in the blast furnace changed[,] consequently the furnace gobbed up. . . . There was one person (David B. Adams) was a thorough practical furnace keeper and when allowed to have his way about managing the furnace, would make the moltin iron run from the furnace as free and almost as thin as water.[96]

As well as organizing the iron council, Snow also admonished Henry Lunt to take care of the company books; further, Snow made Matthew

Carruthers responsible for day-to-day administration of the works when J. C. L. Smith was unavailable.

In addition to documenting the iron council, the minutes of the 12 May meeting are valuable because they explain an otherwise ambiguous reference to a fort that Henry Lunt makes note of in his journal on 14 May: "Went up to the Iron works with bro Snow and look[ed] out a place for to lay off a Fort. He said he empowered me to see to the locating of it, and

---

SHOPPING IN ST. LOUIS
DESERET IRON COMPANY RECEIPTS, JUNE 1853

Eddy, Jameson & Co.	$ 947.08
(fabric, handkerchiefs, needles, buttons, jeans)	
Ellis & Cavender	513.34
(boots and shoes)	
George D. Little	1,499.47
(shirting, flannel, blankets)	
Barnard Adams [2 receipts; totaling:]	29.53
(window glass, hardware, drugs, chemicals)	
William W. Price	73.50
(hardware and cutlery)	
Robert Nicholson	331.12
(sugar, spice, tea, coffee, tobacco, dried fruit)	
St. Louis Coat Company	159.00
(mens apparel)	
E. A. & S. R. Filley	55.68
(dishes, china)	
Amos H. Shultz	92.26
(school books, dictionaries)	
E. R. Violett & Co	42.83
(cast steel, nails)	
Meyer & Braun	160.87
(shoemaking supplies, leather)	
J. T. Dowdall & Co.	51.98
(weaving materials, wool carding cards and combs)	
Charles Rogers	236.48
(cutlery, scissors, door locks, screws, ink, steel pens)	

Source: Palmer Collection, SUU Archives

also to the giving out of the Lots."[97] It was on 14 May 1852, exactly one year earlier, that Lunt had gone walking with Philip Klingensmith, also to "look out a sight" for a new fort. Nothing came of their efforts at that time, as we know, and Lunt does not record the true beginnings of Cedar City's relocation phase until six months later, on 27 October, when he again, this time in the company of George A. Smith and others, "look[ed] out a sight for a city," the future Plat A.

The 1852 events might mislead us into assuming that the 14 May 1853 site review was similar—a premature attempt that produced no results. Indeed, the outcome of this second search for a fort site was the same as the first: nothing happened. But the intention here, in 1853, was more defined and its scope more precise than that of a year ago. This site exploration would probably have resulted in a building project adjacent to the iron works had the town's priorities not been redirected by fears of Indian unrest. The intended 1853 fort was, in fact, the brainchild of Erastus Snow, who appears to have envisioned it as a kind of workers' dormitory, convenient for the men and efficient for the iron works:

> President Snow said he had decided to have a fort built near to the iron works for the brethren to live in who would be constantly employed at the works. He sugested that the lots and entire fort be in the hands of the Deseret Iron Company; he recommended the houses to be built uniform neat and good. He thought of proposing that the brethren turn in the field [presumably West Field] to the company, and for the company to employ a few good hands to farm it.

The workers, however, were not enthusiastic about the idea, the desire seeming to be "for every one to farm his own." Even so, "It was moved and carried unanimously that Bro. Snow select a sight for a field for the Deseret Iron Company."[98] Despite Snow's apparently well-conceived design and his sufficient authority to implement it, neither fort nor field materialized as he intended. Instead, central activities in the township for the next few months focused on securing what already existed against possible Indian attack.

Meanwhile, the newly formed iron council met first on 5 June, to discuss spending the appropriations for roads and coal mines in the canyons, and again on 10 July to discuss ways to move ahead on the iron works and provide food for the workers.[99] On 9 July, Lorenzo Barton asked members of the council for 270 lbs. of iron from the blacksmith shop to build machinery in Parowan but they concluded that, if Barton had "nearly all the wrought Iron that the Iron Co. had on hand," it would slow the progress of the iron works.[100] A meeting between Franklin D. Richards and the "proprietors" was scheduled for 26 July 1853, but due to Brigham Young's warnings regarding Indian difficulties, it was canceled in favor of devoting all energies to settlement defense.[101]

The pioneers had fulfilled the monumental task of relocating their townsite while still maintaining trial runs at the iron works, producing, indeed, the first actual implements. Again, however, the uncertainties of pioneer life interrupted furnace activity. For the rest of the summer, community efforts would be channeled into "forting up," a task which necessarily brought iron production to a standstill.

Endnotes

1. Lunt, diary, 14 May 1852.

2. Jarvis, *Ancestry,* 165. During the October general conference, George A. Smith himself had proposed that Lee start a settlement on the Virgin River where warm-weather produce could be raised.

3. Conway B. Sonne, *World of Wakara* (San Antonio, Tex.: Naylor, 1962), 200–201; S. Lyman Tyler, "The Earliest Peoples," in Poll, Alexander, Campbell and Miller, eds., *Utah's History,* 28–29.

4. Whittaker, journal, 12 and 16 Mar 1852.

5. Lunt, diary, 2 Jul and 7 Aug 1852.

6. Ibid., 7 and 9 Aug 1852; see also Dalton, *Iron County Mission,* 77–78, relating the story with slight variations.

7. Knecht and Crawley, *Early Records,* 121.

8. George A. Smith to Samuel W. Richards, 7 Nov 1852, cited as "Prosperity of Iron County, Deseret" in *Millennial Star* 15 (19 Mar 1853): 188; see also Lunt, diary, 18 Oct 1852.

9. Lunt, ibid., 21 Oct 1852.

10. Brigham Young to Isaac Higbee, 18 Oct 1849, published in Roberts, *Comprehensive History,* 3:458–59.

11. Lunt, diary, 20 Feb 1853.

12. Hancock, "Biography of Charles Willden," 14.

13. Lunt, diary, 1 Nov 1852.

14. Ibid., 2 Nov 1852.

15. LaVon Adams Mons, "History of David Barclay Adams, Pioneer of 1852," typescript, 1–2, copy in Shirts Collection; see also Mary E. Adams, comp., "Diary of David Barclay Adams," typescript, 1, copy in Shirts Collection.

16. Lunt, diary, 13 Nov 1852.

17. Ibid., 11 Nov 1852; Jarvis, *Ancestry,* 166.

18. Lunt, ibid., 27 Oct 1852.

19. George A. Smith to Samuel W. Richards, 26 Dec 1852, published in *Millennial Star* 15 (30 Apr 1853): 286. Smith mentions 200 lots, while William Palmer gives a figure of 120. Palmer, however, was only including those lots north and east of the public square which fell inside the Cedar City (Plat A) fort. See illus. 12-1 incorporating Palmer's drawing of the Plat A Fort; see also Palmer, "Gleanings," Palmer Collection; and Jarvis, *Ancestry,* 166–67.

20. Lunt, diary, 27–28 Oct 1852.

21. See ch. 10, n. 35. Franklin D. Richards verifies that George A. Smith left for northern Utah on 21 Nov, the day after Snow and Richards arrived in Parowan. See Richards, journal, 20–21 Nov 1852.

22. Deed Book A, ca. 28 Jan through 1 Mar 1853.

23. Lunt, diary, 28 Jun, 14 and 26 Oct 1852.

24. Ibid., 1 Nov 1852.

25. Ibid., 5 Feb 1853.

26. Henry Lunt to editor, 26 Feb 1853, published in *Deseret News* 10 Mar 1853, 34.

27. Lunt, diary, 30 Apr 1852 (referring to 29 Apr), 8 and 12 Jun 1853.

28. Ibid., 19 May 1853.

29. Ibid., 11 and 19 Feb, 2 Jun 1853.

30. Ibid., 17 Oct 1852.

31. Ibid., 7 Nov and 25 Dec 1852; 23 Jan and 6 Feb 1853.

32. Ibid., 6 Mar 1853.

33. Ibid., 27 Apr 1853.

34. Ibid., 30 Apr–1 May 1853.

35. Hancock, "Biography of Charles Willden," 15.

36. Several sources on Feargus O'Connor Willden are known. The LDS Church Archives has a "compiled information" file, donated in 1957 by Ione Thompson of West Valley City, Utah. It is distinct from the one-page sheet of notes made by William Palmer about Feargus, titled "Extracts of Biography of Feargus O'Connor Willden Written by Himself" which is now in the Palmer Collection. Here, we cite passages from a typescript about Feargus of which the Shirts Collection has only pp. 3–6 and 10 and the origin of which was long unknown. Late in preparing this book, however, contact was made with Ronald Payne of Spanish Fork and Sharon Rae Payne of Salt Lake City, who made available their Willden family histories for examination. The Shirts Collection pages appear to be taken from a 68-page history entitled "Biography of Feargus O'Connor Willden and Progenitors" of which the Paynes have a complete copy (the location of the original is unknown). We are indebted to them for identifying this source.

37. Lunt, diary, 30 Dec 1852–1 Jan 1853.

38. Ibid., 10 Feb 1853.

39. Ibid., 22 Feb 1853.

40. Zilpha Smith to George A. Smith, 24 Sep 1854, George A. Smith Papers, LDS Church Archives. We are indebted to Jill Mulvay Derr for bringing this letter to our attention.

41. Lunt, diary, 16–17 Dec 1852.

42. Ibid., 30 Dec 1852. See ch. 13, nn. 17–19 in reference to a similar situation in 1854, pointing up a chronic problem within the pioneer smelting process.

43. Ibid., 16 Dec 1852.

44. Ibid., 3 Jan 1853.

45. Ibid., 7 Jan 1853.

46. Henry Lunt to George A. Smith, 7 Mar 1853, published in *Deseret News,* 3 Apr 1853 3d unnumbered page.

47. J. C. L. Smith to George A. Smith, 3 Jan 1853, in *Deseret News,* 5 Feb 1853, 2nd unnumbered page.

48. Lunt, diary, 10 Dec 1852.

49. Ibid., 12 Jan 1853.

50. Deseret Iron Company, Minutes, 7; Lunt, diary, 12 Jan 1853.

51. Lunt, diary, 6 Feb 1853.

52. Ibid., 21 Feb 1853; Deseret Iron Company, Minutes, 7.

53. Deseret Iron Company, ibid.

54. "John Calvin Lazell [*sic*] Smith," 2–3.

55. Deseret Iron Company, Minutes, 7.

56. Matthew Carruthers to Franklin D. Richards, 3 Jan 1853, excerpted in "News from Iron County," *Deseret News,* 5 Feb 1853, 3d unnumbered page.

57. Lunt, diary, 8 Jan 1853.

58. Deseret Iron Company, Minutes, 7; "John Calvin Lazell Smith," 3.

59. Lunt to editor, 26 Feb 1853, published in Deseret News, 10 Mar 1853.

60. Deseret Iron Company, Minutes, 11.

61. Lunt, diary, 13 and 18 Jul 1853.

62. "John Calvin Lazell Smith," 3.

63. Ibid.

64. Lunt, diary, 15 Jan 1853; "An Act, Appropriating Money to promote the manufacturing of Iron in Iron County," 5 Jan 1853, in *Territorial Acts and Resolutions.*

65. William R. Palmer, "Utah's Pioneer Iron Industry," *Sons of Utah Pioneers News* (Salt Lake City: Sons of Utah Pioneers, Aug 1957), B-10, B-11.

66. "Diary of Richard Harrison," 6. The relevant phrases are: (26 Feb) "preparing floor of the foundry"; (28 Feb) "fixing the moulding floor in the foundry"; (1 Mar) "fixing Molding floor"; (2 Mar) "working at a flask & molding

floor"; (21 Mar) "Prepaired the Sand for molding." Lunt's letter of 26 Feb 1853 mentions that about half of the 70 men in and about Cedar City were regularly employed by the Deseret Iron Company.

67. Deseret Iron Company, Minutes, 7; Lunt, diary, 25 Feb 1853.

68. Minutes, ibid.

69. Lunt to Smith, 7 Mar 1853.

70. Lunt, diary, 26–28 Feb 1853.

71. Ibid., 28 Feb 1853.

72. Ibid., 1–4 Mar 1853; Deseret Iron Company, Minutes, 8. Lunt writes that coal was used, while the Minutes refer to charcoal. In his letter to George A. Smith, 7 Mar 1853, Lunt agrees with the Minutes in stating that charcoal was used for this run.

73. Lunt, diary, 10 Mar 1853.

74. Lunt to Smith, 7 Mar 1853.

75. Matthew Carruthers to Brigham Young, 5 Feb 1852, in Journal History.

76. "Diary of Richard Harrison," 17 Mar 1853.

77. Lunt, diary, 17 Mar 1853.

78. "Diary of Richard Harrison," 18–19 Mar 1853.

79. Lunt, diary, 20 Mar 1853; Harrison, ibid., 20 Mar 1853.

80. Lunt, ibid., 21 Mar 1853.

81. Ibid., 22–23 Mar 1853; "Diary of Richard Harrison," 22 Mar 1853; Deseret Iron Company, Minutes, 8.

82. Minutes, ibid.

83. Lunt, diary, 2 and 4 Apr 1853.

84. Ibid., 7 Apr 1853.

85. Conference Report of Apr 1853, *Deseret News,* 30 Apr 1853, 3d unnumbered page, referring to George A. Smith's "Iron Sermon."

86. Crook, "Early Industry and Trade," 59, n. 2.

87. Crook, ibid., 50–51, citing Deseret Iron Company Journal.

88. Deseret Iron Company, Minutes, 9.

89. Lunt, diary, 25 Mar 1853.

90. Deseret Iron Company, "Invoice of goods for Iron County, No. 1," 28 Feb 1853, Palmer Collection.

91. Deseret Iron Company, "Snow & Richards, Invoice No. 2, Deseret Iron Co.," Mar 1853, Palmer Collection.

92. Lunt, diary, 2 May 1853.

93. "Price List of Items in Cedar City Taken from One Sheet of Company's Books, 1853," cited in Crook, "Early Industry and Trade," 60–62.

94. Deseret Iron Company, Misc. Receipts, 8–14 June 1853, Palmer Collection.

95. Erastus Snow and Franklin D. Richards to "Brother Calvin," 5 Sep 1853, Palmer Collection.

96. Chatterley, "History of Cedar City," 5–6.

97. Lunt, diary, 14 May 1853.

98. Deseret Iron Company, Minutes, 11.

99. Ibid., 12; Lunt, diary, 5 Jun, 10 Jul 1853.

100. Lunt, ibid., 9 Jul 1853.

101. Deseret Iron Company, Minutes, 12.

12

Forting Up during the Walker War

1853–1854

Exactly when the decision was made in Cedar City to build a new fort by enclosing part of Plat A with a wall is not known. The fort is not included in Dame's survey and archaeological evidence shows that the wall encircled only the northeast sector of the plat. Most sources indicate this wall was built in response to the growing Indian unrest which culminated in the Walker War.

By 1853, Mormon settlers had outstayed their welcome in Wakara's territory. While the Ute leader initially saw the Mormons as a useful barrier between his people and the Shoshoni and as a market for horse trading, the differing perspectives of settlers and Indians led to constant misunderstandings. On their part, Mormons were not sympathetic to Wakara's raids on weaker tribes, such as the Paiutes, to provide women and children for slave traders. Subsequent antislave-trade acts passed by the territorial legislature displeased the Indians, who felt the newcomers had no right to interfere with tribal economy and traditions. Despite Brigham Young's policy of conciliation, Mormons were continually on their guard whenever they ventured outside their forts. The Indians feared that, proffers of friendship aside, the coming of white settlers to their homeland meant the end of traditional Indian society.[1]

In April 1853, a misunderstanding almost triggered armed hostilities in Parowan. George Braffit missed a pair of fine horses after an emigrant party had passed through en route to southern California. A militia detachment, headed by James A. Little and including James H. Martineau, Priddy Meeks, Samuel Gould and nine other men, started out for Iron Springs, the emigrants' last stop. Wakara and 700 men were camped at Summit Creek and observed this military activity with alarm. A small boy told Wakara's scout that the militia was "going out to fight Walkar." When the posse of settlers arrived at Summit Creek, their behavior was so boisterous that Wakara was convinced the information was correct and had his warriors surround the men. When Little explained they were merely after missing horses, Wakara would not believe him and flatly stated the emigrants hadn't taken the animals.

Colonel Little reportedly said "Well, boys, then let's go home," and led his group through the ranks of suspicious Indians, who turned and pursued the settlers rather half-heartedly for some time. The militia reached Parowan safely but a council was quickly convened and "everyone went to making bullets." A young man named Samuel Lewis volunteered to report this encounter to Brigham Young and ask his advice. Leaving the settlement within the hour, he successfully made the 540-mile round trip in eight days, averaging over 65 miles a day. He returned with "orders to avoid all trouble or conflict, as Parowan was too distant to receive any help." Fortunately, by the time he returned, local tensions had subsided.[2]

Brigham Young was very aware of such dangers, especially to those in outlying colonies. He took advantage of the 4th of July 1853 falling on a Sabbath to reaffirm previous counsel. The content of his Sunday sermon from the Tabernacle to the members at large could not have reached southern Utah for several days at least. Its context, however, shows that initial warnings to prepare against possible Indian attack had been made some weeks before he spoke:

> There seems to be some excitement among the people, and fears are arising in the breasts of many as to the general safety. . . . If the people of Utah Territory would do as they are told, they would always be safe. . . . The word has gone out now, to the different settlements in the time of harvest, requiring them to build Forts. Could it not have been done last winter, better than now? Yes. Do you not suppose people will now wish they had built Forts when they were told? . . . They will learn better I expect by and by, for the people have never received such strict orders as they have got now. I will give you the pith of the last orders issued; (v.z.) "That man or family who will not do as they are told on the orders, are to be treated as strangers, yea, even as enemies, and not as friends."[3]

The same month, Indians and Mormons fought at Springville, Utah County, over how much fish should be traded for how much flour. The minor affair escalated, not ending until violence broke out, leaving one of the Indians dead. Efforts at some form of conciliation on both sides were of momentary effect and on 18 July 1853, Wakara's brother Arapeen (or Arapeen's companion) fatally shot Alexander Keele as Keele stood guard at Fort Peteetneet.[4] In response, Colonel Peter W. Conover, acting on

Brigham Young's orders, left Provo on 19 July, heading for Manti with 150 men, intending to help weaker settlements along the route by displaying strength and resolve to Wakara. But the Indians were "neither idle nor dismayed by the force sent out." In a set of well-directed, simultaneous skirmishes, they surprised the post at Pleasant Creek, stole cattle from Manti and horses from Nephi and wounded a guard in Springville.[5]

On 20 July, Apostle Franklin D. Richards arrived in Parowan to inform the settlers that general fighting had commenced and that they were to take immediate precautions. As governor and ex officio superintendent of Indian affairs, Brigham Young issued General Orders on 21 and 25 July, outlining military measures. An 1852 restructuring of the Nauvoo Legion by the territorial legislature had elevated Daniel H. Wells to the rank of lieutenant general, the first to be given that position since Joseph Smith. Young and Wells now ordered that

> the policy of constructing forts and occupying them be adopted and rigidly enforced—that the commandants of the various military districts in the Territory cause all of the forces under their commands respectively to repair immediately to their posts in their various settlements putting the same in a state of effecient defence, keeping their arms and ammunition in readiness, constructing corrals for stock and stack yards for the grain and taking all possible care of the grain, hay and vegetables.[6]

Apparently believing that Conover had become more punitive of the Indians than protective of the settlers, Brigham Young also ordered a conclusion to his military expedition and forbade "the settlers to retaliate on the Indians or threaten retaliation." In Conover's place, Brigham Young sent his southern Utah specialist, George A. Smith, to take "command of all the Military districts south of Great Salt Lake County, with instructions to enforce General orders No. 1."[7]

Abandoning the Compact Fort, 27 July–11 August 1853

Meanwhile, events in southern Utah were taking on the form and direction Brigham wished. On 26 July, the very day after the second issuance of General Orders in Salt Lake City, George Bowering noted in his journal that, as part of a continuing celebration in Cedar City of the festivities surrounding the 24th, a dance was held in the afternoon.

> ... in the midst of dancing in all the glory thereof. We were called out of the Ball-room in the Bowery to listen to instructions, or orders, from Head Quarters, that is to say from Pres. Brigham Young, Governor of

Utah Territory. The orders were to enforce Martial Law, in consequence of Indian difficulties. And notice given for every man to
reassemble in the Bowery to-morrow morning to hear the General
Orders read[.][8]

Bowering had only been in the Cedar City settlement since 30 April
1853, arriving that Saturday evening with his fellow-travelers, the Robert
Latham family. He expected to be employed herding cattle but was quickly
called to teach school instead. Since he boarded successively with parents
of his students, he did not at first build a home of his own. Starting classes
at 9 A.M. on Monday, 9 May, with nearly 60 pupils, he probably spent
much of his time in the Compact Fort in the "Small log-house called the
schoolhouse." His description might have mildly irked Henry Lunt, who
had just overseen a "comodius" enlargement of the building, completed,
almost certainly, in the hours just prior to Bowering's arrival.[9]

On 27 July, the morning after the dance was interrupted, the men
gathered in the Bowery to hear the reading of General Orders, after which
the battalion was reorganized. Instructions from Salt Lake City were very
clear and, as Bowering reports, were carried out right away:

> The families living South side the creek commanded to move into the
> fort. Peter Shirts came in from Shirts' Creek seven miles south. John D
> Lee came in from Harmony sixteen miles south. The brethren began to
> build up every open place in the fort, and to settle down as well as they
> could, Joel H Johnson and family moved in from his place six miles
> north, The brethren stood guard day and night and things going on
> well under the directions of Elder F D Richards[.][10]

Twenty-six teams and wagons were immediately dispatched to help dis-
mantle Harmony's eight houses, load up the logs and transfer them to
Cedar City. Twelve teams came from Cedar City to Shirts Creek and 20
to Johnson's Spring to help with the move.[11]

Brigham Young sent Lieutenant Colonel William H. Kimball, son of
his counselor Heber C. Kimball, to implement General Orders in the outlying colonies during this period of uncertainty. Kimball, whose
"Southern Expedition No. 1" raised the protective mine breastworks
mentioned in chapter 9, kept a daily journal of their itinerary. On
2 August, Kimball rode into Parowan, noting on the same day that "E. F.
Heap," Superintendent of Indian Affairs (actually E. F. *Beale*) made him
a courtesy call.[12]

On the 3d, Kimball assessed Parowan's military status, pronouncing
all but two of the settlement's firearms in good condition. He praised the

town, saying the pioneers were "in good order for defending themselves," and singled out Captain Hopkins for "having his men under a rigid discipline." Returning to Cedar City, Kimball and his party passed through Johnson's Spring, confirming that the small colony had indeed relocated to the larger settlement.[13] "The Piede [Paiute] Indians at these settlements were very friendly," reported John Lyman Smith who had joined Kimball's expedition. "[T]he settlers left their grain; chickens, &c., in their care."[14]

These reports are complemented by those of E. F. Beale, Kimball's misidentified visitor. Traveling through Cedar City with a small party on 4 August 1853, he recorded the scene in the official journal of the trip:

> The inhabitants are principally foreigners, and mostly Englishmen from the coal districts of Great Britain. At the time of our visit, the place was crowded with the people of the surrounding country seeking refuge from the Indians, and its square was blocked up with wagons, furniture, tents, farming implements, &c., in the midst of which were men, women, and children, together with every description of cattle, creating a scene of confusion difficult to describe.[15]

We know that the fort referred to directly by Bowering and indirectly by Beale is the Compact Fort, because construction of defensive walls in Plat A had not yet begun. Bowering, in fact, provides the information we need to distinguish between the two sites. On 4 August, he records the arrival of George A. Smith, eager to implement the intended "measures for their safety." Between 9 and 12 August, Bowering documents the resulting changes:

> Aug: 9th Monday. . . . Notice given that the fort be vacated on Wednesday next, that the inhabitants move over to the south side of the creek upon the plat appointed for a City and there build a fort half a mile square and when the inhabitants sufficiently strong the fort to be enlarged south and west.
>
> Aug: 11th Wednesday. Early this morning a general pulling down and moving all useable materials and goods unto the New Fort, Soon every house were down.
>
> Aug: 12. Thursday. Finished our move[.][16]

In retrospect, it may seem the leadership was being inefficient in its arbitrary shuffling of people and resources back and forth during the crisis. First, on 27 July, everyone in Cedar City and the outlying colonies was told to move to the Compact Fort, in effect abandoning Plat A, which until that moment had been not only the preferred but the official place of settlement since the authorized relocation several months earlier. Then, only two weeks after the settlers responded by crowding into the Compact Fort, they were told to move back to Plat A and not merely abandon the Compact Fort temporarily but demolish it completely and fort up on Plat A as quickly as possible.

On reflection, however, we can identify the sound logic dictating these unusual population shifts. If the risk of hostile attack were believed to be immediate and intense, it would make sense to bring everyone into the Compact Fort where people could be assigned front-line and support roles quickly and easily if the dangers escalated. Once the imminent threat subsided, however, the Compact Fort's vulnerability to Indian attackers using the Knoll to their advantage would be weighed and a quick remove to a less vulnerable position authorized. This could easily account for the short time the settlers spent in the Compact Fort and the speed and certainty with which they were ordered to move back to (and only to) Plat A. The demolition of the Compact Fort would seem to be a confirmation of this thinking, as the leaders would not have allowed any large building components (however disassembled) to remain behind, providing Native American raiding parties with inadvertent cover.

Evacuating to Parowan

While Cedar City was taking in evacuees from Shirts Creek, Fort Harmony and Johnson Springs, Parowan was hosting settlers from Paragonah. George A. Smith ordered the evacuation of Paragonah's citizens on 3 August 1853. Paragonah means "many springs" or "marshes" in the Paiute tongue. It was originally farmland claimed in 1851 by brothers Job and Charles Hall of Parowan. In 1852, a company led by William H. Dame built rude huts to provide shelter while they began farming; the crop was so successful that many men brought their families and settled permanently.[17]

Although George A. Smith's orders did not call for Paragonah to be razed, it was evidently destroyed as one of the protective measures triggered by the Walker War. On 2 August 1853, two days before E. F. Beale noted the vivid confusions of life in the temporarily crowded Compact Fort, he passed through Paragonah just in time to see it dismantled. As he described it, the town had

> about thirty houses, which, although built of adobes, present a neat and
> comfortable appearance. The adobes are small and well pressed,
> and, are made of a pink-colored clay. The houses are built to form a

quadrangle, the spaces between them being protected by a strong stockade of pine pickets. Outside of the village is an area of fifty acres inclosed within a single fence and cultivated in common by the inhabitants. It is called The Field, and a stream from the Wahsatch Mountains irrigates it, after supplying the town with water. . . .

We did not remain long at Paragoonah; for soon after our arrival, the inhabitants, in obedience to a mandate from Governor Brigham Young, commenced removing to the town of Parawan, four miles to the southward, as he considered it unsafe, with the smallness of their number for them to remain at Paragoona. It was to us a strange sight to witness the alacrity with which these people obeyed an order which compelled them to destroy in an instant, the fruits of two years' labor; and no time was lost in commencing the work of destruction.[18] Their houses were demolished, the doors, windows, and all portable woodwork being reserved for future dwellings; and wagons were soon on the road to Parawan, loaded with their furniture and other property.[19]

Parowan was undergoing changes of its own, if less drastic ones. It is not clear how complete its fort was in the first days of August 1853. We can, in some ways, think of Parowan as "between forts." The original lots surrounding the public square of old Fort Louisa had just been expanded, requiring removal of the pickets that had helped form a complete outer wall. Houses built around the perimeter had been moved to the fronts of their lots. With the influx of settlers from Paragonah, the population would have been near 400. Almost certainly, George A. Smith urged the citizens in August 1853 to make a fort (or at least repair the existing wall), but they seem initially to have relied instead on the strength of their individual houses and their military preparations.

Feuding over the Cattle

While the outlying settlers were being evacuated to the larger townsites, loose stock, according to General Orders, were to be sent to Salt Lake City for protection. George A. Smith rounded up 271 head of cattle and four horses as this "surplus stock," in an effort to comply.[20] The action was taken to deny Indian raiding parties their spoils of war, as well as to protect the pioneers' major investment in the livestock so crucial to their survival. Smith, however, met strong opposition at Cedar City from settlers who refused to send their herds along with the rest. George Bowering's journal entry lends a touch of understatement to a volatile situation:

Aug: 8th Sunday. This morning. The County Commander, Colonel James A Little, Bp P. K Smith and others seperated the cattle to be in readiness to move the surplus. I was told some were opposed unto their cattle going, brought out their Guns, threatened to shoot the man who would touch their cattle. This caused the buisness to be deferred for the present.[21]

Matthew Carruthers, head of the Cedar City militia, chose to resign his commission rather than comply with the order and was replaced by John D. Lee. George A. Smith immediately delegated to Colonel William Kimball the task of persuading the settlers to obey counsel and release the cattle forthwith.[22]

The cattle owners, however, were not ready to be convinced. Their unexpected display of stubborn disobedience brought a flurry of consequences, including meetings to consider the "improper conduct" of the miscreants and a sermon from the equally adamant George A. Smith, speaking "against rebelling and showing the duties of saints." On 9 August, Richard Varley was held "Under trial and aquited," but Joseph Hunter Sr., George Hunter, John Gregory, William Addshead and David Stoddard were found guilty and "put under guard for their rebellion yesterday."[23] Since all this occurred at the very moment of removal to the "New Fort," that goal took precedence. The men remained under arrest until Sunday, the 15th, when, as Bowering noted,

> Elders Geo A Smith and F D Richard[s] held a council with the Authorities[.] At 3 o'clock p m A meeting held out of doors near the house of Elder James A Little. Pres: Henry Lunt and others addressed the congregation on redeeming ourselves from all disgrace that is upon us respecting the cattle. On Motion that we send more cattle away. Carried. On motion that Bp P K Smith and Elder J D Lee be the judges to say what cattle go away and what remain Carried. On motion a Petition be sent to Parowan to redeem our brethren who are prisoners which have gone away Carried.[24]

According to local tradition, the livestock were never returned, even after peace was restored. If true, this was probably not due to intentional misappropriation or neglect. Communal herds faced dangers other than Indian attack. Livestock in Manti, for example, were decimated by wolves and coyotes. Church-owned cattle herds in Cache Valley suffered losses of almost 80 percent during the severe winter of 1855–56.[25] Even so, the social fabric of Cedar City was certainly weakened by this event. Bowering records attending a meeting on 8 October that, although cattle are never mentioned, must have been a reaction to moving the herd:

> As several of the brethren are dissatisfied with things and the government of affairs in the presiding Officers being tyranical in their rule:

they are preparing to go to California and occasionally meet together to arrange their buisness. As I was lodging with Richard Varley and the meeting to night was at his house I took the liberty to remain and stay the meeting. They did not say any thing against the principles of the gospel only against the tyranical rule the Officer took and they could not stand it. Was preparing to arm themselves with weapons of defense. If they were followed by the Officers to try to bring them back they would try the virtue of bows and arrows, that they would not be brought back alive.

This is followed by two brief entries reading "Oct 16th Monday. Some of our California brethren started out to day," and "Oct 17th Teusday. The remainder went to day."[26] By mid-November, ecclesiastical leaders in Cedar City took action against a total of 26 people who had left the settlement in recent weeks for the West Coast, excommunicating all of them and court-martialling seven for "breaches of discipline during the Walker War."[27]

Forting Up the Plat A Site, 11 August 1853–5 January 1854

Elias Morris, a brick mason who reached Cedar City on 30 April 1853, the same day George Bowering arrived, penned a journal entry covering the whole relocation phase, up to and including the construction of a fort wall:

> At this time [the settlement] was a small log cabin fort on the north side of the river. . . . I commenced to build a house inside the fort, had the walls up to eight feet hiegh. . . . Before I could complete my house, an Indian war broke out, and martial law was declared. By order of G. A. Smith who was the commander in chief of the Southern district, we torn down the old fort and moved to the south side of the river where a city was surveyed, half a mile square. In one week all the inhabitants was transferred from the old fort into temporary shantees and dug outs. The first public duty we had to do besides standing guard night and day under military orders was to build a fort wall of adobe ⅓ of a mile square and 8 feet high which was done in a very short time.[28]

The siting of the fort at the northeast corner of Plat A proper is clearly shown on illustration 12-1, the Plat A Fort Layout. Reasons for enclosing only that part of the townsite are sound: (1) the northeast sector was closest to the waters of Coal Creek; (2) that sector was also closest to the Compact Fort survey site and to the iron works; (3) the land was better there, due to rich silt deposits from Coal Creek. According to pioneer property records, 54 of the Plat A city lots claimed by settlers were completely inside the area circumscribed by the wall. Another 16 were either next to or part of the wall on the west and south sides, while 20 were completely outside the wall.

Heeding Brigham Young's counsel and complying with local leaders produced not merely a rush of activity but tangible results on and around Plat A. In a letter of 25 September to Franklin D. Richards, printed in the *Deseret News,* Henry Lunt reported the rewards of obedience:

> The General orders of the Governor are being carried out daily. The amount of labor that has been done since our removal from the old fort, seems to surpass all I ever before saw. There is an immense quantity of hay stacked within our fort. We are now nearly every man engaged in enclosing the fort, principally with an adobie wall, and hope to have it finished soon. We have six men with the herd of cattle daily, well armed, and a strong guard every night around the fort; and as soon as the fort is enclosed, hope to commence the iron work anew.[29]

A month later the settlers were shocked to learn that Pahvant Paiute Indians had killed U. S. Army Captain John W. Gunnison and seven of his company on the Sevier River. Surveying a railroad route, Gunnison had been in the wrong place at the wrong time when the Indians attacked to avenge the murder of a chief's father by a passing immigrant train.[30] Perhaps motivated by this news, Apostles Erastus Snow and Franklin D. Richards decided in November to found a new settlement at Summit Creek, seven miles west of Parowan, to afford the remaining cattle better protection. Even during this period of uneasiness, however, Mormon attitudes toward the Indians were not entirely defensive. The preceding September, as Andrew Jenson noted, "Elder Joel H. Johnson was appointed to teach the Indians farming and other work, and to teach the Gospel to them; all his children to do the same forever after him."[31]

Meanwhile, despite the progress made, construction of the Plat A wall was so slow that by 18 December Bishop Klingensmith asked the settlers to postpone Christmas festivities until the wall was up and the gate hung.[32] By 29 December, Henry Lunt wrote the *Deseret News* that the iron works had "stopped for the last few weeks to enclose the Fort."[33]

Early in 1854, John D. Lee wrote Brigham Young that "On the Sunday before Christmas, the people voted to enclose the city with walls, bars and gates before they should dance and make merry, and from that time on, a general rush was made until the gates were up—which was completed on 5th January."[34] Lee's letter implies a unity more hoped for than true. According to William Palmer, the young people argued that they had worked hard and deserved a Christmas Eve dance. Bishop

Klingensmith refused permission, however, citing the promise everyone had made to forego celebrations until the wall was done.

The would-be dancers next pled their case with Thomas Cartwright, the town fiddler, who yielded and had them move the furniture out of his house to provide room for dancing, but the bishop's sharp ear heard the fiddle. He immediately "bore down upon the revelers, broke up the party, and on the spot cut them all, Brother Cartwright and the caller included, off the Church for breaking their covenants." Cartwright quickly appealed to the high council, who deliberated but could not agree amongst themselves. Stake President J. C. L. Smith had the councilmen join in a prayer circle and then adjourned the meeting, telling them to take one hour and come back prepared to vote. At that point, "a spirit of unity and peace came upon them" and the problem was resolved. Memberships were restored, the hand of fellowship extended to all and everyone agreed to be back on the job the next morning, where they worked diligently until the task was done.[35]

The well-earned sense of accomplishment felt by all at finishing the Plat A fort wall, however, was of short duration. Constructed in haste, some sections of the wall proved weak. On 20 January, as John D. Lee wrote President Young four days later, "a wind storm from the S. W. blew down from 15 to 20 rods of our fort wall, on the N. and S. lines. The storm lasted 24 hours; it was the heaviest wind storm that I ever saw in the mountains."[36] Samuel H. Rogers, newly arrived in Parowan from Utah Valley, was among those recruited to rebuild the wall. On 27 January 1854, he records that he "toock my family to Cedar City, Built my portion of city wall" and then returned almost immediately to Parowan, at the request of the stake president, to help move a newly established cattle herd to the Summit Creek sanctuary.[37]

Even though the push to secure the settlements had depleted their resources, the Mormon settlers were willing to share what they had with a party of explorers who appeared unexpectedly. A Parowan lookout had reported seeing Indians on 6 February, coming from the north about 20 miles away. These travelers proved to be John C. Frémont with nine fellow explorers and 12 Delaware Indians who reached the fort the next day "in a state of starvation." Captain Frémont had attempted to cross the same mountain range which had proved so difficult for Parley P. Pratt's Southern Exploring Expedition four winters earlier and had fared much worse:

> One of [Frémont's] men had fallen dead from his horse the day previous . . . They reported that they had eaten twenty-seven broken-down animals; that when a horse or mule could go no farther, it was killed and

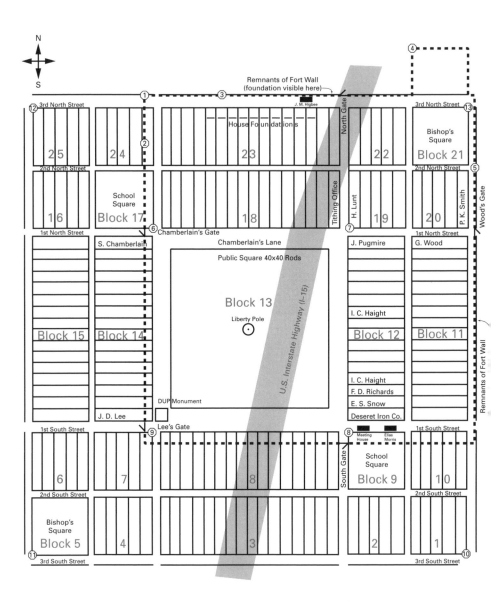

Illus. 12-1. Plat A Fort Layout: this diagram shows (1) fort layout including community squares and gates; (2) representative house lots; (3) block numbers (in gray); (4) brass caps marking fort wall perimeter (in octagonals).

divided out, giving one-half to the Delawares, and the other to the Colonel and his men; the hide was cut in pieces and cast lots for. After the bones had been made into soup, they were burned, and carried along by the men for luncheon. The entrails were shaken, and then made into soup, together with the feet and eyes; thus using up the whole mule. They stated they had travelled forty-five days living on this kind of fair.[38]

Frémont himself wrote to his wife, "We owe our lives to these good Mormons, who not only cared for us for two weeks, but gave us food and new horses to continue our journey."[39]

Features of Cedar City's Plat A Fort

William Chandless, whom Gustive Larson calls "Cedar City's first tourist booster," visited Cedar City during this period and was impressed by the finished fort. He described it as:

> a square of half a mile with almost continuous houses on each side and the hinder wall of these forms the fortifications of the place. The center of the enclosure is used as a farm-yard ground, corrals for cattle, etc., so that the place is very open and with a delightful airiness.[40]

There are differing accounts of the dimensions of the wall itself. Solomon N. Carvalho, traveling with Frémont's party as an artist, described the structure as "an adobe wall twelve feet high, six feet at the base to two and a half at the top."[41]

According to the Charles Willden family history, "The walls of the new fort were to be of adobe, 10 feet high, three feet thick on the stone foundation and taper to one foot thick on the top."[42] Lunt had also reported the walls of his adobe house to be 10 feet high.[43] Andrew Jenson claimed the walls were "8 feet high, built of adobes and washed gravel, cut into chunks."[44] Perhaps wall height varied or perhaps some of the witnesses reported estimations rather than actual measurements.

Illustration 12-1, the Plat A Fort Layout, is derived from three maps, showing the boundary of the wall and features of the fort inside Plat A's perimeter. The component maps are: (1) the Plat A Map with engineering overlay, created by York Jones in 1984 in collaboration with Morris Shirts; (2) William Palmer's drawing of the Plat A Fort, published March 1951 in the *Improvement Era;* and (3) Andrew Jenson's "1853 Plan of Cedar Fort" in his "Manuscript History of Cedar City," compiled around 1910.

He almost certainly based his illustration on Palmer's early interview and research notes, adding a few more details to Palmer's drawings.[45] Both Palmer and Jenson describe the Plat A Fort as being around 100 rods square, very close to the dimensions given by Elias Morris: a walled fort one-third-mile-square (1,760 feet or 106.6 rods). The actual space enclosed by the fort wall (see perimeter marked on illus. 12-1) is closer to 115 rods square.

By correlating illustration 12-1, the Plat A Fort Layout, with illustration 11-1, Dame's 1852 Plat A Survey, and then factoring in data from the Iron County Recorder's Office, we can begin to grasp the layout of the entire settlement, identifying specific lot owners and related community sites. To make this correlation, we need a fixed point. In his journal, Henry Lunt names the location of his house on the new city plat as Lot 5, Block 19 (confirmed by deed of 3 March 1853 in the Iron County Recorder's Office).[46] Dame places this lot on the west edge of Block 19, adjacent to the northeast corner of the public square. Combined, Lunt's deed and Dame's survey provide the required fixed point, allowing us to identify the owners of the other lots in Plat A. These can be found on illustration 12-2, Plat A Lot Owners.

On 30 January 1860 the boundaries of the Cedar City Ward were redrawn as follows:

First Ward: east line and Center of Old Fort
Second Ward: south and west line of Old Fort
Third Ward: two blocks east of New City
Fourth Ward: remaining part of New City

These new boundaries demonstrate that, even this long after the Compact Fort or "Old Fort" was torn down, people were still living on its site, as well as on the "New City" or Plat A site.[47] Collating the various descriptions of and comments about Cedar City's early years leads to several tentative but logical conclusions regarding the development of the growing township.

For instance, three of the gates into the fort seem to be named for adjacent property owners. Wood's Gate, on the east side, is just north of George Wood's lot; Chamberlain's Gate, on the west, is just north of Solomon Chamberlain's property; Lee's Gate, on the southwest, is just south of John D. Lee's two lots. Those responsible for erecting the Daughters of Utah Pioneers monument must have known where to place it, as the inscription correctly marks the south*east* corner of Block 14 as being the John D. Lee Gate, which was sited at the south*west*

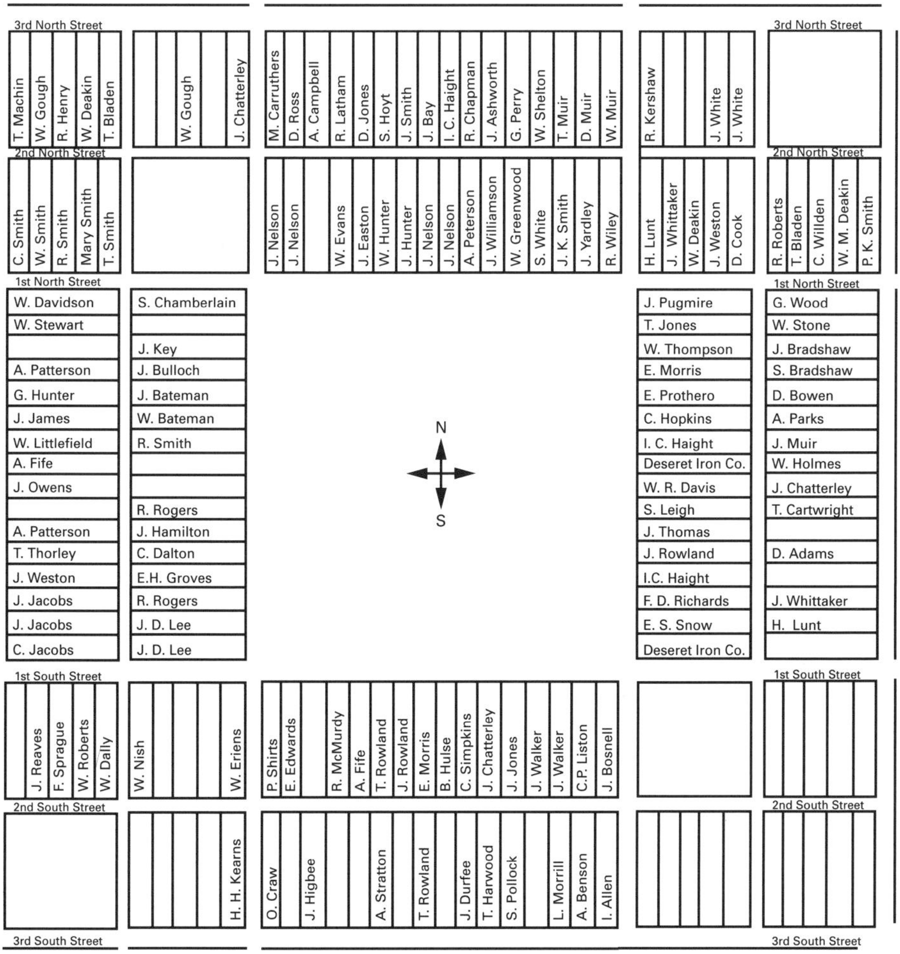

Illus. 12-2. Plat A Lot Owners: William Dame's 1852 Plat A Survey showing individual Cedar City lots, with names of owners superimposed, taken from deed books of the Iron County Recorder's Office. See app. 8.

corner of the public square (see illus. 12-1), the intersection of then-First South and First West.

A second point is that some houses not placed on deeded lots seem to have been built inside the north wall where their foundations can still be seen, but no clear references to these houses have yet been found in writings of the period or in the deed books. Palmer's *Improvement Era* drawing identifies one house as belonging to John M. Higbee, an immigrant who arrived from Utah Valley in the fall of 1853 and who may have built a temporary shelter or even a cabin against the north wall, facing the seven-rod wide street (see illus. 12-1).

The location and ownership of individual lots help us identify the position of the wall relative to the rest of the settlement. Correlating the claimed lots before and after martial law was declared shows that, prior to August 1853, 11 lots were outside the wall, 30 were inside and three were along the wall; after martial law was declared, nine were outside the wall, 24 inside and 13 along the wall. The number of lots along the wall of the fort increased significantly once the likelihood of Indian attack seemed eminent.

No record of owners exists in the Iron County Recorder's Office for lots in the southeast corner of the plat, Blocks 1, 2 and 10 (see illus. 12-1 and 12-2). Almost half of the lots in the southwest corner of the plat were likewise unclaimed (Blocks 4, 6 and 7), possibly because they were difficult to irrigate (not currently the case) or perhaps because they were close to Indian campgrounds or major trails.

The south and west portions of the wall were unusually placed, because they bisected all the lots surveyed along those sides, as the broken line on illustration 12-1 shows, marking the layout of the Plat A fort wall. Had a fort wall been factored into Dame's original October 1852 survey, he would logically have designed it around the entire perimeter of the city lots or down internal streets or alleys. An experienced surveyor, he would not have run sections of wall straight through blocks reserved for schoolhouses, let alone through the home lots of individual settlers.

Two Cedar City ordinances passed in 1855 suggest that the fort wall was fairly flimsy in parts because people were piercing it, possibly to gain access to corrals and gardens on the west and south. The wording suggests that the upkeep of the wall was prorated among the settlers, each family held responsible for a certain section. The first ordinance, approved 7 April 1855, reads: "Be it ordained by the City Council of Cedar City that any Person or Persons refusing or neglecting to put up their Wall when called upon by the overseer shall be liable to a Fine of

Fifty Dollars and the expense of building the Wall before any Court having Jurisdiction." The second ordinance, passed barely two months later, reads:

> Sec. 1. Be it ordained by the City Council of Cedar City that any Person or Persons, who have wooden Pickets in their Portion of Wall shall remove them forthwith and replace them with adobies, where the situation of the place will admit, to the acceptance of the overseer of the Wall.
>
> Sec. 2. No Person or Persons shall cut or make any Hole or Door way through the Wall of this Fort, without making a Door or Shutter Bullet proof and that with the advice and consent of the overseer.
>
> Sec. 3. Any Person having Portions of Wall, that require Propping, shall remove the Props and build the Wall to stand without them, to the acceptance of the overseer.
>
> Sec. 4. Any person refusing or neglecting to comply with this ordinance shall be liable to a Fine not to exceed Fifty Dollars at the discretion of any Court having jurisdiction.[48]

These ordinances clearly imply that the wall was neither cut stone nor neatly mortared brick. Some parts had a rock foundation but the major building material seems to have been adobe brick, supplemented by mud, straw and 4 by 10 inch blocks of silt and gravel, initially deposited as sediment in the flood plain of Coal Creek. Other sections were makeshifts of stick, brush and willow that frequently had to be propped up.

Modern Remnants of Plat A Landmarks

Early deeds and surveys reveal how pioneer Plat A relates to modern Cedar City. The public square, or Block 13, provides an excellent example. The street plotted along the south side of Block 13 aligns well with modern roadways known today as "Pioneer Road" or "Industrial Road" (note the signposts labeled "Old Fort Rd." and "Old Field Rd." above "Industrial Rd." in illus. 12-3). The west side of the street running along the west edge of Block 13 coincides with a modern fence line, while the east side of the street on the east side of the public square lines up with modern commercial property.

Remaining physical evidence confirms that the old fort wall followed the outer perimeter streets on the north and east sides of Plat A. The north side of the north perimeter street coincides today with what is believed to be rubble from the wall that was built there around 1853–54; a section of wall foundation is still visible (see illus. 12–4).

Photograph by Morris A. Shirts

Illus. 12-3. Convergence of streets at 800 West preserves the pioneer connection to modern Cedar City.

Further, a wall foundation was unexpectedly discovered north of the bishop's square, Block 21 (see illus. 12-1), suggesting the wall was extended there beyond the town's original boundary. What may very well be rocks of the east wall of the fort can also be seen for about 30 feet near the north end of the east boundary line. Limited excavation in selected spots on the north side has also revealed remnants of a foundation.

The south side of the south perimeter street on Plat A lines up roughly with the location of modern Cedar City's 400 North (originally 300 South). With reference to the bisected lots, the wall ran completely down Blocks 24, 17 and 14 on the west. It formed the southwest corner of the fort by clipping the north end of Lot 1, Block 7, thence running across all lots in Blocks 8, 9 and 10 before turning to become the east side of the wall. The irrigation ditch, dug to bring water to the pioneer garden plots, aligns extremely well with the west side of the west perimeter street on Dame's Plat A map. Note the sites of the 13 brass caps marked on illustration 12-1. These caps mark the entire perimeter of the fort wall. The photograph of Morris Shirts and York Jones (see illus. 12-5) documents the placing of Brass Cap No. 7, which marks Henry Lunt's Lot 5 on Block 19.

Forting Up in Parowan

As mentioned earlier, Parowan citizens did not completely enclose their town in 1853, despite continuing tensions with the Indians. After several attempts at reconciliation, Brigham Young and Chief Wakara finally concluded a peace treaty on 11 May 1854 at Chicken Creek. On 24 May, Brigham Young visited Parowan accompanied by Wakara, Squash Head and another Indian dignitary named Grosepeen. At least part of the purpose of this joint tour was to graphically demonstrate the end of hostilities, for Young, in a public meeting at which he announced that the war was over, pointed to Wakara and said, "I have the war with me." Nevertheless, he then directed the residents of Parowan to fort up, as the citizens of Cedar City had done. The directive was to surround the city by a wall 12 feet high and six feet thick.[49] Even though it was planting season, the settlers dutifully complied. By 15 July, Martineau reported to the *Deseret News* that "Our wall is very rapidly progressing, considering the enormous weight of labor resting upon our shoulders."[50] He later referred to the wall as " built at a cost of many thousands of dollars."[51]

Although tensions had eased, the colonists must have wondered whether the peace would hold. On Friday, 22 September, an Indian stole a horse from Beason Lewis of Parowan. The thief was soon apprehended. He was held under guard in the schoolhouse while the settlers debated whether to take any action. Members of his tribe, assuming he

Photograph by Morris A. Shirts

Illus. 12-4. Remnants of a rock foundation of the Plat A fort wall, visible along the north side of the north perimeter street.

would be executed, set up ambushes all around the city and planned a general massacre but the Mormons released the man with a stern warning, perhaps not realizing at the time how close they had come to disaster. Four days later, George A. Smith returned from Salt Lake City. He found the Indians insolent and demanding tribute from the settlers. It was unanimously decided to stop all work except grain harvesting and finish the Parowan wall to its full height of 12 feet. According to Martineau, this was an enormous task, "but the people worked with a will, knowing that it would add greatly to their safety. The wall was of dampened earth and straw solidly compacted, and became in time as solid as an adobe."[52]

On 7 November, John Steele reported to George A. Smith that the wall completely encircled the city, although it was not uniform in height: "some of it is five feet high, some ten; and about one half is up twelve feet, the full height. It is six feet wide at the bottom, and two feet and a half at the top."[53] Andrew Jenson gives the only known statistics on the length of the wall, stating that it encircled the old fort "which was 56 rods

Illus. 12-5. Author Morris Shirts (left) and colleague York Jones place Brass Cap No. 7 on the site of Henry Lunt's Lot 5, Block 19.

Photograph provided by Morris A. Shirts

square, with a wall enclosing 112 rods square." His remaining dimensions are identical to Steele's.[54]

On 29 January 1855, only eight months after negotiating peace with Brigham Young, Chief Wakara died at Meadow, just south of Fillmore. David Lewis had visited Wakara only the day before to deliver a letter from Brigham Young, expressing his continued support. Parowan settlers were advised to stay inside the fort until after the funeral ceremonies, since it was feared the Indians might want to provide Mormon "attendants" to escort their chief to the land of the dead.[55] Instead, a Paiute slave girl, two women of the tribe and between 12 and 20 of Wakara's best horses were killed. A young Paiute boy was tied to Wakara's body alive and buried with the chief. In addition to these sacrifices, which were apparently contrary to Wakara's dying wish, he was buried with guns, bows and arrows, blankets, buckskin robes, cooking utensils and the unopened letter from Brigham Young.[56] According to tradition the grave was located high on Pig Mountain east of Meadow Creek near the "eye" of the "old sow," a local landmark.[57]

Modern Remnants of Parowan Landmarks

The exact location of the fort wall built by Parowan's settlers in 1854 is uncertain. However, Ray Morris and Frank Mortensen, both descendants of Parowan settlers and both in their eighties when interviewed in 1982, agreed in general that it ran along the north line of the Karl Morris property at 51 North 300 West. Mortensen recalled that a waterwheel, installed at the northwest corner of the fort, had left an indentation and that, during his lifetime, earth from the old wall was scraped into the depression.

Mortensen stated in 1982 that the south wall ran along the south side of 200 South and that a now-demolished building at 50 West 200 South, used first as Calvin Pendleton's gun repair shop and then as a Presbyterian school, stood just inside the fort wall. Mortensen recalled that William Thornton formed an ad hoc committee of older citizens in the 1950s. Based on their memory of the wall's location, they supervised the installation of three-inch steel posts about three feet high to mark the fort's four corners. Two are still in place. The northwest corner marker is near 70 North 200 West, on the east side of the street near the canal, while the northeast marker is directly east, on the west side of 100 East, near 81 North.

Mortensen remembered the missing southwest corner marker as being near the present southeast corner of 200 South 200 West, due south of the present fire station. He also recalled the southeast corner marker as having been near the present southwest corner of 200 South and 100 East, directly south of the Old Mill monument. He further noted that there were gates in the middle of each of the four walls and that a lane ran through Block 16 to the west wall.

These recollections coincide well with historical data. If the mud wall were 112 rods square, it would lie 56 rods from the center of the Old Rock Church. A remeasurement of the site in the 1980s showed that 56 rods north would align with the northeast and northwest marker posts, a total of 924 feet from the Old Rock Church to the location of the wall, or 132 feet north of the south curb of North Alley and very near the Ray Morris property line (as of the time of his interview).

Going west 56 rods would locate the wall just west of the canal, which would place the canal inside the fort and in line with modern utility poles running north and south along 200 West. Even though Ray Morris and Frank Mortensen stated that the canal was outside the fort, there is considerable evidence that the fort surrounded industrial mills that used water power. Christian Rasmussen had a mill near the northeast corner of the fort, while Calvin Pendleton had a machine works a little farther south and west on Center Street, possibly first owned by Jonathan Pugmire.

Beginning again at the Old Rock Church and moving 56 rods south, the fort wall position can be located two feet beyond the south edge of the sidewalk on the south side of 200 South, corresponding with Mortensen's recollection. Going east the same distance would locate it nine feet east of the west curb of 100 East in front of the county courthouse, lining up, with only an insignificant variation, with the location of the now-missing southeast marker post.

These modern remeasurements prove that constructing fort walls cost the settlers a great deal of time and energy in both Parowan and Cedar City. Even though such defensive projects delayed the prime mission of iron-making, it is clear that those most involved in the Deseret Iron Company continued to press ahead, one way or another. Once fort walls were raised, however, the time and strength of many more settlers could again be called on for use in iron production. This added manpower became an important factor in the furnace runs to come.

Endnotes

1. Merlo J. Pusey, *Builders of the Kingdom: George A. Smith, John Henry Smith, George Albert Smith,* Studies on Western History and Culture Series, no. 1 (Provo, Utah: Brigham Young University Press, 1981), 86–87.

2. Dalton, *Iron County Mission,* 76–77, with no source given. The incident appears, however, in Jenson, "Parowan Ward History," 62. See also Lunt, diary, 14 Apr 1853.

3. Brigham Young, address to the members, 4 Jul 1853, in *Deseret News,* 15 Oct 1853, 1st unnumbered page.

4. Knecht and Crawley, *Early Records,* 131. See also Neff, *History of Utah,* 372. For related sources, see ch. 2, n. 23.

5. Knecht and Crawley, ibid., 131–32.

6. Ibid., 132.

7. Ibid., 132–33.

8. Bowering, journal, 26 Jul 1853.

9. Ibid., 30 Apr–9 May 1853; compare schoolhouse references in Lunt, diary, 4 Sep 1852–1 May 1853.

10. Bowering, journal, 27 Jul 1853.

11. Knecht and Crawley, *Early Records,* 134.

12. Journal History, William H. Kimball's Journal of Southern Expedition No. 1, 25 Jul–3 Aug 1853.

13. Ibid.

14. Knecht and Crawley, *Early Records,* 134.

15. Gwinn Harris Heap and E. F. Beale, and others, *Central Route to the Pacific from the Valley of the Missouri to California, 1853* (Philadelphia: Lippincott, Grambo, 1854), reprinted as *Central Route to the Pacific,* Far West and the Rockies, vol. 7, introduction and notes by LeRoy R. Hafen and Ann W. Hafen (Glendale, Calif.: Arthur H. Clark, 1957), 229 (hereafter cited as Hafen and Hafen, *Central Route*), copy of typescript excerpts (copied by Dale L. Morgan) in Shirts Collection. Note that William Kimball may have confused the identities of the two men who authored the report, or merely mixed up their names inadvertently, since he records the name of his caller in Parowan on 2 August as "E. F. Heap."

16. Bowering, journal, 4, 9–12 Aug 1853.

17. Dalton, *Iron County Mission,* 170–71; *A Memory Bank for Paragonah,* comp. by the Betsy Topham (Paragonah) Camp, Daughters of Utah Pioneers (Provo, Utah: Community Press, 1990), 8–9; Van Cott, *Utah Place Names,* 288.

18. William H. Dame, "Journal of William H. Dame to Iron Co. Utah, 1850–59," SUU Archives. Under "Aug/[18]53," Dame tries to assess the value of the lost settlement: "3 day[,] moved from Red Creek to Parowan[;] cause, Indian War[.] Houses torn down[.] Loss estimated $3,184.00" (cited from hand-copy of photostat of original, made by Della Dame Edmunds in 1970).

19. Hafen and Hafen, *Central Route,* 221–22. Note 123 reads "The prompt and unquestioning obedience of the Mormons to their leader was a striking feature of Mormon life."

20. Knecht and Crawley, *Early Records,* 135.

21. Bowering, journal, 8 Aug 1853.

22. Pusey, *Builders of the Kingdom,* 87–88.

23. Bowering, journal, 8–9 Aug 1853.

24. Ibid., 15 Aug 1853.

25. Campbell, *Establishing Zion,* 66–67, 265.

26. Bowering, journal, 8, 16–17 Oct 1853.

27. Janet Burton Seegmiller, *A History of Iron County: Community above Self* (Salt Lake City: Utah State Historical Society, 1998), 62.

28. Elias Morris, diary, ca. Apr 1853, typescript excerpts supplied by George Q. Morris to William R. Palmer, 18 Mar 1940, Palmer Collection (cited from copy in Shirts Collection).

29. Henry Lunt to Franklin D. Richards, 25 Sep 1853, published in *Deseret News,* under "Items from Iron County," 15 Oct 1853, 4th unnumbered page.

30. Campbell, *Establishing Zion,* 110; Larson, *Erastus Snow,* 249–51.

31. Jenson, "Parowan Ward History," 65.

32. Palmer, "Pioneer Fortifications,"183.

33. Henry Lunt to editor, 29 Dec 1853, published in *Deseret News,* 2 Feb 1854, 1st unnumbered page.

34. John D. Lee to Brigham Young, 24 Jan 1854, published in *Deseret News,* 16 Feb 1854, 3d unnumbered page.

35. Palmer, "Pioneer Fortifications," 183–84.

36. Lee to Young, 24 Jan 1854.

37. "The Journal of Samuel Holister Rogers," 180–81, Perry Special Collections.

38. John Calvin Lazelle Smith to editor, *Deseret News,* ca. 16 Mar 1854, 3d unnumbered page.

39. Dalton, *Iron County Mission,* 5.

40. As quoted in Gustive O. Larson, *Cedar City: Gateway to Rainbow Land* (Cedar City, Utah: privately printed, 1950), 20, copy in Historical Collection, Cedar City Public Library.

41. Carvalho, *Incidents of Travel and Adventure,* 210.

42. Hancock, "Biography of Charles Willden," 15.

43. Lunt, diary, 5 Feb 1853.

44. Jenson, "Manuscript History of Cedar City," 42.

45. The Plat A Fort Layout, created in 1984 by York Jones and Morris Shirts, Shirts Collection. William R. Palmer's description of the layout reads: "The flagpole stood in the center of a 40 by 40-rod public square. Streets were six rods wide and avenues three rods. There were 120 4 by 10-rod lots." "Pioneer Fortifications," 185. Andrew Jenson describes the fort as "100 rods square and all lots measured 4 x 20 rods. The streets were 6 rods wide. The walls were 8 feet high, built of adobes and washed gravel, cut into chunks. There were several bastions built in the wall, and the openings were supplied with heavy gates." Jenson, "Manuscript History of Cedar City," 42.

46. Lunt, diary, 5 Feb 1853; Deed Book A, 49.

47. Minutes of Teachers Meeting—First Division of Cedar Ward (1860), Palmer Collection.

48. Shirts, Morris A., "Summary of Ordinances, Cedar City, 1853–1856" (ordinances approved 7 Apr 1855 and 2 Jun 1855, both repealed at a later but unspecified date), typescript, SUU Archives.

49. Jenson, "Parowan Ward History," 74. The Salt Lake City Council had, in Jul 1853, directed the raising of a wall there,

> built of mud taken from the ditch, and mixed with straw or hay and gravel. . . . This was deemed to be the cheapest and in the end most durable method that could be adopted at that time.
>
> On the 27th [it was recommended that the wall] be made twelve feet high and six feet thick at the bottom, carried up with an equal slope on each face, so as

to be two and a half feet thick at the height of six feet, then carried up the remaining six feet two and a half feet thick and rounded on the top. (Knecht and Crawley, *Early Records,* 131.)

This structure was financed by assessing a tax of $10 per lot plus 5 percent tax on each lot, its improvement and all taxable property.

50. James Martineau to George A. Smith, 16 Jul 1854, published in *Deseret News,* 3 Aug 1854, 3d unnumbered page; also in Jenson, "Parowan Ward History," 73.

51. Jenson, ibid., 76.

52. Ibid., 79.

53. John Steele to George A. Smith, 7–8 Nov 1854, published in *Deseret News,* 30 Nov 1854, 3d unnumbered page.

54. Jenson, "Parowan Ward History," 74.

55. Bancroft, *History of Utah,* 477, n. 72; Sonne, *World of Wakara,* 219.

56. Sonne, ibid., 219–220.

57. Day and Ekins, *Milestones of Millard,* 311–12; Charles Kelly, "We Found the Grave of the Utah Chief," *Desert Magazine* 9 (Oct 1946): 17–19, as cited in Sonne, ibid., 220.

13

The Noble Furnace

1854–1855

The Walker War and the need to fort up against it were not the only events that delayed iron production toward the end of 1853. On Saturday, 3 September, a fierce cloudburst unexpectedly flooded Coal Creek, destroying every canyon bridge and washing out dams the pioneers had labored so hard to build. Eight months after the event, Brigham Young described the swollen creek as a "singular stream," which could sometimes "sweep across the flat, carrying down rocks that would weigh perhaps twenty or thirty tons."[1] The autumn storm sent water rushing three feet deep over the iron works, washing away hundreds of bushels of charcoal (estimated to be worth $500) and scattering stacks of wood. The "Report of Travels" written by Apostles Snow and Richards included an assessment of this flood, ending with the telling statement that "the present site was not the proper one on which to permanently locate the Iron Works."[2] The day after the storm, at the Sunday morning muster, the militia was put to work repairing the dam and soon restored a proper flow of water to the fort.[3] The community suffered another blow at the unexpected death on 10 September of revered settler Joseph Chatterley, who had accidentally shot himself a few days earlier while lifting a rifle from a wagon.[4]

A week after the Cedar City flood, "the first Stake Conference ever held in Iron County convened in Parowan," moving to Cedar City the next day, a Sunday.[5] On Monday, Stake President J. C. L. Smith, in his role as superintendent of the iron works, gathered the proprietors of the company together at Jonathan Pugmire's blacksmith shop to evaluate flood damage. Although acknowledging the canyon bridges were gone, Smith felt the damage to the iron works was minimal and asserted that he "did not see anything in the way of commencing the iron works again." Many of the brethren insisted they were already overwhelmed by the effort to comply with President Young's orders to enclose the fort. It was decided that the leaders themselves would take on the job of gathering up company property washed down the creek by the flood. Several men volunteered to go exploring for fire clay of good quality,[6] a sign of optimism that furnace operations would resume before long.

Pioneer resilience is demonstrated in Snow and Richards's "Report of Travels." Giving a positive spin to the setbacks caused by the flood, they noted that the waters had created a supply of "ready-made adobies:"

> This freshet brought down an immense quantity of well ground material and desposited the same in various depths on the surface, from four to ten inches, which when dried, proved to be a very superior

---

GENERAL CONFERENCE STATISTICAL REPORT

One method of tracking the continuing streams of converts hoping to help build Zion was statistical reporting at each semi-annual general conference. Figures for Parowan and Cedar City, tallied 6 October 1853, are given below:

Parowan (Bishop Tarlton Lewis reporting):

High Priests:	11
Seventies:	38
Elders:	29
Priests:	2
Teachers:	/*
Deacons:	/*
Total Ward Population:	392

Cedar City (Bishop Philip Klingensmith reporting):

High Priests:	12
Seventies:	25
Elders:	48
Priests:	7
Teachers:	12
Deacons:	5
Total Ward Population:	455

Source: *Deseret News*, 15 Oct 1853 (vol. 3, no. 19), 3d unnumbered page.
*The backslash marks appear to represent zero.

material for building wall and houses and has been extensively used for that purpose.[7]

Appointing a New General Manager

The first annual convocation of Deseret Iron Company stockholders began on 10 November 1853 with additional sessions held the 16th, 18th, 27th and 28th. Erastus Snow had a number of concerns that he expressed over the several days of discussion. He was primarily concerned about tightening up the finances of the company. He chastised shareholders for crediting hours of labor toward the unpaid balances on their shares and also condemned the practice of paying debts or ordering goods without authorization from the general superintendent. Probably during the meeting on the 18th, Snow reported the company's assets and debts, balancing $10,704.29 received by the company with $10,440.44 paid out. To the remainder of $263.85, Snow factored in amounts outstanding due to the company plus an estimate of its holdings in merchandise and other property. This resulted in the company having a paper value of $11,374.81 on which to operate.[8]

Two days after the meetings started, a petition signed by 184 Cedar City men, including J. C. L. Smith, John Steele, Tarlton Lewis, Henry Lunt and David B. Adams, was sent to the territorial legislature asking for additional road appropriations. The petitioners pointed out that the strongest bridges their resources could build had been destroyed by the flood of 3 September and that new bridges would cost $800.00 to $1,000.00 each. One alternative would be to cut through canyon rock, creating a route that would avoid the creek, but carving such a road out of the mountain would also be expensive.[9]

It was during this month, November 1853, that Isaac C. Haight (see illus. 13-1) became active in the Iron Mission. Shortly after returning from his mission to England, he was called by Brigham Young to relocate in Iron County. On 8 October 1853, Haight wrote in his journal that "I had much rather have stayed here [Salt Lake City], but am willing to obey the counsel of my Brethren."[10] Leaving on the 20th, he arrived with his family in Cedar City on 1 November. He was officially introduced at the 10 November 1853 shareholders meeting. After opinions were expressed about committing the company's welfare to non-shareholders, Haight demonstrated his commitment to the Iron Mission by volunteering to become a shareholder himself.[11]

On Sunday, 5 November, five days before the shareholder assembly, numerous meetings—religious, military and economic—had been held

Courtesy LDS Church Archives

Illus. 13-1. Isaac C. Haight (1813–86), became general manager of the Deseret Iron Company in late 1853.

throughout the day. As George Bowering's journal records, at a midday public gathering in front of Bishop Klingensmith's house, Erastus Snow "spoke at some length upon various subjects," especially touching on those who had left for California. In his opinion, "they will be loosers by so doing and . . . a blessing unto us they are gone." He then brought up the need to build a "meeting and school house." A motion was quickly made and carried to erect an assembly room 25 by 40 feet to be paid for by subscription.[12]

The urgency of this decision makes sense when we remember that the old schoolhouse, which had just been enlarged on 1 May, was a casualty of the Walker War, being demolished (at the very least dismantled) by 11 August during the pulling down of the Compact Fort. Those now crowding onto Plat A, therefore, had apparently been without a "comodius" building for three months and the continued lack of meeting space had become a priority.

The ongoing shareholders' meetings reconvened on 26 and 27 November 1853 and Isaac C. Haight was appointed general manager of the Deseret Iron Company. This required him to post a bond of $10,000. In addition, since he was also elected one of four company trustees (the others being Vincent Shurtleff, Christopher Arthur and Jonathan Pugmire), he was required to post another bond of $2,000.[13]

Prior to the company meeting on 27 November, Erastus Snow and Franklin D. Richards presided over a stake conference where Isaac Haight and Marius Ensign were appointed to fill vacancies on the high council. Very possibly one of these positions was that formerly held by Matthew Carruthers, who had apparently decided that iron-making in southern Utah could not generate a livelihood. After months of inner debate, he finally relinquished his ties to the community, sometime after 10 November, and returned to his native Scotland.[14]

Before departing for Salt Lake City, Snow and Richards recommended that Cedar City be organized as a municipality, nominating city officers and designating Isaac C. Haight as mayor. On 6 December 1853 the first city election in Cedar City was held, confirming the nominations. John D. Lee, William Miller, George S. Clark and Philip Klingensmith were chosen to serve as aldermen and James Lewis became city recorder.[15] Haight, who had been reluctant to take over the management of the iron works in the first place, now found himself not only a business and ecclesiastical leader but a civic leader as well.

Early Trial Runs of 1854

The iron works stopped while all hands helped to raise the Plat A fort wall. Precisely on 1 January 1854, however, despite severe cold, the pioneers began mining and hauling coal. By 9 January the iron works had been repaired, the furnace charged and the blast put on. The furnace continued blowing until the evening of the next day when the air was so cold the water froze up in the wheel, interrupting the blast and cooling the works, resulting in solidification of the iron. Little iron had been made anyway, because the sulfur in the inferior coal had eaten away at the iron during smelting, leaving it brittle. Work was temporarily put on hold and Haight wrote to Erastus Snow asking him to purchase a steam engine so they need not depend on Coal Creek to power the blast.[16]

Two anecdotal sources add to the evidence that high sulfur content in the coal was interfering with proper smelting. In a missionary reminiscence, John Lee Jones, son of iron worker John Pidding Jones, recalled that the pig iron "was so hard they could not chip it. It was as hard as bissmer [Bessemer] steel on account of so much sulpher in the coal. It ate the carbon out of the iron and left it very hard."[17] William Ashworth, son of iron worker John Ashworth, remembered that "During the time Father worked at the foundry, they made a limited variety of articles, but the metal was so hard for lack of proper fluxing material that it could not be dressed—a fire would not even phaze it."[18]

The furnace was not charged again for over two months. On 27 March the furnace master tried a mixture of half charcoal and half coke (Haight asked that more wood be burned into charcoal) but the furnace still needed to be blown out after three days because of the damage done by the sulfur. Furthermore, the blow-outs had damaged the furnace itself and repairs needed to be made.[19] J. C. L. Smith, Henry Lunt, James A. Little, John D. Lee, Samuel West, James H. Martineau and Silas and Jesse Smith took time to attend April conference in Salt Lake City but without any new iron products to display this year.[20]

By 8 May the furnace was repaired, sufficient charcoal had been processed and the iron workers were ready for another trial run. The first charge produced too little iron, and that of an inferior quality, so furnace master David B. Adams experimented with a combination of six bushels of charcoal, 20 lbs. of magnetite, "20 lbs. of lean ore from the mountain" and 15 lbs. of limestone. Although by the evening of 10 May the furnace had produced 500 to 600 lbs., "a good specimen of model iron," the lining gave way at midnight and the blast was taken off.[21]

Building the Noble Furnace

The furnace was inadequate to the task. When the Deseret Iron Company board met on 23 May 1854, the decision to enlarge the furnace had already been made. To increase the blast in their bigger furnace, Haight recommended that they also enlarge both the waterwheel and the cylinder. A week later, the old furnace was razed and the rubble wheeled away. A foundation for the new furnace, three feet deep and 21 feet square, was dug on the site of the old one and lined with solid rock. The project was considered significant enough to require an architect and Elias Morris, skilled in masonry and building construction, was appointed. Even before it was begun, the pioneers expected it to be a "noble building" and it came to be known as the "Noble Furnace."[22]

Work continued all summer, as we learn from an untitled account book kept by James Whittaker from April to September 1854. It is one of only two bound account books remaining from the Deseret Iron Company. Preserved in the LDS Church Archives, it demonstrates how the iron operation had matured. The workers were well organized and efficient in their own specialties as they cooperated to construct the Noble Furnace.

According to this book, miners James Williamson, John Smith II, Robert Latham, Alexander Patterson, Alexander Campbell, Thomas Rowland and George Parry stopped digging in the coal fields in May to begin quarrying rock for the new furnace.[23] During June and July, joined by James Bullock, William Thomas, Uriel Curtis, Thomas Jones, Thomas Thorley and George Easton, they divided their time between the quarry and the coal mines.[24] In August the miners again focused their efforts on quarrying rock for furnace construction. The account book indicates the more experienced miners were credited $3.00 a day; others earned $2.00 to $2.50.[25]

Teamsters John and Evan Owens, John Hamilton, Alanson Niles, George Wood, Orin Craw, William Lewis, James Farrer, W. W. Willes, Robert Easton and H. H. Kearns hauled rock from the quarry for $1.00 a ton and coal down the steep canyon roads for $5.00 a ton. Over the summer they freighted 560 tons of rock and 115 tons of coal to the iron works. Coal was processed into coke throughout the summer, in anticipation of large runs once the Noble Furnace was completed—Eliezar Edwards, the chief collier, was credited $2.50 a day for coking. Teamsters also carted sand, adobes and lumber to the furnace site.[26]

Masons Robert Wiley, Joseph Clews, Thomas Jones, John Groves, Joseph Hunter and Samuel Bradshaw earned $3.00 a day building the furnace. Elias Morris, the superintending mason, was the highest paid worker at $4.00 a day; however, he volunteered to exchange his wages for a quarter share in the company, which he valued at $635.00.[27] His brother John Morris earned $3.50 a day, also as a mason. Furnace master David B. Adams labored at the iron works five to six days a week all summer for $2.50 a day. In May, he and his assistants were busy "filling" and "keeping" the old furnace before its lining gave way; their "labor at the furnace" in June, July and August presumably referred to helping the masons construct the new furnace, as there are no further references to "filling" and "keeping" at this time.[28]

Richard Harrison, superintendent of the moulding department, lent an extra pair of hands to the construction effort, working all summer as a carpenter for $2.00 a day. H. H. Kearns doubled as both teamster and carpenter. He must have been a skilled woodworker for he earned $3.00 a day. In August, John Ashworth joined the carpenters, working for $2.00 a day. Common laborers who helped build the furnace also earned $2.00 a day credited to their company accounts.[29]

On 19 July, Isaac Haight left for Salt Lake City with a train of empty wagons to bring back merchandise to restock the company store. He returned on 2 September, but supplies from the East had not arrived in Salt Lake City in time to fill his wagon train. He left with a much smaller load of goods than anticipated, disappointing to the men who had worked all summer in hopes of receiving considerable reimbursement from the company store.[30] On his return, Haight would find one of the pillars of the community absent. Henry Lunt, who had devoted so much time and effort to the establishment of the Iron Mission, left in August on a proselyting mission to his native England, wearing the best clothes he owned, "a broadcloth coat, moccasins, and a pair of pants made from one of . . . his wife's blue serge skirts."[31]

In Cedar City, as the furnace neared completion that September, the board of directors met to balance the books and recruit new shareholders, hoping to start iron production in earnest. Thomas Dunlop Brown, an experienced bookkeeper who was also recorder for the Southern Indian

Mission headquartered in Harmony, was engaged to audit the company books. After store goods were distributed to the iron workers, debits of $4,785.96 were balanced with credits in an equal amount. A total of 206 men were listed as having accounts; Catherine Chatterley, widow of shareholder Joseph Chatterley and an otherwise unidentified "Mrs. Randals" were the only women on the list. There were also accounts for the *Deseret News* and for tithing offices in Parowan, Cedar City and Harmony.[32]

On 24 September 1854, Isaac Haight wrote to Franklin D. Richards, then in Liverpool, of the furnace's completion:

> The foundation of a new furnace was . . . laid about the 25th of May, twenty-one feet square, of red sand stone, carried up perpendicularly twelve feet above the ground, then tapered eighteen feet to the top. The tunnelhead is eight feet, making the furnace thirty-eight feet to top of tunnel head. It is six and a half feet in the boshes, three and a half feet at tunnel head inside, and thirteen feet square outside. The lining is of porus sand stone, that will stand the fire well. The cause of lining with rock is that we can get no fire brick that will stand. The hearth is of grey sand stone. It took some six hundred and fifty tons of rock, and cost $3782.45. . . .
>
> We have also enlarged the water wheel four feet, and made circular cylinders three and a-half feet in diameter, which also are completed. They work admirably, and will give a blast of two and a-half pounds to the square inch.
>
> The furnace is also completed, and is said, by those who have seen it, to be as good a furnace as they ever saw in England, or any other country. The blast pipes are not yet finished, but will be by the time the furnace will be heated ready for the blast.
>
> We are also building six coke ovens, of the same kind of rock as the furnace; and after they are finished, I intend to add six more, with which I am in hopes to supply the furnace with good coke, and make good iron[33] (see illus. 13-2 and 13-3).

An itemized list of the building costs for the Noble Furnace shows that $2,027.12 was credited to 28 men who presumably worked directly on furnace construction. According to the list, furnace master David B. Adams received $247.50 and chief mason Elias Morris earned $121.25. The labor required to quarry the rock cost $630.32, hauling rock cost $623.80, hauling limestone $5.00, hauling clay $7.87 and hauling sand $60.50. Since the sandstone itself did not cost anything, the amount paid for materials was minimal, consisting primarily of $25.00 for lumber (most likely from the sawmill in Parowan) and $262.34 for items provided by the blacksmith.[34]

As Haight had requested, the waterwheel was enlarged four feet to provide a larger blast. Two new double-action cylinders, three and a half feet in diameter, constituted the blowing equipment powered by the wheel. The bridge over which the charge would be carried to the furnace was built at a 20-degree incline and included a hoisting device, also run by the waterwheel.[35] Of the large sandstone coke ovens referred to by Haight in his letter to Richards, four were built by January 1855, two were under construction and six more were planned.[36]

A complete inventory, dated 16 September 1854, was taken of all the iron company property. This included the furnace, casting house, bridge house, office, furnace tools, blacksmith tools, wagons and supplies of fuel and iron. The Deseret Iron Company's total assets (excluding company store merchandise) came to $16,168.48. The pioneers had stockpiled 215½ tons of coal at $10.00 a ton, 165 tons of coke at $20.00 a ton, 1,000 bushels of charcoal valued at $210.00, 200 tons of iron ore at $6.00 a ton and an unspecified amount of "Shirts iron ore" (hematite ore discovered by Peter Shirts northeast of the iron works) valued at $206.08. The cost of the wheel and cylinders equaled $896.16.[37] Significantly, the fuel cost more than the iron ore, probably because the latter was more plentiful and accessible. Historian and economist Leonard Arrington suggests that the Iron Mission had access to two hundred million tons of 52 percent iron ore.[38]

Keeping Records in the Deseret Iron Company Journal

The same month the inventory was taken, a new account book was begun, the second of the two complete Deseret Iron Company ledgers to have survived. A gold mine of information about the iron works, it was kept continuously from 6 September 1854 to 16 May 1867. Entries for 1861 to 1867, however, cover only a few pages. Located first in the collections of the Cedar City chapter of the Daughters of Utah Pioneers, then stored in the basement of the federal post office in Cedar City, it is now in the Southern Utah University Archives. This large, leather-bound book is simply marked "Journal" and will be referred to by that name hereafter. The pages measure 9½ by 15 inches and are of pale blue paper with blue lines. Between the pages are small accumulations of sharp dust particles and flakes of charred paper, which might be dust from the operation of the iron works or evidence that the book has survived a fire. The Journal is in fairly good condition, with none of the binding stitches broken. Entries were made by several men, whose hands are quite legible.

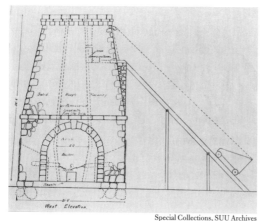

Illus. 13-2. (left) George Croft's 1956 rendering of the Noble Furnace, drawn from specifications found in Deseret Iron Company records.

Illus. 13-3. (below) Another of Croft's 1956 renditions, showing the cross-section at the base of the furnace.

Special Collections, SUU Archives

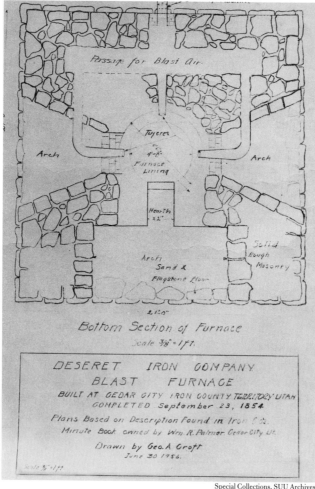

Special Collections, SUU Archives

The bookkeeping system used in the Journal is more complex than that used in the April–September 1854 untitled account book. While that book simply records the credits and debits of the Desert Iron Company as a whole, the Journal divides the company into separate departments, each with its own account. Headings appearing regularly throughout the book include engineering, furnace, furnace no. 2, office expenses, blacksmith shop, moulders cupola, stock, trial furnace, trial furnace no. 2, store house, machine shop, coke ovens, sundries and merchandise. Evidently, the company bookkeepers collected time sheets and charges from each of the foremen at the end of the week and then posted them in the Journal on Monday, to insure the work was done before it was posted. Entries tracking goods from the company store were posted throughout the week. Individual accounts in the Journal are very clearly entered. Because it is unclear, however, exactly how the pioneer iron clerks allocated each worker's labors to the various departments, the entries are sometimes difficult to interpret.

Journal entries for the first few months, late in 1854, record general activities needed to put the renovated iron works in operation. Preparations intensified, leading up to the big furnace runs beginning April 1855. Generally, the men worked in teams organized around their iron-making specialties, although, during peak periods of construction or furnace-tending, everyone helped out wherever needed.

Through fall 1854, over 50 teamsters, making up the largest group of iron workers, hauled coal, wood, rock and lumber. John and Evan Owens continued to be among the most active teamsters, as were John Hamilton and James Farrer, joined by John Nelson, Adam and Peter Fife, John Yardley and Robert Keys. After the Noble Furnace was completed that September, many hours were spent quarrying rock to build the coke ovens. The Owens brothers and others hauled almost 82 tons of rock from the quarry in September, 68 tons in October and 12 tons in November, although this was significantly less than the amount quarried over the summer for the construction of the Noble Furnace. Some of this rock might have gone into the construction of the storehouse, as John Ray and John and Evan Owens also hauled rock there. By the end of October, teamsters had hauled over 9 tons of coal from the Coal Creek mines.[39]

James Williamson, Alexander Patterson, Robert Latham, Alexander Campbell and John Smith II, the miners, continued to work late into the fall. Coal was mined in yards and carried away in tons. The miners received $14.00 per yard for digging coal, comparatively good wages. In November the miners dug 31 yards of coal (the equivalent of 47 tons of coal hauled to the furnace site). In December, they dug 29½ yards but 86 tons of coal were reported to have been hauled away from the canyon. The miners probably stockpiled some of the coal they had mined over the summer and the teamsters were hauling this as well as newly mined coal.[40]

At the same time, William Davidson and William Morgan spent two days exploring for new coal deposits, earning $3.00 a day each. William Thomas, William Evans and David and John Morgan (not on the regular mining crew) worked at the Salt Creek Mine less than a mile up the canyon, northeast of present-day Milt's Stage Stop. The iron workers, especially Henry Lunt, blamed inferior coal for the company's early failures to make iron. Evidently, the pioneers still felt apprehensive about the coal and continued searching for a better-quality source. While the coal miners labored in Coal Creek, George Parry, Andrew Patterson, John Hamilton, John Nelson and the Fife brothers together hauled over 40 tons of iron ore, at $4.00 per ton, from West Mountain to the furnace site.[41]

At the beginning of December 1854, teamster Robert Keys brought 12 loads of sand, two loads of adobes and one load of wood for the continuing construction of the coke ovens. Separate accounts were kept for wood hauled to the storehouse to warm the clerks and wood taken to the furnace site to stockpile for fuel. Both cedar and pine were stocked. A circular-bladed saw attached to the waterwheel gearing cut wood for the furnace.[42]

Elias Morris, who supervised the building of the Noble Furnace, also headed the group of masons who worked on the construction of the coke ovens (an indication the iron workers had advanced beyond the stage of digging coal pits in the ground). Thomas Thorley and George Munroe joined Eliezar Edwards in the coking operation.[43]

As the iron workers geared up for production on a larger scale, the masons built a company office. By spring 1855, they had also built a trial furnace, "moulder's oven" and machine shop. Morris and Wiley received 12½¢ a yard for plastering work on the new office. The masons also built a storehouse of adobe brick, while carpenter Alvah Benson worked on its flooring, a storage bin and a door. Carpenters H. H. Kearns and John Ashworth shingled the storehouse roof for which Jabez Durfee provided 7,000 shingles for $56.00.[44]

The engineers, led by Thomas Bladen, included Wardman Holmes, William Morgan, George Horton and Charles Simpkins. Technically, they were the most ambitious of all the iron workers. Their ingenuity, however, often makes it difficult to tell what mechanical devices they were actually working on. Bladen and Morgan designed some kind of lifting apparatus, while Kearns and Ashworth worked on the "run" and Bladen, Horton and Holmes worked on the "tram" or "charging tram." It appears that the frontier engineers created a mechanized furnace-loading assembly based on an incline plane up which buckets traveled, loaded with charging materials for the furnace. William Morgan dug pits for a "filling machine," possibly preparing a foundation for the mechanized charging tram. Bladen, Horton, Holmes and Samuel Leigh not only worked on the "filling machine" but also constructed water pipes.[45] Andrew Patterson worked in the rock quarry "making a bridge," which might have been either a bridge to cross Coal Creek (which otherwise had to be forded to reach the quarry) or a bridge leading to the top of the furnace.[46]

In November 1854, Joseph Hunter sold the company a lathe for $80.00, and Thomas Bladen spent several days using it. Although the engineers worked mostly with wood, Bladen also spent time in the blacksmith shop making "turning tools." Blacksmith Peter Hanson, assisted by Thomas Corlett as his striker, sharpened coke oven tools, such as picks, drills, hammers and chisels, and made necessary items like coal buckets. Together, Thomas Bladen and Peter Hanson used up 725 lbs. of coal during mid-November.[47]

Journal entries for February and March 1855 indicate that Engineer Charles Simpkins spent at least 12 days "pattern making," credited with $3.00 per day. The term "pattern making" usually referred to moulds used in casting and he could have been planning to make some special parts like cog wheels or spider gears.[48] After the patterns were made, Richard Harrison cast the pig iron into practical items using the moulder's oven. He was assisted at various times by John Pidding Jones, Joseph Walker, Samuel Pollock, C. P. Liston and Thomas Green.

The engineers also repaired and maintained the waterwheel. William Richards and William Morris spent many hours cleaning the tailrace. Thirty-three feet of lumber went to a "water cistern." Perhaps the engineers repaired its tank to insure a constant water supply for the overshot wheel. The Journal also lists 200 feet of lumber for "blast pipes," a necessary part of furnace technology. Later the engineering crew used 126 feet of lumber to add water pipes for cooling purposes near the tuyeres.[49]

As general manager of the Deseret Iron Company, Isaac Haight was well-compensated. According to the Journal, he received $97.50 in October 1854, $100.00 in November and $350.00 for work between 1 December and 24 March. For the next seven months, he earned a standard rate of $125.00 a month, compared to some $50.00 a month for common laborers and $60.00 to $100.00 a month for skilled laborers.[50]

Keeping the Deseret Iron Company Journal was most likely the responsibility of Christopher Arthur and his sons Joshua and Christopher Jr. who served as company clerks. Christopher Arthur, an original shareholder and one of the first four trustees, had immigrated from Wales, arriving in Salt Lake City on 26 September 1853. He bought a farm, intending to settle there, but was recruited by Erastus Snow in March 1854 to run the Deseret Iron Company farm which Snow hoped to establish. Selling his own property "for chips and wetstones," Arthur relocated to Cedar City in less than a month.[51]

Arthur's sons had been well-educated in their Welsh homeland and were prepared to serve in positions of responsibility. The day after the family arrived in Cedar City, Isaac Haight asked Christopher Jr. (Christopher Jones Arthur) to act, in their absence, as deputy secretary for Franklin D. Richards and deputy treasurer for Thomas Tennant.[52] Young Christopher also clerked in the store for $2.50 a day, while his brother Joshua managed the books at the iron works for comparable wages.

Isaac Haight saw his promising clerk, Christopher Arthur Jr., not only as a potential leader, but also as a future son-in-law. One day as Christopher was working in the company store, Haight arrived with a fine carriage and asked him if he would drive Sister Haight and his daughter Caroline from Parowan to Cedar City. Christopher had already noticed the tall, dark-haired girl and readily complied. On the way back, Sister Haight suggested stopping over in Summit, "the ground being covered in a luxurient plat of beautiful grass mingled with flowers," and hinted that Christopher might gather a bouquet for Caroline. When Christopher asked Haight for "the privilege of keeping his daughters company with the design of marriage," he easily received consent. Christopher proceeded to buy a city lot from Elias Morris next to his father's and contracted for the building of a house, while paying "homage to Caroline once and sometimes twice a week." On 30 December 1854, at the marriage of friends, someone hinted that another ceremony might be in the offing. This resulted in a private talk between Christopher and Caroline: the bride's father performed their own wedding that very evening.[53]

Charging the Noble Furnace

Preparations for the first run in the Noble Furnace had intensified early in December 1854. By the 9th, Haight had written George A. Smith about the settlement's most pressing needs. Smith passed this wish list along to the *Deseret News*, which printed it on the 21st:

By a recent letter from Mr. Isaac C. Haight, superintendent of the Iron Company's operations in Cedar City, we learn that one of the principal drawbacks to the iron works in that place, is the want of mechanics who are properly skilled in the different departments of iron manufacture. Two good furnace keepers, two blacksmiths well skilled in engine work, and two good cokers, are very much needed; and we feel, through your columns, to invite such mechanics as are acquainted with the manufacture in iron, to locate themselves in Cedar City, and apply their skill and ingenuity in unfolding to this territory the rich treasures of the mountains. A good furnace is completed. Seven coke ovens are also prepared, and four hundred tons of fuel on hand. The blowing apparatus is of the best quality, and the spell which has so long hung over the iron operations will soon be broken.[54]

Courtesy Daughters of Utah Pioneers
Cedar Cirty, Utah

Illus. 13-4. Christopher Jones Arthur (1832–1918), store clerk and trustee of the Deseret Iron Company, later served as mayor of Cedar City.

Courtesy Daughters of Utah Pioneers
Cedar Cirty, Utah

Illus. 13-5. Caroline Haight Arthur (1837–1874), daughter of General Manager Isaac Haight, married Christopher J. Arthur at age 17.

The pioneers did not let the holiday season go by without notice. Dancing well into the night was a time-honored tradition with the Saints, and the Journal records that William Sears Riggs earned $5.00 for fiddling and Darius Shirts $2.50 for "calling."[55] Although workers accomplished little during the last week of 1854, except for coking and for hauling a considerable amount of cord wood (the latter by John Yardley, William Shelton, John M. Higbee and William Greenwood),[56] by early January, all was ready. James Lewis reported to George A. Smith that "great exertions are being made to give the iron ore a trial in a few days, and things in that quarter appear far more prosperous, preparations having been made upon more scientific principles."[57] Just as they had done the year before, David B. Adams and his crew started operations on New Year's Day. At

9:00 P.M. on Monday, 1 January 1855, they began charging the Noble Furnace with a mixture of three lbs. coke, 99 lbs. "Utah coke," 20 lbs. magnetite, 60 lbs. bog ore and 30 lbs. limestone. The blast was put on at 4:00 in the afternoon the next day and continued to blow until early Wednesday morning when the waterwheel froze. Closing up the furnace tightly to prevent the iron from chilling, the men waited until the afternoon sun had thawed the ice and continued to operate the furnace. On Thursday a connecting rod of the cylinder piston broke but they continued blowing with only one cylinder until noon when they tapped the iron to check its progress and found it "hard brittle and white." The rod was repaired by 5 P.M. and the blast put on again, running until 6 A.M. on the 5th. When the furnace was tapped, iron of a similar constitution was found. The blast continued until 11 P.M. that night with no further improvement.[58]

Late Friday, 5 January, Adams modified proportions in the charge by adding 10 lbs. more magnetite and 10 lbs. less limestone. Heavy snow on 6 January slowed the movement of charges up the inclined plane, but workers continued blasting until the other cylinder went out on Sunday, 7 January. They repaired the blowing machinery and tried to start up the blast on Tuesday but by then the furnace had cooled down so much the iron was chilled. It took nine men nine hours to clean out the furnace

---

ANALYSIS OF PIONEER ORE
BY YORK JONES

Around 1977, York Jones analyzed an iron ore sample taken from the furnace site and found an explanation of the "hard brittle and white" pig. Pioneer iron had 1.02 percent phosphorus compared to modern specifications of about .3 percent. Too much phosphorus causes brittleness, yet its levels in iron are difficult for a furnace master to control. Furthermore, samples of "bog ore" (hematite) taken from an old mining site at the base of Red Hill east of Cedar City had an unusually low iron content, only 15 percent Fe_2O_3, with almost 60 percent silicon dioxide. Ideally ore should have over 40 percent iron and less than 10 percent silicon dioxide. Limestone found at an old pioneer digging near the same site was adequate, but coal from the Webster-Nelson mine near the pioneer mine in Right Hand Canyon had too much sulfur and too little carbon, making it unsuitable for coking.

Source: Jones, "Iron Mining and Manufacturing", 61–62. The MSS is undated, but two hand-written notations, one reading "1976" and the other "5/78," both initialed by Jones, allow us to approximate the date of his study.

and retrieve the "bear" or "salamander," which amounted to about 760 lbs. of iron, valued at $190.00. Furnace repairs were again made, the men hoping for better luck when enough charcoal would be available, leaving them less reliant on "Utah coke."[59] David B. Adams, now receiving $4.00 a day as furnace master, was paid $1.00 a day in overtime for around-the-clock attention to the furnace. The seven men assisting him received 50¢ a day in extra wages during the blasts.[60]

While repairs were being made on the Noble Furnace, some of the iron workers decided to experiment with different combinations of fuel and iron in a smaller trial furnace. On 19 January, they charged the furnace with 50 lbs. of charcoal, no coke, 10 lbs. of magnetite, 15 lbs. of "dry kanyon ore" and 10 lbs. of limestone. Experimenting with a new hot blast technique, however, they burned out the tuyeres, which caused the blast to melt the furnace lining made of sand and fire clay. Although the iron workers had charged the furnace eight times before the lining gave way, the iron ore had been "eaten up." This surprised them, since they usually attributed such results to sulfur in the coal and this time no coal had been used.[61]

On 20 January, they retried the cold blast method, producing iron of a nice grey color. It was lumpy rather than fluid, however, so it was given to the blacksmith to make into nails. The men then decided to line the trial furnace with the same sandstone that lined the Noble Furnace and on 25 January they began experimenting again with various mixes of coal, charcoal and raw pine.[62]

By mid-February 1855, the iron workers were experimenting with a "new cupola," which the Journal designates "trial furnace no. 2." Thomas Bladen and Joseph Walker alternated as furnace masters on the cupola, which may have been even smaller than the first trial furnace. Per day, Bladen received $3.50 and Walker $3.00 for their labors.[63] The iron workers continued trying different proportions of charcoal, wood, magnetite, red ore, limestone and clay. New mixtures were tested each day in batches of 1,000 to 2,000 lbs. Initially the blast was too small and the iron not hot enough to run, but with an increased blast (despite difficulties caused by another snowstorm), the ore ran clear on 16 February and produced the much-anticipated result—"good grey iron."[64] The yield was 530 lbs. of ore worth $132.00.[65] Materials for the charge cost $66.80, mostly for fuel. Labor cost at least $141.40.[66]

Deseret Iron Company Journal entries from the beginning of March show that the colliers had been working furiously throughout February to produce charcoal for another run in the Noble Furnace. H. L. Cook, the head charcoal man, was credited with 1,364 bushels of charcoal at 20¢ per bushel, the largest order to date. Two weeks later, he and his assistants had produced another 371 bushels at 20¢ a bushel for $74.20.[67] Architect and mason Elias Morris was paid $65.00 for improving the Noble Furnace by "opening a new tweer." The amount implies a complex operation, even for the most skilled mason in the company. The furnace men evidently felt they were not getting enough blast from the tuyeres already in use. Usually their furnaces had two tuyeres on opposing sides of the hearth. A third one could be added at the rear, but doing so would require a complete revamping of the blast pipes and the hearth.[68]

The furnace workers put the blast on the renovated "great furnace no. 2" at 5:00 P.M., Saturday, 3 March. The charge balanced coke and charcoal in equal proportions and used three kinds of iron ore: not only magnetite but "red ore" and "lean ore" as well (both probably hematite). Everything went well until Monday afternoon when the waterwheel malfunctioned. After two hours of repairs, the furnace was operated again until Wednesday morning when it "clogged up"—the lining had failed. A new lining of red sandstone was installed within a week and by the next Wednesday, 14 March, the blast was renewed. The new charge was fueled with a proportion of 12 lbs. coke to four lbs. charcoal. The iron flowed well but was ruined by excess sulfur. The charge was modified to increase the charcoal content and 80 lbs. of iron was produced. By 17 March the tymp stone burned out and the Noble Furnace had to be blown out again for repairs.

Meanwhile, construction continued on the "moulder's cupola," using 2,400 adobes. The moulders cast six hot blast pipes (to increase furnace heating power), two pedestals, bed plates and a pinion wheel. At the same time, some of the workers were logging hours on a new (or possibly rebuilt) air furnace, apparently beginning around 19 March.[69] But primary focus stayed on blast furnace preparations. Anticipating Brigham Young's annual visit in the spring, everyone expended the utmost energy on making an impressive run in the Noble Furnace before his arrival. This required hauling coal, sand, iron ore, limestone and "1,000 feet of lumber."[70]

Tasting Success

Once repaired, the Noble Furnace was started up again on 9 April 1855. Months of experimentation finally paid off. The blast was put on at 3:45 in the afternoon and by 6:00 the next morning 130 lbs. of beautiful grey iron poured out. The furnace was tapped again at 12:45 P.M., producing another 165 lbs. of iron. Work stopped early in the evening of 10 April to repair the waterwheel and reproportion the ingredients in the charge but the furnace was back in operation by 12 April and working well. By that evening, 400 lbs. of iron had been produced and another 484 lbs. ran out overnight. On 15 April it was necessary to halt production for five hours to fix the waterwheel again and build a stone wall to support a bridge that had collapsed. The furnace was up again the same day with production figures far exceeding anything the Iron Mission had previously achieved:

April	Charges	Coke	Charcoal	Wood	"Magnite" Ore	"Lean" Ore	Limestone	Proceeds
15	31	125	100	100	45	90	50	1,112 lbs.
16	40	125	100	100	45	90	50	1,714 lbs.
17	58	100	100	150	45	90	50	932 lbs.
18	32	100		300	45	90	50	1,480 lbs.
19	48	100		300	45	90	50	1,419 lbs.
20	49	100		300	45	90	50	1,938 lbs.
21,22	28	100		300	45	90	50	369 lbs.
							TOTAL:	8,964 lbs.

On 20 April the furnace hit peak production with 1,938 pounds of iron. At 2:00 P.M. on the following day, the gudgeon of the waterwheel broke. Work was halted while a replacement part was quickly made. Production started up again at 11:00 P.M. on Sunday, 22 April.[71] The total output for the furnace runs from 9 to 22 April was 10,143 lbs. of pig iron. The 8,964 lbs. produced in the last week alone entered into the accounts of the Deseret Iron Company on 23 April as being worth $2,241.00 or $500.00 a ton.[72]

Around this time, tragedy was averted by the watchful eyes of iron workers who were always mindful of each other's safety. John Lee Jones, the son of John Pidding Jones, recounted a night during one of the furnace runs when the life of James Timmings, a furnace stoker, was put in jeopardy:

> One Night the Wind was Very Rough & Whistled around a great deal. Those who was tending Furnace at Night inquired why Jim had not come down the tramway for near 2 Houres, one of the men went up & found him[.] his Body was Hanging by his Chin over the Curving Stone dangling in the air 38 ft above the ground[.] They immediat ly Took his Body downe thee Tram Way, Dug a Hole in the Ground 12.

> Oclock at Night & Put him with his Head downward & Buried him for
> ½ Hour or So to draw the fumes of Sulpher from his Lungs. He Came
> to Life[?] again but his appearance his Face was ashley White. I can
> remember his Pale look Vividly[.][73]

The method of resuscitation was certainly unorthodox but at least it seems to have worked.

Minutes of the Deseret Iron Company (dictated by either the furnace master or the general manager) do not mention any runs after 22 April and do not state when the furnace stopped operating. An entry in the account book for 28 April, however, credits the furnace with another 6,118 lbs. of iron, valued at $1,529.50 ($500.00 a ton), which implies that operations continued beyond 22 April.[74] According to Isaac Haight's journal, output was even greater than that recorded in the minute book, his entry exulting that "we made some ten tons of good iron."[75] Apparently the run did not stop because of mechanical failure. As stockpiles of traditional fuel disappeared, the pioneers gathered huge quantities of sagebrush to burn, an inefficient source at best.

Nevertheless, with the large amount of iron produced during April 1855, moulders were kept busy transforming pig iron into useful implements, including more hot blast pipes, machine parts, tools, horseshoes, pots, flatirons and nails. William Ashworth recalled later in life that the iron workers "made a few stoves but could not get them smooth enough to be marketable. Some bells for school houses and churches were cast."[76] One of the few artifacts known to have survived from the Deseret Iron Company is one of these bells (see illus. 13-6). It weighs about 150 lbs. and was originally placed in a wooden tower; later it hung in the belfry of a hotel run by Henry Lunt's family. According to local historians, the boys of Cedar City rang it often. "Meetings, schools, funerals, dances, even the time for taking the town herds of sheep and cattle out to feed and their return, were rung by the community bell."[77]

With many technical problems solved—excepting lack of fuel—the greatest need was for still more manpower. George A. Smith, who had led the first settlers to Iron County, enthusiastically called for more recruits:

> One hundred and fifty men are wanted immediately in this county to
> carry on the Iron Works successfully; those most needed are wagoners,
> miners, colliers, lime-burners, lumbermen, quarrymen, brick and stone
> masons, carpenters, joiners, machinists, charcoal burners, and furnace
> men. Fifty additional teams are necessary to keep the furnace supplied
> with fuel and ore. The people are in high spirits on the iron subject; the

Photograph by York Jones

Illus. 13-6. Deseret Iron Company bell, cast in 1855. Photograph taken inside George and Mary Davies Wood cabin. The bell is now on permanent display (as is the cabin) at Iron Mission State Park in Cedar City.

furnace having been kept successfully in operation two weeks satisfied the most sceptical that nothing was wanting but to continue the charge, as the furnace was blown out simply for want of fuel.[78]

George A. Smith's euphoria is understandable. The pioneer iron workers had struggled through a whole range of problems from inadequate natural resources to extremes in climate, improvising techniques to match the peculiar challenges of smelting ore on the American frontier. Now they had prevailed, creating a sustainable iron-making operation. The Iron Mission seemed poised, at last, to become truly successful.

Endnotes

1. Brigham Young, *Journal of Discourses* (27 May 1855), 2:283.

2. Erastus Snow and Franklin D. Richards, "Report of Travels," ca. 6 Dec 1853, published in *Deseret News,* 15 Dec 1853, 3d unnumbered page; Deseret Iron Company, Minutes, 12–13; Arrington, *Great Basin Kingdom,* 125, citing "Manufacture of Iron in Utah." See also Henry Lunt to Franklin D. Richards,

25 Sep 1853, published in *Deseret News,* 15 Oct 1853, 4th unnumbered page; and Bowering, journal, 3 Sep 1853.

3. Bowering, ibid., 4 Sep 1853.

4. Ibid., 10 Sep 1853.

5. Jenson, "Parowan Ward History," 64.

6. Deseret Iron Company, Minutes, 13.

7. Snow and Richards, "Report of Travels."

8. Deseret Iron Company, Minutes, 6, 14–30.

9. "Petition of Cedar City Residents," 12 Nov 1853, document no. 1815, Utah State Archives and Records Service.

10. Haight, journal, 8 Oct 1853. Haight's arrival in Cedar City on 1 Nov 1853 is documented by Bowering, who writes in his own journal of a meeting that Wednesday evening "in the centre of the Fort round a fire" at which "Elder I. C. Haight, Spoke his feelings, and then the meeting dismissed."

11. Deseret Iron Company, Minutes, 15.

12. Bowering, journal, 5 Nov 1853. Snow and Richards give the building's dimensions as 28 x 60 feet (in "Report of Travels," cited in n. 2 above); Jenson gives them as 25 x 60 feet (in "Manuscript History of Cedar City," 37). Bowering's 5 Nov journal entry, cited above, uses the phrases "of building" and "be built," both of which imply new construction. Andrew Jenson, however, in a somewhat ambiguous comment says that the schoolhouse was moved rather than demolished. Referring to the Ross home, which became the school-*cum*-meetinghouse in the Compact Fort after the family left Cedar City, Jenson reports:

> It remained there until 1853 when, on account of Indian difficulties, it was removed to its present location. The meeting house in the second location was an adobe building standing against south wall, about 60 by 28 feet. When the location was changed the house was taken down and moved to the present location, and put up on Block 37, lot 18, east of present Tabernacle, on the same block. It was called the Social Hall. It was used for all public purposes until the present tabernacle was built. It was still standing . . . until 1891 when it was considered unsafe for public use. (Jenson, "Manuscript History of Cedar City," 8)

Jenson appears to be saying the old schoolhouse was still standing when he wrote the manuscript history but was derelict by 1891. The "second location" should be Plat A, the south wall reference putting the building's relocation somewhere near the back edge of one of the 16 lots in Block 8 (see illus. 12-2). Jenson's reference to "present location" should mean Plat B, although Lot 18 of Block 37 on that plat was assigned to William Stewart. If Jenson is correct, the building had an unexpectedly active and varied existence: supposedly the first structure raised in the Compact

Fort, it was originally a family home. It was then expanded and turned into a meetinghouse by Joseph Chatterley, acting privately; expanded again by Henry Lunt, acting publicly as community leader; supposedly dismantled, moved and rebuilt on the south side of the public square in Plat A; and finally moved again, this time to Plat B where it took on new life as the Social Hall. Erastus Snow's remarks "on the necessity" of building a meetinghouse and George Bowering's report of dismantling the Compact Fort, however, substantially weaken the premise that the Social Hall could be the direct descendant of the Ross family cabin.

13. Deseret Iron Company, Minutes, 30, dating Haight's appointment to 26 Nov 1853. Haight's journal entry for the 27th, however, records his being appointed that day "one of the Directors and . . . Manager of the Company's affairs in America."

14. Haight, journal, 27 Nov 1853; Snow and Richards, "Report of Travels"; and Deseret Iron Company, Minutes, 14, confirm that Carruthers was living in Cedar City until at least this date. At the 10 Nov shareholders meeting he is listed as one of five men (the others being David Stoddard, James Williamson, William Stones and Joseph Clews) who "asked leaf to withdraw" as shareholders of the company. The absence of his name in subsequent company documents implies that he left for Scotland not long after this meeting.

15. Snow and Richards, "Report of Travels"; Jenson, "Parowan Ward History," 65; Deseret Iron Company, Minutes, 30. Haight, journal, records that the municipal election was held Monday, 5 Dec, rather than 6 Dec as given in the "Parowan Ward History."

16. Deseret Iron Company, Minutes, 31.

17. "Taken from a Autobiography of John Lee Jones as a missionary," 2-pg. reminiscence in possession of the Alva Matheson family in Cedar City, Utah. Final line of typescript reads "Ella Leigh has the original copy of this paper. Copied October 1965" (cited from copy in Shirts Collection).

18. William Ashworth, "Autobiography," bound typescript, 9 Perry Special Collections.

19. Deseret Iron Company, Minutes, 31.

20. J. C. L. Smith, letter to editor, ca. 1 Mar 1854, published in *Deseret News*, 16 Mar 1865, 3d unnumbered page.

21. Deseret Iron Company, Minutes, 31–32.

22. Ibid., 32.

23. Deseret Iron Company, untitled account book, Apr–Sep 1854, 35–36 LDS Church Archives.

24. Ibid., 42–89.

25. Ibid., 90–124. As already noted in ch. 10, it should be emphasized here that, in almost all cases, amounts earned by workers were actually credits entered against their names in the company books.

26. Ibid., 42–124.

27. Elias Morris, diary excerpts, 2.

28. Deseret Iron Company, untitled account book, 28, 42–124.

29. Ibid., 42–124.

30. Deseret Iron Company, Minutes, 33–34.

31. Lunt, diary, comments following 18 Jul 1853; Jones, *Henry Lunt,* 180.

32. Deseret Iron Company, Minutes, 33–36.

33. Reprinted in "Manufacture of Iron in Utah," *Millennial Star* 17 (6 Jan 1855): 6; more details appear in Deseret Iron Company, Minutes, 37. Very similar descriptions of the furnace occur in all three sources and in Morris, diary excerpts, 2. A comment in the *Millennial Star* article, "The particulars of the furnace, brother Elias Morris, who was the Architect, will give you," suggests that he was the original source of the description.

34. "Furnace Account, cost of erecting, from 30 May to 16 Sept. 1854," Deseret Iron Company, miscellaneous documents, Palmer Collection.

35. Crook, "Early Industry and Trade," 65; Jones, "Iron Mining and Manufacturing," 56.

36. Lucius N. Scovil to editor, 7 Dec 1854, published in *Deseret News,* 4 Jan 1855, 2nd unnumbered page.

37. Deseret Iron Company, inventory, 16 Sep 1854, 2 pp., Palmer Collection.

38. Arrington, *Great Basin Kingdom,* 128.

39. Deseret Iron Company, Journal, 3, 6, 8–9, 13.

40. Ibid., 10–12, 16–17, 25, 37.

41. Ibid.

42. Ibid., 15, 29.

43. Ibid., 13, 18–19.

44. Ibid., 6–9, 12–13, 23, 28, 30, 69, 213.

45. Ibid., 9, 14, 16–17.

46. Ibid., 16–17.

47. Ibid., 10–11, 14–15.

48. Ibid., 55, 80.

49. Ibid., 17.

50. Ibid., 13, 15, 23, 51–55, 57, 82, 212.

51. "C. J. Arthur," unsourced, incomplete biographical typescript, 7 (copy in Shirts Collection).

52. Ibid., 9.

53. Ibid., 9–12.

54. George A. Smith to editor, 9 Dec 1854, published in *Deseret News,* 21 Dec 1854, 3d unnumbered page.

55. Deseret Iron Company, Journal, 24.

56. Ibid., 20.

57. James Lewis to George A. Smith, 26 Dec 1854, published in *Deseret News*, 11 Jan 1855, 2nd unnumbered page.

58. Deseret Iron Company, Minutes, 39.

59. Ibid., 40; Deseret Iron Company, Journal, 76.

60. Deseret Iron Company, Journal, 28.

61. Deseret Iron Company, Minutes, 40–41.

62. Ibid., 41.

63. Deseret Iron Company, Journal, 74.

64. Deseret Iron Company, Minutes, 42.

65. Deseret Iron Company, Journal, 76.

66. Ibid., 74–75.

67. Ibid., 70–71, 81.

68. Ibid., 44.

69. Ibid., 94.

70. Ibid., 96.

71. Deseret Iron Company, Minutes, 43.

72. Deseret Iron Company, Journal, 102.

73. John Lee Jones, single holograph sheet, "The Names of Those Who Run the Blast Furnaces," including report of a life-threatening accident, Palmer Collection (copy in Shirts Collection).

74. Deseret Iron Company, Journal, 105.

75. Haight, journal, Apr 1855.

76. Ashworth, *Autobiography*, 9.

77. Dalton, *Iron County Mission*, 119–120.

78. George A. Smith to editor, 14 Mar 1855, published in *Deseret News*, 30 May 1855, 92.

Part IV

Facing Failure

14

The Iron Works in Decline

1855–1861

O n 19 May 1855, Brigham Young and his company arrived in Cedar City to evaluate the progress of the Iron Mission, having stopped on the way to investigate the abundant coal deposits in Sanpete County. They visited the iron works as soon as they arrived and saw for themselves the recent successes in iron output. Achievements there were matched by increasing growth and stability in both Parowan and Cedar City. The day after his visit to the iron works, Brigham Young presided over a conference making Cedar City, Harmony and Johnson's Spring a new stake, separate from the one at Parowan. Isaac C. Haight was appointed president of the new Cedar City Stake with Jonathan Pugmire and John M. Higbee (see illus. 14-1) as his counselors.

Haight felt burdened with this new responsibility but, as usual, agreed to shoulder the additional load. He commented that the stake presidency "with my other duties, seemed a great task, yet I feel to do as the Lord shall direct or appoint me to do." A week earlier, Haight had been reelected mayor of Cedar City for another two years. On 21 May, President Young returned to Parowan and reorganized the stake there. J. C. L. Smith, who had presided over the original stake, was named president of the now-separate Parowan Stake.[1]

Immediately upon returning to Salt Lake City, Brigham Young addressed the Saints in the Tabernacle, reporting at length on the Iron Mission. In light of recent successful runs in the Noble Furnace, he affirmed that "the brethren have done as well as men could possibly do, considering their impoverished circumstances, and the inconveniences they have had to labor under." He stressed the benefit of running the furnace as long as possible, preventing damaging "blow outs" which cost so much to repair. To this end, he called for 15 good teams and 25 more men to go to Iron County and help meet the increasing demand for iron ore

Courtesy Richard Neitzel Holzapfel

Illus. 14-1. John M. Higbee (1827–1904), counselor in the Cedar City Stake Presidency and major in the territorial militia.

and fuel. He insisted that if they had a mind to, they could keep the furnace running for several months at a time:

> Iron we need, and iron we must have. . . . We have an abundance of the best quality of iron ore. A trial furnace was made, and kept hot for sixteen days, and produced as good pig metal as can be found in the world; this they puddled, and brought forth excellent iron. I believe the castings made from the pigs will be superior to any in the world. I repeat that iron we must have, and we are right on the threshhold of obtaining it; we have our feet on the step, and our hand holds the latch of the door that leads to the possession of this invaluable material.

He also pointed out the difficulty of relying on creek water to power the blast. "[I]n one freezing night it will perfectly close up, insomuch that there will not be enough to water a horse." He noted with anticipation that the iron workers were building an engine that would keep the blast furnace operating through the winter. Because plentiful, high-quality fuel was so important to continuous iron production, President Young revealed that he had considered moving the iron works to the rich coal supplies in Sanpete County. Nevertheless, he had decided against it for the time being.[2]

Contemplating a Third Move

Although Brigham Young was satisfied to leave the iron works in southern Utah, he was not satisfied with the Plat A fort site. At the Cedar City stake conference, he proposed moving the town one more time because of flood danger to Plat A if Coal Creek overflowed. He suggested relocating south of the iron works and east of the Plat A fort. He did not recommend tearing down the fort, which could be used to accommodate newcomers, but encouraged Cedar City residents to move to the new location at their discretion. One week after Brigham Young's visit, Isaac Haight motioned that "the city be located and occupied according to the proposals of President Young." Agreement was unanimous.[3]

By the end of the month, William H. Dame had surveyed the relocation site, designated Plat B, the present location of Cedar City. Dated

30 May 1855, Dame's survey consisted of 40 blocks, the first group of which were 24 by 72 rods, with Blocks 21 to 40 subdivided into lots 8 by 12 rods (see illus. 14-2). Landmarks in modern Cedar City correlate easily with this survey. Block 44 was reserved for the city park. Modern 200 North borders Blocks 31 to 39 on the north, while Center Street borders them on the south. Center Street is north of Blocks 22 to 30, which are bordered on the south by 200 South. Sixth West is adjacent to Blocks 30 and 31 on the west and 300 East is adjacent to Blocks 22 and 39 on the east.

On Sunday, 10 June 1855, Isaac Haight encouraged the settlers to start building on the new site, stating that "if they did not feel to build there they are not as they ought to be in feeling, for the president [said] it was not safe here."[4] On 25 June 1855, over 90 men paid fees for lots in Plat B, many claiming double lots, although the actual move took place more slowly (see app. 10).

Battling the Environment: Grasshoppers and Drought

The greatest challenge that spring, however, was not relocation but the combined effect of drought and insects, which proved almost catastrophic. Farmers were still planting in May because spring warmth had come so late but even worse were the "grasshoppers of small dimensions" which were "far more numerous than the contending armies in the Crimea."[5] George A. Smith wrote Franklin D. Richards on 31 May that "in every settlement I passed through there were myriads of grasshoppers. At Parowan there were none when I arrived there, but in a few days the little fellows began to appear in innumerable hosts."[6] During Brigham Young's trip to the southern settlements that month, as reported in the *Deseret News* of 31 October, he found the Saints "with their crops almost entirely destroyed by the ravages of grasshoppers, rendering their hard exertions and the labors of their hands fruitless."[7] William McDonald planted 20 acres of wheat on his rented farm but the insects attacked his field:

> It came up Nice and was looking fine and the Grasshoppers Hatched out And Swept the ground so Clean there wasent a Green thing left. That stopped My farming that year and it seemed as though there Wood be a famin for the Whole Country Was swept Clean of vegetation and We Were over a thousand Miles from Where We could get aney Help.[8]

The drought was equally uncontrollable, made worse by relentless winds. George A. Smith complained on 18 May that "The wind has blown a gale here for the last four days, dust in the eyes, and every where, that dust can find a resting place, is the result. The farmers have to irrigate

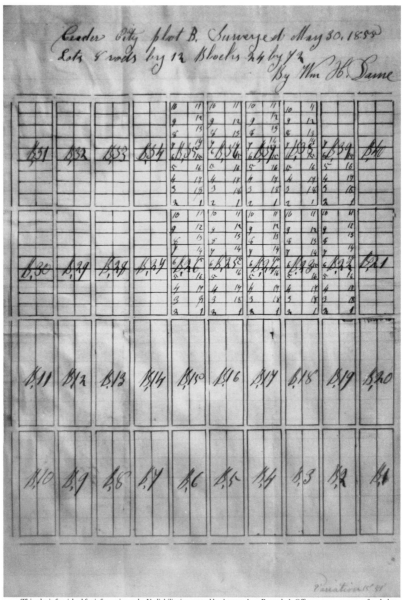

Illus. 14-2. Dame's "Ceader City" Survey of Plat B, dated 30 May 1855, showing individual lots at 8 by 12 rods and city blocks at 24 by 72 rods. This is the site of modern-day Cedar City (see app. 10 for listing of lot owners).

all the land before sowing, the spring has been so dry."[9] James Lewis echoed in the *Deseret News* that "the streams are very low, and we have had no rain this summer, the country is very much parched."[10]

In October 1855, when J. C. L. Smith, Jesse N. Smith, Philip Klingensmith and Thomas Dunlop Brown arrived in Salt Lake City with a party from Iron County, they reported that not over 20 bushels of wheat had been raised at Parowan.[11] The Parowan settlers rationed food but also took an additional precaution, as reported by the *Deseret News* in June of that year:

> The fields look like a desert and every separate bench appears to be hatching out fresh crops of grasshoppers. . . . The water is lower than has ever been known before, and but a small portion of the land resown can possibly be watered. . . . The Public Square at Parowan city (10 acres) has been planted with potatos in the hopes that the united efforts of men, women, and children, chickens, ducks, turkies, &c, &c., may save a sufficiency to have occasionally a little potato soup next winter.[12]

The emergency forced the settlers to abandon their wheat fields outside the fort and ration available water among the garden-sized interior plots. A series of entries in Deed Book B proves the existence of 88 small lots, 18 feet wide and 132 feet long in Block 12, the public square. No survey map is extant, but the number of lots plus the space needed for irrigation ditches and access paths would completely fill the square as it probably existed then. George A. Smith's ironic comment to John Taylor at the time echoes the *Deseret News* report: "Men, women, children, geese, ducks and chickens are all conspiring to try and raise something."[13]

In Cedar City, as in Parowan, crops were light and the pioneers devoted much of their energy to mere survival. Coal Creek ran so low that it could not be divided sufficiently for both farming and iron production. Home building in the new city halted and water levels dropped too low to allow the waterwheel at the iron works to operate. Fires swept through the canyons, destroying not only standing timber but also the bridges the pioneers had built.[14]

Although the Noble Furnace could not function without water, other activities at the iron works continued throughout fall 1855. The men in the blacksmith shop were busy fixing both farm tools and furnace parts. The engineering department continued its efforts—which Brigham Young had noted at the last general conference—to build an engine able to make the iron works independent of Coal Creek. The Deseret Iron Company

Minutes confirm that, when the furnace was idle (as it was for much of 1855), the men always tried to occupy their time as best they could:

> No record being kept from April to Oct. 14th, the following is as near as the clerk at the works can recollect. A pudling furnace and Trip Hammer were put up and some few hundred of scrap iron was heated and drawn out for the lathe, furnace bars and water tweers. The moulders made castings for hot blast, a large lathe and wheels for gearing of the cylinders. A new water wheel was made with cast iron cranks and gudgeons, put in together with the wheel gearing for working the cylinders. One of the cranks bursting by wedging too tight a new one was cast the following day and put in. Several tons of Lean ore were hauled placed upon beds and roasted. A few hundred bushels of charcoal was burned and hauled by D. Gould. Several hundred tons of coal was hauled and burned into coke.[15]

According to the Deseret Iron Company Journal, almost 17 tons of rock were quarried and 54,000 adobes delivered to build a large machine shop.[16] Coal was hauled from the mines, Henry Cook and Samuel Gould processed bushels of charcoal and cords of wood were stockpiled.

The water flowed again briefly and the iron workers made another start with the Noble Furnace toward the end of November. In the week ending 23 November 1855, 24 tons of "lean ore" and 12 tons of "magnetic ore" (magnetite) from West Mountain were hauled in, as well as over 25 tons of coal and approximately 20 cords of wood. Samuel Gould provided 662 bushels of charcoal. In addition to gathering sufficient fuel for another furnace run, the teamsters hauled large quantities of adobe brick for the construction of a foundry.[17] Nevertheless, a severe winter was moving in on the iron works. Erastus Snow reported these problems in a letter written 11 December:

> I learn that the freezing of Coal Creek, a few days since, stopped the blast from the furnace after a few days' successful operation; and the directors have concluded to suspend further operations until spring, except to use up the metal now on hand in casting some mill gearing, &c. It is certain that Coal Creek cannot be relied upon for a motive power in our Iron Works, and that the sooner we have an engine the better. The cost of such a one as we need would not exceed $1500 in St. Louis.[18]

Writing two weeks later, Snow referred to the pioneers "occasionally" succeeding "in running out about a ton a day" of ore through this period. Even so, snow was so deep that coal beds in the canyon were inaccessible and mining stopped as well.[19]

The end of the year brought another and more unexpected calamity. On 30 December 1855, John Calvin Lazelle Smith, Parowan's respected stake president and community leader, died of heart failure after a brief illness but some years of less than perfect health.[20] In a 29 December letter, written from then-state capital Fillmore City, George A. Smith alerted Franklin D. Richards that "President John C. L. Smith of Parowan is reported very sick." After sharing more news, he broke off the completion of his letter until the following 5 January, then noting that a "Brother Wilford, an emigrant from Australia, came in from Parowan last evening, with letters and the melancholy news of the death of Elder John C. L. Smith, the president of the stake. He was a good man and has gone to rest, but his loss will be sever[e]ly felt in that part of the country."[21] J. C. L. Smith was only 33 years and a few months old when he died. The sadness felt by the settlers at his passing intensified on 10 August 1856, not much more than seven months later, at the death of his infant son, little John Lazelle Smith.[22] William H. Dame, the hard-working surveyor of Parowan and Cedar City, became the new stake president on 16 January 1856.[23]

By 3 February, even with snow still on the ground, George A. Smith was encouraging a general relocation to Cedar City Plat B. "We should improve that place as Brigham had said so," he affirmed. He "did not wish to see any more improvement made here [on Plat A] not even on a house worth fifteen dollars."[24] Three weeks later, water ditches on the new townsite were ready and the Saints were again urged to build there.

In spring 1856, new settler Bengt Nelson described the dwellings in Plat B, which reflected the poverty of the pioneers:

> Returning from Iron Springs, the first thing I did was to secure a lot on which to erect a home for myself and wife, the new city, the present site of Cedar, having been surveyed the year before. I secured a city lot from the Bishop and was the third settler in the new city, as the people had not started to move up from what was called the old Fort, but as I was expected to work at the iron works I came direct to the new location as it was much nearer the iron works than the old Fort. I dug a cellar, but having no lumber, I used willows for the roof, then covered them with straw that I obtained from a kind farmer, and then covered that with dirt, but it proved to be a rainy season, and the roof leaked badly. I tore the roof away, made some adobes, walled up the cellar, and built an adobe room on top of it. I succeeded in procuring some old boards for the roof, and covered them with dirt. But not having any boards for the floor, we had quite a time, until I got hold of a few pieces and we made them answer for part of a floor, at least.[25]

Tackling Manpower Shortages and Technical Challenges

The "rainy season," which made it so hard for Nelson to install his roof, was all too brief. In 1856, the Iron County pioneers were again plagued with drought and grasshoppers and some settlers left to find farms in more hospitable country. On 21 May, President Haight wrote Brigham Young that "our prospects in relation to the Iron Works looks to me rather discouraging at present, for want of the necessary help." When he returned from the statehood convention, he asked for volunteers to haul coal, but the men said their teams were too weak to get up to the mines. He noted that

> the prospect looks rather dull for getting much fuel. I expect to Start the Blast furnace some time in June and use up the fuel we have on hand, And so much more as we can get, I feel almost discouraged Some times and ready to give up the Job but as you sent me here to take charge of the Iron Works I intend to continue to do the best I can however discouraging things may appear, until you see fit to appoint another that will take hold and do beter than I have yet been able to do.[26]

A 10-day trial of the "hot blast" furnace, possibly trial furnace no. 1, ran from 20 to 30 June 1856 but produced only 300 lbs. of iron (on the 22nd) before the iron chilled and the furnace had to be blown out.[27] In July, desiring to salvage the iron, Joseph Walker built a small furnace "for running the old bear in to pigs."[28] On 21 July, a company led by Isaac Haight went to West Mountain exploring for iron. Peter Shirts successfully located a deposit and they returned the next day with 2,400 lbs. of high quality metal, which they called "virgin ore." This ore body is believed to be the deposit located about two miles west of Pinto Junction beside Highway U-56, the highway between Cedar City and Newcastle. The explorers wanted to calcine the ore and then try it in a cupola or small furnace. On 28 July, Elias Morris began taking down the old hearth, reducing the boshes and relining the Noble Furnace in preparation for another run.[29]

The shortage of labor prompted Thomas Bladen to go on a mission to "recruit and convert skilled iron workers" in England and he arrived in Liverpool on 7 August 1856. He wrote to John Taylor from New York describing the iron works in glowing terms, going so far as to imply that the coal was of a high quality for coking. As he reported,

> There is an extensive range of buildings for the work shops where a great number of mechanics are employed in almost every branch of the iron trade. Other mechanics will shortly be wanted to assist in carrying

on the work. The company is fast preparing to supply the rising state of Deseret with everything in the iron trade that she will require from a nail to a steam engine.

Brethren who feel an interest in this great work, will do well to arise and assist in rolling on the same, that Deseret may be independent of the nations for the most valuable of all metals—iron. The bees of the hive of Deseret are at work.[30]

Despite Bladen's enthusiasm, iron production was plagued with difficulties in 1856. A furnace run was tried in June, but failed. Thomas Gower, rather than the experienced David B. Adams, was the keeper.[31] The workers were just getting the furnace started up when the blast pipes accidentally burned out. By the time the pipes were replaced, the water shortage in Coal Creek made it difficult to operate the furnace. Another run was attempted in mid-July with David B. Adams as keeper, but it was cut short and the iron chilled.[32] Shortly afterwards, Adams left the works and moved to Beaver County, probably due to the terrible drought. On 4 August, wrote Haight in his journal "We also started the iron works, but for the want of water we had to stop without accomplishing much."[33] The moulder's cupola continued to operate, making castings for individuals and small accounts (such as a business run by Isaac Haight and Charles Simpkins) to supplement iron company work. As with the winter of 1855–56, the iron works essentially shut down over the winter of 1856–57.

Even as they were struggling in near poverty, the iron workers were willing to give assistance to a short-lived attempt to produce lead in southern Nevada. Indian missionaries called to the area in June 1855 had discovered outcroppings of lead 30 miles southwest of Las Vegas. Brigham Young approached Nathaniel V. Jones in February 1856 to lead an expedition of 30 men to investigate and, if possible, found a lead industry. The Iron Mission provided supplies and Bishop Klingensmith traveled with the lead missionaries to Las Vegas to evaluate the deposits. Hauling equipment from Salt Lake City, Jones and his men were able to produce about 9,000 lbs. of lead which the Mormons made into bullets. Lack of nearby water and forage, however, made mining difficult, as did impurities in the lead. The missionaries abandoned the effort and returned to Salt Lake City in March 1857. Ironically, the impurities which had frustrated the smelting process turned out to be silver and "gentile" prospectors discovered a nearby lode in 1861, which became the immensely rich Potosí silver mines.[34]

New hope for the iron works arose in March 1857, however, when Isaac Haight received a letter from Brigham Young offering the use of a steam engine that had originally been imported for the sugar mill and was now being surplused by the paper mill in Salt Lake City.[35] A pair of 30 horse-power engines had been brought south from Salt Lake Valley a year before (March 1856) but had not worked well. The iron company engineers in Cedar City had not been able to build a satisfactory engine themselves, despite newspaper accounts of the iron company casting "some beautiful machinery, intended to supercede the use of Coal creek for motive power." President Young suggested that Haight send a company of trusted men to Salt Lake City to retrieve the new engine but the directors of the Deseret Iron Company wanted Haight himself to supervise the transport.[36] The Minutes record the much-anticipated arrival:

> April 8th, 1857. The engine sent down by Prest. Young arrived in this city 4 P.M. and on the morning of the 9th was taken to the iron works, examined and found correct according to invoice, except cold water pump.[37]

The Deseret Iron Company Journal indicates six months later that $2,181 was paid to Brigham Young for the engine.[38] Setting it up, building an engine house and modifying the furnace was an ambitious project, but it promised to free the iron works from its frustrating dependence on Coal Creek.

The engine was tried on 8 July 1857 but the new technology created its own set of mechanical problems which needed to be solved before the furnace could function properly. At first, the workers could not create a sufficient draft in the chimney for the boiler fire. They tried lining the stack to decrease its diameter, then raising the stack, then running a new flue from the fire box to the stack. As Isaac Haight informed Brigham Young on 25 July, "We are preparing to put the blast on the furnace on Monday[;] wee have been raising our Chimney stack to increase the draft from the Baile [sic] furnace as we use the Old Stack that was built for the Old Air furnace."[39] Finally the draft was strong enough for the engine to power a furnace run on 28 July; however, a leak in one of the flues in the boiler stopped the engine after a 12-hour run. The blast was put on again on 30 July but muddy water from a canyon rainstorm deposited sand in the steam cylinders. The workers then decided to build a reservoir to provide a supply of clear water for the boiler. The small reservoir, 75 feet long and averaging 25 feet wide, was lined with fire clay and gravel.[40]

The engine now worked well, but other problems with the furnace remained unsolved. First a valve on the blast cylinder broke, then the furnace lining proved insufficient for the strength of the blast. When the furnace was put back on, it worked "very middling," yielding "little iron[,]

Illus. 14-3. Daniel H. Wells (1814–91) appointed to lead the territorial militia.

cinder and bogus."[41] Comparing the various Deseret Iron Company records reveals that the number of iron workers continued to decline throughout the coming months. Those who remained worked mostly on repairing equipment and on constructing or improving buildings.[42]

Restructuring the Territorial Militia

Isaac C. Haight, called to the Cedar City stake presidency on 20 May 1855, was elected to the 1855 territorial legislature that August. He left with Jesse N. Smith on 5 December, in freezing weather, to attend legislative sessions in Fillmore, where he was appointed a member of the military committee. There, he worked on a bill to more completely organize the militia.[43] Following a family visit, Haight again headed for Fillmore, leaving on 4 March 1856, this time as delegate to the convention preparing a petition for statehood. He was accompanied by Washington County's representative, John D. Lee, of Fort Harmony.[44]

Although conditions at the iron works had given Haight a temporary rest, he was now kept busy by a second term as territorial legislator. The 1856–57 session met on 8 December 1856 in Fillmore, only to reconvene on 18 December in the Social Hall in Salt Lake City. Haight was again appointed to the military committee. Because there had been no serious military engagement since the Walker War, the legislature took advantage of the time to restructure the Nauvoo Legion, authorizing Lieutenant General Daniel H. Wells (see illus. 14-3) to head a committee to draft a new set of laws and regulations. In February 1857 the committee met to reorganize the militia, as requested. Each division would have two brigades, consisting of 1,000 ordinary soldiers. And each brigade would contain two regiments (of five battalions each). Individual battalions would have 100 soldiers, organized into two companies of 50 men each, while a company would be divided into five platoons of 10 men each who would elect their own platoon leader from within the group. Military district boundaries were redrawn, making a total of 13 for the territory. The "Iron Military District," or Tenth Regiment, included Iron, Beaver and Washington Counties and was to be organized under the supervision of William H. Dame.[45]

During the 1856–57 legislative session, Haight recorded that Heber C. Kimball, Brigham Young's first counselor, presided over a ceremony designed to rededicate the legislators from all over the territory to the work of establishing the Kingdom of God. On 30 December 1856,

> Both houses met in joint session and Prest. Kimball required every member to repent of all their sins and be baptised for the remission of the same before any business could be done. Preparations were then made and all the members repaired to the Endowment House and were baptised in the font, and were confirmed and all were made to rejoice with joy and gladness unspeakable.[46]

This rededication was part of a movement begun earlier in 1856 by Brigham Young's second counselor, Jedediah M. Grant. Grant wanted to reinvigorate the Saints who, he felt, were becoming lax in religious observance after almost ten years in their Great Basin sanctuary. During this Mormon Reformation, local leaders conducted detailed personal interviews with members to evaluate their conduct. Rebaptism followed, renewing spiritual commitment and enthusiasm for the cause of Zion. After witnessing the fruits of the Reformation in Salt Lake City, President Haight was determined to bring this work back home. His diary entry for February 1857 records that he "started the reformation in Cedar City and vicinity," although other pioneer journals indicate the Reformation was already well recognized as far south as Harmony. A constant Reformation theme echoing in Sunday meetings throughout southern Utah was strict obedience to all authorities—both general and local.[47]

Political Maneuvering in the Nation

As if the technical problems of manufacturing iron and the difficulties of surviving the unpredictable climate of southern Utah were not enough, the iron missionaries were about to be embroiled in troubles on a much larger scale. When statehood was deferred and the Territory of Utah was created on 9 September 1850, politically astute Thomas L. Kane warned the Mormons that territorial status came with hidden dangers: federal control of all key administrative positions by using the power of political appointments.[48] In the 1856 presidential election, John C. Frémont, Abraham Lincoln and Stephen A. Douglas, all former friends of the Mormons, became involved in arguing against the "twin evils" of polygamy and slavery. The Democrats won the election and James Buchanan became President, strongly urged by southern constituents to emphasize a national crusade against polygamy over the crusade against slavery. Alarming reports were coming in from disgruntled presidential appointees to Utah, including Judge W. W. Drummond (who was forced from his Utah judgeship for reported immoral conduct). Relying on such reports, President Buchanan became convinced that Utah Territory was in a state of rebellion against federal authority.[49]

Drummond's opinions, for instance, were echoed by Thomas S. Twiss, Upper Platte River Indian Agent, and W. M. F. Magraw, former contractor of mail services between Missouri and Utah. Since 1849, Brigham Young and other leaders had discussed the possibility of creating a Mormon mail and freighting service. They hoped to improve communications among the Saints and tap some of the profits to be made in overland trading and hauling, primarily with those wagon trains headed for California. By 1855–56, a marked decline was observable in eastern mail service and the time seemed right to push Mormon plans forward as a practical alternative.[50]

On 6 August, the *Deseret News* printed a request from Postmaster General James Campbell soliciting bids for the mail route between Independence, Missouri, and Salt Lake City. Church financial backing enabled Mormon contractor Hiram Kimball of Salt Lake City to make the "lowest responsible offer" and he was awarded the route. The first months of 1857 brought flurries of related activity and far-flung correspondence, planning more connections once the central carrier service began. Brigham Young was elated. Then, suddenly, all was over.

In June 1857 the government nullified Kimball's contract, giving as official justification the "non-arrival of the mail within the stipulated time." The true origin appears to be the enmity of W. M. F. Magraw, who, as former mail contractor, disliked the idea of the potentially lucrative government contract going to Mormon bidder Hiram Kimball. Magraw vented his indignation by writing what Andrew Neff calls a "malignant" letter to the President of the United States. In it, Magraw described the Saints "as being in an uncontrolled state of lawlessness, in which murder, rapine and terrorism flourished and which had been superimposed upon a helpless society by a vicious, despotic, self-constituted theocracy at the head of which was Brigham Young."[51]

Without any fact-finding or local investigation to support his actions, Buchanan decided to take a strong stand. He made new appointments, including Alfred Cumming as governor of Utah Territory, Jacob Forney as Indian Superintendent and Delana R. Eckles, Charles E. Sinclair and John Cradelbaugh as federal judges.[52] Mormons were especially alarmed by the appointment of Cumming, former mayor of Augusta, Georgia, because of his connections to Missouri (well remembered for its anti-Mormon hostilities) where he was a successful administrator of Indian lands. On the advice of Secretary of War John Floyd, Buchanan's plan included sending a sizable military expedition along with the new appointees, to enforce their acceptance.

On 28 May 1857, orders were dispatched by General Winfield Scott to assemble a large army at Fort Leavenworth, Kansas, to march to Utah. On 29 June, General Scott appointed General W. S. Harney as commanding officer of this expedition.[53] Harney's appointment was met with trepidation in Utah as he was a tough-minded military officer who had earned the epithet "Squaw Killer" in his battle with the Sioux Indians in 1854. It was reported that Harney planned "to capture Brigham Young and the twelve Apostles, and execute them in a summary fashion, and winter in the Temple of the Latter-day Saints."[54] Before the army left for Utah, however, Harney was reassigned to Kansas to maintain peace between abolitionists and their opponents. Colonel Albert Sidney Johnston, another stern disciplinarian, replaced Harney.

The first contingent of 850 troops left Fort Leavenworth on 18 July 1857 and arrived at "Camp Scott," better known as Fort Bridger, in November. By late that month, the force had increased to over 2,000 men,[55] ultimately reaching approximately 2,500. The total standing U.S. Army at that time was only 13,000 men,[56] which meant that, at peak operation, almost one-fifth of the nation's military manpower was diverted to solve the "Utah problem." Congress was not in session when Buchanan decided to send such a large force; apparently he attempted to execute the entire operation in secrecy. Brigham Young may have learned something of "Buchanan's Army" as early as 7 June 1857, for on that date, in a speech in Salt Lake City, he reportedly expressed the opinion that "trouble was brewing, and that some of the officers who had been sent to the Territory were circulating false rumors about the Latter-day Saints."[57]

On 24 July 1857, approximately 2,600 pioneers assembled at the head of Big Cottonwood Canyon, east and south of Salt Lake City, to celebrate the tenth anniversary of their arrival in the valley. A. O. Smoot, Judson Stoddard and Porter Rockwell, who had been checking out the anticipated Mormon-operated mail route to Missouri, arrived at noon and confirmed Brigham Young's suspicions—U.S. troops were approaching Fort Laramie. The three messengers, in a small springboard wagon with two span of horses, had covered the 500 miles from Fort Laramie in five days to alert Brigham Young as soon as possible. However, the Saints assembled for the anniversary festivities were not given the unsettling news until that evening.[58] In Cedar City, oblivious to the approaching danger, citizens celebrated with a parade in which a "Company of Mechanics from the Iron Works" marched together, "each man bearing machinery representing his branch of industry."[59]

Preparing for War

Brigham Young, who had not yet been officially advised of his replacement, moved to exercise his authority as governor to defend the territory against all enemies. On 5 August, two weeks after the army's approach was confirmed at the 24 July celebration, President Young issued a "Proclamation of Martial Law." The essence of the document was succinctly put in three statements at its end:

> 1st:—To forbid, in the name of the People of the United States in the Territory of Utah, all armed forces, of every description, from coming into this Territory under any pretense whatever.
>
> 2nd:—That all the forces in said Territory hold themselves in readiness to march, at a moment's notice, to repel any and all such threatened invasion.
>
> 3d:—Martial law is hereby declared to exist in this Territory, . . . and no person shall be allowed to pass or repass into, or through, or from this Territory, without a permit from the proper officer.[60]

Two days prior, George A. Smith, who had commanded all the southern militia units during the Walker War, had left Salt Lake City to prepare outlying citizens for anticipated hostilites with approaching federal troops. On 4 August, he directed General Aaron Johnson of Springville to mobilize the local troops; at Nephi, Smith delivered orders to Major George W. Brandley; at Fillmore, he instructed Major L. H. McCullough to prepare. In Beaver, he met with Bishop Philo T. Farnsworth who was captain of a company attached to the battalion at Parowan. Finally, on 8 August, Smith himself arrived in Parowan where he found Colonel William H. Dame already drilling the troops.[61] According to James Martineau:

> This afternoon, at 3 o'clock the 1st Bat. mustered for the first time since its organization, and while on parade, Br. Geo. A. Smith arrived from G. S. L. City bringing information on the approach of an army from the United States to invade the Territory and wage a war of extermination against us. He brought orders from Head Quarters of immediate preparation for defense and for the preservation of grain etc; also instruction from Pres. B. Young to the same effect, and recommending

that the Bishop get possession of all grain not wanted for immediate use and recommending all to live their religion and be prepared for that which <u>may</u> come to pass.[62]

As president of the Parowan stake, William H. Dame was the ranking religious leader. As colonel and commanding officer of the Iron Regiment, to which he had been elected on 28 July 1857, he was also the ranking military leader. The regiment consisted of four battalions, each with a major as its commanding officer. The First Battalion was in Parowan, commanded by Major James Lewis. The Second Battalion was in Cedar City, commanded by Major Isaac C. Haight, who had a dual rank as he was also lieutenant colonel, second in regimental command to William H. Dame. Major John M. Higbee, now first counselor to Haight in the presidency of the Cedar Stake, commanded the Third Battalion, also in Cedar City. Major John D. Lee commanded the Fourth Battalion, located at Fort Harmony (see app. 11).

On Sunday, 9 August, George A. Smith spoke twice to the people assembled in the Parowan Tabernacle, recalling his role in founding the town and appealing to the fighting spirit of the citizens. Because he was so trusted and beloved, his words had heightened impact:

> As a people we have been long harassed and oppressed, driven, slain and plundered. I have got through with it. . . . If we trust in God he will give us power over our enemies. If there are any who are afraid, I wish them to go now, go like gentlemen, all who are not willing to die for their religion.[63]

On 10 August, Smith back-tracked to Paragonah to speak. After working on his property for three days, he traveled to Cedar City, where Colonel Dame had gone to drill the Second and Third Battalions. George A. Smith visited the iron works on 15 August and spoke twice the next day in Sunday meetings. That evening he traveled to Fort Harmony and the next day, as Rachel Lee reported, "the brethren paraded in order to show the Officer of this place how to disiplin their men aright. . . . President G. A. Smith deliverd a discours on the Spirit that actuated the United States towards this people—full of hostility and virulence."[64]

Apostle Smith and Colonel Dame then rode south to Washington City where again Smith preached and Dame drilled the militia. Smith spoke in Santa Clara before returning to Parowan, speaking once more on Sunday, 23 August, encouraging the settlers to destroy their property rather than let it be used by their enemies: "But if the gentiles do come here I hope they will find nothing but a desert."[65] These speeches were inflammatory and obviously designed to prepare the people psychologically for all-out war. Their homes, their lives, their families and their lifestyle were believed to be in jeopardy. Responding to the threat, Colonel Dame reported to Lieutenant General Daniel H. Wells on that same Sunday that the district militia was organized with 200 men, armed and ready for action.[66]

George A. Smith left Parowan for Salt Lake City the next day. "From about this time," Martineau noted, "parties of from three to five men were sent out to explore in the mountains," to search for a hiding place in the south where the Mormons could gather if the army invaded the northern settlements.[67] A letter from Lieutenant General Wells to Colonel Dame, sent on 13 August, again emphasized the need to conserve grain and counseled Dame to "instruct the Indians that our enemies are also their enemies. . . . They must be our friends and stick to us for if our enemies kill us off, they will surely be cut off by the same parties."[68] By mid-August all militia units throughout the territory had held musters and some were in the field. "Observation forces" were sent to Fort Hall and Bear River to guard the northern approaches. One group was sent to observe U.S. Army activities in the Fort Bridger and Fort Laramie areas and to harass the troops whenever possible. Now that martial law was in effect, Iron County units guarded southern approaches to the territory and allowed no one through without a pass.

Disaster at Mountain Meadows

Although a steady stream of emigrants had arrived in Salt Lake City throughout the summer, until the first part of August they had chosen the northern route to California, bypassing southern Utah. The first wagon train to take the southern route that year, rather than risk a possible winter passage over the Sierra Nevada Mountains, was a party of some 40 wagons and considerable ranching stock. Captained by Alexander Fancher and John T. Baker, the group consisted mainly of families from northern Arkansas intending to settle in the San Joaquin Valley.[69] Unaware of the "Proclamation of Martial Law," the Fancher-Baker train moved south without a pass or the sanction of a Mormon escort. As they traveled down the Mormon Corridor, contact with settlers became abrasive. The emigrants were anxious to replenish supplies for the long trek across the desert and objected to the Mormon policy of withholding grain from outsiders, especially for animals. Conversely, by traveling through Utah Territory without permission, the wagon train may have seemed a direct, even willful violation of President Young's edict. Only a few months earlier, Apostle Parley P. Pratt, the beloved Mormon leader who first explored southern Utah, had been murdered in Arkansas.[70] At the very least the Arkansas travelers would have been a galling reminder of this still painful loss.

Later accounts claim that members of the wagon train went even further, threatening the very safety of the Mormons. This harassment supposedly came from a group of "Missouri Wildcats" who had joined the Arkansas families en route. Analysis of the Fancher-Baker company, however, reveals that few of the travelers and none of the 13 single men in the party had Missouri connections.[71] Even so, settlers apparently assumed that some of the company were from Missouri where Mormons had been severely persecuted 20 years earlier. Iron missionary C. Perry Liston, for example, recalled his anxiety when the "large party of emigrants partly from Missouri passed through our quiet settlement" boasting that "Johnsons [sic] Army was coming from the East and from the South and they would kill every mormon in Utah."[72]

The prospect of a wagon train reaching California and inciting the federal troops there to march on Utah Territory would have been especially alarming to the isolated southern outposts. Acting in their military roles, local ecclesiastical leaders met several times in both Cedar City and Parowan to determine how Brigham Young's proclamation of martial law should be applied. Finally, President Haight sent James Haslam, furnace keeper at the iron works and fifer for Colonel Dame's regiment, as an express rider to President Young asking for advice.[73]

A significant part of Mormon defense strategy had been a campaign to convince Native Americans that Mormons were their friends and advancing American forces their enemies. Jacob Hamblin brought several Indian chiefs, including Paiute Chief Tutsegabit, to meet with Brigham Young in Salt Lake City to reinforce the message.[74] In his autobiography William Ashworth recounted that a group of Indians had followed the Fancher-Baker train into Beaver, convinced that they had poisoned a spring at Corn Creek which had made the Indians sick.[75] The 500 to 900 head of cattle belonging to the emigrants could also have tempted the Indians, who, joined by local tribesmen, trailed the wagon train to Mountain Meadows.

Mountain Meadows was a well-known campsite on the California Road. Its luxurious grasses provided a final rest stop for exhausted livestock before the much-feared desert crossing between Utah and California (see illus. 14-4). Given the size of the train, some of the emigrants may have driven loose oxen and cattle another four and a half miles south to Cane Springs, where more pasture was available.[76]

At dawn on Monday, 7 September, the Fancher-Baker train was brought under siege. The party at Cane Springs may have suffered the first Indian attack, survivors retreating to Mountain Meadows. There the emigrants drew their wagons into a circle, chained wheels together, dug firing pits and threw dirt under the wagons, creating a strong defensive barrier. While some emigrants, perhaps as many as seven, were killed and others wounded in the initial assault, the entire group resisted the siege for five days. By Friday, 11 September, however, low on water and ammunition, they were in a desperate state.[77]

The role of the Mormons in inciting the Indians to attack the Fancher-Baker train continues to be debated but there is no doubt that Mormon militiamen from the Second and Third Battalions (Cedar City) and the Fourth Battalion (Harmony) took part in the siege, including at least two high-grade field officers, Majors John D. Lee and John M. Higbee. The Indians were incensed by the casualties they had suffered

Photograph by V. Lee Oertle

Illus. 14-4. Wide-angle view, southwest of Mountain Meadows, overlooking the site of the 1857 massacre of the Fancher-Baker wagon train. Because of severe grazing, drought and flood, sagebrush and weeds have replaced the once-luxuriant grasses.

and the situation was becoming volatile even for the Mormons. If the Indians chose to interpret as a betrayal any mercy shown by the militia toward surviving emigrants, the Indians might turn and attack the Mormons. Seeking for some kind of authoritative solution, the militiamen sent messengers to William H. Dame as Parowan Stake President and head of the Iron Military District and to Isaac C. Haight as Cedar City Stake President and second in regimental command (see app. 11).[78]

James Haslam, the emissary to Brigham Young, had reached Salt Lake City around noon on Thursday, 10 September, leaving immediately after his meeting with President Young and arriving in Cedar City on the 13th. However, before he returned with Young's reply (which contained orders not to molest the wagon train), William Aiden, one of three men from the Fancher-Baker party trying to escape for help, was killed by a Mormon militiaman. At that point, the decision was made to give in to increasingly hostile feelings among the Indians and eliminate the entire wagon train.[79] Exactly who made this decision and when it occurred has never been established.

Most reports concur that, after almost a week of fighting, Major John D. Lee, who claimed to be acting on orders from his superiors, led a negotiation team to the emigrant camp, to lure them from their redoubt, unarmed, on the promise of safe conduct to Cedar City, 35 miles back along the pioneer trail, if they would leave all their possessions to the Indians. Having little choice, the emigrants accepted the conditions and began their trek. The youngest of the children, 17 or 18 of them, were placed in the first wagon, followed by a second wagon containing the wounded, as well as arms and ammunition. These wagons were followed by the women and older children walking in a group. Some distance behind them walked the able-bodied men, each paired with an armed militiaman. After traveling one and one-half miles, these groups were intentionally allowed to string out along the trail, separated from each other by a small rise in the ground and by shrubbery. At a given signal, the accompanying Mormon militiamen, aided by Indians coming out from cover, attacked and massacred the entire train of emigrants, with the exception of the youngest children. These were taken to safety by Bishop Philip Klingensmith.[79]

Within days, the militiamen, appalled by their own deeds, confused about who exactly had ordered the destruction of the Fancher Train and afraid of possible repercussions, attempted to blame the entire episode on the Indians. John D. Lee reported this version of the story to Brigham Young on 29 September when Lee was in Salt Lake City for general conference.[80] Initially, the cover-up was successful, but gradually the involvement of community leaders such as John D. Lee, John M. Higbee, Isaac C. Haight, William H. Dame and Philip Klingensmith became known. Because these men led not only the militia but also the stakes and wards, the civil government and the iron works, they had been greatly trusted. Their status had been reinforced by recent emphasis on Mormon Reformation, which renewed the obligations of Saints to follow their leaders. At the local level, at least, that trust was now broken.

Suspending Iron Operations

Until the ramifications of the Mountain Meadows massacre surfaced, the advancing U.S. Army contingent was still perceived as the primary threat to the well-being of the community. In September 1857, Isaac Haight wrote in his journal that because of that threat, President Young had ordered him to close down the iron works:

> We started the iron works. Had received word to suspend all business and take care of the grain as the United States were sending troops into the Territory to oppress the Saints, and force officers upon us contrary to our wishes and the constitution.[81]

The Deseret Iron Company Journal for 3 October 1857 shows that John P. Jones, Joseph Walker, George Munroe, Joseph H. Smith and John Bradshaw Jr. were paid for melting down the furnace, while George Horton was reimbursed for tending the steam engine during operations. The week ending 12 October appears to be the final week of tangible iron work before Brigham Young's injunction took effect. Planning on the day when they could reopen the works, some of the men continued to labor on the engine house as well as on a shanty in the canyon for the miners. On 12 October, Isaac Haight and Christopher Arthur were reimbursed for their respective services over the past year as general manager and clerk. These payments closed the office expense account.[82] On 23 November, the Cedar City Tithing Office was credited with $2,223.87 from which 38 iron workers drew funds. It is unclear whether any of these "credits" came in the form of cash payouts.[83]

Providentially, an early winter ushered in by severe cold on 17 October halted the approach of Johnston's Army, preventing inevitable hostilities. Although conflict was postponed, the territory remained in a state of alert. Mass meetings were held in various communities throughout the territory to express support for a joint proclamation by Brigham Young and the territorial legislature, chastising the government of the United States for sending an army against the people of Utah. In Cedar City, a resolution was passed that outlined grievances accumulated since the Nauvoo period, which approved Brigham Young's establishment of martial law and pledged lives and property to protect the territory against invasion.[84] William Dame and James Lewis wrote to George A. Smith on 23 December to assure him that the people of southern Utah were continuing their preparations: "The spirit of the south is good and all are on hand to do what they can to roll forth the good work. Bro. Dame has put 60 bushels of wheat into your bin and has stopped the work upon the overshot wheel until orders from you."[85]

As spring 1858 approached, leaders in Salt Lake City realized the need to respond to the U.S. forces that would certainly enter the valley when the weather warmed. The policy of laying waste to the northern settlements and fleeing to the south as the army approached seemed most likely to win the sympathy of the people of the United States. In line with activites begun the previous fall, Brigham Young, on 10 March, wrote Isaac Haight, asking him to "send a company to explore White Mountains to find a place for the Saints to hide from the gentiles."[86] On 21 March, the president called a public meeting in Salt Lake City explaining the evacuation plan. He asked all those who had never been driven from their homes to raise their hands and said that they would be given the opportunity to move first.[87] On 30 March, he again wrote Haight requesting that teams and wagons come to Salt Lake City to move the printing press south.[88]

In April, Brigham Young intensified the search for a safe haven. He instructed William H. Dame to raise a large company "of from 60 to 70 men, 20 waggons with 4 mules to each wagon, 2 Teamsters & a Horseman, with seed, grain, tools, &c., to Penetrate the Desert in search for a resting place for the Saints."[89] Ultimately, it was decided that a move only as far south as Utah County would be sufficiently impressive.

Meanwhile, President Buchanan, under pressure for allowing so many U.S. troops to be deployed on an uncertain expedition, ventured to defuse the situation by issuing, on 6 April 1858, a "full and free" pardon to the "rebellious" Mormons. Feeling that they deserved an apology rather than a pardon, Brigham Young waited until 12 June to officially accept. At that point, the Mormons allowed Alfred Cumming to assume his position as governor of the territory and the federal troops marched peacefully through a deserted Salt Lake City on their way to new headquarters 40 miles away at Camp Floyd.

Starting Back Up on a Smaller Scale

As early as January 1858, iron workers restarted operations, although on a limited scale. On 9 February, Henry Lunt, who had been home from his mission to England since September, wrote Albert Carrington: "Nothing has been done at the Iron works since last fall, but of late some of the brethren have been altering and repairing the blast furnace and preparations are being made for another trial, which I trust will prove successful."[90] On 12 March, Isaac Haight had received formal approval from Brigham Young to "go ahead with the Iron Works."[91] The first entry in the Deseret Iron Company Journal made in five months was on 31 March 1858, crediting several men for working on furnace repairs as far back as 19 January.[92]

Masons and common laborers spent the month of April erecting a new furnace, supposedly on top of a cupola that had just been torn down. This furnace was most likely a reincarnation of "trial furnace no. 2," which may itself have been the demolished cupola. For the new construction, sand, rock and fire clay were hauled to the site and entered under the Journal account for "furnace no. 2." Labor on the new furnace included hauling adobes and calcining ore. The engineering department worked on raising an incline, digging trenches and making and laying blast pipes. The blacksmith shop made bolts, bands and pump valve covers.[93] Haight wrote Brigham Young on 4 May 1858, describing the completion of a "Small furnace 3 feet in the Boshes,"[94] obviously the new "furnace no. 2" referred to in the Journal.

Evidently, the iron workers were going back to the idea of using charcoal in the blast, as a number of men were credited with hauling wood for burning.[95] On 4 May, Haight reported to Brigham Young that he had been searching books on the manufacture of iron, especially Overman's, and had learned "that the Magnetic Ore has to be worked with Charcoal." Haight also claimed that the iron operation was "rather weak handed this Season" because of the number of men who had been sent exploring.[96] (He did not specify whether these explorations were for hiding places for the Saints or for new coal and iron deposits.)

In May, the steam engine was refurbished to power the new furnace. The old flue was torn down and a foundation dug for a "new engine stack."[97] Over 50 tons of magnetite ore were broken by Thomas Thorley and William Roberts and the moulders' cupola was used to fashion 225 lbs. of pig iron into new tuyeres and a dam plate.[98] Journal entries during the first week of June indicate that wood was hauled and chopped, limestone broken and coal and fire clay hauled in preparation for the next furnace run. At least 331 bushels of charcoal were purchased in one week and Jehiel McConnell was credited for another 556 bushels of charcoal the next. This effort appears to have been a bona fide furnace run. Furnace keepers Joseph Walker, Thomas Crowther and Joseph H. Smith worked from 3 to 6 days each. Fillers James Haslam, John Humphries and Joseph Clews kept the furnace charged, while George Horton, Samuel Jewkes and Richard Birkbeck drove the steam engine. Some of the men had to do double-duty, as most of the skilled workers also worked as common laborers and for laborers' wages.[99]

Despite two months of work expended on the new furnace, however, the run was not successful. An entry on 14 June indicates that Joseph Clews was paid for "getting the bear out of furnace" (cleaning up after the failure). Some iron may have been salvaged, as the moulding department paid $275 to the account of furnace no. 2 for 1,100 lbs. of cast iron. The fact that Theodore Turley was sent exploring for ore gives a hint that the iron workers suspected their problems were incident to the quality of ore they had been using.[100]

Aftermath of the Utah War

With Governor Cumming's announcement, on 14 June, that peace had been officially restored to Utah Territory, both Mormon and non-Mormon leaders set about to uncover the truth behind the Mountain Meadows massacre. In July 1858, Apostles George A. Smith and Amasa Lyman traveled to southern Utah. On 29 July, they visited the scene of the massacre, where bones that wolves had disinterred still lay scattered. Complaints against President Haight and Bishop Klingensmith were investigated in Cedar City from 4 to 6 August. Although it is unclear whether these complaints related directly to Haight and Klingensmith's supposed participation in the massacre, it is clear the community had withdrawn its support. As Juanita Brooks points out, "In less than a year after the massacre at Mountain Meadows, the feeling among the people was so strong against their local church leaders that they made a formal complaint against them, an action rare in Mormon society."[101] According to John D. Lee, who was asked to attend the proceedings, Apostles Smith and Lyman "reproved the authorities for the unwise policy which they had adopted to govern the People & told them that they should never over rate their influence amoung the People." They then effectively released the settlers from their commitment to remain in Cedar City, telling the people that "they were at liberty to remove to any settlement where they thought that they could better their condition."[102]

From 10 to 12 August, in Parowan, the two Apostles also investigated charges against William H. Dame.[103] This almost certainly touched on Mountain Meadows, since George A. Smith, on 17 August, wrote a lengthy report from Parowan to Brigham Young about the massacre. Ultimately, Dame was absolved of all complicity. Only John D. Lee, absent from this investigation, was specifically mentioned by George A. Smith as having been at the scene of the massacre with the Indians.[104]

A separate federal investigation began seven months later. In March 1859, Jacob Forney, the recently appointed superintendent of Indian affairs, traveled to southern Utah to collect the small children saved from the massacre. During his visit, he gathered information that he felt implicated Mormon militiamen in the calamity. In April, Judge John Cradelbaugh, associate justice for the southern district of Utah Territory, left for the south with 200 U.S. troops, planning to find and punish those responsible. On 29 April, Isaac Haight, who had been warned of their coming, went into hiding for three weeks, together with John M. Higbee and others. John D. Lee and Philip Klingensmith hid separately.[105] Although some citizens were persuaded to talk privately with Cradelbaugh, he was unable to make any arrests.[106] Advised that the judge and his troops were heading back north, Haight and company started for home. Ironically, they ran right into the search party but were not recognized—a situation Haight attributed to divine intervention.[107]

One Last Try for Iron

Between the time of these two investigations, a new furnace run of considerable size was attempted in late September 1858, using "stone coal" (probably lumps of bituminous coal rather than coke). Entries in the Deseret Iron Company Journal imply that the run was a failure. Possibly the boiler became plugged with sand, requiring the foundation to be dismantled for repairs. Or the foundation could have given way, causing the boiler to settle, disrupting the flow of steam to the engine. In any case, the steam cylinders had to be cleaned and, because the blast was interrupted, the furnace cooled. Cleaning the furnace was no minor operation—a new tymp stone, hearth and dam were installed. Even the funnel head had to be replaced, along with the hearth, to clean out the "bear" and repair the inside of the furnace.[108]

The furnace interior was almost completely rebuilt, the steam engine and boiler readied and the charge prepared by mid-October. The run was a relatively short one; whether it succeeded or failed was not recorded in the Journal.[109] Isaac Haight was more specific, writing dispiritedly in his journal for September–October 1858 that he "Spent the time in procuring material for the furnace. Made two trials in making iron, in both the lining of the furnace gave way, made but little iron."[110]

This run was the last. Haight had received a letter from Brigham Young, dated 8 October, instructing him to close down the iron works:

> We think it would be well to abandon the idea of making Iron for the present, and let all the brethren; [sic] pursue those avocations which they please. Put every thing in as good a condition for preservation as possible, and let it rest. Such fruitless exertions to make Iron seems to be exhausting not only the patience, but the vital energies, and power of the settlement. Hence we consider it best for the present, at least to suspend further operations, in such useless endeavors to produce that important article.

> If however you succeed in your present attempt, which I understand you are now making in producing iron from the ore (which I must confess is hardly a supposable case) of course it would materially alter the case, and I should be very agriably disappointed and wish you to go ahead with the works.[111]

This letter constitutes a huge shift in Brigham Young's attitude, standing as the first evidence of official recognition that the dream of creating a sustainable iron industry in southern Utah was over. The Iron Mission had been created for that purpose but now the iron works had become secondary to the survival of the settlement itself. It would be hard to prove that the loss of public trust in Parowan and Cedar City's ecclesiastical leaders affected Brigham Young's final decision to shut down the iron works but it must have been central to the issues he was wrestling with at this difficult time.

There are postings over the next few weeks in the Deseret Iron Company Journal for items directly or indirectly connected to the iron works. William Davidson was credited for digging lean ore and fire clay for John Urie. William Lapworth built a mud wall on the company's city lot. Isaac Haight was paid for the two and a half months he spent in Salt Lake City, attending various conferences and the territorial legislature. A few entries were made to furnace no. 2, apparently to tally any outstanding labor or equipment charges, to clear all accounts. The company books were audited at the end of October by Martin Slack and J. T. Geary, James

Whittaker preparing the accounts for them. At the end of their calculations, they found that the company suffered a loss of $14,221.15 for 1858.[112] Overall, the Deseret Iron Company owed more than $37,000.00 in accounts payable which did not include thousands of dollars of labor that were never reimbursed.[113] In the final analysis, around $150,000.00 had been spent on the iron works, producing only about 25 tons of pig iron.[114]

This audit officially closed the iron works account, although domestic entries related to the company store continued in the Journal. Entries in November 1858 show that Jehiel McConnell was burning around 1,000 lbs. of charcoal on West Mountain, raising the possibility that the wood near Cedar City had been depleted by iron production. An entry for 10 December lists two gallons of tar for the engine, suggesting that other uses might have been found for the steam engine after the closing of the works. On 22 December, the engineering department was paid for preserving the steam engine for the winter and securing the engine house doors.[115]

In July 1859, George A. Smith traveled south and was importuned by Isaac C. Haight, who wanted to be released from the presidency of Cedar Stake, "as my enemies swore they would destroy me if they could get me. There was little prospect of my being at home much for a time to come, to attend to the duties of my office."[116] Consequently, George A. Smith released the entire stake presidency (Haight, Higbee and Richard Morris), effectively dissolving Cedar Stake. Philip Klingensmith was released as bishop of Cedar City as well and replaced by Henry C. Lunt as "Presiding Bishop." The unusual reorganization continued with Richard Morris being named Lunt's first counselor, as well as "2nd Bishop & clerk to keep the tithing Books." Thomas Jones was named "2nd con. [counselor] & Bishop."[117] Lunt himself, in his diary, draws attention to the unique nature of these callings:

> On Sunday, the 31st of July, 1859 Apostle Geo. A. Smith drove up to my house about noon, dined with us and at two o'clock attended meeting. After the usual exercises he arose and said "The President has instructed me to come and disorganized this Stake of Zion and to make a Bishop and President out of one man, and I nominate Bro. Henry Lunt as that man."[118]

The declining population of Cedar City was undoubtedly a contributing factor in the decision to combine normally separate offices into one. While there had been approximately 1,000 settlers at the time of the most successful furnace run in April 1855, population levels had dropped below 400 (about 55 families) by the 1860 census, after the iron works were closed.[119]

In December 1859, Martin Slack, clerk of the Cedar City Ward, reported on conditions in the smaller Cedar City with cautious optimism:

> Our new city [Plat B] is being built up steadily; there are already several large houses built of brick and a few more in contemplation; it has a much better location than the Old Fort. Two years ago there were about 150 families residing in this place, but through various causes, such as a scarcity of water, poor land and the suspansion of the iron works—some have removed to other parts of the Territory, and a few more families anticipate removing next spring. Although Cedar city is such a remarkably hard place to live in, yet I believe every family raised sufficient breadstuffs to serve them until another harvest and some raised a large surplus; hence we have not a poor person in our midst.

Shortly into the new year, he again wrote, reporting holiday events and mentioning civic projects to come. Henry Lunt was singled out for special praise:

> Bishop Lunt, by the judicious course he is taking, has secured the confidence and esteem of the people over whom he presides; he is zealously and successfully discharging the duties of his calling and takes great interest in the general welfare of the Saints.[120]

During the next two years, and ironically for the citizens of Cedar City and Parowan, the coming of Johnston's Army made home manufacture of iron less crucial because supplies and equipment the army brought west found their way into use throughout the territory. The enterprising duo of Charles Simpkins and Jonathan Walker operated a small foundry at the old iron works, casting scrap iron into useful objects like threshing machines and lathes.[121] In 1861 seven wagon loads of cannon balls surplused from the U.S. troops were hauled to Cedar City. They were melted down by Walker and John P. Jones and made into sawmill and gristmill irons, bells, stove parts and molasses rolls (large bars used to press sugar cane). Eventually, the coming of the Union Pacific Railroad to northern Utah in 1869 brought down the high cost of imported iron, which had been a major reason for establishing the Iron Mission in the first place.[122]

A number of entries in the Deseret Iron Company Journal from 1859 to 1862 indicate that private individuals and small businesses were buying coke, coal, charcoal and cast iron from the company's stock. Brigham Young maintained a personal interest in the steam engine, requesting Henry Lunt to keep it in "a good state of preservation" until further notice.[123] A large auction was held on 19 December 1861. Over 40 of the iron workers, along with groups such as "Leigh Wood & Co." and the Cedar

School trustees, bid on chains, doors, shovels, hammers, wrenches, anvils, wagons, lumber, wheelbarrows, glass, brads, bolts, sandpaper, coke and iron. Joseph Hunter paid $87 for the warehouse and $150 for the storehouse, while George Wood paid $245 for the overshot wheel and $40 for a city lot owned by the Deseret Iron Company.[124]

There were no more auctions, but other transactions occurred between June 1862 and May 1867. They indicate that the remainder of the company holdings were sold directly to individuals and businesses, such as $546 worth of equipment to "Snow & Whipple & Co." A list of men who turned in grain to the Cedar City Tithing Office on 16 May 1867 closes the Journal. The last entry in the books, other than the list of grain transfers, symbolizes the demise of the Deseret Iron Company: "for one bull, small old and scrubby to bishop Lunt 25.00."[125]

A Mission Transformed

Parowan, Cedar City and their satellite communities no longer existed only to support the production of iron. Occupations which had been secondary now became significant. The open ranges of southern Utah were well-suited for raising sheep and cattle and for dairy farming. The settlements provided farms for converts immigrating to the Great Basin and their strategic location along the Mormon Corridor also made them ideal freighting headquarters. Furthermore, they were a strength and resource to outposts further south, founded to work with the Indians, raise winter crops and grow cotton for home use and export. By 1870 the population of Iron County had risen to over 2,000.[126]

Henry Lunt, whose mission to England kept him free from taint by the Mountain Meadows massacre, presided over Cedar City's transformation in his triple role as bishop, stake president and mayor. Even as his eyesight degenerated, he remained a capable leader and prodigious correspondent. The communitarian economic principles he had fostered in the pioneer iron works contributed to the growth of Cedar City's cooperative store, as well as to sheep and cattle cooperatives in the 1860s and 1870s.[127] Bishop Lunt called upon Cedar City's successful freighters, such as the former boy-pioneer David Bulloch, to assist the new Church Immigration Plan, bringing converts over the Great Plains to Zion until the transcontinental railroad, completed in 1869, superseded the old modes of travel.[128] When the Deseret Telegraph Line linked Salt Lake City with St. George in 1867, Henry's wife, Ellen, and his daughter, Henrietta, were among the first telegraph operators.[129]

Early in the Iron Mission years, George A. Smith had built a sawmill in Parowan, to which Samuel Gould added a pair of stones for grinding flour.[130] The trades continued to flourish in Parowan with the addition of a tannery, Calvin Pendleton's gun and machine shop, William Holyoak's saddle and harness shop, Lorenzo Barton's wheelwright shop, Herman Bayles's carpenter shop, Morgan Richards's lime kiln, Thomas Davenport's pottery factory, Thomas Durham's cabinet mill and Peter Mortenson's tub and bucket factory.[131] In 1869, William Dame, still Parowan Stake President, organized the Parowan United Mercantile and Manufacturing Institution (PUMI) to sustain home industry by buying supplies wholesale and bargaining with buyers. The cooperative expanded the tannery into a boot and shoe shop; the professions of tailor, hornmaker, painter, clockmaker, dressmaker and milliner were also added to Parowan's thriving trade center.[132]

Over the years, the Iron Mission had given birth to offshoot settlements along the Old Spanish Trail. In 1852, the same year that John D. Lee and Elisha Groves settled Harmony, former trail captain Anson Call led fifty families to Fillmore, midway along the route from Salt Lake City to Parowan. In 1855, William C. Mitchell, Sydney R. Burton and John Steele helped settle Las Vegas, teaching the Indians there to farm and protecting California-bound travelers.[133] In the 1860s, pioneers seasoned by years of experience in the Iron Mission now became leaders in new enterprises beyond the Parowan-Cedar City hub.

Veteran iron entrepreneur Erastus Snow was called to preside over the cotton-growing communities along the Virgin River in 1861. When war between the states seemed imminent, Mormon experiments in growing cotton gained importance. Ever the champion of self-sufficiency, Snow warned that "with the prospect of general distress through the destruction of the cotton industry of the South[ern States] . . . the question of shirts or no shirts loomed up before the people of Utah."[134] Snow brought equipment auctioned from the Cedar City iron works to St. George, 50 miles south—the town had been named in honor of the first Iron Mission president, George A. Smith. A small cotton mill in the former tub and bucket factory in Parowan processed a portion of the crop grown in Utah's Dixie until mills could be built closer to the fields.[135] In 1870, the Rio Virgin Manufacturing Association was formed, with Erastus Snow as president, to attract investors to the cotton industry much as the Deseret Iron Company had once sought to raise capital for iron production.[136] Acreage devoted to cotton decreased, however, before adequate factories were operational. Desperate cotton missionaries found their yield difficult to market from remote fields and turned to harvests which would feed their own families first. Molasses from sorghum cane emerged as the export which saved the colonies from complete poverty.[137]

Furnace-master David B. Adams, who had moved from Cedar City to Beaver in 1856, became, in the spring of 1862, the founding father of Adamsville, nine miles west. Later, Adams and iron moulder Richard Harrison lent their expertise to a new effort, the 1868 organization of the Union Iron Works in the Pinto-Iron Springs area, west of Cedar City. The Union Iron Works operated three beehive coke ovens and a small furnace on Pinto Creek, producing pig iron destined for the stamp mills of Bullion, Nevada. The company underwent a series of reorganizations to attract new capital, but eventually failed for the same reasons that plagued the Deseret Iron Company: iron ore so hard it was difficult to flux, coal too high in sulfur to easily coke and charcoal increasingly expensive to make.[138]

Mormon efforts to accelerate industrialization in the American West were doomed by the nature of the very resources and technologies they hoped to exploit. Land was so abundant that fur trading, stock raising and agriculture were initially far more attractive to westerners than foundries and factories too capital-intensive to survive. The discovery of gold in California brought prospectors rushing to exploit mineral resources, but few made fortunes in mining until a transportation infra-structure had been developed. Lacking the navigable rivers of the East, western industry could not begin to keep pace with settlement until the final link of the transcontinental railroad was completed. As auxiliary rail lines made the system more accessible, raw materials from distant ports of origin could finally be brought economically to local factories and finished products delivered to markets equally far-flung.

When Brigham Young envisioned a thriving iron industry in south-ern Utah, he wanted to produce the iron implements which would sup-ply an agrarian economy—nails, ploughs and wagon wheels. During the next decade, however, iron processing was transformed by the use of bituminous coal for smelting ore and the development of the Bessemer method of producing steel. After the Civil War, iron and steel not only went into agricultural implements, but made possible the rapid rise of American industry. Demand increased, both for wartime and peacetime pursuits, and the consolidation of small enterprises into larger companies in the latter half of the nineteenth century made financing possible for projects that had only been dreamed of by earlier generations. In the 1880s, President John Taylor, attempting to revive the cooperative ideal, promoted church sponsorship of the Iron Manufacturing Company of Utah. It was not until 1924, however, that the Columbia Steel Corporation brought sufficient capital to the area to build a modern plant at Ironton, between Provo and Springville, becoming the first iron works to reap a profit from the rich ore deposits of southern Utah.[139]

Endnotes

1. Isaac C. Haight, journal, 20 May 1855; Knecht and Crawley, *Early Records,* 157; "Minutes of First Cedar Stake and High Council (1855–56). Original," 1, Palmer Collection.

2. Brigham Young, *Journal of Discourses* (May 1855), 2:281–83 (see app. 9 for full transcript).

3. "Minutes of First Cedar Stake," 3.

4. Ibid., 5.

5. George A. Smith to editor, 14 May 1855, under "Home Correspondence" published in *Deseret News,* 30 May 1855, 92.

6. Jarvis, *Ancestry,* 197, citing George A. Smith to Franklin D. Richards, 31 May 1855.

7. "Thirteenth General Epistle of the Presidency of The Church of Jesus Christ of Latter-day Saints," *Deseret News,* 31 Oct 1855, 268.

8. William McDonald, diary, typescript, 4, Shirts Collection.

9. George A. Smith to editor, 18 May 1855, published in *Deseret News,* 30 May 1855, 92.

10. James Lewis to George A. Smith, n.d., under "Elders' Correspondence" in *Deseret News,* 3 Oct 1855, 238.

11. "Home News," *Deseret News,* 3 Oct 1855, 237, regarding "Prest. J. C. L. Smith and Hon. J. N. Smith of Parowan, Bishop Klingensmith of Cedar, Elder T. D. Brown of Harmony" and others.

12. "Grasshoppers, &c.," *Deseret News,* 27 Jun 1855, 125.

13. George A. Smith to John Taylor (in Taylor's capacity as editor of *The Mormon*), 20 Jun 1855, reprinted in Jarvis, *Ancestry,* 198–99.

14. Lewis to Smith, "Elders' Correspondence."

15. Deseret Iron Company, Minutes, 44. No one named "D. Gould" appears in Iron Mission records. Most likely this is a simple typographical error for "S. Gould."

16. Deseret Iron Company, Journal, 193, 213.

17. Ibid., 226–27.

18. Erastus Snow to editor, 18 Dec 1855, published in *Millennial Star* 18 (19 Apr 1856): 51.

19. Erastus Snow to editor, 15 Jan 1856, published in *Deseret News*, 23 Jan 1856, 368.

20. Jenson, "Parowan Ward History," 88; "History of John Calvin Lazelle Smith," unpublished family history comp. 1959 by great-granddaughter Helen Thurber Dalton, expanded 1975, Shirts Collection.

21. Jarvis, *Ancestry*, 204–5; see also Dalton, ibid., 36 (handwritten numeral "51" on this page in Shirts Collection copy).

22. Jenson, "Parowan Ward History," 93.

23. Ibid., 89.

24. "Minutes of First Cedar Stake," 21.

25. Bengt Nelson Sr., *Autobiography of Bengt Nelson Sr.* (n.p.: privately printed, ca. 1910), ch. 7, par. 1, copy in Perry Special Collections.

26. Isaac C. Haight to Brigham Young, 21 May 1856, LDS Church Archives.

27. Deseret Iron Company, Minutes, 45–46.

28. Ibid., 46.

29. Ibid.

30. Thomas Bladen to John Taylor, 2 Jul 1856, in Journal History.

31. Deseret Iron Company, Journal, 342.

32. Ibid., 347.

33. Haight, journal, 4 Aug 1856.

34. Arrington, *Great Basin Kingdom*, 127–29.

35. Haight, journal, Mar 1857; Arrington, ibid., 115.

36. "Improvements in the South," *Deseret News*, 5 Mar 1856, 413.

37. Deseret Iron Company, Minutes, 49.

38. Deseret Iron Company, Journal, 440.

39. Isaac C. Haight to Brigham Young, 25 Jul 1857, LDS Church Archives. The questioned letter-form appears to be "Baile" but is ambiguous in this context. Deseret Iron Company, Minutes, 49, records that "Engineer wanted the stack raised 20 feet higher, worked at raising stack to 23 July. 27 July. Run a flue inclining about 6 feet from the fire box to the stack, shutting off old flue underground."

40. Deseret Iron Company, Minutes, 49–50.

41. Ibid, 51.

42. Jones, "Iron Mining and Manufacturing," 72.

43. Haight, journal, 15 Dec 1855.

44. Ibid., Feb–Mar 1856.

45. Hansen, "Nauvoo Legion in Utah," 18–19, 22; Whitney, *History of Utah*, 4:621–22.

46. Haight, journal, 30 Dec 1856.

47. Haight, ibid., Feb 1857; Rachel Andora Woolsey Lee, journal, 1856–1860, 9–11, 14–15, 17, original in Henry E. Huntington Library, San Marino, California,

copy made 1970 by Harold B. Lee Library in Perry Special Collections; "The Journal of Samuel Holister Rogers," 156; George K. Bowering to editor, published in *Deseret News,* 3 Dec 1856, 309.

48. Arrington, *American Moses,* 225–26; Anderson, *Desert Saints,* 90–91.

49. Norman F. Furniss, *The Mormon Conflict, 1850–59* (New Haven: Yale University Press, 1960), 63–67, 75.

50. Neff, *History of Utah,* 326–33; Campbell, *Establishing Zion,* 227–29.

51. As quoted in Neff, ibid., 332.

52. Furniss, *Mormon Conflict,* 96–97.

53. LeRoy R. Hafen and Ann W. Hafen, vol. 8 of *The Utah Expedition: 1857–1858,* Far West and the Rockies (Glendale, Calif.: Arthur H. Clark, 1958), 14, 27–34.

54. Furniss, *Mormon Conflict,* 121.

55. Hafen and Hafen, *Utah Expedition,* 174, n. 61.

56. Anderson, *Desert Saints,* 178.

57. Hafen and Hafen, *Utah Expedition,* 179.

58. Arrington, *American Moses,* 251; Bancroft, *History of Utah,* 504; Furniss, *Mormon Conflict,* 60–61; Pusey, *Builders of the Kingdom,* 90. Pusey says that Smoot, Stoddard, Rockwell and Nicholas Groesbeck rode into camp "on the second day of the outing."

59. Martin Slack and George Bowering, report to editor, 24 Jul 1857, in *Deseret News,* 19 Aug 1857, 187.

60. "Citizens of Utah," broadside publication, 5 Aug 1857, as quoted in Arrington, *American Moses,* 254 (reissued 15 Sep 1857 with minor changes; reprinted in Whitney, *History of Utah,* 1:626–27). Sections headed "Preparing for War" and "Disaster at Mountain Meadows" drawn from unpublished draft articles by Morris A. Shirts (copies in Shirts Collection): "Conditions Which May Have Triggered the Mountain Meadows Massacre," Aug 1993; "Mountain Meadows Massacre—Another Look," Mar 1991; "The Old Spanish Trail and the California Road through Mountain Meadows," Jan, 15 Feb and 21 Feb 1990; "Cane Springs: Its Physical and Historical Relationship to Mountain Meadows," 1 May 1989.

61. Jarvis, *Ancestry,* 215; it may be of interest to note that Bishop Philo T. Farnsworth is the grandfather of namesake Philo Farnsworth, the inventor of television.

62. "James H. Martineau Record, Parowan, Utah" (1855–1860), pt. 2, p. 32; typed copy made and proofread by William H. Palmer, Palmer Collection. Likewise, on 8 Aug 1857, Samuel H. Rogers recorded that Smith "brought leters from President Brigham Young and Daniel H. Wells, also other important news respecting the movements of Congress of the United States with regard to Utah, also of the two thousand and five hundres soldiers being in rout for Utah Territory" ("The Journal of Samuel Holister Rogers," 162).

63. "Martineau Record," pt. 1, p. 23.

64. Rachel Lee, journal, 46.

65. "Martineau Record," pt. 1, p. 25; see also Jarvis, *Ancestry,* 216.

66. Dame listed the weapons and ammunition available and noted the condition of the troops:

> The command feel calm, quiet, and willing to act upon any command that may be given and any orders from head Quarters will be cheerfully obeyed—We can place 200 effective men in the field if necessary. Every effort is being made to secure all the grain in every settlement, and your previous orders are being strictly carried out. Every inlet of the District south of Beaver is now guarded. If a hostile force is found to be approaching us we shall immediately express to you, and await your further orders; unless attacked, in which case we shall act on the defensive, and communicate immediately with you. (William H. Dame to Daniel H. Wells, 23 Aug 1857, Territorial Militia Records, series 2210, Utah State Archives and Records Service)

67. "Martineau Record," pt. 1, p. 26. Young erroneously believed that there were hiding places in the southwest deserts capable of supporting a large population, although previous explorations had failed to discover them (Campbell, *Establishing Zion,* 247–48).

68. Daniel H. Wells to William H. Dame, 13 Aug 1857, Palmer Collection.

69. Larry Coates, "The Fancher Party before Mountain Meadows," 22, Brown Library, Special Collections, Dixie State College, St. George, Utah.

70. Juanita Brooks, *Mountain Meadows Massacre* (Norman: University of Oklahoma Press), 57.

71. Coates, "Fancher Party," 27–29.

72. "Autobiography of Commodore Perry Liston, 1821–1879," typescript, Perry Special Collections. Parowan settlers Tarlton Lewis and Isaac Leavy had both been seriously wounded in 1837 when Missouri militiamen attacked a Mormon village at Haun's Mill after Governor Lilburn Boggs ordered Mormons to leave the state or be exterminated. Lewis's brother Benjamin had been among 19 Mormon men and boys who had died as a result of the assault. Elisha H. Groves, Urban V. Stewart and John S. Higbee (father of John M. Higbee, commander of the Iron Regiment's Third Battalion) had all filed petitions for redress from the state of Missouri for losses when they were driven from their homes. See Dalton, *Iron County Mission,* 23–24, and Clark V. Johnson, ed., *Mormon Redress Petitions, Documents of the 1833–1838 Missouri Conflict* (Provo, Utah: Religious Studies Center, 1992), 222–23, 235, 286. See also Marvin Hill, *Quest for Refuge: The Mormon Flight from American Pluralism* (Salt Lake City: Signature Books, 1989), 93–94.

73. Brooks, *Mountain Meadows Massacre,* 62–63.

74. Janet Seegmiller, *A History of Iron County* (Salt Lake City: Utah State Historical Society, 1998), 66.

75. Ashworth, *Autobiography,* as quoted in Brooks, *Mountain Meadows Massacre,* 50–51. (The passage cited is on p. 102 of the copy of the *Autobiography* in Perry Special Collections.)

76. "Martineau Record," pt. 2, p. 34; Joseph Fish, "History of Enterprise," typescript, 10–12, Perry Special Collections; Clive Burgess, interview by Morris Shirts, regarding Burgess family history, 1989–90, notes in Shirts Collection.

77. Morris Shirts, research/correspondence with Lee Oertle and J. K. Fancher Jr., 1988–90, Shirts Collection; see also Ashworth, *Autobiography,* 9.

78. Brooks, *John Doyle Lee,* 210–11.

79. Brooks, *Mountain Meadows Massacre,* 74–75; see reports of 1859 U.S. military expedition to the massacre site in Captain Reuben P. Campbell, interim report to F. J. Porter, 30 Apr 1859, Sen. Ex. Doc. 42, 36th Cong. 1st Sess., 15; Assistant Surgeon Charles Brewer, official report to Reuben Campbell, 6 May 1859, photocopy of holograph, Shirts Collection; Brevet Major James Henry Carleton, special report to W. W. Mackall, Assistant Adjutant General, U.S. Army, San Francisco, California, 25 May 1859, House Doc. 605, 57th Cong. 1st Sess., 26–29.

80. Brooks, ibid., 140–41.

81. Haight, journal, Sep 1857.

82. Deseret Iron Company, Journal, 442–43.

83. Ibid., 446.

84. Resolution drafted in Cedar City, *Deseret News,* 10 Mar 1858, 6. The committee to draft the resolution was chaired by John M. Higbee and included Elias Morris, Theodore Turley, Daniel M. Thomas, Richard Harrison, Ira Allen and Martin Slack, secretary.

85. William H. Dame and James Lewis to George A. Smith, 23 Dec 1857, in Journal History.

86. Haight, journal, 10 Mar 1858.

87. Brooks, *Mountain Meadows Massacre,* 155.

88. Haight, journal, 30 Mar 1858.

89. Lee, journal, as quoted in Cleland and Brooks, *Mormon Chronicle,* 1:158.

90. Henry Lunt to Albert Carrington, 9 Feb 1858, published in *Deseret News,* 10 Mar 1858, 6.

91. Haight, journal, 12 Mar 1858.

92. Deseret Iron Company, Journal, 486.

93. Ibid., 486–89.

94. Isaac C. Haight to Brigham Young, 14 May 1858, LDS Church Archives.

95. Deseret Iron Company, Journal, 486.

96. Ibid., 486–89.

97. Ibid., 489.

98. Ibid., 492–93.

99. Ibid., 494–95.

100. Ibid., 496.

101. Brooks, *Mountain Meadows Massacre*, 164.

102. Lee, journal, quoted in Cleland and Brooks, *Mormon Chronicle*, 1:179.

103. Haight, journal, 10–12 Aug 1858.

104. Brooks, *Mountain Meadows Massacre*, 167–70.

105. Lee, the only participant ever convicted of the Mountain Meadows killings, was executed in 1877, following two trials and 20 years of conflicting testimony about the event. Whatever the degree of his guilt, he enjoyed little peace in the years that followed the massacre. On 5 Mar 1864, for instance, the minute book of the Fort Harmony branch contains the following entry: "Bishop Lunt was present. John D. Lee tendered his resignation as President of the Branch because of much dissatisfaction among the people toward him. Elder James H. Imlay was selected and set apart to succeed him as President. Bishop Henry Lunt set Mr. Imlay apart" (Jones, *Henry Lunt*, 251, citing Harmony Ward Minute Book).

106. Brooks, *Mountain Meadows Massacre*, 172–77.

107. Haight, journal, 29 May 1859.

108. Deseret Iron Company, Journal, 507–09.

109. Ibid., 510–12.

110. Haight, journal, Sep–Oct 1858.

111. Brigham Young to Isaac C. Haight, in Brigham Young's letter book for 1858, 432, LDS Church Archives.

112. Deseret Iron Company, Journal, 512–17.

113. Jones, "Iron Mining and Manufacturing," 74. One iron worker complained, "I was constantly busy for the people both night and day and worked for nothing. . . . I never received one cent, neither from tithing, donation, or gift."

114. Gustive O. Larson, "Bulwark of the Kingdom: Utah's Iron and Steel Industry," *Utah Historical Quarterly* 31 (summer 1963): 253; Arrington, *Great Basin Kingdom*, 127.

115. Deseret Iron Company, Journal, 529–32.

116. Haight, journal, 31 Jul 1859.

117. Lee, journal, as cited in Cleland and Brooks, *Mormon Chronicle*, 1:213.

118. Lunt, diary, entry following 1 Nov 1858 and preceding 25 Sep 1859.

119. Wood and Armstrong, "Abbreviated Sketch," 11; Dalton, *Iron County Mission*, 120.

120. Martin Slack to editor, 19 Dec 1859 and 4 Jan 1860, published in *Deseret News*, 15 Feb 1860, 394.

121. Henry Lunt to George A. Smith, 29 Aug 1860, published in *Deseret News*, 12 Sep 1860, 221; Henry Lunt to editor, 18 Aug 1862, published in *Deseret News*, 27 Aug 1862, 72.

122. Crook, "Early Industry and Trade," 69; Dalton, *Iron County Mission,* 120; Jones, "Iron Mining and Manufacturing," 74; John Lee Jones also refers to his father-in-law, James Simpkins, a "noted machinic," making

> quite a number of Thereshing Machines & Cane Mills. From Cannon Balls, that was brought here to Utah . . . at the time that the Johonston Army was Sent by Prest Beaucannon. to Kill & exterminate all the Mormons The Very weapons, as I have Said before in My Record. That was brought to destroy the Saints of God in these Mountains, was afterwards used in building up Zion, thus the Lord performs his Mighty Works & Wonder among the children of men and turns the wrath of man to praise him." (Jones, Biography of John Lee Jones, 100–101)

123. Brigham Young to Henry Lunt, 10 Feb 1860, Palmer Collection.

124. Deseret Iron Company, Journal, 547.

125. Ibid., 548–51.

126. Seegmiller, *Iron County,* 74.

127. As quoted in Jones, *Henry Lunt,* 278–79.

128. Jones, ibid., 244–45.

129. Ibid., 238.

130. Dalton, *Iron County Mission,* 356.

131. Ibid., 356–62.

132. Ibid., 362–64; Seegmiller, *Iron County,* 83.

133. Dalton, ibid., 198–99.

134. As quoted in Larson, *Erastus Snow,* 316.

135. Dalton, *Iron County Mission,* 358–60.

136. Jones, *Henry Lunt,* 279.

137. Campbell, *Establishing Zion,* 264–65.

138. Larson, "Bulwark of the Kingdom," 253–54. See also Graham D. Macdonald III, *The Magnet: Iron Ore in Iron Co. Utah* (n.p.: privately published, 1990).

139. Larson, ibid., 254–55.

15

In Retrospect:
Why the Iron Works Failed

Given the iron missionaries' determination to succeed, how can we account for their failure to create a sustainable iron industry? Largely through no fault of their own, the iron missionaries faced a number of difficulties they could neither foresee nor surmount. Among these were: (1) geographical problems, (2) unpredictable climate, (3) smelting challenges, (4) insufficient financing, (5) personnel conflicts and (6) security concerns.[1]

Geographical Problems

For the blast furnace to operate efficiently, it had to be located near ample and easily obtainable supplies of iron ore, fuel for the furnace, limestone for flux, a power source for the blast and adequate lumber and stone. Vast supplies of high quality iron ore were available at the first site proposed for the blast furnace, the well-named Iron Springs, eight miles west of Cedar City. Because the iron workers, trained in Great Britain, preferred coke as fuel, the pioneers decided to locate the blast furnace in Cedar City itself, near the coal deposits of Coal Creek Canyon. Even though three of the key ingredients necessary for successful iron production—coal, limestone and water power—were within easy reach, the coal at this site contained too much sulfur for optimum coking. At one point, President Young even considered moving the iron works to the superior coal fields of Sanpete County, but never followed through with the idea.

Locating firm ground on which to build the furnace was also crucial. The foundation of the stack had to support not only the full weight of stack and lining but also the burden of fuel, limestone and iron ore. The Noble Furnace, for instance, contained over 640 tons of stone but was supported by a rock foundation only 21 feet square and three feet thick. Bedrock lay an estimated 30 feet below the surface at this point. As a result, the furnace may have settled, cracking the outer wall and contributing to the instability of the lining.

Daily life in Cedar City gave the pioneers, on separate occasions, compelling reasons to move the settlement itself. When he visited the Compact Fort in May 1852, Brigham Young saw that its location, directly below the Knoll, made the colony vulnerable to attack. After the settlers moved to the second site, Plat A, their experiences with Coal Creek alerted President Young to the dangers of flooding. Consequently, he ordered a move southwest to Plat B, the site of modern Cedar City. Although each reason for relocating the settlement site was sound, the repeated transfers diverted time and energy from the iron works.

Unpredictable Climate

The early settlers of Iron County attempted to build and operate the iron works in a strange, often hostile, environment. Extreme weather proved to be the norm and settlers found it difficult to implement, let alone sustain, a normal planting schedule. During their first winter, temperatures rose to over 80 degrees in February. Having no experience with local seasons, the pioneers promptly planted their crops. At the next cold snap, seedlings froze in the ground. The spring runoff, which looked more than adequate for irrigation, dwindled and disappeared each summer, leaving crops to burn in the fields. Moreover, the crucially important spring-summer farming cycles occurred in the very months when the iron-mongers could hope to run the furnace at full capacity. Thus, the demand for water was highest when its availability, as summer came on and the streams dried up, was least to be trusted.

Early furnace blasts were powered by waterwheels geared to a pumping device. Ideally, a furnace blast had to be evenly maintained. If the blast were interrupted or the furnace shut down, the furnace burden would cool, congealing into a conglomerate mass. Unfortunately for the iron missionaries, such interruptions occurred: (1) when Coal Creek flooded, washing out diversion dams and carrying off fuel, lumber and other supplies; (2) when high water in springtime threatened crops in the fields, requiring all hands to avert the emergency; (3) when low water in late summer imperiled growing crops, requiring a diversion of the water from iron production to save them; and (4) when Coal Creek froze up, often in December or January, locking the waterwheel in ice. While the steam engine sent to the iron workers in 1857 was intended to replace the waterwheel, making the engine operational created a whole new series of technical challenges.

Right after April 1855, when the iron missionaries achieved their greatest success, a summer drought and grasshopper infestation plagued southern Utah. When similar conditions ruined the harvest again in 1856, the community found itself in a fierce and unexpected struggle merely to survive. Under these circumstances, many iron workers, previously dependent on the town's farmers to supply their daily bread, had to abandon their furnace assignments and take up subsistence farming just to keep their own families from starvation. Bowing to reality, many settlers left the area to relocate in more hospitable surroundings. As a result, the iron works suffered manpower losses that drained the young industry of needed expertise.

Smelting Challenges

Processing iron ore required advanced technology and a highly skilled labor force. The ironmongers of England, Scotland, Ireland and Wales who joined the Iron Mission were well-trained but unfamiliar with magnetite ore and other raw materials native to southern Utah. Consequently, they were forced to experiment continually with charge mixtures and furnace structure, rather than devote their efforts to actual production. Foundry records indicate that the iron workers had particular difficulty with the furnace lining and the quality of fuel.

Technical failures in pioneer furnace lining materials often caused problems during iron production. A cracked hearth lining, for example, could allow furnace gas or slag to escape, compromising the smelting process. The bosh lining could collapse, clogging the hearth. The tuyeres, through which air was blown into the furnace, could also be damaged, cooling the furnace burden prematurely.[2] To function properly, the furnace lining required construction materials which could: (1) resist temperatures at least as high as the melting point of iron; (2) endure sudden changes in temperature which would otherwise cause the lining to spall (chip or splinter); (3) survive the physical action of hard, abrasive pieces of iron ore, limestone and coke grinding away as they passed through the furnace and (4) tolerate adverse chemical reactions between ingredients in burden and lining.[3]

Firebrick that contained at least 40 to 45 percent alumina (aluminum oxide) but was low in iron, silica and carbonate was preferred. Such brick was being made in England (known there as Stourbridge brick) and exported to centers of industry in the eastern United States in the 1850s; it was not, however, available on the Western frontier. The only clay the iron missionaries could access did not meet the standard necessary to produce firebrick of sufficient hardness.[4]

An opportunity to directly analyze pioneer furnace lining came in fall 1982 when Cedar City public works crews excavated the intersection of 100 East and 400 North to improve underground utilities (see illus. 15-1). Realizing this was the site of the pioneer iron works, author Morris Shirts collected samples of furnace rubble, including charred brick and sandstone, sending some of the brick to Dr. William T. Parry, professor of geology and geophysics at the University of Utah (see illus. 15-2). Dr. Parry's analyses revealed only a small amount of the desired aluminum oxide content but large amounts of quartz (silica oxide), iron oxide and calcium carbonate, all of which limited the capacity of the lining to withstand high temperatures. He found, in fact, that the brick could melt at around 250 degrees F., well below the melting point of iron.

The reaction of quartz and calcium carbonate during pioneer furnace runs would have created calcium silicate and carbon dioxide gas, producing large bubbles in the brick as it melted under the heat of the burden (see illus. 15-3). Reactions between carbon monoxide from fuel combustion and iron oxides in the brick clay produced metallic iron particles in the brick itself, further undermining its stability. Expansion and compression during heating and cooling had badly spalled the particular samples of lining retrieved for analysis. Later efforts by pioneer iron workers to use sandstone in the lining material (in the 1854 Noble Furnace, for example) were more successful, but high carbonate content eventually caused weakening and spalling even of this stone.[5]

Providing quality fuel for the furnace proved to be as difficult as providing quality lining. Enthusiasm for local coal soon waned when it was found to contain too much sulfur (5.76 percent), resulting in a reaction that produced hard, brittle pig iron. Hoping to find higher quality coal, the pioneers mined at least five different sites in the canyons of Coal Creek, but all proved inferior. As an alternate fuel, hundreds of bushels of charcoal were made from scraggly cedar and pine trees in the immediate area, but supply was limited and could not be quickly renewed. In March and April of 1853, when iron workers were trying desperately to get display samples to Salt Lake City for April general conference, they resorted to charges of raw pitch pine, but this was even more inadequate. The fuel

Photograph by Morris A. Shirts

Illus. 15-1. Cedar City Street Department excavations in fall 1982 uncovered rubble from pioneer blast furnace runs. Author Morris Shirts collected various pieces from the furnace layer and sent them to Dr. William Parry, geologist at University of Utah, for analysis.

problem was never solved well enough to provide long-term, reliable, uninterrupted blast furnace operation.

Insufficient Financing

Although the Deseret Iron Company was created to provide proper financing for the plant, creating a stable economy for the workers, there was never enough operating capital. Stock subscriptions in the company were never completely paid and there was little, if any, circulating currency, especially among the workers. Attempts to attract overseas investors were only partly successful. Cash flow problems afflicted the whole territory but such attempts to help as sending "gold missionaries" to California and organizing special work projects for newly arrived immigrants had little impact on Iron County. The most notable relief came from a territory-wide tax levy. Iron County men had the option of paying their tax assessments by performing some form of labor related to work at the foundry.

Church tithing donations were deposited locally, some designated for the support of needy iron workers. These local contributions were

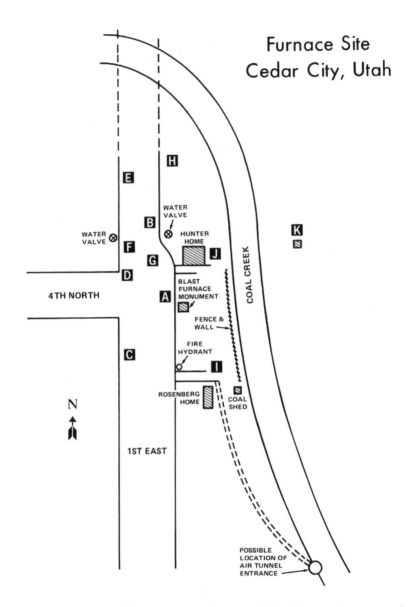

Illus 15-2. Diagram of the Deseret Iron Company's blast furnace site uncovered during street excavations. Recovered specimens are identified at the locations on which they were found: (A) blackened earth and partially smelted iron ore; (B) cinder; (C) ashes, not from the blast furnace; (D) furnace rubble—brick and sandstone; (E) scattered furnace rubble; (F) coke; (G) cinder; (H) cinder, charcoal; (I) coal, charcoal; (J) cast iron pieces; (K) possible location of the first furnace. (See "The Demise of the Deseret Iron Company: Failure of the Brick Furnace Lining Technology," *Utah Historical Quarterly* 56 [Winter 1988]: 31.)

most often collected in the form of farm produce and were administered through the Deseret Iron Company store which served, in reality, as the bishop's storehouse. The Deseret Iron Company also purchased consumer items, often in St. Louis, to meet the settlers' needs. Nevertheless, the company store could not fully support the workers and their families. Since the situation required iron workers to be farmers as well, iron work too often lagged.

Personnel Conflicts

While the strength of Mormon colonizing lay in the willingness of individual Saints to accept difficult assignments without question, it is not surprising that some rebelled against ecclesiastical control. In 1851, four of the original iron missionaries, Samuel Bateman, Thomas Corbitt, Dennis Winn and Hiram Woolsey, returned to Salt Lake City "contrary to counsel," not the only such instance. Some pioneers became disenchanted with the rigors of climate and geography and left for "greener pastures," particularly California. In 1853, during the Walker War, the

Photograph by Morris A. Shirts prepared for Utah Historical Quarterly article referenced at illus. 15-2.

Illus. 15-3. This brick from the Deseret Iron Company coking kilns shows thermal and chemical deterioration. It was partially melted by the heat of the smelting process. In addition, gases evolving from chemical reactions produced bubbles throughout the brick.

unwillingness of local settlers to release their cattle for transport to Salt Lake City as a protective measure against Indian raids actually reached the point where mutinous militiamen leveled rifles at their superior officers.

The settlers least happy about moving cattle north were members of the Scotch Independent Company. Most of the time, however, ethnic disagreements were not sufficiently contentious to undermine the purposes of the Iron Mission. A more serious threat was economic inequality. At the outset of the mission, John Steele felt that prosperous farmers were more likely to complain about the Parowan soil and then abandon the mission at the earliest opportunity.[6] During the winter of 1852–53, Henry Lunt and J. C. L. Smith chided established settlers for selling grain at prices too high for newcomers to afford or, even worse, for stockpiling precious supplies as immigrants starved. While new recruits were often called south specifically for their skills in working iron, their poverty kept them from using those skills to best advantage.

Even less destitute settlers, however, found it difficult to meet their own basic needs while addressing mission priorities. So many crucial tasks demanded attention that the Iron Mission's most troublesome disputes revolved around which to tackle first. Some disagreements were settled amicably through discussion and negotiation. Other differences were resolved by multiple meetings lasting long into the night, draining resources and exhausting emotional energy. Still others were settled by ecclesiastical fiat, an apparently efficient means which tended to suppress dissent only temporarily.

The iron managers were faithful and hard-working men, but their multiple roles often left them overwhelmed and exhausted. J. C. L. Smith, for example, superintended the iron works, served as stake president and worked as a local attorney. His heavy schedule may have aggravated the heart condition which led to his premature death. Isaac C. Haight was simultaneously general manager of the Deseret Iron Company, Cedar City stake president, mayor of Cedar City, major in the militia, local postmaster and representative to the territorial legislature. Although such arrangements centralized leadership, it was impossible for individual men, however capable, to serve effectively in so many capacities. Managers, charged with making critical decisions, lacked time to familiarize themselves with the technical aspects of iron-making. Furthermore, experienced leaders were lost to the region when called on proselyting missions or to other assignments. Apostles George A. Smith, Erastus Snow and Franklin D. Richards, for example, were given major responsibilities elsewhere, which deprived the iron industry of much needed continuity in leadership.

Security Concerns

Mormon settlers and Native Americans were never completely at ease with one another. As towns crowded out wilderness, tribesmen were hard-pressed to sustain themselves by traditional pursuits. Hungry Indians saw the settlers' cattle as a communal source of food. Perceiving Native Americans as wayward children whose behavior would improve under firm parenting, pioneers reacted to the raids on their herds with scoldings, threats and, on rare occasions, whippings. Mormons were anxious to improve the condition of the Indians through proselyting and practical education. Most Indians, however, preferred their own traditions. Many considered baptism and priesthood ordination a matter of diplomatic necessity without sincere conversion. Others could not adapt to the settled life of farming.

Although both sides tried to achieve alliances for mutual benefit, Indians and settlers could not rely on each other's promises. Constant skirmishes left both groups wary and insecure. When the Walker War broke out in 1853, anxieties accelerated, effectively closing down iron production while the settlers built forts in Cedar City and Parowan. Peace was negotiated but the need for constant guard duty continued to draw manpower away from iron production.

The iron missionaries' uneasy relationship with neighboring tribes was overshadowed in 1857–58 by a more uneasy relationship with the United States. The economic and political consequences of the Utah War critically affected the iron works. Brigham Young declared martial law throughout the territory and placed the Iron County militia on special alert to guard the southern approaches to the region. Although specific orders had been issued to avoid bloodshed whenever possible, they were insufficient to prevent the most unfortunate consequence of this political and military imbroglio: the September 1857 massacre, by Mormon militiamen and Native Americans, of all the adults and older children in the Fancher-Baker wagon train. Three-fifths of the Mormon militia at Mountain Meadows were iron workers.

For deeply religious people, no matter the rationale of a possible war of extermination with the U.S. Army, such slaughter was psychologically and spiritually debilitating. The oath of silence taken by the participants in the massacre meant that there was, in effect, no way to talk about it and come to terms with what had happened. The scapegoating, first, of the Indians and, second, of John D. Lee added more lies to the initial cover-up. Furthermore, it fractured the trust and confidence the members had

had in their leaders. Suffering from personal despair and spiritual disaffection, many iron workers moved away. Others withdrew emotionally. Mountain Meadows, in short, cast a pall over the entire settlement which has, in many ways, only begun to lift in recent years.[7]

The Iron Mission Legacy

Although the iron missionaries were never able to supply the territory with adequate iron implements, the benefits they gained by colonizing southern Utah far outweighed their failures. Those sent to the Iron Mission understood they were being called by a prophet representing the will of God. Although some pioneers faltered in the face of overwhelming obstacles, most remained true to their callings and endured the difficult years. Many of their descendants still live in the Parowan-Cedar City area; others helped populate settlements in all six states of the southwest. Even though the Iron Mission never fulfilled initial expectations, permanent settlements there guarded the southern gateway of the Mormon empire and established the southern boundary of the state.

The Iron Mission also powerfully affected the lives of those who joined it. Being a member of the Iron Mission constituted a tremendous challenge to individual iron workers and their families. The Mormons' westward immigration has rightly been compared to the biblical exodus of the ancient Hebrews from Egypt. However, those who served in the Iron Mission, or in similar colonizing projects, did not find rest in the promised land still being created in the valley of the Great Salt Lake. To leave the haven of Salt Lake City, for so long the ultimate goal of their efforts, and move, sometimes shortly after their arrival, to a barren and inhospitable land amidst the dangers of an icy winter, must have been hard to bear. To build a complex industry from the ground up without benefit of a working infrastructure (agriculture, transportation, financial institutions or civic services) was a superhuman task. Each difficulty the iron missionaries faced brought a new test of character and a new trial of their dedication to establish the Kingdom of God in the desert. In the final analysis, floods, drought, technological problems and interpersonal disagreements were insufficient to deter these pioneers from their assigned callings.

One who studies the history of the Iron Mission cannot fail to be reminded of a biblical metaphor that exemplifies the whole enterprise: "Behold, I have refined thee, but not with silver; I have chosen thee in the furnace of affliction" (Isaiah 48:10). The integrity and religious commitment of each iron worker was refined and tested through adversity no less than the iron they smelted. The furnace smoke rising to the sky above Coal Creek represented for them as much a burnt offering, and just as demanding a sacrifice, as the smoke rising above the temple altar in the Hebrews' promised land. The smelting and purifying of iron stood as a daily symbol of the spiritual purification and character refinement that each pioneer experienced by putting aside his or her personal interests to establish a modern-day Zion. Both descendants and students of history can learn a great deal from the commitment of these unfaltering men and women to a vision of overarching importance and take pride in the way they faced and overcame the trials of their faith.

Endnotes

1. Materials in this chapter first appeared in two forms: a presentation at the Mormon History Association annual meeting, St. George, Utah, 1993; and an article, coauthored with William T. Parry, professor of geology and geophysics at the University of Utah, who provided technical information necessary to explain the situation at the company works. The article is titled "The Demise of the Deseret Iron Company: Failure of the Brick Furnace Lining Technology," *Utah Historical Quarterly* 56 (winter 1988): 23–35 (hereafter cited as Shirts and Parry). James D. Norris's *Frontier Iron* and Frederick Overman's *Treatise on Metallurgy* (both cited in the bibliography) are helpful sources on understanding early blast furnaces and metallurgy. Overman's earlier work, *The Manufacture of Iron in All Its Various Branches* (Philadelphia: Henry C. Baird, 1850), is also recommended.

2. Shirts and Parry, 35. See also Deseret Iron Company, Minutes, Book 1, 40–43 (ca. Jan and Mar 1855) and Book 2, 8–11 (ca. Sep–Oct 1858); see also Haight, journal, entry for "April, 1854."

3. Shirts and Parry, 28–30.

4. Ibid.

5. Ibid., 30–35.

6. "Extracts from the Journal of John Steele," *Utah Historical Quarterly* 6 (Jan 1933): 25.

7. Two events of equal importance to the story of this difficult episode in southern Utah history took place in the final decade of the twentieth century. On 15 Sep 1990, a new memorial to the Mountain Meadows victims was dedicated by Gordon B. Hinckley, then a counselor in the LDS First Presidency. Raised on Dan Sill Hill, just above the level stretch of the meadows, it gave a clear view of the whole landscape and was accompanied by a set of plaques that included a list of those in the Fancher-Baker wagon train. Erecting the 1990 memorial and successfully coordinating with Arkansas descendants of the massacre victims were achievements in

large part due to amateur historian Lee Oertle. He made the initial overtures in 1988 to create a proper memorial at the site and quickly recruited Morris Shirts and approximately 30 others, creating the Mountain Meadows Memorial Committee. Their more than two years of untiring effort brought the hope of a new monument to reality. Sadly, after this important step was achieved, both Shirts and Oertle died. The memorial itself was, over the next few winters, severely damaged by water infiltrating between the stem wall and the monument face. (It has since been repaired and is being maintained by the Utah State Parks and Recreation Department.) During a visit in 1998 to Dixie College in St. George, LDS Church President Gordon B. Hinckley visited the Mountain Meadows site and expressed concern over continued deterioration at the 1932 monument marking Brevet Major James H. Carleton's 1859 memorial cairn. Hinckley spearheaded plans not only for repairs but also for a new monument at that site, aided by the Mountain Meadows Association. This memorial was dedicated by President Hinckley on 11 Sep 1999, at ceremonies well-attended by descendants of both Mormon militiamen and Arkansas emigrants.

Appendix 1

Mormon Way-Bill and Advice
to Emigrants

(Table of Distances from Salt Lake City 1851)

From Temple block, G. S. L. City to Willow Creek	25 ⅝
To summit of dividing ridge between Utah and Salt Lake valleys	4 ⅞
To American Creek	9 ¼
To Provo River and fort	11 ½
To Hobble creek, good feed	7 ¼
To Spanish Fork, good feed	6
To Peteetneet, good feed	5
To Salt Creek (several small streams between) good feed	25
To Toola creek ford, no wood, good feed from this to the Sevier, the road is sandy passing over a high ridge	18 ⅝
To Sevier river, feed tolerable and willows for fuel	6 ¼
To Cedar creek, the first stream south of the Sevier, good feed and wood, road rather mountainous and sandy	25 ½
To 4th stream south of Sevier, crossing 2 streams, good feed, wood	17 ½
To Willow flats, the water sinks a little east of the road	3 ⅝
To Spring, good feed and water	25
To Sage creek, wood, feed poor	22 ¼
To Beaver, good feed and plenty of wood	5 ⅛
To North Kanyon creek, in the Little Salt Lake Valley, good feed, no wood, the road rough and steep for 6 miles	27 ¼
To 2nd stream, good feed and wood	5 ⅜
To 3rd stream, good feed and wood	6 ¾
To Cottonwood creek in Iron County, good feed and water	12 ⅞
To Cedar springs, good feed, etc.	9
To Pynte Creek, feed good about one mile up the Kanyon	23
To Road Creek, this is a small rivulet flowing down the Kanyon of the divide, road rough, feed good	9
To Santa Clara, road descending and rough, poor feed, from this point to Cahoon pass, look out for Indians	16

To Camp springs; 1 ½ miles before you come to this spring you leave the Santa Clara, feed good	17 ⅛
To Rio Virgin, crossing over the summit of the mountain dividing the Santa Clara and the Virgin, road good, feed poor	22 ⅞
Thence down the Virgin, crossing it ten times, feed good down the river	39 ⅛
To Muddy, the road ½ a mile very steep and sandy, good feed	19 ⅝
To Los Vagus, good feed, &c, water is sometimes found at the distance of 23 miles from Muddy 2 ½ miles west of road in holes; also some grass about one mile from road	52 ⅝
Thence up to Vagus, good feed	5
To Cottonwood springs, poor feed	17
To Cottonwood grove, no feed, feed and water can be found 4 miles west, by following the old Spanish trail to a ravine—thence travel to the left in the ravine one mile	29 ¾
To resting springs, good feed and water, lay by and rest your animals for the desert	21 ¾
To spring of pure water, left of the road which follows into the Amagoshe [Amargosa] or Saleratus creek; let no animals drink the saleratus water	7
To Salt Springs, no fresh water, poor feed	14 ⅛
To Bitter springs, good road, but poor feed	38 ¾
To Mohave, good road, good feed	30 ¾
To Last ford of Mohave, good feed all the way up the Mohave	51 ½
To the sumit of Cahoon pass	17
To Camp west of Cahoon pass, road bad down the Kanyon	10
To Coco Mongo ranche	11 ½
To Del Chino ranche (Williams)	10
To San Gabriel river	19 ⅜
To San Gabriel Mission	6
To Pueblo De Los Angelos	8 ¼

Advice to Emigrants

We would recommend emigrants who have cattle to shoe them, and we would advise, not to take them further on the route than Fort Hall, or Great Salt Lake, but exchange them there for others, or horses. It is useless for men to start from either of these places with worn out cattle, as they never will get them to their journey's end. Thousands of cattle and horses were sacrificed, because emigrants knew no better last year. The road from the States to Salt Lake or Fort Hall, is comparatively a railroad to the one from thence to California. We would recommend no man to overload his wagon with tools, etc., for spade, shovels, picks, etc., can be purchased cheap in California. Throw away your old yokes, chains, boxes, etc., for you will do so before you cross the desert, no wagon should have more than 800 lbs. with three yoke of cattle.

We wish to impress on the minds of the late emigrants, the danger they are exposed to, if they do not get over the Sierra Nevada mountains, before the 10th of October. Snow falls from the 1st to the 10th of that month, and after it has fallen some days, it is impossible for wagons to overcome the snow; and it will be fortunate for them if they succeed to get over themselves.

Pack animals are the best all the time, and single men had by all means better pack. Hard bread is the best to take from either of these places; also dried beef.

Clothes can be bought in Sacramento and Stockton, as cheap as in the States, and it is useless for men to overload themselves with such articles, to regard their movements, when, if they can get to good diggins which will average from $8 to $16 per day, they can secure all they want, and the kind that is the most useful, with one or two days' work.

Men carrying ploughs, anvils, gold washers, stoves, or any other article of weight, may as well throw them away, or dispose of them; as it is perfectly useless to wear out their cattle, and at last leave the cattle, and goods between this and California.

After the emigrant settles on his winter diggins, he had better secure provisions enough to last him until April; together with pickles, vinegar, etc. as a preventive to the scurvy.

Emigrants had better not dispose of their animals when they are poor, but place them in good hands on ranches; as a poor horse or ox will not fetch over $10 or $15, while a fat ox or horse is worth $100.

Source note: LeRoy R. Hafen and Ann W. Hafen, eds., *Journals of Forty-Niners— Salt Lake to Los Angeles, 1820–1875,* The Far West and the Rockies Historical Series, 1820–1875, vol. 2. (Glendale, Calif.: Arthur H. Clark, 1954), 321–24. A copy of the Way-Bill is in the William Robertson Coe Collection, Beinecke Library, Yale University, New Haven, Conn.

Appendix 2

Iron Missionaries

December 1850–June 1851

Missionaries	Age in 1851	Birth Place	Vocation	Sources and Notes
ADAIR, Joseph				1
ADAMS, Arza				1
ADAMS, Orson B.	36	NY	Engineer	1–5 ["Arza"; variant of "Orson"?]
Susann	32	NY		5 [Listed in JA]
John S.	7	KY		5
ADAMS, William	29	IL	Stonecutter	1–5
Mary A.	29	Ire		5
Charles	8	Ire		5
James J.	5	Ire		5
Arnah C.	1	UT¹		5 [OS:LDR, p. 40, as "Anna Catherine"]
ALGER, John				1
ALGER, Samuel				1
ALLEN, Rufus C.				1
BADGER, John C.	26	VT	Laborer	2–5 [3: age 23]
BAKER, Simon	39			1–3, 5 [GS: express rider: 25 Mar 1851]
son (unnamed)	12			[GS: with express: 25 Mar 1851]
BARLOW, J. M.				1
BARNARD, John P.	47			1–4 [GS: express rider: 17/25 Mar 1851]
Mary (Wife)				[Listed in JA]
Mary (Daughter)				[GS: with express: 25 Mar 1851]
BARTON, Lorenzo	34	MA	Carpenter	1–5
Sarah	24	OH		5 [Listed in JA as 17 years old]
BASTON, Andrew	44	ME	Farmer	2–5 [2: "Barton"; 3 and 4: "Bastin"]
BATEMAN, Joseph	48	Eng	Collier	1–5
Margaret	57	Eng		5

Missionaries	Age in 1851	Birth Place	Vocation	Sources and Notes
BATEMAN, Samuel	18			1–4 [Left against counsel: GS, 28 Apr 1851]
BATEMAN, Thomas				1
BAYLISS, Herman D.	39	NY	Carpenter	1–5 [3, JA: "Bayles"; 4: "A. D. Baylis, "38]
Juliet	34	NY		5 [Listed in JA as "Juliette"]
BAYLISS, Sarah	42	MA		5
Sarah E.	1	UT		5
BENSON, Ezra T.		MA		1
BENSON, Richard	35	Eng	Carpenter	1–5
Phoebe	31	Eng		5
Elizabeth	12	Eng		5
Richard H.	2	IL		5
BLOXHAM, Thomas				2–3 [2: "Bloxom"; 3, IMR: "Bloxum"; JA: "Bloxham"]
BOGGS, Francis	45	OH	Carpenter	1–4 [OS: IMR as "Fr. Boggs"]
BOZARTH, Beverly	28			4 [OS: LDR, p. 40, same spelling]
BRAFFIT, George	47	NY	Cooper	4–5 [OS: ACL as "Bravit"]
Sarah	47	CT		5
Lucretia	15	NY		5
Mary	13	IL		5
Almira	16	OH		5
Joseph	18	OH		5
Horace	21	NY	Cooper	5
Calvin	22	NY	Cooper	5
BRIMHALL, George	36	NY	Millwright	2–5 [3: age 35]
BRINGHURST, Samuel	38	PA	Blacksmith	1–5 [OS: IMR]
Eleanor	34	PA		5
William A.	11	PA		5

Name	Age	State	Occupation	Notes
Anna B.	9	PA		5
Robert	5	IA		5
Samuel (twin)	1	UT		5
Eleanor (twin)	1	UT		1–5
BRINGHURST, William	32	PA	Farmer	1–5 [express rider: 17 Mar 1851; OS:IMR]
Ann D.	27	PA		5
Joseph	3	UT		5
BRINTON, David	25	PA	Blacksmith	1–5 [3, 4 and JA: age 25; 5: age 35]
Harriet W.	28	PA		5
Evans	13	PA		5
Caleb	2	MO		5
David	1	UT		5
BRONSON, Lemon	50	CT	Farmer	1–5 [1,6: "Bronson"; 2, 3, 4, JA: "Brunson"; 3: age 54; 4: age 50]
Nancy	29	KY		5
Clinton	23	OH		5
Martha	17	MI		5
Lorinda	15	MI		5
David O. H.	9	IN		5
BROWN, Benjamin	56	NY		1, 4
BROWN, Ebenezer	49	NY	Farmer	2–5 [OS: IMR]
Phoebe	52	NY		5
Guernsey	25	NY	Farmer	5
Harriet	23	NY		5
Mormon	20	NY	Farmer	5
John	15	NY		5
BURNHAM, Isaac	20	MA	Farmer	1–5 [OS: IMR]
BURR, Charles C.				1
BURTON, John	53	VA	Laborer	2–5
BURTON, R. T.				1 [OS: IMR as "Rich." Burton]
CALL, Anson	41	VT	Farmer	1–5 [express rider: 17 Mar 1851; OS:ACL]
Mary	37	VT		5

Missionaries	Age in 1851	Birth Place	Vocation	Sources and Notes
Maria	18	NY		5
Anson V.	16	OH		5
Mary V.	15	OH		5
Chester	10	IL		5
CANNON, Angus M.	16	Eng		2–3 [3: age 16; OS: IMR as "Canon"]
CARN, Daniel				1
CARRUTHERS, Matthew	39	Scot	Ironmaster	2–5 [2 and 5: "Carruthers"]
Isabella	34	Scot		5 [JA: "Mrs. Carruthers," age 19]
CARTWRIGHT, Thomas	36	Eng		1–5
Jane	32	Eng		5
Sarah A.	11	Eng		5
Ellen	9	Eng		5
Joseph	6	Eng		5
Mary	5	Eng		5
Thomas	3	NY		5
Caroline	1	UT		5
CHERRY, Aaron B.	50	OH	Farmer	1–5 [3 and 4: as 49; 5: as 50; OS: IMR]
Margaret	49	KY		5
Rebecca	22	KY		5
Sarah Jane	20	KY		5
John J.	17	KY		5
Mary M.	15	KY		5
Amelia	13	KY		5
Jesse	11	IL		5
Thomas	10	IL		5
Caroline	8	IL		5

Name	Age	State	Occupation	Notes
Joseph	4	IA		5
CHIPMAN, Steven	22	Can	Farmer	2–5 [2, 4: "Washman"; 3, 5: "Washburn"]
CHIPMAN, Washburn				1 [OS: ACL and IMR]
CLARK, Ezra				1–4 [left against counsel: GS, 28 Apr 1851]
CORBITT, Thomas				1
CRAGAN, James				1
CROSS, Benjamin				
DALY, Nancy M.	21	OH	Surveyor	5 [5: Listed with Gideon Wood family]
DAME, William H.	31	NH		1–5 [Listed in JA]
Lovina	26	OH		5 [JA: "Lovinia A." age 20]
DECKER, Zechariah B.	33	NY	Farmer	1–5 [3: "Zachariah"; 4: "Z. B."]
Nancy	23	MO		5
Eliza	5	IL		5
Zechariah	1	UT		5
DOLTEN, John	49	PA	Blacksmith	1–5 [1, 2, 5: "Dolten"; 3, JA: "Dalton"]
Rebecca	53	PA		5
Ellen	24	PA		5
John	23	PA		3 [Not on 5]
Harvey	22	PA		5
Edward	21	PA		5
Sophia	15	PA		5
DOLTEN, Simon C.				1 [Probable member of Dalton/Dolton clan]
DOLTON, Charles W.	23			2, 4 [2: "Dolten"; 5: "Dolton"; JA: "Dalton"]
DOLTON, Harry	25			4 [OS: ACL as "Dalton"]
Isabel				[Named in LDR, p. 40; unnamed in ACL]
Amanda				[Named in LDR, p. 40; unnamed in ACL]
DRAKE, Orson				1
Betsy				[OS: LDR, p. 39]
DUEL, O. M.				1
DUNCAN, Chapman	39	NH	Farmer	1, 4–5 [OS: ACL]
Martha	38	VT		5 [OS: ACL, unnamed]

Missionaries	Age in 1851	Birth Place	Vocation	Sources and Notes
Ellen J.	11	IA		5 [OS: ACL, unnamed]
Emely Deseret	1	UT		5
DUNCAN, Homer				1
EABY, John				1
EDWARDS, Hope				2 [3: "Edward Hope"]
ELDREDGE, John				1
ELMER, Elijah	41	VT	Millwright	1–5 [In 3, 5 and JA: age 40]
Mary	41	KY		5
Elizabeth	18	IL		5
Annis	13	IL		5
Lucy	9	IL		5
Elijah	1	UT		5
EMPEY, William Y.				1–3 [2: "Wm. Y."; JA: "William"; GS: express rider, named 17 Mar 1851, left 25 Mar 1851]
ENSIGN, Marius	29	CT	Farmer	2–5 [4: "Merius"; JA: "Marius"]
Eliza A.	18	PA		5 [OS: LDR, p. 18: "Eliza McKee," age 20]
FAHRAR, James	28	Eng	Farmer	1–5 [JA: "Farrer"]
FARR, Aaron F.	32	VT	Farmer	1–5 [5: "A. F."; OS: IMR]
Persis	30	NH		5
Celestia Ann	4	IL		5
Persia A.	2	UT		5
Aaron F.	6 mo	UT		5
FIFE, Peter M.				1, 4 [OS: Fife family in Anson Call list]
FITZGERALD, Perry				1
FOOTE, Timothy B.				1
FROST, Burr	35	CT	Blacksmith	1–3, 5 [JA; OS: IMR]

Name	Age	Origin	Occupation	
Mary E.	35	CT		5
Emeline	12	CT		5
Edwin	11	CT		5
Burr	1	UT		5
FULMER, Almon L.	34	PA	Yeoman	1–5 [3: age 33; 5: "Fuller"; in JA; GS: express rider, named 17 Mar 1851, left 25 Mar 1851]
Sarah	25	NY		5
Almon L.	6	IL		5
Sarah	2	UT		5
Buckley M.	6 mo	UT		1
GARDNER, Elias				1
GATES, George				1
GOODALE, Isaac N.	36	NY	Farmer	1–5 [Listed in JA]
Maria	23	NH		5
Maria	2	UT		5
Louisa	2 mo	UT		5
GOULD, Samuel				1 [GS: arrival noted, 8 Apr 1851; OS: IMR]
Fanny				[OS: LDR, p. 39]
John				[OS: LDR, p. 39; John, William as children of earlier marriage]
William				
GRANT, David			Tailor	1
GREEN, Alphonzo				[ACL as "Alphonzo"; IMR as "Alphonso"]
GREEN, Robert	44	NY	Farmer	1–5 [3: age 45; 5: age 44]
Eliza	30	NY		5 [JA: "Eliza Green," age 22]
Elizabeth	11	NY		5
Caroline	9	NY		5
Lidia Jane	1	UT		5
GREGORY, Albert				1
GROVES, Elisha H.	53	KY	Farmer	1–5
Lucy	43	MA		5
Marah Leah	14	MO		5

Missionaries	Age in 1851	Birth Place	Vocation	Sources and Notes
Samuel	12	IL		5
Patience	18	IL		5
Lucy	2	UT		5
HALL, Charles	28	ME	Cooper	2–5 [4: entry present but scored through]
Elizabeth C.	21	KY		5
Charles	2	UT		5
Thomas	2 days	UT		5 [5: Thomas, 2 days old; no Margaret] [OS: McG: birthdate 11 May 1851]
Margaret A.	2 days	UT		2–5 [JA and LDR (p. 17) give middle name as "Pitcher"]
HALL, Job	30	ME	Cooper	5
Mary E.	23	NY		5 [5: birthplace given as "Miss."]
Job	2	MS		5
Mary E.	8 mos	UT		5
HAMBLETON, Samuel	18	Ire		1–3, 5 [2, 3: "Hamilton"]
HAMMOND, F[rancis] A.				1 [1: "F. A. Hammond"]
HANCOCK, Charles				1
HANCOCK, Levi W.				1
HARMISON, James	31	PA	Farmer	1–4 [JA; express rider:17 Mar 1851]
HARPER, Charles A.	34	PA		1–5 [JA; express rider:17 Mar 1851]
Lovina W.	32	IL		5
Harvey	8	UT		5
Charles	2	UT		5
HARRISON, Richard	43	Eng	Iron Moulder	1–5 [4: "Rich. Harrison"; listed in JA]
Mary A.	39	Eng		5 [JA: "Mrs. Harrison," age 25]
John	5	IL		5
Mary A.	10 mos	UT		5
HENDERSON, John	19	MO		2–3, 5 [Listed in JA]

Name	Age	Place	Occupation	Notes
HENDRICKS, Daniel	49	MA	Farmer	1–5 [1, 3, 5, JA: "Hendricks"; 2: "Hendrix"; 4: initial letter of name obscured by paper tear, otherwise, entry clearly reads "[D]anl H. Endrix"]
Lucy	38	CT		5
Amaranda	2	UT		5
Henrietta	4 mos	UT		5
HOFHEINS, Jacob	38	Ger	Bricklayer	1–5 [3: "Hoffines"; listed in JA]
Mary A.	40	MD		5 [OS: ACL as "Sister Hofheins"]
Laman	7	IO		5
HOLBROOK, Chandler	43	NY	Farmer	1–5 [JA: "Pres. of Sev[enties]."]
Eunice	40	NY		5 [OS: ACL as "Unice"]
Mary	15	MO		5
Eunice	13	MO		5
Orson	9	IL		5
Joseph	7	IL		5
Lafayette	1 mo	UT		5
HOLLINGSHEAD, Nelson S.	26	Can	Joiner	1–5 [4: "N. S. Hollingshead"; listed in JA]
HOPE, Edward				3 [JA: "Heap, Edward"; see "Edwards, Hope"]
HORNE, Joseph	39	Eng	Farmer	1–5 [JA; OS: IMR as "Horn"]
Mary	32	Eng		5
Henry	13	MO		5
Joseph S.	10	IL		5
Richard	7	IL		5
Elizabeth	5	IL		5
Leonora	2	UT		5
HOVEY, Joseph G.	39	MA	Stonecutter	1–5 [3: age 38; OS: IMR]
Sarah	18	MA		5 [JA: "Mrs. Hovey," age 24; OS: IMR]
HOWD, Simeon D.	37	NY	Farmer	1–4 [4: name variant[2]; JA: "Simeon D."; OS: IMR]
Lucinda	31	IL		5
Martha	7	IL		5
Permelia	3	UT		5

Missionaries	Age in 1851	Birth Place	Vocation	Sources and Notes
Lucinda A.	1	UT		5
HOYT, Israel				1
HULSE, Benjamin R.	35	NY	Ship joiner	1–5 [In JA; 1: "Hultz"; 4: "Hults"; 5: age 36]
Jane	34	NY		5 [JA: "Mrs. Hulse," 23; OS: ACL]
Anna	3	NY		5
Angelina	1	UT		5
HUNTER, George	22	Scot	Miner	1–5 [5: age 23; listed in JA]
JARVIS, Norman	32	NY	Farmer	[OS: ACL]
JOHNSON, Benjamin F.	33	MA		1 [Former secretary to Joseph Smith]
JOHNSON, Joel H.	49	OH	Farmer	2–4 [Listed in JA]
JOHNSON, Nephi	17		Farmer	2–4
JOHNSON, Sextus E.	21			
JUDD, Zadok K.	22	Can	Tailor	2–5 [4: "Zedoc Judd"; listed in JA] [OS: DesNews, 8 Feb 1851, p. 206]
JONES, William				1
KELSEY, Stephen	21	OH		
LAWSON, James	30	Scot	Machinist	1–5 [Listed in JA; OS: IMR]
Mercy	35	Eng		5
Mary I.	10	MO		5
LEANY, William	35	KY	Wheelwright	1–5 [5: JA and IMR]
Elizabeth	26	IN		5
Sarah Ann	6	IA		5
William	4	UT		5
Elizabeth E.	1	UT		5
LEAVITT, George	22	Can	Farmer	2–4 [4: "Levitt"; JA; OS: IMR as "Leavitte"]
Emeline				[JA; OS: IMR as "Emily Leavitt"]
LEE, John D.	37	IL	Farmer	2–5 [5: Age 37; listed in JA]

Name	Age	Birthplace	Occupation	Notes
Mary Vance (Polly)	33	TN		5 [In JA as Polly Lee, age 26]
Elizabeth	ca. 3 wks	UT		[OS: McG: birthdate, 24 Apr 1851]
Lovinia	15[3]	TN		5 [JA: Lovina Lee, age 27]
Lemuel (Indian child)	12	TN		5 [5: probably born in UT; may be younger]
[? "John Alma"]	9	IL		5 [see note[4] below]
[? "John David"]	ca. 9 wks	UT		[GS: birth reported: 19 Mar 1851]
Sarah	3 days	UT		5 [unknown except in census]
LEMMON, James W.		ME	Teacher	4 [OS: ACL as "James W. Lemon and wife"]
LEWIS, James	37	MA		1–5 [5: Age 38]
Emily	20	UT		5 [JA: "Mrs. James Lewis," age 29]
Elizabeth	3	UT		5
Emely	2	UT		5
James	1 day	MO		5 [OS: McG: birthdate 21 May 1851]
LEWIS, Jesse	25	SC	Laborer	2–3, 5 [Listed in JA]
LEWIS, Philip B.[5]	46	KY		2–4 [4: "P. B."; in JA, same age]
Mrs. Philip B.				[JA: "Mrs. Philip B.," age 28]
LEWIS, Tarleton	45	IL	Carpenter	1–5 [2, 4, "Tarlton," 5: age 46]
Melinda	40	IL		5
Beeson	15	IA		5
Melinda	7	UT		5
Tarleton	4			5
Martha	2			5
LISH, Peter				2–3 [JA: "Peter Leish" (no age given)[6]]
LITTLE, James A.	28	NY	Teacher	1–5 [1: "Jas. Little"]
Mary J.	18	OH		5 [JA: "Mary Jane Lytle Little," age 30]
Lucy	2	UT		5 [See note[7] below]
LOVE, Andrew	42	SC	Farmer	2–5 [Listed in JA]
Nancy	36	NY		5 [Listed in JA]
Elizabeth	8	IL		5
Mary E.	1	UT		5
LUNCEFORD, Joseph	22	IL	Farmer	2–3, 5 [in JA; 2: "Lunceford"; 5: "Luntsford"]

Missionaries	Age in 1851	Birth Place	Vocation	Sources and Notes
LUNT, Henry	26	Eng	Storekeeper	1–5 [Listed in JA]
LYTLE, John M.				1
MARTINEAU, James H.				[OS: LDR]
McGUFFIE, James	23	Eng	Coal Merchant	1–5 [1: "M'Guffie"; 5: "McGuffey"; in JA]
MEEKS, Priddy	36	SC	Physician	4–5 [4: "P. Meeks," age 53]
Sarah	55	KY		5 [OS: ACL "Priddy Meeks, wife and child"]
Margaret J.	49	IL		5
MILLER, Daniel A.	13	NY	Farmer	1–5 [JA; OS: IMR]
Hannah	41	NY		5
Lovisa	31	VA		5
Jacob	15	IL		5
James	14	IL		5
Susanna	12	IL		5
Jane	10	IL		5
Joseph	8	IL		5
Isabel	5	UT		5
Emeline	3	UT		5
Sarah	1	UT		5
MILLER, Reuben	3 mos			1
MILLER, Robert E.	23	Scot	Ship Carpenter	1–5 [5: age 25; in JA as age 23]
Eliza	20	NY		5
Elizabeth	1 mo	UT		5 [OS: McG: birthdate, 25 Mar 1851[8]]
MILLET, Joseph	18	Can	Teamster	3–5 [4: "Millit"; JA, age 16; OS: IMR]
MILLS, William				1
MITCHELL, William C.	44	Eng	Brickmaker	2–5 [Listed in JA]
Louisa	28	Eng		5

Name	Age	Origin	Occupation	Notes
William C., Jr.	15	Eng		2–5 [Listed in JA; 4: age 16]
Enoch	1	UT		5
MOGGREDGE, Henry	23	Eng	Shoemaker	4–5 [OS: ACL]
MOORE, George[9]				2–3 [2: "Moor"; 3 and JA: "Moore"]
MORSE, Gilbert	35	PA	Farmer	4–5 [OS: ACL: Morse, wife, 3 children]
Cynthia A.	27	OH		5
Mary	7	OH		5
Lidia	3	UT		5
Cynthia M.	4 mos	UT		5
MORSE, William A.	64	NBruns	Physician	1–5 [2, 4: "Wm. A. Morse"; listed in JA]
Sarah	50	PA		5 [JA: "Mrs. William Morse"]
MULFORD, Munson				1
NEWMAN, Elijah	53	VA	Laborer	1–5 [4: "E. Newman"; listed in JA]
OWENS, Robert	33	MD	Farmer	5[OS: ACL "Robert Owens, wife and child"]
Catherine	32	VA		5
Jerome	12	IN		5
Nephi	7	KY		5
Sarah	2	UT		5
Robert	4 mos	UT		5
Martha Allen	27	KY		5 [Presumably a plural wife]
Margaret	6 mos	UT		5
PARKS, James	20	Can	Laborer	2–5 [5: age 21; listed in JA]
PECK, Martin H.				1
POTTER, E. G.				4
PUGMIRE, Jonathan	28	Eng	Blacksmith	2–5 [5: age 51; JA; OS: IMR]
Joseph A.	52	Eng	Laborer	2–5 [2: "Joseph H."; listed in JA]
RAY, Paul[10]	18	France	Teamster	2–3
RICE, William	28			1 [4: "Wm. R. Rice" (or "Wm. K. Rice")]
RIGBY, Seth				1
ROBINSON, Joseph L.	46	VT	Farmer	1–5 [4: age 46; 5: age 40; listed in JA]
Susan	42	KY		5 [Listed in JA]

Missionaries	Age in 1851	Birth Place	Vocation	Sources and Notes
William P.	14	KY		5
Sidney	12	MO		5
Mary J.	2	UT		5
SABIN, Ara	28	NY	Chairmaker	2–5 [2, 3 "Asa"; 4: "A. W."; 5, IMR: "Ara"; JA]
Nancy A.	23	E. TN		5
Ara	3 mos	UT		5
SANDERSON, John	40	Eng	Woolen Man^r	2–5 [5: age 45; listed in JA]
SHAW, James				1
SHAW, Michael	27	Eng	Sailor	4–5 [OS: ACL as "Micheal"]
SHEETS, Elijah F.	29	PA	Blacksmith	1–5 [5: age 30; listed in JA]
Susannah	22	PA		5
Nephi	1	UT		5
SHIRTS, Peter	42	OH	Fisherman	2–5 [Listed in JA as "Peter Shurtz"]
George	19	OH	Fisherman	2–3, 5 [Listed in JA as "George Shurtz"]
Darius	18	OH	Fisherman	5
Don Carlos	16	OH	Fisherman	2–3, 5 [Listed in JA as "Don Carlos Shurtz"]
Saria	12	IL		5
Ann E.	2	IA		5
SMITH, George A.	34	NY	Yeoman	1–5 [4: age 36; 5: age 33; listed in JA]
Zilpha	32	NY		5 [Listed in JA]
Peter A.[11]	15	PA		2–3, 5 [Listed in JA]
Ruth (Indian child)	4			5
SMITH, John C. L.[12]	28	PA	Laborer	1, 4 [i.e., John Calvin Lazelle Smith]
SMITH, Jonathan	38	PA	Farmer	2–5 [Listed in JA]
SMITH, Thomas S.	34	NY		1–5 [3 and 4: 32; 5: 38; in JA, IMR]
Polly	33	CT		5

Name	Age	Place	Occupation	Source
Alma J.	8	MI		5
Alvira	4	IA		5
Thomas	6 mos	UT		5
STEELE, John	30	Ire	Farmer	1–5 [Listed in JA]
Catherine	34	Ire		5 [JA: "Catherine Steele," "two children"]
Mary	9	Ire		5
Elizabeth	4	UT		5
Moroni	2	UT		5
Susannah[13]	11 days	UT		5 [OS: McG: birthdate, 28 Apr 1851]
STEWART, Urban	34	TN	Farmer	2, 4 [4: "Herben B. Steward," age 33]
TAYLOR, Allen				1
THOMPSON, Robert				1
TOPHAM, John, Jr.	25	Eng	Butcher	1–5 [5: "John Jr.," age 26; listed in JA]
Betsey	16	NY		5
TOWN, Chester				2–3 [Listed in JA]
VANCE, William P.	28	TN	Farmer	1–5 [2: "Wm. P."; 4: "W. P."; listed in JA]
WALKER, Joseph	38	Eng	Forgeman	2–5 [Listed in JA]
Betty	38	Eng		5
John	17	Eng	Laborer	5
William	15	Eng		5
Thomas	13	Eng		5
Mary	11	Eng		5
Simeon	6	Eng		5
Hyrum	2	MO		5
WATTS, Benjamin	30	MA	Currier	2–5 [2: "Benjamin Watt"; JA as "Watts"]
Mrs. Benjamin Watts				5 [JA as "Mrs. Benjamin Watts"]
WEBB, Charles Y.	32	NY	Joiner	2–5 [4: "Charles Webb"; JA; OS: IMR]
Margaret	26	NJ		5
Willis	8	NY		5
Jennette	5	IA		5
WEBB, John				1

Missionaries	Age in 1851	Birth Place	Vocation	Sources and Notes
WEST, Chauncey	19	IL	Interpreter	1
WHEELER, Thomas S.	46	VT	Tinman	3, 5 [2: "Thomas J. Wheeler"]
WHIPPLE, Edson	27	PA		1–5 [3: "Edwon Whipple"; JA as "Edson"]
Mary Ann	2	NJ		5 [Listed in JA (first wife)]
Mary				5
Harriet				[Listed in JA (second wife)]
WHITNEY, Francis T.	45	ME	Blacksmith	1–5 [4: "F. T."; 5: age 46; listed in JA]
Clarissa	21	OH		5 [Listed in JA with "five children"]
New Samuel	2 mos	UT		5 [OS: McG: birthdate, 1 Mar 1851]
WILEY, Robert	41	Eng	Bricklayer	1–5 [Listed in JA]
William	12	OH		5 [5: presumably Robert Wiley's son]
WILLIAMS, Edward	30	Eng	Tailor	2–5 [Listed in JA: age 29]
WILLIAMS, Rice				1
WINN, Dennis[14]	25	AL	Farmer	2–3 [Listed in JA]
WOOD, Daniel				1
WOOD, George	28			1–4 [Listed in JA]
Mary				[Listed in JA]
WOOD, Gideon D.	42	NY		2–5 [Listed in JA; OS: IMR]
Hannah	41	NY		5
Lyman S.	17	OH		5
Electa	16	OH		5
Elizabeth	10	IL		5
WOOLF, John A.	45	NY	Shoemaker	2–5 [4: "John A. Wolf"; JA as "Woolf"]
Sarah Ann	36	NY		5
Absalan	18	NY	Farmer	5
Sarah Ann	16	NY		5

Name	Age	State	Occupation	Source
James	14	NY		5
Eliza	12	NY		5
Isaac	10	NY		5
John	8	NY		5
Andrew	6	IL		5
William	4	UT		5
Phoebe E.	4 mos	UT		5
WOOLLEY, Samuel A.	25	PA	Storekeeper	1–5 [3 and IMR: "Wooley"; 4: "S. A."; JA]
Catherine	24	PA		5
Samuel H.	3	IA		5
Mary Permelia	1	UT		5
WOOLSEY, Hyrum[15]	25			2–3 [Listed in JA]
WRIGHT, Jefferson	25	MA	Farmer	1–5
Sarah	19	RI		5
Sarah E.	5 mos	UT		5
YOUNG, George	28	Scot	Iron Moulder	1–3, 5 [variant spellings[16]]

Sources

1: "Call List," *Deseret News*, 16 Nov 1850.

2: "Departure List," *Deseret News*, 11 Jan 1851.

3: Lunt List, Diary, typescript, 15–18.

4: Elders' Quorum List, 9 Feb 1851.

5: May 1851 Utah Census (Zabriskie and Robinson).

JA: Jenson's Arrival List, "Parowan Ward History," 17–23.

GS: Excerpt from George A. Smith, official journal entries.

OS: Other sources (as given in explanatory notes).

Explanation of Appendix II

Main Sources. Data in this table is based primarily on the sources coded in the appendix as numbers 1 through 5:

Source 1. "Names of the company and their outfit for Little Salt Lake," *Deseret News*, 16 Nov 1850. Because it is the first document listing names of those called to serve as iron missionaries, it is designated the "call list."

Source 2. "Names of persons over 14 years of age, on 21st December [1850], gone to Iron county, led by elder George A. Smith," *Deseret News*, 11 Jan 1851. Since this article reports those already underway for the Iron Mission, it is designated the "departure list."

Source 3. "Names of the Pioneers who came to Parowan under the leadership of Apostle George A. Smith . . .," listed in Henry Lunt's diary, pp. 15–18, giving male members of the company by name, with the number of women and children accompanying the party summarized. This source is designated the "Lunt list."

Source 4. "Elders' Quorum List," a hand-written list of names dated 9 Feb 1851, listing many of the male members of the Iron Mission, their current ages and priesthood callings. The source used here is an LDS Church Archives microfilm of the original.

Source 5. "1851 Utah Census," begun 12 May 1851 as per Brigham Young's instructions. The version used here is Zabriskie and Robinson's published transcript of the Washington, D.C., original, with minor errors in the transcript corrected after consulting LDS Church Family History Library microfilm of original (film 0,025,540).

Lists of names given in the primary sources are not, as expected, identical. For instance, some names which appear on the "call list" appear nowhere else. Depending on how each list is interpreted, there are

21 or 22 names on Source 3, the "Lunt list," which do not appear on Source 4, the "Elders' Quorum list." Conversely, 22 or 23 names on the "Elders' Quorum list" do not appear on the "Lunt list." Spelling of names in this appendix follows Zabriskie and Robinson.

Inconsistencies are often difficult if not impossible to reconcile—explanations have been included if possible. Recording, reading, transcription and/or typographical mistakes are common. Therefore, spelling variants have been noted where known. Journalists and clerks depended heavily on oral sources and nineteenth-century spelling practices were far more flexible than ours.

Zabriskie explained that the Iron County census was not taken until 1851 (as part of the National Census of 1850), first, because the act creating Utah Territory was slow to arrive in Salt Lake City and, second, because proper forms had not arrived from Washington. Thomas Bullock, under the direction of Brigham Young, had made an unofficial enumeration of the population which did not include essential information required in the census. (This may be the 1 Apr 1851, "Census of Utah Territory" now in the LDS Church Archives, Salt Lake City.) The official census began on 12 May 1851 in Iron County, two days after Young's arrival on his first trip to assess the well-being and progress of the Iron Mission. The federal record is difficult to read and interpret. Letter forms for *es*, *as* and *os* are often identical, as are forms for *ns*, *rs*, *us* and *vs*. Zabriskie also notes misstatements of fact (especially ages), including some cases where persons are misnamed and/or placed in wrong families. These have been corrected here, wherever found.

Additional Sources. In addition to the five sources noted above, two other primary sources are used: excerpts from George A. Smith's journal and excerpts from Andrew Jenson's "Parowan Ward History, 1849–1900." The former is coded to "GS," the latter to "JA." In addition, several other sources ("OS") are cited, including:

ACL. The "Anson Call list," taken from Smith's journal, entry of 31 May 1851, comprising men and women who journeyed under Anson Call's leadership to Parowan, arriving a few days before Brigham Young's larger party reached the Iron Mission.

LDR. Any "Luella Dalton reference" in this appendix is to her *History of Iron County Mission, Parowan, Utah,* especially to persons arriving there on 8 May 1851 (pp. 39–40). Dalton often neglects to cite specific sources. Therefore, she is included here as a secondary, not primary, source.

IMR. This LDS Church Archives document, labeled "Iron Mission Record," is explained in ch. 3, n. 45. The list being used here identifies those who returned with Brigham Young to Salt Lake City, after the president's visit south in May 1851. It is *not* clear whether *all* of those who returned to Salt Lake City at this time are included in this list.

McG. The "MacGregor list" is identified in ch. 2, n. 104. Some of the newborns listed on it appear in appendix 2; some do not. Likewise, some of the newborns reported in the census do not appear in the MacGregor list.

The Iron County population was shifting at the time of Brigham Young's visit, just as the census and other records were being created. Many families of missionaries arrived at this same time. Appendix 2 attempts to indicate these additional arrivals where possible.

Notes

1. All births listed as in "Utah" are listed in census as occurring in "Deseret."

2. Source 4 microfilm shows paper tear; assuming "Simeon" is now-unreadable word, rest of entry reads "F. Houd."

3. Lovinia possibly listed as age 15 in census to disguise status as plural wife.

4. "John D." (Jr.) possibly confused with unnamed son, born 19 Mar 1851.

5. Philip left to join Iron Mission on 15 Apr 1851 (as per *Deseret News* of 17 May 1851 [vol. 1, no. 33], p. 259.

6. One of three men leaving for California by permission (see GS: 21–27 Apr 1851).

7. Author's note: not their child; their first child born 10 Jun 1851.

8. Source 5: age 14, born in Deseret, is a misreading of "14 da[ys]" in original.

9. One of three men leaving for California by permission (see GS: 21–27 Apr 1851).

10. Actually John D. Lee's teamster, Frenchman Paul Royls. Joseph Millett records his nickname as "Pull Wah."

11. Sometimes referred to as "Peter A. Dibble" (see chapter 2).

12. GS reports arrival of "C. L. Smith" on 8 Apr 1851.

13. Source 5: "Susan A."; OS: McG records Susannah's parents as John and Elizabeth Steele.

14. Leaves for Salt Lake City on 28 Apr 1851, "contrary to counsel."

15. Leaves for Salt Lake City on 28 Apr 1851, "contrary to counsel."

16. 1: "George A."; 2: "G. C."; 3: "George C. Yong"; 5: "George Young"; JA: "George C."

Examples of Lots Assigned in Fort Louisa/Fort Parowan

1851–1853 (based on Surveys by William H. Dame)
(see illus. 4-1, 5-1 and 5-4)

Part 1: House Lots

Records of these property transactions appear in Deed Book A, Iron County Recorder's Office, Parowan. As discussed in Chapter 5, Dame's initial survey created city (i.e., house) lots that were two rods by four rods (33 by 66 feet). Although the first deed of this type does not appear in Deed Book A until p. 13, the entire group is among the earliest of the lot allocations, being created from Dame's first general lot survey of 1851. The 10 lots given below comprise a distinct set of entries. The corresponding deeds have no range and block numbers, probably because the lots were all located in Range 1, making repetition unnecessary. Here, giving both ward and lot number sufficed to legally describe each lot. Also, since these lot dimensions were given as rods and/or feet, there was no need to include acreage, routinely noted in the deeds for small or large farm lots.

The entry numbers given for the first two lots on p. 13, ("1") and ("2"), indicate non-sequential numbering. The deed just before these is no. 72; the deed immediately after them is no. 73. Why they were designated 1 and 2 is unclear. Throughout the appendix, original spelling, phrasing and punctuation have been retained, even where there are evident errors. The "fee date" appears to be the date on which Dame is paid for surveying the lot (in some cases it may prove to be the date on which he <u>completed</u> the survey of that lot). The "filing date" is the date on which the lot and its owner are officially registered with James Lewis, the first recorder of the county.

Page (Entry)	Fee Date	Filing Date	Name of Owner	Ward No.	Lot No.	Survey Name
13("1")	02 Jun 51	03 Jun 51	Daniel Hendricks	1st	11	Parowan

Entry reads: [Lot 11] ". . . being 33 feet front by 66 feet deep. also Lot 11 in said Ward's private Caral, being 29 feet front by 4 Rods deep."

| 13("2") | 02 Jun 51 | 03 Jun 51 | Leman Brunson | 1st | 13 | Parowan |

Entry reads: [Lot 13] ". . . being 33 feet front by 66 feet deep."
Superimposed diagonally: "Transfered to Samuel Gould Decr. 2 1851. Recorder Page 19. No 104."

| 17(94) | 02 Dec 51 | 03 Dec 51 | Solomon Chamberlin | 4th | 10 | Parowan |

Entry reads: [Lot 10] ". . . being 33 feet front by 66 feet deep. also Lot 10 in said Ward's Private Caral, being 14 feet 8 inches front by 4 Rods deep."

| 17(95) | 02 Dec 51 | 03 Dec 51 | Solomon Chamberlin | 4th | 13 | Parowan |

Entry reads: [Lot 13] ". . . being 33 feet. front by 66 deep, also Lot 11 [*sic*] in Said Ward's Private Caral, being 14. feet 8 inches front by 4 Rods deep."

| 19(103) | "paid" | 08 Dec 51 | John L. Smith | 1st | 07 | Parowan |

Entry reads: [Lot 7] ". . . being 33 feet by 66 feet."

| 19(104) | "paid" | 08 Dec 51 | Samuel Gould | 1st | 13 | Parowan |

Entry reads: [Lot 13] ". . . being 33 feet by 66 feet. Said Lot Transfered from Leman Brunson" [see 13(2) above].

| 20(112) | 21 Jan 52 | 21 Jan 52 | Jacob Hofheins | 2nd | 21 | Parowan |

Entry reads: [Lot 21] ". . . being 33 front by 66 deep. also Lot 21 in 2d Wards Private Caral, 29 ft front by 4 Rods deep—also South half, Lot 22, in Second Ward of Fort Parowan, also North half, Lot 21, in 2d Ward Private Coral. 11 feet front by 4 Rods deep."

| 25(138) | 15 Jan 52 | 29 Mar 52 | William A. Morse | 3rd | 02 | Parowan |

Entry reads: ". . . Lot 2, private Caral. 29 feet front by 4 Rods.—Also Lot 2/ & 3 in <u>fourth</u> Ward. Parowan Fort. also Lots 2 & 3 in private Caral. 14 feet 8 inches front Each by 4 Rods deep."

Page (Entry)	Fee Date	Filing Date	Name of Owner	Ward No.	Lot No.	Survey Name
25(140)	03 Apr 52	06 Apr 52	Benjamin Jones	4th	05, 06	[--]

Entry reads: ". . . Lots 5 & 6, fourth Ward, also Lots 5 & 6 Private Caral 29 ft 4 inches by 4 Rods."

Page (Entry)	Fee Date	Filing Date	Name of Owner	Ward No.	Lot No.	Survey Name
27(151)	10 Apr 52	02 Jul 52	Herman D. Baylis	1st	08	Parowan

Entry reads: ". . . Lot 8 First Ward Parowan Fort also Lot 8 1st Wards Private Carall 20 feet front by 4 Rods deep."

Part 2: Small and Large Farm Lots

A detailed discussion of the farm lots occurs in chapter 4. The set given below is a sample and is listed chronologically, containing the first three pages of entries from Deed Book A. Note that five-acre or small farm lots fall in Ranges 1NW to 4NW, while 10-acre or large farm lots begin in Range 4NW and extend out as far as Range 11NW. "Block" numbers should not be confused with city blocks; here, they represent the horizontal coordinates which, with the vertical ranges, create the grid Dame used for his surveys. Since the filing dates all occur within 1851, each of these deeds represents a lot created by Dame's initial survey. The fact that they occur in Deed Book A prior to the house lots may indicate that farm lots were surveyed and allocated even before individual city lots were assigned to the settlers.

Page (Entry)	Fee	Filing Date	Name of Owner	Range No.	Block No.	Lot No.	Survey Name (& acres)
1(1)	"paid"	07 Feb 51	Francis T. Whitney	01	01	16	Centre Creek (5)
1(2)	"paid"	07 Feb 51	George A. Smith	01	01	01	Centre Creek (5)
1(3)	"paid"	07 Feb 51	James Lewis	05	01	08	Centre Creek (10)
1(4)	"paid"	24 Feb 51	Zedick Judd	04	01	11	Centre Creek (5)
1(5)	"paid"	24 Feb 51	Zedick Judd	08	06	01	Centre Creek (10)
2(6)	"paid"	24 Feb 51	Zedick Judd	08	06	08	Centre Crick (10)
2(7)	"paid"	24 Feb 51	George Brimhall	01	01	09	Centre Crick (05)
2(8)	"paid"	24 Feb 51	George Brimhall	10	07	02	Centre Creek (10)
2(9)	"paid"	27 Feb 51	Philip B. Lewis	03	01	10	Centre Creek (05)
2(10)	"paid"	27 Feb 51	Peter Shirts	11	06	01	Centre Creek (10)
2(11)	"paid"	27 Feb 51	Peter Shirts	11	06	07	Centre Crick (10)
3(12)	"paid"	16 Mar 51	Jefferson Wright	10	06	01	Centre Creek (10)
3(13)		16 Mar 51	Elisha H. Groves	02	01	04	Centre Creek (5)
3(14)		16 Mar 51	Elisha H. Groves	04	01	13	Centre Creek (10)
3(15)	"paid"	11 Apr 51	Wm. C. Mitchell	05	01	04	Centre Creek (10)
3(16)	"paid"	11 Apr 51	Wm. C. Mitchell	02	01	06	Centre Crick (5)
3(17)			Thomas Corbitt	01	01	04	Centre Crick (5)

Part 3: "Special" Lots

A number of unique lots appear in Deed Book A. Some of these are unusual because of size or location; some are interesting because of the assigned lot owner. Together, they provide an example of the variety of land transactions occurring in outlying settlements of the pioneer era.

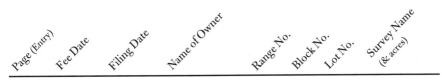

Page (Entry)	Fee Date	Filing Date	Name of Owner	Range No.	Block No.	Lot No.	Survey Name (& acres)
4(18)	"paid"	12 Apr 51	Parley P. Pratt	--	--	--	Centre Crick (132)

This unusually large "lot" begins at NE corner, Block 1, Range 3SW; the acreage falls more across foothills than it does across farm land. Dame surveyed the lot at Pratt's request on Pratt's birthday, during a stopover in Fort Parowan on his way to California to take ship for an overseas mission.

| 14(77) | 19 Aug 51 | 19 Aug 51 | Wm H Dame | 06 | 06 | 01 | Centre Crick (80) |

This sizable farm lot appears to be the "payment-in-kind" which Dame received in lieu of a salary for his professional surveys of the settlement.

| 15(81) | -------- | | Elijah Elmer | -- | -- | -- | Centre Creek |

This entry is a Quit Claim Deed dated 8 Nov 51, in which Elijah Elmer vacates his *undivided Third of a Grist Mill Situated on Centre Creek* to George A. Smith. It contains one of the few direct references to the gristmill known to be operating in Parowan because of many journal references to flour-grinding there.

| 19(106) | 23 Dec 51 | 26 Dec 51 | William C. Mitchell | 02 | 01 | 04 | Coal Creek (20) |

This is the first deed recording a property transaction at Coal Creek, modern Cedar City.

| 19(107) | 08 Jan 52 | 08 Jan 52 | James A. Little | 14NE | 06, 07 | 03 | Red Crick (324) |

This is the first deed recording a property transaction at Red Creek, modern Paragonah.

| 25(141) | "paid" | ---- | Brigham Young | [As described] | | | ------ |

Entry reads: ". . . the property (To Wit) one log House one adobie House and fort Lot and two five acre Lots, Viz. Lots 14. &. 15. Block one, range Three Once owned by me [Isaac B. Kirby], the same is hereby assigned to Gov. Brigham Young."

Appendix 4

Cedar City Settlers

11 November–31 December 1851

Names of Settlers	Military Company[1]	David Bulloch[2]	John Chatterley[3]	James Whittaker[4]	Secondary Sources[5]
Adams, David				b	
Anderson, James			b		
Baird, James	F				
Barton, Lorenzo				x	
Bateman, William	C			x	
Bladen, Thomas			a	x	
Bosnell, James			a		
and wife			a		
Bulloch, James	F	b	a		
and wife			a		
Bulloch, Robert					b
Campbell, Alexander			a		
and wife					a
Carruthers, Matthew			a	x	b
Cartwright, Thomas	F		a		a, b
and wife			a		
Cassell, George	F				
Chatterley, John	F		b		a
Chatterley, Joseph	C		a	x	a
and wife			a		
Deakin, William			a		
Easton, Alexander	C	a, b	a		
and wife		a, b	a		
Easton, George	C	b	a		
and wife			a		

Names of Settlers	Military Company[1]	David Bulloch[2]	John Chatterley[3]	James Whittaker[4]	Secondary Sources[5]
Easton, James		b	a		
and wife		b			
Easton, John	C	a, b	a		
and wife		a, b			
Easton, Matthew		b	a		
Easton, Robert	C	a, b			
and wife Mary		a, b		x	
Evans, William	F				
Fife, Peter M.	C				
Filanque, Peter			a, b		a
Gould, Samuel				x	
Gregory, [unnamed]			a		
and wife			a		
Harrison, Richard	F		a		a, b
and wife			a		
Henderson, William		a	a		
Henry, Robert	F				
Hulse, Benjamin			a		b
Hunter, George		b*			
Hunter, Joseph			a		
and wife			a		
Hunter, William			a	x	b
and wife			a		
Johnson, N.	C			x(?)	
Johnson, S.	C			x(?)	
Keir, Alexander	F	a, b	a	x	
and wife		a, b	a	x	
Klingensmith, Philip			a		b
and wife			a		
Lewis, Jessie (Mr.)			a		
Lunt, Henry	F	b*	a, b	x	a
Martineau, James	F				
Mitchell, William Sr.					a
Mitchell, William Jr.	F				a
Parks, Arthur			a		
and wife			a		

Names of Settlers	Military Company[1]	David Bulloch[2]	John Chatterley[3]	James Whittaker[4]	Secondary Sources[5]
Pugmire, James			a		
and wife (1)			a		
and wife (2)			a		
Pugmire, Jonathan					b
Ross, Alexander	C				
Ross, Daniel	C		a	x	
Ross, Duncan	F		b		
Rowland, Thomas	F				
Shirts, Peter			a, b		a
Slack, William	F		a	x	
and wife			a		
Stoddard, John Sr.	(F?)	a, b			
and wife		a, b			
Stoddard, John Jr.	(F?)	a			
Stoddard (Grandmother?)		a			
Stone, William	F				
Thorpe, James	F				a
Tout, John	F			x	
Walker, Joseph		b*	a	x	
and wife			a		
West, Samuel	F				
Whittaker, Ellen				x	a
Whittaker, James Sr.	F		a	x	a
and wife			a		
Whittaker, James Jr.	F			x	a
Williams, Edward	F				
Williamson, James	F	a, b		x	
and wife		a, b			
Wood, George		b*	a		b
and wife (1)			a		
and wife (2)			a		
Wood(s), William	F		a		
and wife			a		

Sources

1. Military Companies: The designation "C" represents a member of the mounted (cavalry) company [Territorial Militia Muster Rolls of 1851–1867 for Iron County, document no. 3287, acc. no. 014279, Utah State Archives and Records Service]. The designation "F" represents a member of the infantry (foot) company [identical source; document no. 3285]. "John Stoddard" is listed as a member of Company F, but the muster roll does not indicate whether this is the father or the son.

2. Bulloch Sources: The designation "a" refers to "Life Sketch of David Bulloch" [full cite at ch. 6, n. 10]; designation "b" refers to "Facts Furnished by David Bulloch" [full cite at ch. 6, n. 24]. The four names given an asterisk in this column (George Hunter, Henry Lunt Sr., Joseph Walker, and George Wood) are mentioned in "Facts Furnished by David Bulloch" prior to the list of first settlers. These men are described (with "many others") as having "come over from Parowan" to start the "first Old Fort corral," distinguishing them from those grouped together later in the document as a cohesive party of original settlers.

3. Chatterley Sources: The designation "a" refers to a list of first settlers of Cedar City, passed down from John Chatterley, its author, to his daughter Nancy Walker [see ch. 6, n. 63]; the designation "b" refers to Chatterley's "History of Cedar City."

4. Whittaker Source: An "x" in this column refers to the Journal of James Whittaker. In several entries, Whittaker refers to two men with the "Johnson" surname. One is called "Bishop Johnson," the other "Bro. Johnson." No first names are mentioned. The relevant dates are 30 Nov 1851, 6 Mar 1852 and 6 Jun 1852.

5. Secondary Sources: The designation "a" refers to Andrew Jenson's "Manuscript History of Cedar City;" the designation "b" refers to Gladys McConnell's untitled talk on Cedar City history.

Brigham Young's Address to the Saints in Parowan and Cedar City

May 1852

The source of this epistle is a draft document in Brigham Young Papers, Outgoing Correspondence, LDS Church Archives. The text, in William Clayton's hand, was signed by Brigham Young and Heber C. Kimball and is believed to have been read by James Ferguson at the close of a church conference held in Parowan in May 1852. The notation "Oct. or Nov. 1851" appears on the back of the document, in the hand of Thomas Bullock, Brigham Young's clerk. As Cedar City was only settled on 10–11 November 1851, however, the draft could not have been written as early as October. More convincing is Henry Lunt's journal entry of 12 May 1852 in which he records copying out the entire epistle after hearing it read.

To the Saints in Parowan and Cedar Cities and the regions
around about in Iron County

Beloved Brethren having visited among you and witnessed your labor in promoting the cause of truth by the establishment of permanent settlements in the vallies of the Mountains wherein our Brethren from afar can find rest with us while the Indignation of the Lord shall be poured out upon the Nations and feeling an ardent desire for your welfare and the wellbeing of the Enterprize in which you have enlisted considered that a word of instruction and Counsel left with you might be useful in reminding you of some things which when absent might be forgotten. Brethren in your midst our hearts have been made to rejoice and our souls refreshed in the union of spirit and effort the good order and industry which so eminently characterises your exertions and the love of which so richly abides in you[.]

It is with regret that we observe there are some among you who seem disposed to scatter out from the Forts thereby hazarding their own lives and the peace of the whole Territory[.] We are located in the midst of savage tribes who for generations untold have been taught to rob plunder and kill and the gratification of every lustful appetite for Blood and revenge[,] success in which among themselves paves the way to destinction and influence. They are moreover ignorant and degraded living in the lowest degree of filthiness practicing extreme barbarity to all such as unfortunately fall into their hands[;] under circumstances peculiar we have been shown into their midst[.] They are of Israel so are we[. O]ur position among them furnishes abundant opportunities of doing good[.] We can here become saviors in very deed saviors of our brethren[.] Even those who through the transgression of their Fathers are weltering under the heavy penalties incured through disobedence [*sic*][.]. It is a privelege as well as a duty thus to use our influence and exertion to bring them back to the Fold of Christ for the promise is unto them of whom the Lord said a remnant should be saved[.]

While therefore we extend our Charity and good feelings unto them, let us, not condescending to their level, seek to Elevate them in the scale of beings seek to bring them to a Knowledge of their Fathers and our Fathers their God and our God, while we thus seek to do them good[. I]t is obvious that we should not place our selves in their power subject ourselves to the caprice of their Savage Nature which through causes unknown to us may at any moment become excited and arrayed against us. Then follows colision [*sic*] and warfare and even though we may be successful in the first event yet embittered feelings are engendered which may last for years. Let us then be wise and avoid every measure that gives them any advantage over us[.] To those Brethren who have gone from the Fort and settled south of Cedar City We say return and remain with your Brethren subjecting yourselves to the counsel of those who are placed in authority and set to govern and control. The settlement at Elk horn Springs should be maintained as a herd ground and the Brethren at that point should build a Fort and be susteined by a few more families sufficient to strengthen the place against any surprise and those who dwell there should always be on the alert with their horses and equipments ready at any moment to go or come or defend themselves. They should never leave the Fort destitute of sufficient Men to defend it if it should prove necessary neither should you hold the life of an Indian as Equivalent for the Loss of a few cattle. It is far cheaper for us as a people to feed them all than to defray the expenses of an expedition against them. Though it should prove successful and none of the lives of our Brethren be lost It is well known that they are always hazarded upon such occasions.

Therefore Brethren in all your intercourse with them be mild yet firm generous yet Economical and use diligence, patience and perseverence in inducing them to return to habits of Industry by giving them Employment which meets with an ample and sure reward[.]

The Lord has been merciful with you be ye merciful with them of the rich abundance of his store he has imparted unto you impart you unto them not only food and raiment but of the spirit of grace and forbearance virtue and truth of the which ye have become partakers through the manifold mercies and blessings of our God. We are stewards only over all that we possess for the Earth is the Lord's and the fullness thereof. Therefore let us be wise stewards and not neglecting to put to usury our means and increasing our substance yet so order our course that we shall be able to given an account of our stewardship that shall prove creditable to ourselves and advantageous to the cause which we have espoused, that our Faith may be made Manifest by our Works and our whole lives and existance bear to be tested at the shrine of truth and Knowledge of Wisdom and righteousness towards our God[.]

To the Brethren at Cedar City we wish to say a few words[:] we have formed an organization for the purpose of bringing out the Iron[. I]t is unnecessary for us to add that this is and has been the principle object of locating the settlements in Iron County[. Y]ou have the ore, the coal, the Timber: in rich abundance you have in your midst a supply of grain and need have no fears of a scarcity of food[.] You will gradually be strengthened in number as the Emigration shall arrive[.] Everything conspires to accomplish this most desirable object, the manufacture of Iron.

Brethren shall it be done, shall the people of this Territory be no longer dependant upon foreign and distant countries for their Mill Irons, ~~and~~ [sic] Machinery, and Stoves, their pots and Kettles, their plows and every other useful and necessary implement which is composed of Iron, or shall we be disapointed in our expectations and still labor under the present disadvantage of precarious and expensive transportation and continual drain of our money or do without those articles which are so necessary and which are so easily furnished by a little well directed industry and perseverence in our midst You have raised your hands in solemn covenant that you will do all that lies in your power to accomplish this object; and we now leave you with the fullest expectation that you will bend your united and untireing Efforts to this purpose with the fullest assurance that but a few weeks shall roll around before the cheering intelligence will salute our Ears,—"send your orders we are prepared to fill them. The Iron is piled up in our houses and in our streats send your teams and carry it away." You Brethren have been selected for this purpose and set apart to this mission. Let no influence swerve you from this duty. Let no selfish interest intervene betwixt you and the accomplishment of your duties but let a devoted magnanimity for the Public interest blended with a oneness of untireing Efforts characterize all your exertions in whatsoever you shall put your hands to do[;] do it in a spirit of oneness and of faith believing, and the happiest results will be most likely to follow[:] so shall you accomplish the object of your mission and subserve the Public good.

It is a gentile custom to sell Knowledge. This principle is utterly opposed to the Principles of Salvation[;] by it no person would ever to be able to Enter the Celestial gate. [H]ad the savior of the world required remuneration for disclosing his knowledge of the way to obtain Eternal life made manifest by his words and atoning blood at the hands of the Children of Men, who could have been saved? [S]urely not the poor fishermen who followed him while living and bore testimony of his death and resurrection which testimony they also sealed with their blood[. H]aving also been made partakers of the good word of life they also shared in his sufferings, after having freely proclaimed the same to all people. The Jew first and also unto the gentile. "Ho Every one that thirsteth come drink of the waters of life freely and whosoever will let him come without money and without price" was the proclamation. Did the almighty require a fee or charge per diem or Mileage for opening up again the way of life and salvation in this last dispensation and was not the gospel brought to you by the servants of God without reward from you? If these things are so then how reasonable to suppose that not only our Knowledge but our talents our capacity, be it they great or small should be devoted to the cause of God in what Ever calling we may be engaged in, that is conducive to its interest[.]

"If I had been called upon to manage the affair I would have been successful but he Knows nothing about it"[—]how common the sentiment and yet how destitute of sense and detestable the principle, fools that they are who act upon this principle[;] do you not know that all you possess of knowledge of wisdom of Judgement yea of existance is lent and given you of the Lord, Again it was said by our Savior, "Let him who would be the greatest among you become the least of all" and how truly exemplified is this principle in the life and sufferings of our redeemer who decended [*sic*] below that he might arise above all things. Brethren are these true principles and will we not act upon them[? A]re these the truths of Eternity and we give heed to them. [W]ill we enwrap ourselves in the folds of selfishness and self importance in unyielding aristocratic feelings and withhold the little Knowledge that we may chance to possess from our brethren and from our common cause, God and the building up of his Kingdom, and the promoting of his cause upon the Earth, should be our theme by day and by night; and how we can best subserve its interests our most anxious enquiry to yield forth our most earnest contributions in faith in Knowledge in works or in anything which we possess[,] is but our reasonable service and is justly due to our sacred cause[.] If we ever attain unto a celestial Glory we may expect to seek for it with willing hearts and with all our might mind and strength. The work in which you are engaged, in the manufacture of Iron at this juncture is one branch of the Kingdom of our God and should be pursued with all the vigor and Energy that has hitherto characterized your Exertions in tbse vallies, should be pursued as regardless of the consequences pertaining to pecuniary considerations as preaching the gospel[. I]t is as sacred as any other Mission and when was the time and where the place that a faithful Elder who trusted in God did not find food and clothing sufficient to supply his necessities. We do not recommend that you neglect to enclose your field, water your grain, and harvest the same, this is all necessary to save and secure the labor which you have performed and the seed which you have put into the ground, but be generous with one another and not permit any influence foreign to your Mission to intervene and thwart the purposes thereof[.]

The Church does not desire to engage in any Enterprise foreign to its legitimate functions nor divert the funds from their proper objects, and much prefers that individuals should engage in every kind of domestic Manufacture. She has enough to do in spreading the Gospel, building Temples, and preparing the way for the salvation of the Living and the dead. It is true that she has extended assistance in many instances and thereby become involved in manufactories and Enterprises of various Kinds[.] This has been permitted because of our anxiety to have operations of this Kind commenced and the poverty of the people not enabling them to sustain themselves until the Enterprise itself should prove lucrative, but i[t] is not desirable to do so and it always proves detrimental to her interests.

In relation to the extent of assistance which we expect to render your Enterprize you have been instructed and your President and Bishop will see carried into effect[. I]t Comprises the produce and labor tithing only of residents here and orders on the funds need not be drawn with any expectation of having them answered. Commence upon a small scale and produce the Iron before you go into any great expense and then you can increase your operations as circumstances will permit and justify[. L]et your improvements be of a permanent nature that your labor be not lost[;] do not be discouraged in your experiments if the first should fail. In new and untried localities that would be an incident most likely to occur and yet a subsequent trial prove more successful. [B]ut enough has been said upon this subject[;] words will not accomplish the desired object but united and persevering efforts will.

We therefore close our Epistle praying God our heavenly Father in your behalf that his blessings may ever rest down upon you and all the faithful saints who shall essay to perform his will upon the Earth until a more perfect day shall usher in the brighter dawning of a glorious inheritance among the blood washed throng in [the] presence of Hyrum & Joseph[,] our Redeemer and our God.

Brigham Young

Heber C. Kimball

Shareholders and Officers in the Deseret Iron Company

Names	1	2	3	4	5	6	Comments
ADAMS, David B.	¼			x			Subscribed, Nov 1852; appointed furnace master, Nov 1852; withdrew, Nov 1853
ALLEN, Ira	¼			x		x	Referred to as shareholder in 1855
ARTHUR, Christopher Sr.	1		x			x	Subscribed, 1852; elected trustee, Nov 1853; elected secretary pro tem, Nov 1854
ARTHUR, Christopher Jr.	¼			x			Trusteeship, ¼ share transferred from Vincent Shurtleff, May 1854; withdrew as trustee, Nov 1855
BARTON, William	¼					x	Withdrew, April 1853
BOSNELL, James	¼			x	x	x	Listed as member, Nov 1853
CARRUTHERS, Matthew	¼			x			Subscribed, Nov 1852; withdrew, Nov 1853
CARTWRIGHT, Thomas	¼			x	x	x	Subscribed, Nov 1852; withdrew; left area
CHATTERLEY, Catherine					x		Widow of Joseph

Names	1	2	3	4	5	6	Comments
CHATTERLEY, Joseph	½			x	x	x	Subscribed, Nov 1852; died, Sep 1853; transferred to Catherine Chatterley
CLEWS, Joseph	¼			x			Subscribed, Nov 1852; withdrew, Nov 1853; transferred to Jonathan Pugmire
COOK, Henry	¼					x	Requested release, 1857
CORAY, George	¼					x	First mention Oct 1856
DALTON, Charles W.	¼			x	x	x	Listed as member, Nov 1853; transferred to S. D. White
EASTON, Alexander	¼			x			Subscribed, Nov 1852; withdrew, Nov 1853
ENSIGN, Merius	¼					x	Divided ¼ share with Benjamin Hulse
FIFE, Peter M.	¼			x		x	On balance sheet, 1854
HAIGHT, Isaac C.	¼			x	x	x	Subscribed, Nov 1853; elected trustee, Nov 1853; elected president pro tem, Nov 1854
HALL, Job P.	¼			x		x	On balance sheet, 1854
HARRISON, Richard	¼			x	x	x	Subscribed, Nov 1852; made moulding superintendent, Nov 1852; withdrew, Nov 1853
HULSE, Benjamin R.	¼			x	x	x	Subscribed, Nov 1852; transferred to Merius Ensign, Oct 1856
JONES, Elias	1		x	x		x	Subscribed, 1852
JONES, John	1		x	x		x	Subscribed, 1852

Names	1	2	3	4	5	6	Comments
JONES, Thomas	1	x	x	x		x	Subscribed, Apr 1852
KEIR, Alexander				x			Withdrew by Nov 1853
KERSHAW, Robert	¼			x	x	x	Received from Samuel Kershaw, Nov 1853
KERSHAW, Samuel	¼			x			Subscribed, Nov 1852; withdrew; transferred to Robert Kershaw, Nov 1853
LITTLE, James A.				x	x		Listed as member, Nov 1853; withdrew, Nov 1854
LISTON, C. Perry	¼			x		x	Withdrew, Nov 1858
LUNT, Henry	¼			x	x	x	Subscribed, Nov 1852; appointed clerk, Nov 1852
MORRIS, Elias	¼					x	Elected trustee, Nov 1858
POLLOCK, Samuel	¼			x		x	On balance sheet, 1854
PUGMIRE, Jonathan	½			x	x	x	Subscribed, Nov 1852; ¼ received from Joseph Clews, Nov 1853; elected trustee, Nov 1853-Oct 1856; withdrew ¼, Nov 1854
RICHARDS, Franklin D.	1	x	x	x		x	Secretary of organizing committee, Apr 1852; compensated with subscriber's share, Apr 1852; elected secretary, Nov 1853
REID, Robert	¼					x	
SHELTON, William	¼			x		x	On balance sheet, 1854
SHURTLEFF, Vincent	¼	x		x	x	x	Purchasing agent, May 1852; elected trustee,

Names	1	2	3	4	5	6	Comments
							Nov 1853; trusteeship, share transferred to Christopher Arthur, Jr., May 1854
SMITH, George A.				x	x		Subscription date unknown; withdrew: Nov 1854, Oct 1856, Nov 1857 (final)
SMITH, J. C. L.	¼			x		x	Appointed superintendent pro tem, Nov 1852; died, Oct 1856; share withdrawn
SMITH, Philip K.	1			x		x	On balance sheet, 1854
SNOW, Erastus	1	x		x		x	Chairman of organizing committee, Apr 1852; compensated with subscriber's share, Apr 1852; elected president, Nov 1853
STEELE, John	¼			x		x	On balance sheet, 1854
STEWART, Urban V.	¼			x			
STODDARD, David	¼			x			Subscribed, Nov 1852; withdrew, Nov 1853
STONES, William	¼			x			Subscribed, Nov 1852; withdrew, Nov 1853
TENNANT, Thomas	4	x	x	x		x	Treasurer of organizing committee, Apr 1852; subscribed, Apr 1852; elected treasurer, Nov 1853; died Oct 1856; shares kept by estate
Utah Territory	2					x	Paid for by Perpetual Emigrating Fund, Oct 1855

Names	1	2	3	4	5	6	Comments
WALKER, Joseph	¼			x	x	x	Subscribed, Nov 1852; elected trustee, Nov 1855
WESTON, John	1	x	x	x			Subscribed, Apr 1852
WILLIAMS, George				x			
WILLIAMSON, James				x			Withdrew, Nov 1853
WOOD, George	½			x	x	x	Subscribed, Nov 1852; withdrew ¼ share, Nov 1854; elected trustee, Oct 1856
YOUNG, Brigham	2					x	As trustee-in-trust for LDS Church (shares paid for by Cedar City, Parowan, and Harmony tithing offices, May 1855 and Cedar City tithing office, Oct 1855)

Note: James Whittaker is mentioned in the company minutes under 6 Nov 1854 as proxy for Henry Lunt (then on his mission) and also for the Chatterley estate.

Source Codes:

1: Number of shares (each worth £500 English sterling or $2,420).
2: Original organizing committee member.
3: Original shareholder in England.
4: Listed in Deseret Iron Company Minute Book (pp. 14–49). The 1854 balance sheet covers pp. 35–36.
5: Listed in Share Register 1853, Book A.
6: Listed in John Crook's thesis: roster of "additional subscribers" (p. 49).

The above list of shareholders should be considered incomplete, as other Deseret Industry Company records may exist (or may not have survived), containing additional names.

Articles of Incorporation of the Deseret Iron Company

1852 and 1853

A set of Articles of Incorporation, handwritten in blue ink on light blue paper, is in the William R. Palmer Collection, SUU Archives, Cedar City, Utah. Basic text is emended by holograph corrections, deletions and additions. Typed versions, quoted in various publications, differ from this "original." Its paragraphs have been confusingly numbered; although still the earliest-known version, it is evidently a working copy. Paragraph 2, for example, is unnumbered, but "(2)" has been penciled in and the following numerals advance, ending in two paragraphs numbered "6." Both sets of numbers are included in the transcript below:

Articles of Incorporation

Deseret Iron Company 1852

(1) 1. We the undersigned do hereby unite ourselves in a Firm Company to be known as the

Deseret Iron Company

(2) The design of said company is to procure a tract or tracts of land in Utah Territory containing Iron-Ore, Coal, Water privileges &c. and thereon to erect works for the manufacture of Iron and all such articles made of Iron as the wants of that community and the wisdom of the company may determine.

(3) 2. The Members of the Company shall constitute a board of Directors from whose number shall be appointed a President, Secretary & Treasurer.

(4) 3. The Capital Stock of the Company may be increased by the sale of Shares to one Million Pounds Sterling £1,000,000.

(5) 4. The amount of each share composing the Capital Stock of said Company shall be five hundred Pounds (£500).

(6) 5. Each share of the Company's Stock shall be represented by a certificate of the same signed by the President, Secretary, and Treasurer.

(7) 6. No person shall be allowed to withdraw Stock from the company or transfer the same to another without the consent of three fourths of its members.

6. All unpaid stock shall be charged 5 per cent interest from the 1st day of May 1852 until the first day of January 1853 after which 10 per cent shall be the rate of interest until other wise ordered by the Company.

7. No certificate of stock shall be issued until the full amount of a share is paid into the treasury, but the Treasurer's receipt countersigned by the Secretary shall represent any portion of said shares until the full amount is paid and a Certificate thereto issued.

8. The company shall hold their general meetings annually the first which shall be held in the Territory of Utah on the third Monday in September 185[3], the particular place to be fixed by the president and due notice thereof to be given in the Deseret News.

9. It shall be the duty of every member to represent himself at each general meeting of the Company either in person or by proxy, and each proxy shall present his credentials from the person he represents, to the meeting until the Company shall appoint from am[on]g the members a boa[r]d of Directors to manage its affairs.

10. Until the Company shall elect a Board of Managers or Directors to controul its affairs, each member shall in all its business affairs be entitled to as ma[n]y votes as he owns share tickets and one vote only for shares past paid.

11. The President and Secretary (or board of directors when such board shall have been constituted) shall cause the books of the Company to be properly audited and a dividend of the profits of the Company declared at or before each annual meeting and provide for the payment of such dividends to the holders of Share Tickets or Treasurer's receipts.

12. That Erastus Snow & Franklin D. Richards for and in consideration of services rendered in procuring the organization of the company, and to be rendered in directing the business of the company, untill the Machinery necessary for the erection of the works shall be transported to Utah Ter[ritory] or untill the first general meeting of the company as heretofore Provided for, and in selecting a suitable location for the erection of the works and securing to the Company at least 640 acres of land for that purpose, and procuring the company charted by the legislature of Utah, shall be entitled to one share in the capital stock company.

13. Erastus Snow is hereby appointed President[,] Franklin D. Richards Secretary, and Thomas Tennant Treasurer for the company until its first general meeting in Utah Territory, as contemplated in Article 8, or until others shall be duly appointed.

14. The President and Secretary shall be active agents and managers of the Company's affairs until its first general meeting as above and shall have power to adopt such measures and empl[o]y such help as they may find necessa[r]y to advance the designs of the Company.

15. The Treasurer shall appropriate no funds of the Company except on the order of the President and Secretary.

As members of the Deseret Iron Company we here by subscribe to the foregoing Articles and agree to take the amou[n]ts of Stock severally attached to our names.

NAMES	No. of Shares	Amounts
Thomas Tennant	4 shares	£2,000
Thomas Jones	1 share	500
Erastus Snow	1 share	500
Franklin D. Richards	1 share	500
John Weston	1 share	500[17]

An eighteenth article was added to the above set about a week after they were adopted. It is explained and reproduced in ch. 10, p. 258–59.

In order to officially charter the Deseret Iron Company, George A. Smith submitted a bill to the territorial legislature, establishing the Deseret Iron Company as a legal entity. The act also clarified the role of the board of directors and set terms of office for president, secretary, treasurer and four trustees. The House of Representatives passed the bill on 17 Jan 1853; it was signed by Governor Brigham Young.

An Act
To Incorporate the Deseret Iron Company

Sec. 1. *Be it enacted by the Governor and Legislative Assembly of the Territory of Utah,* That Erastus Snow, Franklin D. Richards, Thomas Tennant, Geo. A. Smith, Matthew Carruthers, John C. L. Smith, and Joseph Chatterly, their associates and successors, be, and they are hereby created a body corporate, to be known by the name and style of *Deseret Iron Company,* for the purpose of erecting Furnaces, Mills, Machinery, &c., for the manufacture of Iron and

Steel, and all such articles made of Iron and Steel, as the wants of the community, and the wisdom of the company may determine.

Sec. 2. Said company shall have power in their corporate name, to sue and be sued, to defend and be defended, in all courts of law and equity; to hold, lease, rent or convey property, real or personal; and shall have perpetual succession for the term of fifty years, and may have a corporate seal, which they may use and alter at pleasure.

Sec. 3. Each share of capital stock of said company shall consist of two thousand four hundred and twenty dollars, ($2420.00,) or five hundred pounds sterling, (£500.)

Sec. 4. The company may increase their capital stock as their business shall require, to carry out the purpose and objects contemplated in the first section of this act.

Sec. 5. Each share of the company's stock shall be represented by a certificate of the same, and they may issue certificates, for half and quarter shares, all which shall be signed by the President, Secretary and Treasurer.

Sec. 6. Each stock holder shall be entitled to four votes for each share which may have been paid: *Provided*, that no stock holder shall be entitled to more than twenty votes: *Provided also*, that any subscription of stock shall be entitled to one vote of each quarter share paid thereon.

Sec. 7. For the government, regulation and internal policy of the company, there shall be elected from among the stock holders a President, Secretary, Treasurer, and four Trustees, which shall constitute a Board of Directors.

Sec. 8. The President, Secretary, and Treasurer may hold their offices two years, and until their successors shall be elected and qualified.

Sec. 9. At the first general meeting, the Trustees shall be elected as follows: one for one year, one for two years, one for three years, and one for four years; after which the vacancies may be filled as they occur annually, each Trustee to hold his office four years.

Sec. 10. The Board of Directors shall have power to fill any vacancies which shall occur, until the next annual meeting of the company, and should circumstances occur, which in their opinion render it necessary, they may call a special general meeting; they may also make, ordain, and establish such rules and regulations for the government of the company as they shall deem proper: *Provided*, that no such rules and regulations shall be incompatible with the Constitution and laws of the United States, or the laws of this Territory; *Provided also,* that a majority of the Board present, shall constitute a quorum to do business.

Sec. 11. Absent members shall be permitted to vote by proxy and shall authorize their proxies by writing, which when presented to the meeting shall entitle them to vote.

Sec. 12. If the Deseret Iron Company, now in operation in Iron County, shall at their general meeting, accept, and adopt this charter, and organize under the provisions thereof; then the previous acts of the company and of their officers and agents, under the instructions and provisions of their present constitution, shall be valid and in good faith.

Sec. 13. The first general meeting of the company, shall be held on the third Monday of September, eighteen hundred and fifty three, or as soon after as convenient, after which their annual meeting shall be held at such time and places as they shall determine.

Sec. 14. The officers and agents of the company shall be required to give bonds, with approved securities, which shall be filed with the Clerk of the court of the county in which they shall be executed.

Sec. 15. The officers shall cause the books of the company to be properly audited, and a balance sheet or exhibit of business to be made out, also a dividend of the profits arising from the same to be declared, at or before each annual meeting.

Sec. 16. The books of the company shall be subject to the inspection of the stock holders at all times.

Sec. 17. Nothing in this charter shall be so construed as to authorize or imply banking powers to the Deseret Iron Company.

Approved, Jan. 17th, 1853.

W[illard] Richards
President of the Council

J[edediah] M. Grant
Speaker of the House of Representatives[76]

Cedar City Lot Entitlements, Plat A
(see illus. 12-2)

The following list, organized chronologically, reflects city lot filings on "Plat A," the area first chosen for city expansion after initial settlement on the "Old Fort" site, itself later replaced by the more permanent remove to an area designated "Plat B" (see app. 9). According to Deed Book A, Iron County Recorder's Office, from which the entries below are taken, each lot was H acre in size (4 by 20 rods in measurement). Several of the entries merely note "fees paid" in lieu of the actual date. Entries shown here occur between 1853 and 1855; original spellings and abbreviations are retained. The sequence in which they appear in the deed book is also retained, even though dates are occasionally nonconsecutive.

Date Fees Paid	Date Filed	Owner of Record	Lot No.	Block No.	Page No.
28 Jan 53	01 Mar 53	William Stone	15	11	45
28 Jan 53	01 Mar 53	Job Rowland	05	12	46
28 Jan 53	01 Mar 53	John White	01	22	46
28 Jan 53	01 Mar 53	John White	02	22	46
28 Jan 53	01 Mar 53	James Whitaker	04	19	46
28 Jan 53	01 Mar 53	Thomas Machen	05	25	47
[fees paid]	01 Mar 53	John Easton	12	18	47
28 Jan 53	01 Mar 53	Silas Hoyt	11	23	48
28 Jan 53	01 Mar 53	Andrew Petersen	07	18	48
28 Jan 53	01 Mar 53	Arthur Parks	11	11	48
28 Jan 53[a]	01 Mar 53	Robert Henry	03	25	48
28 Jan 53	01 Mar 53	Henry Lunt	05	19	49
28 Jan 53	01 Mar 53	Phillip K. Smith	01	20	49
28 Jan 53	01 Mar 53	Mathew Caruthers	16	23	50

Date Fees Paid	Date Filed	Owner of Record	Lot No.	Block No.	Page No.
28 Jan 53	01 Mar 53	Charles Willden	03	20	51
28 Jan 53	01 Mar 53	Samuel Bradshaw	13	11	51
28 Jan 53	01 Mar 53	John Bradshaw	14	11	51
28 Jan 53	01 Mar 53	John Chaterly	01	24	52
28 Jan 53	01 Mar 53	William Gough	03	24	52
28 Jan 53	01 Mar 53	Thomas Bladen	01	25	52
28 Jan 53	01 Mar 53	William Deaken	02	25	52
28 Jan 53	01 Mar 53	Thomas Smith	01	16	52
28 Jan 53	02 Mar 53	Mary Smith	02	16	52
[fees paid]	02 Mar 53	Richard Smith	03	16	52
28 Jan 53	02 Mar 53	William Smith	04	16	52
28 Jan 53	02 Mar 53	Charles P. Smith	05	16	52
28 Jan 53	27 Oct 53	Samuel Leigh	07	12	68
28 Jan 53	27 Oct 53	Jerremiah Thomas	06	12	69
28 Jan 53	01 Nov 53	Elias Morris	13	12	72
28 Jan 53	01 Nov 53	Walter Muir	01	23	72
28 Jan 53	04 Nov 53	Robert Chapman	07	23	73
21 May 53	22 Sep 53	David Muir	02	23	66
21 May 53	22 Sep 53	Thomas Muir	03	23	66
24 Nov 53	25 Nov 53	Benjiman R. Hults	08	08	76
24 Nov 53	02 Dec 53	Isac C. Haight	04	12	76
24 Nov 53	02 Dec 53	John Nelson	09	18	76
24 Nov 53	02 Dec 53	John Nelson	08	18	77
24 Nov 53	02 Dec 53	John Key	14	14	77
24 Nov 53	02 Dec 53	William R. Devis	08	12	77
24 Nov 53	02 Dec 53	William Bateman	11	14	77
24 Nov 53	02 Dec 53	Robert Gallispie	16	14	77
24 Nov 53	02 Dec 53	Joseph Chatterly	06	11	77
24 Nov 53	02 Dec 53	David Jones	12	23	77
24 Nov 53	02 Dec 53	David D. Bowen	12	11	77
24 Nov 53	02 Dec 53	Wm Eavans	13	18	77
24 Nov 53	02 Dec 53	Eleazor Edwards	15	08	77
24 Nov 53	02 Dec 53	Edward Pretharro	12	12	78
26 Nov 53	03 Dec 53	Franklin D. Richards	03	12	78
26 Nov 53	03 Dec 53	Erastus Snow	02	12	78
26 Nov 53	03 Dec 53	Erastus Snow (on behalf of Deseret Iron Company)	01	12	78
15 Dec 53	17 Dec 53	Isac C. Haight	08	23	79

Date Fees Paid	Date Filed	Owner of Record	Lot No.	Block No.	Page No.
[transfer]	17 Dec 53	Isac C. Haight (from Job Rowland, for $10)	05	12	79
[transfer]	18 Dec 53	Jacob Hofheins (from Isac C. Haight, for $15)	05	12	79
22 Dec 53	01 Jan 54[b]	Isac C. Haight	10	12	79
22 Dec 53	01 Jan 54[b]	Erastus Snow (on behalf of Deseret Iron Company)	09	12	80
22 Dec 53	01 Jan 54	Elisha H. Groves	04	14	80
22 Dec 53	01 Jan 54	Charles W. Dolton	05	14	80
22 Dec 53	01 Jan 54	John D. Lee	01	14	80
22 Dec 53	01 Jan 54	John D. Lee	02	14	80
22 Dec 53[c]	08 Jan 54[c]	Robert Kershaw	05	22	81
22 Dec 53	08 Jan 54	Richard Smith	10	[ ][d]	81
22 Dec 53[c]	08 Jan 54[c]	Joseph Bateman	12	14	81
22 Dec 53	08 Jan 54	John Smith	10	23	81
22 Dec 53	08 Jan 54	H. H. Kearnes	01	04	82
22 Dec 53	08 Jan 54	Wm Deakin	03	19	82
22 Dec 53	08 Jan 54	Wm Thomas	14	12	82
22 Dec 53	08 Jan 54	Johnathon Pugmire	16	12	82
22 Dec 53	08 Jan 54	Wm Shelton	04	23	83
22 Dec 53	14 Jan 54	Elias Morris	09	08	84
22 Dec 53	14 Jan 54	Wm Roberts	02	06	84
22 Dec 53	14 Jan 54	Festus Sprague	03	06	84
22 Dec 53	21 Feb 54	George Perry	05	23	85
22 Dec 53	21 Feb 54	Wm Gough	04	25	86
22 Dec 53	21 Feb 54	David Cook	01	19	86
22 Dec 53	21 Feb 54	Job Rowland	10	08	87
22 Dec 53	21 Feb 54	Soloman Chamberlain	16	14	87
22 Dec 53	21 Feb 54	Christaphor Jacobs	01	15	89
22 Dec 53	21 Feb 54	John Owans	08	15	89
22 Dec 53	22 Feb 54	Orrin Craw	16	03	89
22 Dec 53	22 Feb 54	John M. Higbee	14	03	90
22 Dec 53	22 Feb 54	Peter Shirts	16	08	90
22 Dec 53	22 Feb 54	Ira Allen	01	03	91
28 Feb 54	01 Mar 54	James James	11	15	91
01 Mar 54	18 Mar 54	Waldo Littlefield	10	15	92
[transfer]	12 Apr 54	Calvin Moor (from Robert Gallispie, for $75)	16	14	93

Date Fees Paid	Date Filed	Owner of Record	Lot No.	Block No.	Page No.
01 Mar 54	12 Apr 54	Laban Morril	03	03	94
01 Mar 54	12 Apr 54	Jabaz Deirfee	07	03	95
01 Mar 54	12 Apr 54	George Wood	16	11	95
01 Mar 54	12 Apr 54	Robert Keys	08	11	95
01 Mar 54	12 Apr 54	Thomas Cartwrite	07	11	95
01 Mar 54	12 Apr 54	Joseph Walker	03	08	96
01 Mar 54	12 Apr 54	Joseph Walker	04	08	97
[transfer]	22 Apr 54	John Groves	07	23	97
		(from Robert Chapman, for $20)			
01 Mar 54	22 Apr 54	David Adams	05	11	97
01 Mar 54	22 Apr 54	Comadore P. Liston	02	08	97
01 Mar 54	22 Apr 54	Wm Dally	01	06	98
[transfer]	08 May 54	James A. Little	05	19	98
		(from Henry Lunt, for $25)			
20 Apr 54	16 May 54	John Weston	02	19	99
20 Apr 54	16 May 54	John Weston	14	15	99
20 Apr 54	25 May 54	Robert Wiley	01	18	103
24 May 54	26 May 54	Thomas Bladem	04	20	103
24 May 54	26 May 54	James W. Bay	09	23	103
03 Jun 54	03 Jun 54	John Yardly	02	18	107
12 Jul 54	10 Jul 54	Roberts Roberts [sic]	05	20	108
11 Sep 54	15 Sep 54	Henry Lunt	02	11	110
11 Sep 54	15 Sep 54	James Whitaker, Sen.	03	11	110
11 Sep 54	15 Sep 54	Alvey Benson	02	03	110
11 Sep 54	15 Sep 54	Thomas Jones	15	12	110
11 Sep 54	15 Sep 54	John P. Jones	05	08	110
11 Sep 54	15 Sep 54	Robert McMerdy	13	08	110
[transfer]	18 Sep 54	Ira Allen	15	11	111
		(from William Stones, for $200)			
[transfer]	25 Sep 54	Isac C. Haight	02	12	114
		(from Erastus Snow, for $60)			
[transfer]	08 Oct 54	Christafer Arthur	13	12	116
		(from Elias Morris, for $250)			
[transfer]	09 Oct 54	Wm Stewart	04	12	116
		(from Isac C. Haight, for $25)			
[transfer]	08 Dec 54	Charles Hopkins	16	08	123
		(from Peter Shirts, for $200)			

Date Fees Paid	Date Filed	Owner of Record	Lot No.	Block No.	Page No.
[transfer]	23 Dec 54	Samuel D. White	07	23	124
		(from John Groves, for $55)			
17 Nov 54	14 Feb 55	Russel Rogers	03	[ ]d	127
17 Nov 54	14 Feb 55	Robert McMurdie	07	[ ]d	127
[transfer]	14 Feb 55	Anthany J. Stratton	05	14	128
		(from Charles W. Dolton, for $400)			
13 Feb 55	15 Feb 55	John Hamilton	06	14	128
13 Feb 55	15 Feb 55	Wm Eriens	01	07	129
13 Feb 55	15 Feb 55	Wm Nish	05	07	129
13 Feb 55	15 Feb 55	Wardman Holmes	09	11	129
13 Feb 55	15 Feb 55	Alexander Campbell	14	23	129
13 Feb 55	15 Feb 55	Robert Lathem	13	23	129
13 Feb 55	15 Feb 55	Daniel Ross	15	23	129
13 Feb 55	15 Feb 55	James Bosnell	01	08	129
13 Feb 55	15 Feb 55	Thomas Harwood	06	03	130
13 Feb 55	15 Feb 55	Thomas Rowland	11	08	130
13 Feb 55	15 Feb 55	Thomas Rowland	09	03	130
13 Feb 55	15 Feb 55	Samuel Pollock	05	[ ]d	131
13 Feb 55	15 Feb 55	Peter M. Fife	09	14	132
13 Feb 55	15 Feb 55	Samuel D. White	04	18	132
13 Feb 55	15 Feb 55	Wm Stewart	15	15	132
13 Feb 55	15 Feb 55	William Davidson	16	15	133
13 Feb 55	15 Feb 55	Thomas Tharley	05	15	133
13 Feb 55	15 Feb 55	John H. Willis	04	15	133
13 Feb 55	15 Feb 55	Alexander Paterson	13	15	133
13 Feb 55	15 Feb 55	Alexander H. Loveridge	06	15	133
13 Feb 55	15 Feb 55	John Muir	10	11	134
13 Feb 55	15 Feb 55	James Bullock	13	14	134
13 Feb 55	15 Feb 55	John K. Smith	03	18	134
13 Feb 55	15 Feb 55	Charles Hopkins	11	12	135
13 Feb 55	15 Feb 55	Josiah Reaves	04	06	135
13 Feb 55	15 Feb 55	Wm Greenwood	05	18	135
13 Feb 55	15 Feb 55	John Jacobs	02	15	136
13 Feb 55	15 Feb 55	Swen Jacobs	03	15	136
13 Feb 55	15 Feb 55	John Chatterly	06	08	136
13 Feb 55	15 Feb 55	Charles Simkins	07	08	136
13 Feb 55	15 Feb 55	John Nelson	15	18	137
13 Feb 55	15 Feb 55	John Nelson	16	18	137

Date Fees Paid	Date Filed	Owner of Record	Lot No.	Block No.	Page No.
13 Feb 55	15 Feb 55	James S. Williamson	06	18	137
13 Feb 55	15 Feb 55	Adam Fife	12	08	138
13 Feb 55	15 Feb 55	Adam Fife	09	15	138
13 Feb 55	15 Feb 55	Joseph Hunter	10	18	138
13 Feb 55	15 Feb 55	Wm Hunter	11	18	139
13 Feb 55	15 Feb 55	George Hunter	12	15	139
13 Feb 55	23 Feb 55	John Ashworth	06	23	140
13 Feb 55	23 Feb 55	Anthony Stratton	13	03	140

Notes

a. Deed Book entry gives this fee date as "January 25/53" but preceding and following entries all give 28 Jan 1853, making this entry almost certainly an inadvertent error.

b. Date is miswritten as "January 1/1853."

c. Both dates are miswritten in the original. The fee date has been overwritten to read "1854" but should read "1853"; the filing date is written "1853" but should read "1854."

d. The block number is inadvertently omitted in this entry.

Excerpts from an Address by President Brigham Young, Delivered in the Tabernacle, Great Salt Lake City

27 May 1855

We have visited the Iron works in Cedar city, Iron county, and as far as I am capable of judging, I will say, that the brethren have done as well as men could possibly do, considering their impoverished circumstances, and the inconveniences they have had to labor under. They have probably progressed better than any other people would upon the face of the earth. They are without sufficient capital to rapidly accomplish so great a work, and many are without suitable clothing, and almost destitute of bedding, and other things necessary to supply the common comforts of life for themselves and families. Although they have been thus destitute, yet in the midst of all that, they have progressed almost equal to men of capital in the older states.

I am not familiarly acquainted with the fluxing or separating the metal from the ore, but those who understand building furnaces and their operations, are aware that it is very injurious for a large and expensive furnace to blow out, as they call it, hence policy requires the blast to be continued as long as possible. I have learned, of late, from men of experience in these matters, why it is desirable to continue the heat—it is because no furnace can be heated up for two or three weeks, and then blow out, or stop, without risk of spoiling the furnace, or destroying its lining; and it frequently so injures the furnace, that it has to be rebuilt, or at least a portion of it. Hence, when it costs from one to five thousand dollars to prepare a furnace to bear a long blast, it is a great loss to any company to have it blow out in a short time.

Our brethren who have been operating in Iron county, have a very fine furnace, but they are so weak handed as not to be able to continue the blast over fourteen days, and I have learned that they want help. This is the main object of my speaking upon this subject, and my mind inclines in favour of their having it, and I want to see whether the brethren will turn out with their teams and help them. The Church has done much for them, and we are still intending to aid. Our last winter's operations have helped them; the Territory took two shares, and the Trustee in Trust, two; still they are not able to carry on the business profitably. Iron we need, and iron we must have. We cannot well do without it, and have it we must, if we have to send to England for it. We have an abundance of the best quality of iron ore. A trial furnace was made, and kept hot for sixteen days, and produced as good pig metal as can be found in the world; this they puddled, and brought forth excellent iron. I believe the castings made from the pigs will be superior to any in the world. I repeat that iron we must have, and we are right on the threshhold of obtaining it; we have our feet on the step, and our hand holds the latch of the door that leads to the possession of this invaluable material.

From the time I first went to Iron county until now, I had thought that perhaps the brethren were dilatory—my feelings were tried; I would not say, however, that I had suspicions pertaining to the doings of the Iron Company there; but let that be as it may, it is all right with me now, the iron we must have. From the time I went to San Pete, and saw that beautiful coal bed, averaging eight feet thick, with its stony strata of nine, five, and three inches, which probably will give out, and learned that iron ore was close by the coal bed, I took into consideration the distance from Cedar City to this place, and the distance from here to San Pete. When I had weighed all the circumstances, my mind balanced in favor of the works at Cedar City for the present; and if I can get brethren to join me, I will send one or two teams myself, with teamsters. We want fifteen good teams, with men with them who are willing to take hold and quarry out the ore and the coal, and get wood, and lime, or anything else that is wanted. Twenty or twenty-five men, besides these teamsters, are wanted, and we wish to send them now, in the fore part of the season. If we will do this, and we can if we have a mind to, I suppose that in two or three weeks after they arrive there, the blast furnace can be kept running for several months, or until they are obliged to stop in consequence of the deficiency of water. There is a large stream of water there, but it is a singular stream, sometimes it will sweep across the flat, carrying down rocks that would weigh perhaps twenty or thirty tons, and appear as though it would sweep everything before it; and when the cold weather comes, and you would naturally think that you were going to have water to turn a mill wheel, or to create the blast for the furnace, and every use for which it might be needed, in one freezing night it will perfectly close up, insomuch that there will not be enough to water a horse.

That is a singular feature, but it is the way it operates. The brethren are now making an engine, so that they can continue their blast through the winter. If any are disposed to forward this work, I call upon them to lend their aid, to send the men and teams, and we can have the iron.

The distance from here to the iron works is about 290 miles. This should not deter us from bringing iron from there, though it could be quicker come at if iron works were established at San Pete, which is not much over 100 miles from here. I have this to say, if any of the brethren feel disposed (as the grasshoppers have taken their crops, and they have not much to do) to go there, I think it would be a good course to pursue. There is plenty of grain there; I could have bought wheat, I do not know but thousands of bushels, at a dollar per bushel; but as sure as you send men there, it will be raised to three dollars; that is incorrect policy, and, as Jesus said, the children of this world are wiser than the children of light.

I have asked this people not to sell their grain, but to preserve it to a day of need, but sell it they would. I have then said, "Will you sell it for a dollar and a quarter per bushel, and let that be the standing price?" "No, we will have two dollars per bushel for it." I then said, "Well, brethren, will you keep it at two dollars, and not sell it to Gentiles cheaper than that?" "No, I will not, but I will have no more than a dollar and a quarter of a Gentile." This is a great mistake in the dealings of the people one with another.

I will bring my remarks to a close on this subject. . . .

. . . Above all things else let this people be faithful to their God and their religion, keep their vows and covenants, and walk humbly before Him, that we may receive the blessings we anticipate, which may God grant, for Christ's sake. Amen.

Source:

Excepts taken from full address, as printed in *Journal of Discourses,* 26 vols. (Liverpool: F. D. Richards, 1855–86), 2:279–84.

Cedar City Lot Entitlements, Plat B

(see illus. 14-1)

The following list, extracted chronologically from entries in Deed Book B, contains city lot filings on "Plat B," the third and permanent area chosen for city expansion after initial settlement in the Compact Fort and interim relocation to "Plat A" (see app. 8 for Plat A filings). Note that lot sizes have expanded, each lot now measuring 8 by 12 rods. Entries here occur between 1855 and 1857; original spellings and abbreviations have been retained. Partial lot transfers, of which there are several, are not included in this tally.

Date Fees Paid	Date Filed	Owner of Record	Lot No.	Block No.	Page No.
25 Jun 55	18 Jul 55	James Anderson	12	38	37
25 Jun 55	18 Jul 55	Isaac C. Haight	10	38	37
25 Jun 55	18 Jul 55	Joseph Balm	13	38	37
25 Jun 55	18 Jul 55	James Farrar	18	39	37
25 Jun 55	18 Jul 55	Joseph Walker	16	39	37
25 Jun 55	18 Jul 55	Elias Morris	05	38	37
25 Jun 55	18 Jul 55	Robert Wiley	06	38	37
25 Jun 55	18 Jul 55	John Morris	04	38	38
25 Jun 55	18 Jul 55	Isaac C. Haight	09	38	38
25 Jun 55	18 Jul 55	Richard Harrison	08	38	38
25 Jun 55	18 Jul 55	Richard Harrison	07	38	38
25 Jun 55	19 Jul 55	Erasmus Anderson	06	39	38
25 Jun 55	19 Jul 55	Robert Keys	10	24	38
25 Jun 55	19 Jul 55	Wm Smith	13	26	38
25 Jun 55	19 Jul 55	John Morgan	03	39	39
25 Jun 55	19 Jul 55	Wm Leigh	02	24	39
25 Jun 55	19 Jul 55	Thomas Thorly	13	[ ][a]	39

Date Fees Paid	Date Filed	Owner of Record	Lot No.	Block No.	Page No.
25 Jun 55	19 Jul 55	John Baugh	09	24	39
25 Jun 55	19 Jul 55	John K. Smith	15	24	39
25 Jun 55	19 Jul 55	John Gerber	17	23	39
25 Jun 55	19 Jul 55	Wm. Roberts	12	24	39
25 Jun 55	19 Jul 55	Samuel Leigh	03	37	40
25 Jun 55	19 Jul 55	John Gerber	18	23	40
25 Jun 55	19 Jul 55	John Adams	14	24	40
25 Jun 55	19 Jul 55	Joseph Clews	11	24	40
25 Jun 55	20 Jul 55	Alexander Loveridge	04	36	40
25 Jun 55	20 Jul 55	Alexander Jacobs	06	36	40
25 Jun 55	20 Jul 55	Wm. Richards	07	36	40
25 Jun 55	20 Jul 55	David Adams	09	36	41
25 Jun 55	20 Jul 55	Charles Simpkins	12	36	41
25 Jun 55	20 Jul 55	Andrew Patterson	10	36	41
25 Jun 55	20 Jul 55	Joab Rowland	03	38	41
25 Jun 55	20 Jul 55	James Farrer	15	39	41
25 Jun 55	20 Jul 55	Thomas Bladen	02	38	41
25 Jun 55	20 Jul 55	George Wood	01	38	41
25 Jun 55	20 Jul 55	Charles Willden	07	39	42
25 Jun 55	20 Jul 55	John Hamilton	05	39	42
25 Jun 55	20 Jul 55	John Hamilton	04	39	42
25 Jun 55	20 Jul 55	Thomas P. Smith	11	23	42
25 Jun 55	20 Jul 55	Charles P. Smith	12	23	42
25 Jun 55	20 Jul 55	John Woodhouse	10	23	42
25 Jun 55	20 Jul 55	John Gerber	01	23	42
25 Jun 55	20 Jul 55	Charles Woodhouse	09	23	43
25 Jun 55	20 Jul 55	John M. Higbee	10	25	43
25 Jun 55	20 Jul 55	Thomas Jones	08	25	43
25 Jun 55	20 Jul 55	Wm Williams	16	36	43
25 Jun 55	20 Jul 55	John McFarland	15	36	43
25 Jun 55	20 Jul 55	John Chatterly	14	36	43
25 Jun 55	20 Jul 55	Charles Simpkins	13	36	43
25 Jun 55	20 Jul 55	John Jacobs	05	36	44
25 Jun 55	20 Jul 55	Wardman Holmes	01	25	44
25 Jun 55	20 Jul 55	John Yardly	16	24	44
25 Jun 55	20 Jul 55	Samuel McMurdy	09	22	44
25 Jun 55	20 Jul 55	David Stoddard	10	22	44
25 Jun 55	20 Jul 55	Wm Bateman	15	38	44

Date Fees Paid	Date Filed	Owner of Record	Lot No.	Block No.	Page No.
25 Jun 55	20 Jul 55	James Whittaker, Jun.	13	37	44
25 Jun 55	20 Jul 55	James Whittaker, Sen.	14	37	45
25 Jun 55	20 Jul 55	Thomas Green	16	38	45
25 Jun 55	20 Jul 55	George Wood	18	38	45
25 Jun 55	20 Jul 55	Peter Nelson	09	26	45
25 Jun 55	20 Jul 55	William Thomas	02	39	45
25 Jun 55	20 Jul 55	John Urie	16	37	45
20 Jul 55[b]	20 Jul 55	John Bohn	14	38	45
25 Jun 55	20 Jul 55	John Ashworth	03	36	46
25 Jun 55	20 Jul 55	Andrew J. Stratten	02	36	46
25 Jun 55	20 Jul 55	George Perry	01	36	46
25 Jun 55	20 Jul 55	John Grawes[c]	18	35	46
25 Jun 55	20 Jul 55	James Bosnel	10	26	46
25 Jun 55	20 Jul 55	Peter Anderson	08	26	46
25 Jun 55	20 Jul 55	Comodore P. Liston	07	26	46
25 Jun 55	20 Jul 55	Crismas Rasmuson	05	26	47
25 Jun 55	20 Jul 55	George Horton	17	25	47
25 Jun 55	20 Jul 55	Wm Morgan	07	35	47
25 Jun 55	20 Jul 55	John Walker 2nd	04	26	47
25 Jun 55	20 Jul 55	Wm Davidson	05	35	47
25 Jun 55	20 Jul 55	John Smith 2nd	01	35	47
25 Jun 55	20 Jul 55	Joseph Hunter	03	35	47
25 Jun 55	20 Jul 55	Henry Lunt	15	37	48
25 Jun 55	20 Jul 55	Wm Shelton	11	36	48
25 Jun 55	20 Jul 55	Wm C. Stewart	18	37	48
25 Jun 55	20 Jul 55	John P. Jones	17	37	48
25 Jun 55	20 Jul 55	John Bradshaw	01	39	48
25 Jun 55	20 Jul 55	George Bowing[d]	04	35	48
25 Jun 55	20 Jul 55	Wm Moore	15	26	48
25 Jun 55	20 Jul 55	Samuel D. White	09	25	49
25 Jun 55	20 Jul 55	Alexander Campbell	15	35	49
25 Jun 55	20 Jul 55	Peter M. Fife	17	35	49
25 Jun 55	20 Jul 55	John Bradshaw	02	35	49
25 Jun 55	20 Jul 55	Joseph Walker	17	39	49
25 Jun 55	20 Jul 55	James Williamson	06	35	49
25 Jun 55	20 Jul 55	Robert Lathan	12	26	49
25 Jun 55	20 Jul 55	Robert Lathan	11	26	50
25 Jun 55	20 Jul 55	Catherine Chatterly	01	37	50

Date Fees Paid	Date Filed	Owner of Record	Lot No.	Block No.	Page No.
25 Jun 55	20 Jul 55	James Haslam	06	37	50
25 Jun 55	20 Jul 55	John Humphries	09	37	50
25 Jun 55	20 Jul 55	Christopher Arthur	12	37	50
25 Jun 55	20 Jul 55	Joshua Arthur	10	37	50
25 Jun 55	20 Jul 55	James Haslam	07	37	50
25 Jun 55	20 Jul 55	Samuel Bradshaw	14	35	51
25 Jun 55	20 Jul 55	Adam Fife	13	35	51
25 Jun 55	20 Jul 55	Adam Fife	12	35	51
25 Jun 55	20 Jul 55	Alexander Patterson	11	35	51
25 Jun 55	20 Jul 55	Daniel Ross	09	35	51
25 Jun 55	20 Jul 55	Philip K. Smith	10	35	51
25 Jun 55	20 Jul 55	Erasmus Hansen	04	26^e	51
25 Jun 55	20 Jul 55	John Weston	01	26	52
25 Jun 55	20 Jul 55	John Weston	02	26	52
25 Jun 55	20 Jul 55	James Haslum	08	37	52
25 Jun 55	20 Jul 55	W. W. Richards	16	25	52
25 Jun 55	20 Jul 55	Joel W. White	12	25	52
25 Jun 55	20 Jul 55	John Kay	04	37	52
25 Jun 55	20 Jul 55	Joshua T. Willis	11	25	52
25 Jun 55	20 Jul 55	George Hunter	05	37	53
25 Jun 55	20 Jul 55	John Ashworth	18	36	53
25 Jun 55	20 Jul 55	Thomas Williams	17	36	53
04 Aug 55	04 Aug 55	George P. Peay	08	35	53
04 Aug 55	04 Aug 55	Jorgen Hansen	06	26	53
04 Aug 55	06 Aug 55	George Munro	08	36	54
[transfer]	03 Jan 56	Henry L. Cook (from John Hamilton, for $5)	05	39	56
[transfer]	03 Jan 56	Brier Baugh (from James Haslum, for $10)	08	37	57
[transfer]	03 Jan 56	Henry L. Cook (from John Hamilton, for $5)	04	39	57
[transfer]	03 Jan 56	John Baugh (from James Haslum, for $30)	06	37	58
[transfer]	03 Mar 56	Isaac C. Haight & James Simpkins (from Deseret Iron Company, for $100)	01	12	66
[transfer]	31 Mar 56	John White (from John Smith 2nd, for $60)	10	23	71

Date Fees Paid	Date Filed	Owner of Record	Lot No.	Block No.	Page No.
[transfer]	31 Mar 56	[blank] Owen (from Job Rowland, for $10)	03	38	73
24 May 56	19 Jun 56	William Nish	06	25	75
24 May 56	19 Jun 56	John Jacobs	15	25	75
24 May 56	19 Jun 56	Swen Jacobs	14	25	75
24 May 56	19 Jun 56	Elliot Wilden	03	22	76
24 May 56	19 Jun 56	William Memmot	02	22	76
24 May 56	19 Jun 56	John Memmot	01	22	76
24 May 56	19 Jun 56	Charles Wilden	04	22	76
24 May 56	19 Jun 56	Wm S. Riggs	07	22	76
24 May 56	19 Jun 56	William Sansberry	12	22	76
24 May 56	19 Jun 56	John Gerber	11	22	76
24 May 56	19 Jun 56	Thomas Walker	13	22	76
24 May 56	19 Jun 56	Nephi Johnson	13	25	77
24 May 56	19 Jun 56	John Stoddard	07	25	77
24 May 56	19 Jun 56	Seth Dodge	04	25	77
24 May 56	19 Jun 56	Robert Nish	05	25	77
24 May 56	19 Jun 56	John Gerber	01	23	77
24 May 56	19 Jun 56	John Sherret	03	24	77
24 May 56	19 Jun 56	Thomas Crowther	06	24	78
24 May 56	19 Jun 56	John Weston	07	24	78
24 May 56	19 Jun 56	John Weston	08	24	78
24 May 56	19 Jun 56	Erasmus Nickerson	17	24	78
24 May 56	19 Jun 56	Seth Dodge	03	25	78
[transfer]	20 Oct 56	John Groves (from Joseph Hunter, for $13.50)	03	35	80
04 Mar 57	05 Mar 57	Philip K. Smith	11	22[f]	93
23 Mar 57	22 Apr 57	Jehiel McConnell	17	26	94
23 Mar 57	22 Apr 57	Benjamin Smith	18	25	94
23 Mar 57	22 Apr 57	John Jacobs	15	25	94
23 Mar 57	22 Apr 57	Daniel Huchinson	17	38	95
23 Mar 57	22 Apr 57	Robert Easton	06	25	95
23 Mar 57	22 Apr 57	George A. McConnel	16	26	95
23 Mar 57	22 Apr 57	Swen Jacobs	14	25	95
23 Mar 57	22 Apr 57	Nephi Johnson	13	25	95
23 Mar 57	22 Apr 57	John Bradshaw	03	25	95
23 Mar 57	22 Apr 57	Robert Nish	05	25	95
23 Mar 57	22 Apr 57	John Sherrett	03	24	96

Date Fees Paid	Date Filed	Owner of Record	Lot No.	Block No.	Page No.
23 Mar 57	22 Apr 57	John Muir	07	24	96
23 Mar 57	22 Apr 57	David D. Bowen	08	24	96
23 Mar 57	22 Apr 57	Rasmus Nicklason	17	24	96
23 Mar 57	22 Apr 57	Thomas Crowther	05	23	96
23 Mar 57	22 Apr 57	Geo. Corey	08	23	96
23 Mar 57	22 Apr 57	Robert Easton	07	25	96
23 Mar 57	22 Apr 57	Wm Thomas	01	24	97
23 Mar 57	22 Apr 57	Wm S. Riggs	07	23	97
23 Mar 57	22 Apr 57	Deseret Iron Company	11	37	97
23 Mar 57	22 Apr 57	Philip K. Smith	03	26	97
23 Mar 57	22 Apr 57	John Weston	11	38	97
02 Aug 57	25 Aug 57	Jonathan Pugmire	11	33	101
02 Aug 57	25 Aug 57	John Woodhouse	06	34	101
02 Aug 57	25 Aug 57	Samuel Pollock	02	34	101
02 Aug 57	25 Aug 57	Samuel Pollock	03	34	101
02 Aug 57	25 Aug 57	Wm S. Riggs	05	34	101
02 Aug 57	25 Aug 57	Richard Birkbeck	12	34	102
02 Aug 57	25 Aug 57	Jesse B. Lewis	07	34	102
02 Aug 57	25 Aug 57	James Simpkins	08	34	102
02 Aug 57	25 Aug 57	John Morris	11	34	102
02 Aug 57	25 Aug 57	Josiah Reaves	04	34	102
02 Aug 57	25 Aug 57	John Sherrett	14	34	102
02 Aug 57	25 Aug 57	Thomas Cartwright	10	34	103
02 Aug 57	25 Aug 57	James Bosnell	09	33	103
02 Aug 57	25 Aug 57	James Bosnell	10	33	103
02 Aug 57	25 Aug 57	James Bullock	16	34	103
02 Aug 57	25 Aug 57	James Williamson Jun.	15	34	103
02 Aug 57	25 Aug 57	Christopher Arthur Sen.	13	34	103
02 Aug 57	25 Aug 57	John P. Jones	08	33	104
02 Aug 57	25 Aug 57	David Stoddard	17	34	104
02 Aug 57	25 Aug 57	David Stoddard	18	34	104
02 Aug 57	25 Aug 57	Charles Hopkins	02	33	104
02 Aug 57	25 Aug 57	Charles Hopkins	03	33	104
02 Aug 57	25 Aug 57	Samuel Jackson	11	27	104
02 Aug 57	25 Aug 57	Thomas Harwood	10	27	104
02 Aug 57	25 Aug 57	Samuel Jewkes	07	33	105
02 Aug 57	25 Aug 57	John Stoddard	01	34	105
02 Aug 57	25 Aug 57	John White	11	28	105

Date Fees Paid	Date Filed	Owner of Record	Lot No.	Block No.	Page No.
02 Aug 57	25 Aug 57	John White	12	28	105
02 Aug 57	25 Aug 57	William Bateman	01	33	105
02 Aug 57	25 Aug 57	William Bateman	18	33	105
02 Aug 57	25 Aug 57	Daniel McFarland	12	33	105

Notes

a. Block number inadvertently omitted in original entry.

b. As the many entries before and after this all bear a 25 Jun 55 fee date, this is probably an unintentional duplication of the filing date.

c. Possibly "John Groves" or "John Greaves" with an inadvertent extra minim on the *v*, creating the appearance of a *w*.

d. Presumably an incomplete spelling of "Bowering."

e. The lot and block numbers on this entry are identical to those on the entry of John Walker 2nd (Deed Book B, p. 47, 4). A missing transfer between the men is possible, but a miswritten lot or block number is more likely.

f. This entry records the same lot and block as that allocated a year earlier to John Gerber (Deed Book B, p. 76, 7), identical to the problem referred to in the note just above.

Appendix 11

Utah Territorial Militia (Nauvoo Legion): 10th Regiment Battalion and Company Muster Rolls

10 October 1857

This appendix reconstructs the original muster of Oct 1857, once owned by Daniel H. Wells, now housed in the Utah State Archives and Records Service. Taken just a month after the Mountain Meadows Massacre, the tally provides an effective census of much of the male population of the region. Original spelling has been retained, even if other sources use more familiar forms. Faded ink and unclear penmanship make some readings difficult. In the few truly doubtful cases, dashes and/or question marks within brackets are used. If first names appear as initials but the person is well documented elsewhere, the full Christian name appears in brackets; likewise, if an abbreviated form is likely to confuse, it is expanded within brackets. Standard superscriptions used here include:

Alex^r, Ale^r	Alexander	Ja^s	James
Chas, Ch^s	Charles	Rich^d, Richr^d	Richard
Chris^r, Christ^r, Chrs^t	Christopher	Robt	Robert
D^d	David	Saml, Sm^l	Samuel
D^l	Daniel	Thos	Thomas
Edwd	Edward	W^m	William
Hez^h	Hezekiah		

REGIMENTAL STAFF, PAROWAN
William H. Dame, Col.
Commander James H. Martineau, Adjt
Calvin C. Pendleton, Surgeon
James H. Haslam, Pvt., Music

1ST BATTALION, PAROWAN
James Lewis, Major
Zechariah B. Decker, Adjt.

Company A, Beaver
Philo T. Farnsworth, Capt.
Ross R. Rogers, Adj.
Joseph Gough, Fifer
John Bohn, Drummer

Company B, Parowan
S[ilas] S. Smith, Capt.
David Cluff, Adj.
Thomas Durham, Fifer
James McGuffie, Drummer

Company C, Parowan
Jesse N. Smith, Capt.
Wm Adams, Adjt.
Morgan Richards, Fifer
Wm C. Mitchael, Drummer

2ND BATTALION, CEDAR CITY
Isaac C. Haight, Major
John M. Macfarlane, Adjt.

Company D, Cedar City
Joel W. White, Captain
Daniel S. Macfalane, Adjt.
James H. Haslum, Fifer
James Whittaker, Drummer

Company E, Cedar City
Elias Morris, Captain
Richd V. Morris, Adjt.

3RD BATTALION, CEDAR CITY
John M. Higbee, Major
John Urie, Adjt.

Company F, Cedar City
Wm Taite, Captain
John Woodhouse, Adjt.
John S. Humphries, Fifer
David Stoddart, Drummer

Company G, Cedar City
Eliezar Edwards, Capt.
Christopher J. Arthur, Adjt.
James Timmins, Fifer
John Stodart, Drummer

4TH BATTALION, FORT HARMONY
John D. Lee, Major
W. R. Davis, Adjt.

Company H, New Harmony
Alexander G. Ingram, Capt.
J[ohn] R. Davies, Adjt.

Derius Shirts, Fifer
Jno. [John] Alma Lee, Drumr
Company I, Washington
Harrison Pearce, Capt.
George Spencer, Adjt.
John M. Adair, Fifer
Alfred [-]. Johnson, Drummer

Company A, Beaver
First Platoon
E[dward] W. Thompson, 2nd Lt.
Joseph Betterson, Sgt.
Privates
    Elisher Hoops
    Mathew McEwen
    James Farrer
    Robert Thimbleby
    S[imeon] F. Howd
    Joseph Hoops
    John Morgan
    John Bough
Second Platoon
Seth Dodge, 2nd Lt.
Graham Douglass, Sgt.
Privates:
Andrew Patterson
    John M. Davis
    William O. Shelton
    Samuel Kershaw
    Thomas Green
    William Greenwood
    John Ashworth
    Robert Patterson
Third Platoon
James Low, 2nd Lt.
Charles C. Woodhouse, Sgt.
Privates:
    James P. Anderson
    Orson Tylor
    Robert Kershaw
    William Evans
    John Yardley

James Adams
John Knowles
W[ilson] G. Nowers
Fourth Platoon
James Duke, 2nd Lt.
David B. Adams, Sgt.
Privates:
  Dennis Nelsen
  Benjamin Worldly

Company B, Parowan
First Platoon
J[oseph] P. Barton, 2nd Lt.
S[tephen] S. Barton, Sgt.
Privates:
  O[rson] B. Adams
  W[illiam] E. Jones
  J. Prothero
  B[enjamin] Watts
  J. S. Barton
  Wm Roberts
  H. M. Alexander
  John Adams
Second Platoon
J[ob] P[itcher] Hall, 2nd Lt.
J. R. Roberson, Sgt.
Privates:
  M[arius] Ensign
  J[ohn] Topham
  W. E. A. Roberts
  H[ans] Y. Mortensen
  J[ames] Williamson
  Wm Williamson
Third Platoon
S[amuel] H. Rogers, 2nd Lt.
T[homas] Davenport, Sgt.
Privates:
  U[rban] V. Stewart
  L[orenzo] Barton
  W[illiam] C. Mcgregor
  H[erman] D. Bayles
  U[riah] R. Butt

Wm Holyoak
A. S. Hadden
Fourth Platoon
C[harles] Y. Webb, 2nd Lt.
J[ohn] S. Hyatt, Sgt.
Privates:
  S[idney] R[igdon] Burton
  J[ames] Guymon
  L. Guymon
  E[lijah] Newman
  J[enkin] Evans
  T[homas] Evans
  H[enry] Holyoak
Fifth Platoon
C[harles] Hall, 2nd Lt.
S[ilas] Hoyt, Sgt.
Privates:
  John Eyre
  Wm Talbot
  J. Nelson
  A[nders] Y. Mortenson
  A. Smith
  J. Smith
  J[ames] McGuffie Sen.
  Rubin Carter

Company C, Parowan
First Platoon
Edwd Dalton, 2nd Lt.
Samuel Lewis, Sgt.
Privates:
  Barnabus Carter
  Chas Carter
  Atha Carter
  Beason Lewis
  John H. Henderson
  Thos Lafevre
  Ja^s H. Dunton
  Chas Adams
Second Platoon
John Steele, 2nd Lt.
Wm Leany, Sgt.

Privates:

    Charles Okey

    Wm Devinport

    Joseph Fish

    Wm M. West

    David Ward

    Wm Lafevre

    John Gould

Third Platoon

Wm Barton, 2nd Lt.

Saml West, Sgt.

Privates:

    Tarlton Lewis

    Wm Carter

    John Carter

    David Carter

    Paul Smith

    Jesse Louder

    Geo. Holyoak

    Edwd Harbour

Fourth Platoon

F[rancis] T. Whitney, 2nd Lt.

Luke Ford, Sgt.

Privates:

    Andrew Baston

    Saml Gould

    John Wardell

    Jacob West

    Edwd Ward

    Wm Row

    Wm H. Asten

    Edwin Knott

Fifth Platoon

Elijah Elmore, 2nd Lt.

N[elson] S. Hollinghead, Sgt.

Privates:

    Geo. Holyoak Jun.

    Morgan Jinkins

    Predy Meeks

    James Woods

    M. Anderson[1]

    Wm Anderson

    J. Roley

    Horice Fish

Company D, Cedar City

First Platoon

Robert Lathem, 2nd Lt.

George Hunter, Sgt.

Privates:

    Philip K. Smith

    James Whittaker Sen[i]or

    John Morris [Senior]

    Charles C. Hopkins

    James Williamson

    Charles Lord

    Samuel W. White

    George Sant

Second Platoon

Nephi Johnson, 2nd Lt.

Seth Johnson, Sgt.

Privates:

    Labin Morriel

    James Dalley

    William Dalley

    James Bay

    Joseph Pugmire

    Alex^r Orton

    Samuel Orton

    Thomas Smith

Third Platoon

Jehiel McConnel, 2nd Lt.

[-----] McConnel, Sgt.

Privates:

    George McConnel

    Soloman Chamberlin

    Thomas Hunt

    Alva Benson

    William Hunter

    Chrs^t Arthur Senr.

    Peter Nelson

    Robert McMurdy

Fourth Platoon

George Wood, 2nd Lt.

Ben[ji]man Arthur, Sgt.

Privates:

    Thomas Cartwright

    Morton Chartley

David Savage
John Owens
Briah Baugh
Thimothy Adams
Alexander Campbell
James Corlet

Fifth Platoon
Pery C. Liston, 2nd Lt.[2]
Thomas Thorley, Sgt.
Privates:
William More
John V. Adams
Peter Adams
John Kays
Hez[h] Simpkins
Joseph Hunter
William Hunter
David Muir

Company E, Cedar City
First Platoon
E[zra] H. Curtis, 2nd Lt.
Sam[l] Pollock, Sgt.
Privates:
W[m] Riggs
W[m] Williams
Tho[s] Harwood
Jabez Durfie
Thomas Williams
Joseph Simpkins
John Memmott

Second Platoon
A[nthony] J. Stratton, 2nd Lt.
Sam[l] McMurdie, Sgt.
Privates:
Sam[l] Jewkes
John Key
Thomas Collett
W[m] H. Bateman
James Wiley
Sam[l] Baugh

Third Platoon
Rich[d] Harrison, 2nd Lt.

Rob[t] Wiley, Sgt.
Privates:
Rich[d] Smith
John X. Smith
John Parry Sen[r]
J[ames] W. Bosnell
Tho[s] T. Willis
R[ichard] R. Birkbeck
Jonathan Pugmire
Peter Mackleprang

Fourth Platoon
Sween Jacobs, 2nd Lt.
Josuah Arthur, Sgt.
Privates:
Chris[r] Jacobs
John Jacobs
Christ[r] Rasmuson
George Hanson
Rasmus Mickleson
Bank [Bengt] Nelson
Hyrum Davidson

Fifth Platoon
Ira Allen, 2nd Lt.
Andrew Allen, Sgt.
Privates:
Simeon Allen
Tho[s] Jones
Jos. [Joseph] Bohn
Yence Anderson
Alwise Bower
Moroni Benson
Sam[l] Woods
Joseph Woods

Company F, Cedar City
First Platoon
W[m] C. Stuart, 2nd Lt.
John Western, Sgt.
Privates:
Ja[s] Simpkins
Wardman Holms
John Groves
Thos. Crowther

John Chaterly
Daniel D. Cook
Joseph H. Smith
Joseph Clews

Second Platoon
Andrew S. Gibbons, 2nd Lt.
George K. Bowering, Sgt.
Privates:
    Erasmus Hanson
    John Muir
    David D. Bowen
    George Perry
    Wm Morgan
    David Hutchinson
    Ch^s Chamberlain

Third Platoon
Joshua T. Willis, 2nd Lt.
Ale^r H. Loveridge, Sgt.
Privates:
    Henry L. Cook
    Wm Middleton
    Jessie B. Lewis
    Ja^s Williamson Jn^r
    John Middleton
    Thos Campbell
    Ch$^{[s]}$ Wilden Jn^r
    Wm Smith

Fourth Platoon
Martin Slack, 2nd Lt.
Francis Webster, Sgt.
Privates:
    Wm Lapworth
    Saml Bradshaw
    John Bradshaw
    Wm Treehorn
    Ellott Wilden
    Wm Haslam
    Saml. Jackson

Fifth Platoon
John Hamilton Jn^r, 2nd Lt.
Saml L. Hamilton, Sgt.
Privates:
    John Hamilton Sn^r

John Hunter
Wm Hunter Jn^r
Pieter Jenson

Company G, Cedar City
First Platoon
John H. Willis, 2nd Lt.
Henry Higgins, Sgt.
Privates:
    John White
    Josiah Reeves
    Lemuel Willis
    David Williams
    Evan Owens
    John Harris
    Benjamin [?Ro]wland
    David Morgan

Second Platoon
Samuel Leigh, 2nd Lt.
George Horton, Sgt.
Privates:
    George Munro
    William Thomas
    William W. Richards

Third Platoon
John P. Jones, 2nd Lt.
D^l Simpkins, Sgt.
Privates:
    Thomas Gower
    Benjamin Smith
    William Walker
    John S. Walker
    Joseph Walker
    John Lee Jones
    Charles Simpkins Jun.

Fourth Platoon
Peter M. Fife, 2nd Lt.
William Bateman, Sgt.
Privates:
    Chas. Wilden Sen.
    Fergus Wilden
    Thomas Muir
    Robert Easton

John Wilden
Chas. P. Smith
Robert Bullock

Fifth Platoon
Wm W. Willis, 2nd Lt.
George Coray, Sgt.
Privates:
James Bullock
Jno. Bradshaw Sen.
Henry Helliker[3]
William Davidson
Joseph Hunter
Thos Willis

Company H, New Harmony
First Platoon
Jacob Hamblin, 2nd Lt.
Thales H. Haskell, Sgt.
Privates:
R[ufus] C. Allen
Dudly Levatt
Thos Eccles
Prime Colman
Ira Hatch
D^d Tullis
Lemuel Levitt
Duane Hamblin

Second Platoon
Oscar Hamblin, 2nd Lt.
Z[adok] K[napp] Judd, Sgt.
Privates:
Sm^l Knight
Francis Hamblin
Jeremiah Lovett
Fredrick Hamblin

Third Platoon
Richr^d Robinson, 2nd Lt.
A. G. Thornton, Sgt.
Privates:
Benj. Knell
Benj. R. Hults
Rob[er]t Dickson
Lemuel Lee

George Williams
Joseph Littlefield

Fourth Platoon
Don Carlos Shirts, 2nd Lt.
Sm^l E. Groves, Sgt.
Privates:
Benj. Platt
Thos Riddle
Isaac Riddle
Sydney Littlefield

Fifth Platoon
Henry Barney, 2nd Lt.
Jas. G. Davies, Sgt.
Privates:
E[lisha] H. Groves
Waldo Littlefield
Gilbert Morse
Peter Shirts
Robert Richey
John Blackburn

Company I, Washington
First Platoon
Robert L. Lloyd, 2nd Lt.
Louis L. Matheney, Sgt.
Privates:
Robert D. Covington
John Couch
John M. Couch
William Duggin
Jonathan B. Regan
Joseph Smith
Baylus E. Sprouse
William Free[man?]

Second Platoon
James H. Mathews, 2nd Lt.
William T. Hawley, Sgt.
Privates:
Thomas Adair
James Adair
William W. Da[----]
Stephen Duggins
James A. Mowery

James D. Mccullough
John Garber
Lewis Gerber

Third Platoon
John W. Freeman, 2nd Lt.
William Slade, Sgt.
Privates:
    John Freeman
    John W. Clark
    Elijah A. Sprouse
    Leborn[?] Sp[---]
    Thomas Smith
    Jefferson Slade
    William R. Slade
    John Price

Fourth Platoon
John P. Thomas, 2nd Lt.
George Hawley, Sgt.
Privates:
    John M. Adair
    Samuel Adair
    Samuel N[ewton] Adair
    William H[inton] Crawford
    Joshua Holden
    James M. Mangum
    John Mangum
    Alfred T. Johnson

Fifth Platoon
Gabriel B. Coley, 2nd Lt.
John Hawly, Sgt.
Privates:
    George W. Adair
    Joseph Adair
    James Elsworth

Evan Edderts[?]
Jabus Nordin[?]
James Pearce
Umpstead Rencher
Oscar Tyler

Sixth Platoon
Sixth Platoon 2nd Lt.
Joseph Hadfield, Sgt.
Privates:
    Willis Young
    Thomas Clark
    Enos Dodge
    Thomas J. Pearce
    Joshua Neale [Meade?]
    William Y. Young

Notes

1. A "Morton" Anderson appears in Company C of the Parowan muster rolls of 1852; however, since there are also references to a "Miles" Anderson in contemporary sources, "M. Anderson" could refer to either man.

2. Numerous contemporary references confirm that this entry refers to "Commodore Perry" Liston.

3. This is a variant of "Heinrich Elliker," brother of Philip Klingensmith's plural wife, Margarethe. Their father, Heinrich Sr., died of cholera on the passage west (as did several siblings), so the reference can only be to the son.

Bibliography

List of abbreviations used in this bibliography follow:

Cedar City Library:	Historical Collection, Cedar City Public Library, Cedar City, Utah.
Iron County:	Iron County Records, Iron County Recorder's Office, Parowan, Utah.
LDS Church Archives:	Archives Division, Historical Department, The Church of Jesus Christ of Latter-day Saints, Salt Lake City.
Perry Special Collections:	L. Tom Perry Special Collections, Harold B. Lee Library, Brigham Young University, Provo, Utah.
Sherratt Library:	Special Collections, Gerald R. Sherratt Library, Southern Utah University. The William R. Palmer Collection, within Special Collections, is frequently cited herein. Entries from the Special Collections at large will be cited as "Sherratt Library"; entries within the Palmer Collection will be cited as "Palmer Collection."
Utah State Archives:	Utah State Archives and Records Service, Salt Lake City.

PRIMARY SOURCES

Corporate Documents

Deseret Iron Company. Untitled account book, Apr–Sep 1854. LDS Church Archives.

———. Journal, 6 Sep 1854–5 Jan 1867. Sherratt Library. In microfilm collection, see "Daughters of Utah Pioneers No. 1402, Deseret Iron Company Financial Ledgers, 1854–1869."

———. Minutes. Original in LDS Church Archives; typescript in Palmer Collection.

Deseret Iron Company. Miscellaneous Documents. Palmer Collection. Includes: "Articles of Incorporation, 1852"; Charles Jordan to Erastus Snow, undated letter (ca. 1852); Charles Jordan to "Dear Sir," 27 Apr 1852; "Design of a Blowing Machine and Framing for the Same," ca. 1852 (misdated "1854" by penciled notation); Erastus Snow and Franklin D. Richards to Vincent Shurtleff, 1 May 1852; Erastus Snow and Franklin D. Richards, to "Beloved Brethren of the Deseret Iron Company," 8 May 1852; James Bulloch, shipping list, Salt Lake to Coal Creek, Nov 1852; Bill of Sale, 30 Nov 1852; Share Register, 1853, holograph, Book A; "Invoice of Goods for Iron County, No. 1," 28 Feb 1853; "Snow & Richards, Invoice No. 2, Deseret Iron Co.," Mar 1853; misc. receipts, Jun 1853; Ledger, 1853–1854; "Furnace Account, Cost of Erecting, from 30 May to 16 Sep, 1854"; Inventory, 16 Sep 1854.

Iron Works Account Book. Dec 1851–Nov 1852. Palmer Collection.

Journals, Diaries and Biographies

Ashworth, William. "Autobiography." 2 vols. Bound typescript. Perry Special Collections.

Bowering, George K. Journal. Original in possession of Bernon Auger, Salt Lake City. Copy in LDS Church Archives (restricted by family).

Dame, William. "Journal of William H. Dame to Iron Co. Utah, 1850–59." Sherratt Library.

"Diary of Richard Harrison, 1838–1867." Bound typescript. Perry Special Collections.

"Extracts from the Journal of John Steele." *Utah Historical Quarterly* 6 (Jan 1933): 2–28.

Fish, Joseph. "Journal of Joseph Fish." Bound typescript. Perry Special Collections.

Haight, Isaac C. Journal. Part 1: 7 Jun 1842–Aug 1852; Part 2: 9 Aug 1852–Jan 1862. Original in possession of Herbert Haight, Cedar City, Utah. Typescript copy in Sherratt Library.

"Journal of George A. Smith, President of the Iron County Mission." Vol. 1 (7 Dec 1850–7 Apr 1851) and vol. 2 (8 Apr 1851–ca. 18 Nov 1851). LDS Church Archives.

"The Journal of Samuel Holister Rogers." 2 vols. Perry Special Collections.

Lee, John D. "Journal of the Iron Co. Mission." Original in LDS Church Archives. Published as "Journal of the Iron County Mission, John D. Lee, Clerk, December 10, 1850–March 1, 1851." Gustive O. Larson, ed. *Utah Historical Quarterly* 20 (Apr 1952): 109–34; (Aug 1952): 253–82; (Oct 1952): 353–83.

Liston, Commodore Perry. Autobiography, 1821–1879. Typescript. Perry Special Collections.

Lunt, Vern, and Rachel Petty Lunt, comps. *Life of Henry Lunt and Family, Together with a Portion of His Diary.* Original in possession of Paul Lunt, Cedar City, Utah. Typescript in Perry Special Collections.

Morris, Elias. Diary. Palmer Collection.

Nelson, Bengt, Sr. *Autobiography of Bengt Nelson Sr.* N.p.: privately printed, ca. 1910. Copy in Perry Special Collections.

Pratt, Parley P., Jr., ed. *The Autobiography of Parley P. Pratt.* 4th ed. Salt Lake City: Deseret Book, 1985.

Richards, Franklin D. Journal. "May 1852 and Onward." LDS Church Archives.

Whipple, Edson. Journal. Typescript. Perry Special Collections.

Whittaker, James, Sr. Journal. Occasional entries by James Jr. Sherratt Library.

Family and Local Histories

Baker, Edith L. *Tales of the Fore-Bears* [Woolf family history]. Bountiful, Utah: privately published, 1989.

"Biography of Chapman Duncan: 1812–1900." In "Mormon Diaries," Perry Special Collections.

Bulloch, David. "Life Sketch of David Bulloch." Typescript. Cedar City Library.

Chatterley, John. "History of Cedar City." Undated typescript. Cedar City Library.

———. Unsourced, undated list of Cedar Fort pioneers. Cedar City Library.

Fish, Joseph. "History of Enterprise." Typescript. Perry Special Collections.

Hancock, Jennie Jensen. "Biography of Charles Willden, 1806–1883." Unpublished typescript in family records of Ronald Payne, Spanish Fork, Utah, and Sharon Rae Payne, Salt Lake City. Similar version, "History and Diary of Charles Willden Sr.," in Palmer Collection.

"Iron Mission Record." 1850–59. Working title assigned by Morris Shirts to hand-written MS (anonymous, undated, unpaginated, untitled and missing front page[s]). LDS Church Archives.

"James H. Martineau Record, Parowan, Utah." 1855–1860. Palmer Collection.

Jarvis, Zora Smith. *Ancestry, Biography, and Family of George A. Smith.* Provo, Utah: Brigham Young University Press, 1962.

Jenson, Andrew. "Parowan Ward History, 1849–1900." Microfilm of typescript. Sherratt Library.

———. "Manuscript History of Cedar City Ward." LDS Church Archives.

John Anthony Woolf Family Life Histories: John Anthony Woolf and Sarah Ann Devoe, Their Children and Grandchildren. Salt Lake City: Woolf Family Organization, 1965.

"John Calvin Lazell [*sic*] Smith." Unattributed family history. Typescript. Palmer Collection.

Jones, Evelyn K. *Henry Lunt: Biography and History of the Development of Southern*

Utah and Settling of Colonia Pacheco, Mexico. Provo, Utah: Privately printed, 1996.

Jones, John Lee. "Biography of John Lee Jones: Principal Residences: Cedar City and Enoch, Utah; Mission to England." Bound typescript. Perry Special Collections.

"History of John Calvin Lazelle Smith." Unpublished family history, comp. 1959, expanded 1975, by great-granddaughter Helen Thurber Dalton. Copy in Shirts Collection, Perry Special Collections.

Macfarlane, Kate Palmer. "Facts Furnished by David Bulloch concerning Settlement of Cedar City. Dictated by David Bulloch January 25, 1920. . . Recorded by Kate Palmer Macfarlane." Palmer Collection.

Martineau, James H., as Stake Historian. Parowan Stake Minutes, 11 Aug 1859 to 13 Feb 1860. Microfilm Collection, LDS Church Family History Library, Salt Lake City.

A Memory Bank for Paragonah. Compiled by the Betsy Topham Camp, Daughters of Utah Pioneers (Paragonah). Provo, Utah: Community Press, 1990.

Millett, Joseph. "Brief Account of Artemus Millett & Family." Holograph in possession of Nanon (Mrs. John Reed) Corry, Cedar City, Utah. Copies in Sherratt Library and Perry Special Collections.

"Minutes of First Cedar Stake and High Council (1855–56). Original." Palmer Collection.

"Minutes of Teachers Meeting—First Division of Cedar Ward (1860)." Palmer Collection.

Palmer, William R. "First Forts at Cedar City, as told by David Bulloch." Palmer Collection.

———. "Gleanings." Palmer Collection.

———. "History of Joseph Walker and Sons." Palmer Collection.

Tennant, Thomas. Estate Papers. Filed under Utah District Court (Salt Lake County): "Probate Records, Estates and Guardianship, 1852–1910: An Index to Book A through F." LDS Church Family History Library, Salt Lake City.

Urie, John. "Early History of Cedar City and Vicinity." Multiple versions of this document exist: four, respectively, in Cedar City Library; Utah State Historical Society; Palmer Collection and Perry Special Collections. Fifth, the key quotation appears in Andrew Jenson's "Manuscript History of Cedar City." Sixth, a version appears in Kate Carter, *Our Pioneer Heritage;* seventh, another in Evelyn K. Jones and York F. Jones, *Mayors of Cedar City;* and eighth, another in Evelyn Jones, *Henry Lunt Biography.*

Willden, Feargus O'Connor, sources: see "compiled information file" on Willden family in LDS Church Archives (material donated 1957 by Ione Thompson, West Valley City, Utah). A sheet of notes made by William Palmer, entitled "Extracts of Biography of Feargus O'Connor Willden Written by Himself" in Palmer Collection. Copies of unpublished "Biography of Feargus O'Connor Willden" in family records of Ronald Payne, Spanish Fork, Utah, and Sharon Rae Payne, Salt Lake City.

Public Records

Brewer, Charles, Assistant Surgeon. Official Report to Reuben Campbell, 6 May 1859. 36th Cong. 1st Sess., 1860. S. Ex. Doc. 42.

Campbell, Reuben P., Capt. Interim report to F. J. Porter, 30 Apr 1859. 36th Cong. 1st Sess., 1860. S. Ex. Doc. 42.

Carleton, James H. Carleton, Brevet Major. Special Report to W. W. Mackall, Asst. Adj. Gen., 25 May 1859. 57th Cong. 1st Sess., 1902. H. Doc. 605.

Dame, William. "Coal Creek Survey Iron Co. U. T. [Utah Territory], 1853–4." Old Survey Book. Iron County.

Deed Book A (7 Feb 1851–28 Feb 1855); Deed Book B (28 Feb 1855–15 Sep 1863); Deed Book D (12 Aug 1863–16 Sep 1874). Iron County.

Laws and Ordinances of the State of Deseret (Utah). Compilation 1851, Salt Lake City: Shepard Book, 1919. Microfilm copy, Utah State Archives.

Martineau, James H. 1881 Survey, Township 36 South, Range 10 West. General Land Office, Bureau of Land Management, Cedar City, Utah.

Mining Location Notices. Book A. Iron County.

"Petition of Cedar City Residents." 12 Nov 1853. Doc. no. 1815. Utah State Archives.

Shirts, Morris A. "Summary of Ordinances, Cedar City, 1853–1856." Typescript. Sheratt Library.

Territorial Acts and Resolutions Passed at the Second Annual Session of the Legislative Assembly of the Territory of Utah. Great Salt Lake City, George Hales, Printer, 1853. In Register of the Laws of the State of Utah, 1851–. Microfilm in Utah State Archives.

Territorial Militia Muster Rolls (1851–1867). Iron County. Doc. no. 3285 and no. 3287, acct. no. 014279. Utah State Archives.

Territorial Militia Records. William H. Dame to Daniel H. Wells, 23 Aug 1857. Microfilm. Utah State Archives.

Zabriskie, George O., and Dorothy Louise Robinson. "U.S. Census for Utah, 1851." *Utah Genealogical Magazine* 29 (Apr 1938): 65–72; (Jul 1938): 130–42. Original in Census Bureau, Washington, D.C., as "U.S. Federal Census, 1850, Utah . . ." Copy in LDS Church Family History Library, Salt Lake City.

Secondary Sources

Books and Theses

Anderson, Nels. *Desert Saints: The Mormon Frontier in Utah.* 2nd ed. Chicago: University of Chicago Press, 1966.

Arrington, Leonard J. *Brigham Young: American Moses.* New York: Alfred A. Knopf, 1985.

———. *Charles C. Rich: Mormon General and Western Frontiersman.* Provo, Utah: Brigham Young University Press, 1974.

———. *Great Basin Kingdom: Economic History of the Latter-Day Saints, 1830–1900.* Lincoln: University of Nebraska Press, 1968.

Baugh, Alexander L. *A Call to Arms: The 1838 Mormon Defense of Northern Missouri.* Dissertations in Latter-day Saint History. Provo, Utah: Joseph Fielding Smith Institute for Latter-day Saint History and BYU Studies, 2000.

Britsch, R. Lanier. *Unto the Islands of the Sea: A History of the Latter-day Saints in the Pacific.* Salt Lake City: Deseret Book, 1986.

Brooks, Juanita. *John Doyle Lee: Zealot, Pioneer Builder, Scapegoat.* Glendale, Calif.: Arthur H. Clark, 1962.

———. *Mountain Meadows Massacre.* Norman: University of Oklahoma Press, 1974.

Campbell, Eugene E. *Establishing Zion: The Mormon Church in the American West, 1847–1869.* Salt Lake City: Signature Books, 1988.

Carter, Kate B., comp. *Our Pioneer Heritage.* 20 vols. Salt Lake City: Daughters of Utah Pioneers, 1958-77.

Carvalho, Solomon. *Incidents of Travel and Adventure in the Far West with Col. Frémont's Expedition.* New York: Derby and Jackson, 1857.

Cleland, Robert Glass, and Juanita Brooks, eds. *A Mormon Chronicle: The Diaries of John D. Lee, 1848–1876.* 2 vols. San Marino, Calif: Huntington Library, 1955. Reprint, Salt Lake City: University of Utah Press, 1983.

Crook, John G. "The Development of Early Industry and Trade in Utah." Master's thesis, University of Utah, 1926.

Dalton, Luella Adams. *History of the Iron County Mission, Parowan, Utah.* Parowan, Utah: Privately published, 1970.

Day, Stella H., and Sebrina C. Ekins, comps. *Milestones of Millard: 100 Years of History of Millard County 1851–1951.* Springville, Utah: Art City Publishing, for Millard County Daughters of Utah Pioneers, 1951.

Dixon, Madoline Cloward. *Peteetneet Town: A History of Payson, Utah.* Provo, Utah: Press Publishing, 1974.

Ellsworth, S. George. *The Journals of Addison Pratt.* Salt Lake City: University of Utah Press, 1990.

Fish, Rick J. "The Southern Utah Expedition of Parley P. Pratt, 1849–1850." Master's thesis, Brigham Young University, 1992.

Furniss, Norman F. *The Mormon Conflict, 1850–59.* New Haven: Yale University Press, 1960.

Hafen, LeRoy R., and Ann W. Hafen. *Old Spanish Trail: Santa Fe to Los Angeles.* Vol. 1 of The Far West and the Rockies Historical Series, 1820–1875. Glendale, Calif.: Arthur H. Clark, 1954.

———, eds. *Central Route to the Pacific.* Vol. 7 of The Far West and the Rockies Historical Series, 1820–1875. Glendale, Calif.: Arthur H. Clark, 1957. Reprint of Gwinn Harris Heap and E. F. Beale, and others, *Central Route to the Pacific from the Valley of the Missouri to California, 1853.* Philadelphia: Lippincott, Grambo, 1854.

———. *Journals of Forty Niners—Salt Lake to Los Angeles.* Vol. 2 of The Far West and the Rockies Historical Series, 1820–1875. Glendale, Calif.: Arthur H. Clark, 1954.

———. *The Utah Expedition: 1857–1858.* Vol 8 of The Far West and the Rockies Historical Series, 1820–1875. Glendale, Calif.: Arthur H. Clark, 1958.

Hansen, Ralph. "Administrative History of the Nauvoo Legion in Utah." Master's thesis, Brigham Young University, 1954.

Johnson, Clark V., ed. *Mormon Redress Petitions, Documents of the 1833–1838 Missouri Conflict.* Provo, Utah: Religious Studies Center, 1992.

Jones, Evelyn K., and York F. Jones. *Mayors of Cedar City and Histories of Cedar City.* Cedar City: Southern Utah State College, 1986.

Knecht, William L., and Peter L. Crawley. *Early Records of Utah: History of Brigham Young, 1857–1867.* Berkeley, Calif.: MassCal Associates, 1964.

Larson, Andrew Karl. *Erastus Snow: The Life of a Missionary and Pioneer for the Early Mormon Church.* Salt Lake City: University of Utah Press, 1971.

Larson, Gustive O. *Cedar City: Gateway to Rainbow Land.* Cedar City, Utah: privately printed, 1950.

Lyman, Edward Leo. *San Bernardino: The Rise and Fall of a California Community.* Salt Lake City: Signature Books, 1996.

Macdonald, Graham D., III. *The Magnet: Iron Ore in Iron Co. Utah.* N.p.: Privately published, 1990.

Neff, Andrew L. *History of Utah: 1847–1869.* Salt Lake City: Deseret News Press, 1940.

Norris, James D. *Frontier Iron: The Maramec Iron Works, 1826–1876.* Madison, Wis.: State Historical Society of Wisconsin, 1964.

Overman, Frederick. *The Manufacture of Iron in All Its Various Branches.* Philadelphia: Henry C. Baird, 1850.

———. *A Treatise on Metallurgy.* 3rd ed. New York: D. Appleton, 1855.

Poll, Richard D., Thomas G. Alexander, Eugene E. Campbell and David E. Miller, eds. *Utah's History.* Logan: Utah State University Press, 1989.

Pusey, Merlo J. *Builders of the Kingdom: George A. Smith, John Henry Smith, George Albert Smith.* No. 1 of Studies on Western History and Culture Series. Provo: Brigham Young University Press, 1981.

Seegmiller, Janet. *A History of Iron County*. Salt Lake City: Utah State Historical Society, 1998.

Smart, William B., and Donna T. Smart. *Over the Rim: The Parley P. Pratt Exploring Expedition to Southern Utah, 1849–50*. Logan: Utah State University Press, 1999.

Sonne, Conway B. *World of Wakara*. San Antonio, Tex.: Naylor, 1962.

Temin, Peter. *Iron and Steel in Nineteenth-Century America: An Economic Inquiry*. Boston: MIT Press, 1964.

Walker, Ronald W., and Dean Jessee. "First Contacts in Utah" and "Settling Parowan." In *Brigham Young's Indian Correspondence*. Provo, Utah: Brigham Young University Press, forthcoming publication.

Whitney, Orson F. *History of Utah*. 4 vols. Salt Lake City: George Q. Cannon & Sons, Publishers, 1892.

Articles and Unpublished Papers

Coates, Larry. "The Fancher Party before Mountain Meadows." Brown Library, Special Collections, Dixie State College.

Janetski, Joel. "150 Years of Utah Archeology." *Utah Historical Quarterly* 65 (spring 1997): 100–133.

Jones, York, comp. and ed. "Iron Mining and Manufacturing in Iron County, Utah, 1850–1975." Undated typescript. Shirts Collection.

Larson, Gustive O. "Bulwark of the Kingdom: Utah's Iron and Steel Industry." *Utah Historical Quarterly* 31 (summer 1963): 248–61.

Morgan, Dale L. "State of Deseret" *Utah Historical Quarterly* 8 (Apr/Jul/Oct 1940): 67–239.

Palmer, William R. "Pioneer Fortifications." *Improvement Era* 54 (March 1951): 148–50, 183–87.

———. "Utah's Pioneer Iron Industry." *Sons of Utah Pioneer News* (Aug 1957).

Shirts, Morris A. and William T. Parry. "The Demise of the Deseret Iron Company: Failure of the Brick Furnace Lining Technology." *Utah Historical Quarterly* 56 (winter 1988): 23–35.

Index

*The numbers for pages with illustrations appear in **boldface**.*

Adair, Joseph, 425, 498
Adams, David Barclay
 Cedar City settler, **293, 331**, 451, 476, 484
 founds Adamsville, 401
 furnace master, 231, 250, 267, 274, 299–300,
  302, 308, 347–50, 357–59, 379, 461
 iron work in Scotland, 289
 iron work in Utah, 211, 269, 306, 345
 leaves Iron Mission for Beaver, 379
 organizes Union Iron Works, 401
 sergeant in militia, 493
 shareholder, 270, 273, 461
Adams, John, 238, 484, 493, 495
Adams, Mary A., 425
Adams, Mary E., 311n. 15
Adams, Orson B., 27, 35, 128, 211, 269, 425, 493
Adams, Susann, 425
Adams, William, 70, 425, 492
Adobe bricks, 64n. 95, 132, 213, 243, 276, 294,
  300–301, 322, 344, 354, 376, 393
Adobe houses, 69, 171, 295, 322, 354, 364n. 12
Adobe walls, 170–71, 325–26, 329, 333, **335**
Adshead, James, **293**
Adshead, William, 211, 269, 492
Aiden, William, 390
Air furnace, 262–66, 271, 300–301, 360, 380
Allen, Ira, 272, **331**, 406n. 84, 461, 475–76, 495
Allen, Rufus C., 10, 108, 275, 425, 497
Allred, Galen, 182–83
Allred, Jay, 190n. 41
American iron industry, 4, 196, 231, 401
Ammomah, 11, 115n. 45
Amon, 110, 115n. 45, 155, 175
Anderson, Erasmus, 483
Anderson, James, 151, 155, 451, 483, 492
Anderson, Miles, 211, 269
Anderson, Peter, 485
Andirons, 20, 304–6, **304**
Arapeen, 286, 318
Armstrong, Belle, 164, 245, 250n. 82
Arrington, Leonard, 351
"Arrival list," 19, 120, 442
Arthur, Caroline Haight, 356, **357**
Arthur, Christopher
 company trustee and clerk, 279, 346, 356,
  391, 461

lot holder, 486, 488
 militia member, 494
 original shareholder, 256–58, 260, 283n. 52
Arthur, Christopher Jones, 272, 283n. 54,
  356–57, **357**, 461, 492
Arthur, Joshua, 356, 486, 495
Ashworth, John, **293, 331**, 347, 349, 354, 478,
  485, 486, 492
Ashworth, William, 347, 362, 388
Badger, John C., 425
Baird, James, 150, 155, 175, 451
Baker, John T., 387
Baker, Simon, 26–27, 36, 40, 43–45, 50,
  54–55, 57, 70, 74, 76, 425
Balm, Joseph, 483
Barnard, Isaac, 82
Barnard, John P., 27, 48–49, 74, 76, 96n. 91,
  108, 111, 120, 425
Barnard, Mary, 425
Barton, Lorenzo, 170, 310, 400, 425, 451, 493
Barton, Sarah, 425
Barton, William, 272, 286, 461
Baston, Andrew, 99, 133, 425, 494
Bateman, Joseph, 211, 269, **293, 331**, 425
Bateman, Margaret, 425
Bateman, Samuel, 110, 415, 426
Bateman, William, 150, 210, 227, 243, 268,
  293, 331, 451, 484, 489, 495–96
Baugh, Brier, 486, 495
Baugh, John, 484, 486, 492
Bay, James W., 276, **293, 331**, 476, 494
Bayles, Herman D., 90, 400, 426, 447, 493
Bayliss, Juliet, 426
Bayliss, Sarah, 426
Beale, E. F., 320–22, 339n. 15
Beaman, Louisa, 95n. 73
Beaver, **30**, 307, 379, 381, 385, 388, 401, 405,
  421
Bells, 362, **363**, 398
Benson, Alvah, **331**, 354, 476, 494
Benson, Alvin, 86
Benson, Ezra T., 16, 19, 118, 139, 426
Benson, Heber, 86
Benson, Phoebe, 426
Benson, Richard, 51, 87–88, 91, 106, 129, 211,
  269, 302, 426

Berner, James, 145, 158n. 25
Bernhisel, John M., 73, 122
Big Field. *See* Cedar City; Fort Louisa
Birkbeck, Richard, 394, 488, 495
Bishops
  Cedar City, 124, 216–27, **328**, 344, 397
  Fort Louisa/Parowan, 122–24, 131, 216–17,
    344
  traveling company, 26, 43, 56, 58n. 6
Bladen, Thomas
  Cedar City settler, 156, 179, **206, 331**, 451,
    474, 484
  engineer, 267, 299, 302, 305, 354–55
  controversy over trying ore, 205–8, 221n. 21
  furnace master, 264, 359
  iron worker, 210, 212, 268, 306
  iron works leadership, 224, 245–46, 261,
    283n. 54, 308
  makes blast furnace model, 232, **232**
  recruits iron workers in England, 378–79
Blowing machine, Charles Jordan's, 258–60,
  259, 270
Bloxom, Thomas, 119–20, 426
Boggs, Francis, 119–20, 426
Bohn, John, 485, 491, 495
Booth, William, 144, 158
Bosnell, James, 156, **179**, 180, 210, 224, 243,
    268, 272, 277, **331**, 451, 461, 477, 485,
    488, 495
Bowen, David D., **331**, 474, 488, 496
Bowering, George, 176, 178, 229, 319–21,
    323–25, 346, 364n. 12, 485, 496
Bozarth, Beverly, 426
Bradshaw, John Jr., **293, 331**, 391, 474, 485,
    487, 496
Bradshaw, Joseph, 289
Bradshaw, Samuel, **293, 331**, 349, 474, 486, 496
Braffit, George, 110, 317, 426
Braffit, Sarah, 426
Brimhall, George, 82, 102, 426, 448
Bringhurst, Ann D., 427
Bringhurst, Eleanor, 426
Bringhurst, Samuel, 27, 41, 43, 48–49, 112, 426
Bringhurst, William, 108, 118–19, 427
Brinton, David, 91, 120, 427
Brinton, Harriet W., 427
Bronson, Lemon, 70, 121, 427
Bronson, Nancy, 427
Brooks, Juanita, 394
Brown, Benjamin, 427
Brown, Ebenezer, 70, 91, 119, 427

Brown, Isaac H., 10, 71, 111
Brown, James S., 22n. 11
Brown, Phoebe, 91, 427
Brown, Thomas Dunlop, 275, 283n. 54, 349, 375
Buchanan, James, 382–84, 392
Bulloch, Christina, 143, 145, 158n. 24
Bulloch, David
  arrives on Coal Creek, 155
  emigrates from Scotland, 142–45, **143**
  hauls freight, 399
  interviewed by William Palmer, 163–65,
    168, 171, 174, 176, 181
  lists settlers of Cedar City, 451–54
  maps of Cedar City settlement, **165, 174, 181**
Bulloch, Isabella Dunn, 142
Bulloch, James, 142, 145, 150, 158n. 14, 268,
    276–77, **331**, 451
Bulloch, Matt, 190n. 41
Bulloch, Robert, 145, 158n. 24, 451, 497
Bulloch, Thomas, 8, 17, 117–18, 152, 443, 455
Burgess, Clive, 406n. 76
Burnham, Isaac, 119, 427
Burt, Andrew, 145, 158n. 25
Burt, John, 145, 158n. 25
Burton, John, 121, 427
Burton, R. T., 120, 427
Burton, Rich [*sic*], 119
Burton, Sydney Rigdon, 400, 493
Busby, Mona, 145
California
  deserters to, 155, 175, 228–29, 302, 325,
    346, 415
  gold fields, 6, 8, 71, 401
  Mormon settlements in, 3, 16, 108, 114n. 32
  trailblazers to, 4–8, 26, 54
  Wakara's trade to, 11, 111
California Road, 5–7, 157n. 1, 194, 228, 300,
    388
Call, Anson
  bishop in Parowan, 122–24
  captain of "1st 50," 26–27, **27**, 36, 40, 48,
    53–54, 56–57, 427
  civic activities, 74, 78, 93, 99, 104
  explores Center Creek, 70, 72
  founds Fillmore, 400
  leads new arrivals, 110, 115, 117, 120, 443
Call, Mary, 110, 427
"Call list," 18–19, 60n. 26, 109, 119–20, 442
Campbell, Alexander, 156, **331**, 348, 353, 451,
    477, 485, 495
Campbell, Robert L., 10, 13

Cane Springs, 389, 404n. 60

Cannon, 9, 37, 55, 70, 77, 86–87, 93n. 32, 111, 117, 128

Cannon, Angus M., 119–20, 428

Cannon, George Q., 79, 275

Cannon balls, recast, 398, 408n. 122

Cardon, Alfred, 144

Carn, Daniel, 19, 118, 428

Carrington, Albert, 146, 214–15, 393

Carruthers, Isabella, 428

Carruthers, Matthew
 acting superintendent, 229, 305, 309
 Cedar City settler, 147, 152, 156, 159n. 34, 175, 331, 428, 451
 "contrary" behavior, 170, 205, 227–29, 324
 dispute with Bladen, 206–8, 212, 221
 emigrates, 33–34, 85, 123, 142–43
 iron works activities, 209–10, 213, 229, 243, 267–69, 300, 303
 militia duties, 148–49, 152–53, 324
 returns to Scotland, 229, 346, 365n. 14
 second counselor ("presiding elder" over Cedar City), 124, 146, 153–54, 175, 205, 304
 serves on iron and high councils, 216–17, 224, 227, 229, 308
 shareholder, 270, 273, 461, 469

Cartwright, Jane, 428

Cartwright, Thomas
 Christmas dance fiddler, 327
 company blacksmith, 244, **244**, 246, 300, 306
 iron worker and shareholder, 210, 213, 224, 268, 270, 272–73, 461
 lot owner, 488, 494
 settlement activities, 9, 51, 107, 119, 150, 156, 178–79, 225, 428, 451

Carvalho, Solomon N., 52, 63n. 78, 329

Cassell, George, 150, 451

Cattle, livestock
 cooperatives, 399
 herds established, 104, 113n. 18, 127, 182, 326, 362, 456
 ordered to Salt Lake City, 323–25, 416
 protected on trail, 35, 45, 51, 422

Cedar City (Little Muddy, Cottonwood or Coal Creek)
 area explored, 4, 8, 13, **14**
 bastions, 171, 187, 340n. 45
 Big Field, 167–68, **169**, 176–83, **179**, 190n. 41, 224–26, 228, 295
 city government, 122, 243, 346–47

Compact Fort, 165–83, **169**, **174**, **181**, 204, 207, 215, 226, 228–32, 240, 285–92, **291**, 294–97, 319–22, 325, **328**, 330, 364n. 12, 410, 487
 cooperatives, 399
 corral, "southside," 148, 163, 165–68, 170–71, 174–76, 178, **181**
 council house, 242
 garden lots, **169**, 240, 292, **293**
 historic names, 22n. 12, 147–48
 Knoll, 70, 151–52, 163, 167, **169**, 173, 176, 181, **181**, 183, 232, 286, 290, 322, 410
 Old Fort plat, 168, **169**, 175, **179**, 181, 290
 pioneer remnants, 333–34
 Plat A, **169**, 188n. 7, 285, 289–92, **291**, 294–97, 310, 312n. 19, 317, 321–22, 325–35, **328**, **331**, 340n. 45, 372, 377, 410, 473, 487
 Plat A Fort, **169**, 290, 312, 325–30, **328**, 332, **335**, 340, 347, 372
 Plat B, **169**, 372–73, **374**, 398, 410, 483–89
 Red Hill, **169**, 176, 189n. 29, 194, 278, 358
 site evaluated, 75–76, 80, 140–41, 147–48
 survey of, 147–48, 150, 167, **169**
 Wagon-Box Camp, 163–68, **165**, **167**, **169**, 170–71, 187–88
 western fields, **169**, 176–77, 180, 292

Census, Iron County, 19–20, 24, 34, 36, 107, 110, 117, 119–22, 141, 143, 146, 397, 425–44

Center Creek (river), **30**, 31, 57, 69–71, 74–80, 82, 88–89, 91, 93, 102, 104–5, 119, 127, 129, 140

Center Creek (settlement). *See* Parowan

Chalk Creek. *See* Fillmore

Chamberlain, Solomon, **328**, 330, **331**, 446, 494

Chandless, William, 329

Charcoal, 4, 46, 64n. 95, 75, 82, 195–96, 198, 200, 206, 230–32, 236, 251, 300, 302–3, 305, 343, 347–48, 351, 359–62, 376, 393–94, 397–98, 401, 412, **414**

Charcoal ovens, 195, **196**, 231

Chatterley, Catherine, 272, 283n. 54, 461, 485

Chatterley, John
 lists first settlers in Cedar City, 155–56, 161n. 63, 166, 451–54
 lot owner, **179**, **293**, 484
 militia member, 150–51, 496
 writes Cedar City reminiscences, 143, 151, 164, 168, 174–75, 185–86, 229, 308

Chatterley, Joseph
    buys Ross home, 174–75, 364n. 12
    Cedar City settler, 150, 155–56, **293, 331**, 343, 451, 474
    iron worker and shareholder, 203, 210, 268, 270, 272, 350, 462
    serves on iron and high councils, 216, 224
Cherry, Aaron B., 27, 44, 55, 70, 77, 119, 428
Cherry, Margaret, 428
Chicken Creek, **30**, 31, 39–40, 60n. 33, 334
Chipman, Washburn, 119, 429
Choir, 51, 89, 109, 294
Church of Jesus Christ of Latter-day Saints,
    The. *See* Bishops; Elders quorum;
    First Presidency; High council;
    Missionaries; Quorum of the Twelve
    Apostles; Seventies; Stakes; Tithing;
    Wards and branches
Clark, Ezra, 110, 120, 429
Clark, George S., 214, 346
Clerks and bookkeeping. *See* Deseret Iron
    Company
Clews, Joseph, **179**, 210, 213, 268, 270, 349, 365n. 14, 394, 462, 484, 496
Coal
    anthracite, 239, 244, 258
    bituminous, 239, 258, 395, 401
    as furnace fuel, 195–96, 198, 206–7, 230, 244–45, 258, 303, 347–49, 351, 353–54, 360, 376–78, 394–95, 398, 401, 412, 480
    high sulfur content of, 196, 347, 401, 409, 412
    "stone coal," 110, 114, 232, 236, 239, 245–46, 248, 303, 395
Coal Creek (river), **14**, 76, 80, 140, 168, **169, 181**, 176–77, 223, 242, 290, 295, 343, 410
Coal Creek (settlement). *See* Cedar City
Coal Creek Canyon, 14, **169**, 176, 197, 213, 234, 236–37, 409
Coal Creek Canyon road, 122, 140, 168, 206–7, 232–36, 241, 345
Coal deposits, 110–12, 114–115n. 42, 140, 223, 232, 234, 236–39, 241, 244, 245, 371, 376, 393, 409, 457, 467, 480
Coal mines, 203, 232–34, **235**, 236–39, 270, 302, 310, 348, 353–54, 376
Coke, 195–98, 200, 230–32, 238–39, 347, 349–51, 353–55, 357–61, 376, 395, 398–99, 401, 409, 411, **414**
Coke ovens, **196**, 350–51, 353–54, 357, 401

Compact Fort. *See* Cedar City; Fort Louisa
Conover, Peter W., 318–19
Cook, David, 288, **293, 331**, 475
Cook, Henry, 96n. 83, 272, 376, 462, 486, 496
Coray, George, 272, 462, 488, 497
Corbitt, Thomas, 70, 102, 110, 415, 429, 448
Corlett, Thomas, **293**, 355
Cotton Mission, 400–401
Cottonwood. *See* Cedar City
Cottonwoods, The, **14**, 180, 234
Council of Fifty, 94n. 47
Cove Fort, **30**, 31, 50, 56, 62nn. 69, 74
Cradelbaugh, John, 383, 395
Craw, Orin, **331**, 348, 475
Croft, George, 352
Crook, John G., 272, 283n. 54, 465
Crowther, Thomas, 394, 487–88, 495
Cumming, Alfred, 383, 392, 394
Cupola, 202, 258, 299, 304–5, 353, 359–60, 378–79, 393
Curtis, Uriel, 348
Dally, William, **331**, 476, 494
Dalton, Amanda, 429
Dalton, Charles W., 65, 70, 74, 78, 110, 272, **331**, 429, 462, 475, 477
Dalton, Edward, 86, 211, 269, 493
Dalton, Harry, 110, 429
Dalton, Isabel, 429
Dalton, John, 70, 74, 120, 123, 429
Dalton, Juliette, 65, 110
Dalton, Luella, 23n. 45, 86–88, 93n. 32, 107, 287
Dalton, Rebecca, 429
Daly, Nancy M., 429
Dame, Lovina, 429
Dame, William H.
    absolved of complicity, 395
    civic activities, 77, 123–24, 127, 339
    commands Tenth Regiment, 381, 385–87, 390–92, 405, 491
    exploring party member, 70–73, 99, 263
    high counselor, 216
    organizes Parowan Cooperative, 400
    Parowan Stake president, 125, 377, 386, 390
    settles Paragonah, 322
    surveys Big Field, 178–81, **179, 181**, 190
    surveys Cedar City, 147, 167, **169**, 175–76, 188, 278
    surveys Fort Louisa/Parowan, 82, 98, 100, 103–4, 129, **130**, 133, **134**, 445–49
    surveys Plat A, 289–90, **291**, 292, **293**, 330, **331**, 332–34

surveys Plat B, 372–73, **374**, 483–89
traveling camp leader, 27, 35, 429
Dancing, 128, 187, 242, 296, 319, 326–327, 357
Darby, Abraham, 196
Dart, John, 110
Dart, Phoebe, 128
Davenport, Thomas, 400
Davidson, William, **331**, 354, 396, 477, 485, 497
Davis, William R., **331**, 474, 492
Deakin, William, 156, **331**, 451, 474
Decker, Nancy, 429
Decker, Zechariah, 55, 64, 70, 78, 119, 429, 491
"Departure list," 19, 109, 119, 141, 442
Deseret General Assembly (provisional state
    legislature), 9, 34, 73, 79, 84
Deseret Iron Company
    Articles of Incorporation, 256–57, 259,
        277–79, 467–69
    assets, 345, 351, 361
    board of directors, 256, 273, 278–79,
        348–49, 380, 467–70
    clerks and bookkeeping, 274, 348–50, 353,
        356, 391, 399
    iron council, 299, 308–9
    legal status, 278–79, 469–71
    organization of, 253–60, 285
    shareholders, 256–58, 270–73, 278–80,
        283n. 54, 308, 345–46, 365n. 14,
        461–65
    stock, **257**, 260, 270–71, 273, 413
    stock certificate, **257**
    store, merchandise, 273–78, 306–8, 415
    successor to "pioneer iron works," 215,
        267–71
    trustees, 272, 279, 346, 356, 461, 463–65,
        469–70
Deseret Iron Company Journal, 238, 351, 356,
    359, 376, 380, 391, 393–96, 398–99
Dibble, Peter A. *See* Smith, Peter A.
Ditch-digging contest, 186, 206
Dodge, Seth, 487, 492
"Dog irons." *See* Andirons
Dominguez, Francisco, 4–5
Dominguez-Escalante party, 3–5
Drake, Betsy, 429
Drake, Orson, 108, 429
Dramatic association, 86, 218, 275
Drummond, W. W., 383
Duncan, Chapman, 19, 110, 127, 212, 244,
    249n. 78, 429
Duncan, Homer, 10, 430

Duncan, Martha, 429
Dunton, James H., 211, 269, 493
Durfee, Jabez, **331**, 354, 495
Durham, Thomas, 400
Durham, Wilford, 133
Easton, Alexander, 145, 150, 156, 158n. 24,
    179, 211, 269–70, 273, **293**, 451, 462
Easton, George, 145, 150, 156, 348, 451
Easton, James, 145, 156, **179**, 210, 243, 268,
    277, **293**, 452
Easton, John
    captain of Scotch Independent Co., 143–45
    Cedar City leadership, 124, 154, 205, 224,
        228, 240
    Cedar City settler, 150, 156, **293**, **331**, 452,
        473
    iron worker, 210, 268
Easton, Mary, 145, 452
Easton, Matthew, 145, 210, 212, 269, **293**, 452
Easton, Robert, 145, 150, 158n. 24, **179**, 210,
    212, 348, 452, 487–88, 496
Economic independence, 3, 251, 280, 307
Edwards, Eliezar, **331**, 349, 354, 492
Edwards, Hope, 430, 433
Egan, Howard, 8, 26
Elders quorum, 122–23, 129, 344, 442–43
Elmer, Elijah, 35, 119, 132, 136, 244, 249n. 78,
    430, 449, 494
Elmer, Mary, 430
Empey, William, 43, 96n. 91, 108, 120, 430
Engine. *See* Steam engine
Enoch. *See* Johnson Springs
Ensign, Eliza, 430
Ensign, Marius, 70, 272, 346, 430, 462, 493
Eriens, William, **331**, 477
Evans, William, 150, **331**, 354, 452, 474, 492
Fancher, Alexander, 387
Fancher-Baker Company, 387–91
Fancher, J. K., Jr., 406n. 77
Farming. *See also* Irrigation
    Big Field, Cedar City, 167–**169**, 176–83,
        179, 190n. 41, 224–26, 228, 295
    Big Field, Fort Louisa, 97–104, **103**
    drought, 202, 373, 375, 378–79, 411
    early planting, 90, 104–6
    grasshoppers, 373, 375, 378
    harrowing, **105**
Farnsworth, Philo T., 385, 404, 491
Farr, Aaron F., 78, 112, 119, 140, 430
Farr, Persis, 430
Farrer, James, 10, 348, 353, 430, 483, 484, 492

Ferguson, James, 214–15, 218, **218**, 455

Fife, Adam, **331**, 353–54, 478, 486

Fife, Otto, 234

Fife, Peter M., 19, 110, 149–50, 272, 353–54, 430, 452, 462, 477, 485, 496

Filanque, Peter, 155, 239, 248n. 57, 452

Fillmore (Chalk Creek), 15–16, **30**, 31, 46, 61n. 56, 62n. 60, 146, 289, 336, 381, 385, 400

First Presidency, 3, 16, 26, 251, 256, 419n. 7

Fish, Joseph, 193, 222n. 41, 494

Flake, J. M., 6

Flooding, 129, 177–78, 220, 233, 343–44, 480

Forney, Jacob, 383, 395

Fort Harmony, **14**, 28, 322, 381, 386, 407, 497

Fort Louisa. *See also* Parowan
bastion, 82, 84–87, 90, 94n. 63, 109, 131
Big Field, 97–104, **103**, 127, 129
compact fort, 80
corral, 82, 84–86
council house, 80–82, 84–87, 89, 94n. 63, 109, 118, 122, 131–32
garden lots, 84–85, 97
Mortenson drawing of, **85**
naming of, 89, 95n. 73, 126
school and bowery, 106–7
second survey as Parowan, 129–33, **130**, **134**
survey of, 82–84, **83**, 98, 129

Fort Peteetneet (Payson), **30**, 33–34, 38, 318

Fort Utah (Provo), 9, 15–16, 18, 25–27, 29–32, **30**, 87, 213

Freighting, 126, 244, 307, 383, 399

Frémont, John C., 123, 327, 329, 382

Frost, Burr, 46, 69, 88, 112, 119, 202–3, 430

Frost, Mary E., 431

Fulmer, Almon L., 20, 35, 42, 70, 72–75, 78, 89, 99, 108, 431

Fulmer, Sarah, 431

Furnace. *See also* Cupola; Noble Furnace; Trial furnace
bellows, 198, 206
Bladen's model of, 232, **232**
blast pipes, 350, 355, 360, 362, 379, 393
blow out, 200, 202, 347, 378, 479
bosh or slope, **200**, 201, 350, 378, 393
casting house, 201, 302, 305, 351
charging bridge, 201, **201**
charging tram, 355
chimney, **200**, 201
dam stones, 202, 230, 393, 395
foundation, 230, 240, 244, 301, 348, 350, 393, 395, 409–10
firebrick, 200–201, 241, 301, 412
hearth or crucible, 198, **200**, 202, 263, 303, 350, 360, 378, 395, 411
lining, 198, **200**, 201, 338, 348–50, 359–60, 380, 396, 409–12, 414, 419, 482
mouth, tunnel-head, trundle-head or funnel head, **200**, 201, 350
sandstone walls, 198, 200–201, 350–51, 359–60, 412, **414**
site of, 230–32, **414**
stack or chimney, **200**, 201, 243–44, 300–301, 380, 393, 403, 409
tuyeres, 200, **200**, 300, 303, 359–60, 393
tymp stones, 202, 360, 395

Furnace fuels. *See* Charcoal; Coal; Coke; Pine wood

Furniture-making, 184

Gallisby, Robert, 110, 128, 211, 474–75

Garcés, Francisco, 5

Gardner, Elias, 36, 60n. 26, 431

Geary, J. T., 396

Gerber, John, 238, 484, 487, 498

Goodale, Isaac Newton, 35, 82, 85, 127, 431

Goodale, Maria, 431

Gorlinski, Joseph, 183, 190

Gough, William, 211, **293**, **331**, 474

Gould, Fanny, 109, 431

Gould, John, 109, 431, 494

Gould, Samuel, 10, 88, 109, 119–20, 126, 146, 289, 300, 317, 376, 400, 402n. 15, 431, 446, 452, 494

Gould, William, 109, 431

Grant, Jedediah M., 74, 118, 284n. 76, 382, 471

Grant, John, 142

Great Britain
Deseret Iron Co. financing from, 253–56
iron industry, 4, 193, 196
recruiting iron workers in, 378–79

Greaves, John, 210, 269

Green, Alphonzo, 110, 119–20, 431

Green, Eliza, 431

Green, Robert, 112, 431

Green, Thomas, 355, 485, 492

Greenwood, William, **293**, **331**, 357, 477, 492

Gregory, John, 156, 288, 324, 452

Griffith, John, **293**

Grimshaw, Hunter, 230, 232

Gristmill, 88, 244, 398, 449

Groves, Elisha H.
bishop and high counselor, 26, 70, 216
civic duties, 78, 81, 97, 101, 128, 149

gives patriarchal blessings, 275
Iron Mission president, 124, 129, 146, 154, 205, 217, 431
lot owner, 85, 102, **331**, 448, 475
militia member, 497
territorial legislator, 122, 146, 205, 207
Groves, John, 349, 476–77, 487, 495
Groves, Lucy, 431
Gunnison, John W., 326
Guns, pioneer, 185
Haight, Isaac C.
    Cedar City mayor, 346–47, 372–73
    Cedar Stake president, 371, 390, 397
    commands Second Battalion, 386, 388, 390–91, 492
    complaints against, 391, 394–95, 397
    Deseret Iron Co. general manager, 124, 345–51, **346**, 364–65, 378–80, 393, 396
    high counselor, 346
    lot owner, **328, 331**, 483, 486
    overlapping leadership roles, 416
    released from stake presidency, 397
    shareholder and trustee, 272, 279, 462
    Southern Exploring Expedition, 10–11, 13, 15–16, 23
    territorial legislator, 381–82
Hall, Charles, 65, 78, 90, 322, 432, 493
Hall, Elizabeth C., 65, 110, 432
Hall, Job Pitcher, 90, 110, 432, 462, 493
Hall, Mary E., 110, 432
Hamblin, Jacob, 275–76, **276**, 388, 497
Hamilton, John, **331**, 348, 353–54, 477, 484, 486, 496
Hamilton, Samuel L., 432, 496
Hamilton Fort, **14**
Hancock, Clarissa, 120
Hansen, Erasmus, 486, 496
Hansen, Jorgen, 486
Hanson, Peter, 355
Harmison, James, 70, 108, 432
Harmony. *See* Fort Harmony
Harper, Charles A., 70, 74, 108, 432
Harper, Lovina W., 432
Harrison, Mary A., 432
Harrison, Richard
    Cedar City settler, 156, 178–79, 432, 452, 483
    civic and military activities, 51, 123, 150, 225, 243, 406n. 84, 495
    iron moulder, 267, 302, 304–5, 308, 313n. 66, 355, 432, 462
    iron works activities, 210, 213, 216–18, 224, 228, 234, 268, 270, 272, 308, 349

iron works superintendent, 215, 218, 223, 225–26, 230, 240–41, 243–46, 261, 264
    organizes Union Iron Works, 401
Harwood, Thomas, **331**, 477, 488, 495
Haslam, James, 388, 390, 394, 486, 491–92
Henderson, John H., 432, 493
Henderson, William, 156, 452
Hendricks, Daniel, 120, 433, 446
Hendricks, Lucy, 433
Henry, Robert, 150, 211, 269, **293, 331**, 452, 473
Hewit, William, **293**
Higbee, Isaac, 18, 29
Higbee, John M.
    Cedar Stake counselor, 125, 371–72, 386, 397
    commands Third Battalion, **372**, 386, 389, 391, 395, 492
    settlement activities, 332, 357, 475, 484
    writes grievance resolution, 406n. 84
High council, 216–18, 224, 227–29, 241, 244, 327, 346
Hofheins, Jacob, 35, 70, 77, 111, 133, 433, 446, 475
Hofheins, Mary A., 110, 433
Holbrook, Chandler, 82, 85, 120, 433
Holbrook, Eunice, 110, 433
Holidays
    Christmas, 41, 47, 170, 296, 326–27
    July 4th, 128
    July 24th, 128, 141, 242, 319, 384–85
    New Year's, 46–47, 298
Hollingshead, Nelson S., 433, 494
Holmes, Wardman, **293, 331**, 354–55, 477, 484, 495
Holyoak, William, 400
Homestead Act of 1862, 133
Hope, Edward, 430, 433
Hopkins, Charles, 10, 62n. 66, **331**, 476–77, 488, 494
Horne, Joseph, 10, 26, 36, 40, 48–50, **49**, 53, 62n. 74, 70, 74, 119, 145–46, 433
Horne, Mary, 433
Horton, George, 354–55, 391, 394, 485, 496
Hosanna cheer or shout, 242, 245, 304
House-building, 170–73, 184–85
Hovey, Joseph G., 70, 119, 433
Hovey, Sarah, 433
Howd, Lucinda, 433
Howd, Simeon D., 114n. 42, 119, 433, 492
Hoyt, Silas, **331**, 473, 493
Huchinson, Daniel, 487, 496
Hulse, Benjamin R., 96n. 88, 106, 156, 210, 268, 270, 272, **331**, 434, 452, 462, 474, 497

Hulse, Jane, 110, 434
Humphries, John S., **293**, 394, 486, 492
Hunt, Jefferson, 5–6, 26–27, 54, 63n. 85,
    71–74, 76–79, 92n. 25, 135n. 10
Hunter, Charles R., 182
Hunter, George, **179**, **293**, 324, 434, 452, 454,
    478, 486, 494
Hunter, Joseph, 156, **293**, 324, **331**, 349, 355,
    399, 452, 478, 485, 495, 497
Hunter, William, 156, **179**, 208, 210–12, 269,
    452, 478, 494–95
Hyde, Orson, 16, 139, 252
Indians. *See* Native Americans
Iron, nails of, 37, 56, 110, 185, 193, 195, 202–3,
    253–54, 276, 309, 359, 362, 401
Iron, scrap, 185, 193, 202–3, 228, 398
Iron County
    elections, 74, 76–78, 122
    organization of, 34, 59n. 21, 73–74
Iron County militia. *See* Militia
Iron deposits, 3, 6, 8, **9**, 13, 48, 72, 75,
    114–15n. 42, 243, 251, 253, 265, 351,
    378, 394, 409
Iron manufacturing
    "bear" or "salamander," 197, 359, 378,
        394–95
    blow out, 200, 202, 347, 378, 479
    charge or burden, 195, 197, 202, 245, 300,
        302–3, 305, 347–48, 351, 358–63, 396
    process of, 3–4, 196–202, 218–19, 280, 411–13
    slag or cinder, 197, 201, 230, 302, 381, 414
    flux, 196–97, 201, 300, 303, 401, 409, 479
Iron Manufacturing Company of Utah, 402
"Iron men," 209–11
Iron Mission
    Brigham Young's assessment of, 479–81
    Brigham Young's instructions to, 34–35,
        218–19, 455–60
    George A. Smith's instructions to, 26, 39,
        51, 55–57, 80, 90, 101
    "Iron Mission Leadership" chart, 124–25
    military organization of, 34–35
    recruitment for, 16–18
    traveling organization of, 26–27
Iron Mission State Park, 172–73, 195, 363
Iron Mission traveling company
    "1st 50," 26–27, 29, 32, 36–41, 43–50, 53–57
    horse teams, 27–28, 39, 41–46, 48–50, 53
    ox teams, 27–28, 36, 39, 41–45, 48–52, 56
    "2nd 50," 26–27, 29, 32, 36–41, 43–45, 53–57

Iron missionaries
    arrivals and departures, 108–10, 117–21,
        288–89, 297
    census of, 119–21, 425–44
    deserting to California, 155, 175, 228–29,
        302, 325, 346, 415
    deserting to Salt Lake, 38, 58, 65, 110, 415
    economic inequality among, 297–99, 416
    ethnic background of, 51, 121, 128, 142–46,
        148, 152, 171, 206, 231, 275, 280, 288
    occupations of, 17, 19–20, 400
    refined through adversity, 418–19
Iron ore
    hematite, 4, 194, 200, 263, 265, 300, 302,
        351, 358, 360
    "lean ore," 348, 360–61, 376, 396
    magnetite, 4, 194, 200, 265–66, 302, 348,
        358–60, 376, 393, 411
Iron production
    final trials, 393–94, 395–96
    first andirons cast, 304
    first furnace charge, 231, 245–46
    most successful run, 361–62
    Noble furnace first charged, 356–59
    pig iron for conference, 245–46, 251–52
    priority over farming, 224–29, 242
    production resumes at, 343, 347, 393–94
    reasons for shut-down, 231, 396, 409–19
    threat of war interrupts, 311, 391
Iron products
    cast iron, 193–95, 202–3, 251, 258, 303–06,
        308, 362, 376, 394, 398–99, 414
    pig iron, 194–96, **195**, 202, 246, 251–52,
        263, 300, 347, 355, 361–62, 393, 397,
        401, 412, 480
    wrought iron, 194–95, 258, 310
Iron Springs, 8–9, 72, 75, 77, 79, 111, 140, 215,
    230, 317, 377, 409
Iron workers
    blacksmiths, 17, 19, 21, 100, 109, 193, 195,
        202–3, 210, 212, 216, 240, 244, 246, 276,
        310, 350–51, 353, 355, 357, 359, 375,
        393, 426–27, 429–30, 437–38, 440
    carpenters, 17, 21, 100, 109, 276, 349, 354,
        362, 425–26, 435
    colliers, 19, 195–96, 300, 349, 359, 362,
        376, 425
    engineers, 19, 245, 267, 353–55, 380, 393,
        403, 425
    furnace masters and keepers, 197, 206,

231–32, 250, 261, 267, 280, 289, 302–3, 347–50, 357–62, 376, 394, 401, 439, 461

masons, 17, 19, 100, 211, 240, 276, 281, 325, 348–50, 360, 354, 362, 393

miners and quarrymen, 19, 212, 232, 281, 348, 353–54, 362, 425, 433–34, 480

moulders, 17, 215–16, 240, 267, 304, 308, 349, 353–55, 360, 362, 376, 379, 393, 401, 432, 441

teamsters, 21, 211, 233–34, 348–50, 353–54, 357, 360, 362, 376, 393, 436–37, 444, 480

Iron Works Account Book, 208–12, 221n. 24, 222n. 27, 229, 249n. 80, 267–69

Irrigation. *See also* Farming

  at Center Creek, 76, 81–82, 85, 87, 105, 127

  at Coal Creek, 76, 80, 140, **169**, 176–78, 223, 242, 290, 295, 343, 410

  at Red Creek, 127–28

Jackson, Samuel, 488, 496

Jacobs, Alexander, 484

Jacobs, Christopher, **331**, 475, 495

Jacobs, John, **331**, 477, 484, 487, 495

Jacobs, Swen, **331**, 477, 487, 495

James, James, 263–66, 271, 280, 300–301, 303, 307, **331**, 475

James, Thomas, 4

Jarvice, Norman, 110, 434

Jenson, Andrew, 19, 120, 155, 159n. 35, 217, 326, 329, 335, 364n. 12, 443, 454

Jewkes, Samuel, 394, 488, 495

Johnson, Benjamin F., 118, 434

Johnson, Joel H., 123, 127, 210, 216, 265, 269, 320, 326, 434

Johnson, Nephi, 91, 434, 452, 487, 494

Johnson, Sixtus E., 85, 91, 121, 434, 452

Johnson Springs (Enoch), 14, 210, 320

Johnston's Army, 384–88, 387–88, 391–92, 398, 408n. 122

Jones, Dan, 9–10

Jones, David, **331**, 474

Jones, Elias, 257, 283n. 52, 462

Jones, Hyrum, 173

Jones, James, 258

Jones, John, 257, 283n. 52, 462

Jones, John Lee, 175, 347, 361, 408n. 122, 496

Jones, John Pidding, 173, 175, **331**, 347, 355, 361, 485, 488, 496

Jones, Nathaniel V., 379

Jones, Thomas (financier), 255–56, 260, 280–81, 283, 463, 469

Jones, Thomas (miner and mason), 125, 230, 280–81, 306, **331**, 348–49, 397, 463, 476, 484, 495

Jones, William, 38, 58, 65, 434

Jones, York, 230, 329, 334, **336**, 358

Jordan, Charles, 258–60

Judd, Zadock K., 102, 129, 133, 265, 434, 448, 497

Kane, Thomas L., 382

Kanosh (chief), 62n. 66, 146, 286

Kay, John, 214–15, 296, 486, 495

Kearns, H. H., **331**, 348–49, 354–55, 475

Keele, Alexander, 318

Keel, Karl, 190n. 41

Keir, Alexander, 142, 145, 150, 156, **179**, 180, 210, 212, 226, 243, 268, 283n. 54, **293**, 452, 463

Keir, Mary, 145

Keir, Robert, 145

Kelly, Charles, 341n. 57

Kershaw, Robert, 272, **331**, 463, 475, 492

Kershaw, Samuel, 210, 269–70, 463, 492

Key, John, **293**, **331**, 474, 495

Keys, Robert, 353–54, 476, 483

Kimball, Heber C., 74, 108, 118, 139, 146, 214, 252, 320, 382, 455, 460

Kimball, Hiram, 383

Kimball, William H., 237, 320, 324, 339n. 15

Kingdom of God

  building up of, 20, 80, 153–54, 219, 280, 382, 418

  iron manufacture as a branch of, 219, 459

Kinkead & Company, 244, 307

Klingensmith, Philip (Smith, Philip K.)

  Cedar City bishop, 124, 216–17, 223–25, 240, 246, 261, 326–27, 344, 375, 397

  Cedar City settler, 156, **215**, 221n. 25, **293**, **328**, **331**, 452, 486, 487, 488

  civic activities, 215, 285, 290–91, 346–47

  evaluates Lead Mission deposits, 379

  iron works activities, 210, 236, 239, 272, 464

  Mountain Meadows involvement, 390–91, 394–95, 397, 494

Lapworth, William, 396, 496

Larson, Gustive, 36, 77, 329

Las Vegas, 5, 379, 400

Latham, Robert, 320, **331**, 348, 353, 477, 485, 494

Lawson, James, 35, 70, 74, 119, 434
Lawson, Mercy, 434
Lead Mission, 379
Leany, Elizabeth, 434
Leany, William, 40, 119, 123, 204, 434, 493
Leavitt, Emeline, 434
Leavitt, George, 114n. 42, 217, 434
Lee, John D.
    civic and ecclesiastical activities, 74, 78,
        120, 123, 126, 216, 346–47, 381
    in Fort Harmony, 139, 285, 320, 381, 400,
        407n. 105
    on Iron Mission trek, 18, 26–29, **28**, 36
    iron-related activities, 207–8, 211, 269, 306
    lot owner, **328**, 475
    militia advancement, 149, 324, 386, 492
    Mountain Meadows involvement, 389–91,
        394–95, 407n. 105, 417
    regional travels of, 120–21, 149, 207, 347
    settlement activities of, 81–82, 85, 99–106,
        103, 109, 122, 187, 242, 286–87,
        326–27, **328**, 330, **331**, 434
Lee, John Alma, 435, 492
Lee, Lovina, 47, 89, 120, 435
Lee, Mary Vance (Polly), 47, 65, 89, 435
Lee, Rachel Andora Woolsey, 386
Leigh, Samuel, 258, **331**, 355, 474, 484, 496
Leigh, William, 483
Lemmon, James W., 65, 110, 269, 435
Lemmon, Susannah, 65
Lewis, Beason, 335, 493
Lewis, David, 336
Lewis, Emily, 65, 435
Lewis, James
    called on mission to China, 244
    civic and military activities, 35, 82, 212,
        386, 491
    county recorder, 74, 78, 94, 99, 188, 204,
        347, 357, 375, 392, 445
    family and occupation of, 65, 107, 435
    lot owner, 132, 448
Lewis, Jessie, 156, 435, 452, 488, 496
Lewis, Melinda, 435
Lewis, Phillip B., 78, 102, 435
Lewis, Samuel, 318, 493
Lewis, Tarlton
    bishop in Parowan, 95, 122, 124, 216–17,
        227, 344
    captain of "2nd Ten," 27, 40, 55, 57
    civic duties, 123, 127, 212, 227, 289, 345, 494
    explores Center Creek, 70, 76, 78, 81–82
    family of, 119, 435

Lewis, William, 348
Liberty poles
    at Cedar City, 165–66, 175, 242, **328**
    at Fort Louisa (Parowan), 70, 82, **83**, 287
    at Little Salt Lake Valley, 13
Limestone, 195–98, 201, 230, 302–5, 348, 350,
        358–61, 394, 409, 411
Lish, Peter, 55, 64, 110, 435
Liston, Commodore Perry, 272, **331**, 355, 388,
        463, 476, 485, 495
Little, James A.
    builds road to coal, **213**, 232, 236
    civic and ecclesiastical duties, 78, 107, 147,
        212, 216, 265, 347
    militia activities, 35, 149, 317, 323–24
    settler and lot owner, 435, 449, 476
    shareholder, 272, 283n. 54, 463
Little, Mary J., 435
Little Muddy. *See* Coal Creek; Cedar City
Little Salt Lake Valley (Parowan Valley), 11, 13,
        14, 16–18, **30**, 31, 54–55, 57, 63n. 85,
        64n. 93, 69, 72–73, 123, 126, 135n. 10
Littlefield, Waldo, **331**, 475, 497
Log houses, 31, 170–73, 175, 295, 320
Love, Andrew, 27, 45–46, 140–41, 435
Love, Nancy, 435
Loveridge, Alexander H., **331**, 477, 484, 496
Lowe, Elmer, 86
Lowe, John, 155, 175, 492
Lunceford, Joseph, 435
Lunt, Ellen Whittaker
    Cedar City settler, 155, 294–95, 453, 454
    operates telegraph, 399
    struck by lightning, 295–96
    visits Salt Lake City, 305
    wedding of, 164, 186–87, **187**
Lunt, Henrietta, 399
Lunt, Henry
    authority conflicts, 152–54, 218, 227–28,
        240, 244, 324
    Cedar City settler ("president of traveling
        company"), 147, 149–55, 452, 454
    community and home chores, 177, 184,
        219–20, 224, 287, 294–95
    conference trips, 303–5, 347
    Deseret Iron Co., clerk and shareholder,
        215, 267–68, 270, 272, 274, 463
    distributes city lots, 290–91
    ecclesiastical callings, 124–25, 205, 212,
        216–17, 223, 397–99, 407n. 105
    evaluates fort sites, 147, 215, 285

expands schoolhouse, 296–97, 320

handles settlement problems, 170, 182, 287–88, 298–99, 416

Iron Mission, member and clerk, 23n. 45, 25–26, **26**, 28–29, 156, 436, 455

lot ownership, 178–79, **293**, **328**, 330, **331**, 334, **336**, 473, 476, 485

marriage and family, 164, 186–87, 294–96, 399

military titles, 149–53

mission to England, 349, 393, 399, 465

oversees Big Field fencing, 224–25, 228

preaches iron sermons, 244, 265, 304

supervises iron works, 30, 217–18, 223–24, 227–30, 239–46, 262–67, 271, 277, 299–305, 308–10, 326, 345, 398

Lunt, Henry, Jr., 238

Lyman, Amasa M., 6, 16, 108, 277, 306, 394

Macfarlane, Daniel, 489, 492

Macfarlane, John, 484, 492

Macfarlane, Kate Palmer, 158n. 24, 164

Machin, Thomas, 211, 269, **293**, **331**, 473

Magraw, W. M. F., 383

Major, William W., **85**, 214

Manti, 9, 110, 123, 319, 324

Maramec Spring Iron Works, 4, 143, 196, **199**, 245–46, 274

Martineau, James H., 121, 235, 238, 317, 385, 436, 452, 491

Matheson, Alexander, 152, 163–64

Matheson, Alva, 152, 163

McConnell, George A., 487, 494

McConnell, Gladys, 155, 164, 454

McConnell, Jehiel, 394, 397, 487, 494

McCune, Alice, 60n. 28

McDonald, William, 373, 402n. 8

McGregor, William C., 65, 493

McGuffie, James, 120, 436, 493

McMurdy, Robert, 476, 477, 494

McMurdy, Samuel, 484, 495

Meeks, Priddy, 110, 123, 263, 317, 436, 494

Meeks, Sarah, 436

Meetinghouse, 80, 82, 97, 165, 168, 171, 174–75, **181**, 182, 188n. 11, 212, 215, 296–97, 346, 364–65n. 12

Memmot, John, 487, 495

Memmot, William, 487

Memorial plaques, 231–32, 419–20n. 7

Militia

camp military organization, 34–35

Cedar City (Second and Third Battalions), 149–52, 171, 226, 343, 385–91, 492, 494–96

Company C (horse company), 149–52, 160, 167, 202

Company F (foot company), 149–52, 160, 167, 190, 202, 206, 226

Iron County (Tenth Regiment) muster roll, 491–98

organized in Parowan, 148–49

restructured by legislature, 319, 381

role in Mountain Meadows massacre, 385–91, 394–95, 405n. 66

Miller, Daniel A., 91, 104, 113n. 6, 119, 122, 124, 436

Miller, Eliza, 65, 436

Miller, Hannah, 436

Miller, Robert E., 65, 133, 436

Miller, William, 346

Millett, Joseph, 25, 47, 90–91, 106, 119, 436

Mining

coal, 203, 232–34, **235**, 236–39, **238**, 244, 270, 310, 348, 353–54, 376, 480

lead, 379

silver, 379

Missionaries

cotton, 400–401

gold, 6, 413

to Indians, 275, 287, 326, 400

iron. *See* Iron Missionaries

lead, 379

proselyting, 101, 110, 186, 244

Missouri redress petitions, 405n. 72

Mitchell, Louisa, 436

Mitchell, William C., Jr., 51, 106, 150, 152, 437, 452, 492

Mitchell, William C., Sr., 27, 51, 102, 106, 152, 178, **179**, 400, 436, 449, 452

Moggredge, Henry, 110, 437

Mons, LaVon Adams, 311n. 15

Moor, Calvin, 475

Moore, P. George, 110, 437

Moore, William, 485, 495

Morgan, Dale, 79

Morgan, David, 354, 496

Morgan, John, 354, 483, 492

Morgan, William, 354–55, 485, 496

Morley, Isaac, 9, 108

Mormon Battalion, 5, 71

Mormon Corridor, 3, 22, 31, 387, 399

Mormon Reformation, 382, 391

Mormon Way-Bill, 8, 22n. 16, 421–23

Morrill, Laban, **331**, 476, 494

Morris, Elias

  captain in militia, 492

  chief mason for Noble furnace, 211, 348–50, 354, 360, 378

  coauthors grievance resolution, 406n. 84

  describes Plat A fort, 325, 330

  lot owner, **291, 331**, 356, 474–76, 483

  shareholder, 272, 463

Morris, John, **293**, 483, 488, 494

Morris, Ray, 337

Morris, Richard, 125, 397, 492

Morris, William, 355

Morse, Cynthia A., 437

Morse, Gilbert, 110, 437, 497

Morse, Sarah, 437

Morse, William A., 82, 85, 99, 123, 219, 437, 446

Mortensen, Frank, 337

Mortenson, Bart, 85

Mortenson, Peter, 400

Mountain Meadows massacre, **14**, 387–91, **389**, 394–95, 399, 417–20, 491

Muir, David, 288, **293, 331**, 474, 495

Muir, John, **331**, 477, 488, 496

Muir, Thomas, 288, **293, 331**, 474, 496

Muir, Walter, 288, **293, 331**, 474

Munroe, George, 354, 391, 486, 496

Mustard, Sandy, 145

Native Americans

  assist settlers, 13, 287, 321

  Brigham Young's advice concerning, 287, 456–57

  cultivate Corn Creek, 48

  guide Frémont, 327–28

  Navajos, 286

  Pahvants, 286–87, 326

  Paiutes, 11, 111, 286–87, 317, 321–22, 326, 336, 388

  role in Mountain Meadows massacre, 387–90, 395, 417

  Shoshoni, 11, 29, 111, 317

  slave trade of, 5, 11, 317

  taught farming, 11, 111, 129, 326, 399–400

  tensions with pioneers, 31–32, 42–43, 71, 80, 155, 175–76, 218, 286–88, 290, 306, 317–19, 335, 417

  Timpanogos Utes, 4, 9, 29

  Utes, 4, 5, 9, 11, **12**, 29, 32–33, 36, 38, 72, 111, 146, 286, 317, 334, 336

  weapons, 81–82, 185

Nauvoo Legion, 34–35, 59n. 19, 149–50, 160n. 43, 171, 213, 226, 319, 381, 403n. 45, 495

Neff, Andrew L., 236, 383

Nelson, Bengt, 377–78, 495

Nelson, John, **293, 331**, 353–54, 474, 477, 493

Nelson, Peter, 485, 494

Newman, Elijah, 27, 40, 46, 76, 112, 123, 216, 437, 493

Nickerson, Erasmus, 487, 488

Niles, Alanson, 348

Niles, Alonso, 211

Nish, Robert, 487

Nish, William, **331**, 477, 487

Noble Furnace, 348–51, **352**, 353–62, 371, 375–76, 378, 409–10, 412

Norris, James D., 4

Oertle, Lee, 419–20n. 7

Old Rock Church, 85–86, 121, **131**, 337–38

"Old Sow Cannon," 77, 93n. 32

Old Spanish Trail, 4–8, **7**, 21n. 5–6, 63n. 85, 71, 400, 404n. 60, 422

Ouiwonup, 287

Overman, Frederick, 194, 197, 393

Owens, Catherine, 437

Owens, Evan, 348, 353, 496

Owens, Jerome, 204

Owens, John, **331**, 348, 353, 475, 495

Owens, Robert, 110, 204, 244, 437

Pace, James, 33, 36, 39

Page, Daniel, 133

Palmer, Richard, 304

Palmer, William R., 48, 164–67, 171, **174**, 176, **181**, 250n. 82, 272, 302, 304, 312n. 19, 340n. 45

Paragonah (Red Creek), **30**, 31, 55–56, 64n. 95, 117, 263, 322–23, 339n. 17, 386, 449

Parks, Arthur, 85, 156, 211, 269, **293, 331**, 452, 473

Parks, James, 437

Parowan (Center Creek). *See also* Fort Louisa

  city government organized, 121–23, 126

  explorations of Center Creek, 11, 13, **30**, 31, 57, 70–73

  "forting up," 334–36

  growth of trades, 400

  name of, 123, 126

  pioneer remnants in, 131–33, 135, 337–38

  property allocation, 101–4, **103**, 445–49

  suitability of soil at, 57, 69, 97–102, 416

  surveys of, 88, 129, **130**, 131–33, **134**, 135

Parowan Canal Co., 127
Parowan City Council, 141
Parowan Iron Company, 215, 262–67, 277–78, 280
Parowan United Mercantile and Manufacturing Institution (PUMI), 400
Parowan Valley. *See* Little Salt Lake Valley
Parry, George, **293**, **331**, 348, 354, 475, 485, 496
Parry, William T., 412–13
Patriarchal blessings, 275
Patterson, Alexander, **331**, 348, 353, 486
Patterson, Andrew, 354–55, 484, 492
Payson (Fort Peteetneet), 31, 33–34, 36–38, 41, 58, 73, 79, 119, 139, 153
Peay, George P., 486
Pendleton, Calvin C., 125, 337–38, 400, 491
Peteetneet (chief), 72–73, 81–82, 111, 286
Petersen, Andrew, **293**, **331**, 473
Phelps, W. W., 10, 139
Pine wood, 196, 245, 300, 305
"Pioneer iron works," 205–13, 217–18, 223–32, 239–46, 266–71, 277, 280, 399
Pitt, William, 214
Pollock, Samuel C., 272, **331**, 355, 463, 477, 488, 495
Polygamy, 120, 139, 382
Potter, E. G., 437
Potter, L. W., 110
Pratt, Addison, 8
Pratt, Parley P.
    death in Arkansas, 388
    leads Southern Exploring Expedition, 8–11, 13, 15–16, 20, 26–27, 31, 43, 45–46, 61, 70, 73, 145, 327
    meets Chief Wakara, 9, 11
    recommends Center Creek, 76, 147
    visits Parowan prior to mission, 101–3, 108–9, 113, 449
Proclamation of Martial Law, 385, 387–88
Prothero, Edward, **331**, 474
Provo. *See* Fort Utah
Puddling furnace. *See* Air furnace
Pugmire, James, 156, 453
Pugmire, Jonathan
    blacksmith, 129, 184–85, 203, 338, 343, 437
    Cedar City settler, 453, 475, 488
    Cedar Stake first counselor, 125, 371
    iron worker, 119, 210, 268, 306, 437
    lot owner, **293**, 488
    militia member, 405

son's accidental death, 204
    trustee and shareholder, 270, 272, 279, 346, 462–63
Pugmire, Jonathan, Jr., 204
Pugmire, Joseph A., 437, 494
Quorum of the Twelve Apostles, 6, 8, 16–17, 245–46, 253–55, 384
Railroads, 79, 398–99, 401
Randals, Mrs., 350
Rasmuson, Crismas, 485
Rasmussen, Christian, 337
Ray, John, 353
Reaves, Josiah, **331**, 477, 488, 496
Red Creek. *See* Paragonah
Rees, Watkin, 238
Reid, Robert, 272, 463
Resurrection Camp, 15, 43
Rice, William, 437
Rich, Charles C., 6, 8, 16, 34, 108, 277, 306
Richards, Alma, 136n. 46
Richards, Franklin D.
    civic and ecclesiastical leadership, 206, 253, 319–20, 324, 326, 328, 346, 377, 474
    coauthors iron report. *See* Erastus Snow
    implements Deseret Iron Co., 245–46, 264–72, 278
    leadership of Deseret Iron Co., 276–77, 279–80, 282, 301, 307–8, 311, 343–44, 356, 463, 468–69
    lot owner, **328**, 474
    organizes Deseret Iron Co., 206, 253–61, **255**, 285
Richards, Joseph, 133, **134**
Richards, Levi, 255–56
Richards, Morgan, 132, 136n. 46, 400, 492
Richards, Samuel W., 142, 255
Richards, William W., 355, 484, 486, 496
Riggs, William Sears, 357, 487–88, 495
Rim of the Basin, 92n. 16, 189n. 27
Rio Virgin Manufacturing Association, 400
Roberts, Roberts, 476
Roberts, Ross, 133
Roberts, William, 211, **331**, 393, 484, 493
Robinson, Joseph L., 85, 99, 104, 121–22, 124, 146
Robinson, Susan McCord Burton, 121, 437
Rock quarries, 20, 62n. 60, 82, 197, 348–50, 353, 355, 376, 483
Rogers, Russel, **331**, 477
Rogers, Samuel H., 327, 493

Rogers, Seth, 133

Rollo, Alex, 179, 190n. 41

Ross, Alexander, 150, 174–75, 453

Ross, Daniel, 150, 156, 174–75, 185–86, **293**, **331**, 453, 477, 486

Ross, Duncan, 150–51, 155, 174–75, 186, 453

Ross house. *See* Meetinghouse

Rowland, Benjamin, **293**, 496

Rowland, Job, **293**, **331**, 473, 475, 484, 487

Rowland, Thomas, 150, 269, **293**, **331**, 348, 453, 477

Royls, Paul, 47, 437, 444

Sabbath observance, 38–39, 56, 79, 81, 91, 245

Sabin, Ara W., 35, 119, 438

Sabin, Nancy A., 438

San Bernardino, 5–6, 16, 107–8, 277, 288

Sanderson, John, 51, 438

Sanpete Valley, 9, 11, 108, 372, 480–81

Sansberry, William, 487

Sawmills, 82, 86–89, 109, 118, 123, 132, 211, 350, 398, 400

Schoolhouse. *See* Meetinghouse

Scotch Independent Company, 142–46, 149–50, 155–56, 157–58n. 10, 205, 416

Self-sufficiency. *See* Economic independence

Seventies (priesthood quorum), 18, 344

Shaw, Michael, 110, 438

Sheets, Elijah F., 27, 35, 438

Sheets, Susannah, 438

Shelton, William O., 272, **293**, **331**, 357, 463, 485, 492

Sherrett, John, 487–88

Shipps, Jan, 20

Shirts, Belana Pulsipher, 142

Shirts, Darius, 20, 120, 155, 357, 438, 497

Shirts, Don Carlos, 20, 438, 497

Shirts, George, 20, 155, 438

Shirts, Margaret Cameron, 142

Shirts, Morris A.
    assigns titles to records, 93n. 45, 208
    collaborations, 329, **336**, 412–13
    excavates furnace site, 412–13
    inspects mill site, 88
    interviews with Cedar City residents, 190

Shirts, Peter
    builds outside fort, 218
    in exploring parties, 46–48, 70, 77, **112**, 114–15, 126, 129, 151–52, 234, 239, 265–66, 320, 351, 378
    guides to Coal Creek, 140–41, 151–52, 155
    iron work, 211, 269, 275, 306
    marries Belana Pulsipher, 142
    militia member, 497
    Parowan and Cedar City settler, 151–52, 156, **331**, 438, 448, 453, 475–76
    settlement activities, 20, 91, 102, 104, 106–7, 136, 141, 146, 157, 244

Shirts Creek, 140, 244, 286, 320, 322

Shurtleff, Vincent, 255, 259–60, 272, 279, 282, 307, 346, 463

Simpkins, Charles P., **331**, 354–55, 379, 398, 484, 496

Simpkins, James, 408n. 122, 486, 488, 495

Slack, Martin, 396, 398, 406n. 84, 496

Slack, William, 150, 156, 170, 210, 268, 453

Smith, Benjamin, 487, 496

Smith, Charles P., 211, 269, 275, **331**, 474, 484, 497

Smith, George A.
    called to lead Iron Mission, 16, **17**, 124, 438
    commands southern Utah militia, 319, 321–25, 335
    concern for oxen (Old Balley, Bright), 42–44
    debates Big Field location, 97, 99–100
    establishes Fort Louisa, 76–82, 84, 87–91, 101–02, **103**, 104–07
    explores Center and Coal Creeks, 69–75
    governs Parowan, 122–23, 126–28
    hosts Chief Wakara, 110–11
    incites against federal troops, 385–87
    investigates Mountain Meadows massacre, 394–95
    Iron County chief justice, 34, 59n. 21, 73–74, 122
    leads camp to Little Salt Lake Valley, 25–29, 32–36, 38–58
    orders cattle to Salt Lake, 323–24
    organizes militia, 34–35, 148–49
    oversees fort relocation, 285, 289–91
    plows first furrow, 90, 104
    preaches iron sermons, 214, 251, 306
    promotes Parowan Iron Co., 262–64
    proposes Cedar City site, 139–40, 147–48
    recruits volunteers, 18, 362–63
    reports on drought, 373, 375
    St. George named after, 400
    sawmill of, 87–89, 126, 146
    shareholder, 283n. 54, 464
    Utah Stake president, 146, 213

Smith, J. C. L.
    goes to Salt Lake City, 129, 245, 261, 305, 347
    illness and death, 377, 416

oversees pioneer iron works, 124, 217, 227–
    29, 241–43, 262, 264, 267, 416, 438
Parowan Stake president, 125, 371, 375
presides over "Stake of Zion," 124, 216–17,
    264, 287, 298, 327, 416
superintendent of Deseret Iron Co., 267,
    271–73, 276–77, 280, 289, 299, 301,
    307–9, 343, 345, 464
Smith, Jesse N., 125, 132, 347, 375, 381, 492
Smith, John, II, **293**, 348, 353, 485–86
Smith, John K., **331**, 477, 484
Smith, John Lyman
    controversy over trying ore, 205–7, 212
    first counselor, Iron Mission, 124, 146–47,
        159, 202, 204–5, **207**, 211–13
    leaves for territorial legislature, 217
    returns with Col. Kimball, 321
Smith, John P., 238
Smith, Jonathan, 438
Smith, Joseph, city of Zion plan of, 3, 98, 290,
    292
Smith, Joseph H., 391, 394, 496
Smith, Lucy Meservy, 108
Smith, Mary Amelia, 132, **331**
Smith, O. K., 6
Smith (Dibble), Peter A., 25, 47, 91, 101, 104,
    106, 139, 438
Smith, Philip K. *See* Philip Klingensmith
Smith, Polly, 438
Smith, Ruth, 91, 438
Smith, Sarah Ann Libby, 108, 127
Smith, Silas, 347, 491
Smith, Thomas, 35, 70, 72, 74, 76, 89, 119,
    331, 438, 474, 484, 494, 498
Smith, William, 238, **331**, 474, 483, 496
Smith, Zilpha Stark, 25, 47, 89, **89**, 128–29,
    132, 299, 438
Snow, Erastus
    community leadership, 326, 343–47, 356, 376
    implements Deseret Iron Co., 245–46,
        264–73
    leadership of Deseret Iron Co., 229, 236,
        276–80, 282, 301, 306–10, 376, 464,
        468–69
    lot owner, **328**, 474–76
    mission president in Denmark, 254
    organizes Deseret Iron Co., 206, 253–61,
        255, 285
    presides over Cotton Mission, 400–401
    remarks on iron manufacture, 220 n. 2
    "Report of Erastus Snow and Franklin D.
        Richards"

as "Manufacture of Iron in Utah," 189n.
    17, 254–55, 279–80, 281n. 14, 284n.
    78, 366n. 33
    as "Report of Travels," 343–47,
        363–64nn. 2, 7, 12; 365nn. 14, 15
Snow, Lorenzo, 16
Snow, Zerubbabel, 146, 251
Soap-making, 185
Southern Exploring Expedition, 8–10, 20,
    21nn. 1, 4; 31, 45–46, 61n. 53, 145, 327
Southern Indian Mission, 275–76, 349–50
Southern route. *See* California Road
Sowiete, 11, 286
Spaniards, 4, 11, 155, 175, 215
Spanish Trail. *See* Old Spanish Trail
Spiers, John, 306
Sprague, Festus, 305, **331**, 475
St. George, 13, 399–400
St. Louis, 7, 142–43, 196, 245–46, 258, 275,
    307, 309, 376, 415
Stakes
    Cedar City, 71, 125, 217, 371–72, 397
    Parowan, 125, 371
    "Stake of Zion," 124, 216–17, 267, 343
Steam engine, 347, 379–80, 391, 393–94,
    396–98, 410–11
Steele, Catherine, 439
Steele, Elizabeth, 65, 444
Steele, John C.
    complains of other farmers, 416
    counselor in stake presidency, 124, 216–19,
        227, **241**, 287, 439
    describes Parowan wall, 335–36
    iron works activities, 212–13, 241–44, 272,
        300, 345, 439, 464
    militia activity, 35, 493
    promotes Parowan Iron Co., 262–66
    settles Las Vegas, 400
Stewart, Urban V., 272, 405n. 72, 439, 464, 493
Stewart, William, **331**, 364n. 12, 477, 485, 495
Stoddard, David Kerr
    drummer in militia, 492
    emigrates from Scotland, 142–46
    iron worker, 210, 212, 269
    lot holder, **293**, 484, 488
    refuses to release cattle, 324
    shareholder, 270, 273, 365n. 14, 464
Stoddard, Janet Kerr, 142
Stoddard, John, 145, 150, 158n. 14, **293**,
    453–54, 487–88, 492
Stoddard, Mary Williamson, 145

Stones, William, 150, 210–12, 269–70, **293**, **331**, 365n. 14, 453, 464, 473, 476

Stratten, Andrew J., 485

Stratton, Anthony, **331**, 478, 495

Sulfur, 195–96, 347, 358–60, 401, 409, 412

Summit, 109, 122, 326–27, 356

Taugunt, 111

Taxes, 123, 275, 302, 413

Taylor, John, 245, 253, 375, 378, 401–02

Taylor, Stephen, 10, 16, 118

Telegraph, 399

Tennant, Thomas, 255–56, 258, 279, 283n. 52, 464, 469

Thomas, Daniel M., 406n. 84

Thomas, Jerremiah, **293**, **331**, 474

Thomas, William, **331**, 348, 354, 485, 488, 496

Thompson, Edward W., 133

Thorley, Thomas, 211, 238, **331**, 348, 354, 393, 477, 483, 495

Thornton, William, 337

Thorpe, James, 150, 453

Three Peaks, The, **14**, 231

Timber or lumber, 76–77, 79–82, 87–91, 239–41, 355

Timmings, James, 361–62, 492

Tithing

    donations, 153, 219, 256–57, 264, 292

    method of recording, 275, 397

    uses of, 4, 182, 203, 210, 407n. 113, 413, 459

Tithing offices, in Cedar, Parowan and Harmony, 272, 275, 350, 391, 399, 465

Topham, Betsy, 65, 439

Topham, John, 65, 76, 211, 269, 439

Tout, John, 150, 206, 453

Towne, Chester, 110, 439

Trial furnace, 206–7, 353–54, 359, 393, 480

Turley, Theodore, 406n. 84

Tutsegabit, 388

Tyler, S. Lyman, 311n. 3

Union Iron Works, 401

Urie, John, 147–48, 164, 396, 485, 492

Utah Territorial Legislature

    buys shares in Deseret Iron Co., 271–72, 283n. 54, 464

    chastises federal government, 392

    incorporates Deseret Iron Co., 278–79, 469–71

    involvement in Mormon Reformation, 382

    iron appropriations, 236, 301–3, 345

    passes anti–slave trade acts, 317

    restructures militia, 319, 381

Utah Territory

    federal appointees to, 382–84, 394–95

    organized, 61, 71, 382, 443

    stakes created in, 217

Utah War

    aftermath of, 394–95

    federal troops sent during, 384–85, 388, 391–92, 404n. 62, 405n. 66

    tensions leading to, 139, 382–85, 417

Vance, William P., 10, 439

Varley, Richard, 210, 240, 262, 269, 324–25

Vélez de Escalante, Silvestre, 4–5

Wagon-Box Camp. *See* Cedar City

Wakara. *See also* Walker War

    burial of, 336

    camps near Coal Creek, 70–72

    comes to Fort Louisa, 110–11, 123, 126

    invites Mormons to settle, 11

    horse and slave trade of, 11, 286, 317

    negotiates peace, 334

    settles Utes in Sanpete Valley, 9, **12**

    in Walker War, 36, 317–19

Walker, Betty, 186, 439

Walker, Emma Smith, **205**

Walker, John, II, 485

Walker, Jonathan, 398

Walker, Joseph, 156, **179**, **205**, 205–6, 270, 272, **331**, 439, 453, 465, 483, 485

Walker, Nancy, 156, 161n. 63, 454

Walker, Thomas, 487

Walker War, 36, 63n. 78, 237, 317–23, 325, 327, 334–35, 343, 346, 381, 385, 415

Ward, Barney, 32, 215

Ward, David, 186, 494

Wards and branches

    Cedar City, 125, 330, 344

    Fort Louisa (Parowan), 84, 122, 131–32, 344, 443, 445–47

Warner, Ted J., 21n. 4

Waterwheel

    flume, 198, 302

    maintenance of, 299–300, 347–48, 350–51, 355, 360–61, 376

    millrace, 88, 127, 198, 242, 302

    overshot, 198, 242, 302, 355, 399

    preparation of, 207, 239–40, 258

    replaced by steam engine, 410–11

    undershot, 198, **199**, 242

Watts, Benjamin, 85, 120, 439, 493

Webb, Charles Y., 119, 439, 493

Webb, John, 70, 439
Webb, Margaret, 439
Webster, Lou, 239
Wells, Daniel H., 118, 146, 213–15, 218, 319, **381**, 387, 405n. 66
West, Chauncey, 10, 15, 440
West, Samuel, 150, 216, 263, 347, 453
Weston, John, 255–57, 283nn. 52, 54, **331**, 465, 469, 476, 486–88
Wheeler, Thomas S., 29, 43, 70, 72, 74, 81, 92n. 25, 101, 106, 111, 121, 440
Whipple, Edson, 35, 46, 52, 65, 69, 78, 85, 90, 99, 120, 153, 399, 440
Whipple, Harriet, 65, 440
Whipple, Mary Ann, 65, 440
White, Joel W., 486, 492
White, John, 210, 269, 286, **293**, **331**, 473, 486, 488–89, 496
White, Samuel D., 272, **331**, 462, 477, 485
Whitney, Clarissa, 65, 120, 440
Whitney, Francis T., 65, 85, 102, 110, 216, 440, 448, 494
Whittaker, James, Jr., 150, 453, 485, 492
Whittaker, James, Sr.
    Cedar City settler, 150, 152, 155, 156, 220, 292, **293**, 295, **331**, 453, 465, 473, 476, 485, 494
    describes daughter's wedding, 186–87
    describes early Cedar City settlement, 164, 168, 170, 175–76, 178–79, 182, 184–85, 206, 209, 213, 232–33, 286
    iron worker, 210, 224, 269
    keeps iron works account books, 209, 266, 268, 348, 396–97
Wilcox, William, 133
Wiley, Robert, 51, 89, 91, 123, 139, 154, 175, 177–78, 225, 292, **293**, **331**, 349, 354, 440, 476, 483, 495
Willden, Charles, 62n. 69, 175, 288, **293**, 297, 329, **331**, 474, 484, 487, 496
Willden, Elliot, 487, 496
Willden, Feargus O'Conner, 297–98, 496
Willes, W. W., 348, 497
Williams, Edward, 150, 182, 190n. 46, 211, 243, 269, 307, 440, 453
Williams, George, 283n. 54, 465, 497
Williams, Thomas, 486, 495
Williams, William, 484, 495
Williamson, James S., 142, 145, 150, 158n. 24, 210, 212, 226, 243, 268, 283n. 54, 348, 353, 365n. 14, 453, 465, 485, 493–94
Willis, John H., 477, 496

Willis, Joshua T., 486, 496
Wimmer, Peter, 132
Wood, George, 51, 70, 74, 172–73, 210, 213, 224, 239, 246, 268, **293**, **328**, 348, 363, 399, 440, 453–54, 476, 484–85, 494
Wood, Gideon D., 44, 70, 119, 429, 440
Wood, Hannah, 440
Wood, Mary Davies, 51, 172–73, 440
Wood, Rhoda Matheson, 164, 166, 188n. 6, 245, 250 n. 82
Woodhouse, Charles C., 484, 492
Woodhouse, John, 484, 488, 492
Woodruff, Wilford, 118, 215
Woods, William, 150, 211, 453
Woolf, John A., 123, 140–41, 440
Woolf, Sarah Ann Devoe, 141, 440
Woolley, Catherine, 441
Woolley, Samuel A., 35, 78, 119, 441
Woolsey, Hiram, 110, 415, 441
Wright, Jefferson, 102, 441
Wright, Sarah, 441
Wynn, Denis, 110, 415
Yardley, John, **293**, **331**, 353, 357, 476, 484, 492
Young, Brigham
    appointed governor of Utah Territory, 71
    assesses settlement sites, 215, 285–86, 288, 372, 410
    conference report of, 371–72, 479–81
    instructs iron missionaries, 34–36, 217–19, 455–60
    iron financing of, 253, 271–72, 465
    names Iron County, 73
    offers steam engine, 379–80
    organizes Parowan City, 122–23, 126
    organizes stakes, 217, 317
    prepares for Utah War, 384–85, 388, 390–92
    prepares for Walker War, 318–20
    relations with federal government, 139, 382–85, 392, 417
    relations with Native Americans, 11, 287, 334, 336, 456–57
    summons iron leaders to Salt Lake, 245–46
    suspends iron production, 391, 396
    visits Iron Mission, 39, 108, 111, 117–23, 126, 285–86, 371–72
Young, George, 441
Young, Joseph W., 255
Young, Lorenzo Dow, 118, 139, 288
Zion
    establishing, 20–21, 51, 72, 75, 186, 280, 419
    plan for city of, 3, 98, 289–92

Morris A. Shirts earned his Ed.D. at Indiana University. He taught at Brigham Young Unversity and at Southern Utah University, where he served as dean of the college of education. He coauthored *Silver, Saints & Sinners: A History of Old Silver Reef, Utah*, and was a founding member of the Mountain Meadows Monument Committee.

Kathryn H. Shirts is the daughter-in-law of Morris Shirts. After receiving her bachelor's degree in history at Stanford, she obtained master's degrees from Harvard Graduate School of Education and Harvard Divinity School, where she studied American religious history.

Cover art: A detail of a painting by R. D. Adams depicting the pioneer iron works beside Coal Creek during the first iron run on 29–30 September 1852. The painter's grandfather was furnace master David Barclay Adams, who showed him where various buildings were located at the old iron works site. His great-grandfather was iron missionary Peter Shirts. Courtesy Special Collections, Gerald R. Sherratt Library, Southern Utah University.